Pacific Crucible

ALSO BY IAN TOLL

Six Frigates: The Epic History of the Founding of the U.S. Navy

Pacific Crucible

War at Sea
in the Pacific,
1941–1942

IAN W. TOLL

W. W. NORTON & COMPANY
New York   London

Copyright © 2012 by Ian W. Toll

For information about permission to reproduce selections from this book,
write to Permissions, W. W. Norton & Company, Inc.,
500 Fifth Avenue, New York, NY 10110

For information about special discounts for bulk purchases, please contact
W. W. Norton Special Sales at specialsales@wwnorton.com or 800-233-4830

Manufacturing by RR Donnelley, Harrisonburg, VA
Book design by Helene Berinsky
Production manager: Anna Oler
Maps by Loren Doppenberg

Library of Congress Cataloging-in-Publication Data

Toll, Ian W.
Pacific crucible : war at sea in the Pacific, 1941–1942 / Ian W. Toll. — 1st ed.
p. cm.
Includes bibliographical references and index.
ISBN 978-0-393-06813-9 (hardcover)
1. World War, 1939–1945—Campaigns—Pacific Area. 2. World War, 1939–1945—
Naval operations, American. 3. World War, 1939–1945—Naval operations, Japanese. I. Title.
D767.T65 2012
40.54'26—dc23
2011028907

W. W. Norton & Company, Inc.
500 Fifth Avenue, New York, N.Y. 10110
www.wwnorton.com

W. W. Norton & Company Ltd.
Castle House, 75/76 Wells Street, London W1T 3QT

1 2 3 4 5 6 7 8 9 0

To Henry,
who will read this later.

CONTENTS

LIST OF MAPS

PROLOGUE

Oh, East is East, and West is West, and never the twain shall meet,
Till Earth and Sky stand presently at God's great Judgment Seat;
But there is neither East nor West, Border, nor Breed, nor Birth,
When two strong men stand face to face, tho' they come from the
ends of the earth!
——RUDYARD KIPLING, *The Ballad of East and West*

It has been observed that if a sailor had climbed into a time machine in the year 1850, and was randomly transported through time, he would have found himself more at home as a foremast jack in the Spanish Armada, which had sailed against England in 1588, than in one of the big steel battleships of 1900. In those latter fifty years of the nineteenth century, a period brief enough to span one man's career, the Industrial Revolution had utterly demolished and recreated the hardware and technology of naval warfare. Even so, there was to be no intermission, no respite in the pace of change. At the turn of the twentieth century, the world's navies stood on the verge of parallel revolutions in ship design, engine design, weapons systems, communications, and doctrine. Turbine engines would replace inefficient reciprocating engines. Fuel oil would replace coal. Fire director systems would allow one man to train all of a ship's guns on a target, and to correct for the pitch and roll of the ship. The self-propelled torpedo, designed to strike an enemy ship at the waterline, was improving in range and dependability. Radio communications would link fleets at sea to their shore-based commands. Several nations were experimenting successfully with submarines. In 1903, the Wright brothers made their historic first flight at Kitty Hawk, and farsighted officers could envision the future possibilities of these new "flying machines." In 1906, Great Britain launched a new battleship, the HMS *Dreadnought*. She had 12-inch guns and a 21-knot cruising speed, and from the day she slid down the ways every other battleship in the world was obsolete.

All the ranking American admirals of the Second World War began their naval careers during that era of stupendous technological change. Between about 1900 and 1910, as fresh-faced teenagers leaving home for the first time, they entered the U.S. Naval Academy in Annapolis, Maryland. To win admission, they had passed punishing entrance examinations and survived a ruthless selection process. They were Protestant and middle class, almost to a man. There were no blacks, no Jews, and precious few Catholics. A few were "navy juniors," following in the footsteps of fathers or grandfathers. They came from every region of the country, but within a year or two their accents and dialects were wrung out of them, and they spoke in an efficient, superregional version of English, so that their family and friends at home would shake their heads in wonder at the changes the navy had wrought. "Now he belongs to his country," his parents were told, and the implication was clear—their influence over him was all part of the past. He had crossed a threshold into a new life, from which there was no return except by the disgraceful act of failing and flunking out.

At Annapolis they entered an austere, inward-looking, highly regimented social order, hermetically sealed off from the cacophonous civilian society in which they had been raised. From reveille at six-thirty to lights-out at nine-thirty, their days were parceled out in exacting increments of time. They drilled and marched for hours in all kinds of weather on the academy grounds, and conducted physically exhausting amphibious drills in open boats on the Chesapeake. Plebes learned to "double time down the corridor, change directions at sharp right angles, and sit rigidly at attention while sitting on the forward two inches of [their] chair." Wayward behavior was kept in check by a combination of stern discipline and social pressure. Demerits were assessed against a long list of violations—tardiness, talking in ranks, smoking, failing to "square away" one's room, or sneaking into town for a beer. They learned basic seamanship, first by practicing on rigging and spars erected in a drill hall, later by cruising in old schooners and cutters on the Severn River.

Academic coursework emphasized seamanship, navigation, gunnery, tactics, and engineering. The key to a high class ranking lay in rote memorization of data supplied in classroom lectures and textbooks, followed by regurgitation on command. There was little occasion for analysis or independent thought, and the midshipmen were not encouraged to grapple too daringly with the major naval-military-technical-doctrinal issues of the day. The great emphasis was on character. Referring both to West Point and Annapolis, President Theodore Roosevelt told the Congress: "We do not need to have these schools made more scholastic. On the contrary we should never lose sight of the fact that the aim of each school is to turn out a man who shall be above everything else a fighting man . . . the best part of the education is the high standard of character and of professional morale which it confers." What was imperative, in those first years of a naval career, was to cultivate the right set of attitudes, the correct personal bearing, to cut a good figure in dress blues or whites, immaculately turned out in fore-and-aft hat and crisp white gloves, with a ceremonial sword at the hip. In short, to be well-liked: to fit in.

The past was always present. They were never allowed to forget that they were heirs to a proud warrior tradition; that they were charged personally and collectively with upholding the honor of their flag. The halls at Annapolis were decorated with tattered ensigns and faded oil paintings depicting naval scenes of the American Revolution and the War of 1812, the age of "wooden ships and iron men," when the ancient heroes—Jones, Perry, Decatur, Preble, Stewart—had won and defended the nation's independence at sea. Heavy emphasis was laid on the social graces. The young men were taught to cultivate good manners, to balance teacups in a parlor, to compose a handwritten letter that would not embarrass the sender or recipient, and to dance a passable waltz without treading on a lady's toes. They were encouraged to speak a little French and earn at least a nodding acquaintance with the classics. As naval officers they would perform quasi-diplomatic roles in ports of call around the world, and it was thought important that they should carry themselves with grace and confidence in every social setting, and never risk being looked down upon by any man or his wife, be they civil or military, foreigners or Americans.

Above all, Annapolis functioned as an engine of assimilation. Those who would not or could not fit in were spat out. Those who stayed and saw it through were bonded to each other and to the navy, with a deeply felt *esprit de corps*, overpoweringly and for life.

As for the big doctrinal questions of fleet strategy, these were the glory days of Alfred Thayer Mahan, the American naval officer–turned–historian and strategic guru whose doctrines had been embraced and put into practice by every major navy in the world. Mahan had been catapulted into international fame with the publication in 1890 and 1892 of his first major work, *The Influence of Sea Power Upon History*. In these and subsequent books and essays he set forth the three "Mahanian dogmas" that governed the thinking of naval strategists right up until the beginning of the Second World War—the cult of the big gun battleship, the iron rule of concentration, and the annihilation of the enemy fleet in a single decisive battle.

In looks, Mahan was the caricature of a bookish intellectual—tall, lanky, and spare, with posture very erect; his face sallow and sad, with pale blue eyes, a weak chin concealed under a graying beard, and a bulbous forehead merging into a majestic bald dome. He was abstemious, self-disciplined, pious, and reserved with strangers even to the point of seeming shy. He had graduated Annapolis in 1859 (when the institution was only fourteen years old) and entered the old wooden-hull sailing navy in time for the election of Lincoln and the secession of the southern states. He passed the four years of the Civil War in uneventful blockade duty off the rebel coast. In the postwar period his duties took him around the globe, with cruises on various ships throughout Europe, the Middle East, Latin America, and Asia. By 1884, Mahan had twenty-five years of honorable but otherwise unremarkable naval service behind him. He was a forty-five-year-old captain with no great hope of attaining flag rank (admiral). There was nothing to stop him drifting along for twenty more years and retiring with a comfortable pension. But he was heartily tired of the sea, where he had spent more than half his career, and keen to try a new direction. So when he was offered a position as history lecturer at the newly founded U.S. Naval War College in Newport, Rhode Island, he took the job at once.

Mahan believed himself to be utterly unqualified for the job—"profoundly ignorant," as he put it. But he had a voracious appetite for knowledge and a monastic temperament that suited him to long hours of solitary study. He pillaged bookshops, haunted libraries, and bored through hundreds of years of history—the ancient Greeks and Romans, the colonial rivalries of Britain, Holland, France, and Spain, the rise and fall of Napoleon. "I tackled the job much as I presume an immigrant begins a clearing in the wilderness, not troubling greatly which tree he takes first," he later wrote. "I laid my hands on whatever came along, reading with the profound attention of one who is looking for something." One afternoon in the fall of 1885, while working in the library of the English Club in Lima, Peru (where his ship had put in), Mahan was engrossed in a history of the Punic Wars of Rome and Carthage in the second and third centuries BC. A question entered his mind, arriving with the force of a revelation. What if Hannibal had invaded Italy by sea, rather than by the long overland route through Spain and the Alps? Would Rome have fallen and the entire course of Western history been diverted? "The light dawned first on my inner consciousness," he wrote, "that control of the sea was an historic factor which had never been systematically appreciated and expounded." His mind took hold of the idea and did not let go, and soon afterward he began to write. The press of time required that he complete his Naval War College lectures for the fall of 1886, and the trial of putting his ideas into words forced him to clarify his essential thesis. As the pages flew, he recalled, "Every faculty I possessed was alive and jumping." The lectures were committed to paper by September 1886, and subsequently published by Little, Brown under the famously stilted title: *The Influence of Sea Power Upon History.*

The timing was propitious. Industrialization and technological change had prompted many nations to begin overhauling their fleets. National rivalries and imperial ambitions, especially among the great powers of Europe, threatened to provoke the mother of all naval arms races. The world was grasping toward a better understanding of seapower. What was it? What was its value? How was it attained? How should it be used? Mahan was not the first to ask those questions, but he framed them cogently and elegantly, and set out to answer them in a methodical way, with examples taken from the naval wars of the past.

Above all, Mahan preached the importance of "capital ships," or heavily armed battleships of the largest class. Frigates, cruisers, and destroyers might perform useful supporting roles, such as scouting, or protecting convoys—but a nation lacking big ships armed with big guns could never be more than a second-rate naval power. Mahan was adamant that this fleet of battleships must act at all times as a single, concentrated unit. To divide or disperse the fleet was the classic and recurring error of naval strategy—again and again, throughout the pages of history, a united fleet had hunted down and destroyed the scattered elements of a divided fleet. To those Mahan added a third precept: an emphasis on the *offensive*. The battle fleet should not be deployed as a kind of coast guard, to be kept close to one's harbors. A navy's supreme purpose, he declared, must be to range across the oceans, relying upon secure overseas bases if necessary; to hunt and destroy the enemy fleet. "War, once declared, must be waged offensively, aggressively. The enemy must not be fended off, but smitten down." The enemy must be met and destroyed in a "decisive battle," like those of Salamis, Actium, Lepanto, the Nile, or Trafalgar—an engagement in which the victors sink or capture all (or substantially all) of the enemy's ships, putting an end to his ability to wage naval war. Big ships with big guns, concentrated into a single, undivided battle fleet, and infused with an overriding purpose to wipe the enemy off the face of the sea—that was Mahan's formula for seapower.

Recognition came quickly and globally. Reviews were adulatory, and admiring letters poured in from around the world. *Influence* and his subsequent works were swiftly translated into French, German, Japanese, Russian, and Spanish. Two years after he had broken into print, Mahan was acclaimed as the most influential scholar of seapower ever to have picked up a pen, and a foreign policy sage whose statements were parsed and pondered and brooded over as if they had been handed down from Mount Olympus. "From 1892 on, everyone quoted him," wrote an admiring Frenchman, "and those who debated the subject endeavored to show their views were in agreement with his." In Britain, it was said that every officer in the Royal Navy had either read the book or was pretending that he had. Prime Minister William Gladstone labeled *Influence* "the book of the age," and in the Houses of Parliament Mahan's name was thrown around in such a way as to cut off all debate. In 1894, Mahan received honorary degrees from both Oxford and Cambridge, and at a Royal Navy Club banquet a toast was offered: "We owe to [Captain Mahan] the three million pounds sterling just voted for the increase of the navy." In Germany, Kaiser Wilhelm II reported to a friend: "I am just now not reading but devouring Captain Mahan's book and am trying to learn it by heart. It is a first class book and classical in all points." The Kaiser ordered his naval minister, Alfred von Tirpitz, to place translated copies of *Influence* aboard every ship in the German navy, and to let it be known that every officer was expected to read it. The Anglo-

German naval arms race that preceded (and by some lights provoked) the First World War unfolded under the deep influence of Mahan.

But in no nation did Mahan's writings make so deep and lasting an impression as in Japan. Mahan himself believed that to be the case: he remarked that "more of my works have been done into Japanese than into any other one tongue," and said no other country had showed "closer or more interested attention to the general subject." In 1894, *Influence* was translated and distributed through the association of Imperial Japanese Navy officers. Both the navy and army staff colleges adopted it as a textbook. Copies were presented to the Meiji emperor and the crown prince, Yoshihito. The Japanese Naval Staff College attempted (unsuccessfully) to recruit Mahan to join its faculty. Mahan's doctrine of the "decisive battle" echoed Miyamoto Musashi, the great samurai philosopher and swordsman of the sixteenth century, who had extolled the power of "total absorption in a single telling blow." Admiral Heihachiro Togo wrote in his own brush-hand, in exquisite calligraphy, a tribute: "Naval strategists of all nations are of one opinion that Mahan's works will forever occupy the highest position as a worldwide authority in the study of military science. I express my deep and cordial reverence for his far-reaching knowledge and keen judgment."

As Japan's political elites fell under the sway of Mahan's ideas, its navy's never-ending crusade for a greater share of the national budget gained momentum and adherents. Japan was an island-nation like Britain, declared the admirals: and like Britain, Japan could be attacked only by enemies who must come from over the sea. The army's imperial ambitions would come to nothing unless troops could be delivered safely to the Asian mainland. The Japanese navy, they insisted, should hold status equivalent to that of the British Royal Navy—it should be reconstituted as the primary branch of the nation's military forces, with a prior claim on policy-making influence and state funding.

In his own country, Mahan's most ardent champion was Teddy Roosevelt, who upon finishing the first volume of *Influence* in May 1890 wrote to congratulate the captain: "During the last two days I have spent half my time, busy as I am, in reading your book, and that I found it interesting is shown by the fact that having taken it up I have gone straight through and finished it." Roosevelt published an admiring review in the *Atlantic Monthly*, reserving special praise for Mahan's conclusion that the United

States should build a new fleet of heavy battleships. Their partnership grew more intimate in 1897–98, during Roosevelt's stint as assistant secretary of the navy, when the two collaborated in planning the fleet deployments that would lead to a quick American victory in the Spanish-American War. During Roosevelt's presidency (1901–09), Mahan was one of an inner circle of the president's advisers, allies, and fellow imperialists, a group that included John Hay, Elihu Root, and Massachusetts senator Henry Cabot Lodge. Roosevelt sometimes lifted passages out of Mahan's essays and wove them into his speeches nearly word for word. Mahan was "only too glad" that his work should be put to use in that way: he told the president, "The question of credit in such connection is to me quite immaterial."

Roosevelt was a brilliant, vociferous, combustible man, not the type who ordinarily reaches the presidency. In his whirlwind career, which had taken him from college to the White House in less than twenty years, he had been many things: a historian, lawyer, ornithologist, minority leader of the New York State Assembly, boxer, ranchman, New York City police commissioner, naturalist, hunter, civil service reformer, prolific author, devoted husband and father, voracious reader, assistant secretary of the navy, war hero, empire builder, advocate of vigorous physical exercise, governor of New York, and vice president of the United States. He was a big, broad-shouldered, barrel-chested man, with tan, rough-textured skin. His hair was close-cropped and reddish-brown in color, with bristles around the temples beginning to show gray, and his almost impossibly muscular neck looked as if it was on the verge of bursting his collar-stays. He wore pince-nez spectacles with a ribbon that hung down the left side of his face. When he smiled or spoke, he revealed two very straight rows of teeth, plainly visible from incisor to incisor, their gleaming whiteness sharply accented by his ruddy complexion.

No president since John Adams had campaigned so vigorously to expand the American navy. In 1903, he had shouted to an audience of 5,000 Chicagoans: "There is a homely old adage which runs, 'Speak softly and carry a big stick,' you will go far. If the American nation will speak softly, and yet build, and keep at a pitch of the highest training, a thoroughly efficient navy, the Monroe Doctrine will go far." That doctrine, a promise to ward off new European encroachments in the western hemisphere, was "as strong as the United States Navy, and no stronger." The United States had once faced one great ocean; now it faced two, and its long, sparsely populated

Pacific coastline presented both opportunities and dangers. "In the century that is opening," he told an audience of San Franciscans that year, "the commerce and the command of the Pacific will be factors of incalculable moment in the world's history." The president was determined to cut a canal through the Central American isthmus, and did not flinch from fomenting a revolution to detach Panama from Colombia. In Roosevelt's mind, the Panama Canal was above all a military necessity, for it would make possible a rapid transfer of naval power between the Atlantic and the Pacific. By 1906, digging on a vast scale was underway.

The Spanish-American War had left the United States with a far-flung assortment of overseas territories. That was not a development relished by all Americans, who had been steeped in an anti-imperialist, revolutionary heritage since 1776. But the immediate practical problem could not be ignored—Cuba, the Philippines, Hawaii, and the other islands of the Caribbean and Pacific that had fallen into the American lap could not be defended except by a navy. "The enemies we may have to face will come from over sea," Roosevelt told an audience of naval officers; "they may come from Europe, or they may come from Asia." Roosevelt saw Germany, with its territorial ambitions in South America, as a dangerous rival in the Atlantic and Caribbean. Yet the German threat was kept in check by the Royal Navy, the most powerful in the world, and in the foreseeable future the Anglo-German face-off would maintain a favorable balance of power on the Atlantic flank. But Japan, recent victor of the Russo-Japanese War, was a formidable naval power with great geostrategic advantages in the western Pacific. "In a dozen years," Roosevelt predicted in 1905, "the English, Americans and Germans, who now dread one another as rivals in the trade of the Pacific, will have each to dread the Japanese more than they do any other nation."

During his first term in office, using the "bully pulpit" of the presidency (a term he coined), President Roosevelt convinced Congress to build ten battleships, four armored cruisers, and seventeen smaller vessels. Naval spending rose nearly 40 percent, surpassing $100 million. It was the largest peacetime naval expansion in American history. By 1906, the United States had more battleships afloat than any other naval power except Britain.

The expanded fleet had to be manned, and thousands of new officers were urgently needed to man it. The Naval Academy at Annapolis held the key to the future of Roosevelt's navy, and he lavished his presidential attentions on the institution. Under his impetus, the academy was undergoing a spectacular makeover, and the campus was a sprawling construction site. Hammers, saws, and shouting workmen disturbed the peace six days a week. Old dilapidated wooden and redbrick buildings were being pulled down to make way for new Beaux-Arts edifices constructed of granite, marble, and gray brick. A new chapel, with an imposing terra-cotta dome and massive bronze doors, would be completed in 1908. President Roosevelt often caught the morning train from Washington to deliver speeches, cut ribbons, or cheer the football team. The president also turned up at the academy for commencement ceremonies, where he would look each graduating midshipman in the eye, crush his right hand in his vicelike grip, and hand him his diploma.

To the academy's reigning brass, Roosevelt's close interest was a mixed blessing. The commander in chief was a meddler. When the Naval Academy football team was abolished because the players were neglecting their studies, the president intervened to restore the team, and also insisted that the annual Army-Navy Game be played. "I greatly admire football," he explained. "I believe in rough, manly sports." In February 1906, Roosevelt pardoned a midshipman who had been convicted of hazing, dismissing the practice as "some exuberance of animal spirits." He arranged to have *judo* (Japanese wrestling) taught at the academy, remarking that it was "not physical exercise so much as it is an extraordinarily successful means of self-defense and training in dexterity and decision." When the program was subsequently cancelled, Roosevelt blamed the decision on the academy fathers, those "elderly men of a routine habit of mind."

The admirals and captains at the top of the naval hierarchy in those years had begun their careers before the Civil War. They had ascended the ranks through the slow grind of clocklike promotions, and in their last few halcyon years before retirement they were in no mood to be disturbed by changes foisted upon them by younger and more energetic men down the chain of command. The navy bureaus in Washington were bastions of conservative opinion, top-heavy with time-serving officers. Technological progress met with their prolonged interference simply because it was new and unfamiliar. Innovators, reformers, and iconoclasts were exiled to isolated billets until they resigned in frustration. Proposals to force the early retirement of older officers, a practice decried as "plucking," brought their fierce opposition. Even by 1906, when the expansion of the service was well underway, the U.S. Navy was still an older man's navy. The youngest captain in the service was twenty years older than his British counterpart. The British navy could hold up several examples of officers who had been promoted out of the enlisted ranks, but in the putatively more egalitarian United States there was not one such man.

Contemptuous of the "old-style naval officers of the kind who drift into positions at Washington," President Roosevelt announced his intention to "encourage the best among them by sharply discriminating against the worst." Since its founding the navy had been governed by a principle of seniority, and officers of every rank remonstrated bitterly against promoting younger men over their heads. But in Roosevelt's navy, men would advance according to merit, allowing for the early and rapid promotion of deserving younger officers. Lazy, complacent, or incompetent men would no longer be permitted to languish in the middle ranks for decades on end—an "up or out" principle would require that they win promotion on the merits or face compulsory retirement. Line officers had always looked down on engineers as an inferior caste—but now all were merged into one integrated corps, with equivalent ranks, uniforms, wardroom privileges, and berthing facilities.

To the chagrin of the brass and even his own secretary of the navy, the commander in chief carried on a direct correspondence with the "young Turks," mid-level officers who campaigned for reform from within the ranks of the service. With Roosevelt in power, that type of officer, who had not thrived in the navy perhaps since the days of the War of 1812, could dare to believe that his ideas would be implemented, that his talent would be rewarded with early promotion. The president was only too happy to short-circuit the chain of command, to intervene in the normal course of naval business to encourage innovation and new technology, as when he ordered that men engaged in testing submarines be given additional pay to compensate them for the extreme hazards involved. Aboard battleships, emphasis on "spit and polish"—pomp, pageantry, and the outward appearance of the ship—was curtailed, and the time thus saved was devoted to gunnery drills. Gun crews practiced hitting targets, with the results carefully recorded. One ship was pitted against another in gunnery competitions, and officers whose ships did not make the grade had to answer for the deficiency. On the qualities required of naval officers, Roosevelt was outspoken: "They must have skill in handling the ships, skill in tactics, skill in strategy . . . the dogged ability to bear punishment, the power and desire to inflict it, the daring, the resolution, the willingness to take risks and incur responsibilities which have been possessed by the great captains of all ages, and without which no man can ever hope to stand in the front rank of fighting men."

ON THE AFTERNOON and evening of May 27, 1905, in the gray, gloomy waters of Tsushima Strait in the Sea of Japan, the main battle force of the Imperial Japanese Navy met and annihilated a Russian fleet under the command of Admiral Zinovy Rozhestvensky. The Battle of Tsushima, as it came to be known in the West, was one of the most lopsided in the history of naval warfare. It drew comparison to the Battle of Trafalgar, the great British victory over Napoleon's navy that had been fought almost exactly a century earlier. Of the twelve battleships brought into action by the Russians, none escaped; four were captured and eight sent to the bottom. More than 4,000 Russian officers and seamen lost their lives; nearly 6,000 were taken prisoner. The Japanese fleet, under the command of the great Admiral Heihachiro Togo (crowned as "Japan's Nelson" in the Western press), lost only three small torpedo boats and suffered casualties of just 117 killed and 583 wounded.

The wipeout at Tsushima was the closing act of the Russo-Japanese War, a vast and bloody conflict that had raged for two years across Korea and Manchuria and on the adjoining seas. At the time, it was one of the largest and most destructive wars that had ever been fought, involving the clash of armies numbering in the hundreds of thousands. It was the first major war of the twentieth century, the first to be fought by armies equipped with advanced machine guns and modern artillery, dug into long trench lines and supplied by rail transportation on a large scale. In all those respects it foreshadowed the First World War.

It was a war no one had expected Japan to win. Tsar Nicholas's Russia was a major imperial power with three times Japan's population and fifty times its territory. Japan was a remote and enigmatic East Asian island-state that had remained aloof from the rest of the world until the 1850s. The Japanese infantryman was physically smaller than his Russian counterpart and not as well equipped, but he fought with skill and tenacity, had greater self-sufficiency and initiative, marched faster, showed greater endurance in unforgiving conditions, and appeared to possess an almost preternatural lack of fear. At the great battle for Mukden in February and March 1905, the Japanese troops stormed the Russian trenches in unrelenting waves, and the Russians were aghast at the sight of their foes charging across the field with bayonets fixed and beatific smiles on their faces, as if elated by the chance of a noble death. For the first time in the modern era, since perhaps the Battle of Poitiers in 732, an Eastern power had triumphed over a Western one.

Japan's two-generation rise from feudal and pre-industrial origins to the status of a major economic and military power was more than remarkable—it was (and remains) unprecedented in the entire course of human history. The Meiji Restoration was always a bit of a misnomer, in that there had been an unbroken line of emperors prior to their "restoration," and even after the fact the emperor did not wield supreme power. But there was something appealing in the notion that the Japanese were reaching back to find something essential in their national headwaters, rather than merely conforming to the ways of the West. The real shift in political power was to an urban merchant class and to a handful of powerful samurai clans from the Satsuma and Choshu provinces of southwest Japan. They provided the governing elites, who recognized (with impressive foresight) that Japan would fumble away its independence unless it could build up national institutions and industries capable of resisting the encroaching power of the West. The samurai leaders of the Meiji period hung up their swords and stepped comfortably into the roles of administrators, bureaucrats, political leaders, and visionaries; they instituted reforms from the top down, using strong, centralized government institutions to carry out their program. They bought off the feudal grandees with rich pensions and left the traditional hierarchies largely intact. Political parties emerged but often ran up against countermeasures aimed at curbing their power and influence. The Japanese people cast votes to elect representatives of the Diet, or parliament—but the legislature never grew powerful enough to confront the supreme power of the bureaucracy. There was never, in any sense, civilian control of the military, which remained supreme in both name and fact, and enjoyed a special direct advisory relationship with the throne.

Most striking to Western observers of the Russo-Japanese War, Japan's armed forces on both land and sea had behaved with qualities of grace and humanity that put the Russians to shame. The "Imperial Rescript to Soldiers and Sailors," issued by the Meiji emperor in 1882, had peremptorily forbid-

den atrocities against civilians or prisoners. "If you affect valor and act with
violence," Meiji had warned, "the world will in the end detest you and look
upon you as wild beasts. Of this you should take heed." Twenty years later,
Japanese soldiers and sailors were still taking heed. Western war correspondents' reports were replete with examples of the kindness shown by Japanese
soldiers and sailors to prisoners of war, who were given plenty of good food,
medical care, clean clothes, cigarettes, Russian books and newspapers, even
wine. At sea, the Japanese fleet flew their ensigns at half-mast to observe
the death of a Russian admiral. Admiral Togo personally visited wounded
Russian prisoners, and General Maresuke Nogi paid his respects in person
to a memorial to Russian dead in Port Arthur. Only about 1 percent of Russian prisoners died in Japanese captivity, and all were buried with painstaking attention to military honors. The Japanese Red Cross mounted a relief
effort that fed and cared for tens of thousands of displaced Korean and Chinese civilians in the war zone. Many had fled from territory occupied by the
Russian army, where looting, rape, murder, and mayhem had gone largely
unpunished. By contrast, the Japanese army did not tolerate such crimes
and punished offenders in its ranks with the utmost severity.

That Japan had beaten a European army in the field was surprising. That
it had crushed a European navy at sea was astounding. That it had behaved
with greater chivalry than Russia was dumbfounding, because it upended
the Western premise that the East was a barbarous place populated by barbarous people. As the editors of the *Illustrated London News* put it on January 14, 1905: "Europe has not recovered from the shock of finding out that
the Japanese are a great people."

Roosevelt was pleased by the Japanese triumph. For years he had been
personally fascinated with Japan and all things Japanese. "The Japs interest me and I like them," he told Cecil Spring-Rice, a British diplomat who
was the president's close friend. In his autobiography he wrote, "I believe in
them; I respect their great qualities; I wish that our American people had
many of these qualities." During his presidency, Roosevelt read deeply in
Japanese history, literature, and philosophy. He especially admired *Bushido:
The Soul of Japan*, a book written by Inazo Nitobe, a Japanese educator
and diplomat: the president purchased sixty copies and distributed them
to friends and colleagues. When he read Admiral Togo's message to the
Japanese fleet after its victory at Tsushima, Roosevelt was moved to tears
and ordered that it be distributed to every ship and station in the Ameri-

can navy. He maintained a close friendship and correspondence with his old Harvard schoolmate, Kentaro Kaneko, who spoke English fluently and had made it his life's work to promote Japanese culture in America and American culture in Japan. In 1904, Roosevelt began training in *judo* under the grandmaster *sensei* Yoshiaki Yamashita. The president enlisted a dozen members of his entourage as fellow students, and during twice-weekly training sessions the White House hallways rang with the sounds of men grunting and hurling each other to the floor. "My right ankle and left wrist and one thumb and both great toes are swollen sufficiently to more or less impair their usefulness, and I am well mottled with bruises elsewhere," Roosevelt wrote his son in March 1905. "Still I have made good progress, and since you have left [Yamashita] has taught me three new throws that are perfect corkers."

As a historian, Roosevelt saw in Japan a vindication of one of his favorite theories: that certain "races" were endowed with superior "fighting stock." Such peoples were destined to dominate their neighbors, vanquish their enemies, spread their language, religion, and culture beyond their borders, and advance the cause of civilization through achievements in commerce, science, and the arts. It had been true of the ancient Greeks and Romans, and later the Goths. It had been true in subsequent centuries of the Spanish, the French, the Dutch, and the British. More recently it was true of the Germans, the Americans, and the Japanese. But no other nation, Roosevelt believed, had ascended as rapidly or as dramatically as Japan. Since Commodore Perry's black ships had sailed into Tokyo Bay half a century earlier, he said, "the growth of Japan has been literally astounding. There is not only nothing to parallel it, but nothing to approach it in the history of civilized mankind."

Mahan was no less taken aback by Togo's victory. It was an event, he wrote, that had "fairly startled the world." Mahan was one of a handful of Westerners who had personally witnessed the turmoil of the Meiji Restoration. He had first visited the country in 1867, as a twenty-eight-year-old lieutenant commander on the USS *Iroquois*. While the ship was anchored off Kobe, a pair of samurai sought refuge there from enemies on shore. Mahan was impressed by their intense, martial bearing and obvious physical strength—he observed that they were "as thick almost as blackberries"—but they were also helpless landsmen, incapable of keeping their feet in the boat that brought them out to the anchorage. Thirty-eight years later, on hearing the news of Tsushima, Mahan was reminded of the sight of those dispossessed swordsmen as they had stood on the deck of the *Iroquois*, "cold, wet, and shivering," and he marveled at the rise of Japan. "Were not our shaking morning visitors of the same blood, the same tradition, and only one generation in time removed from the soldiers and seamen of the late war?"

After Tsushima, both combatants in the Russo-Japanese War had good reasons to seek an end to hostilities. Russia was on the verge of revolution, and Tsar Nicholas was forced to keep his best troops near St. Petersburg to suppress a general uprising. Japan had financed the war with foreign borrowing, but its ongoing deficits were vast and unsustainable, and bankers in London and New York were shutting off the spigots. When Roosevelt offered to mediate peace talks in Portsmouth, New Hampshire, both sides readily agreed. After prolonged, angst-ridden negotiations, the Russians agreed to sign over leasehold rights to Port Arthur, cede the southern half of Sakhalin Island, withdraw their troops from Manchuria, and acquiesce in Japanese domination of Korea—but they flatly refused to pay a war indemnity, which the Japanese had earlier demanded as a sine qua non. Moved by a personal appeal from Roosevelt, and keen to avoid a collapse in the talks, the Japanese negotiators at last dropped their demand for an indemnity, and the Treaty of Portsmouth was signed on September 5, 1905.

The treaty was a triumph of American diplomacy, and Roosevelt would be rewarded with the Nobel Peace Prize in 1906. But when the transpacific telegraph cable carried the news to Tokyo, hours after the signing, the Japanese people exploded in rage and incredulity. Having rejoiced at the sweeping victories of their army and navy, and fallen under the sway of an inflammatory press, public opinion had anticipated a fat war indemnity and the annexation of all of Sakhalin Island. Learning that they would have no indemnity, and only half of Sakhalin, many Japanese supposed the Western imperial powers had closed ranks to deny them their hard-won spoils of war. In Tokyo, the American legation was attacked and set on fire by rioters carrying Japanese flags draped in black crepe. Thirteen Christian churches were vandalized, looted, or burned to the ground. There were public calls for the assassination of the Japanese envoys who had signed the treaty, and in Hibiya Park, crowds marched behind brass bands, chanting: "The war must go on!" Armed mobs charged and trampled police barriers; police stations were attacked and occupied; hundreds were arrested.

When the riots came to an end two days later, a thousand people had been wounded or killed.

The violent public reaction fit a pattern that would continue until 1941. Western diplomacy was suspected as an elaborate conspiracy to encircle, suppress, and persecute Japan. International treaties were scrutinized obsessively, not only by governing elites but in the press and among citizens at large. The Japanese people received little candid or useful information about the world beyond their shores. There was a tendency to go hard on the diplomats, men who had traveled widely, learned foreign languages, and affected Western dress and manners—they were distrusted as a fifth column, as men who had fallen under insidious foreign pressures and were no longer authentically Japanese. Nowhere in the Tokyo newspapers was it reported that Russia was moving reinforcements into Manchuria and was evidently willing to fight on rather than meet the terms demanded, or that Japan was tottering on the verge of national bankruptcy. Truthful appraisals of Japan's limitations were rarely aired in public, and that was another part of the tragic pattern that would lead to the Second World War.

Unpopular as it was, the treaty won ratification in Tokyo, and the whole imbroglio might have blown over quickly if a second provocation had not burst into the headlines the following year. It occurred in San Francisco, California, in the aftermath of the devastating earthquake and fire of April 1906, which killed some 3,000 people and left the city a charred and rubbled wasteland. Two weeks after the holocaust the School Board decreed that ethnic Japanese students would be forced into a segregated school, so that white children "should not be placed in any position where their youthful impressions may be affected by association with pupils of the Mongoloid race." Henceforth, Japanese children residing throughout the stricken city would be forced to make their way through streets still littered with smoking wreckage and swarming with hooligans to an "Asians-only" school in Chinatown.

It was the latest affront in a long campaign of persecution against California's immigrant Japanese. The movement had been ginned up by local and state politicians, union bosses, and the fiercely nativist press—most infamously, by the *San Francisco Chronicle*, which seized on the issue to gain an edge in its cutthroat circulation battle with its archrival, the *Examiner*. The *Chronicle's* editorial pages returned to the subject almost daily, shouting (for example) that "The danger to American institutions from the flood of Japs must be apparent to every thinking man." "Brown men," it warned, were "an evil in the public schools," and a "menace to American women." A headline on March 1, 1905, read: "Unclean Practices of Orient Bringing Degradation and Debasement in the Train of Unrestricted Immigration." An editorial four days later: "Japan sent us not her fittest, but her unfittest; she has sent us the scum that has collected up on the surface of the boiling waters of her new national life, the human waste material for which she herself can find no use."

Post-earthquake San Francisco was a desperate and lawless place, in which local authorities could do little to stop a surge of looting, robbery, armed thuggery, and mob violence. San Francisco's Japantown (*Nihonjin-machi*) had been devastated in the earthquake, and thousands of homeless refugees were forced to spread out into adjacent neighborhoods in search of shelter, bringing them into collision with hostile whites who had also been burned out of their homes. City officials and the police were suspected of tacitly encouraging an anti-Japanese pogrom. Japanese were chased and beaten in the streets; rocks were thrown through the windows of their homes; and Japanese-owned businesses were plastered with signs warning, "White men and women: Patronize your own race."

Japan had donated $246,000 in disaster relief for the stricken city, exceeding the combined relief pledges of every other nation in the world. When a prominent Japanese seismologist arrived from Tokyo to lend his expertise to the rebuilding effort, he was waylaid in the streets and beaten by a mob.

Events in San Francisco received headline coverage in the Tokyo press, and some of the more flamboyant broadsheets called for the recently victorious Japanese navy to stage a rescue mission. "It will be easy work to awake the United States from her dream of obstinacy when one of our great Admirals appears suddenly on the other side of the Pacific," the *Hochi Shinbun* declared on October 22, 1906; "We should be ready to strike the Devil's head with an iron hammer for the sake of the world's civilization." The government of Japan lodged angry protests with the Roosevelt administration, claiming that the measures enacted in California were a breach of the Japanese-American treaty of 1894. Secretary of State Elihu Root suspected that Japan had held secret talks with the government of Colombia to establish a base on the South American mainland. A *New York Sun* correspondent based in Tokyo told his editors that Japanese public opinion was not easily aroused by events so far from home, "but the exclusion of Japanese children from the public schools of California cuts this child-loving nation to the quick."

President Roosevelt was disgusted, not only because the Californians had embarrassed the nation by their troglodytic behavior, but because most of the state's representatives in Congress had opposed the president's naval buildup. As the president saw it, the state's leaders were foolishly provoking Japan "while at the same time refusing to take steps to defend themselves against the formidable foe whom they are ready with such careless insolence to antagonize." Roosevelt sent a cabinet member to San Francisco with hopes of persuading the School Board to reverse its decision. When the overture was spurned, *Harper's Weekly* published a cartoon on its cover depicting the city of San Francisco as a mischievous-looking boy with a slingshot, and suggested that Japan should open a school of manners for white Californians. "The feeling on the Pacific slope," the president wrote Lodge, "is as foolish as if conceived by the mind of a Hottentot."

In a fervently worded passage of more than 1,200 words in his Annual Message to Congress, Roosevelt denounced the segregation order as a "wicked absurdity" enacted by a "small body of wrongdoers." The Japanese, he declared, "have won in a single generation the right to stand abreast of the foremost and most enlightened peoples of Europe and America; they have won on their own merits and by their own exertions the right to treatment on a basis of full and frank equality." He added: "We have as much to learn from Japan as Japan has to learn from us; and no nation is fit to teach unless it is also willing to learn."

The president's dogged diplomacy led to the "Gentlemen's Agreement" of 1908, in which the San Franciscans agreed to rescind the segregation order in exchange for a Japanese promise to limit emigration of its citizens to the United States. But negotiations took place amid a series of sensational war scares. Digging was proceeding at a furious pace in Panama, but the canal would not be completed until 1914: in the meantime the main fleet of the U.S. Navy could reach San Francisco only by a grueling 13,000-mile journey around Cape Horn. The Japanese fleet at Yokohama lay just half that distance away. Would it strike now, when the canal was unfinished and the American navy powerless to intervene? Rumors flourished, especially in the newspapers of William Randolph Hearst—a Japanese fleet had been sighted offshore; a secret Japanese base was under construction in the Aleutians; Japanese envoys were seeking a hostile alliance with Mexico; local Japanese women had been enlisted as "breeding machines" in a slow but sure demographic conquest, so that their offspring would eventually engulf the region. Dime store novels imagined the "Yellow Peril," a lurid scenario in which Asian hordes descended on the west coast and pushed the whites east of the Rockies.

Roosevelt had done his best to defuse the crisis, and his efforts had not been entirely unsuccessful, but there was no doubt in his mind that Japan posed a threat. "I had been doing my best to be polite to the Japanese," he later wrote, "and had finally become uncomfortably conscious of a very, very slight undertone of veiled truculence in their communications in connection with things that happened on the Pacific Slope; and I finally made up my mind that they thought I was afraid of them." More than the security of California was at stake. Hawaii was not much closer to North America than it was to Japan, and it was home to a large and growing community of immigrant Japanese. Guam was unfortified and defenseless, lying 5,800 miles from San Francisco and a quarter of that distance from Japan. The Philippines, an archipelago of some 7,000 islands with a combined coastline as long as that of the entire United States, lay right on Japan's southern doorstep. The Japanese navy could easily blockade Manila, wipe out the feeble U.S. Asiatic Fleet stationed there, and land an invasion force at any one of a thousand beachheads on the main island of Luzon. "The Philippines form our heel of Achilles," Roosevelt told War Secretary William Howard Taft in August 1907, and the analogy was fitting: every candid strategic-military study concluded that the islands would quickly fall to a determined Japanese naval-amphibious attack.

Confounded by the various complications and contradictions, and hoping to keep a lid on the Japanese crisis until the work in Panama was completed, Roosevelt devised a plan to send the main U.S. battle fleet on a goodwill tour around the world. If a war broke out with Japan, he told Lodge, the navy "would have a good deal to find out in the way of sending the fleet to the Pacific." A practice run would allow the navy to discover "all failures, blunders, and shortcomings in time of peace and not in time of war." The Great White Fleet (so-called because the ships were painted white) would comprise sixteen battleships and a large number of auxiliary vessels, manned by about 18,000 men. It was a technically and logistically demanding exercise, and it was also unprecedented—no nation had ever dispatched its entire navy to circumnavigate the globe.

On December 16, 1907, the fleet departed from Hampton Roads with crews manning the rails and bands striking up tunes, and fired a 21-gun salute in honor of Roosevelt, who watched from the presidential yacht, the *Mayflower*. "Did you ever see such a fleet?" Roosevelt asked. "Isn't it magnificent? Oughtn't we all feel proud?" The long line of ships stretched for seven miles across the sea. They rounded Cape Horn and touched at several ports of call in the Pacific, including Yokohama, Japan. In Tokyo, the American officers were received by the emperor at the Imperial Palace. In a voyage of fourteen months, the fleet touched at six continents, returning by the Suez Canal and the Mediterranean. In an American newspaper cartoon, one of the battleships was done up as a likeness of Roosevelt himself. The president's face was represented as her bow, with the brim of his Rough Rider's hat as her foredeck; his open mouth was swallowing the advancing sea. The fleet returned from its 46,000-mile voyage in the days just before Roosevelt left office. Again he watched from the deck of the *Mayflower*, and again he received 21 guns from each ship. In his speech, given afterward on the flagship, he congratulated the officers and men: "This is the first battle fleet that has ever circumnavigated the globe. Those who perform the feat again can but follow in your footsteps." The cruise of the White Fleet, said Roosevelt, demonstrated that "the Pacific was as much our home waters as the Atlantic."

IN JANUARY 1914, the first ship passed through the Panama Canal. In July of that year, Europe plunged into the Great War. In December, Alfred Thayer Mahan died in his bed, aged seventy-four.

The future U.S. admirals of the Pacific War had reached their late twenties and early thirties. They had risen to the rank of lieutenant or lieutenant commander. Having already been marked as officers destined for high command, they were sent off to the Naval War College in Newport, where they would study, debate, and plan for prospective future naval wars. Scenarios were played out on tabletop game boards, with model ships to represent the contending fleets and throws of the dice to decide the fortunes of battle. The place was said to be haunted by the ghost of Mahan, and the games assumed that the forthcoming war would climax in a clash of battleships in the western Pacific, in one of Mahan's archetypal "decisive battles."

"War Plan Orange," the American playbook for a war in the Pacific, envisioned that "Orange" (code name for Japan) would strike suddenly and with devastating success, overrunning the Philippines, Guam, and possibly Hawaii. The small U.S. Asiatic Fleet, based at Subic Bay in the Philippines, would destroy its shore facilities and all supplies it could not carry away, and flee to safer waters. Within a week of the war's breaking out, the main battle force of the U.S. Navy, probably stationed on the east coast, would raise steam and put to sea in a grand odyssey of conquest and liberation. Passing through the Panama Canal, it would push on across the interminable wastes of the central Pacific, occasionally anchoring in the lagoons of desolate atolls to replenish fuel and provisions. Arriving months later in the western Pacific, the fleet would hunt down and annihilate the main battle fleet of the Japanese navy. The victorious American fleet would blockade Japan's home islands and throttle its trade, forcing capitulation.

The flaws in the plan were plain to see. Roosevelt's White Fleet had proven only that a fleet of battleships could sail around the world in a peaceable goodwill tour. To repeat the performance in wartime, in hopes of vanquishing the formidable Japanese fleet in its home waters, was a different prospect. Under optimal conditions, a battleship of that era might sustain a long-distance cruising speed of 10 or 12 knots. A chain of well-stocked and properly defended fuel stations would have to be maintained along the way. As the weeks at sea wore on, wear and tear would accumulate and crew efficiency and morale could be expected to deteriorate. Drawing closer to the war zone, the fleet would need to remain hypervigilant to the danger of surprise attack. At any moment, with little or no warning, the officers and men might be called upon to fight and win the all-determining battle for which they had traveled so far. They would be pitted against an enemy fleet that had been biding its time, lying in wait within easy reach of its major bases, with officers and crew rested and ready and ships in good repair. War Plan Orange seemed to recap the dismal career of the Russian fleet under Admiral Rozhestvensky in 1905, and who could say with confidence that the result would not be the same?

Only a handful of iconoclasts guessed that airplanes and submarines would rewrite all the rules of naval warfare, that by the late 1930s battleships would be worse than useless (because of the money and manpower they diverted), and that Mahan's three dogmas were sinking rapidly into obsolescence. The First World War revealed glimpses of the future. The German U-boats proved that submarines could menace seaborne supply lines. The war in Europe hinted at the possibilities of airpower, and by the end of the war the British had demonstrated that airplanes could take off from and land on ships. Jutland, the largest naval battle of the conflict, neither bore out Mahan's doctrines nor completely refuted them. But none of the lessons of the First World War could break the power of the battleship cult, whose acolytes dominated the ranks of all the world's major navies until the opening salvos of the next war.

TEDDY ROOSEVELT, failing to reclaim the presidency on the third-party Bull Moose ticket in 1912, entered his political afterlife as a writer, speechmaker, and crusader on behalf of his favorite causes. As always, he preached that friendly and peaceable relations with Japan should be "one of the cardinal principles of our foreign policy." He returned to the same nostrums he had prescribed since the California schools crisis in 1906—to lavish courtesy and flattery on the Japanese, in hopes of soothing their delicate sense of national honor; to avoid senseless provocations, both in California and in Asia; and to remain prepared, at all times and at the drop of a hat, to send the main battle fleet of the U.S. Navy to the western Pacific. Roosevelt also continued to suspect the Japanese were "bent upon establishing themselves as the leading power in the Pacific." War might yet be inevitable, but American foreign policy should be aimed at postponing the day of reckoning as long as possible. The Philippines were largely indefensible, and would remain so even if Congress could somehow be persuaded to pour tens of millions of dollars into their defense. The only hope of forestalling Japanese aggression was a credible naval deterrent. Roosevelt returned again and again, with stridency verging on apoplexy, to the theme of "naval preparedness." It was one of his favorite watchwords, a term he coined—"preparedness"—and he hammered it home in speeches, letters, and articles. The navy was the nation's right arm, he wrote in the *New York Times*, and "woe to our country if we permit that right arm to become palsied or even to become flabby and inefficient." Americans, if they failed to prepare for war, would have a "bitter awakening; and if ever that bitter awakening comes, I trust our people will remember the foolish philanthropists and the recreant congressmen and other public servants at whose doors the responsibility will lie."

As Woodrow Wilson took office in 1913, he named to the post of assistant secretary of the navy a thirty-one-year-old former New York state senator named Franklin Delano Roosevelt. Franklin was Theodore Roosevelt's fifth cousin, and had married the latter's niece, Eleanor. (TR had given the bride away at their wedding in 1905.) Though FDR was a Democrat, and would be working for a president who had just defeated TR in a national election, he was also a dyed-in-the-wool navalist and a disciple of Mahan. On his fifteenth birthday, in fact, Franklin had received from Theodore a gift-wrapped copy of *The Influence of Sea Power Upon History*. According to FDR's mother, the boy had "practically memorized the book." FDR would run the day-to-day operations of the navy during his stint in office, as TR had done when he held the same post in the McKinley administration.

In May 1913, TR wrote to congratulate the younger man on his appointment, and also to offer unsolicited guidance. Never permit the fleet to be divided between the Pacific and the Atlantic, he warned, and added: "I do not anticipate trouble with Japan, but it may come, and if it does it will come suddenly."

The words were prophetic but twenty-eight years too early. When the "bitter awakening" came, on a bright Hawaiian morning in 1941, it came more suddenly than all but the most ardent pessimists had imagined. FDR, having followed in TR's footsteps through the offices of assistant navy secretary and governor of New York, would be serving in his ninth year as president of the United States. In ironic fulfillment of Mahan's law of concentration, the battleships of the Pacific Fleet would be moored in a double file in the East Loch of Pearl Harbor, bow to stern and beam to beam, as neat as a team of horses harnessed to a stagecoach. But they would not be prepared.

Pacific Crucible

The Pacific, 1942

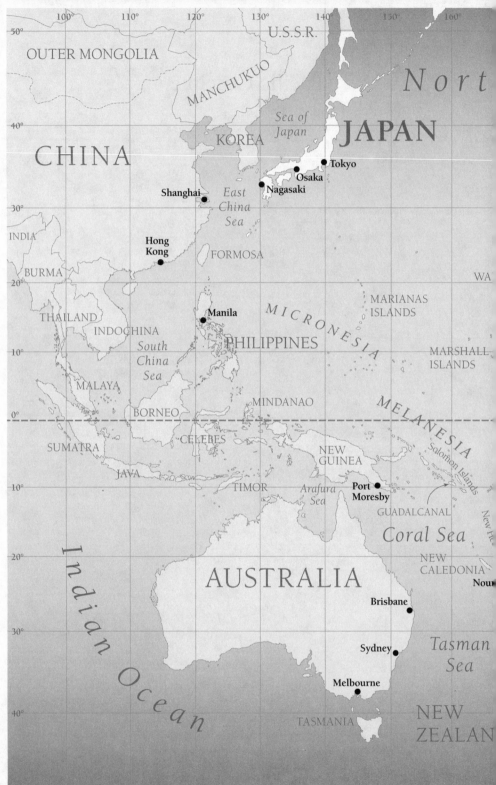

Chapter One

F OR THE INHABITANTS OF OAHU, THERE WAS NOTHING UNUSUAL IN
being jerked out of sleep by guns and bombs and low-flying aircraft.
The island was crowded with military bases, and live-firing drills were
commonplace. In early 1941, as the danger of war had seemed to grow, the
services took to conducting "simulated combat exercises"—mock battles
pitting the army against the navy, the navy against the marines, the
marines against the army. On these days, a colossal amount of ammunition
was thrown up into the air, and the island's lightly built wood-frame houses
would shake and rattle as if an earthquake had struck. So when the familiar
racket started up, at a little before eight in the morning on that first Sunday
in December 1941, most of the residents pulled a pillow over their heads, or
turned back to their coffee and comic strips and radio programs, and tried
to ignore the deep concussive thuds of distant bombs, the heavy booming of
antiaircraft batteries, and the faint *rat-a-tat-tat* of machine guns.

But it was soon clear that these were no ordinary exercises. Floors shook,
windows rattled, airplanes roared low overhead, and empty machine-gun
casings fell on rooftops like hail. In Honolulu, civilians emerged from their
homes, many still wearing pajamas and nightshirts. Explosions could be
heard in the city, and smoke rose above King Street in the McCully district.
Sirens blared, and to the west, above Pearl Harbor and Hickam Field, a gigantic pall of oily black smoke boiled thousands of feet into the sky. Looking up,
observers on the ground could see a small armada of dive-bombers circling
at high altitude in lazy figure-eight patterns. Every so often, a group of the
aircraft would coalesce into an orderly attack formation; and then individual
planes would peel off, one by one, to begin their dive-bombing runs.

The spectators were impressed: the flyboys were putting on a terrific show. Twelve-year-old Dan Kong, still in his pajamas, remarked to his brother, "Wow, spectacular maneuvers." The two climbed an avocado tree in their family's backyard for a better view. "I had to admit it was very realistic," another civilian witness recalled. A sailor at Pearl Harbor pronounced it "the best goddamn drill the Army Air Force has ever put on!" The heavy smoke over Pearl Harbor was thought to be "smoke bombs"—or perhaps, as Honolulu mayor Lester Petrie supposed, a "practice smoke screen . . . I thought that was a perfect demonstration."

At four minutes past eight, KGMB interrupted its regular Sunday morning radio broadcast of organ music carried live from the First Baptist Church of Waikiki. The announcer, Webley Edwards, read a brief statement recalling all military personnel to their bases and stations. Normal programming then resumed, but new interruptions followed every few minutes, with announcements calling firemen, doctors, rescue workers, and disaster wardens to work. At 8:40 a.m., Edwards came back on the air: "We interrupt this broadcast to bring you this important news. Please pay attention. The island is under attack. I repeat, the island is under attack by hostile forces." Skeptical listeners refused to take the news seriously, assuming that the announcement was another element of an unusually vivid practice alert. Some recalled the panic caused by Orson Welles's fictional *War of the Worlds* broadcast three years earlier. Shortly before nine, Edwards returned to the air. In a quavering voice he pleaded with his listeners to believe him: "This is no maneuver. Japanese forces are attacking the island. This is the real McCoy!"

Even seasoned military men found it difficult to believe what they were seeing, and admitted to feeling bewildered and disorientated as the attack unfolded. The notion that an actual raid was underway was slow to enter their minds. In the eyewitness accounts, that pattern of belated comprehension is repeated again and again. A plane approaches. ("Why are those planes flying so low?") American ground-based antiaircraft guns fire at the intruder. ("Why are the boys shooting at that plane?") A bomb drops. ("What a stupid, careless pilot, not to have secured his releasing gear.") It explodes. ("Somebody goofed big this time. They loaded live bombs on those planes by mistake.") As the plane turns upward, the Japanese "Rising Sun" insignia comes into view on the underside of the wings. ("My God! They're really going all-out! They've even painted the rising sun on that plane!") An American ship explodes. ("What kind of a drill is this?") Even then, some men refused to believe that a war had begun that morning—perhaps, as Commander A. L. Seton of the light cruiser *St. Louis* first guessed, the attacker was "a lone, berserk Japanese pilot who somehow had gotten to Pearl and now would be in trouble with his navy and ours."

On the street outside the YMCA in downtown Honolulu, sailors were piling into buses, jitneys, taxicabs, and private cars. Military trucks roared down the main thoroughfares, crammed with "armed soldiers wearing tin helmets, looking skyward." Fire trucks, rescue units, and policemen on motorcycles raced toward the fires burning in several parts of the city. Sirens screamed; rubber shrieked on pavement. No one observed the speed limits. On the two-lane blacktop highway to Pearl Harbor, recalled Lieutenant Commander Lawson Ramage, "every conceivable vehicle was loaded with sailors—buses, taxis, and everything else—rushing to get out there."

For many witnesses, the first direct confirmation that an actual attack was underway came as their vehicles were strafed by low-flying enemy planes. "We heard what sounded like the clicking of typewriter keys," said Seaman Larry Katz, who was sharing a cab with several other sailors. "I looked out the back window . . . and saw a plane coming down the highway with fire coming out of its wings or engine. It was tracer bullets coming down the highway at all the cars, including ours." Jack Lower, a civilian electrician, was riding with several other men in the back of an open truck. Each time a plane approached for a strafing run, the men pounded their fists on the roof of the cab, the driver stomped on the brakes, and the passengers dove into the roadside foliage for cover. As the aircraft passed, they clambered back into the truck and continued. Navy Lieutenant Clarence Dickinson recalled seeing sparks leap up from the pavement just ahead of the car in which he was riding as a passenger. Moments later, the car ahead was hit with a burst of 20mm cannon. "Suddenly from the shock of bullets that sedan rocked and was enveloped in a cloud of yellow dust," he wrote. "We watched the car careening and bumping crazily on empty tires . . . I had time to register an impression of small holes of rain-drop size along that car, like stitches."

By 8:10 a.m., just fifteen minutes after the first bombs and torpedoes had struck the ships lying in Pearl Harbor, the main battle force of the Pacific Fleet was crippled. Along the eastern shore of Ford Island, in the anchorage known as "Battleship Row," the battleships lay smashed, burning, and blackened, their masts and superstructures leaning over the harbor at 45-degree angles. So much thick black smoke was billowing out of the stricken ships that observers could barely tell which had been hit. The *California* was half-sunk, her keel resting on the bottom, her hull ripped open by Japanese torpedoes; the *West Virginia* was smashed and blazing, her paint charred and bubbling, with enormous volumes of smoke pouring from her stricken port side; the *Maryland* and the *Tennessee* were in better shape, but both ships were jammed against the mooring dolphins, immobilized and out of action. *Oklahoma*, hit by a barrage of torpedoes, had actually capsized, turning 150 degrees off the vertical, her long keel pointed up toward the sky.

The battleship *Arizona*'s forward magazine had detonated in "a mighty thunderclap of sound, deep and terrible," sending a ball of fire mushrooming into the sky to a height of several thousand feet. Seconds after the explosion, burning debris began raining down on the decks of nearby ships. It continued to fall for an improbably long time. "There were steel fragments in the air, fire, oil—God knows what all," Seaman Martin Matthews of the *Arizona* recalled, "pieces of timber, pieces of the boat deck, canvas, and even pieces of bodies. I remember lots of steel and bodies coming down. I saw a thigh and leg; I saw fingers; I saw hands; I saw elbows and arms." Much of the *Arizona* was simply gone—the ship had been turned inside out, as it were—and the surviving portion of the hull sank to the harbor floor, leaving only a portion of the superstructure and the muzzles of three guns from Turret Two showing above the surface. Her tower and cranes leaned steeply toward the channel, and dead men hung upside down from the ladders. The blast had killed more than 1,000 of the *Arizona*'s crew in an instant, and many of the survivors were so badly burned that their shipmates did not know how to help them. "These men were zombies, in essence," recalled Marine Private James Cory, who served aboard the *Arizona* and survived the attack. "They were burned completely white. Their skin was just as white as if you had taken a bucket of whitewash and painted it white. Their hair was burned off; their eyebrows were burned off. . . . They were moving like robots. Their arms were out, held away from their bodies, and they were stumping along the decks."

But for many who witnessed the events of December 7, 1941, the most unforgettable image of all was the sight of the enemy airplanes, diving out of the sky in such numbers that the morning had seemed to dim, as if a cloud had passed across the sun. Before that morning, Americans had been led to

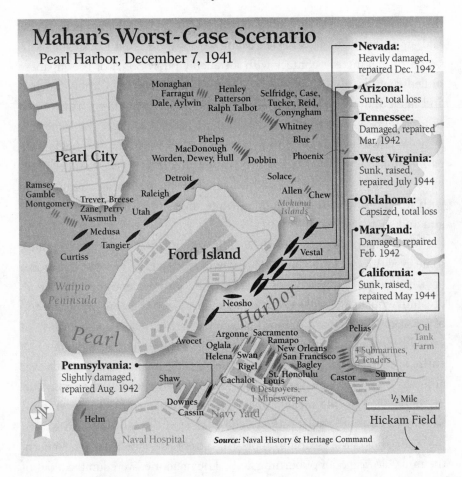

Mahan's Worst-Case Scenario
Pearl Harbor, December 7, 1941

Nevada:
Heavily damaged, repaired Dec. 1942

Arizona:
Sunk, total loss

Tennessee:
Damaged, repaired Mar. 1942

West Virginia:
Sunk, raised, repaired July 1944

Oklahoma:
Capsized, total loss

Maryland:
Damaged, repaired Feb. 1942

California:
Sunk, raised, repaired May 1944

Monaghan
Farragut
Dale, Aylwin
Henley
Patterson
Ralph Talbot
Selfridge, Case,
Tucker, Reid,
Conyngham
Whitney

Pearl City

Phelps
MacDonough
Worden, Dewey, Hull
Dobbin
Blue
Phoenix

Detroit
Solace
Ramsey
Gamble
Montgomery
Trever, Breese
Zane, Perry
Wasmuth
Utah
Raleigh
Allen
Chew
Mokunui Islands

Medusa
Tangier
Curtiss

Ford Island

Vestal

Waipio Peninsula

Neosho

Harbor

Pearl

Pelias
Oil Tank Farm

Argonne
Avocet
Oglala
Helena
Sacramento
Ramapo
New Orleans
San Francisco
Bagley
St. Honolulu
Louis
4 Submarines,
2 Tenders

Swan
Rigel
Cachalot
Castor
Sumner

Pennsylvania:
Slightly damaged, repaired Aug. 1942

Shaw

6 Destroyers,
1 Minesweeper

½ Mile

Downes
Cassin
Navy Yard
Helm

Naval Hospital
Source: Naval History & Heritage Command

Hickam Field

believe that Japanese naval airpower was a joke, an assortment of second-rate airplanes piloted by third-rate aviators. But these planes were handled brilliantly. The dive-bombers planted their bombs with pinpoint accuracy; the torpedo planes came in low and made textbook drops; the Zeros roared in on the tails of the bombers and made deadly strafing runs. If not for the carnage on the ground and in the harbor, the entire spectacle could have been an air show. Witnesses were amazed at how low the attackers flew—so low (as one person remarked) that you could have thrown a baseball and hit a Japanese airplane; so low that witnesses on the third floor of the Navy Yard Hospital looked *down* on the torpedo planes as they began their runs on the American battleships. The Japanese pilots were plainly visible in their cockpits, many with canopies open; witnesses could see their "cat's-eye" flight goggles, their windblown scarves, their brown aviators' helmets, their white headbands—"Hell, I could even see the gold in their teeth," said an army officer at Wheeler. Many witnesses recalled the strange sensation of making eye contact with an enemy pilot. Some of the Japanese smiled ruefully, almost apologetically; a few even waved. Others laughed and made taunting gestures. "They were so low you could see them grinning, you know," remarked machinist's mate Leon Bennett of the *Neosho*. "I mean, really, they were laughing, all smiles; they were having a field day, a ball." A marine reported seeing a rear-seat gunner "let go the handles of his gun, clasp his hands high above his head and shake them in that greeting with which American prize fighters salute their fans. Then he grabbed his gun and shot some more."

Watching the diving planes, the falling bombs, and the exploding ships, some eyewitnesses were reminded of newsreel footage of the war in Europe, or a big-budget Hollywood production. The entire scene had an unreal, dreamlike quality. "I still expect to awaken from a bad dream or see the end of a war movie," wrote Captain Elphege Gendreau, a fleet surgeon, several weeks afterward. Theodore Mason, seaman of the *California*, agreed: "The entire scene had the flickering two-dimensional quality of a B-grade war film." In many cases it was the non-visual senses that left the most lasting impression on the memory—the terrified screams of the men trapped belowdecks; how the steel rungs of the ladders in the burning ships seared into the palms of the escaping sailors; the bitter taste of fuel oil in the mouth; the rank, cloying odor of burning flesh. The memories were jumbled, out of sequence; but they were also vivid, indelible, even after the passage of many years. The terrible suddenness of the raid, the abrupt transition from peace to war, the immense scale of the carnage, the almost incomprehensible fury and malevolence of the attackers—"It was like being engulfed in a great flood, a tornado or earthquake," said Chief Petty Officer Charles Russell. "The thing hit so quickly and so powerfully it left you stunned and amazed." For Signalman John H. McGoran of the *California*, the experience of being at Pearl Harbor on December 7, 1941, was simply impossible to describe. "If you didn't go through it, there are no words that can adequately describe it; if you were there, then no words are necessary."

FRANKLIN DELANO ROOSEVELT had been passing a tranquil Sunday afternoon in his Oval Study on the second floor of the White House. Not to be confused with the larger and more formal Oval Office, located downstairs, the study was a part of the president's official residence; a set of double doors on the west side of the room led directly to his bedroom and private bath. In past presidential administrations, the study had been known as the "Yellow Room" or "Oval Parlor," and had been used variously as a sitting room, a library, and a place for the storage of unwanted furniture and files. President Harding had played poker here with his friends and cronies, and the Hoovers had used it as a screening room for silent films.

By December 1941, Roosevelt had occupied the study for nine years, and it had acquired a cluttered, lived-in, and slightly dingy appearance, much like his house at Hyde Park, in the Hudson River Valley of New York. Nearly every square inch of the walls was occupied with photographs and paintings of many different shapes, sizes, and themes. There were not enough bookcases to accommodate all of the president's books, so volumes were jammed horizontally above the rows on the shelves, or stacked on the floor against the walls and in the corners. Heavy drapes blocked the natural light from the windows, giving the room a gloomy aspect; but the darkness helped obscure the fraying corners of the upholstery, the threadbare patches in the carpet, and the black cords that snaked along the floor from the lamps to the wall sockets. The ashtray on the president's desk was often overflowing with spent butts, and the room smelled deeply of cigarettes. If the decor had any unifying theme at all, it was nautical. There were perhaps two dozen of Roosevelt's beloved collection of Currier & Ives prints, depicting wooden sailing ships at sea; there were half a dozen ship models on the tables and bookcases, protected under glass display cases; and on one of the walls, next to a picture of the president's own mother, hung a portrait of John Paul Jones, naval hero of the American Revolution.

For Roosevelt, the Oval Study was a refuge of sorts, his inner sanctum. Often he spent his entire day here, seated in his wheelchair, behind his desk, his back to the large south-facing windows with their view of the Ellipse and the Washington Monument. Much of the substantive work of his presidency was done at this desk. Here he read reports, dictated letters and memoranda, spoke on the telephone, and received aides and visitors. But this was also the room in which Roosevelt liked to relax, as he was doing on this particular Sunday afternoon. Dressed in an old gray turtleneck sweater and flannel slacks, he was tinkering with his stamp collection while carrying on a desultory chat "about things far removed from war" with his closest aide and good friend, Harry Hopkins. The two men had eaten lunch in the study, on trays. Earlier, the president had sent word that he would be unable to join First Lady Eleanor Roosevelt and about thirty guests at a luncheon in the Blue Room. Eleanor would subsequently tell the disappointed visitors (a mixed group of friends, relatives, and government officials) that her husband had been detained by the crisis unfolding in the Pacific, but that was not strictly true: Roosevelt had sent his regrets before the raid had even begun. He was tired and he wanted to relax. He would have no such luck.

The black telephone on his desk rang at 1:40 p.m. (Washington time). It was Secretary of the Navy Frank Knox, who advised Roosevelt that an alert had just been transmitted from Pacific Fleet headquarters: "Air raid Pearl Harbor. This is no drill." Knox could offer no further details, but promised to call back as soon as he knew more.

Hopkins was incredulous. Japan, he said, would not and could not attack Hawaii; the report must be wrong. Roosevelt did not agree—he said he believed the report was "probably true," and remarked that "it was just the kind of unexpected thing the Japanese would do."

Within minutes, Admiral Harold R. "Betty" Stark, the chief of naval operations, called to confirm the appalling news. Stark and Knox had been on the phone with Rear Admiral Claude C. Bloch, commandant of the Fourteenth Naval District in Hawaii, who had given them a real-time eye-witness account of the raid while the second wave of enemy planes was over the base. A few minutes later, the president took a call from Joseph B. Poindexter, the territorial governor of Hawaii, who requested and was granted authority to declare martial law in the islands. During this brief conversation, Poindexter's voice rose to a frantic pitch. The president turned to Hopkins and the other aides who had crowded into the study and exclaimed, "My God, there's another wave of Jap planes over Hawaii right this minute!"

The news passed quickly through the White House. Eleanor was told by one of the White House ushers just as she was seeing her luncheon party off. The visitors "stood around in stupefied knots," one later wrote; "—there was nothing to say—it was absolutely incredible. The guests seemed to melt away—nobody bothered to say goodbye to anyone." The first lady went upstairs and slipped into the president's study, but the room was already crowded with aides, and she soon realized that her husband "was concentrating on what had to be done and would not talk about what had happened until this first strain was over." She withdrew to her sitting room and went to work on her correspondence.

Throughout the afternoon, updates poured into the White House. Grace Tully, the president's chief secretary, took several calls from Admiral Stark. She made shorthand notes of what he told her, then quickly typed the information into memos and handed them to Roosevelt. "The Boss maintained greater outward calm than anybody else but there was rage in his very calmness," Tully wrote. "With each new message he shook his head grimly and tightened the expression of his mouth." A steady stream of aides was entering the study, and soon the din of loud voices made it impossible for her to work. She moved out to the hallway, and then to the private telephone in the president's bedroom. While she was typing, members of the staff hovered behind her and peered over her shoulder. She later wrote: "The news continued to come in, each report more terrible than the last, and I could hear the shocked unbelief in Admiral Stark's voice as he talked to me. At first the men around the president were incredulous; that changed to angry acceptance as new messages supported and amplified the previous ones."

Seated behind his desk at the center of the storm, Roosevelt remained calm and composed. He spent much of the afternoon on the telephone, attending to troop movements, dictating a news release for the press, setting up new security procedures for ports and strategic installations, ordering measures to observe or detain enemy nationals. Dozens of executive orders were required; Roosevelt told his aides to execute the orders immediately, and bring them to him for a signature later. One by one, the president's leading military and foreign policy advisers arrived in the study and took a seat—Secretary Knox, Admiral Stark, Secretary of War Henry Stimson, Secretary of State Cordell Hull, Army Chief of Staff General George C. Marshall. The president asked hard questions. How could the attack have succeeded? How bad was the damage? What were the Japanese likely to do next? It was still not clear what was happening in Hawaii. The radiotelephone connection to Oahu was lost several times, cut off in midsentence, and at one point there was a period of several hours in which no connection could be obtained. Were the air strikes continuing? Each new report suggested that the destruction was worse than previously believed.

As the meeting adjourned, about 4:30 p.m., it was agreed that the full cabinet would be summoned to meet at the White House at eight-thirty that evening, with the congressional leaders to follow at nine.

Many of the people around Roosevelt judged that he was, in a sense, relieved. The waiting and uncertainty were finished. The American people had been bitterly divided over the prospect of war, but now (as Secretary of War Stimson put it) "a crisis had come in a way that would unite our people." Eleanor agreed: "I thought that in spite of his anxiety Franklin was in a way more serene than he had appeared in a long time. I think it was steadying to know finally that the die was cast."

As the last of the Japanese aircraft headed back out to sea, the East Loch of Pearl Harbor was littered with flotsam of every description, much of it blackened by the flames: clothing, shoes, books, life vests, mattresses, accommodation ladders, lifeboats, barrels. There was an almost indescribably foul combination of odors—the oppressive fumes of fuel oil; the vast billowing clouds of black, acrid smoke; the sickly-sweet smell of charred flesh. Millions of gallons of oil had erupted into the harbor from the torpedoed battleships. "People who have never seen this at sea cannot imagine what oil is like once it is exposed to cool seawater," said Private Cory. "It becomes a globlike carpet about six inches thick, gelatinous." Sailors who leapt from the burning ships, or were blown off the decks by explosions, found themselves swimming through congealed oil. It was exhausting and dangerous. Seaman Mason of the *California* tried to swim beneath the surface, but when he came up for air, the "gummy black oil was clogging my nose and ears, burning under my eyelids. The rank, sweet taste of the stuff made me want to vomit."

The wind was blowing hard, about 25 knots; photographs taken that morning show flags flapping hard on their poles. Inevitably, the fires on the battleships, fanned by those powerful gusts, spread to the harbor. Survivors described a conflagration advancing toward them across the water, how it engulfed the heads of other men; the brief, agonized screams from behind the curtain of flames, and then silence. Even from a distance, the heat radiating from the vicinity of Battleship Row was almost unendurable, but motor launches and whaleboats plowed directly into the maelstrom in the attempt to rescue survivors. The crew of one boat tried to douse the fires using handheld CO_2 extinguishers: "Each time this was done the sides of the boat broke into flames, which had to be put out before the next run," said Lieutenant Ephraim P. Holmes. "The heat was so intense that the men in the boat had to lean way over the unexposed side to protect themselves." Swimmers found salvation in a boathook, as they were seized by the belt or collar and hauled into a boat. These rescued men were choking on oil, spitting oil, vomiting oil; many were so thoroughly drenched in oil that it was difficult to determine whether they had been wounded. "I remember one sailor that I pulled out of the water, and I took my handkerchief and wiped the oil from his face," said Marine Private Leslie Le Fan; "I couldn't tell if he was a black man or a white man or a Chinaman." They were laid in the bottom of the boats, said Seaman Ed Johann, until each boat "was loaded with the wounded, all pressed together, all in great pain."

At "Ten-Ten Dock," across the harbor from Ford Island, wounded men were lifted on stretchers from the boats. The scene was chaotic. Sailors and officers who had spent the night ashore pressed forward, hoping to find a boat that could take them back to their ships. Sirens screamed; medical corpsmen shouted to clear a way for the stretchers; dead and wounded men were laid in rows on the concrete pier. Private cars and ambulances were arriving in great numbers, immobilizing traffic. The wounded were administered a shot of morphine and offered a drink of water. Their faces were blackened by smoke or soot, their eyes almost smashed shut; some had lost all of their hair and much of their skin. It was necessary to strip the burn victims of their clothing, but oil-soaked fabric had seared into the flesh, and when it was removed, long ribbons of skin came off with it. "I was trying to put some petroleum jelly on them and trying to cover them with gauze," said Shipfitter third class Louis Grabinski of the *West Virginia*, who lent a hand with the wounded. "But that wasn't helping; it seemed to be taking their skin off. It seemed like it was better to just leave the skin open instead of putting something over it. They wanted to tear the gauze off, or if they had a skivvy shirt, they wanted to tear that goddamn thing off, because they were blistered, burnt."

Emergency treatment centers were set up in several locations throughout the Navy Yard and Ford Island, including the Marine Barracks, the Dispensary, and the Bachelor Officers Quarters (the "BOQ"). All were soon overwhelmed with casualties. At the Ford Island mess hall, wounded men were laid on all of the tables, and newly arriving stretchers had to be left on the patio outside. "Some of these men looked beyond help, burned flesh and

bone showing through the oily mess," said Seaman Victor Kamont. "Some of
these men were half clothed, raw meat just hanging from their bones. Some
cried like babies, babbling for their mother, father or loved ones. It was a sickening sight." Lightly wounded men were wandering around in a daze, refusing to respond when spoken to, resisting violently when others tried to lead
them into the centers for treatment; there were men who were completely
naked but seemed unaware of their nakedness, even in the presence of civilian women or Red Cross nurses. Carl Carlson, a sailor who was fortunate
to escape from the *Arizona* with minor wounds, recalled meeting one of his
shipmates in the sick bay at Ford Island. The man was "laying across from
me . . . and he was holding his intestines in with his hands. And he looked
up at me, and he said, 'War sure is hell, isn't it, shipmate?' and I said, 'Yeah,
it is.' And I wasn't bleeding anywhere so I got up and walked out of there."

On the docks and landings, the dead were being laid in two rows, with
a walkway down the center. The heads in each row pointed inward, so that
the bodies could be identified, either by their faces or their dog tags. Some of
the dead men's faces had an unnaturally dark pallor, but their bodies showed
no visible wounds: that indicated that they had been killed by the concussive force of one of the huge explosions, shattering the blood vessels without
breaking the skin. Seaman Nick Kouretas of the USS *Raleigh* spent several
hours searching for his brother: "I would run along the aisle and, knowing
my brother's characteristics, look for him. He chewed his nails. I knew where
he had a wart; I knew every little mark on his body. I would get so far, and
I'd say: 'Well, this guy looks like him,' but I couldn't see a face. I'd pick up the
hand, and I'd say: 'No, that's not him,' and then go on." Eventually, sheets
or blankets were brought to cover the bodies. "I'll tell you one thing," said
Seaman William Fomby of the *Oklahoma*. "When you see all these people in
bed sheets laying out stacked up like cordwood, it takes all the glamour out
of war. You really realize that something bad is going on."

The Ford Island airfield was a ghastly sculpture garden of twisted, burning clots of aluminum wreckage, the remains of aircraft wiped out on the
ground. Thirty-three out of seventy planes had been destroyed in the raid.
At the southeast end of the island, Hangar Six lay gutted and smoking: it
had been struck by at least three Japanese bombs. On the seaplane ramp,
the strafed and burning fragments of the big PBY Catalina seaplanes were
scattered among the ubiquitous palm trees. Concrete surfaces throughout
the island were littered with shrapnel and pocked with large craters, each

marking the spot where a 550-pound bomb had landed. Sailors who had been ordered to abandon their ships were milling around in confusion, their uniforms smeared with blood and oil. "There was a lot of us there in limbo, just standing around," Seaman Elmo Rash remembered. "I started thinking about everything that had happened, and I started to shake. I walked around for a while until I was feeling better." Men were in various states of undress, and some plundered the abandoned barracks and dependents' housing for clothing. There were reports of men wearing bizarre get-ups: a sailor's cap and a lieutenant's dress blue jacket; a tuxedo with bare feet; a bathrobe and boots; seaman's dungarees with a swallow-tailed coat and a "fore and aft" admiral's hat. Gangs of sailors roamed the island, bandoliers of ammunition slung over their shoulders, like bandits in a western film. In the Ford Island administrative building, said Bosun's Mate Howard French, "There was mass confusion. . . . There was no order, no control, no authority. People were milling around like so many lost sheep."

The Marine Barracks, a massive concrete building in the Navy Yard, was hastily converted into a receiving and billeting center for these itinerant sailors. Men who had crawled out of the harbor were instructed to strip off their oil-soaked clothing and place it in garbage cans, and then stand in line for a hot shower. In many cases, the sludge oil had penetrated so deeply into the men's pores that it was nearly impossible to get clean. "You wiped off as much as you could with towels and whatever rags you could find, but there was no way in the world to get it all off," said Seaman Jim Lawson of the *Arizona*. Soap and water did not do the trick—it was necessary to scrub the oil-stained skin with alcohol or gasoline. Some men went so far as to actually bathe in gasoline; but even those who managed to remove the visible stains complained for weeks afterward that they were coated head to foot in a thin film of oil, that their eyes smarted from the gasoline, or that they were plagued by intense headaches and blurred vision.

The marine quartermaster sergeant issued clean, dry dungarees, underwear, socks, a toothbrush, toothpaste, a razor, and a ditty bag to any man who needed them. Paperwork was ignored; no one was required to sign for anything. The marine mess sergeant did his best to feed any hungry sailor who walked into the mess hall, and the chow line was continuous, with men lining up for lunch behind others still waiting for breakfast. It was feared that the drinking water may have been poisoned by saboteurs, so men drank beer, soft drinks, Kool-Aid, and water drawn from swimming pools. One sailor remembered that he and his mates were grateful to be served "dry sandwiches and coffee made from chlorinated swimming pool water. We were hungry so it was delicious."

A check-in station for sailors was set up on the first floor of the Marine Barracks. The name of each abandoned ship was stenciled on the wall behind a table staffed by a junior officer. Sailors and officers checked in and were told to wait for reassignment. Many were ordered to join cleanup details on the ships and around the base. On Ford Island, teams of sailors removed debris from the hangars and pushed wrecked aircraft off the runways. Others carried fire extinguishers and put out dozens of small brush fires that had sprung up in the grasslands around the airfield. Men were given buckets and ordered to pick up shrapnel and scrap metal. There was so much shrapnel on the ground that "you could walk out on the parking lot and scoop it up with your hands." The public works staff of the Fourteenth Naval District was hard at work laying a new 16-inch water main from Hospital Point to Ford Island, and other workers were getting the dry docks back into working order. Sailors returned to the stricken battleships with galvanized steel buckets, and began the grisly task of collecting the remains of their slain shipmates. "I recall finding severed knee joints as well as shoulder fragments and torn, burning body torsos, all unidentifiable because of their burned condition," remembered Seaman Charles Sehe of the *Nevada*.

Though the shock of the raid was still fresh in everyone's minds, the survivors made a concerted effort to raise their collective morale. Music helped: on the waterfront at Ford Island, a jukebox blared "I Don't Want to Set the World on Fire," and on the battleship *Maryland*, the ship's band performed on deck while the repair teams worked. The crew of the *Nevada* agreed on a new nickname: the "Cheer-Up Ship." Signs on her deck proclaimed: "We'll Fight Again" and "Cheer Up the Cheer-Up Ship." The crisis tended to bring out the best in the malingerers, the lazy men, even the prisoners in the brig, who were ordered out of their cells and put to work. Everyone pitched in. "Things were so bad at Pearl Harbor," Seaman Mason recalled, "that even the chiefs were working."

ADMIRAL HUSBAND E. KIMMEL, Commander in Chief of the Pacific Fleet (CINCPAC), was staggered by the number of things he did not know. He did not know where the enemy aircraft had come from. He did not know where they had gone. Had they been launched from aircraft carriers? Or from Japanese air bases in the Marshall Islands, several thousand miles to the southwest? The latter seemed implausible, given the great range—but if they were carrier-borne aircraft, where had the enemy carriers gone? North, south, west? Were they running for safety, or preparing another airstrike? Above all, had the Sunday morning raid been the opening move in a planned sequence of attacks, perhaps to be followed by troop landings? Was Oahu about to be invaded?

Kimmel's CINCPAC headquarters was in a three-story white stucco building with an Art Deco facade, lined with coconut palms and fronted by a neatly kept lawn. His windows offered a panoramic view of the carnage in the harbor. The staff officers were doing what they could to pull themselves together, but the stark reality that the entire Pacific battle force had been knocked out of action had left them stunned and speechless. "Kimmel seemed calm and collected," recorded Lieutenant Commander Edwin T. Layton, an intelligence officer on the CINCPAC staff. "But he looked shocked by the enormity of the thing that was happening to his command and by the fact that his world was blowing up around him." As the admiral watched his precious battleships burn, he occasionally muttered, "What a doleful sight!" Officers who had abandoned the stricken ships streamed into the headquarters, their white uniforms stained with fuel oil; many seemed dazed. Although no one was willing to admit it at the time, a heavy pall of fear had settled over the headquarters. Layton recalled that his yeoman's hands shook visibly as he handed the commander an intelligence log, and Lieutenant Walter J. East stated flatly that "people were frightened and if they say they weren't, they're damned liars."

In those first desperate hours after the raid, Kimmel's problem was not so much that he lacked good intelligence about the enemy's whereabouts. His problem was that his headquarters staff were overwhelmed by reports that were ambiguous, contradictory, garbled, or altogether wrong. His initial instinct (which would prove accurate, but not in time to do anything about it) was that the enemy carriers had approached from the north. A squadron of U.S. Army bombers arriving that morning from the mainland had spotted Japanese planes headed north after the raid, and a radar station at Opana, on northern Oahu, had also tracked aircraft headed northward. But the Japanese raid had destroyed or immobilized most of Oahu's long-range patrol planes, both army and navy, so the American commanders were unable to launch a proper air search. At 9:42 a.m., Kimmel warned the U.S. carrier *Enterprise*, at sea about 200 miles west of Oahu, that there was "some indication" of a Japanese carrier force northwest of the island. Within minutes, however, new contact reports pointed south. (In every case, as it would eventually become clear, those reports proved to be U.S. ships misidentified as enemy.) One faulty alert put two Japanese carriers southwest of Barbers Point. The cruiser *Minneapolis*, which was near the reported coordinates (and had probably been mistaken for the phantom enemy force), attempted to send a dispatch correcting the report. But the ship's radio operator made a transmission error, with the result that the message went out as "two enemy carriers" instead of "no enemy carriers" in sight. The *Enterprise* turned east to give chase, and launched fifteen Douglas Dauntless SBD dive-bombers to search the zone southwest of Oahu. Six Curtiss SOC-3 seaplanes were launched from her accompanying cruisers to search north and northeast. Both flights found only American ships, but in some cases the pilots mistook them for enemy ships, adding new layers of confusion to the scene. The CINCPAC diary noted: "The view was held for some time that carriers were both north and south of the island."

On Ford Island, those few PBYs that had emerged unscathed from the morning's raid were ordered into the air. Soon the big amphibians were roaring down the channel between Ford Island and Hospital Point and staggering into the sky. Getting them aloft was a dangerous prospect, because the East Loch (which served as their runway) was littered with wreckage and overlaid with a carpet of heavy sludge oil. Twenty-nine-year-old Lieutenant Thomas H. Moorer, a seaplane pilot (and future chairman of the Joint Chiefs), left a vivid description of what it was like to drive his aircraft down the channel, with the row of burning battleships just off his wingtips, his pontoons bucking violently over the wakes left by the boats, and oily water splashing up onto his windshield, "with the result that I never did see anything until I was well clear of the island. It was a one hundred percent instrument take-off after we got hit with the oil."

Throughout the Navy Yard and Ford Island, it was broadly assumed that a Japanese invasion was underway. Sailors deprived of their ships felt a peculiar sense of vulnerability, as they had received no training in land fighting. Defenses were hastily organized. On Ford Island, gangs of sailors were set to work digging trenches, filling sandbags, and setting up .30- and .50-caliber machine guns on tripods. Craters left by the Japanese bombs were surrounded with piles of sandbags and converted into foxholes. Rifles were handed out from the back of trucks, generally at random, including thousands of Browning automatic rifles and some thoroughly obsolete bolt-action 1903 Springfields. No one was asked to sign for the weapons they received. "Somebody handed me two hand grenades," said Seaman Warren G. Harding of the *California*. "I said: 'What do I do with them?' He said: 'Never mind! Don't pull this!' That's all the instruction I had." Sailors were seen carrying butcher's knives and meat cleavers. Navy radioman Joseph Ryan was issued a .30-caliber rifle and ammunition and told, "You guys stay right here on 10-10 dock, and when the Japanese come in, get as many of them as you can before they get you."

SUNDAY AFTERNOON WAS RADIO PRIME TIME, when highly rated programs aired simultaneously across America on NBC and CBS network affiliates. Beginning at about 2:30 p.m., news announcers broke in over regular programming to report that Pearl Harbor had been attacked by Japanese aircraft. The scene was much the same all across the nation: families congregated around their big cabinetlike radios and listened breathlessly to the first reports. Children who asked questions were shushed. If the radio's vacuum tubes burned out, people sat in their cars and listened to their car radios.

"I had no real sense of where Hawaii was," recalled a civilian, Scott Leesberg, who heard the news from a ham radio operator in Oberlin, Ohio. "I knew it was in the Pacific." That was a very common reaction. Pearl Harbor? Oahu? Honolulu? They were not familiar names. Hawaii had been the setting for a few movies in the 1930s, and most Americans at least understood that it was a United States territory located somewhere in the Pacific. Atlases and maps were pulled off the shelves and studied carefully. For the majority of Americans who lived east of the Mississippi, Hawaii was more distant than Europe, where war had been raging for more than two years. But it was American soil, and it was an attack that had sunk American ships and killed American servicemen. The public had seen plenty of newsreel footage of devastated cities, both in Europe and in China. Bombs falling from the sky had seemed a distant nightmare, and further evidence that the ancient civilizations of the world were irredeemably barbaric places, from which the New World must always remain aloof. Now, with terrible suddenness, it seemed at if it *could* happen here. In neighborhoods all across the country, people stepped out of their homes and looked skyward, as if expecting a fleet of Japanese planes to appear suddenly overhead.

Children and adolescents, with no direct memory of the Great War, tended to shrug the news off. Some assumed that the United States would simply bomb Japan back; and that Japan, having been taught a proper lesson, would refrain from any further aggression. When it was reported late Sunday afternoon that a Japanese submarine had been sunk off Oahu, ten-year-old James Erickson of Chicago rejoiced, assuming that the war was as good as won and Japan would surrender by the end of the day. Nineteen-year-old Iris Bancroft, also of Chicago, confessed to feeling exhilarated and even elated by the coming of the war. "My life to date had been relatively uneventful. So had my future," she recalled years later. "Now, suddenly, I knew anything could happen. The new possibilities ahead were impossible to ignore. . . . I felt as if I were the heroine in a romantic movie." The older generations reacted differently, especially those with sons or nephews of draft age. Pat Vang, nine years old, heard the news over the radio in her father's grocery store. She asked her father, "Is it real bad, Daddy?" He replied, "Yes baby, very, very bad. A lot of good men will die."

British prime minister Winston Churchill was at Chequers, his official country residence in Buckinghamshire, with two American houseguests—John "Gil" Winant, the U.S. ambassador, and Averell Harriman, the Lend-Lease coordinator. At nine o'clock that evening, the prime minister turned on his portable radio for the BBC news broadcast. Only after several items on the Russian front and the British army in Libya did the broadcaster mention a report of Japanese attacks on American and British targets in the Pacific. Churchill strode down the hall to his office and asked his staff to place a transatlantic radio-telephone call to the White House. In three minutes the connection was successfully made, and the two leaders were on the phone.

"Mr. President, what's this about Japan?" Churchill asked.

"It's quite true," Roosevelt replied. "They have attacked us at Pearl Harbor. We are all in the same boat now."

Churchill informed Roosevelt that Japanese troops had landed in Malaya, and promised to go before the House of Commons the following day and ask for a declaration of war. "This certainly simplifies things," Churchill told the president, and added, "God be with you."

The prime minister's reaction to the news was unequivocal. He rejoiced.

"So we had won after all!" Churchill wrote years later, in the now-famous passage of his war memoirs. "England would live; Britain would live; the Commonwealth of Nations and the Empire would live. . . . Hitler's fate was sealed. Mussolini's fate was sealed. As for the Japanese, they would be ground to powder. All the rest was merely the proper application of overwhelming force." Since the war in Europe was not going particularly well at that moment, it was a daring prediction; and Churchill's comment to Roosevelt that Japan's sudden entry into the war "simplifies things" flew in the face of many perplexing complications. Eighteen months had passed since the fall of France, and Hitler was the seemingly invincible master of continental Europe. In June 1941, 148 divisions of the German Wehrmacht had poured across the Russian border, and by December they had advanced to within artillery range of Moscow. Britain had been at war for more than two years; it had stood alone against Germany for a year; and though it had absorbed the punishment of the Luftwaffe's bombing campaign and escaped, for the moment, the threat of a cross-Channel invasion, there was every risk of a renewed assault in 1942, especially if the Soviet Union should collapse.

Would Japan attack Russia in the east, freeing Hitler to transfer forces to the west? Would Japan overrun British colonies in Asia—Hong Kong, Malaya, Singapore, Burma, perhaps even India? Would the Axis armies achieve a dreaded link-up in the Middle East? Would the sparsely populated nations of Australia and New Zealand be swallowed up? Perhaps even more alarming, would the United States channel its entire energy into the war against Japan, thereby starving Britain and Russia of tanks, airplanes, transports, weapons, and other vital war matériel?

Churchill was vividly aware of all of those hazards, and yet he had the absolute conviction that Pearl Harbor, by jolting the United States out of its isolationist lassitude, would secure ultimate victory for the Allies. He recalled the words of Sir Edward Grey, thirty years earlier, concerning the entry of the United States into the First World War. America was like a gigantic furnace, Grey had said: "Once the fire is lighted under it there is no limit to the power it can generate." With these heartening reflections in mind, Churchill went to bed and "slept the sleep of the saved and thankful."

IN WASHINGTON, at four in the afternoon, traffic at major intersections was blocked by trucks carrying troops of the District of Columbia National

Guard. The telephone system was paralyzed by incoming calls, as members of the public sought news of the attack; additional operators were called in to work, but it was difficult to get a line anywhere, local or long distance. Machine-gun nests had been hastily set up on the front steps and rooftops of public buildings. Marines were called out to guard the Capitol, and uniformed provost marshal guards, wearing steel helmets left over from the First World War era, appeared suddenly outside the War and Navy departments on the corner of Seventeenth Street and Constitution Avenue.

At the Japanese Embassy on Massachusetts Avenue, a large, sullen crowd was gathering on the sidewalk outside the gates. At one point, a man climbed out of a taxi and began throwing bottles at the building. Members of the embassy staff, reported the *Philadelphia Inquirer*, were seen to carry "baskets of documents into the garden and began setting fire to them." Masuo Kato, a Japanese journalist, left the complex at about 4 p.m. Looking up to the sky above the roof, he noted that "white puffs were curling upward in the air." More documents were being burned on the roof. The crowd outside grew uglier, with several men cursing and shouting threats. As Kato made his way outside, the crowd surged toward him menacingly. They did not touch him, but one man said: "You are the last son of a bitch we're going to let out." District of Columbia police and an FBI detail soon arrived and restored order.

At the White House, where blackout restrictions had not yet taken effect, floodlights suffused the building and grounds in brilliant white light. Traffic on Pennsylvania Avenue slowed to a crawl as drivers stared; they seemed to crane their necks in the hope of catching a glimpse of the president or his men through the windows. Hundreds of spectators had gathered on the sidewalk outside the iron fence. A few men carried children on their shoulders. Police officers and Secret Service agents tried to keep them moving, but more arrived constantly throughout the late afternoon and early evening hours. Eventually they stood three or four deep. Some began to sing: "God Bless America" and "My Country, 'Tis of Thee." About fifty or sixty reporters and photographers were clustered under the portico. One journalist, Merriman Smith, wondered if President Roosevelt "could hear those unrehearsed songs coming spontaneously and from the hearts of the little people across his back lawn."

Secretary of the Interior Harold Ickes, as he entered the White House gate, noted that the crowd was "quiet and serious" and seemed to be "responding to that human instinct to get near the scene of action even if they could see or hear nothing." Seventy-four-year-old Secretary of War Henry Stimson stepped out of his limousine and (said a witness) "bounded up the steps like a mountain goat." Glen Perry of the *New York Sun* recorded: "It was very cold and a light mist somewhat obscured the moon. Lights blazed in the State Department, and clerks just called to duty kept running across the sidewalk past the ancient cannons into the building."

Shortly after nightfall, Grace Tully entered the president's office. He was alone, smoking a cigarette and sifting through the papers on his desk. "Sit down, Grace," he told her. "I'm going before Congress tomorrow. I'd like to dictate my message. It will be short." He inhaled deeply and let the smoke out. He began speaking, Tully recalled, "in the same calm tone in which he dictated his mail. Only his diction was a little different as he spoke each word incisively and slowly, carefully specifying each punctuation mark and paragraph." The speech began: "Yesterday, December 7, 1941, a date which will live in world history, the United States of America was suddenly and deliberately attacked by naval and air forces of the Empire of Japan." When he had finished speaking, Tully was sent off to type the draft, which ran to some 500 words. When she brought it back for his review, the president drew a line through the phrase "world history" and wrote "infamy."

THE WHITE HOUSE PRESS ROOM, which normally accommodated no more than two dozen people, was jammed with more than a hundred reporters, cameramen, and photographers. A long line of reporters waited for a turn at each of half a dozen telephones. The floor was littered with cigarette butts and a tangle of black cables running to the cameras and microphones. A battery of klieg lights bathed the scene in a harsh electric glare. The room, observed BBC correspondent Alistair Cooke, "already had that air of tobacco-choked energy that is the Washington odor of panic." "The press room was a madhouse," recalled Glen Perry. "Hilmer Baukhage, Fulton Lewis, Ted Wingo and other broadcasters were set up there, typing scripts and then reading them into their microphones with the crowd talking and working in the background." Roosevelt's press secretary, Stephen Early, had issued the first of several announcements at 2:30 p.m. Glistening with sweat and squinting into the lights, Early had acknowledged that the navy had suffered "doubtless very heavy losses." Updates had followed every fifteen or twenty minutes, and each time he arrived with a new statement, the room fell to a hushed silence and the reporters bowed over their notepads. It was the biggest story any journalist in the room had ever covered.

At about eight o'clock, the members of the cabinet began filtering into the Oval Study. They sat in chairs arranged in a semicircle facing the president's desk. Behind the desk sat Roosevelt, who had changed into a rumpled dark suit, and was smoking a cigarette. Secretary of State Cordell Hull sat on a Chippendale armchair in front of the desk. Secretary of the Navy Frank Knox stood hunched over the president, speaking to him in a low voice. Harry Hopkins, looking pale and gaunt, was the only non-member of the cabinet present. One of Roosevelt's naval aides briefed the cabinet secretaries on what had happened at Pearl Harbor. According to Labor Secretary Frances Perkins, press secretary Early was "rushing back and forth saying, 'They've had another telephone conversation with Admiral "So-and-So." Things are worse than were reported earlier.'"

At about nine o'clock, when all had arrived, Roosevelt began to speak. He remarked that the cabinet was meeting under circumstances more dire than at any time since 1861, at the outset of the Civil War. The president's face, according to Perkins, was drawn and gray, with the muscles around his mouth showing tension and anger. Uncharacteristically, he did not offer so much as a quip or a halfhearted smile. Several of the secretaries, particularly those whose departments did not touch upon defense or foreign affairs, were not entirely sure what had happened in Hawaii. "We just got scraps of information, an episode here and there," wrote Perkins. "We got a picture of total confusion. Still, nobody knew exactly what had happened. Nobody knew where the planes had come from. This young naval aide had said they were from a carrier, but he was only assuming."

Several times, in response to telephoned updates confirming the extent of damage to the fleet, Roosevelt groaned audibly. His anguish left a deep impression on the cabinet members. Whatever the commander in chief thought of the army, the Army Air Forces, or the marines, he was a navy man in his bones. The feeling could be traced back to his childhood, when he had watched his distant and much-admired cousin, Theodore Roosevelt, champion a major naval building program. He had read the works of Alfred Thayer Mahan diligently and cited them in debates and term papers at Groton and Harvard. He had learned to sail in the fog-shrouded waters off Maine and New Brunswick, and was by far the most proficient yachtsman ever to occupy the White House. He had personally amassed one of the world's largest collections of early American naval prints, paintings, documents, and ship models. He had served for eight years as assistant secretary of the navy in the Woodrow Wilson administration (his longest tenure in any job other than the presidency itself) and had taken direct responsibility for getting the navy on a war footing in 1917–18. As president, he had signed major naval expansion bills in 1938 and 1940, aimed at building a navy capable of fighting and winning simultaneous wars in the Atlantic and Pacific. "It was obvious to me that Roosevelt was having a dreadful time just accepting the idea that the navy could be caught off guard," Frances Perkins recalled. "His pride in the navy was so terrific that he was having actual physical difficulty in getting out the words that bombs had dropped on ships that were not in fighting shape and prepared to move, just tied up. I remember that he said twice to Knox, 'Find out, for God's sake, why the ships were tied up in rows.' Knox replied, 'That's the way they berth them.'"

As the cabinet listened in rapt silence, Roosevelt read aloud the short speech he had dictated earlier that afternoon, which he planned to deliver to a joint session of Congress the following day. When he had finished, Hull and Stimson immediately raised objections to the limited scope of the speech, which (in Stimson's words) "represented only the just indignation of the country at Japan's treachery in this surprise attack and not the full measure of the grievances we have against her as a confirmed law breaker and aggressor." Nor did it connect Germany with the attack. Hull, wrote Harold Ickes in his diary, "pressed his point so hard that the president finally became a little impatient." Roosevelt was firm: he preferred the short version. He wanted to channel the full force of the American people's fury, which would tend to unite them and put the bitter debates of the isolationists and interventionists behind them. Nor did the president want to mention Germany, since (as the isolationists would surely point out) there was no hard evidence of collusion between Hitler and Japan. Roosevelt's draft was accepted as written.

At about ten, congressional leaders joined the group. The cabinet members surrendered their chairs and stood against the walls, so that the study was now very crowded. To the congressmen and senators, the president gave a short summary of what was known about the attack. In response to a congressman who asked how the Japanese could have achieved such complete surprise, Roosevelt revealed his keen understanding of naval tactics by explaining that enemy carriers could have approached to within several hundred miles of Oahu under cover of darkness, foiling any American air patrols, and launched the airstrike before dawn. He admitted that it was not yet clear how seriously the American fleet had been damaged, but concluded, "the principal defense of the whole west coast of this country and the whole west coast of the Americas has been very seriously damaged today."

"The effect on the Congress was tremendous," Stimson wrote in his diary. "They sat in dead silence and even after the recital was over they had very few words." Someone asked if the president would be requesting a declaration of war, but Roosevelt would not reply directly, indicating that he had not yet made up his mind. (He had, but did not want the news leaked in advance.) Several congressmen flared up in anger that the U.S. Navy had been caught so badly off guard. Senator Tom Connolly of Texas asked, "How did it happen that our warships were caught like tame ducks in Pearl Harbor? How did they catch us with our pants down? Where were our patrols?" Roosevelt replied, "I don't know, Tom. I don't know."

As the congressmen filed out at 10:45 p.m., Roosevelt left them with an unsettling thought. While they slept that night, it would be daytime in Japan, the Philippines, and throughout East Asia. "They are doing things and saying things during the daytime out there, while we are all in bed." One of the congressmen remarked, "We are in bed too much." As they left the White House, the congressional leaders were intercepted in the stone portico by a crowd of reporters. They all avowed total, bipartisan unity. Congressman Joseph Martin, the House minority leader, told a *New York Times* reporter, "There is no politics here. There is only one party when it comes to the integrity and honor of the country."

The lights on the second floor of the White House burned well past midnight, as the president refined drafts of his message. He was helped into bed by his son James, at about one in the morning.

FIVE TIME ZONES TO THE WEST, darkness fell over Pearl Harbor. A soft rain was falling. A bugler sounded evening colors. Throughout the base, men stopped whatever they were doing, stood to attention, and saluted the flag as it came down. Strict blackout conditions had been ordered and no lights were permitted to show from buildings, ships, cars, or even flashlights. But the East Loch was illuminated by the orange glow of the still-burning *West*

Virginia and *Arizona*, and by the intense white light of the acetylene torches cutting into the upturned hull of the *Oklahoma*, where survivors had been heard tapping. A gibbous yellow moon rose in the east, bright enough to cast shadows. Searchlights probed for enemy aircraft; flares and red rockets shot up here and there; and intermittent bursts of tracer fire drew geometric patterns across the sky.

Night brought with it a heavy sense of foreboding. Rumors circulated quickly, and evolved through repeated retellings—there were said to be enemy submarines in the harbor; there had been troop landings at Barbers Point, Diamond Head, or Kaneohe Bay; spies and saboteurs were operating within the base itself. One of the most persistent reports, not conclusively refuted until Monday, was that enemy paratroopers had landed in the mountainous interior of Oahu. They were said to be wearing blue coveralls with red "Rising Sun" patches on their shoulders. Americans wearing blue uniforms stripped them off to avoid being mistaken for the enemy. In the darkness, imaginations ran wild and every sound seemed grotesquely amplified. Marine Lieutenant Cornelius C. Smith, stationed at the Marine Barracks, recalled that his men were even spooked by noises that were recognizable and familiar. "A laundry cart rumbles across the asphalt patch out behind the bakery. With all of that weight and those tiny skate wheels, it sounds just like a machine gun. A messman drops a bench end on the concrete deck. A rifle shot. The short wave set crackles with static. More machine guns."

Everywhere, constantly, all night long, men fired their weapons. The target might be a noise, a struck match, a lit cigarette, the headlights of a distant car. Conscientious sentries, when they heard or saw a movement, would shout: "Halt! Who goes there? Advance and be recognized!" Others simply aimed and pulled the trigger. Guards opened fire on the men who had arrived to relieve them. "You couldn't go five feet because somebody would start shooting," said Radioman Ryan, who was assigned to run messages that night. "You wore your whites so that you could be seen in the dark, and you whistled the 'Star-Spangled Banner' so you'd be known as an American. Boy, it was risky; I could easily have been shot." Antiaircraft batteries opened fire on lights in the sky, then fell silent as the gunners realized they were shooting at stars. Much of the shooting was merely cathartic, a way to soothe the nerves. At the Navy Yard tank farm, a large complex of steel tanks which held the navy's main fuel reserves in the Pacific, someone accidentally threw the main switch that turned on the floodlights. A voice cried, "Shoot those lights out!" Dozens of weapons opened fire. Across the fence, in Hickam Field, the army guards thought they were under attack and fired back. It was not just a few stray shots, Army Lieutenant Charles Davis recalled, but "a genuine firefight with a good amount of volume to it." Surprisingly, no casualties were reported.

The *Enterprise* and her screening ships (together they were designated Task Force 8, under the command of Vice Admiral William F. Halsey) had made a long, fruitless search to the south. Having found no enemy ships, the *Enterprise* aircraft turned back, their fuel reserves running low. Most of these planes tracked the blacked-out *Enterprise* by picking up and following her long phosphorescent wake, and landed safely (a fine accomplishment, as the pilots had not been trained for night landings). But Halsey ordered a squadron of six F4F Wildcat fighter planes, under the command of Lieutenant (jg) Fritz Hebel, to return directly to the naval air station on Ford Island.

The squadron approached Oahu from the south at 10:45 p.m. Hebel radioed the Ford Island control tower and requested landing instructions. The tower gave him clearance to land and specified that the six planes should approach the base with their running lights fully illuminated. It was perfectly obvious to everyone on the ground that the antiaircraft batteries were manned by nervous (and in some cases inexperienced) gunners, and the risk of a friendly fire incident was very great. The Ford Island tower broadcast a notice to "all ships present and army antiaircraft units," advising them of the approach of American planes. The broadcast was repeated a second time—an unusual step, showing the tower's anxiety for the safety of the planes—and the word was passed haphazardly through the antiaircraft batteries to hold fire.

From the ground, the six Wildcats were plainly visible as they made their slow approach, losing altitude gradually, their green and red running lights shining brightly. Commander Allen Quynn of the *Argonne* understood that those were American planes—what sort of enemy pilot would fly over the base at night with his aircraft running lights on?—but he also feared for them, given the number of itchy trigger fingers at Pearl Harbor. "Will anyone smack them?" he wondered.

The firing began as the first plane made its final turn to line up with the runway, at an altitude of about 1,000 feet. One of the aft antiaircraft batteries on the battleship *Pennsylvania*, flagship of the battle force, opened fire; an instant later, hundreds of guns were blazing away. "It looked like the Fourth of July, with everybody shooting up there," said Gunner's Mate Curtis Schulze of the *Downes*. "They had tracers. Mostly, it was small arms fire." From the control tower radio came frantic cries to hold fire, but there were too many guns in too many places. The men on the ground were exultant. "By God," said Seaman Mason of the *California*, "this time we were going to shoot back! . . . We took aim at the lights and opened fire with a fierce kind of joy. . . . We were striking back the foe who had so humiliated us." The notion that the planes were American seemed never to enter their minds. "We had gotten addicted to shooting at everything that flew during the day, and I guess that it was automatic what we did," said Seaman Fomby.

Lieutenant Hebel, over the radio, was heard to cry: "My God, what's happened?" Two planes were hit immediately, crashing into the channel west of Ford Island and into a tavern named the Palm Inn in Pearl City. Ensign Eric Allen bailed out successfully but was machine-gunned while floating down in his parachute. A fourth pilot, James Daniels, dove low, swooped over the floodlights near the southern edge of the runway, then cut hard left toward Barbers Point. Hebel's plane was hit several times—he pulled away and tried an emergency landing at Wheeler, but his plane skidded into a cane field near Aiea. He was badly injured, and died the following morning. Two other pilots crashed or bailed out, both surviving with minor injuries. Only Daniels managed to land his plane without injury to himself or damage to his aircraft.

There was so much antiaircraft fire, so many bright red tracer patterns in the sky, that men on the ground were momentarily blinded. As the guns fell silent and the shell bursts faded, Seaman Carl Schmitz of the USS *Castor* recalled, "the sky turned so dark you had a hard time seeing ten feet in front of you."

Chapter Two

NEW SENTRY BOXES WERE ERECTED OUTSIDE THE WHITE HOUSE THAT night, and at dawn the grounds were swarming with plainclothes Secret Service agents and soldiers wearing trench helmets. The president rose early on Monday, having taken just four hours of sleep. He drank his coffee and ate his breakfast while reading the latest dispatches. He dressed, with the help of his valet, in a dark suit and his old blue naval cape. At about eight that morning, news was carried over the radio that Britain had declared war on Japan. "We can only feel that Hitler's madness has infected the Japanese mind," Churchill had told the British people in a BBC broadcast, "and that the root of the evil and its branch must be extirpated together."

A few minutes after noon, Roosevelt was wheeled out the main entrance of the White House and lifted into his limousine. A ten-car motorcade, which included three cars identical to the one carrying the president, roared down Pennsylvania Avenue at twice the speed limit. Men armed with Tommy guns crouched on the running boards. At 12:20 p.m., the convoy pulled up at the south entrance to the Capitol. Roosevelt emerged, unsmiling. In the car he had put on the heavy steel braces that enabled him to stand erect on his ruined legs, and he was able to walk, arduously, on the arm of his son James, a marine captain. The president barely acknowledged the crowd, described by the *Washington Evening Star* as "a tense, grim throng." The building had not been so heavily guarded since the Civil War. "Marines with bayonets on their rifles were posted at entrances," the *Star* reported, "and the Capitol police, out in full force, formed a secondary line. Cables were stretched along the sidewalks around the House and to hold back the crowd waiting for a glimpse of the president." One congressman, having forgotten his identification, pushed his way through a phalanx of soldiers and was very nearly shot.

The cabinet, as "solemn as owls," filed into the House chamber. They were followed by the entire Senate and the nine members of the Supreme Court. The galleries were packed with reporters, photographers, and cameramen. At 12:29 p.m., Speaker Sam Rayburn brought his gavel down on the rostrum and shouted: "The President of the United States!" BBC correspondent Alistair Cooke, observing the scene from the press gallery, described a long, nervous interval as Roosevelt made his way to the dais. The clicking of the president's leg braces could be plainly heard as he edged up the ramp to the podium, with "one arm locked in his son's, the other hand feeling every inch of the long sloping rail." The cameras would not roll until the president was safely behind the podium, his disability primly hidden away—but every soul in the crowded chamber had seen his pained exertions, and the metaphor was too palpable to be missed. Cooke wrote: "Before we heard his confident tenor and listened to the sincere automatic applause, we saw him walk and thought of the wounded battleships slumped over in Pearl Harbor."

Eleanor Roosevelt, dressed in black with a silver fox fur, sat in the galleries near Edith Wilson, who had sat in this chamber twenty-three years earlier to hear her husband, President Woodrow Wilson, ask for a declaration of war against Germany. "Now the president of the United States was my husband," wrote Eleanor, "and for the second time in my life I heard the president tell the Congress that this nation was engaged in a war. I was deeply unhappy. I remembered my anxiety about my husband and brother when World War I began; now I had four sons of military age."

The president stood at the podium, leg braces locked, and gripped the sides of the rostrum for support. He put on his glasses, opened a black loose-leaf notebook, and began to speak: "Yesterday, December seventh, nineteen forty-one—a date which will live in infamy—the United States of America was suddenly and deliberately attacked by naval and air forces of the Empire of Japan." The timing of the raid, Roosevelt declared, left no doubt that it had been planned and executed while the Japanese and American governments were engaged in recent diplomatic negotiations, and that Japan had thus "deliberately sought to deceive the United States by false statements and expressions of hope for continued peace." He detailed all of the attacks

Japan had launched in the previous twenty-four hours—Midway, Wake, Guam, the Philippines, Hong Kong, Malaya—and concluded, "Japan has, therefore, undertaken a surprise offensive extending throughout the Pacific area. The facts of yesterday speak for themselves. . . . No matter how long it may take us to overcome this premeditated invasion, the American people in their righteous might will win through to absolute victory."

Congress, the *Evening Star* reported, was "solemn and angered" as the president delivered his address; but several lines were punctuated by thunderclaps of powerful applause and foot-stamping. With his concluding words, "we will gain the inevitable triumph, so help us God," the entire chamber rose to their feet and presented a deafening ovation. Roosevelt raised a hand and left the podium, escorted once again by his son. The speech had lasted a mere five minutes, and the phrase "a date which will live in infamy" was the only line that most Americans would ever remember; but it had attracted the largest audience in the history of radio: 60 million, according to the ratings. He had written it entirely himself, without contribution from his speechwriters. The playwright and presidential aide Robert Sherwood remarked of Roosevelt, "I do not think there was another occasion in his life when he was so completely representative of the whole people."

An hour later, a declaration of war passed both houses, with one dissenting vote in the House and none in the Senate.

ROOSEVELT WAS STILL ON THE RADIO as the sun rose over Pearl Harbor. A soft rain was falling over the half-sunken, still-blazing battleships *West Virginia* and *Arizona*. Fireboats continued to work them over with hoses, and immense columns of greasy, black, evil-smelling smoke continued to roll into the sky. On Ford Island, men stumbled into the mess halls for coffee and breakfast, "their eyes puffy, faces drawn, unshaven, and dirty." Few had slept at all, and many had neglected to eat since the previous morning's attack. For twenty-four hours they had been fueled by nervous energy and adrenaline, and were only now realizing that they were exhausted and wolfishly hungry.

At the Naval Hospital, a handsome stucco building wreathed in palm trees along the Navy Yard side of the harbor, the short-handed staff had been working without respite since the previous morning. It had been a long and petrifying night. Small arms and antiaircraft fire kept up a constant din, persuading the doctors and nurses that a battle was raging outside the windows. Surgeons struggled to keep their hands from shaking while bent over the operating tables. At about eleven o'clock, when an exploding flak shell blew out many of the windows of the upper floors, doctors, nurses, corpsmen, and patients had cried out all together in fright. The nurses had worked relentlessly, mechanically, without relief, doing what they were trained to do—sterilizing trays of instruments, giving shots, setting up intravenous feeds, changing dressings. Observing strict blackout conditions, they worked with flashlights covered with blue carbon paper to dim the light. It seemed obvious that a Japanese invasion was underway. Having been warned of how the Japanese would treat female prisoners, some of the nurses carried pocketknives and resolved to slash their wrists if the hospital was taken. Dawn brought a puissant sense of relief. "No one could imagine what daylight meant to us," said Lieutenant Ruth Erickson, a nurse at the hospital. "We could now see outside. Even the air was cleaner, purer. There was a feeling that we had made it. Our material possessions meant nothing. The fact that we were alive—that was the full meaning. We had prayed many times, and we were grateful that our prayers had been answered."

With daylight, casualties continued to arrive at the hospital in great numbers. As the wards filled, the corpsmen pushed the beds closer together to make room for more. The burn cases were the worst. The standard weekend uniform at Pearl Harbor was shorts and shortsleeve shirts, leaving exposed skin on the arms and legs. A witness described the wounds as "charred, crisp skin like bacon rind, black and oozing." Burns were treated with a variety of dressings—mineral oil sprays, sulfanilamide powder, tannic acid, boric acid. But not much could be done for the men in the burn wards, except to keep them heavily dosed with anesthetic. The smell of burnt flesh permeated the hospital, especially at night when the blackout curtains prevented air from circulating. "I can still smell it," recalled Lieutenant Erickson, many years afterward, "and I think I always will."

The dead were placed in white canvas body bags and moved out to the lawn in front of the hospital. Not all of those who had been declared dead were actually dead: witnesses were horrified to hear muffled groans from within some of the bags. "I started to go back and see," recalled Vivian Hultgren, an army wife, "and then my reasoning said, 'Well, they must be so badly damaged that they can't be helped. They must just be on their last legs. So what can I do?' And that just really haunted me." In the harbor, dozens of bodies were floating to the surface, and motor launches were assigned to bring them to Aiea Landing for identification and burial. At first the crews hauled the bodies into the boats, said Seaman Jack Kelley of the *Tennessee*, but it "got to where, if we pulled them into the boat, they would bust open and run all over the bottom of the boat. So we would just tie a little piece of rope around their leg or their arm or whatever you could get a hold of and get you a string of them and tow them over rather than trying to pull them into the boat." Another sailor assigned to that grisly duty remembered, "The worst part was when the body would start to disintegrate, and we would have to stop in the middle of the tow and re-lash."

On the previous afternoon, civilian lumberyards in Honolulu had been ordered to build as many pine coffins as they could, and these were transported to Pearl Harbor by the truckload. At Aiea Landing, medical corpsmen wearing rubber gloves took dental impressions in the effort to identify the dead. Identified bodies were placed in a numbered box, and a record made of the dead man's name. But many bodies or parts of bodies could not be identified, and these were distributed at random into boxes. Trucks were loaded with coffins and driven to Oahu Cemetery, where bulldozers were digging 150-foot-long trenches. It was necessary to get the dead under the ground as soon as possible: many coffins were leaking blood and oil, and men handling them had to wear masks to cover the odor. It was a gruesome task. "One flatbed truck came up, stopped abruptly, and a box fell off," said Marine Private Le Fan, who spent several days working at the cemetery. "It hit the concrete and burst. There was the trunk of a man, three arms, and one leg in this particular box." For weeks after the attack, funeral ceremonies were held continuously. When a dead man could not be identified, a priest, a rabbi, and a minister would sometimes preside over a single burial. An honor guard would sound "Taps" and place a wooden stake over each grave. In a newspaper photograph of one such ceremony, held shortly after the attack, civilians and uniformed naval officers stand with heads bowed while a trio of grass-skirted Hawaiian women play ukuleles and sing (according to the caption) "Aloha Oe."

Throughout the base, there were alternating scenes of jubilation and grief as men discovered who among their shipmates had survived and who had not. Survivors described a kaleidoscope of contradictory feelings. Some were relieved at having escaped with their lives and limbs intact. Seaman Theodore Mason remembered a peculiar celebration in the shower of the

CINCPAC administration building, as a number of sailors were scrubbing the oil from their bodies. "A feeling of elation possessed me," he remembered. "I was alive! The other men in the shower shouted and laughed and sang. I joined them." Hard on the heels of that curious euphoria came a crushing sense of guilt and shame. "How many of my shipmates were dead, wounded, hideously burned?" Mason asked himself. "Why was I singing? It took years, and additional combat experience, before I forgave myself."

Most of the enlisted men and junior officers at Pearl Harbor were young, in their late teens and early twenties; and they admitted feeling confused about the causes of the war. Many were not in the habit of reading the newspapers, except the comic strips or sports pages, and had not paid much attention to the deterioration of U.S.-Japanese relations in the last months before the war. Japan, and all of Asia, had seemed remote and not particularly important to their lives or to the lives of their families and friends at home. Virtually no one had taken Japan seriously as a military threat. Now, as the Pacific battle force lay in ruins, they felt a pervasive sense of collective disgrace. "Friends back home used to ask about the Japs," recalled Marine Lieutenant Cornelius C. Smith, Jr. "[I answered] 'Hell, we could blow them out of the water in three weeks!' but here we are with our pants down and the striking force of our Pacific fleet is settling on the bottom of East Loch, Pearl Harbor. Who wouldn't be ashamed?" Seaman Nick Kouretas wondered how he could ever face his family again. "What am I going to say to them?" he asked himself. "How can I explain this?"

As terrible as the fate of the *Arizona* had been, many witnesses were even more shaken by the sight of the *Oklahoma*. After being hit by a barrage of aerial torpedoes, she had listed to starboard and then rolled nearly vertical, leaving her gigantic steel hull pointed up to the sky and her superstructure buried in the soft mud bottom of the harbor. Three generations of officers and enlisted men had been taught to believe that every battleship was a fortress, permanent and impregnable. For such a ship to roll over like a toy boat in a bathtub seemed ludicrous, almost inconceivable. But there she was. Gunner's Mate Third Class George E. Waller of the *Maryland* recalled: "We had been told all of our lives that you couldn't sink a battleship, and then to see one go upside down. . . . It was heartbreaking."

But the carriers had survived. At least the carriers had survived.

Admiral William F. Halsey's Task Force 8—the *Enterprise* and her accompanying cruisers and destroyers—had been safely at sea on the morning of the attack. They had been due back in Pearl Harbor on Sunday morning, but on Saturday afternoon, northwest of Oahu, a line dropped by a destroyer had managed to wrap itself around one of the propeller shafts of the cruiser *Northampton*. It was the kind of familiar mishap that routinely beset ships operating in close formation at sea, usually prompting savage recriminations, blame-trading, and fusillades of profanity. The entire task force had lingered as divers worked to unravel the fouled line. When news of the air raid arrived by radio the next morning, the ships had steamed hundreds of miles south in a long, fruitless search, thereby avoiding Vice Admiral Nagumo's carriers, which had withdrawn to the north. Had Halsey chased north, he would have thrust his two carriers into striking range of Nagumo's six, and with such overpowering force the combat-hardened Japanese aviators might easily have sent both the *Enterprise* and *Lexington* to the bottom.

At sunset on Monday, with seven destroyers following in a single file, the *Enterprise* crept down the long outer channel into Pearl Harbor. She inched around the stern of the crippled battleship *Nevada*, which lay beached on the western edge of the channel with her bow thrust into a grove of algaroba trees. In the failing light, men stationed on the carrier's bridge, flight deck, and catwalks took in enough to understand what had happened in their absence: the charred remains of seaplanes and hangars on Ford Island; the smell of fuel oil and roasted paint; the fires still burning in the half-sunken ships; the columns of smoke still spewing into the sky. One of the *Enterprise*'s own dive-bombers, shot down the previous evening by friendly fire, was half-awash in the shallows near the channel. Passing Ten-Ten Dock, they saw the half-sunken remains of the minesweeper *Oglala*, plugged with three Japanese torpedoes apparently intended for the *Enterprise*. A heavy blanket of black fuel oil lay across the water of the harbor—boats motoring through it raised barely a wake, lifting the oil-water surface, a sailor recalled, "in sullen little folds that fell back at once into the overall black melancholy." The base was mostly dark and silent, observing strict blackout conditions for the second night of the war, but a few sarcastic voices called out to the gaping crew of the *Enterprise* as she crept past the stricken battleships: "Where in hell were *you?*" and "You'd better get out of here or the Japs will get you too."

Ordnanceman Alvin Kernan, observing the carnage from the flight deck, reflected that "In a violent way the attack had announced that the day of the battleship was gone." The *Enterprise* and a handful of other air-craft carriers had been unwittingly thrust into the vanguard of the naval war. To men who had learned their trade in a fleet dominated by battleships that was a sobering prospect, but now the war must be waged by the carriers or not at all, because "there wasn't anything else." Admiral Halsey, watching with gritted teeth from the *Enterprise* flag bridge, was heard to mutter, "Before we're through with them, the Japanese language will be spoken only in hell." Whatever their misgivings, whatever evils the war might bring, their longing for vengeance would nourish and sustain them.

As soon as the carrier's dock lines were secured to a Ford Island berth, Halsey descended into a launch that would take him to see Admiral Kimmel at CINCPAC headquarters on the other side of the loch. The boat was fired upon as it motored toward the Navy Yard landing, and it was only the darkness of the night that saved Halsey from being shot. He found Kimmel and his staff haggard and unshaven, still wearing their Sunday whites, which were crumpled and stained with blood, dirt, and oil. As he sat with Kimmel, new and far-fetched rumors circulated through the headquarters. One, a report that Japanese troops had been seen landing in gliders, prompted Halsey to chuckle. "What the hell is there to laugh at?" demanded Kimmel. Halsey said the report was obvious bunk: gliders did not have the range to fly from any Japanese island base, and the Japanese carriers would never waste deck space on "any such nonsense." His reasoning was unassailable. As a carrier admiral he intuited what Kimmel by then suspected: that the Japanese were long gone, and the ongoing contact reports were products of mass hysteria. The previous morning's attack had been a hit-and-run carrier air raid, and the enemy flattops were now well on their way back toward Japan.

As the *Enterprise* berthed, the fuel lines were hauled aboard from a waiting tanker and inserted into her tanks. Refueling and reprovisioning continued at a hurried pace through the small hours of the morning: all wanted to be safely back to sea by first light. A long line of sailors snaked from the dock up a gangway through the hangar deck and down the ladders to the magazines and galleys, and through those hundreds of pairs of hands were passed the rounds of ammunition and victuals to replenish the *Enterprise*'s stores. New crew members reported aboard, many bringing nothing but the uniforms on their backs, because their sea bags were entombed on Battleship Row. By four in the morning, the *Enterprise* had drunk her fill of fuel oil and loaded all the ammunition and stores she could carry. Admiral Halsey came aboard without ceremony. Provisions were stacked on her hangar deck in unseamanlike fashion, waiting to be properly stowed below, but there was no time to lose: dawn was imminent.

Her lines were cast off and she retraced her route past the wrecked battleships, Hospital Point, the seaplane base, then made a slight course adjustment a few points to starboard, and headed back toward the beached *Nevada*, marking the passage to the open sea. Leaving the miserable waste of Pearl Harbor behind, recalled Alvin Kernan, the *Enterprise* sailed "down the channel, through the nets, and into the blue water, picking up speed as she went, the sun rising, the water beginning to hiss alongside, and the smell of oil, charred paint, bodies, and defeat left far behind. The planes landed aboard later and the war had begun."

IN WASHINGTON, the first chaotic stages of mobilization had been set in motion. Alistair Cooke was reminded of a silent film of the vaudevillian era, "when the resting firemen, grown amiable on undisturbed sessions of beer and games of pinochle, are electrified by the alarm and, diving headlong down the greasy pole, start to clomp importantly in every part of town." Military units in trucks seized major intersections, causing monumental traffic jams on both Monday and Tuesday. Machine-gun nests and antiaircraft units were set up on the roofs of public buildings. This being December, darkness fell in late afternoon, and as a precaution against enemy air raids, the city's streetlights and the huge floodlights which normally lit up the Capitol dome were left dark. Air-raid wardens waved down cars and shined flashlights into the eyes of motorists and pedestrians, asking impudent and idiotic questions. Four cherry trees on the Washington Mall were chopped down by some zealous patriot, presumably because they had been a gift from the Japanese government. Fear and confusion were everywhere evident. A downtown building caught fire, and when the fire engine sirens sounded, residents assumed that hostile planes were overhead. As in communities all around the country, there was a panic of buying, as people hoarded food and other consumer goods in anticipation of rationing or shortages. "By nightfall on December 8," the journalist David Brinkley wrote of Washington, "the markets looked as if a high wind had blown them clean."

There were a quarter of a million government workers in Washington,

D.C., up from 38,000 in 1917; that number would more than double during the war. Secretary of War Henry Stimson ordered the entire U.S. Army into uniform, numbering about 1.6 million men. The navy quickly decided to reinforce Pearl Harbor and set up a new aerial search pattern to guard against a renewed air raid. In cities throughout the country, police were placed on twenty-four-hour duty, guarding defense plants and bridges and water supply facilities against sabotage. Ports throughout the country were closed to all foreign shipping. All weather reports by radio broadcast were halted, as they might prove useful to the enemy in choosing air-raid targets. A nationwide strike of 125,000 welders was summarily called off by the union leaders, who cited "the situation in the Pacific."

Looking back from the present it is practically impossible to reconstruct the terror of those early days of the war, when it was not at all obvious that the American mainland would be spared enemy air raids. On Monday, the radio waves and newspapers were full of reports of air raids over American cities. Associated Press tickers reported an unknown plane off Montauk Point, Long Island, and air-raid sirens wailed in the streets of Manhattan. The *Brooklyn Eagle* reported: "Enemy planes were approaching Long Island—from New England and then from the Virginia coast. Bombers, apparently, were heading for the Brooklyn Navy Yard, for Mitchell Field and other points. . . . Air raid sirens are sounded. Schools were closed. Employees were sent home. Police warned pedestrians to keep off the crowded streets." On the west coast, men armed with shotguns and hunting rifles piled into cars and drove toward the beaches, eager to do battle with the Japanese landing forces. In San Francisco, the switches were pulled on street and bridge lights, but otherwise the city's hills glittered almost as brightly as they had on December 6. Air-raid sirens blared throughout the night, and were repeated by ferry horns; eventually, it seemed the ferry horns were leading and the air-raid sirens answering. Vigilantes took baseball bats to automobile headlights, and threatened to smash the windows of merchants and homeowners who did not observe the blackout order.

Numerous reports had Japanese planes patrolling about 100 miles off the coast, and on Monday night it was confidently reported by the Army Air Forces that sixty Japanese planes had appeared over the Golden Gate Bridge, and were beaten off by American fighters. Asked how he knew the planes were Japanese, General William Ryan replied, "Well, they weren't army planes, they weren't navy planes, and you can be sure they weren't civilian planes." When, on Tuesday, there were suggestions (later proven accurate) that there had been no Japanese planes over the bay, Lieutenant General John DeWitt replied angrily:

> Death and destruction is likely to come to this city at any moment.
> The people of San Francisco seem unable to appreciate that we are
> at war in every sense. . . . Those planes were over our community for
> a definite period. They were enemy planes. I mean Japanese planes.
> They were tracked out at sea. Why bombs weren't dropped I do not
> know.

The general might have stopped there, but apparently could not help himself:

> It might have been better if some bombs were dropped to awaken this
> city. We will never have a practice alert. We will never call an alert
> unless we believe an attack to be imminent. . . . If I can't knock these
> facts into your heads with words I'll turn you over to the police and let
> them knock them into you with clubs.

Americans depended on radio and newspapers to keep them informed, but both were full of wild rumors. Military and civil officials were quoted faithfully and respectfully, but it was apparent that the confusion, fear, and disorientation went to the top. The quick clampdown of military censors in Hawaii only amplified the rumormongering. The Japanese had control of the Pacific; California was indefensible; the army was preparing to meet the invader in the Rocky Mountains or perhaps on the eastern bank of the Mississippi River. Admiral Stark, chief of naval operations, briefed congressional leaders at the Navy Department on Tuesday, December 9. The briefing was strictly classified, but reporters waiting on Constitution Avenue needed only to study the dark expressions on the faces of the emerging congressmen to deduce that the news was very bad. "The atmosphere in the Capitol was on the narrow edge of hysteria," wrote the journalist Marquis Childs. The crippling losses suffered at Pearl Harbor were the worst-kept secret in town: "Each senator by nightfall had told ten other persons and they had told ten others, the story losing nothing in the telling."

Partisan politics were, for the moment, deeply out of favor; and congressional leaders of both parties avowed unity in the face of the emergency. For the navy this development was a mixed blessing, however, as the unanimous rage of Democrats and Republicans was unleashed against the culprits who had allowed the cherished battleships, built over many years with elephantine budget appropriations, to be blindsided in the heart of the nation's great Pacific stronghold. Who was to blame for the travesty? On Monday, Democratic congressman John Dingell of Michigan called for an investigation, suggesting that the navy must have been grossly incompetent. The demand for answers was echoed angrily in the press, and on Tuesday, Congress announced a formal inquiry. Heads were obviously going to roll, and by Wednesday it seemed that one of those heads might belong to Navy Secretary Frank Knox. With timing that could not have been any worse, in the week immediately before the war, Knox had launched a media offensive to reassure the country that the navy had nothing to fear from the Japanese. He had been interviewed by *Collier's* magazine, a week before Pearl Harbor, in an article lamentably titled "The Navy Is Ready." If it came to war, he had predicted, the navy would need no more than six months to "knock Japan out of the water." Secretary Knox had granted another interview to *The American Magazine*, whose January issue landed on newsstands the same day Japanese bombs landed on Battleship Row. The day after the attack, the story was still being advertised in newspapers across the country:

Equipped with amazing, new, secret, deadly devices that no enemy
will ever know about (till it's too late)—the biggest, toughest, hardest-
hitting, straightest-shooting navy in the world is primed and ready to
write "finis" to aggressors . . . Let 'em come—from both sides, if they
want to—"WE CAN WIN ON TWO OCEANS!" says Secretary of the Navy
Frank Knox, in the January *American Magazine*—"NOW OUT!"

The humiliated secretary shrewdly made himself absent from Washington in the first week of the war, flying to Pearl Harbor to assess the catastrophe in person.

Aiming to soothe the collective hysteria that seemed to have possessed the country, the White House announced that Roosevelt would address the American people by radio in his twentieth "fireside chat." Presidential speechwriters Bob Sherwood and Sam Rosenman had been hard at it since Sunday evening, and they tinkered with new drafts until minutes before the broadcast at ten o'clock Tuesday night. More than 60 million Americans would tune in, repeating the size of the previous day's radio audience for the "infamy" speech to Congress.

The president was an acknowledged master of radio, having used the medium since the 1920s to advance his career, enact his agenda, and hammer down his opponents. His sonorous, lilting voice carried well over the airwaves. He had a thespian's natural feeling for cadence, pace, and emphasis. Above all, he employed a deft common touch that belied his sheltered upbringing as a scion of the Hudson Valley gentry. He did not try to disguise the aristocratic inflections in his voice, knowing perhaps that the attempt would expose him as a fraud, but he managed to be warm and plainspoken without sounding patronizing or insincere, and he used a laid-back, conversational tone that created, in the listener's mind, an uncanny intimacy. It is often said that Americans liked Roosevelt because they felt they knew him as a neighbor or a friend. That was especially true of Americans middle-aged or older, for whom broadcasting was still a novelty. Never having heard radio until reaching adulthood, they were less inclined to take it for granted than were their children, who had listened to it all their lives. When the president came over the airwaves, they were more susceptible to the unconscious illusion that he was really there—that his presence, and not just his voice, had come into their living rooms; that he was not just speaking but in a sense conversing with them.

Tuesday night's broadcast was made from a large room on the first floor of the White House. Radio engineers set up their microphones on a wooden desk, on which also sat a reading lamp, an ashtray, a pitcher of water, and a glass. Fifty or sixty people sat in rows on wooden folding chairs. At about ten minutes before ten, the president was wheeled into the room and behind the desk. He opened his looseleaf notebook and shuffled through the pages of the speech. He smoked a cigarette; he stubbed it out. At ten o'clock, the radio announcers each spoke into their microphones, introducing the president. He began: "My fellow Americans."

It was about as angry a speech as Roosevelt ever delivered, a hard-hitting Philippic against the Japanese militarist regime, whose "sudden criminal attacks," he said, "provide the climax of a decade of international immorality." He returned again and again to the theme that Japan and its Axis accomplices were a league of thugs who had to be stopped by the decent and law-abiding nations of the world. "Powerful and resourceful gangsters have banded together to make war upon the whole human race. . . . We must be set to face a long war against crafty and powerful bandits. . . . There is no such thing as security for any nation—or any individual—in a world ruled by the principles of gangsterism." He defined the war as a defense of "our right to live among our world neighbors in freedom, in common decency, without fear of assault." There should be a massive increase in war production, with a seven-day week in all war industries, to support not only American military forces but also those of America's allies. Acknowledging that the American people and the press wanted to know what was happening in the Pacific, he insisted that it was necessary to conceal the full truth from the enemy. As for Pearl Harbor, he admitted the damage was "serious" but would say no more. Guam, Wake, and Midway were under attack and might fall; the Philippines were "taking punishment, but defending themselves vigorously." Wartime secrecy would be a burden for the American people, but he warned them not to believe half the rumors they were hearing—"These ugly little hints of complete disaster fly thick and fast in wartime"—and asked the press to exercise restraint in printing unconfirmed reports.

He did not deny the success of the Japanese attack: "We may acknowledge that our enemies have performed a brilliant feat of deception, perfectly timed and executed with great skill. It was a thoroughly dishonorable deed, but we must face the fact that modern warfare as conducted in the Nazi manner is a dirty business. We don't like it—we didn't want to get in it—but we are in it and we're going to fight it with everything we've got."

When the president had finished and been wheeled back into the Oval Study, Sam Rosenman went to see him. He found him alone, behind his desk, smoking a cigarette and poring over his beloved stamps. It was a rare man who could deliver such a speech, on the third day of a war that had started so badly, and then head back to his office to tinker with his stamp collection. He was serene, apparently content, clearing his mind of the day's work so that he could sleep soundly and awake the next day fresh. "He knew by this time all the damage that had been done to us at Pearl Harbor," Rosenman wrote. "Yet I felt, as I looked at him, that he was confident that ultimate victory, as he had said, was certain."

To CRITICS HOWLING for the heads of the men responsible for Pearl Harbor, FDR had offered an oblique reply: "There is no such thing as impregnable defense against powerful aggressors who sneak up in the dark and strike without warning." The same could not be said for Allied commanders in positions west of Hawaii, who failed to put up any meaningful resistance to enemy planes that struck later the same day. Beginning just hours after the raid on Pearl Harbor, as dawn broke over the western Pacific, land-based bombers and fighters of the Imperial Japanese Navy launched a tightly choreographed aerial *Blitzkrieg* against American and British bases throughout the region, and by the third day of the war the local Allied air forces had been reduced to mincemeat. That was a defeat more ruinous in its consequences than the raid on Pearl Harbor, because it led directly to the fall of the Philippines and Malaya. It also gave the lie to the theory, bandied around by those unwilling to admit they had underestimated Japan, that Pearl Harbor had been a lucky "sucker punch" that could never be repeated.

At dawn on December 7 (December 8 west of the International Date Line), medium G3M and G4M bombers, accompanied by Japan's sleek single-seat fighter plane, the A6M "Zero," lifted off from airfields on the island of Formosa and set out across the China Sea to pulverize American air bases in the Philippines. Others took off from newly constructed airfields in Indochina to strike British air bases in Malaya, Burma, and Hong Kong. Still more roared north from the remote atolls of the Marshall Islands to attack Wake Island. A small carrier task force, built around the *Ryujo*, sailed from Palau to launch strikes on Legaspi, on the southern coast of the Philippine island of Luzon; and then turned south to pummel the U.S. naval base of Davao, on the island of Mindanao.

General Douglas A. MacArthur, the U.S. Far East commander, had received several hours' warning of the raid at Pearl Harbor, but his Manila headquarters was thrown into a state of dazed confusion in the first hours of the war, ensuring that the initial Japanese air raids scored with overwhelming success. Much of the blame would later be fixed on General Richard K. Sutherland, MacArthur's chief of staff, who seemed determined to keep subordinate officers away from his boss. The upshot was that American air forces were effectively paralyzed for lack of orders. At midday, Japanese bombers appeared suddenly over Clark Field (the principal American air base in the Philippines, located about forty miles northwest of Manila), and dropped their sticks of bombs from 18,000 feet. From the ground, these appeared as columns of evenly spaced silver glints falling diagonally behind the planes. They grew steadily larger, and Americans on the ground dove for foxholes. A procession of cataclysmic explosions fell across the heart of the air base, among the hangars and maintenance shops and parked planes. Every bomb released fell within the base, and not one structure in the vicinity was left unscathed. An American pilot looking down at the scene could not even see the airstrip, because "the whole area was boiling with smoke, dust and flames. In the middle was a huge column of greasy black smoke from the top of which ugly red flames billowed intermittently."

No sooner had the bombers passed over than the Zeros roared in at rooftop altitude, locked in compact three-plane formations, and strafed the parked planes that had not been finished off by the bombs. None of the American planes caught on the ground at Clark that day would ever fly again. By the end of that first day of the war, half the airpower defending the Philippines was gone. Twelve B-17s and thirty P-40s were totally destroyed; five more B-17s were damaged. That initial disaster guaranteed that more would follow, as the Americans had lost the ability to mount counterstrikes on Japanese air bases or to put up any effective fighter resistance to the wave of air raids that would inevitably follow.

The truth about MacArthur's weird malfunctioning on that day remains shrouded in mystery even now. It is possible he was unwilling to order a strike on Japanese bases from Philippine territory, hoping that the Japanese offensive might otherwise spare the islands. Not only would the general escape scrutiny and censure for his inexplicable failures, no less ignominious and more avoidable than those at Pearl Harbor, but he would be adopted by the American people as a much-loved war hero, the preeminent Allied celebrity of the Pacific War.

In Malaya, the British air defenses fared no better. RAF fighters engaged enemy bombers and Zeros in a pitched air battle over Kota Bahru on the northeast coast, where a Japanese invasion force was put ashore on the first morning of the war. The result was a lopsided victory for the Japanese, as several Royal Air Force Bristol Blenheim and Lockheed Hudson bombers went down in flames. Meanwhile, Japanese G3M bombers from bases in Indochina, more than 600 miles away, appeared suddenly in the skies over Singapore and dropped sticks of bombs on RAF runways and base installations. The raid came as a bolt out of the blue, for the British had never imagined that the Japanese were capable of mounting air strikes across such great distances. An RAF aerodrome at Kota Bahru was abandoned in a state approaching panic, with men lighting out for the hills, ignoring the threats and imprecations of their officers, and allowing food, fuel, weaponry, and the best airstrip in northern Malaya to fall into the hands of the enemy.

British air defense plans had placed too much faith in the Brewster Buf-falo, an obsolete fighter purchased from the United States. A pilot who detested the aircraft said it looked "a lot like the racing planes of the 1930s: all engine, a barrel fuselage, stubby wings, a large canopy, and almost no tail." The underpowered Buffalo suffered fuel delivery problems that limited its rate of climb; it had a flawed landing gear, which often caused serious damage on landing; and its .50-caliber guns were prone to jamming, par-ticularly in the humid weather of the tropics.

In both the Philippines and Malaya, the sudden onslaught pushed the Allied air forces into combat conditions for which they were not adequately prepared, multiplying their non-combat losses. Dozens of American and British aircraft crashed due to engine failures, accidents, or midair collisions with other planes in their squadrons. Planes were shot down by friendly antiaircraft fire when attempting to return to base; planes were forced to ditch when they ran out of fuel; planes managed to land safely but had to be scrapped because of heavy damage. To the Japanese, a crashed Allied airplane was as good as one shot down—perhaps even a little better since it involved no expenditure of ammunition. If the aircrew went down with it, so much the better.

In the years before the war, the Americans and British had taken comfort in a widely held conviction that Japanese airpower was not to be viewed seriously. That impression was nourished by quackish, pseudo-scientific theories proposed by "experts" of various fields. The Japanese would always make bungling pilots, the authorities patiently explained, because they suffered from innate physiological defects. They were cross-eyed and nearsighted, possibly a symptom of their "slanted" eyes. As infants, they had been carried on the backs of their mothers, causing their heads to wobble in a way that threw off the balance in the inner ear. Japanese cultural norms emphasized conformity and obedience; therefore, their young men must lack the aviator's traits of individualism and self-reliance. Western aviation journals cited statistics (of dubious origin) purporting to show that Japan had the highest aviation crash rate in the world. It was acknowledged that Japan had developed a self-sufficient aircraft manufacturing industry—and that was a surprising achievement, admittedly—but the idea that Japanese-built planes could be any good was simply beneath consideration.

Only after the shocking losses of December 1941 did it begin to dawn on the Allies that they had seen only what the Japanese had wanted them to see. "If he [your enemy] is arrogant," Sun-Tzu had written, "behave timidly so as to encourage his arrogance."

In fact, the Japanese naval aviators were among the very best pilots in the world. They had been selected in highly competitive recruiting programs, and earned their wings by surviving long, intense training regimens. They were, on average, far more seasoned than their Allied counterparts. Many had flown more than 100 aerial combat missions over China since 1937, accruing an average of 500 to 600 flight hours in the cockpit. They were intensely motivated and eager to correct all the misimpressions that the West had held of them. They showed resourcefulness and adaptability; they worked supremely well together; and they were ruthless in attacking any weaknesses.

The Mitsubishi A6M Zero was a dogfighting champion, an aerial acrobat that out-turned, out-climbed, and out-maneuvered any fighter plane the Allies could send against it. It was armed with two 7.7mm machine guns (synchronized to fire through the propeller) and two powerful wing-mounted 20mm cannons licensed from the Swiss arms manufacturer Oerlikon. It excelled in relatively low-speed, low-altitude "tail-chasing," because its tight turning radius allowed it to get behind any Allied fighter plane or even to flip over on its back and kill the enemy with a short, accurate burst from above. The Japanese pilots spoke reverently of the airplane's responsiveness to the slightest pressure on the controls. "She handled like a dream," said fighter pilot Saburo Sakai, who flew in the first attack runs against the Philippines. "Just a flick of the wrist—she was gone! I went through all sorts of aerobatics, standing the Zero on her tail, diving, sliding off on the wings." Allied pilots who attacked the Zero using classical dogfighting techniques—chasing and maneuvering to get on the enemy's tail—were shot down almost to a man. Those lucky enough to escape into a cloud, or parachute to the ground, were full of horrified expletives at the shocking capabilities of this mysterious fighter.

The Zero had been placed in service in the summer of 1940, almost eighteen months before Pearl Harbor. Operating from bases on Formosa and along the Chinese coast, Zeros had accompanied bombers on long-range missions into the heart of China. By the standards of the era, the aircraft's range was extraordinary. Manipulating fuel mixtures and propeller speeds, the Japanese had shown it was possible to fly this single-seat plane more than 1,000 miles on a single tank. Pilots were accustomed to the taxing work of such long missions, sometimes even setting the trim to level flight and dozing off in the cockpit. The Zero had chewed up Chiang Kai-shek's Chinese Nationalist air force—in 1940 and 1941, not a single Zero was downed in air-to-air combat over China.

The arrival of this deadly plane had not escaped the attention of General Claire Lee Chennault, commander of the "Flying Tigers," an American volunteer group that fought for the Chinese air force. One of the Tigers, in his diary entry for November 21, 1941, noted that General Chennault had coached the P-40 pilots on how to fight the Zero, offering the same tactical advice that navy fighter jocks would later develop independently—dive from altitude, stick to your wingmen, set up passing shots, and "never try to dogfight a Zero, particularly in turning combat. Hit and run! Hit and run, dive, and then come back to altitude. Of course, always try to stay in groups of at least two. As soon as you find yourself alone, search the skies to rejoin someone." But Chennault's intelligence reports were simply ignored in Washington. The Americans could not bring themselves to believe that Japan could have built and manufactured a machine with a climb rate of 3,000 feet per minute. For a year and half, the Zero remained almost completely unknown in Allied aviation circles, and the American and British pilots were forced to learn about this lethal athlete the hard way. It was yet another example of the fatal hubris of the West in the face of plentiful evidence of the Japanese threat, an attitude that would cost hundreds of planes and aircrews in the early months of the Pacific War.

ON WEDNESDAY, DECEMBER 10, an armada of more than fifty Japanese bombers crossed the China Sea and cruised serenely over Manila Bay at an altitude of 20,000 feet. Nothing could be done to stop them—a few P-40s had tried to intercept them off the coast of northern Luzon, but had been brushed aside by the escorting Zeros, and the U.S. Navy's 3-inch antiaircraft guns could not even reach that height. Untroubled by resistance or opposition, the bombers circled the target-rich panorama below "like a flock of well-disciplined buzzards," as one witness recalled. They were obviously drawing a bead on the Manila waterfront, the ships moored at the wharves, and the U.S. naval base at Cavite, the navy's principal base west of Pearl

Harbor. When they finally let go of their payloads, the bombs cut a swath of carnage through the heart of Cavite, wiping out the repair shops, the warehouses, the machine shops, the barracks, and the power plant. Several barges and tugboats were destroyed at their berths, and one submarine, the *Sealion*, was a total loss. Fires raged out of control. Strong winds swept off the bay and fed the flames, and the firefighters could do little to stop them because much of their equipment had been destroyed. Lieutenant John Buckley, a PT-boat skipper, was appalled at the sight. "They'd flattened it," he said of Cavite; "there isn't any other word. Here was the only American naval base in the Orient beyond Pearl Harbor pounded into bloody rubbish."

Admiral Thomas C. Hart, commander in chief of the Asiatic Fleet, watched the scene from the roof of his fleet headquarters building. His reaction is unrecorded. He might have had some premonition that the army's air defenses would not stand, because he had taken the wise precaution of sending most of his ships away to the south before the outbreak of the war. Now his main base, with all its supporting facilities and munitions, was a smoking hole in the ground. Most damaging, perhaps, was the loss of 230 torpedoes. At this point it was Hart's awful duty to abandon the Philippines, to send all remaining ships of the U.S. Asiatic Fleet south, where they might join up with British and Dutch units for the defense of the Dutch East Indies.

A WEEK BEFORE THE WAR, against the recommendation of his admirals, Prime Minister Churchill had ordered a powerful naval squadron to Singapore in hopes of deterring Japanese aggression against the colony. "Force Z," as it was called, was built around two of Britain's finest and most prestigious ships of war, the battleship *Prince of Wales* and the battlecruiser *Repulse*. The fate of those ships, even more than the loss of the American battle line at Pearl Harbor, was to mark the turning of a new page in naval history.

On December 8 (local date), just hours after the attack on Pearl Harbor, Admiral Tom Phillips had ordered his force to sea to intercept and destroy a Japanese invasion force sighted in the South China Sea. The British had no aircraft carrier in the theater, and the RAF was already in disarray, so the squadron was obliged to sail without air support. Phillips recognized the danger but hoped that the operation could "finish quickly and so get away to the eastward before the Japanese can mass a formidable scale of attack against us."

From the first, Force Z had a great deal of difficulty in even locating the Japanese fleet. They headed northwest into the Gulf of Siam, toward the Japanese beachhead at Kota Bahru in northern Malaya, then chased a false report of a Japanese landing at Kuantan, farther down the coast.

Despite the lack of air cover, the officers and crews of the great British warships were upbeat—whatever they had heard of the shocking result of the air battles over northern Malaya, they remained confident that the Japanese were no match for two of the best and most powerful ships of the Royal Navy. Bert Wynn, able seaman of *Repulse*, recalled that among his mates "the main topic of conversation was how long would it take us to sink the Japanese warships felt to be in attendance around the coast of Singora. I still remember the feeling of absolute confidence running throughout the ship . . . the outcome of such an engagement was felt to be a formality." When, on the afternoon of December 9, a Japanese surface force was sighted by a British patrol plane, a flag deck officer of the *Repulse* remarked to CBS radio correspondent Cecil Brown (who was on board as a press observer), "Oh, but they are Japanese. There's nothing to worry about."

That night over dinner in the officers' wardroom, Brown raised a provocative question. In light of what had happened at Pearl Harbor, were the British too confident? The British officers chewed the question over thoughtfully, and one conceded that it was "wrong" to underestimate the enemy. But the prevailing feeling among them was summed up in another officer's reply: "We are not overconfident; we just don't think the enemy is much good. They could not beat China for five years and now look what they are doing out here, jumping all over the map instead of meeting at one or two places. They cannot be very smart to be doing that."

The air attack on Force Z began shortly after 11 a.m. on Wednesday, December 10. It was pressed home by three waves of twin-engine G3M "Nell" and G4M "Betty" bombers of the 22nd Air Flotilla, based in Indochina, near Saigon. The attackers had crossed the South China Sea, had been in the air for about five hours, and were nearing the point of no return. British lookouts spotted a cluster of ominous black dots high above the horizon in the west, and the marine buglers sounded the call to quarters. As the incoming G3Ms came into range, at an altitude of about 12,000 feet, the gunners opened up and the sky was peppered with black antiaircraft bursts.

Remaining in close formation, the bombers dropped several 250-kilogram bombs. Turning and twisting violently, heeling sharply to starboard and then to port, the *Repulse* dodged all but one bomb, which struck her seaplane deck, killing perhaps two dozen men, but otherwise not impairing the maneuverability or defenses of the ship.

About twenty minutes later, Force Z radar sets picked up a flight of nine torpedo-armed G3Ms coming in from the west. They approached virtually on the wavetops and pressed home their attack against the flagship *Prince of Wales*, diving in groups of two and three to less than 100 feet altitude and attacking on both bows. She was hit twice near the stern, jamming her rudder and flooding her engine rooms. The crippled leviathan steamed helplessly in a jagged circle, flames and smoke spewing behind her into the sky.

A third attack, by torpedo-armed G4Ms of the Kanoya Air Group, descended on the *Repulse*. Spared in the first barrage, the *Repulse* maneuvered to save herself, and managed to avoid almost twenty torpedoes, but at last she was caught in an "anvil" attack, with torpedoes dropped simultaneously on each of her bows. "For me," wrote Cecil Brown, who watched from the flag deck and recorded his impressions in a notebook, "this whole picture—orange flame belching from the 4-inchers, white tracers from pompoms and Vickers guns, and gray airplanes astonishingly close, like butterflies pinned on blue cardboard—is a confusing, macabre game." *Repulse* was struck twice (possibly as many as four times) and immediately began to take on water. "Suddenly there was a massive explosion," one of her crew recalled. "I immediately knew we'd lost *Repulse*, for within seconds she took on a frightening list to port, so rapid no amount of counter flooding would save her." Her captain ordered abandon ship, shouting, "You've put up a good show, now save yourselves."

The men had to jump into the sea, where many drowned and others treaded water for hours, their faces blackened by fuel oil. At 12:23 p.m., *Repulse* rolled over and sank stern-first, her huge hull protruding vertically from the sea, her bow pointed straight up to the sky. Destroyers circled cautiously, picking up survivors.

With the *Repulse* gone, a new wave of Japanese bombers turned to the easier task of putting away the crippled *Prince of Wales*. At 12:44 p.m., she was struck between the stacks by a 500-kilogram bomb dropped from altitude by a G4M bomber, and began to sink immediately. Many men were trapped belowdecks when the ship rolled over and began to sink. The

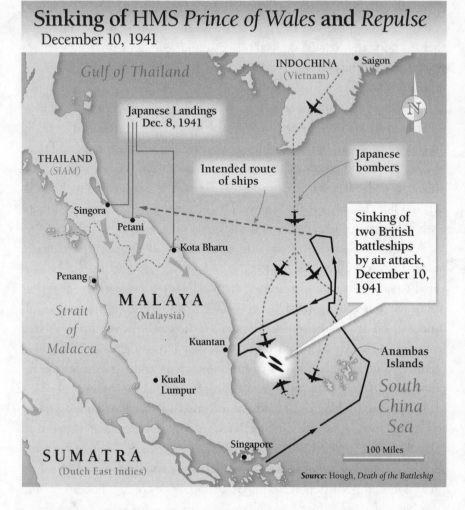

Sinking of HMS *Prince of Wales* and *Repulse*
December 10, 1941

Gulf of Thailand

INDOCHINA
(Vietnam)

• Saigon

Japanese Landings
Dec. 8, 1941

**Japanese
bombers**

N

THAILAND
(SIAM)

**Intended route
of ships**

Singora •

Petani •

**Sinking of
two British
battleships
by air attack,
December 10,
1941**

• Kota Bharu

Penang •

MALAYA
(Malaysia)

Strait
of
Malacca

Kuantan •

**Anambas
Islands**

South
China
Sea

• Kuala
Lumpur

Singapore •

100 Miles

SUMATRA
(Dutch East Indies)

Source: Hough, *Death of the Battleship*

destroyers circled and picked up as many swimmers as they could. A Japanese plane overhead flashed a bravura taunt in plain English: "We have finished our task now. You may carry on."

A handful of RAF fighter planes arrived just as the *Prince of Wales* was going down, but they could do nothing but circle and watch. One of the pilots recalled the sight of the men in the water: "After an hour, lack of petrol forced me to leave, but during that hour I had seen many men in dire danger waving, cheering and joking, as if they were holiday-makers at Brighton waving at a low-flying aircraft. It shook me, for here was something above human nature."

The battle claimed the lives of 47 British officers and 793 men. The Japanese, amazingly, had lost only three planes in the action. The attack, the British had to admit, had been carried out in textbook fashion. "The enemy attacks were without doubt magnificently carried out and pressed well home," wrote the captain of the *Repulse* after the battle. "The high level bombers kept tight formation and appeared not to jink." It had been a finely choreographed one-two punch, with the high-level bombers arriving first and distracting the gunners, followed closely by the torpedo bombers that came in low and dropped their deadly fish in perfectly executed "anvil" attacks.

On the morning of December 10, Churchill was awakened by a telephone call from Admiral Sir Dudley Pound, the first sea lord, who gave him the appalling news that Japanese bombers had sent both ships to the bottom. "Are you sure it's true?" the prime minister asked. "There is no doubt at all," Pound replied. As he put the receiver back in its cradle, Churchill later wrote: "I was glad to be alone. In all the war I never received a more direct shock. . . . As I turned over and twisted in bed the full horror of the news sank in upon me. . . . Over all this vast expanse of waters Japan was supreme, and we everywhere weak and naked." It meant that the last vestige of British seapower in the Pacific had been broken; it meant that even India could now be threatened by sea, as it soon would be; it meant that the Indian Ocean sea-lanes were vulnerable. Both ships, but the *Prince of Wales* especially, had held immense significance to British naval prestige. She was one of the newest and most formidable battleships in the fleet. The previous August, she had carried Churchill to Placentia Bay, Newfoundland, to meet Roosevelt in the flesh for the first time since either man had come to power, and her sweeping teak decks had provided the dramatic setting for that first wartime Anglo-American summit.

Three days earlier, Japanese airplanes had blindsided the American battleships in their anchorage; but never before had such ships been sunk by air attack while operating at sea in full combat readiness. The fate of Force Z was something new in the annals of naval war, and it settled old and bitter arguments. Though it was a Japanese victory and a painful Allied defeat, it was also a conceptual triumph within naval circles all over the world for the cause of aviation, and did more than even Pearl Harbor to undermine the power of the Mahanian "big gun club." Fleet doctrine would be hastily rewritten: battleships would now be relegated to a support role within task forces built around aircraft carriers. Their antiaircraft weaponry would be doubled, tripled, and finally quadrupled, until they were bristling with AA guns of every caliber, and better able to defend both themselves and the carriers against enemy air attack. Their huge 14- and 16-inch main batteries would be employed mainly for shore bombardment, in support of amphibious troop landings. These doctrines were swiftly adopted by the U.S. Navy, and to a lesser extent by the Royal Navy; but they would be slower to penetrate the upper ranks of the Imperial Japanese Navy, where hopes for a decisive clash of battleships at sea would be cherished almost to the end of the war.

THE JAPANESE OFFENSIVE ADVANCED SOUTHWARD by a leapfrogging pattern. Land-based Zeros and medium bombers attacked suddenly and across unexpectedly long distances, clearing the skies over the beaches for the invasion forces that followed. Columns of Japanese troopships, unmolested by air attacks, put troops, tanks, and weapons ashore. From those beachheads the Japanese forces advanced inland, swallowing up territory and capturing airfields, usually intact. Air groups flew into the captured airfields and prepared for the next series of attacks further south. New hammer blows then fell on Allied positions with startling rapidity, before the defenders could pull themselves together. The Philippines, Guam, Hong Kong, Malaya—all were scenes of Japanese triumph and Allied distress. American and British airfields were strewn with twisted, smoking clots of wreckage, the remains of aircraft wiped out on the ground. Mechanics had been killed, hangars damaged or gutted, spare parts destroyed on the ground or fallen into enemy hands. By Thursday morning, four days into the war, Allied pilots and ground support personnel were swimming in a state of confusion, fear, denial, and shock. Scenes of chaotic and panicked retreat added the onus of disgrace to the agony of defeat. At Iba in the Philippines, American personnel fled their posts without orders. At Clark Field, the runways were cratered and unusable, and most of the buildings and hangars had been flattened. The remains of dead airmen were strewn over the base, and would not even be collected and buried until a week had passed. Civilians and military officials, shocked by the speed and scale of the disaster, now seriously doubted that they could hold back the attacking tide.

IT IS OFTEN SAID that Japan's attack on Pearl Harbor was worth the cost in U.S. ships, planes, and men lost, because it galvanized the American people when they had seemed hopelessly divided over the coming war. The judgment is accurate, but incomplete. Hitler finished the job on Thursday, four days after the Japanese attack, by declaring war on the United States when he had the option of doing nothing at all.

In secret prewar communications with the British, Roosevelt had committed the United States to a "Europe-first" strategy. The military logic of "Europe-first" was unassailable, but the policy was never popular with the American people, who felt (after Pearl Harbor) that they had a personal score to settle with the Japanese. On Sunday afternoon, Secretary of War Stimson had proposed a preemptive declaration of war against all three Axis partners, but Roosevelt had rejected the suggestion out of hand, saying he did not want to cleave American opinion at the very moment it had finally been incited to war. Even after Pearl Harbor, Roosevelt could not have obtained a declaration of war against Germany except perhaps by a sharply divided vote in Congress. But without such a declaration, there was a danger that America's productive output would be sucked into the vortex of the Pacific emergency, leaving Russia and Britain on the verge of collapse.

Pearl Harbor had caught Hitler by surprise, no less than anyone outside Japan's ruling circle. When the news reached the Wolf's Lair, the Führer's eastern headquarters in the Masurian Woods of East Prussia, he was exultant. "The turning point!" he declared to members of his assembled staff. "We now have an ally who has never been vanquished in 3,000 years!" The surprise attack seemed likely to tie the United States down in the Pacific, and prevent for the time being its providing effective aid to Germany's enemies. The Japanese onslaught promised to deprive Britain of its Eastern empire, perhaps even India. Propaganda minister Joseph Goebbels shared the Führer's misguided optimism, noting in his diary: "A complete shift in the general world picture has taken place. The United States will scarcely now be in a position to transport worthwhile material to England, let alone the Soviet Union."

On the morning of December 11, Benito Mussolini spoke from a balcony overlooking the Piazza Venezia in Rome, declaring to a rapturous throng that the "powers of the pact of steel" would prevail over the democracies. Hitler spoke before the Reichstag that afternoon at 3 p.m. The Führer's speech was typically strident and convoluted, a ninety-minute performance laced with sarcasm, paranoia, invective, menace, and plaintive appeals to Germany's victimhood and good intentions. Paragraphs were expended in bile directed against the Soviet Union and Great Britain. He spoke at length on the Wehrmacht victories on the eastern front in the first six months of the Nazi-Soviet War, without admitting to the recent setbacks in the siege of Moscow.

When he turned to the United States, Hitler fastened his wrath on the figure of Roosevelt as a member of the "Upper Ten Thousand," a representative of "the class whose path is smoothed in the Democracies . . . this meddling gentleman . . . this honest warmonger . . . the man who is the main culprit of this war." The war, declared the Führer, had been arranged and provoked by a small circle of bankers and plutocrats, mostly American and Jewish, who had employed Roosevelt as their agent. Hitler congratulated Japan on having been "the first to take the step of protest against his historically unique and shameless ill-treatment of truth," for the attack on Pearl Harbor had filled "the German people, and I think, all other decent people in the world, with deep satisfaction."

The declaration of war came in roundabout fashion, well over an hour after Hitler had taken the rostrum. "I have therefore arranged for his passports to be handed to the American Chargé d'Affaires today, and the following . . ." and at this point the expectant deputies drowned the Führer's words in applause. "The American President and his Plutocratic clique have mocked us as the Have-nots—that is true, but the Have-nots will see to it that they are not robbed of the little they have." The Axis powers, the Führer announced, had concluded an agreement which bound the three partners not to lay down their arms until they had subjugated and destroyed "the Anglo-Saxon–Jewish–Capitalist World."

In Washington, the counterdeclarations came quickly and without debate. The vote was unanimous in both houses of Congress. In signing the measures, Roosevelt said that the Allies were engaged in a single, integrated, global conflict across land and sea in every corner of the world. "The forces endeavoring to enslave the entire world now are moving towards this hemisphere." The war would require a long, hard struggle against "the forces of savagery and barbarism."

The Axis propagandists had caricatured America as helplessly splintered by race, ethnicity, class, and creed; as a pampered, luxury-loving society in which the only cause that aroused the people was the pursuit of the almighty dollar; as a nation of loafers and malingerers, overpaid, overfed, and over-enfranchised, in which politicians went with hats in hand to receive the benediction of union bosses. To their eyes, the United States was a sprawling, individualistic, leisure-loving nation, strung out on jazz, movies, baseball, comic strips, horse racing, and radio comedies—anything but work, and certainly not the work of marching off to war. It was a nation enfeebled by divided government, with power impotently shared by the president and Congress and law courts, all constantly put upon by an insolent, unbridled press. Americans were a parochial, self-absorbed, inward-looking people, who could not care less about the rest of the world, who would never consent to spill a drop of blood to defend England, the villainous oppressor of their revolutionary heritage; or Russia, the nerve center of global communism; or any part of Asia, a place so distant and alien it could have been in another galaxy.

The critique was shallow and disingenuous, a collage of crude stereotypes and half-truths. But even in America one heard self-criticism along similar lines, and the nation was clearly unprepared to confront the Axis in 1941. The American people did not like the naked aggression of Germany and Japan, and a majority favored Roosevelt's policy of providing munitions and material support to their victims. But entering the war was a very unpopular prospect. In a Gallup poll taken less than two months before Pearl Harbor, only 17 percent of Americans had favored war with Germany. There was open talk of mass desertions from the army, encapsulated in the mutinous acronym "OHIO," or "Over the hill in October." In August, the House had voted to extend the peacetime draft by the 1-vote margin of 203 to 202. The isolationist movement actually grew stronger in the weeks leading up to Pearl Harbor, with its leaders shouting to packed public halls that Roosevelt was conspiring to foment war with the Axis. By 1941, the president saw that war was coming but could do nothing more than he had already done to change the temper of the American people. He could only wait for some inciting incident or provocation.

"The turning point," Hitler had called the Japanese attack on Pearl Harbor. "A complete shift in the general world picture," Goebbels had concluded. They were right, but not in the sense they intended. Before December 7,

1941, the American industrial economy, lying completely beyond the reach of Axis bombers or armies, had been the single best hope of the embattled Allies. Only by militarizing that economy, harnessing it entirely to war production, could the power of the Axis be destroyed. But the sprawling republic would never be mobilized or militarized without the consent of the American people. "There was just one thing that they [the Japanese] could do to get Roosevelt completely off the horns of the dilemma," wrote the presidential speechwriter Bob Sherwood, "and that is precisely what they did, at one stroke, in a manner so challenging, so insulting and enraging, that the divided and confused American people were instantly rendered unanimous and certain." If the Second World War could be said to have pivoted on a single point, it was not the Battle of Britain, or El Alamein, or Stalingrad, or the fall of Italy. Pearl Harbor, by giving Roosevelt the license to do what needed to be done, sealed the fate of both Germany and Japan.

Chapter Three

I N JAPAN, NEWS OF PEARL HARBOR HAD BEEN BROADCAST OVER THE radio: "News special, News special. . . . Beginning this morning before dawn, war has been joined with the Americans and British." Throughout that bitter cold winter day, traditional patriotic anthems such as the "Battleship March" were interrupted by announcers breaking in with updates. Radios blared from shops and houses: to know the latest, one only had to walk the streets and listen.

To millions of ordinary Japanese, it felt as if heaven and earth had been torn asunder. Even the date, December 8 (a day later than in the United States), seemed to hold transcendent meaning and power. This was *Rohatsu*, a day of special significance to Buddhists—the eighth day of the twelfth month, the day Buddha had gazed up at the morning star and realized enlightenment. Even decades later, when recalling the moment, many Japanese harkened back to an intense physical sensation—"as if my blood boiled and my flesh quivered," said Koshu Itabashi, a middle school student. "I felt like someone had poured cold water on my head," recalled Lieutenant Toshio Yoshida of the Naval General Staff. "A chill cut right through me. I can feel it now."

There was no hint, in the first reports, that the raid on Pearl had been a smashing success, and the voices of the broadcasters were shrill and edgy. Forces were engaged, hostilities had begun; that was the only news at first. Many felt consternation. The United States and Britain were powerful industrialized nations. It seemed improbable that Japan could hold its own against either. But against both simultaneously? With the war in China yet unresolved? "Is it all right to fight a war against such countries?" wondered

Ei Hirosawa, a student in Yokohama: "Can we possibly win? What would victory mean? . . . I couldn't imagine. That was the way I felt as a boy of seventeen." But doubts soon gave way to growing certainty as the day's tally was broadcast—the U.S. battle fleet was smashed, sunk, or burning, and Japanese airplanes reigned supreme over the Philippines and Malaya. Later in the war the Japanese news reports would grow increasingly divorced from reality, but in those early days no deception was necessary: the plain facts were as triumphant as whatever fabrications could have been dreamed up in a propaganda office.

There was elation and exulting—"Victory! Victory!" they shouted to one another—but perhaps the most conspicuous feeling was one of relief. For almost a year the Japanese people had hung in suspense, poised on the brink of war, as the news referred confusingly to various diplomatic transactions. Now there was decision, clarity, unity. "I was thrilled," said Ryuichi Yokoyama, a cartoonist for the *Asahi Shinbun*, one of Tokyo's major newspapers. "Happy. All the indecisive gloom cleared off just like that." The war in China had never rallied the Japanese as this war would rally them. China was an Asian neighbor, the source of Japan's written language, the homeland of Confucius, the cradle of Eastern Buddhism. The war against Britain and the United States was different, or so it was easy to believe—it would be a campaign of liberation against colonial oppressors on behalf of all Asians. It elevated the meaning of the war. Someone, finally, had laid down the gauntlet against the Western imperialists who had always had their way in Asia. "Never in our history had we Japanese felt such pride in ourselves as a race as we did then," wrote Takao Okuna, a literary critic.

The emperor Hirohito was dressed for the day in his navy uniform. Upon receiving the news (according to the diary entry of Koichi Kido, the lord privy seal), he was "perfectly calm, unmoved, and self-possessed." He issued a formal declaration of war in the form of an "imperial rescript," blaming Britain and the United States for "disturbing the peace of East Asia." Japan's long and weary efforts to preserve the peace had been thwarted by the ambitions of the Western powers, who had shown "not the least spirit of conciliation," but had instead "intensified the economic and political pressure to compel thereby Our Empire to submission. . . . Our Empire, for its existence and self-defense, has no other recourse but to appeal to arms and to crush every obstacle in its path." The prime minister, General Hideki Tojo, addressed the nation over the radio. He emphasized that the war would be long and hard. "In order to annihilate this enemy and to con-struct an unshakable new order of East Asia, we should anticipate a long war." But there was no doubt Japan would prevail. "For 2,600 years since it was founded, our Empire has never known a defeat." The day ended with a huge rally outside the walls of the Imperial Palace.

At the Navy Department in Tokyo, said Lieutenant Yoshida, men "were swaggering up and down the halls, swinging their shoulders. Full of pride." A special celebratory sweet red-bean soup was served out to the officers on the Naval General Staff. Throughout the fleet and shore stations of the Imperial Japanese Navy, at home and overseas, officers and men crowded into radio rooms to hear the latest updates from the theaters of combat, and let out savage cries of triumph upon hearing each fresh victory report. "To be perfectly honest," wrote airman Masatake Okumiya, "I personally was astounded at the enemy's inexplicably weak resistance. We expected our forces to fight hard and to achieve a certain minimum of successes, but prior to the attack no one would have dared to anticipate the actual results of our initial assaults." Men posted in the home islands fretted that the war might be over before they could get into it, and clamored for combat assign-ments with a vehemence that bordered on menace. "We could not disabuse these overenthusiastic youngsters of their belief that the war would end too quickly for them to try their mettle against the enemy," added Okumiya. "Our junior pilots were fully convinced that the war would end too soon to enable them to participate."

Admiral Isoroku Yamamoto, commander in chief of the Combined Fleet, was on his flagship, the battleship *Nagato*, anchored off Hashirajima Island in Hiroshima Bay. He had remained awake through the night and morning of the Pearl Harbor attack, hovering in the operations room, playing *shogi* intermittently with his administrative officer, Captain Yasuji Watanabe. As the attack unfolded, his radio operators had intercepted messages directly from Japanese planes, and others from the Americans on Oahu. "Surprise attack successful. . . . Enemy warships torpedoed; outstanding results." Members of the crew, in a celebratory gesture, were permitted to purchase sake at the canteen. Each message brought a fresh burst of rejoicing from the gathered officers, but Yamamoto remained stoic, expressionless. He was disappointed that Admiral Nagumo had withdrawn his carriers after only two attack waves, believing that he should have stayed and pressed the advantage—but the C-in-C shrank from issuing a preemptive order for a

third attack, knowing that to do so would humiliate his subordinate. Yamamoto's chief of staff, Admiral Matome Ugaki, wrote bitterly in his diary that
Nagumo's premature withdrawal was nothing more than "sneak thievery
and contentment with a humble lot in life."

Pearl Harbor had been Yamamoto's brainchild. The Naval General Staff
had approved the operation only reluctantly and in the face of Yamamoto's
threatened resignation. He had not intended a sneak attack. Indeed, Japanese historians have convincingly documented that the admiral was deeply
bothered by Japan's failure to declare war before the bombs fell. He had
repeatedly asked the Foreign Ministry for reassurances that the "14-Part
Message" would be delivered to the U.S. State Department before the strike,
and had received such assurances. The delay in decoding the message at the
Japanese Embassy in Washington was to blame for the delay, though most
Americans would know nothing of that imbroglio until after the war.

The success of the daring operation in the teeth of the Naval General
Staff's opposition strengthened Yamamoto's hand. As a proponent of naval
aviation, he believed in the striking power of his carriers, and in the vulnerability of surface ships to air attack. When he had learned of the arrival
of the *Prince of Wales* and *Repulse* in Singapore, he had personally ordered
thirty-six torpedo-armed G4M "Betty" bombers to reinforce the 22nd Air
Flotilla, and urged them to hunt down the British battlewagons. He had
even placed bets that the two ships would be sunk. The destruction of Force
Z was a personal triumph for Yamamoto and for Japanese naval airpower;
it was also a cause of mighty chest-beating by the nationalist press. "Like a
once-bitten stray dog," declared the editors of a magazine, the *New Order in
Greater East Asia*, "the British Navy must turn around and run as it barks."
In other publications, aerial photos of the *Prince of Wales* slipping beneath
the waves were paired with Western file photos taken the previous August
at the Anglo-American summit in Placentia Bay, depicting Roosevelt and
Churchill bowed in prayer at a religious service on the quarterdeck of the
same ship. Pearl Harbor and the sinking of the British ships raised Yamamoto to a position of supreme influence within the Japanese naval hierarchy. Now he could dictate his wishes to the Tokyo admirals, and would
continue to do so until the defeat at Midway, six months later.

Mitsuharu Noda, a yeoman on the *Nagato*, recalled that Yamamoto
received thousands of telegrams and letters of congratulations in those
early weeks, and was punctilious in replying to each one in his own exqui-

site calligraphy. "He ordered me to have extra-large name cards made up bearing the inscription: 'Combined Fleet Commander-in-Chief Yamamoto Isoroku,'" Noda recounted. "On each, he wrote in his own brush hand, 'I swear I shall conduct further strenuous efforts and shall not rest on this small success in beginning the war.'" It was typical of Yamamoto to bear even the mantle of his own fame as a solemn duty. He seemed well aware that he was the most renowned military man in Japan, except perhaps General Tojo himself, and certainly the most famous admiral since Heihachiro Togo, under whom he had served at Tsushima thirty-six years earlier.

Even in those heady early days of the war, when the navy was scoring victories beyond the wildest hopes of the Japanese, Yamamoto was strangely glum. He felt a sense of heavy foreboding. "A military man can scarcely pride himself on having 'smitten a sleeping enemy,'" he wrote a friend; "it is more a matter of shame, simply, for the smitten. . . . I would rather you made your appraisal after seeing what the enemy does, since it is certain that, angered and outraged, he will soon launch a determined counterattack." To another correspondent he warned of the air raids on Tokyo to come, prophetically deploring "the mindless rejoicing at home. . . . It makes me fear that the first blow on Tokyo will make them wilt on the spot."

WILLIAM MANCHESTER, THE AUTHOR, biographer, and Pacific War veteran, famously called Yamamoto "the greatest admiral since Lord Nelson." At first glance, the comparison seems ridiculous. The British admiral Horatio Nelson (1758–1805) won an unbroken series of one-sided naval victories that left the Royal Navy in sole command of the world's oceans. Yamamoto was directly responsible for Midway, one of the most cataclysmic defeats in all of naval history, and for the equally costly failure of Japan's four-month sea-air-land campaign to recapture the island of Guadalcanal. So much damaging criticism has been directed at Yamamoto's performance in the Pacific War, much of it by his own officers, that it is an awfully long stretch to call him a great admiral, let alone the greatest since Nelson.

But in another sense there is much to be said for the analogy, because the parallels are numerous and striking. Each man possessed an indefinable "presence," an extraordinary natural charisma or force of personality that commanded the fanatical loyalty and deep affection of his subordinates. Each man rose from humble origins, and was especially loved by the enlisted

men of the "lower deck." Each practiced a warm, collegial style with his fellow officers, and went out of his way to attend to the small comforts of his
shipmates. Each had been wounded in action and wore the scars to prove
it—Nelson had lost an arm and the sight of one eye; Yamamoto was missing
two fingers of his left hand. Each man loved a woman who was not his wife,
and in each case the affair caused a public scandal after his death. Each
possessed an innate spirit of audacity that favored all-or-nothing aggression
on the attack, when their more prudent colleagues would have played the
odds and remained content with partial victories. For a time, until the tide
of war turned against Japan, Yamamoto's boldness brought him the same
kind of glory that Nelson accrued throughout his career. Each was slain
in action, and afterward semi-deified in grand public funerals; in each case
their loss caused a public feeling of consternation or even dread, as if the
death of one man could leave an entire nation at the mercy of its enemies.
To an island people, enclosed on all sides by the sea, the quintessential
great fighting admiral occupies a peculiar place in the national imagination.
No corresponding archetype quite exists in a continental nation like the
United States. Yamamoto was lifted up by the Japanese people as a spiritual
defender of their islands in a dire emergency. In that sense he was great,
maybe even as great as Nelson.

He was a short man even by contemporary Japanese standards, standing just five feet three inches tall, and in his later years, having lived an
admiral's sumptuous, sedentary life, his waistline expanded and he could
be called portly. But he carried the extra weight well for a man of his small
stature: he was bull-necked and broad-shouldered, and in his confident, easy
stride there was the mark of a born athlete. In a posed photograph, circa
1940, he sits upright with perfect military posture and yet appears wholly
relaxed. He looks at least ten years younger than his fifty-six years. He stares
back at the camera with large, placid eyes; his skin is dark and smooth; his
hair is close-cropped, emphasizing the noble shape of his head. His shoulders and chest are intricately festooned with gold braid and rows of medals.

He had been born Isoroku Takano, in the city of Nagaoka, in the prefec-
ture of Niigata, on the coast of the Sea of Japan. His father was an impov-
erished former samurai of a defeated clan, but in 1916, at age thirty-two,
Isoroku was adopted into the Yamamoto family and took that name. Such
arrangements were traditional and unexceptional in Japan. He graduated
from the Japanese Naval Academy at Etajima in 1904—one year before

his opposite number, Chester Nimitz, graduated from Annapolis. He served with Togo's fleet at the Battle of Tsushima, and was wounded when a cannon under his command on the cruiser *Nisshin* burst. Some 120 separate pieces of shrapnel were removed from his midsection and legs, leaving them badly pockmarked and scarred; he also lost the index and middle fingers of his left hand.

Yamamoto ascended quickly through the ranks, completed the Naval Staff College course, and was twice posted to the United States, where he studied English at Harvard University for two years (1919–21) and later served as naval attaché in the Japanese Embassy in Washington (1926–27). At a young age he was marked as an officer destined for high rank. He was respected for his powerful intellect and his close attention to technical details, and in naval policy debates he had a talent for persuading both peers and superiors with well-reasoned arguments that cut against the grain of conventional thinking. He possessed the "un-Japanese" quality of being singularly independent-minded and never shrinking from controversy. Sadao Asada, a historian of the Japanese navy, writes that Yamamoto's "pronounced individuality was so rare among Japanese navy men that one former officer remarked that he was almost a 'product of mutation.' He was bold and original, never compromised his principles, farsighted, and known for charismatic leadership."

At a time when gunnery and battleships were still the safest route to promotion, Yamamoto was early to cast his lot with aviation. As a captain in the mid-1920s, he had asked for and received an appointment as second in command of the Kasumigaura Naval Air Training Corps, and thereafter had held several important jobs in the aviation branch of the service. He more than any other man erected the apparatus for recruiting and training Japan's crackerjack airmen, and he personally oversaw the development of an independent, self-sufficient, and highly advanced military aircraft industry. For fifteen years he was recognized as the Japanese navy's chief advocate of airpower, and was one of the first admirals to voice the heretical view that battleships were "white elephants."

He was an internationalist who traveled widely overseas and often represented the navy at disarmament talks. He learned enough English to carry on rudimentary conversations and to read with ease: he claimed to have often skimmed the headlines of forty American newspapers per day. While at Harvard, Yamamoto spent little time in classes but actually stretched his modest budget to travel widely throughout the country, often skipping meals to save funds. He deliberately isolated himself from other Japanese to force himself to master the language. He saw enough of the United States to develop a healthy respect for the size and military potential of its industrial base. "Anyone who has seen the auto factories in Detroit and the oil fields in Texas," he once remarked, "knows that Japan lacks the national power for a naval race with America." He loved gambling and games of chance. He won large sums at the poker, blackjack, and craps tables, and joked that Japan could balance its national budget by staking him and sending him to Monte Carlo.

Yamamoto's travels gave him perspective to observe his country from a distance, to judge its strengths and weaknesses dispassionately. It was a capacity that many of his colleagues in the navy (and even more so in the army) not only lacked but actually rejected as a kind of spiritual corruption. Perhaps the most important part of his legacy was not his naval career at all, but the part he played in the unruly politics of prewar Japan. Yamamoto was convinced that the Japanese army was run by half-wits and lunatics, and he treated the generals with good-natured contempt until it became clear, in the mid-1930s, that the army was taking over the country. As civilian statesmen and elected officials were pushed to the margins of power, and militarist cliques gained ascendancy in every aspect of Japanese politics and society, Yamamoto emerged as one of Japan's leading advocates of a moderate foreign policy. He carried the torch for the "Treaty faction" of the navy, which supported the deeply unpopular disarmament treaties that would restrain the growth of the fleet. He campaigned persistently and at great personal risk to scuttle the alliance with Nazi Germany and to push Japan off its disastrous path toward war with the United States. Once the war was joined against his wishes, he continuously urged the government to seek a peace settlement. But he also did his duty, led the navy in many electrifying victories, and died well, like a samurai. When Japan lay in ruins after 1945, the memory of Yamamoto's dogged efforts before 1941 to stop the slide toward war would enhance his historical standing. In a sense he was vindicated by Japan's defeat.

JAPANESE PSYCHOLOGY AND SOCIAL BEHAVIOR are often explained in terms of *tatemae* and *honne*. *Tatemae*, meaning "front" or "facade," refers to the face one shows the world, the opinions one expresses in public, or the role one is obligated to play based on one's rank or position. *Honne* describes "the truth" or "honest feelings," shared only within a trusted circle of family and friends. To let slip the mask, revealing *honne* to another, is a signal of intimacy or trust; it is tantamount to an offer of friendship. These ideas are hardly unique to Japan, and versions of *tatemae* and *honne* are alive and well in the West. But in the Japanese way of thinking, it is perfectly natural that *tatemae* and *honne* should be at odds, and no one need agonize over the discrepancy, or go out of his way to put them to rights.

Like any correctly functioning Japanese, Admiral Yamamoto took great care to fulfill his obligatory public role. Newsreel footage depicts him stepping onto the deck of his flagship, immaculately turned out in white uniform, chrysanthemum-crested epaulettes on his shoulders, acknowledging his crew with a meaty right hand held to the visor of his uniform cap; or standing on a balcony in Tokyo, acknowledging a cheering crowd in the Japanese fashion, by waving his cap in small circles. On those occasions his face remained hard-set, rigid and expressionless. Even those who knew him well emphasized that he could be "taciturn and extremely uncommunicative" or that he had "a muscularly austere, almost forbidding side." Upon his appointment to the fleet in 1939, a Tokyo headline proclaimed: "Yamamoto, the Stern, Silent Admiral."

On his flagship he lived as a fleet commander was expected to live—in ostentatious luxury, eating multi-course meals at a lavishly set table in a cavernous wardroom, entertained by a forty-piece band that played for his pleasure on the afterdeck. "Yamamoto was every inch the perfect military figure," an officer remarked, "and conducted himself on all occasions with military reserve and aplomb. Even at Rabaul or Truk, he suffered the intense heat of the tropical sun impeccably attired in the pure white Navy officer uniform. This figure of the commander in chief, oblivious to heat, tropical humidity, and insects, never failed to impress every officer and enlisted man. Yamamoto was not merely an admiral, he was the personification of the navy."

But Yamamoto also seemed to take an almost impish delight in letting the mask slip. He had a penchant for disarming candor. A Zen priest from his home district of Nagaoka said that "when one was seated opposite him at a table, one had the feeling that he was laying all his inner workings in front of you and saying, 'Here, take what you want.'" He was a favorite of the

Tokyo newspapers, not only because he was willing to provide off-the-record glimpses of what was happening behind the scenes, but because he invited reporters into his house and plied them with whiskey and cigars. One news-paperman said he was one of the few men in high office "who would tell you straight out what he was thinking without mincing matters," and that he was "forthright to the point of seeming rather eccentric." (Naturally, those sessions did no harm to his public image—like Nelson, Yamamoto appreciated the usefulness of popular fame.) The admiral's candor was evident even to foreigners. "I viewed him as a very human, very real, and very sincere man," said Edwin Layton, who served as a naval attaché in the U.S. Embassy in Tokyo before the war. "Many Japanese are hard to 'get to.' They are quite reserved, sometimes to the point of being aloof. One sometimes has the impression that they are like actors in a drama, wearing false faces or masks to suit their roles. With Yamamoto, I got to feel that on social occasions he did not wear his false face." The admiral eschewed *tatemae*; he let his *honne* shine.

He was a free spirit who took pleasure in sloughing off the obligatory formalities of his rank. He had a boyish streak and a wicked, deadpan sense of humor—an admiral senior to Yamamoto called him a "mischievous devil." It was a side of his personality most likely to emerge ashore, especially when he was out of uniform and showing off for geishas, with whom he was very popular. He would buy a bag of toasted beans from a street vendor and eat them as he walked, tossing them high into the air and catching them in his upturned mouth. Without warning or explanation, he would do a handstand. He would hail a taxi by holding up a single gloved hand, a gesture the driver interpreted as an offer of 50 sen, a generous fare. At the end of the ride the admiral would pay only 30 sen, and in reply to the driver's complaint exclaim, "Don't be silly—look!" and hold up his now-ungloved hand with its two missing fingers. He had a vaudevillian's comic instincts for high silliness and physical comedy. In early 1941, when the fleet was anchored in Sasebo Harbor, Yamamoto dined in a restaurant ashore with one of his geisha girlfriends. Afterward he amused her by impersonating the bowlegged, pigeon-toed, clenched-buttocks, cane-twirling saunter of Charlie Chaplin. He walked in that manner for several hundred yards on a public thoroughfare swarming with the officers and sailors of the fleet. The geisha overheard an exchange between two incredulous sailors. "Hey, that's the C-in-C!" exclaimed the first. "Come off it," his mate replied: "You don't think the C-in-C would go around like that, do you?"

Yamamoto did not drink at all. Gambling and women were his vices. Mitsuharu Noda recalled that the admiral, when playing cards or other games of chance, "sometimes lost his whole uniform at the table," but he seems to have won more often than he lost. He was a master at *shogi* (Japanese chess), and sought out opponents who could play up to his level. He scrutinized the face of his opponent, and if he saw any sign of hesitation, he launched an all-out attack, sacrificing many of his pieces in pursuit of a quick victory. While in Europe and the United States, he studied bridge and poker and became highly skilled at both. He haunted the casinos of the nations he visited, using a high-low betting system that he believed could beat the house odds. He seems to have done well enough that he even spoke of quitting the navy and moving abroad to become a professional gambler. He bet on anything and everything. As navy vice-minister, he bet that he could push a lighted match through the hole of a 10-sen coin. During gunnery exercises with the fleet, he once wagered 3,000 yen, a prodigious sum, that a target vessel would not be sunk. He lost that one, and years later he was still paying installments on the debt. Historians have often connected Yamamoto's passion for gambling to the risky operations he championed as a fleet commander, and indeed, the admiral himself drew analogies to *shogi* when he discussed the merits of proposed operations.

Yamamoto had married at age thirty-four, but it seems he never loved his wife; he had chosen her, he said, because she was "strong as a horse" and seemed capable of putting up with hardships. She and their four children lived in the Akasaka district of Tokyo, but while ashore Yamamoto spent much of his time with the geishas of the Shinbashi district, who nicknamed him "Eighty Sen." (The price of a manicure was 1 yen, equivalent to 100 sen; since he had only eight fingers he demanded a discount.) He grew personally close to several geishas without necessarily taking them as lovers; indeed, in his later years he seems to have regarded them almost as a kind of surrogate family.

Geishas had no counterparts in the West. Perhaps it is necessary to call them prostitutes, inasmuch as every geisha's body was sooner or later sold to a client; but sex was only one of the services a geisha provided, and once she had achieved a certain status, she was largely free to choose whether she would provide it, and to whom. Whatever else they were, geishas were paragons of beauty and grace: they had been trained through long apprenticeships and at great expense as artists, performers, musicians, fashionistas, and conversationalists. They did not live in the shadows, and the most successful became celebrities, their photos adorning posters and magazine covers. Like modern pop stars, they were known by a single name. They were paid chiefly for their company, by the hour. They poured sake, told stories, flirted, danced, and sang to groups of men at teahouses or private residences. Through their connections to powerful men, and by controlling the livelihoods of younger apprentices, some geishas became very wealthy, and were probably the most influential Japanese women of their time.

As a military officer, Yamamoto did not have the financial means to compete with the aristocrats and business elites who usually monopolized the services of the leading geishas. But the women seem to have liked him and lavished attention on him nonetheless. When traveling abroad he bought perfume, cosmetics, and clothing to bring them as gifts. Yamamoto was permitted to make himself at home in the geisha houses even in off-hours: on a weekday afternoon the admiral sometimes showed up at a house in Shinbashi, dressed in uniform, and napped in a spare room, his face smashed against the tatami mat. The geishas looked after him, darning his socks and laundering his underwear. As his biographer speculates, "presumably it stimulated their motherly instincts."

In the mid-1930s, Yamamoto fell in love with a famous beauty named Chiyoko Kawai, who worked under the professional name of Umeryu ("Plum-dragon"). Her colleagues at the Nojima-ya geisha house in Shinbashi were amazed that she would make so much time for a man who obviously could not afford her. Their relationship had begun in a platonic friendship: he often referred to her as a "younger sister." Only after a lengthy courtship did she ask Yamamoto (using an old turn of phrase) to "take her hair down with his own hands." By 1935, she was his closest confidante. He would call her and sing over the phone to her. He would sometimes meet her at a country inn, checking in under a false name. He poured his heart out to her in letters, declaring that he felt a sense of "misery" and "worthlessness" when he reflected that he was "an object of your affection. The more I see of you, so beautiful and beguiling, the more miserable I feel. Please don't think too badly of me. . . . In theory, it was *I* who wanted to be of help to you and to relieve your loneliness, and as a man I feel ashamed to find myself, on the contrary, weakly wanting to cry on your bosom. . . . This is the first time I've told anyone about these feelings of mine."

After Yamamoto was given command of the Combined Fleet, a party of geishas including Chiyoko visited the flagship *Nagato*, moored off Yokosuka Naval Base in Tokyo Bay. The women seemed to feel "oppressed" by the strict military formalities of the ship, by the phalanxes of officers and men who snapped to attention in the presence of the C-in-C. But the admiral remained perfectly at ease. They ate a multi-course lunch in the wardroom while the band played popular folk dances for their amusement. "If the army had ever seen that, it would have caused quite an incident!" remarked his yeoman, Mitsuharu Noda, who added that the scene left him with the impression that the admiral was "really a worldly man, flexible, and approachable."

Yamamoto shrugged off concerns of a public scandal. When warned by a group of younger officers that his dalliances were unseemly, he replied, "If any of you doesn't fart and shit, and has never screwed a woman, I'll willingly hear what he has to say!" During his time in America Yamamoto had read several biographies of Abraham Lincoln, whom he admired as a man born into poverty who became a champion of "human freedom." In 1927, he told a fellow naval officer, Yoshitake Miwa, that Lincoln's flaws only enhanced his appeal:

> A man of real purpose puts his faith in himself always. Sometimes he refuses even to put his faith in the gods. So from time to time he falls into error. This was often true of Lincoln, but that doesn't detract from his greatness. A man isn't a god. Committing errors is part of his attraction as a human being; it inspires a feeling of warmth toward him, and so admiration and devotion are aroused.

No less true of Isoroku Yamamoto.

THE RISE TO POWER of Japan's ultranationalist right was a gradual process that defies easy narrative. It did not repeat the pattern of German or Italian fascism, in which a single magnetic leader rode to absolute power on the back of a disciplined political party. It was a fractious and decentralized movement, a loose confederation of shifting, secretive, like-minded nationalist societies that briefly gained prominence and just as soon dissolved or splintered. The ideological emphasis varied, but often had surprisingly anti-capitalist overtones, with some groups calling for the "return" of all private property to the emperor. Many wanted to do away with all vestiges of Western-style democracy. Others wanted to confront the West and expand Japan's overseas territories. If the movement had a center of gravity, it was in the Japanese army, or rather cliques of predominantly mid-level officers within the army. But it drew supporters from many different walks of life, including scholars, artists, writers, students, clergymen, politicians, bureaucrats, colonial adventurers, martial arts gurus, naval officers, merchants, and members of the court aristocracy. As in Europe, the movement did not lack for mass public support in the early years of the Great Depression, and by the mid-1930s it was no longer safe to hold dissenting views.

The twenties had been the era of "Taisho Democracy," in which the prevailing political climate was moderate and tolerant. It was an era of parliamentary democracy, the heyday of civilian statesmen and Western-educated diplomats who sought friendly relations with the United States and Britain, and were willing to sign treaties that restrained Japan's imperial ambitions in Asia. Political and intellectual elites set out to make Japan more worldly and cosmopolitan. Downtown Tokyo was rapidly assuming the look of a modern Western city, with tall office buildings, streetcars, automobiles, and neon signs—change the writing on the billboards and you might have been looking at Chicago or Philadelphia. There was a craze for all things Western, especially among the city's huge population of university students. Young men (and even more scandalously, women) wore Western clothing and Western hairstyles, smoked Western cigarettes and drank Western cocktails. They whiled away the hours in cafés and night-clubs. They listened to jazz and learned how to dance. They watched the films of Charlie Chaplin and Buster Keaton. They steeped themselves in Western literature and philosophy. They argued the merits of alien creeds like feminism and Marxism.

The times were tumultuous. Riots were endemic in both the cities and the country, usually prompted by wages, food prices, or rents. Landlords and employers were often targeted by death threats, and in turn hired gangs of thugs to break strikes and enforce contracts. Upstart business tycoons flaunted their recently won riches, and surreptitiously deployed their wealth to sway elections. International setbacks injured national pride. At the Versailles Conference, Japan had failed to obtain a racial equality clause (it had been opposed by the United States, among other countries). The U.S. Congress enacted the Johnson-Reed Immigration Act of 1924, which cut off immigration of ethnic Japanese into the United States. Disarmament treaties prompted the reduction of the Japanese army and navy, stunting the ambitions of younger officers whose frustrations were quick to metastasize into revolutionary violence.

Many Japanese were scandalized by the chaos, strife, and indecorum of Taisho Democracy—by the corruption, the vote-trading, the strident rhetoric, the vulgar flaunting of wealth, the Western-style bohemian degeneracy, and the intentional cleaving of society into rival camps. Those trends seemed irreconcilable with *Nihonshugi*, or "Japanism"—the cherished principles of Confucian harmony, filial piety, and reciprocal obligations between superiors and inferiors. No, all men were *not* created equal; no, political legitimacy was *not* derived from the consent of the governed; and no, ordinary people did *not* possess inalienable rights. If dissent existed, it could only be the symptom of a disorder. The Meiji emperor had given the Japanese people a quasi-democratic constitution as a "gift." But he had also emphasized a political order based on national harmony, on serene interactions between the fixed echelons of society. In his Imperial Rescript on Education (1890), a document tantamount to scripture in prewar Japan, he had decreed: "Our Imperial Ancestors have founded Our Empire on a basis broad and everlasting and have deeply and firmly implanted virtue; Our subjects ever united in loyalty and filial piety have from generation to generation illustrated the beauty thereof. This is the glory of the fundamental character of our Empire, and herein also lies the source of Our education." Democratic institutions could not easily grow and thrive in this soil. Autocratic government is a much more natural fit, and when push came to shove, there were simply not enough Japanese willing to put everything on the line to defend their democratic experiment.

The alternative was a theocracy known as *Kodo*, "the imperial way." It was a vision of Japan as a family state, with the *Tenno* (or emperor) as father figure, godhead, and dictator. Its advocates declared that the nation could be reborn by harnessing the power of the *Tenno* against all the ills in society, defined variously as capitalist greed, the chaos of democratic politics, and the humiliations and abuses of foreign powers. That was an act of purification, for "Liberalism and individualism are the dirt which must be

removed." To millions of ordinary Japanese, there was something transcendent and sublime in the notion of subsuming themselves into the identity
of the emperor; as the ultranationalist writer Ikki Kita put it, all of the
"small selves" of the Japanese people would be absorbed into the "larger
self" of the *Tenno*. The *Tenno* was the lineal descendant of the Sun Goddess, Amaterasu-Omikami; he was the "supreme and only God of the universe, the supreme sovereign of the universe," wrote Lieutenant Colonel
Goro Sugimoto, in one of his many prewar tracts; "everything in the universe is a manifestation of the emperor . . . including even the insect chirp-
ing in the hedge, or the gentle spring breeze." His throne had been created
when the heavens and earth first separated, and the first emperor descended
from heaven. The Meiji Constitution of 1889 held that "The Empire of
Japan shall be reigned over and governed by a line of Emperors unbroken for
ages eternal" (Article I) and added, "The Emperor is sacred and inviolable"
(Article III). He was the embodiment of all that was perfect in the Japanese
people, but possessed none of their flaws; it was inconceivable that he could
fail, or misconstrue his role in the hierarchy. He was infallible, by defini-
tion incapable of doing wrong: whatever morality existed in the world had
emanated from his throne.

The *Tenno* was the only national monarch who was also a god. In fact,
he was the ultimate god. It followed that his children, the racially pure and
homogeneous people of Japan, were the world's only divine race. *Kodo* bred
contempt for all foreign races, relegating them to the status of lesser beings.
In conquering them, Japan was also consecrating them, allowing them to
bask in the sacred light of their holy sovereign.

Hirohito, who would ascend to the throne in 1926, was an unlikely can-
didate to be transmuted into a Japanese man-god. He had been born in
1901, the eldest son of the crown prince Yoshihito and grandson of Mut-
suhito, the Meiji emperor. As an infant he had been taken out of the hands
of his parents and brought up in carefully guarded isolation, under the influence of court handlers and military officers. The boy was shy and studious,
weak-chinned, nearsighted, and slight of build; he spoke in a weedy and
skirling voice. He was highly impressionable and eager to please—a trait
that suited those tasked with his upbringing but could leave him vulnerable to manipulation once he took the throne. His education was largely
controlled by major figures in the army and navy, including the two most
renowned heroes of the Russo-Japanese War—first General Maresuke Nogi,

later Admiral Heihachiro Togo. From early childhood, Hirohito was incul-
cated with the seapower teachings of Alfred Thayer Mahan. He was also
steeped in the doctrines of divine descent and State Shinto, though he
seems never to have taken the dogma of his own divinity seriously. He was
rarely allowed beyond the moats and high stone walls of the imperial compound, a 240-acre expanse of grand buildings and parklike land in the heart
of Tokyo—but when he did venture out, he did so in a military uniform.

As Hirohito grew older, some in the court circle began to suspect that
his childhood had been too sheltered, that he had not developed the requisite personality or leadership skills. He remained shy and socially awkward,
and preferred to stay completely mute at court gatherings. He had a disturbing habit of talking to himself. He was watched carefully for any sign of
psychological imbalance, for his father, Yoshihito, who became the Taisho
emperor in 1912, had once, at a public function, rolled an official parchment
into a tube and held it up to his eye as a telescope; he was thereafter shut
away in monastic seclusion where his behavior could not distress the public.
While in middle school, the boy took a deep interest in natural history, particularly marine biology. He worshiped Darwin, whose bust he had installed
in his study, and he had a private laboratory installed in his palace. Here
he was happiest, studying and categorizing his specimens. He found solace
in science, and that was taken as evidence of an inquisitive and empirical
mind. One biographer, Herbert Bix, observes, "Specimen collection and the
study of taxonomy without question fitted Hirohito's methodical nature.
And certainly during his most active years, when surrounded by great disorder, by problems to which all solutions were hard and uncertain, science
was a steadying, relaxing constant in his life."

As a young man, the crown prince leaned toward relatively liberal and
moderate policies. He embraced the causes of parliamentary government,
arms limitation, and diplomatic cooperation with the Western colonial
powers. Those tendencies were reinforced by leading members of the *genro*
(elder statesmen) and royal court, including Prince Saionji and the major
characters in his entourage, the lord keeper of the privy seal and grand
chamberlain. In 1921, at age twenty, the future emperor traveled to Europe.
The trip was unprecedented and caused considerable unrest among right-
leaning Japanese, who feared not only for the prince's safety but also that he
would come under the dangerous influence of foreign ideas. He was hosted
by royalty in several capitals, including the Windsors in London; Hirohito

seems to have been bowled over by the relatively free and easy dealings of
the British royal family with their servants and friends. In France he visited
sites of the recent cataclysmic battles of the Great War, and was appalled
by the scale of the carnage; the experience redoubled his determination to
preserve the peace of Asia.

Upon his return to Japan, the prince took a more confident tone with
his advisers and began to assert his personal freedom. He went skiing in the
mountains of northern Honshu; he took up golf; he went out on the town
with his school chums. All of that came to an abrupt end in 1923, when a
would-be assassin took a shot at the prince as he rode through the streets
of downtown Tokyo in his car. The bullet did not penetrate the vehicle,
but the court suddenly closed ranks and Hirohito found himself boxed in,
a virtual prisoner in his palace, his access to those outside his inner circle
strictly curtailed. The "Toranomon Incident," as it was known, considerably
empowered the ultranationalist right, for it reinforced the godlike separa-
tion of the soon-to-be *Tenno* from his subjects, and cut the young man off
from sources of information and perspective that might have stiffened his
spine against the hidebound, reactionary impulses of his court and military
advisers. Daikichi Irokawa writes that "Crown Prince Hirohito, who had
returned from Europe imbued with the ideals of freedom, had to return to
the life of a caged bird, far removed from ordinary life."

Hirohito inherited the throne in 1926, upon the death of his father. The
official enthronement ceremonies, comparable in scale to a modern-day
Olympic Games, would last the entire year of 1928. Major new construction
and public works projects were commenced in towns and cities throughout
the country. There was a seemingly endless succession of banquets, rice-
growing ceremonies, Shinto rites, flag parades, and lantern processions.
Japanese received lavish gifts or awards or new titles of nobility, said to
have come from the emperor himself. Prisoners were freed in magnanimous
gestures of amnesty in his name. Hirohito performed obscure and secretive rites at the tombs of his ancestors, dressed head to toe in white silk
garments and assisted by high Shinto priests. All throughout, these pro-
cesses were explained to the Japanese people in the newspapers and over
the new medium of radio; scholars and clergymen explained the essence of
the Japanese *kokutai* (political order). All year long, the Japanese people's
ears rang with the rhetoric of an omnipotent and benevolent *Tenno*; and
by December, when the imperial regalia were transferred to Hirohito, the

nation had been fully indoctrinated, to a degree unknown in past Japanese history, with the cult of the emperor as a living man-god. It was said that all Japanese had now been fused into "one mind united from top to bottom." Shortly thereafter, on Tokyo Bay, a huge naval pageant was performed for the new emperor, who stood rigidly on an elevated platform as more than 200 ships and 130 naval aircraft passed in review. The new era was designated *Showa*, meaning "brightness" and "harmony" or "illustrious peace." Hirohito was now *Showa Tenno*; few Japanese had ever heard the name he had been given at birth.

The new era coincided with a crackdown on dissent. The Peace Preservation Law of 1925 clamped down on suspected Communists and other radicals. The dreaded *Kempei Tai*, or "Thought Section" of the Criminal Affairs Bureau, began surveillance of liberals in the media and academia and in suspected political parties. Staff, resources, and power grew steadily. With the approach of the Second World War, the organization and its networks of spies touched the lives of almost all Japanese, especially through the peculiar local institutions known as *tonarigumi* or "neighborhood associations." Agents of the *Kempei Tai* were perfectly willing to use prison and torture against dissidents, but to a surprising degree they often relied on a softer touch, on moral suasion; it seemed they were genuinely more interested in curing, converting, reforming, and rehabilitating wrong-headed Japanese rather than merely repressing or punishing them. From 1933 to 1936, according to the *Japan Times*, some 59,013 people were arrested and charged with "dangerous thoughts." Of those, fewer than 5,000 went to trial and only about half of those trials resulted in a prison sentence. The successful agent would note with pride not the number of convictions he had won but the number of Japanese who had fallen under the sway of foreign or radical ideas whom he had, with "tact and skill," somehow managed to coax back into the fold.

LIKE ANCIENT ROME, Japan had built its empire gradually. Like Rome, its foreign territories were added opportunistically, and by different means— some by outright conquest, some through creative diplomacy, some by taking advantage of turmoil in neighboring countries, by sending in troops to "restore order." As with Rome, every war had enlarged Japan's empire, and every enlargement had merely whetted its appetite for more.

Japan's remarkable rise was said to be preordained, the will of the gods. The same had been said of Rome's. But Japan, unlike Rome, had never suffered a defeat.

In 1875, Japan absorbed the desolate Kurile Islands north of Hokkaido; in 1876, the Bonin Islands, south of Japan; the Ryukyu Islands, including Okinawa, in 1879. Japan fought and defeated China in 1894–95, and Russia in 1904–05. Those victories brought control over Formosa (Taiwan) and Korea, annexed in 1910. In the Great War, Japan sided with the Allies and was subsequently awarded with several former German colonies of Micronesia—the Carolines, the Marshalls, and the Marianas (not including Guam, a U.S. territory).

Among Japanese nationalists it was an article of faith that the United States, the British, and to varying degrees the other Western imperial powers were secretly in league against Japan. Their anger conflated a long litany of complaints, reaching decades back into the past, into a single grand conspiracy to rule over Asia. The West had forced Japan to sign humiliating "unequal treaties" governing its foreign trade and extending extraterritorial jurisdiction over Japanese soil. Anti-Japanese agitation in California was believed to have been deliberately fomented to arouse the American public, and to mobilize the country for war against Japan. At Versailles, after the Great War, the Western powers had rejected a proposed "racial equality" clause in the Covenant of the League of Nations. The United States had enacted the Immigration Act of 1924, which restricted Japanese immigration and (worse) dumped the Japanese into the same class as Chinese and other lesser nations. There was deep suspicion that the United States and its European co-conspirators were plotting to reverse Japan's commercial and territorial gains in China.

The United States, according to a view that was steadily gaining adherents, was a rapacious, duplicitous, and malevolent nation that had bent every fiber of its strength to the subjugation and exploitation of all Asian nations, while deceitfully spreading the rhetoric of freedom, democracy and self-determination. No more stark example of this hypocrisy existed than the enforcement of a "Monroe Doctrine" in the Americas, claiming a sphere of influence throughout a neighboring continent, while insisting on an "Open Door" in China, which was really just doublespeak for the right of Americans and their British cousins to exploit China's riches while preventing others from doing so. Throughout every stage of the rise of Japan, they believed, the United States had conspired to thwart Japan's noble ambitions, attempting by devious means to reverse its military conquests, working behind the scenes to dissolve the Anglo-Japanese Alliance of 1902, using arms control diplomacy to check the growth of Japanese seapower.

Nothing got under the skin of the ultranationalist hard-liners so much as the naval limitation treaties. In the Washington Naval Conference of 1921–22, Japan had agreed to cap the aggregate tonnage of its battleship fleet to 60 percent of the U.S. and British totals, expressed as a 5:5:3 ratio. The treaty reflected a post–First World War consensus that the great powers must shun another costly naval arms race. Japan's lower cap was justified by its lack of commitments elsewhere than the Pacific: Japan could maintain its entire fleet close to home, while the Americans and British had to worry about the Atlantic. The 5:5:3 ratio was confirmed by the London Naval Disarmament Treaty of 1930, and extended to auxiliary ships as well. Until the early 1930s, most Japanese elites—including Hirohito, his court entourage, civilian ministers, and even most of the senior admirals of the navy—supported the treaty system as a means of restraining the superior industrial and shipbuilding potential of the Western powers. Even those with dreams of further Asian conquests saw the sense in buying time, in building up Japan's power gradually and deliberately. The navy could adhere to treaty limits while enhancing its human capital through recruitment and aggressive training, and the downsized battleship program would allow emphasis on categories outside the treaty provisions, including carrier aviation and submarines. Most of all, the treaties spared Japan the economic burden of a naval arms race at a time when its industrial economy was still fragile and emergent. Naval spending had ballooned to some 31 percent of Japan's budget in 1921; the treaty brought that down to 21 percent in 1923. Before the treaty, Japan was literally verging on bankruptcy; military and naval disarmament offered badly needed fiscal relief in the 1920s.

Japan's hard-liners did not find the economic arguments at all interesting or relevant, and the treaty supporters were slow to understand how disarmament was crystallizing the wrath of the hard right. Resentment grew against civilian parliamentary government, with its emphasis on economy and its ability to ram through defense cuts that seemed, in the critics' eyes, to compromise Japan's ability to protect its overseas interests. Some 1,700 commissioned and warrant officers and 5,800 petty officers were dismissed from the navy. Nine out of ten vice admirals were forced against their will to retire. The entering class of the Japanese Naval Academy at Etajima in 1922 was one fifth the size of the prior year's class. It seemed that the navy, which had been one of the most prestigious career paths in Japan, was suddenly a dead end. The treaty put an end to the navy's cherished plans for an "eight-eight fleet"—a fleet of eight battleships and eight heavy battle cruisers. It dealt a heavy blow to the shipbuilding industry, one of Japan's largest and most advanced: the sudden cancellation of naval contracts coincided with a downturn in the private market, forcing shipyards to shut their gates and lay off thousands of workers—perhaps as many as two thirds of the total that had been employed at the peak. Japan's major shipbuilding centers, such as Nagasaki, were devastated. A brand-new 40,000-ton battleship, the *Tosa*, had to be scuttled. As some 50,000 Nagasaki shipyard workers and their fellow citizens watched, a small fleet of tugboats towed the great shape of the newly launched steel hull out to sea. She went to Kure to suffer the penultimate ignominy of serving as a target for gunnery tests. Then her derelict remains were sunk in the Tosa Gulf, the body of water for which she had been named. A generation of Japanese regarded the fate of the *Tosa* as a farce, an atrocity, and an unconscionable betrayal, and they would acclaim her as a martyr to the gutlessness and corruption of Japan's diplomats.

The 5:5:3 ratio was extended for six more years by the London Naval Treaty, signed on April 22, 1930, at the Court of St. James's. Opponents in Japan campaigned against ratification. Admiral Kanji Kato declared: "It is as if Japan were bound hand and foot and thrown into jail by the Anglo-American powers!" It was not an abstruse debate, carried on above the heads of the Japanese public—from 1930 on, the 5:5:3 ratio was an incendiary popular cause, with the capacity to mobilize the Japanese "street." That was due in no small part to a disciplined corps of ultranationalist journalists, scholars, and military officers who took up their pens and their radio microphones to rail against the hated formula as symbolic of the persecution of Japan by the Western powers. Since Perry's arrival in 1853, Japanese foreign policy had been shaped by a quest for international respect, with the ultimate aim of being accepted as an equal by Britain and the United States. To a degree perhaps unique throughout the world, the Japanese people regarded treaties not as mere foreign policy expedients, but as cosmic measurements of their rank in the hierarchy of nations. Sixty percent? Was that all Japan was worth?

On October 1, 1930, the emperor's privy council ratified the London

Treaty. For Japanese liberals, it was a Pyrrhic victory. The day was a turning point in Japanese history; it unleashed sinister forces that would not be fully vanquished until 1945. Within the navy it incited a deadly feud between the senior officers who had traditionally supported the treaty limits (the "Treaty faction") and a rising cohort of hard-liners (the "Fleet faction"). (Isoroku Yamamoto's loyalties would remain with the Treaty faction, though he was politically astute enough to survive the periodic purges of like-minded officers in the 1930s.) Admiral Kato complained of the American proposals in London: "It is a most high-handed proposal, offering us, as it were, only the crust of a pie without the filling." The revered Admiral Togo, hero of the Russo-Japanese War, agreed that the treaty would impose an "irreparable loss" on Japan. In both the navy and the army there was a feeling that civilian statesmen and diplomats were infringing on terrain that fell under the rightful purview of the military. Critics charged treaty supporters with having fallen under the influence of the West; or worse, having been secretly bought by the West. By any means necessary, the civilians had to be put back in their places. By any means necessary, the military must reclaim control over the nation's destiny. It was no doubt the emperor's will.

On September 18, 1931, units of Japan's Kwantung Army launched the imperial adventure known to history as the "Mukden Incident." Troops seized and occupied the city of Mukden, and soon thereafter poured across the entire length and breadth of Manchuria, a land rich in raw materials, including coal, iron, and copper. The action would be depicted as an emergency response to insurgent attacks along the route of the South Manchurian Railway by "bandits" or "terrorists" linked to local Chinese Nationalist groups. In fact the entire operation, including the bombing attacks on the railroad, had been meticulously plotted in advance by mid-level officers on the Army General Staff, with the passive knowledge of dozens and perhaps even hundreds of senior military and civilian officials in Tokyo. In 1932, the region was reconstituted into a putatively independent country named "Manchukuo," and Pu-yi, the last emperor of China's Qing Dynasty, was installed as a puppet emperor, channeling the orders of the Japanese Kwantung Army.

When the League of Nations condemned that annexation, Japanese representatives walked out in protest. That left Japan in a state of international diplomatic seclusion, which was exactly what the ultranationalist right had intended, for it opened the way to a path of further aggression and conquest.

Hirohito may have been privately appalled by the behavior of the army but declined to punish the perpetrators and passively acquiesced in the seizure of Manchuria so long as the army delivered military successes. The cabinet and the *genro* (elder statesmen) advised the emperor to tolerate the Mukden Incident as a fait accompli, and he did. It was a short-term expediency to stabilize the domestic political situation; but over the longer term his failure to act was disastrous, because it only encouraged the conspirators in the army to plan further aggression, both at home and abroad. Daikichi Iro-kawa convincingly writes, "If, as Hirohito later stated, he had desired to be a constitutional, peace-loving monarch at that time, he should have taken a stand by 1933, when the aggression was beginning in earnest. Soon after it became extremely difficult to take any action against the militarists."

The tragic pattern of Japan's "dark valley" was now set. Secretive cliques of mid-level military officers would take control of Japan's major domestic and foreign policy choices through intimidation, assassination, and violent provocations, both at home and abroad. They would take action and then bully their superiors into acquiescing in the consequences. There was a name for that—*gekokujo*, "those below overcome those above," and it had a vener-ated place in Japanese history. (In centuries past, lower-ranking samurai in unstable fiefdoms had used similar means to manipulate their superiors.) The insurgent officers of the 1930s often behaved like gangs of criminal thugs, hoodlums in uniform, speaking reverently of the emperor, issuing threats in his name, then demanding bribes under the title of "loans" in order to spare potential victims. The major *zaibatsu* (business groups), such as Mitsui, Mit-subishi, and Sumitomo, financed those groups, and it is impossible to say whether those funds were paid in order to advance the interests of the firms in the army-controlled territories on the mainland, or whether they were in fact payments to protect leading industrialists from the threat of assassina-tion. Perhaps both motives were present. In Manchuria, gangs with links to the army practiced blackmail, extortion, racketeering, and kidnapping: their victims were predominantly Chinese but sometimes included their own countrymen. In 1930, Minister Osachi Hamaguchi came to power with the support of Hirohito, who was exasperated by General Giichi Tanaka's inability to curb the military and bring it under civilian control; but Hama-guchi was shot dead at the end of the year. In 1931, two attempted coups were put down, but the ringleaders got off with halfhearted reprimands. No charges of treason were ever brought, and the leaders maintained their freedom, even lounging with geishas at teahouses in Tokyo and boasting freely of what they had done. Ultranationalist intellectuals provided the rhetoric and ideas to justify their program; an entire apparatus of radio, film, and newspaper propaganda rushed to defend and glorify them.

They would brook no opposition. They gunned down any man who stood in their way, and that included the highest-ranking civilian ministers of the Japanese government. On May 15, 1932, a gang of naval officers, all wearing their uniforms, broke into the home of the seventy-seven-year-old Prime Minister Tsuyoshi Inukai and shot him dead. His offense had been to warn the emperor that the military was now operating outside any responsible authority. (By murdering him, of course, they only proved his point, but still Hirohito could not bring himself to punish the conspirators.) Confederates attacked and occupied other private homes as well as the Tokyo police headquarters, the Rikken Seiyukai Party headquarters, and several banks. They had hoped to depose the civilian government altogether, and spoke of a "Showa Restoration" in which the emperor would take all power and property unto himself, presumably with policy implications that would favor the military. The navy high command had some wind of the event but, as usual in those cases, took no action to stop it.

With the May 15 incident, a Rubicon had been crossed. The assassination effectively marked a new era of military domination of the Japanese government. Parliamentary party democracy was said by the insurgents to be basically "un-Japanese." The slain prime minister's political party was driven into extinction. From that point on, the Japanese government would no longer function as a parliamentary government. The leader of the majority party in the Diet would no longer be entitled to serve as prime minister. Indeed, the prime minister and other cabinet heads would generally not be selected from the Diet at all, but from the ranks of the military or the court aristocracy. In December 1933, when parliamentary leaders publicly questioned the military budget requests submitted for the year 1934, the Army and Navy ministries issued press releases denouncing their critics as Communist conspirators. For politicians to criticize the military in such a way was unacceptable, one such statement declared: "Such a movement—to separate the public mind from the military—is an attempt to disturb the harmonious unity of the public mind, the essential basis of national defense; and the military authorities cannot overlook it." Any and all civilian statesmen, bureaucrats, aristocrats, or business kingpins who had opposed the

Manchurian operation or higher military spending were put on "death lists." Often the threat was enough to silence them; if not, a bullet would do the trick.

Liberals and moderates found themselves operating within a shrinking perimeter. They could do little more than defuse each successive crisis, using the time-honored techniques of passive resignation and appeasement, always hoping that the storm would abate and the militant nationalists would fade into impotence. To wait, to survive, to avoid inflaming the opposition, to trust in the future—that was the course chosen by Japanese liberals in the 1930s. They supposed the pendulum, given enough time, would swing back in their direction, but it never did. Indeed, they were forced to recant their past heresies, to mouth the slogans of the ultranationalists and the high priests of *Kodo*. It was not just repression but, strangely, a kind of moral suasion. Prosecutions were selective. Dr. Tatsukichi Minobe, a retired law professor, had once (in a twenty-year-old law article) made the mistake of referring to the emperor as an "organ of the state." The old man was pilloried and forced to resign from the House of Peers. In Orwellian fashion, all of his past books and articles were hunted down and destroyed. His colleagues kept quiet. Prime Minister Keisuke Okada, asked to come to Minobe's defense, replied in the spirit of the times: "We cannot afford to make a mistake. There is no alternative but to assume a passive attitude."

Repression was not entirely necessary. The ultranationalist program enjoyed plenty of popular support. The young officers appealed to Japan's romantic imagination. They were celebrated as spiritual descendants of the "Ronin," the masterless samurai of the nineteenth century, proud warriors cast adrift by the collapse of feudal fiefdoms, who wandered like tramps from town to town, penniless, hungry, and humiliated. "In Japan there is a tradition of sympathy for those who strike out against overwhelming odds, even if their idealism or zeal is misplaced," explained Akio Morita, who grew up in the 1930s and went on to found the Sony Corporation. "Many of Japan's folk heroes are men who died trying to accomplish the impossible." Whether their actions were right or wrong, they were thought to be animated by *chūkin*, or "zealous devotion to the emperor," the purest and noblest of virtues. They might break the law, they might execute cabinet ministers, they might engineer military adventures overseas without authority—but by the logic of prewar Japan, they were never entirely wrong if their motive was to serve and aggrandize the *Tenno*.

As in Europe, the Great Depression aggravated all the nation's internal economic pressures and converted Japanese society into a cauldron of the aggrieved and dispossessed. The country was sent into chaos by poverty, famine, mass unemployment, landlord-tenant disputes, industrial strikes, a wave of bank failures and bank runs, and the demise of many small local firms and factories that had employed a large percentage of Japanese. In 1930, at about the same time the London Naval Treaty won ratification, the bottom fell out of rice and silk prices, and in remote northern reaches of Honshu entire families took to the roads. They were wraiths in rags, driven to the edge of starvation, drifting without any sure destination, shunned and abused by the people of the villages along the way. Parents, despairing of feeding their children, sold them into slavery by the thousands. According to statistics collected by the Japanese government, in the northeastern provinces hit hardest by the decline in farm prices, 58,173 girls were sold by their families between 1932 and 1934. They became servants, maids, waitresses, and prostitutes: a few would become geishas. Hundreds of thousands of young men enlisted in the army.

With a population of some 70 million, Japan was the most densely populated country in the world. Its birthrate in those years was almost double that of the United States. It had 2,900 inhabitants per square mile of arable land, and it was widely believed that any further growth in the population would have to occur overseas. Japan was poor in natural resources, requiring imports of oil, rubber, and minerals; and it needed access to foreign markets for its manufactured goods. The seizure of territory in Asia was offered as an outlet, in the same way Hitler spoke of the need for *Lebensraum*, or living space, for Germans. Millions of Japanese, especially from the small towns of the rural interior, emigrated to Korea, Manchuria, and Formosa in pursuit of better living standards. A foreign empire was a vital necessity for Japan, as the Japanese imperialists saw it, and any attempt to deny them that amounted to a foreign conspiracy to bottle up the large Japanese population to the point of starvation and critical overpopulation.

On February 26, 1936, a group of young officers of the army's First Division, stationed in Tokyo, attempted a coup d'état. The move was triggered by an order sending the division to Manchuria. Before dawn, about 1,400 troops departed their base and spread out through Tokyo. They seized or laid siege to major government buildings in the city center, including the Diet, Ministry of War, and police headquarters. The main building of the *Asahi*

Shinbun was attacked and its press equipment vandalized. They invaded the homes of the prime minister and several members of Hirohito's court: they assassinated several officials, including the lord keeper of the privy seal, the inspector-general of military education, and the finance minister. In a manifesto distributed to the newspapers, the rebel leaders declared their purpose to break the grip of the business tycoons, the political party mandarins, and the elderly civilian statesmen, and to acclaim the emperor as supreme ruler, unencumbered by constitutional limitations—in a phrase, to effect a "Showa Restoration." "Japan now confronts a crisis," it announced. "Therefore it is our duty to take proper steps to safeguard our fatherland by killing those responsible. On the eve of our departure to Manchuria we have risen to attain our aims by direct action."

They had counted on inciting a popular revolution, or at least hoped for the backing of the army and navy. There is considerable evidence that their goals were popular, and the insurgents seem to have been considered heroes by many of their countrymen. For three days, Tokyo hung in suspense: the generals did not move to suppress the rebellion, perhaps waiting to see if it would spread. Hirohito was incensed, and was apparently the only man in Tokyo willing to call the uprising what it was—a mutiny. When his cabinet tried to resign, he refused to accept their resignations, telling his ministers they were duty-bound to stay in office and deal with the problem even at the risk of losing their own lives. At last Hirohito issued a peremptory order for the troops to return to their barracks, sucking the life out of the movement, and the navy was sent in to restore order. On February 29, after failing to gain entrance to the imperial compound, where the insurgents hoped to appeal directly to the emperor, the uprising was finished. Several ringleaders were arrested and several others took their own lives. Those arrested were tried in secret and later executed, shouting "Banzai!" to the emperor as they died.

The immediate crisis had passed, but as in 1932 the emperor was quick to let bygones be bygones, and the entire affair only empowered the military and emboldened the ultranationalist right. The new government agreed to demands that all cabinet appointees be approved by the army and navy ministers. Political parties were now completely emasculated. It emerged that the plot, like so many others of that period, had been a poorly kept secret throughout the upper ranks of the army. Even members of the royal family apparently had known of the plot in advance and sympathized with its objectives. None of the leaders was above the rank of captain, but higher-ranking officers knew about it in advance and sat on their hands. Indeed, there is reason to suspect that many had pledged to support the coup if the emperor appeared to give it his support. However, none of those ranking sympathizers was severely punished. General Terauchi, minister of war in the Hirota government, later remarked of the events in 1936: "In connection with this Incident there are those not directly involved but who knew that such plans were afoot. Yet they kept quiet. Some directly incited the men to action; others kept quiet. A really disgraceful group of men were gathered together. And yet if all who were thus involved resigned it would be difficult to find men to take their places."

The conspirators enjoyed broad public sympathy, if not outright support. Their manifesto, demanding economic justice for the rural poor and an end to political corruption, was thought worthy of admiration, both in its composition and its sentiments. When several of the surviving assassins went on trial, a year after the fact, calls for amnesty were raised in the press. The ringleaders of the failed coup were lauded as the conscience of the nation, as honest patriots targeting corruption and timidity in the high councils of government, and as the guardians of *chūkin*.

The army made its long-anticipated move into China on July 7, 1937. Like the invasion of Manchuria, the action was touched off by an "incident"—in this case an exchange of gunfire between Chinese and Japanese troops in Lukouchiao, near a Hun River bridge crossing about ten miles west of Peking (now Beijing). The fighting quickly escalated, and Japanese troops poured across the border into China's northern region. Japan's more efficient army won victory after victory, and in the air the Japanese reigned supreme; but no matter how much territory fell to the invaders, the Chinese Nationalist troops fought on and Mao Tse-tung's Communist guerrillas put up dogged resistance behind the lines. Rapid movements of Japanese troops followed, without authorization from Tokyo. Units were landed up and down the coast, and in December, Japanese troops fell upon the city of Nanking in one of the most ghastly scenes of the twentieth century. They slaughtered perhaps 100,000 Chinese troops and civilians (possibly many more: no one can say for sure). Japanese soldiers, whipped up into a frenzy by reckless officers, committed the crimes of rape, torture, and mass murder on a scale that caused even Hitler's local diplomatic representatives to wince.

IN THE MID-1930s, while the West merrily imagined that Japanese air-power amounted to a few obsolete, cast-off European airplanes piloted by crash-test dummies, the Imperial Navy toiled in obsessive secrecy to develop a homegrown aircraft industry and an elite corps of aviators. The leaders did not make the mistake of ignoring their prospective adversaries. Naval atta-chés in the United States and Europe traveled to air shows, scanned avia-tion magazines, and struck up friendly conversations with foreign pilots and engineers. Whenever possible, the Japanese government purchased Western aircraft and transported them to Japan. They built European airplanes under license, steadily improving their manufacturing capabilities. In 1935, the Jap-anese navy built a full-size mock-up of the U.S. carrier *Saratoga* and practiced aerial attacks on her. For years Japan had studied and borrowed from West-ern technology, but by the early 1930s the domestic industry had developed enough engineering expertise to design and build new aircraft, and by 1936, a quartet of industrial firms—Mitsubishi, Aichi, Nakajima, and Kawanishi—were secretly building some of the best naval fighters, bombers, and seaplanes in the world. Even so, the industrial base was still very small and emergent, relying on a tiny, hard-driven coterie of trained engineers and machinists, a scattered network of subcontractors making hand-tooled components, and a handful of large research centers and assembly plants in Nagoya, Yoko-suka, Musashino, Ota, Kure, and Kawanishi. That the Japanese were build-ing such fine airplanes was remarkable, a testament to their ingenuity and ambition—but the industry was not designed to scale up for mass produc-tion. The problem would grow acute after the first year of the Pacific War. If a picture is worth a thousand words, perhaps nothing was so eloquent as the image of a sleek new fighter plane, gleaming brilliantly in the sun, hauled by a team of oxen over a rutted dirt road, passing unhurriedly over rice fields and through tumbledown villages, from the Nagoya factory where it had been built to the Kagamigahara airfield where it would be tested. It was a practice that would continue through the end of the war.

By 1937, the year of the China Incident, the Japanese navy had achieved near-complete autonomy from Western aviation technology. What is more, the navy had placed into service two Mitsubishi-built airplanes that were at or near the forefront of military aviation throughout the world. The A5M Type 96 (Allied code name "Claude") was the first monoplane fighter placed into service by any air force in the world. It was a sleek aluminum acrobat with a maximum speed of 250 miles per hour, a fast climber, and it proved a champion dogfighter, routinely slaughtering the Soviet-built I-16 fighters of the Chinese air force. The second was a twin-engine, land-based medium bomber, the G3M (Allied code name "Nell"), which could carry either a torpedo or a bomb payload of 1,764 pounds, and had a range of 2,365 nautical miles. The G3M was succeeded by the G4M ("Betty"), which carried the same payload capacity while increasing its flight range to more than 3,000 nautical miles. Two superb carrier-based attack bombers were developed for the Japanese navy between 1937 and 1941. A dive-bomber, the Aichi D3A1 Type 99 ("Val"), went into production in December 1939. Its fixed landing gear made it easy to recognize even at a great distance (and by 1941 gave it the guise of obsolescence, as retractable gear was by that time *de rigueur* in aviation circles). But the Val was a perfectly serviceable dive-bomber, with a range of more than 900 miles: it maintained stability through an attack angle of up to 80 degrees, allowing for good bombing accuracy. In the hands of the more seasoned Japanese carrier aircrews, it was a fearsome weapon. The Nakajima B5N2 Type 97 carrier attack plane, or "Kate," could be configured as a high-altitude horizontal bomber or a torpedo bomber, but always did its most devastating work in the latter role. A big, low-wing monoplane with a long, greenhouse-style canopy, the Kate had a range of more than 600 miles and a maximum airspeed of 235 miles per hour. In 1941, it was without question the best torpedo attack aircraft in the Pacific, far superior to its obsolete American counterpart, the Douglas TBD Devastator. And it was armed with the Type 91 800-kilogram aerial torpedo, the best and most reliable weapon of its kind in the world.

The story of the development of the Zero fighter, successor to the A5M Type 96 ("Claude"), is one of the great tales of aviation history. Finding itself in need of a new fighter plane that could accompany the medium bombers on long-range missions into the heart of China, the Japanese navy demanded of Mitsubishi a new machine with seemingly unattainable specifications for speed, maneuverability, range, and rate of climb. After doubting that such an aircraft could ever be built, the brilliant aeronautical designer Jiro Horikoshi and his team managed to find a way to build a fighter that actually exceeded every one of the desired specifications. The Zero's control surfaces were consummately responsive; pilots learned to love the plane because of its fingertip maneuverability, often remarking that it felt as if the plane was an extension of their bodies. Introduced into com-

bat over the China mainland in 1940, the Zeros wiped the skies clean of
their opponents. In dogfights they usually scored clean kills—that is, they
shot down their adversaries without being struck by enemy fire. In those
conditions the Zero's greatest weakness—its lack of defensive armor and
self-sealing fuel tanks—did not much matter. The Zero was light, fast, long-
legged, supremely maneuverable, and armed with a heavy punch—in other
words, perfectly suited to the needs of the air war over China.

Isoroku Yamamoto could claim a lion's share of the credit for those
achievements. He had staked his career on the future of aviation in the
comparative dark ages of 1924, when, as a forty-year-old captain recently
returned from the United States, he requested and was granted the job
of executive officer of the Kasumigaura Naval Air Training Center, the
"Japanese Pensacola," near the city of Tsuchiura, about fifty miles north of
Tokyo. Thereafter he held a series of important aviation jobs, both at sea
and at a desk: captain of the carrier *Akagi*, 1928–29; chief of the Technical
Department of the Naval Air Command, 1930–33; commander of the First
Aircraft Carrier Division, 1933–34; director of the Naval Air Command,
1935–36. Throughout his career, even as a vice admiral, Yamamoto made
a point of flying as a passenger in naval aircraft of every type, even during
the most hazardous training missions. By exposing himself personally to
the risks of those wild pioneering days of aviation, Yamamoto established
an emotional bond with the pilots of the Japanese navy, one that would last
until the admiral's death in 1943 (fittingly, in an airplane).

In demanding aggressive practice routines, Yamamoto was conscious
that the lives of many aircrews would be cut short, but remained adamant that such sacrifices were necessary. As captain of the *Akagi*, he had
ordered that the names of the ship's dead airmen be inscribed on a wall in
his wardroom. His shipmates sometimes found him reading the names with
tears in his eyes. But he did not relent for safety's sake. "The naval air corps
will probably never be really strong until the whole wardroom is plastered
with names like these," he told his pilots. "I want you to be resigned to that
idea in your work. The first thing I propose you do today is go up and do five
or six loop-the-loops with your instructors; and when you're finished, you
can come and report to me."

Naval Academy graduates sometimes went directly into flight training,
as in the United States—but in Japan, a much larger ratio of airmen were
recruited from the ranks of enlisted men and petty officers already serving

in the fleet. Commissioned officers were always a privileged minority of the naval air corps, and Etajima graduates an even smaller percentage. Most of the Japanese aces were non-commissioned officers, and as Osamu Tagaya observes, "It was they who did most of the flying, the fighting, and the dying." Beginning in the late 1920s, teenaged boys aged fifteen to seventeen were recruited directly into naval flight training out of Japanese schools through a program known as *Yokaren.* To arouse interest in the program the navy staged school fly-overs. The students (even the youngest) stood at attention in the schoolyard as the planes roared low over the rooftops, dipping their wings in salute. Hideo Sato recalled one such demonstration over his school in the suburbs of Tokyo. The pilots dropped rubber balls attached to small parachutes. He was eight years old. "I guess they did it to draw us children into the war effort," Sato said. "Whatever the facts, I only know I was in ecstasy when it was my turn to go up to receive my very own ball."

The prewar navy was obsessed with building a small, elite corps of flyers, and selection criteria were almost prohibitively exclusive. Less than 1 percent of *Yokaren* applicants passed the initial written exam, and many of the fortunate few who made that initial cut would then be weeded out during rigorous physical exams. The select few who remained were sent into basic training. Here each day began with reveille at 5 a.m., followed by a forced immersion in cold water. The recruits rushed out to the parade ground, bowed in the direction of the Imperial Palace, recited an oath of loyalty to the emperor, and were led through a punishing calisthenics routine. Everywhere, throughout the day, they were expected to run, not walk. Meals were Spartan, consisting of rice mixed with barley, or miso soup and pickled vegetables, occasionally some fish or meat. Parade ground drills and basic combat training alternated with classroom instruction in math, science, engineering, reading, and writing. A contemporary photograph depicts pilot-trainees sitting on benches at a long table, listening intently to an instructor. They are dressed in identical crisp white uniforms with oval name tags. Their hair is close-cropped, their faces rapt and hard-set. Each had to maintain a minimum grade average or face expulsion, and class standing was always determined by academic rank. They slept in hammocks slung from the walls of their barracks, like jack-tars on the lower deck of an eighteenth-century man-of-war.

Takeshi Maeda, who would go on to fly a torpedo bomber at the Battle of Midway, went through basic training at Yokosuka Naval Base on Tokyo

Bay. Each day he and his fellow recruits spent hours on the bay, rowing an open boat in all kinds of weather. "Because of the friction between my body and the seat, my pants were covered with blood," he recalled. "After that your flesh became infected, and it produced yellow pus. . . . I would go to the infirmary, and they treated my wounds by applying ointment and gauze. The following day, when I did cutter boat training, the same thing would happen again, and my old wounds would reopen, which was very painful."

Recruits were subjected to unremitting brutality by upperclassmen, instructors, and officers. Any infraction, shortfall, wrong answer, or complaint brought instant retribution, ranging from a casual slap across the cheek to a sudden punch in the face to a savage beating with a baseball bat. A recruit might be forced to stand on his tiptoes for an hour or more, or stand rigidly at attention while a petty officer smashed him repeatedly in the face, or bend over while his tormentor repeatedly belted him on the buttocks with a club. Kicks and blows often persisted after a man had fallen to the ground. No cries or moans of pain were permitted. Often an entire squad was subjected to a brutal beating for one man's imagined transgressions. If any bones were broken, the injured man was sent off to the hospital; once healed he would be re-inducted with a subsequent class.

Saburo Sakai, who went on to become one of the most celebrated fighter pilots of the Pacific War, was once dragged out of his hammock in the dead of night and beaten in front of his shocked mates while they rubbed the sleep from their eyes. The petty officer forced Sakai to bend over: "with that he would swing a large stick of wood and with every ounce of strength he possessed would slam it against my upturned bottom. The pain was terrible, the force of the blows unremitting. There was no choice but to grit my teeth and struggle desperately not to cry out. At times I counted up to forty crashing impacts into my buttocks. Often I fainted from the pain. A lapse into unconsciousness constituted no escape however. The petty officer simply hurled a bucket of cold water over my prostrate form and bellowed for me to reposition, whereupon he continued his 'discipline' until satisfied I would mend the error of my ways." After watching one of his fellow recruits subjected to a similar beating, Takeshi Maeda remembers feeling a surge of bitterness: "How could a human being hit another with a baseball bat?"

Such beatings were a fact of military life in Japan. Indeed, they were generally much worse in the army. Unabashed sadism had a lot to do with it, no doubt; but there was also a school of thought, prevalent in the army and to a slightly lesser degree in the navy, that the beatings did the men good, served to harden and toughen them, groomed them for combat. Military men were convinced, said Katsumi Watanabe, who was beaten savagely as an army draftee, that "beatings were a form of education"—indeed, the beatings were often called "lessons." The cumulative violence, wrote Sakai, transformed the recruits into "human cattle" who "never dared to question orders, to doubt authority, to do anything but immediately carry out all the commands of our superiors. We were automatons who obeyed without thinking." Naval policy seemed not just to tolerate but to encourage such brutality; Takeshi Maeda observed that the most violent instructors were rewarded with promotions. Recruits could not fight back, nor file formal complaints; they could not quit, and they dared not risk being discharged. To be drummed out of the service would bring shame on their families— and not the kind of shame we talk about in the West. A failed recruit's entire family might suffer social ostracism and even persecution. It was a staggering burden, and no surprise that many young men resolved the dilemma by taking their own lives.

Those who survived basic training were assigned to flight training at Kasumigaura. The base had two long runways, 3,000 and 2,200 yards long, and a huge complex of hangars housing hundreds of aircraft. The road to the main gate was lined with a magnificent stand of mature cherry trees, with views of Lake Kasumigaura beyond the airfield. The daily routines of a first-year flight student remained exactingly regimented, and he would continue to suffer the occasional slap or fist punch—but here at least he was permitted (at prescribed times) to smoke, to drink, even to spend a Saturday afternoon in Tsuchiura. The specter of dismissal at any time for any reason hovered over his head. The initial weeks of the program involved a full day of classroom instruction, with a greater emphasis on such practical skills as over-water navigation, engine maintenance, and radio communications. Students pressed their noses into the books for two hours each night before lights-out; many slipped surreptitiously from their cots in the small hours to study by flashlight. The program was designed to function as a ruthless screen for weaker performers. Even those trainees who demonstrated good aptitude in both the classroom and the cockpit were often expelled for trivial offenses. Of Sakai's entering class of seventy students, forty-five were gone before the end of the initial ten-month course, and he noted that expulsion "was feared far more than any mere savage beating."

Kasumigaura aimed to create a cadre of super-athletes, men endowed with superior physical traits honed in a punishing training regimen. The students trained in gymnastics and acrobatics to improve strength, balance, coordination, and physical reaction time. They walked on their hands and balanced on their heads for five minutes; they ran for miles in full gabardine flight suits in the sweltering heat of high summer; they leapt from a tower, somersaulted in the air, and landed on their feet. They were required to hang by one arm from an iron pole for ten minutes. Those who could not swim had a rope tied around their waists and were thrown into the lake; if they sank, they were finally hauled to the surface. Every man was eventually required to swim 50 meters in less than thirty seconds, to swim underwater for a distance of at least 50 meters, and to remain underwater for at least ninety seconds.

Men were pitted against one another in vicious wrestling matches. After each round, the victor was permitted to walk away, while the exhausted loser was required to remain on the mat to take on the next man. A weak or undersized trainee, losing three or four consecutive contests, might be drained of all his remaining strength; nonetheless, he was obligated to continue until he had pinned a man to the mat, or had been pinned in turn by every man in the class. If the unlucky perpetual loser could not get back on his feet, he was dismissed from the program. "With every pilot-trainee determined not to be expelled from the flyer's course, the wrestling matches were scenes of fierce competition," recalled Sakai. "Often students were knocked unconscious. . . . They were revived with buckets of water or other means and sent back to the mat."

They trained to improve their eyesight. They were required to identify objects and symbols that were flashed before their eyes for a fraction of a second. They learned to recognize and describe objects in the outermost corners of their peripheral vision. Sakai writes that he and his fellow students were taught to find and identify stars in broad daylight. "Gradually, and with much more practice, we became quite adept at our star-hunting. Then we went further. When we had sighted and fixed the position of a particular star we jerked our eyes away ninety degrees, and snapped back again to see if we could locate the star immediately. Of such things are fighter pilots made." Reaction times were shortened by such exercises as sitting still while a fly was buzzing in a room; the student was expected to reach out and seize it in his fist. At first, Sakai recalled, few could do it, "but after several months a fly which flew before our faces was almost certain to end up in our hands."

Instructors used the ancient principles of *kendo*, or Japanese swordsmanship, to teach the trainees how to attack and defeat an opponent. The aviators sat through long and mostly silent sessions with Zen priests, in which they were instructed to set their attention in the lower abdomen, to evacuate the mind, to experience combat as a series of effortless acts, in which the hands and feet on the cockpit controls moved without the intrusion of conscious thought.

A year after having entered basic training, the trainees reached a milestone that none would ever forget. They left the earth for the first time in a Type-3 Primary Trainer—a two-seat, dual-control, open-cockpit biplane, powered by a 130-horsepower, five-cylinder engine. An instructor sat in the forward cockpit, the trainee behind. A voice tube ran from the forward seat back to the trainee's flight helmet, allowing for one-way communication. Once the aircraft was aloft, the trainee was tested for basic flight aptitude. How was his hand-eye coordination? How confidently did he take the controls? Could he maintain straight and level flight? The most natural flyers were permitted to handle the aircraft in takeoffs and landings, and a select few were even permitted to solo for the first time. Based on those first assessments, the class was subdivided and the future course of each man's aviation career was decided. Some would become pilots, some aircrew; some would be sent into land-based aircraft, others into floatplanes.

Having mastered the rudiments, the trainees were introduced to a more powerful intermediate trainer known as the Type 93 biplane, or *Akatombo*, the "red dragonfly." The *Akatombo* was powered by a 300-horsepower, nine-cylinder radial engine. Here the trainee sat in the front cockpit, providing an unobstructed view forward but also allowing the instructor to clout him on the back of the head. (Takeshi Maeda recalled that his instructor often shouted through the voice tube, "You're so stupid!" and walloped him with a wooden stick. To protect his skull, Maeda wrapped a towel under the lining of his leather flight helmet. Realizing he was being cheated, the instructor waited until the plane had landed, ordered Maeda to stand at attention with head uncovered, and meted out the accumulated backlog of punishments.) In the *Akatombo*, the student mastered basic flight aerobatics: rolls, spins, loops, stalls. He took his first long overland solo flight, cruising in his open cockpit at an altitude of 15,000 feet or higher: he often found his way home using Mount Fuji's majestic cone as his point of orientation. He would be introduced to the art of formation flying in a three-plane *shutai*, then in a nine-plane *chutai*. He learned to fly using his instruments alone, in a cockpit covered by a canvas hood.

At the end of this intermediate training period, the trainee was subjected to a grueling battery of tests. If he passed, he was awarded his coveted "wings," an insignia patch sewn on the left sleeve: a pair of wings superimposed on an anchor under a cherry blossom. Although his training was far from complete, he could now call himself a naval aviator.

Five or six months of "extended education" followed in operational aircraft, usually obsolete models that had been taken out of front-line service. (Mercifully, men with aviator's wings rarely suffered beatings. Not so mercifully, the newly minted flyers were entitled to beat others junior to themselves, and often did.) The men were divided into carrier and twin-engine land-based programs, and the carrier men were further subdivided into fighter, dive-bomber, and torpedo bomber units. Now their training would emphasize gunnery, bombing, dogfighting, formation flying, and over-water navigation. Fighter pilots practiced firing at drogues towed behind another plane, with results captured by a gun camera. Bombers attacked targets on the ground, with the results measured and scored vigilantly. Pilots destined for carrier squadrons progressed from practice landings on short segments of a runway, to low-speed, low-altitude approaches over an aircraft carrier, to "touch and go" landings (touch the deck and take off without cutting the engine). Finally, they were cleared to lower their tailhooks and put their birds down on a carrier flight deck for the first time.

Having logged an average of about 500 flight hours, they were assigned to a front-line unit, either an air base or an aircraft carrier. Noncommissioned officers and enlisted airmen were promoted to the rank of airman first class; officers were promoted to lieutenant. Here they completed the last phase of their training side by side with veteran aviators. Training schedules were intense. The new flyboys flew constantly: morning, afternoon, sometimes at night. A popular song celebrated the navy's intense pace of training in the years leading up to the war with Britain and the United States. Weekends were a thing of the past, went the refrain; now the days of the week were "Monday, Monday, Tuesday, Wednesday, Thursday, Friday, Friday."

"You can't go home again," wrote Thomas Wolfe, and he might as well have been writing about the newly minted Imperial Japanese Navy aviator, resplendently clad in blue and brass, returning home to visit his family. Of course his parents and siblings were overjoyed to see him, and he them. He had done them a great honor, lifting the status of his entire clan in the eyes of neighbors, colleagues, and friends. He was bigger, stronger, tougher, older, wiser. But his homecoming was inevitably poignant, and more than a little strange. He might have dreamed of home every night he was away, clasping it in his imagination as a sanctuary from the brutality of his tormentors and the unremitting toil of his training. Once there, however, he was inevitably taken aback by the comfort, the ease, the disorder, the aimlessness. The reality of home had steadily diverged from the image he had carried in his mind. It contrasted too sharply with the harsh, purposeful life to which he had grown accustomed. He loved his family as much as he ever had, and they loved him as much as they ever had, but he was aghast at how much space had grown between them. They could never fully understand what he had done and endured, or what he had become. That was a secret known only to his classmates, his fellow survivors, who had shared in the long crucible of his training—the fatigue, the humiliations, the beatings, the deprivations, the chronic dread of expulsion, the ecstasy of flight, and the inconceivable joy he had felt upon receiving those blessed wings. He might never admit it, but his fellow airmen were closer to him now than his own kin. He belonged with them. He could not go home again because now the navy was his home.

THE NAVAL AIR CORPS demonstrated its growing range and power over the skies of China between 1937 and 1941. For four years it maintained air supremacy over a vast expanse of southern China. With growing confidence, aviation officers argued that the Japanese navy should reduce its emphasis on battleships and devote the bulk of its resources to building more airplanes and aircraft carriers. Minoru Genda, a head-turning fighter pilot who made a name for himself by leading a barnstorming air circus, was a persistent critic of the "big gun club." In mock air battles Genda and his team routinely trounced the planes and pilots of the Japanese army, a source of immense pride in a service that tended to regard the army as an insufferable rival. He had helped perfect the deadly "turning in" maneuver that the Japanese Zeros would use to kill so many opponents in the opening months of the Pacific War.

While on a tour of duty at the Naval General Staff in Tokyo in 1936, Lieutenant Commander Genda wrote a paper brusquely asserting: "The main strength of a decisive battle should be air arms, while battleships will be put out of commission and tied up." Genda wanted not only to stop building new battleships but to get rid of existing ones, provocatively suggesting that they "should be either scrapped or used as hulks for jetties." That was heresy, sacrilege, profanation. It contradicted the master strategist Alfred Thayer Mahan. It flew in the face of the navy's basic Battle Instructions: "The battleship squadron is the main fleet, whose aim is to attack the enemy's main fleet." Genda's rivals spread the rumor that he had literally lost his mind.

Blunt criticism was unusual in Japan, but it was also typical of the culture of Japanese aviation. In the mid-1930s, few aviation-minded officers occupied senior posts in the naval command structure, and not a single qualified aviator had reached flag rank. The prime movers were younger and lower-ranking men, who found that they could not make themselves understood except by resorting to "un-Japanese" modes of forcefulness and candor. (Perhaps frank criticism directed upward in the ranks was a trait common to naval aviators of all nations. They, more than their ship-bound brothers, were compelled to rely on themselves at an early age.) Genda found a patron and partner in Admiral Yamamoto, who made sure that the younger man was given the assignments he wanted, and brought him into the Combined Fleet as one of his principal staff officers in 1940. Yamamoto also picked up the cudgels of the anti-battleship campaign. He rejected the notion that there was any such thing as an unsinkable ship, and argued that the longer range of aircraft, and their steadily growing offensive striking power, would sooner or later put an end to the reign of the battleship. "I don't want to be a wet blanket, and I know you're going all out on your job," he told Rear Admiral Keiji Fukuda, a battleship man, "but I'm afraid you'll be out of work before long. From now on, aircraft are going to be the most important thing in the navy; big ships and guns will become obsolete."

Of course, the gun club had no intention of letting a mob of impertinent flyboys take control of the Japanese navy. Anticipating that Japan would abrogate the London Naval Treaty upon its expiration in 1936, the Naval General Staff planned to build and launch a fleet of "superbattleships." These leviathans would weigh some 64,000 tons, about 50 percent larger than the largest battleships in the U.S. Fleet. They would mount a main battery of monstrous 18.1-inch-caliber guns. With weapons of such power and range, they argued, superbattleships would dominate any fleet engagement no matter how many ships were arrayed on either side. If the keels were laid immediately upon expiration of the treaty, and the ships built in closely guarded secrecy, perhaps the Japanese could gain a four- or five-year lead on their American and British rivals. Moreover, even if the United States built battleships of matching dimensions, they would be too broad-beamed to pass through the locks of the Panama Canal. The Americans would be thrown back on the horns of the same dilemma that Theodore Roosevelt had faced thirty years earlier. Setting out from Yokosuka or Kure, the Japanese superbattleships could be in San Francisco Bay before their Atlantic-based American counterparts had even rounded the Horn.

In 1936, the navy placed initial orders for two superbattleships, to be built at Kure and Nagasaki; two more were to be built later at Sasebo and Yokosuka. The shipbuilders were astounded by specifications they received. "We've got to go through with it," said one of the Nagasaki ship architects. "The Navy trusted our engineering expertise enough to give us this project." The ships were to be 263 meters long, 38.9 meters on the beam, and displace more than 72,000 tons when fully loaded. Their massive steam-turbine engines, housed in cavernous 640 square-meter boiler rooms, would develop 150,000 horsepower, driving the great vessels through the sea at a peak speed of more than 27 knots. They would have an effective action radius of 7,200 nautical miles, requiring them to carry 6,300 tons of fuel. Their crew would number 2,500 men. They would be "unsinkable" (or so it was often said, until they were sunk in 1944 and 1945). Shells fired by an enemy ship, or bombs dropped from above, would make no impression on their 40-centimeter-thick "honeycomb" steel armor plating. Their hulls would contain 1,147 separate watertight compartments, all capable of being sealed off to contain flooding. If they took ten torpedo hits, or twenty, or thirty, the damage could be contained, and judicious counterflooding would keep them on an even keel.

So it was said.

The ships, which would be named *Yamato* (built in Kure) and *Musashi* (Nagasaki), were shrouded in obsessive secrecy, because it was feared that if the Americans learned of them they would immediately begin construction on similar lines. On the other hand, it was no simple task to conceal projects of that scale on the teeming urban waterfronts of Kure and Nagasaki.

Large fences were erected around the shipyards, but nothing could be done about the new gantry cranes that towered over the surrounding rooftops. The navy was so touchy about security that it refused to allow any plans or documents to leave its offices. Engineers were not permitted to look at blueprints; contracts had to be settled with a handshake; mock-ups of any kind were strictly forbidden. Engineers who asked too many questions were singled out for police interrogation. In Nagasaki, a city of hills, the entire shipyard was plainly visible from any one of a thousand vantage points. Police swarmed the streets, threatening to arrest any person who seemed to cast a glance in the direction of the elephantine *Musashi*. Watch posts were erected within the yard itself, and guards posted on them with high-powered binoculars to scan the hills. Ferry windows were painted over so that commuters crossing the harbor could not peer into the yard. Eventually, the shipyard hung vast hemp-rope screens, 75,000 square meters altogether, to shield the great ship from prying eyes.

The interior of the *Musashi* was a vast maze, a seemingly endless progression of passageways, ladders, and warrens, and very few men actually knew their way around the ship. No plans were provided to the workers by the security-obsessed architects, so they had to make do with their own crude hand-drawn maps, which had to be destroyed at the end of each work day. Many were reluctant to descend too deeply into the obsidian labyrinth, fearing they might never again emerge. The fear was well placed, for shipyard workers often did lose their way. Some carried pieces of chalk to leave trail marks, and the working parties took roll calls at quitting time to be sure than none was missing. Electrical engineers were brought in to install eight 600-kilowatt generators and a network of electrical cables that could have carried electricity to a large portion of rural Japan.

The *Yamato* was launched without incident on August 8, 1940. The launch of the *Musashi*, three months later, was a more difficult and dangerous proposition. Nagasaki's harbor was small and narrow, surrounded on all sides by steeply ascending land. When the ship entered the water she would be traveling at about 15 knots, and unless her momentum was checked she would run into the opposite shore, only 740 yards away, destroying an entire neighborhood and possibly herself. The problem was solved by running steel cables from harbor moorings to her hull, and dragging heavy chains on one side to turn her once she entered the harbor. Her launch was so secretive that only thirty guests were invited to witness it, all high-ranking officials of the navy and government. The residents of Nagasaki were ordered to stay inside their homes until given an all-clear. Curtains were to be drawn across all harbor-facing windows. Even the police officers who were sent to patrol the streets were ordered to turn their own backs at the moment of launch.

As the hull moved down the slipway, blue sparks leapt up from the concrete, the rails under the hull emitted white smoke, and the onlookers shouted: "Banzai! Banzai!" As the vessel plunged into the water, it raised a wave that traveled across the harbor and crashed on the opposite shore, flooding several of the buildings along the waterfront and capsizing dozens of boats. But the launch had succeeded; the great battleship was afloat and in one piece. The engineers and workers fell to the ground, laughing and weeping and shouting thanks to the heavens.

At the navy's main anchorage off Hashirajima Island, the *Yamato* and *Musashi* dwarfed the other battleships of the Japanese fleet. The *Nagato*, *Mutsu*, and *Kirishima*, traditional battleships with dimensions similar to those of their American and British counterparts, looked like cruisers when anchored alongside their titanic new sisters. As big as the superbattleships were, however, they were beautifully well proportioned, with broad beams tapering to long, sleek, sharp bows. Their decks were covered with polished cypresswood planking, unpainted; fittings were painted judiciously in black, white, yellow, and brown tones; their names stood out in handsome gold *kanji* across their sterns; and finely detailed chrysanthemum crests were mounted on their bows. Their superstructures were hundreds of feet high, with intricate arrays of decks, balconies, ladders, antiaircraft guns, and cranes of various sizes and functions. From the broad plate glass windows of the bridge, so far above the sea, the officers looked down on a parade ground–sized foredeck, and men stationed there must have looked like street pedestrians viewed from the top of a tall office building. Even the main anchor, weighing 15 tons, must have looked no larger than a cuff link. The "sun and rays" battle flag, raised each morning on the ensign staff at the stern, was nearly 25 feet long.

Yamato's first sea trial was on October 20, 1941, six weeks before Pearl Harbor. She performed beautifully in every respect. Her giant engines ran smoothly, and she had no trouble achieving her maximum speed of 27 knots. She carved an easy path through heavy seas, smashing waves right and left off her bows. In the *Musashi's* first outing several weeks later, the 18.1-inch guns were tested for the first time. These colossal weapons fired armor-piercing projectiles weighing 1.5 tons each, about 50 percent heavier than the largest shells thrown by American battleships. Their maximum range was 42 kilometers. A shell fired at that extreme range, with the guns elevated to 45 degrees, climbed from sea level to the altitude of Mount Everest and back to sea level in a flight lasting about a minute and a half. Accuracy was poor at that range, but it was at least theoretically possible to strike enemy ships beyond the horizon. A single hit could put any battleship in the world out of action, and any other class of ship would be literally blown out of the water.

So great was the blast pressure of the 18.1-inch guns that it was not safe for any man to remain in an unbroken sight line to the muzzles. Crewmen on the *Musashi*, stationed on the bridge or belowdecks, or crouched behind the turrets on the other side of the ship, were instructed to wear earplugs and find a handhold—even so, the blast caused them to feel as if their "guts had suddenly been thrust upwards into their throats." Guinea pigs left in cages on deck near the guns were "blown apart" by the shock. As the men peered out from behind their shelters, there was an improbably long pause as the shot traveled through the air. At last they saw the distant tower of water, hundreds of feet high but appearing as no more than a white speck on the horizon. After another long wait, the hollow thud of the faraway explosion reached their ears.

TWICE IN TWO YEARS the army (or rather, factions within the army) had challenged the emperor, while acting in his name. The "*Kodo* faction" had planned the botched coup attempt in 1936, and the "Control faction" had masterminded the China Incident in 1937. In each case, the emperor's halfhearted gestures of resistance had only emboldened and empowered the militarists. After 1937, discovering that they would not be checked from above, the army and the ultranationalist right moved swiftly to consolidate their grip on the country. The National Mobilization Law of 1937 enacted labor conscription to support defense and munitions industries. Rationing of food and basic consumer goods was ordered. Farms were required to turn over their rice harvests at a preset price. Parliament, already weakened, was now completely emasculated.

The Japanese people were instructed how and what to think through autocratic control of every available source of information, including radio, newspapers, newsreels, movies, posters, music, and cartoons. Dissenting views were suppressed as "radical" or "communist," and those who had voiced liberal opinions in the past were driven from public life and forced to recant on pain of imprisonment or worse. Correct thoughts and beliefs were hammered into the minds of the Japanese through official slogans: "I won't desire anything until the war is won" . . . "100 million people, one mind" . . . "Support neighborhood associations" . . . "Beware of spies" . . . "We'll never cease fire till our enemies cease to be!" Lachrymose ballads played day and night on the radio, glorifying the war overseas: "Departing Ship," "Samurai Japan," "Tears and the Flight of Migrating Birds."

In the cinema, Western films mostly disappeared, to be replaced by Japanese feature films about the campaigns in China and Manchuria. Scenes of Japanese forces overrunning enemy positions were often followed by scenes of soldiers grieving over the bodies of their fallen comrades and breaking into tearful renditions of *Kimigayo*, Japan's national anthem. The features were interspersed with newsreels, which opened with martial orchestral music and an animated sequence of the Japanese golden eagle spreading its wings to cover a map of the earth. War news described the latest victories of Japanese troops overseas. A home-front report showed how ordinary Japanese were pitching in to support the war effort. If there was a segment on "Imperial Family News," a bold order was first spelled out across the screen: "Remove your hats!" The audience was required (on pain of arrest) to stand erect, remove their hats, and face the screen. Film footage of the Imperial Palace walls or the emperor's motorcade might follow, with voice-over narration in the abstruse, archaic Japanese reserved for imperial occasions— but never did the emperor himself appear on screen.

Hatred of the West was encouraged as a means of arousing the national spirit. In state-approved surround-sound propaganda, it was often said that the United States and Britain had conspired to deny Japan its sacred right to expand in Asia, and war with both was inevitable: it was only a matter of time. Western cultural influences were denounced as a form of spiritual corruption; it was the goal of the regime to "purify" or "cleanse" Japan of those foreign viruses. A popular slogan was "To hell with Babe Ruth!" and baseball itself was attacked as "a sport of the decadent democracies." In a popular newsreel, a *judo* master vanquished an American boxer, and as the audience cheered, the camera suddenly cut to scenes of Japanese army victories in Manchuria. It was no longer safe to play jazz in the nightclubs of Tokyo, and eventually it would no longer be safe to play Western records even at home. As part of a nationwide anti-luxury campaign called the "National Spiritual Mobilization," women were pressured to do away with jewelry and cosmetics, as well as Western-style clothing and hairstyles: they were urged to wear shapeless work trousers called *monpe*. Men were pressured to cut their hair short or even to shave their heads. Tokyo's popular Western-style dance halls were visited by surly officials who declared, "'You can't dance this,' 'You can't dance that.'" In October 1940, a government decree required all dance halls to shut their doors for good. On the final night at one of the Tokyo dance halls, Kiyoshi Hara recalled, the band ended its last set with "Auld Lang Syne," bringing tears to the eyes of the regular patrons.

Schoolchildren were taught that the emperor had descended from the gods, and that his divine blood ran in the veins of all his subjects. His portrait hung in every school, and was made the object of organized compulsory daily veneration. The Meiji emperor's Imperial Rescript on Education was often read aloud to the students, and if a teacher or school principal should ever stumble over a phrase in the hallowed document, he was forced to resign. Hideo Sato recalled that one of his teachers had explained that "His Imperial Highness" was descended from Amaterasu-Omikami, goddess of the Sun; the teacher "told the story so convincingly and dramatically that we kids sat there, eyes round with wonder, and felt in our heart of hearts that it must be true." The children were cautioned never to use old newsprint to wrap food without first confirming that no photograph of His Highness was included in the pages therein, lest grease or food besmirch his image. The progress of the war was followed closely in the classrooms. Students sometimes pasted Japanese flag markers on maps to signify advances and victories. "I was crazy about geography from the time I was young," recalled Sato. "I really memorized the map of Asia all the way up to India. Places like the 'Malay Peninsula' and 'North Borneo' rang with hidden meaning. I could draw them all in the air back then."

As pathetic as it may seem in retrospect, the imperialist program included a strain of heartfelt, messianic idealism. Conquest overseas was held to be a sacred mission, to be undertaken for the sake of all the benighted and ill-treated peoples of Asia (and perhaps beyond). It was Japan's purpose and destiny to push out beyond its islands and unite *Hakko ichiu*—the "eight corners of the world"—under the care of the "emperor's benevolent heart."

As the only nation in the world that had not separated the spheres of religion, politics, morality, patriotism, and family, Japan's social and political order (*kokutai*) was manifestly superior to that of any other civilization. It offered a Confucian order based on harmony, filial piety, reciprocal obligations between superior and inferior, and deep ties connecting the individual into the collective whole. It offered to advance the lot of lesser peoples by bringing them under the care and guidance of the emperor, the only sovereign who was also a god, and the only god who was also a sovereign: "As in the heavens the sun is not double, so on earth there exists but one *Tenno*." It offered the last best hope for all of humanity, the salvation of a turbulent and unhappy world. It gave the Japanese people a reason to believe they were fighting for something more than national aggrandizement. "If Japan had declared it was fighting only to add territory," remarked Koshu Itabashi, a student at the outset of the war, "I don't believe we ever could have gone as far as Borneo."

Moreover, added the charlatans who flogged their theories with the regime's approval, Japan had once ruled the world in the distant past and was merely seeking to restore that ancient order. "Excavations of ancient relics carried out in various regions of the world testify to the authenticity of the descriptions of the Japanese annals," wrote Professor Chikao Fujisawa. "They brought to light the wonderful fact that in the prehistoric age, mankind formed a single worldwide family system with the Japanese emperor at its head. Japan was highly respected as the land of parents, while all other lands were called the lands of children, or the branch lands. . . . Eminent scholars are unanimous in concluding that the cradle of mankind was neither the Pamir plateau nor the banks of the Tigris-Euphrates, but the middle mountainous region of the Japanese main island." The ancient Japanese people had spread over China and the rest of Asia, bringing the fruits of their civilization; they had even reached Europe under the name of "Huns." But their utopian global order had tragically collapsed after a series of natural disasters, and the world had plunged into a dark age in which "all mankind became estranged geographically and spiritually from the parent-land of Japan, to the detriment of world peace." With dissenting voices drowned out, no rhetoric was too silly or cartoonish, so long as it supported the program. There was only one ocean, declared Professor T. Komaki of Kyoto Imperial University, and Japan ruled it: "The Pacific, Indian and Atlantic were considered separate Oceans, but were thus considered only by Europeans. There are no seven seas: only one sea exists, and it is connected to Japan, where the sun is rising. All waters are connected to Japan. All the ocean is to be recognized as the great Japanese sea."

Japan would drive the white, Christian colonial interlopers out of Asia once and for all, and lead its poor Asian cousins back onto the one true path of Buddhist and Confucian principles. Here the Japanese ultranationalist program found fertile ground, for it could justifiably point to a long history of Western repression, greed, exploitation, and hypocrisy. The West had taken what it wanted from Asia, while giving nothing back, the ultranationalists said—it had kept wages down and prevented industrial development in order to exploit Asia's markets and steal Asia's natural resources. The Japanese, by contrast, envisioned a "Greater East Asia Co-Prosperity Sphere," which would work for the "mutual existence of nations in which one is not exploited by others or vice versa." Japanese found a receptive audience in Asia for its message that "the colored races constitute two-thirds of the world's population but control only one tenth of the earth's surface," and that Japan alone, among the non-white races, was strong enough to cast the West out of Asia. The promise of liberation would be betrayed by Japanese behavior in the territories they occupied—too often they left the locals feeling nostalgic for the old boss—but early in the war, Japan's spectacular victories indubitably raised Asian self-consciousness and aroused a deep yearning for independence.

If Japan was a fundamentally moral country with a divine mission, it followed that Japan's wars were nothing less than pure, ennobling, and just. Enemies who stood in the way of the *kokutai* were "unruly heathens" or bandits, or perhaps even demons with inconceivably evil designs. In any case, they must be slain for the cause of peace. Buddhism taught compassion and pacifism, but the Zen priests who had survived the purges of the past two decades lent their full moral authority to Japan's wars. When Japan fought, declared the Buddhist scholar Daisetz T. Suzuki, it was an "expression of Buddha's compassion." As for the war in China, the cradle of Eastern Buddhism, a book entitled *The Buddhist View of War* published in 1937 explained that China had brought the war on itself by its "defilements," and would ultimately benefit by having "its unreasonableness corrected and an opportunity to reflect on its conduct." Or, if that explanation did not satisfy, perhaps it was enough to grant absolution. Acknowledging that Zen taught "the gospel of love and mercy," Suzuki asserted that the true practitioner of Zen, drawn into war for reasons unrelated to his own ego, was not responsible for the behavior of the sword he wielded. "For it is really not he but the sword itself that does the killing. He had no desire to do harm to anybody, but the enemy appears and makes himself a victim. It is as though the sword performs automatically its function of justice, which is the function of mercy."

Year after year, Japan kept winning battles in China, but could not find a way to win the war. The army seized the coast, the big river valleys, and several of China's largest cities, including Peking, Shanghai, and Nanking. But the conquerors discovered they could not impose their will even in the territories in which they were strongest: the rural hinterlands always remained lawless and ungovernable. Chinese political and military power had long been impotently parceled out among regional warlords, but nothing aroused nationalist passions like the long-term presence of marauding foreign troops. Mao's Communist guerrillas turned their guns on the invaders, pledging to put off their revolution until the "eastern devils" had been driven out. In 1939, fighting broke out along the Soviet-Manchurian border at Nomonhan. Local Japanese generals, acting (as usual) without authorization from Tokyo, moved substantial reinforcements into the area, but the Japanese forces were pulverized in a powerful Russian counterattack. The setback came as a great shock, though it remained largely under wraps: neither side had declared war. Chiang Kai-shek's Nationalist government, safely withdrawn to Chungking, deep in the interior and beyond the reach of Japanese troops, steadfastly refused to capitulate or negotiate. Eventually, a full thirty-eight Japanese infantry divisions, totaling about 750,000 men or some three quarters of the army's entire troop strength, were tied down in China and Manchuria.

Growing rage at China's obstinacy, stoked by effective guerrilla attacks behind the lines, prompted the Japanese army to commit civilian atrocities on a grand scale. The rural pacification campaign was carried out under the army's "Three-All" policy—soldiers were ordered to "Burn All, Seize All, and Kill All." Those were the wretched years of Japan's chemical and biological warfare attacks; horrific medical experiments practiced on prisoners; the rounding up of women and girls to be funneled into a vast system of sexual slavery; the rounding up of men and boys as slave laborers to be worked to death; the mass beheadings and bayoneting of prisoners; the slaughter of perhaps as many as 10 million Chinese civilians all told. "I had already gotten to where I lacked pity," admitted Yoshiro Tamura, who tested bacteriological agents on Chinese prisoners as a member of the notorious Unit 731. "After all, we were already implanted with a narrow racism, in the form of a belief in the superiority of the so called 'Yamato Race.' We disparaged all other races. . . . If we didn't have a feeling of racial superiority, we couldn't have done it." Shozo Tominaga, a young second lieutenant assigned to China in 1941, recalled meeting the infantry veterans he would command. "When I looked at the men of my platoon, I was stunned," he said. "They had evil eyes. They weren't human eyes, but the eyes of leopards or tigers. . . . The longer the men had been at the front, the more evil their eyes appeared." Newly arrived Japanese conscripts were forced to bayonet Chinese prisoners. The victims were blindfolded and tied to stakes. In some cases a circle was drawn around the heart and the soldiers told to *avoid* striking it, so as to prolong the victim's agony. Soldiers who flinched from the macabre initiation ritual were kicked, beaten, and prodded by their officers. "Everyone became a demon within three months," said Tominaga. "Men were able to fight courageously only when their human characteristics were suppressed. So we believed. It was a natural extension of our training back in Japan. This was the Emperor's army."

Western sympathies lay with the Chinese, whose suffering was depicted vividly in newsreel footage. President Roosevelt was personally disgusted, his doctor recalled, and "commented with deep bitterness on the inhumanity of the Japanese." It was also true that major American business interests in China—some of which were overrun or ordered shut down in occupied areas—were directly threatened by the Japanese invasion. Britain and the United States funneled military aid to the Nationalists via the Burma Road. An American gunboat, the *Panay*, was sunk by Japanese air attack in the Yangtze River in December 1937. Relations deteriorated and the specter of war loomed. Creative Japanese propagandists, taking a cue from their soon-to-be German allies, declared Roosevelt the stooge of a Jewish capitalist plutocracy. Those same Jews, they said, had arranged for anti-Japanese lies to be spread through the American media. The United States and its European allies feared and resented Japan's spectacular rise as an Asian power and were conspiring to reverse it. The Japanese press often complained of the "encirclement" of Japan by the Western powers.

But where did obtuse truculence end and foreign policy begin? It was a peculiar tragedy of Japan's ultranationalist psychodrama that the men best qualified to deal with the West were shunted to the margins of power. Japan did not lack for experienced and worldly diplomats, men who had studied at Harvard, Princeton, or Oxford, spoke fluent English, cultivated foreign friendships, and were practiced in the ambassadorial arts. The Foreign Ministry at Kasumigaseki was stacked with them. Many were perplexed and anguished by the drift toward war. But they were powerless to do anything about it, because the militarists who controlled the country had successfully discredited them as a fifth column. Some were murdered outright. Others were forced from office, or exiled to foreign embassies where they were kept in the dark. The military connived to have generals and admirals appointed as foreign ambassadors, or even (in 1941 and again in 1942) as foreign minister. The army set up an in-house office to deal directly with foreign governments, circumventing Kasumigaseki altogether. "The diplomats in fact had become a corps d'elite, a class apart in the public service, or, to put it more cynically, peacocks in a gilded cage," wrote Toshikazu Kase, a chief secretary to the foreign minister throughout the war years. In the turmoil of Japan's "dark valley," the left hand never knew what the right hand was doing—and why would it, when there was no functioning brain center to send coherent instructions to either hand? Professional diplomats sensed that war with the United States was coming, but felt as if nothing could be done to stop it. "Events sometimes overwhelm you, surge around you, and carry you along," wrote Kase. "You can't always move them. One man's will alone is not enough to do anything. War has a life of its own."

Isoroku Yamamoto was unwilling to assume such a passive attitude. He took a stand. He did not conceal his contempt for the shrill, vociferous style of the ultranationalist right, nor the rigidly dogmatic, mindlessly antagonistic politics they championed. He did not approve of their efforts to regulate the dress, tastes, opinions, thoughts, and daily routines of the Japanese people. He publicly undermined some of the goals of the "National Spiritual Mobilization," such as the proposal that all Japanese men should shave their heads. "What does it all matter?" he replied, when asked his opinion by a group of reporters. "I myself have worn my hair short for years. . . . On the other hand, a slob is a slob, however close-cropped he may be. So either's OK, surely?" He dismissed the army brass as a pack of "damn fools," and he never liked their war in China, regarding it as a costly drain of manpower and military resources. Hiroyuki Agawa describes a meeting in which an army officer seated next to the admiral rose to his feet "and began to harangue those assembled at interminable length." Yamamoto stealthily edged the man's chair back several feet. When he had finished speaking and tried to sit down, the officer missed the chair and fell sprawling on the floor. The admiral kept a straight face, looked straight ahead, and continued the meeting as if nothing had happened. In a speech given in his hometown in April 1939, he said the talk of a "national emergency" was overblown, and the government should lower its tone: "I have serious doubts as to whether it is desirable that everyone in the nation, high and low, old and young alike, should be constantly strung up to such a pitch. If you pull a piece of elastic to the point where it will stretch no more, it loses its ability to function as elastic."

In 1937, Yamamoto was appointed vice minister of the navy. There he would serve under Admiral Mitsumasa Yonai, a former commander in chief of the Combined Fleet who was also a political moderate, aligned with the navy's Treaty faction. Together they were determined to crack down on insubordinate ultranationalist naval officers, and to stop the headlong slide toward a disastrous war with the United States. "Orders must naturally come from the top to the bureau chiefs . . . " Yamamoto wrote, "and the subordinates are to devise merely means of implementing these policies." Ensconced in his Navy Ministry office, a dimly lit room lined with bookshelves, Yamamoto opposed the army's attempts to have the Japanese Diet dissolved in 1937 and worked behind the scenes to bring civilian statesmen and scholars back into circles of influence. Yonai was personally close to U.S. Ambassador Joseph Grew, and wanted to renew arms limitation talks with the Western powers to avoid a costly new arms race. After the sinking of the *Panay* in 1937, Yamamoto had presented himself at the U.S. Embassy in Tokyo with a humble (and by some reports, tearful) apology and offered a cash indemnity of $2.2 million. But the political climate in Tokyo would not allow for a return to disarmament. Both Yonai and Yamamoto were marked for assassination by ultranationalist goons, many of whom aired their threats publicly and without fear of arrest. In 1939, the conflict between the army and navy seemed to verge on civil war. Naval police were brought in to guard the homes and offices of senior officers whose lives were believed to be in danger. The ministry ordered fleet units into Tokyo Bay and prepared to bring detachments of sailors and marines into Tokyo to put down a rumored insurrection.

The great foreign policy question of the day was the Tripartite Pact, the German-Italian-Japanese alliance that marked the formal creation of the Axis. The ultranationalist right found much to admire in the military-authoritarian model of Nazism, although they found its Aryan master race ideology troubling and tended to ignore it. German influence was strong in the army: German military texts were taught at the Army Staff College and many mid-level officers had done tours of duty in Germany. Hitler was presented in Japanese newsreels as a heroic figure; *Mein Kampf* was sold in translation (with unflattering references to Asians edited out) and was an immensely popular bestseller. "Japanese youth at that time adored Hitler and Mussolini and yearned for the emergence of a Japanese politician with the same qualities," recalled Harumichi Nogi, a student at Nihon University. "We wanted decisive action." The military triumphs of Nazi Germany in 1939 and 1940 did no good for the Japanese advocates of a cautious foreign policy. The European democracies looked impotent before Hitler's juggernaut, and the army was frantic to obtain an alliance with Germany before the (presumably imminent) fall of Britain. With such an alliance in place, Japan would be well placed to seize British colonial territories in Asia.

A right-wing ambassador in Berlin, bypassing his higher-ups in the Foreign Ministry and working furtively with the army staff, negotiated a draft treaty with German foreign minister Joachim von Ribbentrop and sent it to Tokyo for ratification. Yonai and Yamamoto threw the entire weight of the navy against ratification, but the rapid disintegration of France in May 1940 cut the ground out from under their feet. Yamamoto warned that signing the Tripartite Pact would put Japan on the road to a potentially ruinous war with the United States, and "given the existing state of naval armaments, especially in naval aviation, there is no chance of winning a war with the United States for some time to come." Japan, poor in natural resources, relied on areas controlled by the United States and Britain for four-fifths of its vital imports of oil and steel. At a navy conference in September 1940, he addressed the pact's proponents directly: "I want you to tell us quite clearly what changes have been made in the materials mobilization program in order to make up for the deficiencies." They declined even to answer. The single most important objective of Japan's foreign policy, Yamamoto often declared, was to avoid war with the United States at all costs. But the government was drifting into precisely such a war, while refusing to come to grips with most of the fundamental strategic problems it presented. He remarked that Prince Konoye, the prime minister who approved the pact, would someday be "torn into pieces by the revengeful Japanese people."

Each day men dressed in formal kimonos arrived at the redbrick building of the Naval Ministry and demanded to see Yamamoto. They carried
formal complaints written in fine calligraphy on handmade parchment,
and spoke of the impending punishment of heaven: "We are prepared to
take other measures, so be forewarned." Oddly, no action seems to have
been taken against those menacing envoys. Yamamoto sometimes perused
the threatening letters, making margin comments in red ink—"Stupid!"
"Bunch of fools!" "Insulting!"—but given the recent history of Japan, the
threats could not be ignored. When the cabinet of Prime Minister Kuchiro
Hiranuma fell in August 1939, Yonai was named the new prime minister (a
thankless office, with little power), and Yamamoto, whose life was thought
to be in imminent danger, was sent back to the Combined Fleet as the new
commander in chief, a post he would hold until his death. The Tripartite
Pact was signed in Berlin on September 27, 1940.

As Yamamoto had predicted, the Roosevelt administration began to
tighten the economic screws. An oil trade agreement expired in January
1940, and the United States declined to extend it. Japan had previously
imported 80 percent of its oil from the United States or U.S. territories,
and now it appeared that that entire source might be cut off. That same
month, the United States cut off sales of aviation fuel and scrap metal to
Japan. Gradually the noose was tightened, as new categories of materials were added to the embargo lists. Negotiations opened in Washington
between Secretary of State Cordell Hull and Japanese ambassador Kich-
isaburo Nomura. In July 1941, when Japan invaded southern Indochina at
the expense of the Free French, the British and Dutch announced that no
further exports of oil to Japan would be permitted, and all Japanese assets
in the United States were frozen. That brought events to a head, because
although Japan had stockpiled enough oil for about two years of operations,
that did not provide for the army or for Japanese industry, and the navy
alone was consuming about 400 tons of the stuff every day.

The sixty-one-year-old Admiral Osami Nagano was appointed navy
minister in March 1936. He seems to have accepted that war was inevitable, even if not desirable, and made no real effort to stop it. He allowed
himself to be pressured and manipulated by younger officers. Vice Admiral
Yorio Sawamoto reflected on the reasons why the navy allowed itself to be
pressured into a war that it was not really prepared to fight. The reasons
had to do with "a competition of mediocrities; there was no outstanding

leader of outstanding ability. Pressure from subordinates was the order of the day. Younger officers would not respect their seniors and this made the matter even more difficult. . . . Everybody wanted to evade responsibility and no one had the grit to sacrifice himself to do his duty . . . The atmosphere was such that it put a premium on parochial and selfish concerns for either the army or the navy; considerations of the nation and the world were secondary."

From his flagship, usually anchored at Hashirajima, Yamamoto continued to lobby for accommodation with the United States. He foresaw that a naval war in the Pacific would not be decided by a single "decisive battle" in the pattern of Tsushima, but would evolve into a long war of attrition. He challenged his more bellicose colleagues to acknowledge the size and latent potential of the American industrial economy, and he foresaw that Japan's densely inhabited cities were vulnerable to air raids. The admiral had no confidence in the traditional Japanese war plan of "interceptive operations" to reduce the strength of the American fleet as it advanced across the vast wastes of the central Pacific. He correctly predicted that the Americans would not play into Japanese hands by sending a fleet to rescue the Philippines in the first phase of the war, but would take as much time as needed to build up overwhelming naval and air power, and then return by way of a methodical island-hopping campaign.

Again and again Yamamoto made his views known to Tokyo. On December 10, 1940: "It is too late now to be surprised, enraged, and distressed by America's economic oppression. It is like a schoolboy who lives for the moment and behaves thoughtlessly." The war would be a "calamity," he wrote, and must be avoided at all costs. On October 14, 1940, he wrote Kumao Harada, secretary to Prince Saionji: "To fight the United States is like fighting the whole world. But it has been decided. So I will fight the best I can. Doubtless I shall die on board *Nagato* [his flagship]. Meanwhile Tokyo will be burnt to the ground three times." Yamamoto was willing to go to great lengths to preserve the peace with the United States: he favored abrogating the Tripartite Pact and even withdrawing all Japanese troops from China. When asked directly by Konoye about Japan's chances, he replied, "If we are ordered to do it, then I can raise havoc with the Americans for the first six months or a year, but I have absolutely no confidence as to what would happen if it went on for two or three years."

After the Nakajima Type 97 torpedo bombers performed brilliantly in

1940 fleet exercises, Yamamoto mused to his chief of staff, "It makes me wonder if they couldn't get Pearl Harbor." There lay the germ of his plan to launch a sudden carrier air attack on the American stronghold. It was one of the rich ironies of Yamamoto's career that he simultaneously opposed war with the United States, even to the extent of risking his own life, while also insisting on the attack on Pearl Harbor, even to the extent of resigning his command. "What a strange position I find myself in," he wrote a friend on October 11, 1941, "having been assigned the mission diametrically opposed to my own personal opinion, with no choice but to push full speed in pursuance of that mission. Alas, is that fate?" Lieutenant Commander Genda, then serving on the staff of the First Naval Air Wing, had been studying the possibilities of massed carrier airpower since seeing a cinema newsreel about an American fleet review. The footage had depicted four aircraft carriers sailing in a single file. Genda realized that concentrating multiple carriers into a single task force would allow a huge air armada to be launched in one coordinated strike.

The raid on Pearl Harbor was an eleventh-hour revolt against more than thirty years of war planning, which had envisioned a decisive fleet battle in the western Pacific. In the traditional scenario, submarines, airplanes, and destroyers might peck away at the American fleet as it advanced across the ocean ("attrition operations"), but the killing blow would be delivered by the battleships, concentrated in orthodox Mahanian fashion, after lying in wait for the Americans in Japan's home waters. But Yamamoto now asked: What if the American fleet did not play its part? What if it refused to repeat the around-the-world odyssey that had led Admiral Rozhestvensky to his doom at Tsushima? What if the Americans prudently chose to bide their time and build up their strength before coming to the rescue of the Philippines? How would Japan then score the decisive victory it needed?

Rear Admiral Takijiro Onishi, asked by Yamamoto to make a thorough study of the proposed attack, concluded that there were two significant problems. First, to make the torpedoes run in the shallow waters of Pearl Harbor. Second, to achieve surprise. The shallow-run torpedo problem was solved by devising an ingenious set of wooden fins. As for surprise, Onishi estimated the chance of success at about 60 percent. Others, including Genda, put the odds higher. (For the sake of the navy's honor, Yamamoto asked that Japan's declaration of war precede the attack by at least one hour.) When some of his fellow officers urged that the plan was too risky,

Yamamoto replied, "Don't keep saying, 'It's too much of a gamble,' just because I happen to be fond of playing bridge and shogi. . . . Pearl Harbor is my idea and I need your support."

Several hundred handpicked pilots were sent to Kagoshima Bay, a place that resembled the topography and appearance of Pearl Harbor, to practice the shallow, short-run torpedo drops that the mission would require. The raid on Pearl Harbor would be carried out by a task force of twenty-three ships, including six aircraft carriers, commanded by Vice Admiral Chuichi Nagumo. While negotiations dragged on in Washington, Yamamoto demanded that the Naval General Staff approve his plan. When he was refused, he replied, "Unless it is carried out, the Commander in Chief Combined Fleet has no confidence that he can fulfill his assigned responsibility." That last constituted a direct threat to resign, and Nagano gave in, saying, "If he has that much confidence, it's better to let Yamamoto go ahead."

The Combined Fleet chief had decided on his opening gambit in the war, but remained adamant that the wiser course was not to fight at all. On September 29, 1941, with the fleet preparing to sail for their rendezvous in the Kurile Islands, Yamamoto told Nagano bluntly that the pending war would be a catastrophe. He saw the entire picture clearly, and laid it out with devastating clarity. "It is obvious that a Japanese-American war will become a protracted one," he said:

> As long as tides of war are in our favor, the United States will never stop fighting. As a consequence, the war will continue for several years, during which materiel will be exhausted, vessels and arms will be damaged, and they can be replaced only with great difficulties. Ultimately we will not be able to contend with [the United States]. As the result of war the people's livelihood will become indigent . . . and it is not hard to imagine [that] the situation will become out of control. We must not start a war with so little a chance of success.

Evidently that was a view shared by all or nearly all of the top-ranking officers of the navy, but most were reluctant to say so. They felt pressure from below, from hotheads and hard-liners in the middle ranks—and they were vividly aware that agents of the radical right would gun down any man who stood in the way of Japan's "imperial destiny." But there was a third dimension, perhaps the most important of all: the rivalry between the army and navy. The two services were pitted against each other in an eternal brawl over funding, political influence, and the allocation of resources. Competition between military branches was hardly unique to Japan, but the Meiji Constitution placed both services in a direct advisory relationship with the emperor, with mechanisms freeing them from parliamentary or cabinet control. In practice, by the late 1930s, either service could effectively veto any national budget or depose any prime minister. Conceivably the emperor could be asked to resolve a deadlock between them, but so long as the admirals and generals reached a consensus, he was expected not to interfere. In other words, there was no one in Japan—no office, no agency, no legislature, no dictator, no commander in chief—who could overrule the army or navy when their institutional priorities did not fit into a coherent national policy. The predictable upshot was that both services got what they wanted.

Since 1923, the Japanese navy had identified the United States as its principal "hypothetical enemy." This meant fleet expansion plans were based on a premise that Japan must be prepared to fight and defeat the U.S. Navy. Whatever its merits, that conceptual framework had supplied the admirals with potent leverage in budget negotiations. For nearly two decades, it had secured their funding priorities. It did no harm so long as it was understood as a bargaining posture, but in 1940, American sanctions brought the essential questions of war and peace out of the realm of long-term planning and into the sphere of immediate decision. Navy leaders did not want war with the United States, but could not bring themselves to kill the goose that laid the golden eggs. "Inwardly we felt we could not fight with the Anglo-American powers, but we could not unequivocally say so," admitted a staff officer at the Navy Ministry. "We had called ourselves an invincible navy and we had been telling the army that we could take on the United States. . . . So, we could not say we lacked confidence now. We were afraid that the army would say, 'If the navy can't fight, give us your materiel and budget.'" Another officer added, "If we say we shall absolutely never fight the United States, the army will grasp Japan's total national strength and financial power for its own purposes." Navy Vice Minister Sawamoto was sensitive to the army's oft-repeated taunt that "a navy that cannot make war is worse than useless."

On November 1, 1941, Navy Minister Shigetaro Shimada met with Tojo and expressed his "war determination," but in the same breath asked for an

Principal Ports and Naval Bases of Japan

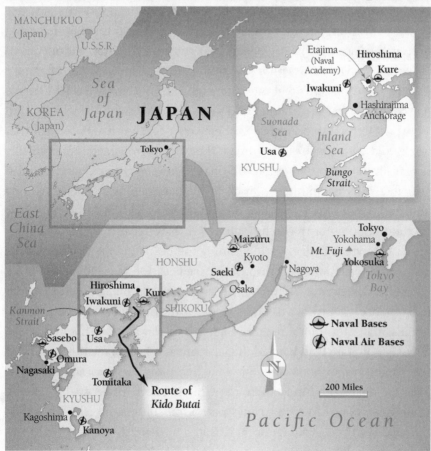

increase in the navy's 1942 steel allotment. Seeking clarity, Army Chief of Staff Hajime Sugiyama asked, "Will you decide for war, Shimada-san, if the navy gets the steel it demands?" Shimada nodded: 300,000 tons of steel would buy the navy's support for the war it did not really want to fight. It is hard to quarrel with the army staff officer who left his reaction in the Confidential War Journal: "How pathetic the navy is!"

Negotiations in Washington dragged out through 1941, but there was never any serious prospect of a settlement. Secretary of State Hull did not waver from his position that the sanctions would continue until Japanese troops were pulled out of China. Hirohito and his closest advisers were opposed to war, but the emperor did not go beyond frequent exhortations to his cabinet to "do your best to achieve a peaceful solution." The Foreign Ministry carried on talks, but did so largely in the dark—the Japanese envoys in Washington had no idea that should their efforts fail, Japan would open immediate hostilities. General Tojo, the army minister, was unequivocal in declaring that a withdrawal from China was impossible. "I cannot yield to this. America's real intention is to control the Far East. Therefore one concession by Japan would lead to another, and so on."

At an Imperial Conference on September 6, 1941, it was decided that war would begin in October unless the Washington talks unexpectedly bore fruit. In October, Tojo forced Prince Konoye out of office and assumed the office of prime minister himself (while maintaining the office of army minister). Under his leadership, he said, there would be "no compromise on the stationing of troops in China." On November 5, Yamamoto's Top Secret Operation Order No. 1, outlining the Pearl Harbor attack plan, was distributed to commanders throughout the fleet. On November 26, the six big aircraft carriers of Nagumo's carrier group *Kido Butai*, observing strict radio silence, slipped out of Hitokappu Bay in the remote northern Kurile Islands, and set sail for a rendezvous north of Hawaii. On that same date, Secretary of State Hull handed the Japanese ambassador a letter reiterating the American position: sanctions would be lifted upon withdrawal of all Japanese forces from Indochina and China. The impasse was apparently irresolvable. Tojo described Hull's note as an ultimatum, though it had included neither a deadline nor a threat. The general was now the dominant figure in Japanese politics, and he was determined to take the country to war: "Sometimes people have to shut their eyes and take the plunge."

The ears of the Japanese people were ringing with propaganda calculated to arouse them to war, and they never heard a dissenting point of view. They heard that Japan was a nation of destiny, with a divine mission to liberate Asia. They were told that the spiritual power of the Japanese people, when fully mobilized, would overcome any material deficiency in conventional military power. They were assured that the Western democracies had grown soft and decadent from easy living, and lacked the stomach to fight. Under the relentless barrage, even well-educated Japanese found it difficult to think clearly. "I did have doubts at times," recalled Harumichi Nogi of the years immediately before the war, "but on such occasions I believed that these thoughts surfaced in my mind because I was lacking in patriotic fervor and spirit. I felt I had to drive myself forward. If a nation decides to take action, everyone must move along with the decision!" Yes, everyone, even the leadership. As much as they might have liked to procrastinate, to wait and watch, the men who ruled the country did not believe they had the luxury of time. The oil embargo amounted to a slow strangulation of the Japanese economy: with each passing day the stockpiles ebbed. The United States had begun a massive naval buildup, and the longer Japan waited to strike, the more formidable the enemy would become. Their Nazi allies were on the move in Europe, and if Japan did not seize the day, would it forever miss the chance to secure its rightful share of the spoils?

By the fall of 1941, no one in Japan could stop the slide, except possibly the emperor, and he had always acquiesced in whatever fragile consensus the ruling circle presented to him. In the end, whatever their doubts and misgivings, no member of the cabinet could find the moral courage to tell the truth and face the consequences. Their recommendation for war was unanimous. Hirohito said, after 1945, "I held the view that being a monarch of a constitutional state, I had to approve the unanimous opinion of the government and the Supreme War Council. If I failed to do so, Tojo would resign and there would be a major coup d'etat, and the completely reckless advocates of war would gain control." Though self-serving, Hirohito's supposition was probably accurate. Tojo had stated that the army was "straining at the leash," and navy leaders believed that the alternative to a foreign war might be a civil war. The leaders of Japan shared a sense that the coming crisis was an external force, beyond their control, like an earthquake or tsunami. It was happening *to* Japan. "The arrow has left the bow," the generals and admirals told each other, and the time had come for each to revert to his proper place in the military hierarchy. With a shared sense of relief, the men who ruled Japan turned away from the great issues of foreign policy and bent to the more familiar task of launching a war, as if it were a mission that had been assigned to them and not one they had chosen.

Chapter Four

U.S. NAVY HEADQUARTERS, OR "MAIN NAVY," WAS HOUSED IN A massive concrete-asbestos edifice on the Washington Mall. The three-story, grime-streaked complex was connected by a covered walkway to a similar structure called the Munitions Building.* Together, they occupied a third of a mile along Constitution Avenue immediately north of the Reflecting Pool, with nine wings branching to the south and running to the edge of the pool itself. The building was one of a dozen "tempos," built hastily and on the cheap in 1918, during the First World War. These crumbling monstrosities had been thrown up on the Mall, between Capitol Hill and the Lincoln Memorial, with the understanding that they would be demolished once the emergency had passed. After the war, the path of least political and bureaucratic resistance had been to leave them standing. Their occupants were content to remain in such a desirable location, so close to the White House and Capitol Hill, and Congress was content not to pay to tear the buildings down and erect replacements.

An officer remembered the prewar Navy Department as a somnolent place, in which "unadorned offices of standard size stretched interminably along dreary corridors." The floors were faded linoleum, the overhead lighting dim and sickly yellow, and windowless wooden doors were identified only by stenciled acronyms or numbers. After December 7, the pace of life suddenly accelerated: an officer arriving a few days after Pearl Harbor described the headquarters as "an ant hill with the top kicked off." The

---

* The building was torn down in 1970 and the land reclaimed as a handsome public park, which today includes the site of the Vietnam Veterans Memorial.

lights burned all night as officers worked around the clock. Many did not physically leave the building in the first week of the war. Cots were rolled into offices, and food brought in on trays. All officers had been ordered to report to work in uniform beginning on Monday, December 8. Prior to the war, it had been the practice of many officers billeted in administrative posts to work in civilian clothing, so in the first few days many senior officers appeared in mismatched, outdated, or ill-fitting uniforms. A young lieutenant recalled seeing several officers wearing uniforms that could not be buttoned, because they had gained weight since having last put them on. "Rear Admiral John Wainwright, one of my favorite Admirals, was evidently missing his raincoat and overcoat. He had on his Admiral's cap, and below it was a very loud Scottish tweed coat."

Marines in steel helmets, bayonets fixed on their rifles, demanded identification from anyone wishing to enter or exit, including high-ranking officers in uniform. A few days after Pearl Harbor, BBC correspondent Alistair Cooke walked into the department through a side door, where he found no guards. He visited the officer he had come to see, but when he tried to leave the building, "a guard lowered his rifle and barred the way." Cooke had been ensnared in one of those distinctive military-bureaucratic paradoxes that Joseph Heller would later describe as a "catch-22." "The theory," Cooke wryly observed, "was that if you were not wearing a visitor's button, you never in the first place came in and were technically not present. This was reasonable but uncomfortable to anybody who hoped soon to resume his life in the world outside the Navy Department." After appealing to an admiral in a nearby office, the Englishman was let out.

Depression-era officers had been schooled in the virtues of parsimony, proper administrative channels, and meticulous execution of paperwork; and that was especially true among those who handled the navy's money, equipment, and materials. Should they fail to account for every item or dollar consumed or spent, their careers would suffer. But on December 8, the service was overtaken by a collective sense that all of that must change. Velocity was paramount. "We were busy as bird-dogs in those weeks following the attack," said a gunnery training officer. "It's hard to describe just how much the workflow moved up." Men up the chain of command were too swamped to answer every request for instructions, so officers and enlisted men of every rank had to assume a wider scope of authority. They sensed, even if they were not actually told, that no one could afford to hesitate when authority to act was uncertain. The new mood lent itself to peremptory action, leaving paperwork and legal authorization to be sorted out in good time. When Rear Admiral Ben Moreell, chief of the Bureau of Yards and Docks, was asked for funds to build a new antiaircraft gunnery training center, his reply was very much in the new spirit. "Hell," he said, "I'll give you all the money you want. I don't give a goddamn what the law says."

Navy Secretary Knox, having flown to Pearl Harbor to assess the devastation firsthand, was back in Washington on the evening of Sunday, December 14. On Monday morning, he held a press conference at his office on the second "deck" (floor) of the Navy Department. "An enormous crowd turned out, the biggest he'll ever have," wrote Glen Perry of the *New York Sun*. "His office was packed, and it took a long time to get credentials checked out. He waited, puffing calmly at his pipe." Frank Knox was an old protégé of Theodore Roosevelt, and had ridden in the "Rough Riders" regiment in the Spanish-American War. In 1930, he had become publisher and part owner of the *Chicago Daily News*. Though he was personally loyal to FDR, Knox's paper had been a tenacious critic of the New Deal, and he himself had been the Republican Party's vice-presidential nominee in 1936. He had taken over the Navy Department in 1940, at the same time that another prominent Republican, Henry Stimson, assumed the post of secretary of war. The two accepted Roosevelt's invitation to join the cabinet because they opposed their party's isolationist platform in the 1940 election campaign.

As a veteran newspaper editor, Knox knew how to make reporters lie down like lambs, and his performance was a tour de force. He surprised them, and sapped their prosecutorial ardor, by revealing more of the truth than they expected to hear. He admitted that the *Arizona* and the *Utah* were destroyed, as well as three destroyers and a minelayer; he also admitted that the *Oklahoma* had capsized, but predicted that she would be righted and returned to service. He allowed that other ships had been damaged "in varying degrees which will require repairs ranging from those which can be done immediately to work covering a period of months." As for casualties, he described the losses as "heavy," and when pressed by the reporters, he admitted that there had been close to 3,000 men killed. Knox conceded that the Japanese attack had been "very cleverly organized and carried out with great skill," but he insisted that morale in Pearl Harbor was very high (which was not entirely true) and added, "I wish the bastards would come back." He emphasized the heroic efforts of the sailors caught up in the raid, and eulogized the dead for having given their lives to a higher cause. News coverage picked up his well-placed cues and followed in the same spirit.

Still, the disagreeable questions remained: How was the U.S. Navy caught so utterly off guard? Who was at fault and who was going to be called to account for the catastrophe? There had been angry rumblings in Congress, demands for the court-martial of the local commanders, even demands for the resignation of Secretary Knox himself. In his brief visit to Hawaii, Knox's pointed questions to Admiral Kimmel left no doubt that the Pacific Fleet commander had been selected as the inevitable scapegoat. To the assembled reporters, Knox would say only that a "formal investigation" would be launched to determine if there had been "any dereliction of duty." But he also stated outright that "the land and sea forces were not on the alert," thus fixing the impression in the minds of the public that the local commanders were chiefly to blame. Kimmel and his army counterpart, General Walter Short, would be relieved of duty, unjustly pilloried in the press, and condemned to spend the rest of the war running an obscene gauntlet of investigations rigged to deflect blame away from Washington.

Kimmel's successor would be Rear Admiral Chester W. Nimitz, the fifty-six-year-old chief of the Bureau of Navigation. The decision was Roosevelt's and was rendered without hesitation. "Tell Nimitz to get the hell out to Pearl and stay there until the war is won," he told Knox on Tuesday morning. Shortly afterward, the phone in Admiral Nimitz's office was answered by Lieutenant H. Arthur Lamar, the admiral's devoted flag secretary. The caller asked to be put through to "Chester." Lieutenant Lamar did not recognize the low, stentorian voice on the other end of the line, and felt "insulted that anyone should be calling my admiral by his first name." He asked for the caller's name. "This is the president," came the brusque reply. "Put him on the phone."

Nimitz spoke to the president briefly, then hurried out to his car for the three-block drive to the White House. Two hours later he returned and told Lamar, "I am going to the Pacific."

Descriptions of Chester Nimitz usually resort to the term "towheaded," because he had a dramatic shock of white hair that stood in contrast to his keen blue eyes and ruddy complexion. His eyebrows were as white as his hair, and combined they gave him gravitas, the look of an elder sage. His eyes were powerfully expressive, alternately broadcasting warmth, skepticism, regret, mirth, or anger, even when the rest of his face gave nothing away. They earned him a nickname among his staff: "the man with the blue eyes." He had good bones. As a young man, Nimitz had been as handsome as a movie idol—a brawny athlete with perfect posture, a strong jaw, and a square, honest face. At fifty-six he retained his good looks. He kept himself fit with long walks and vigorous bouts of tennis.

This was the second time Nimitz had been offered command of the U.S. Pacific Fleet. In early 1941, he had declined the offer on the grounds that he was too junior on the admiral's list. To accept the job would have sent him leapfrogging over the heads of more than fifty admirals who stood above him on the duty rolls. His appointment would have incurred their resentment, said Nimitz, and made it difficult to do the job properly. Now, with the nation at war, no one was quite so concerned with the niceties of the naval pecking order, and in any case the assignment had come in the form of a command.

Like most of his colleagues at the Navy Department, Nimitz had been working around the clock. In the first seventy-two hours of the war he slept on a couch in his office, eating nothing but soup brought to him in a thermos by his wife. After the third day of the war he went home after midnight, crawled into bed for three or four hours of sleep, then rose at dawn and returned to work. The Bureau of Navigation, notwithstanding its name, was actually the navy's personnel department, and the onset of war had saddled Nimitz and his staff with an immense workload. The phones had been ringing almost without interruption, and a daily tidal wave of telegrams washed in through the varnished wooden doors of Nimitz's suite of offices. Officers killed in action had to be replaced; officers whose ships had been knocked out of action had to be reassigned; officers had to be sent out to man a rapidly mobilizing fleet. To the bureau fell the grim, indispensable task of tabulating accurate casualty lists and notifying the families of men killed in action. There were moments, in those early days, when Nimitz seemed on the verge of succumbing to the general epidemic of despair that had swept through the ranks. To a captain in his bureau he remarked, "We have suffered a terrible defeat. I don't know whether we can ever recover from it." He later confided to a friend: "From the time the Japanese dropped those bombs on December 7th until at least two months later, hardly a day passed that the situation did not get more chaotic and confused and appear more hopeless."

The admiral walked home to his apartment at 2222 Q Street and found his wife, Catherine, in bed with a cold. He told her the news. "You always wanted to command the Pacific Fleet," she said: "You always thought that would be the height of glory." "Darling," he replied, "the fleet's at the bottom of the sea. Nobody must know that here, but I've got to tell you." She helped him pack two suitcases with his white and khaki uniforms. He did not take his blues, as they were generally not worn at all in Hawaii's tropical climate.

On December 18, the newspapers carried the news of Kimmel's relief and Nimitz's appointment. The stories ran alongside Nimitz's official navy photograph, depicting a hatchet-faced admiral with a straight, hard mouth and cold, pale eyes. As CINCPAC, Nimitz would receive a two-rung promotion, from rear admiral to full admiral. The *New York Times* described him as "a tanned, white-haired Texan," and gave details of his naval career, dwelling at some length on his heroic act, while a lieutenant in 1912, of saving a sailor from drowning. Glen Perry of the *New York Sun* confided in his diary, "Washington reaction is that this is a smart move, and that public confidence will be greater as the result." Because Nimitz was almost totally unknown outside the navy, and instinctively shunned publicity, an impression took hold in the public mind that he was a "sundowner"—a hard man and a harsh disciplinarian, ill-humored and remote. That impression was badly mistaken, but for the time being it did no harm. It was an image suitable to his rank and profession, especially during wartime. In truth, though he was punctilious in observing naval etiquette, and could throw daggers with a glare or a low tone of voice, Nimitz's natural leadership style relied to a great degree on personal warmth.

Only a week and a half had passed since the attack on Pearl, but it seemed as if the war had been going on for a month or more. Nimitz had been going flat-out for ten days, and he was physically and mentally exhausted. Secretary Knox had ordered that a navy plane be readied to fly the new C-in-C to the west coast, where he would catch another for Hawaii. But Nimitz put his foot down—he needed a few days, as he put it, "to catch up on my sleep and collect my thoughts." What he had in mind was a three-day journey by rail to California, in a comfortable Pullman sleeping car, during which he would replenish his strength and study the briefing reports that had piled up in his inbox. He would leave on Friday, December 19, and arrive in California three days later.

He worked late into the night on Thursday, but devoted Friday morning to his family, going to see one of his daughters, Mary, perform in a school Christmas pageant. His wife, son, and other daughter did not know how long he would be gone, but they were a navy family, and long separations were an ordeal they had learned to expect and endure. No tears were shed. "At no point did I break down," Mrs. Nimitz later recalled. "I was brought up by my mother to take what's coming, and you don't weep over it. You have to go through things." At Union Station, where the platforms were swarming with servicemen and holiday travelers, Nimitz boarded the Baltimore & Ohio Railroad's "Capitol Limited" for the overnight journey to Chicago. He was accompanied by his trusty squire, Lieutenant Lamar, who had been ordered to see that Nimitz ate properly and got plenty of rest. Admiral James O. Richardson, chairman of the Naval General Board, had given Lamar two bottles of Old Granddad, and told the lieutenant to pour "two good slugs" for Nimitz each night before dinner. For the sake of security, the two men traveled incognito, in civilian clothing and under false names. Nimitz's ticket identified him as "Mr. Freeman"—his wife's maiden name.

The train rolled out of Washington and into the patchwork corn fields of rural Maryland. Darkness fell in late afternoon, and Lamar broke out the whiskey. With a drink or two in him, Nimitz revealed more of himself to Lamar than he ever had while at the office. He bantered contentedly and told off-color jokes. He tried to teach the lieutenant the rules of cribbage, but the younger man could not seem to wrap his mind around the game, and Nimitz soon gave up and played solitaire. Later, they went to dinner. That night, as they slept like dead men in their swaying bunks, the train rolled through the industrial heartland of the upper Midwest—Pittsburgh, Youngstown, Akron, Gary—and the next morning, with the skyscrapers of Chicago looming in the distance, Nimitz awoke "really refreshed and feeling that I could cope with the situation."

THE FUTURE FLEET ADMIRAL had been born in 1885, in a cramped limestone cottage in Fredericksburg, Texas, a German immigrant enclave in the hill country west of Austin. He had been raised under the roof of the small, redbrick Nimitz Hotel on Fredericksburg's Main Street—the hotel built by his grandfather and run by his father and uncle (who after his father's death married his mother and became his stepfather). His ancestors were Saxon-Germans of the titled warrior-gentry class: the von Nimitz family could trace its lineage back to the twelfth century, and had once borne a coat of arms. In the mid-nineteenth century, however, Nimitz's great-grandfather had fallen on hard times. Forced to abandon what remained of the family estates, he sought employment as a merchant sea captain. In 1840, he immigrated to America.

As a boy, Chester was never allowed to forget his German heritage: at home, and around town, he spoke as much German as English. In tribute to his great-grandfather's seafaring career, the Nimitz Hotel had been built to resemble a steamship in shape and appearance, and the interior detail was nautical-themed. When Chester was six, the family moved down the road to Kerrville, where they managed another hotel, the St. Charles. It was a poor country inn, never turning much of a profit, and the entire family bore a hand in keeping it running. Chester was never a stranger to hard work. Even as a child he rose before dawn to begin his chores—cleaning, mopping, dusting, chopping wood, lighting fires, hauling garbage. From about the age of twelve he delivered meat for a local butcher, earning a dollar a week. In the warmer months he wore no shoes. At night he often manned the hotel's front desk until ten o'clock. Then he fell into bed and was up again before dawn.

Nimitz did not expect to go to college; his family was too poor to afford it. But in the summer of 1900, when he was fifteen years old, two U.S. Army lieutenants spent a night at the hotel. They gave him the encouraging news that West Point was free of tuition to all who could win admission. He wrote the local congressman, and was told that all of the district's West Point appointments for that year had already been made, but there was one Annapolis appointment still available. It would be made on the basis of a competitive entrance exam to be given the following spring. He would be applying in his junior high school year, one year early, so he had not yet had all the relevant coursework. Nimitz rose at three each morning and cracked the books in the predawn darkness. He was popular around town, known to all as "Cottonhead," so when he announced his intention to take the exam, many in his little community were keen to help. A local teacher tutored him in algebra, geometry, history, geography, and grammar; his high school principal helped him with mathematics. In the spring of 1901, Nimitz passed the exam with the highest marks of all the district's applicants, and won his place in the Naval Academy class of 1905.

From the start, it was clear that Nimitz had chosen the right profession.

The daily routine was austere and exhausting, but no more so than his life in Texas. The midshipmen rose early, but not as early as Nimitz had risen at home. They lived in a drafty, crumbling wooden annex, but Nimitz had never experienced luxurious living and never expected anything else. He was poor, but that made no difference at the academy: he was always popular with his classmates, and emerged as a natural leader. He never struggled in the classroom. The only subject that gave him any trouble was mathematics, but even in that subject he stood near the head of his class. He won three stripes and was named commander of the Eighth Company, a high honor. At graduation, Nimitz stood seventh in his class of 114.

"A man he seems of cheerful yesterdays and confident tomorrows. . . . Possesses that calm and steady-going Dutch way that gets to the bottom of things." That was the tribute written to twenty-year-old Chester W. Nimitz by the editors of the *Lucky Bag*, the Naval Academy yearbook of 1905. The quote, from Wordsworth's *Excursion*, was apt: it got at Nimitz's qualities of serenity, humility, and good-fellowship. He had a pleasant face and an easy manner. He was comfortable in his own skin. He was one of those rare souls who managed to be both supremely confident and genuinely modest.

In the early years of his naval career, Nimitz served in many capacities—afloat and ashore, on gunboats, submarines, destroyers, cruisers, and battle-ships, in recruiting, personnel management, and war planning. As a young officer he served with the U.S. Asiatic Fleet in East Asia. In 1905, when he was billeted on the battleship *Ohio*, the ship put into Tokyo Bay. There he met the great Japanese admiral Heihachiro Togo. Beginning in 1909, Nim-itz served in the navy's fledging submarine service. In 1912, he received the Silver Lifesaving Medal for saving the life of W. J. Walsh, Fireman second class, who was swept off the deck of the submarine *E-1* and carried away by a strong tide. The twenty-six-year-old lieutenant dived into the sea and went after the man, who could not swim—he kept Walsh afloat until they were rescued by a boat. Later that year, Nimitz, still a lieutenant, was given command of the Atlantic submarine force. He became a recognized expert in submarine tactics: in 1912, he published an article on the subject in the *Naval Institute Proceedings*, the trade journal of the naval officer corps. He emerged as the navy's foremost expert in diesel submarine engines.

During the First World War he served in the office of the chief of naval operations in Washington, and later as executive officer of the battleship *South Carolina*. He attended the Naval War College, a ticket that every officer on his way to flag rank had to punch. Here he was indoctrinated in War Plan Orange and the likely scenarios for a war against Japan in the Pacific; later he was to say: "I was asked once how we were able to fight the war in the Pacific, and I said that we fought it just as we had fought it all on paper in the Naval War College. I fought the whole war of the Pacific when I was there in 1923."

In 1912, Lieutenant Nimitz proposed marriage to Catherine Vance Freeman, daughter of a Massachusetts ship broker. "If you love me at all," he wrote his mother, "I want you to congratulate me on becoming engaged to Catherine. . . . You may accuse me of not knowing my mind because two years ago I wanted to marry someone else. Well, two years is a long time and I am no longer the vague-minded person I was then. . . . Now, if you want to make me happy, please write this young lady a nice letter, for my sake." They were married in April 1913. A trip home to Texas followed, in which Nimitz's mother was charming, but his aunts were less than convivial. They murmured darkly among themselves in German, leaving Catherine with the impression that they were not entirely happy to welcome a non-German northerner into the clan. Southern identity remained strong in Texas; the Civil War was still well within the living memory of the older generation. At dinner one night, one of Nimitz's aunts asked, "Chester, if there was another war between the North and the South, which would you fight for?" He replied, "Why, I'd stay by the Union, of course." Catherine took it as a pledge of loyalty, not only to the nation but to her.

They had a girl, Catherine Vance, then a son, Chester Junior, who would follow his father to the Naval Academy and then serve a career in submarines; and two more daughters, Anne Elizabeth and Mary Manson. Chester was a devoted father, making as much time for his children as his duties would permit. In the first decade of their marriage, the Nimitzes lived in Connecticut, Germany, Belgium, Brooklyn, Washington, D.C., Pearl Harbor, and Rhode Island. Catherine did not seem to mind the life of a naval family, the constant packing up and moving from one part of the world to another, the rootlessness. She and the children accepted that the navy was their home.

During the layover in chicago, Admiral Nimitz took a cab to the old Navy Pier and the Naval Reserve Midshipman's School, where he made small talk with old acquaintances and sat for a haircut. While there, he learned that Wake Island was holding out against a new barrage of Japanese airstrikes. That afternoon he and Lieutenant Lamar were back at Dearborn Station to catch the Los Angeles–bound "Super Chief," flagship of the Santa Fé Railway, one of the most celebrated passenger trains of those glory days of long-distance rail travel. With the help of the porters they moved into adjoining compartments in one of the plush Pullman cars. The Super Chief rolled out of Chicago in the fading afternoon light, through a gray winter landscape of stone embankments, bridges, culverts, catwalks, and rooftops, and the city dissolved gradually into the suburbs, and then into the broad plains of western Illinois—"through lovely rolling country," wrote the admiral to Catherine, "nice farms and wide vistas and far off horizons." Lamar poured two strong whiskeys and then both men went to bed.

Awakening refreshed, Nimitz wrote again: "As I get more sleep and rest, things are looking up and I am sure that by the time I reach Pearl Harbor I will be able to meet the requirements of the situation." The admiral spent long hours gazing out the window at the Great Plains, a region of farming and stock-raising, of cement plants, flour mills, grain elevators, and small towns devoted entirely to shipping livestock, grain, corn, and poultry. They passed through Kansas City, a prosperous metropolis and the hub of a dozen rail trunk lines; they continued on through grandly monotonous plains where the corn fields stretched all the way around the horizon; through Dodge City, one of the most infamous towns of the old frontier, where Wyatt Earp and Bill Tilghman had earned their names and outlaws were still buried up on Boot Hill. Crossing into southeast Colorado, a rich agricultural district of dairy farms and alfalfa fields, passengers were advised to set their watches back an hour. More farmland, miles of it: onions, cantaloupes, sugar beets, and other crops; and as the Super Chief rolled on across the plains, the snow-encrusted Rocky Mountain peaks came into view in the distant northwest. It was an arid region, and they passed over irrigation canals that carried precious water to the fields of sunflowers and alfalfa, the broad flat fields of pinto beans and sugar beets; and now, in the little towns along the way, the dwellings and buildings were built of sun-dried adobe bricks.

Lamar had been entrusted with a canvas bag that included highly classified photos and a detailed briefing on the situation at Pearl Harbor. "Don't let this out of your possession," he was told, "and do not open it until you are well along the way outside of Chicago. Then show Admiral Nimitz what's inside." As he perused the contents, Nimitz's mood turned dark. Though he had been briefed by Knox before leaving Washington, he had not imagined the full scale of the carnage. Lamar recalled that the photographs of the scene at Battleship Row "were simply ghastly," and expressed better than words "the complete havoc that was Pearl Harbor." Very few people on the American mainland had seen these images, even those at the highest levels of government. The worst was a shot of the *Arizona*, her great hull totally submerged and her smashed superstructure leaning drunkenly over the harbor, a pall of ugly black smoke still spewing from her remains. Nimitz had come up through the ranks of the battleship navy. Three years earlier, when he had commanded a division of battleships, the *Arizona* had been his flagship. He had known her well. Nimitz thought of Kimmel, whose job he had been offered earlier in the year and by a lucky dodge had turned down. "It could have happened to me," he remarked to Lamar. "It could have happened to any commander."

For a man like Nimitz, who had given forty years of his life to the navy, the defeat at Pearl Harbor felt like a personal reproach. He believed in the navy, had made it his life's work, and had never imagined it could be caught so completely unprepared by Japan or any other nation. He had kept faith with the "navy way"—the red tape, the punctilio, the stolid pace, the unbending discipline—because he believed it was all part of a purposeful design. In 1930, writing for the twenty-fifth anniversary yearbook of his class of 1905, he had written, "My life in the Navy has been very happy and I know of no other profession for which I would forsake my present one." Those were no idle words: Nimitz could have made himself a rich man by leaving the navy for the private sector. In 1915, when he was a lieutenant stationed at the Brooklyn Navy Yard, and living with his wife and two infants in a cramped apartment on Flatbush Avenue, a diesel engine company in St. Louis offered to hire him at an annual salary of $25,000. At the time, the navy was paying him $288 per month. "No thank you," he told the recruiter. "I do not want to leave the navy." "Money is no obstacle to us," insisted the recruiter: "Write your own ticket." "No," Nimitz said. "I don't want to leave the navy."

Chester Junior recalled another conversation in the mid-1930s, when his father confessed that he would someday like to reach the highest rank in the service—that of chief of naval operations, or CNO. Asked how he planned to achieve the goal, Nimitz said that he would do his best, as he always had, and that "he was convinced that in the navy one got what one deserved."

"Dad was a people man entirely," Chester Junior told his father's biographer. "He really wasn't interested in the guns and technology of the navy." The judgment was a little unreasonable—Nimitz had at one point been the navy's foremost expert on diesel engines. But it was certainly true that in the latter half of his career, when he was being groomed for high command, Nimitz concerned himself with the general discipline of leadership. He had closely observed the best of his commanders and consciously modeled himself after them. His specialty, if he could be said to have one, was in nurturing and managing the navy's human capital. His real genius was as a leader, a manager, a judge, and a motivator of men. In the late 1920s, he was appointed to teach at Berkeley as a professor of naval science and tactics. There he spent much of his time recruiting students to the Naval Reserve program, a program that he always held close to his heart. He found great satisfaction in "working with young and extremely independent young men with untrammeled minds—and trying to introduce a little discipline into their thinking and actions."

In 1935, he took the first of two tours of duty at the Bureau of Navigation, the navy's personnel department, responsible for "procurement, training, promotion, assignment, and discipline of officers and enlisted personnel in the Navy." He had a special talent for identifying talented officers and putting them in positions in which their talents would shine. The bureau gave him jurisdiction over the two major feeders for naval officers, the Naval Academy and Naval Reserve Officer Training Corps (ROTC), as well as all the boot camps and other special training schools and programs. He championed the controversial policy of eliminating any differences in the uniforms worn by reservist and regular navy officers. The policy, intended to bolster the authority of the reservists, was unpopular among many in the "Annapolis clique." But it avoided the discrepancy that existed in the British navy, in which reserve officers wore wavy gold stripes (from which sprung the derogatory nickname "the wavy navy"). As chief of the Bureau of Navigation, Nimitz sent out an "ALNAV"—a message to all admirals on all ships and stations—directing them all to take reservists as their personal aides and release their Naval Academy graduates for sea duty. Mahan's dictum that good men and bad ships make a better navy than bad men and good ships was always near Nimitz's thoughts. He was an Annapolis man, but never tolerated blinkered parochialism when it ran against the interests of the service.

Under Roosevelt's administration there had been a tremendous fleet buildup. Major naval spending acts in 1934, 1938, and 1940 created a voracious appetite for officers and enlisted men at all ranks. (The "Two-Ocean Navy" act of 1940 aimed to build two fleets large enough to operate independently without sinning against Mahan's law of concentration. It authorized a 70 percent expansion of the fleet for a then-stupefying price tag of $4 billion.) Nimitz, more than any man in the service, had provided the needed manpower. He introduced the practice of advertising naval recruiting campaigns in newspapers and magazines. The basic training period for enlisted recruits was shortened from eight to six weeks. The Naval Academy class was enlarged by 25 percent, and the academic course shortened from four to three years. New ROTC programs were founded at universities across the country. To carry out the administrative and clerical tasks of the expanding service, he pioneered the hiring of thousands of women as yeomen (F) or yeomanettes.

He was not an aviator and had never served on a carrier, but he had spent much of his career at sea—as all naval officers were expected to do—and his seagoing billets were appropriately varied between destroyers, cruisers, and battleships. He had held a series of important staff jobs; he had engaged in war planning, commanded a cruiser division, and commanded a battleship division. At sea he always assumed that his subordinates knew their jobs until confronted with clear evidence that they did not. He did not affect the "blood and thunder" style of command. He gave his men plenty of scope to act and came down on them only when they had revealed themselves as complacent or incompetent. In such cases he spoke in a low voice, and in polite but blunt terms told a man that his performance had fallen short. "Admiral Nimitz never raised his voice and I never heard him curse during the many years I served with him," wrote Lamar. "But he had a calm and cool manner of dressing down an ensign or even Admiral Halsey when and if he needed it. He never showed displeasure publicly, and I could only tell when he was upset by seeing him biting his lips. Then his steely blue eyes would flash." He was not a slave driver, and he looked after the welfare of his men. Lamar recalled that the admiral "never failed to ask me, whenever we went out, whether his orderlies and drivers had had their chow." But he did not lack the ruthlessness required of all military commanders in wartime. Later, when losses mounted during the Pacific offensive in 1943–44, he would say: "This is one of the responsibilities of command. You have to send some people to their deaths."

As he studied the photographs and briefing reports on board the Super Chief, Nimitz contemplated the full dimensions of the challenge lying ahead of him. He would be inheriting a shattered command, a crippled fleet, and a deeply demoralized staff. He would arrive in Hawaii at a time when it was generally feared that the islands might be overrun by the enemy. He would be in charge of the largest naval war that had ever been waged, and hold command over a war theater that was larger, in square miles, than any other presided over by any military commander in history. The fleet that would destroy the Japanese navy and take the war into the western Pacific would be of a size and scale fundamentally unlike any force ever before assembled. It would require mobilizing the entire American economy and the entire American people. On Sunday, Nimitz again wrote to Catherine, and this time his tone was more guarded. "Had a fine sleep and awoke much refreshed, but after spending most of today reading reports and estimates I find it difficult to keep on the cheerful side. Perhaps when I actually arrive and get over the first shock, things will be better."

They rolled on through miles of painted desert, an epic landscape of mesas and red sandstone cliffs. Navajo women sold blankets and jewelry at the stations of the little towns along the way. Nimitz again tried and failed to teach Lamar how to play cribbage. In Arizona, the landscape continued much the same, with abandoned Hopi pueblos sometimes visible from the train windows, and solitary cacti standing here and there on the hills, and at Seligman their watches were set back another hour. They crossed the Colorado River into the California town of Needles, and continued on through the forbidding plains of the Mojave Desert, where forlorn, sun-baked mountain ranges sat in the distance. Gradually the land grew more fertile as they entered the heart of California. Soon there were apple, peach, and cherry orchards, then a sea of orange and lemon groves. They passed through Fontana, where in two years' time Henry Kaiser would build the first integrated steel mill west of the Rockies. Further westward the palm-lined bungalow communities grew larger and more numerous, and billboard-lined highways stretched away on either side of the tracks; then suddenly there were warehouses, canning sheds, and refrigeration plants towering over the fenced lettuce fields; and everywhere were canals, culverts, and ditches bringing water to make the produce grow. Through tunnels, over bridges, into Pasadena, and on Monday morning the Super Chief rolled into the City of Angels.

Nimitz shook hands with Lamar, who was to fly back to Washington, and boarded a connecting train for San Diego, arriving the afternoon of December 22. There he spent the night as a guest of the local naval air station commander. He was to fly to Oahu in a PB2Y-2 Coronado flying boat, but stormy weather on December 23 made for a rough takeoff attempt. One of the wingtips dragged under the water, and the plane taxied back to base, defeated. The following day, Christmas Eve, the weather was more cooperative. The admiral expressed regrets to the pilot and aircrew for separating them from their families on the holiday. Before his departure Nimitz wrote his wife, closing with the thought: "I only hope I can live up to the high expectations of you and the President and the Department. I will faithfully promise to do my best." At four in the afternoon, the big seaplane, heavily laden with fuel for the long haul to Pearl Harbor, roared down the channel and wobbled into the sky.

FOR TWO DESPERATE WEEKS, the little garrison on Wake Island had held out against relentless Japanese sea and air attacks. The atoll was one of the most remote places on earth, a V-shaped tendril of sand, scrub, and coral rock, 2,300 miles from Oahu, 2,000 miles from Tokyo, 600 miles north of the only slightly less godforsaken atolls of the northern Marshall Islands and the Japanese airfields from which the daily bombing raids had come. Wake and its two small sister islets of Wilkes and Peale, comprising about three square miles all told, were remnants of the partly submerged rim of an ancient volcano. They encircled a shark-infested, cobalt blue lagoon, too shallow and thickly strewn with coral heads to accommodate ships of any draft. With a peak elevation of 20 feet, the islands were so close to the sea that ships might pass within a dozen miles and never know they were there. They had no palm trees, no freshwater sources, produced no food other than fish, and were populated only by flightless birds, hermit crabs, and rats that had deserted some visiting ship decades or possibly centuries earlier. A primitive scrub clung to the parched coral soil. Waves broke across a fringing coral reef, and the din of booming surf was Wake's everlasting background music. The sound was not unpleasant but very loud, so much so that men had to raise their voices to make themselves heard, and (perilously) the engines of approaching airplanes could not be detected until they were immediately overhead.

Wake's sole value was as a way station, a link in the chain of islands connecting the United States to Asia through the axis of Oahu, Midway, Guam, and the Philippines. It had been annexed in 1899, first to serve as a cable relay on the transpacific telegraph, later as a coaling station and a refueling stop for the Pan-American China Clipper Service, whose big four-engine passenger seaplanes landed in the lagoon twice a week. In January 1941, the navy had constructed a 4,500-foot crushed-coral airstrip, and had been working with what little manpower and material resources were on hand to improve defensive installations and ground support facilities for aircraft. The lagoon's small sea-channel was being dredged and coral heads dynamited with the intention of developing an anchorage for large ships. About 1,000 civilian construction workers were converting the Pan-Am facilities on Peale Island into an expanded air station. Two military camps, each with barracks, offices, and storehouses, stood at opposite ends of Wake. A garrison of 450 officers and men of the 1st Marine Defense Battalion was stationed at the shore batteries and defensive works along the southern beaches of Wake and Wilkes islands; many of those men were quartered in tents. The atoll's entire air force consisted of the twelve F4F-3 Wildcats of Marine Fighting Squadron 211 (VMF-211), which had flown in from the carrier *Enterprise* four days before the war.

At noon on December 8 (local date), just hours after the raid on Pearl, Wake was attacked by thirty-four G3M medium bombers operating from the island of Roi in the Marshall Islands. They glided in from the south, under the clouds, at altitude 1,500 feet. No one saw or heard them until less than a minute before the first bombs fell. Four of the Wildcats were patrolling at 12,000 feet, but did not spy the enemy bombers 10,000 feet beneath them. Two more planes had been ordered into the sky but had not yet taken off. Eight new blue-gray marine fighters, two thirds of Wake's entire air strength, were parked almost wing to wing on the edge of the strip. They were not properly dispersed because there was very little room on the cramped airfield to disperse them. The G3Ms roared overhead in a tight "Vee-of-vee" formation and dropped their sticks of 60-kilogram fragmentation bombs with lethal accuracy: they fell directly among the parked aircraft and adjoining machine shops. At the same time the Japanese gunners strafed the pilots and ground crews who were caught out in the open. Dozens of men were cut down in their tracks as they ran across the airfield. The attack unfolded very quickly; the bombers were there and then they were gone. They banked left to attack Camp 2 and the Pan-Am Terminal on Peale Island, wiping out several of the buildings and facilities in that area, and killing ten Pan-Am employees. Then they banked left again and raced away to the south. Neither the marine antiaircraft gunners nor the four planes in the air were able to react in time, and the attackers made a clean escape.

Wake's senior officer, Commander Winfield Scott Cunningham, learned of the attack when a line of bullet holes walked across the ceiling of his Camp 2 headquarters. He leapt into his pickup truck and raced down the main road to the airfield. There, through a shimmering heat haze, he saw the charred hulks of eight precious Grummans, "flames licking over them from end to end." Two large aviation fuel tanks had taken direct hits and detonated, and drums of gasoline along the airfield perimeter were ablaze. Oily black smoke boiled up from the fires and carried away to leeward. Tents had been shredded by machine-gun fire: the aerial gunners had missed nothing. Strewn across the hard-packed coral surface of the airstrip were "broken bodies and bits of what had once been men."

As in the Philippines and Malaya, the initial Japanese airstrikes had come quickly, over a shockingly long range, and were conducted much more skillfully than the Allied airmen had expected. "Our planes on the ground were like targets in a carnival shooting gallery, stationary targets that could not shoot," wrote one of the surviving pilots, Lieutenant John Kinney. Seven of the eight Wildcat fighters at the airfield were destroyed; the eighth was badly shot up but by a heroic patch-job was made airworthy. That left just five fighters to contest the ensuing waves of airstrikes. The strafing and bombing had taken a terrible toll on both the air and ground crews. Of VMF-211's fifty-five men on the ground, twenty-three were killed and eleven wounded. Not a single aircraft mechanic escaped injury. The squadron had suffered more than 50 percent casualties in the first few minutes of combat.

Cunningham and his officers correctly guessed that the attack had come from Roi or one of the other airstrips of the northern Marshall Islands. Assuming the Japanese bombers would not fly at night, they worked backwards to deduce that another attack would fall the next day at midday. Pilots and mechanics, including several walking wounded, worked on repairing damage to the five serviceable planes. Bulldozers borrowed from the civilian contractors dug crude revetments in which to park those survivors. The remaining aviation fuel tanks were dispersed far away from the airfield. The wounded were transported to the Camp 2 hospital on the back of trucks. The Pan-Am seaplane, anchored in the lagoon, had been hit several times, but luckily none of its vital systems was beyond repair. The company asked for and received Cunningham's permission to send the plane to Hawaii with as many of its employees as it could carry. (To Cunningham's disgust, all of the company's non-white employees were left behind.) For the sake of morale and common decency, the dead had to be removed from the field before they were swarmed by the island's rapacious crabs. Burial details held back the crustacean horde until a dump truck arrived and transported the bodies to Camp 2, where they were placed in a refrigerated storehouse alongside ham hocks and sides of beef.

As anticipated, the next day's air raid arrived shortly before noon, but this time the twenty-seven attacking G3Ms bombed from high altitude, about 12,000 feet. Again the bombing was alarmingly accurate, leaving many of the remaining buildings of Camp 2 in smoking ruins. An antiaircraft battery at Peacock Point was knocked out, and the fire control equipment for one of the 5-inch shore guns was damaged. All of the surviving Wildcats were in the air to receive the enemy, and managed to send one of the Japanese bombers flaming into the sea. The marine antiaircraft batteries also opened up and shot down one of the attacking planes, and another was observed with smoke trailing as it fled to the south. The airstrip suffered no serious damage, but as Lieutenant Kinney observed, "The destruction in the vicinity of Camp 2 was devastating. Barracks buildings, both civilian and navy, were riddled, machine shops and warehouses flattened. The most devastating aspect of that day's raid, however, was the damage done to the civilian hospital at Camp 2. All of the wounded from the first day's attack were there when the bombs started falling again. The hospital took at least one direct hit, probably several, and quickly burst into flames." The patients and medical corpsmen were moved into two empty magazines, dark and airless chambers where at least they could count on some protection against bomb shrapnel.

The besieged garrison dug in for a long campaign, with grim hopes that the navy would come to the rescue. Airstrikes continued almost daily, usually arriving about midday. The pilots and mechanics, lacking maintenance manuals, spare parts, and tools, did their best to keep their handful of Wildcats flying by cannibalizing parts from the wrecked planes at the airfield. From about ten each morning, four fighters patrolled the skies above the atoll. On the 10th, they shot down two enemy bombers, and the antiaircraft gunners put up plenty of flak that appeared to damage two more. But the twin-engine Mitsubishis dropped a bomb directly onto a Wilkes Island storage shed that held 125 tons of dynamite (used by the civilian engineers to dredge the lagoon's sea-channel). The colossal blast dismounted one of the antiaircraft guns, destroyed a searchlight truck half a mile away, and detonated all of the marine ammunition (both 3- and 5-inch) within a quarter mile. Range-finding equipment for one of the shore batteries was destroyed. Casualties, surprisingly, were limited to one killed and four wounded, but the garrison was so small that it could hardly afford to lose a man.

At three in the morning on December 11, marine lookouts detected faint silhouettes moving on the southern horizon. "They were like black ghosts slowly moving around out there on the ocean," recalled Sergeant Charles Holmes. Studying them intently in the light of a half moon, the observers soon concluded they were a column of ships. Commander Cunningham was alerted. Some hoped that they might be friendly ships, a relief force from Pearl Harbor, and a few of the civilian contractors actually ran down to the beach with bags in hand, hoping to be among the first to be taken on board. Either Cunningham or the marine garrison commander, Major James Devereux, decided to keep the searchlights dark and hold fire until the ships had closed to within close range. (Both men claimed credit for the decision, leading to hard feelings after the war.) If the column included cruisers (as it did) their guns would probably be of larger caliber and longer range than Wake's 5-inch shore guns. If so, the enemy could elect for a long-range artillery duel in which the Americans would be gravely disadvantaged. Devereux gave strict orders not to fire, but rather to "Stand quiet till I give the word to do anything." As the ships advanced, anxiety grew among the marines: those suspenseful hours before dawn were harder on the nerves than actual combat. "We were scared to death," Corporal Bernard Richardson later confessed. "We could see what was going to happen to us. We seemed to be surrounded . . . we could see that we were about to get it."

The invasion force had sailed two days earlier from Kwajalein in the Marshall Islands, under the command of Rear Admiral Sadamichi Kajioka. There were thirteen ships in the column: six destroyers, three light cruisers,

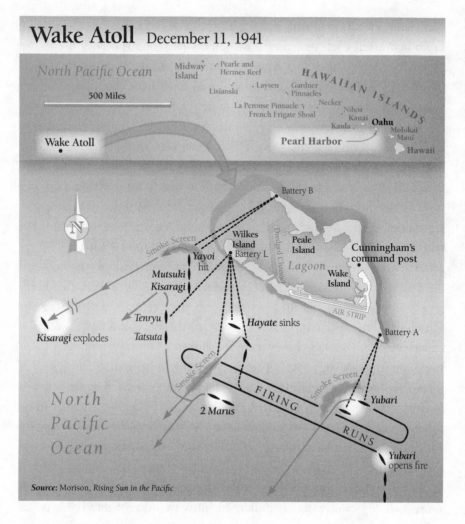

Wake Atoll December 11, 1941

North Pacific Ocean   Midway Island   Pearle and Hermes Reef   HAWAIIAN ISLANDS

500 Miles   Lisianski   Laysen   Gardner   Pinnacles   La Perouse Pinnacle   Necker   Nihoa   Kauai   Oahu   French Frigate Shoal   Kaula   Molokai   Maui

Wake Atoll   Pearl Harbor   Hawaii

Battery B

North   Wilkes Island   Peale Island   Cunningham's command post
    Battery L   Dredged Channel   Lagoon   Wake Island
Smoke Screen   Yayoi hit
Mutsuki
Kisaragi   Tenryu   AIR STRIP
Kisaragi explodes   Tatsuta   Hayate sinks
    Battery A
North   Smoke Screen   Smoke Screen
Pacific   FIRING   Yubari
Ocean   2 Marus   RUNS
    Yubari opens fire

Source: Morison, *Rising Sun in the Pacific*

and four transports carrying 450 troops. Kajioka brought his ships directly in, close under the southern beaches; he apparently assumed the shore guns had been knocked out of action by the airstrikes of the past three days, and had no inkling that he had been spotted and was being led into an ambush. At 5 a.m., with the blue glow of dawn breaking in the east, and the column about four miles off Peacock Point, the cruiser *Yubari*, Kajioka's flagship, turned port and ran parallel to Wake's southern beach. Her companions followed astern. A few minutes later, the cruisers opened fire. From that range the shells came in at a low trajectory, rumbling and whining in the ears of the American defenders. No direct hits were scored on any of the beach guns, still hidden beneath camouflage netting, and the marines remained snug in their bunkers and foxholes, but two oil tanks in the vicinity of Camp 1 were set ablaze. The Japanese transports hung back, and began transferring the landing parties into their boats.

At 6:15 a.m., when it seemed to the marines as if they had been waiting for hours, Major Devereux gave the word to open fire, and the 5-inchers on shore came to life. Battery A, at Peacock Point, opened up on the *Yubari*. The first salvo sailed high but struck a destroyer farther south; the gun crews depressed the elevation and scored four quick hits on *Yubari* at range 5,700 yards. Smoke boiled out of ugly holes torn in the flagship's starboard side, but she was fortunate in that all of the shells had struck above the waterline, and she could still make way at diminished speed. She turned south and fled for safety. Battery L, on Wilkes Island, commanded by Lieutenant John A. McAlister, had a clear field of fire on almost the entire column, but aimed its first salvo at the first and closest of three destroyers advancing in a single column at range 7,000 yards. That was the *Hayate*, and she was soon to be no more.

The battery's targeting equipment having been ruined in the previous day's bombing run, McAlister had to find the range by the time-honored technique of firing and spotting the splashes made by the falling shells. With help from another position connected by telephone, Battery L "walked" its successive splashes toward the target. The *Hayate* charged into the teeth of those hostile salvos and turned port to bring her entire broadside to bear. The spirited approach only exposed the brave little "tin can" to the full brunt of Battery L's next salvo, which struck home amidships and touched off her magazine. A jolt, a white flash, a thunderclap, and the *Hayate* was torn apart—her bow floated one way, her stern the other, each section bobbing pitifully on the sea, and then both quickly sank, taking 168 men down with them. The battery's crew let out a full-throated cheer. "Knock it off, you bastards, and get back on the guns!" bellowed Platoon Sergeant Henry Bedell. "What do you think this is, a ball game?"

McAlister trained his guns onto the *Oite*, the next destroyer in the column, already turning south to flee. She laid down a smoke screen to conceal her retreat, but Battery L managed to land two hits on her upper works. McAlister lobbed several shots at two transports, much further to the east. Though the range was nearly two miles, he scored one hit on the *Kongo Maru*. Finally, McAlister trained his weapon on one of the light cruisers and struck her after-turret; she ran for safety, smoke trailing behind her.

"Nothing could bother Battery L this morning," Commander Cunningham later wrote gratefully. "Battery L was red hot."

On Peale Island, Battery B took aim on the second column of destroyers, running north to pass west of the atoll, and scored a hit on the *Yayoi*, topsides near her stern. The Japanese gunners responded quickly and with great accuracy, landing shells close to the battery on every side and severing a fire control cable to a nearby spotting tower. "Their deflection was perfect from the very first but since they too were firing flat trajectory weapons, they found our low lying position difficult to hit in range," Lieutenant Woodrow M. Kessler explained. "At first their shells burst with greenish-yellow picric acid blobs in the lagoon directly in front of us. Then they went over us to land on the north beach. Then they split the straddle and we were in the middle of their pattern. It was unbelievable to see so many shell bursts in the battery position and yet to suffer no casualties." Taking local control of the gun, the crew fired several more salvos, eventually scoring a second hit on the *Yayoi* and possibly one on the *Mutsuki*. The destroyers turned south, blowing plenty of smoke as they went. Now the entire task force was on the run. At 7 a.m., Admiral Kajioka cancelled the landing and signaled a general retreat back to Kwajalein.

Soon the retiring ships were beneath the southern horizon, but the marines were not yet finished with them. The four remaining flyable F4F Wildcats had been circling high above the atoll, remaining at altitude to receive any Japanese airstrikes that might arrive in coordination with the invasion fleet. "Well, it looks as if there are no Nips in the air," radioed the VMF-211 commander, Major Paul A. Putnam. "Let's go down and join the party."

The Grummans streaked south in chase. Being fighters and not bombers, they were not designed to sink ships, but they had been jury-armed with two small 100-pound bombs each, and they could strafe the enemy decks with their .50-caliber machine guns. Those four planes flew nine consecutive sorties, attacking the retreating task force and then returning to Wake over the gradually widening range for fresh bombs and more ammunition. The squadron's air attacks knocked out a torpedo tube on the cruiser *Tenryu*, wiped out the radio shack on the cruiser *Tatsuta*, strafed the transport *Kongo Maru* and set her on fire, and sank a second destroyer, the *Kisaragi*, by lighting up a rack of depth charges in her magazine. The planes were hit by flak and machine-gun fire, and although none was shot down, all were shot up. One Grumman's bullet-riddled engine lost so much oil on its return leg that the pilot was forced to crash-land on the beach; he walked away, but his plane would never fly again.

The gun crews and aviators had damaged nine of the thirteen ships in Kajioka's invasion force, sinking two. Japanese losses were never reported, but were probably in the range of 500 dead and twice that number wounded. Remarkably, only one American had been killed and only four wounded. That was the sole instance in the entire war to come in which shore batteries turned back an amphibious invasion force. The marines were exultant. "When the Japanese withdrew, you'd have thought we'd won the war," said one Battery L gunner. It had been a remarkable victory, especially after the ruinous bombing raids of the past three days, and was the only such performance of any Allied unit during the initial Japanese offensive. "I am very certain every man on that island grew a good two inches at least," wrote a sergeant assigned to Devereux's staff. "Several people stopped by and congratulated Devereux. We had some kind of hope. We felt great. We were Marines, weren't we?"

But Wake could not hold out much longer. Only two aircraft remained in service. The island was short of critical equipment, ammunition, and manpower. It needed to be reinforced, rearmed, and resupplied—or failing that, evacuated and abandoned to the enemy. "They had no illusions about the future and expected the enemy to return in greater force," wrote Samuel Eliot Morison, "but they assumed that the Navy would make an earnest attempt to relieve them."

With governor poindexter's declaration of emergency on the afternoon of December 7, Hawaii had come under martial law. General Short, before he was relieved, had issued a statement warning civilians to obey all orders "instantly and without question. . . . Avoid the slightest appearance of hostility either in words or in act. . . . All citizens are warned to watch their actions carefully, for any infraction of military rules and regulations will bring swift and harsh reprisals."

A blackout and curfew were strictly enforced: lights-out at six, everyone off the streets at six-thirty. Curfew violators played the nocturnal game of "dodge the police," running through yards and hiding behind bushes and under parked cars, and more than a few of those adventurers were shot. All through the night, blackout wardens roamed the darkened streets, and everywhere their cries were heard: "Lights! Lights! Put out that light!" Blackout offenders were arrested and hauled before the army provost marshal in Honolulu. They entered a plea and made a brief statement, then heard the verdict. Violators were generally fined $100 (a month's wages for the average citizen) or sentenced to one hundred days in prison. For minor violations, such as lighting a cigarette in one's backyard, the offender was sometimes ordered to donate a pint of blood.

Civilians were required to wear identification tags around their necks or wrists, and to carry bulky gas masks on their persons at all times. All had to be fingerprinted and immunized. Stores closed their doors each day at 3:30 p.m. No liquor sales were permitted, and padlocks appeared on all the bars and taverns. Food, medicine, and cigarettes were suddenly scarce, and there were long lines each day at the grocery stores until the shelves were swept completely bare. Gasoline was rationed, 10 gallons per car per month. Ham radio operators were required to turn in all their equipment, and no photographs could be developed without a special permit. Phone calls to the mainland were monitored from the telephone company's switchboard. If a caller violated any rules—speaking in any language other than English, making small talk about the weather in Oahu—the censor would either cut the connection or (more disconcertingly) break into the conversation and sternly admonish the speaker. "No one has much aloha for censorship," wrote a local journalist. "It is accepted, rather gracelessly in some cases, as one of the evils of the war."

Banks of sandbags were placed around the doorways of public utilities and other important buildings. Camouflage patterns were painted on roofs, buses, even the landmark Aloha Tower on the Honolulu waterfront. Lei makers were put to work making camouflage netting to cover gun emplacements, trucks, and aircraft. The word HAWAII was overprinted on all paper currency—in the event of invasion the U.S. Treasury would declare the bills worthless. National Guardsmen, stationed at intersections and bridges, carried rifles with fixed bayonets, but many of the civil defense volunteers who stood alongside them were armed only with the weapons they had brought from home, including knives, clubs, and machetes. Beaches were cordoned off by trenches, pillboxes, and coils of barbed wire. Crude bomb shelters were dug in public parks and private yards, often nothing more than a trench lined with cardboard and covered with a panel of tin siding. During the frequent air-raid warnings, all civilians were ordered to get to a shelter and stay there until the all-clear sounded. Peggy Hughes Ryan, whose husband was a submarine officer stationed at Pearl, recalled that her backyard bomb shelter was overrun with toads and scorpions. "We absolutely refused to go there during air raid warnings, preferring bombs to crawling, jumping things."

Hawaii was home to a large population of ethnic Japanese, including both citizens and foreign residents. They numbered about 158,000, or 37 percent of the territory's population. There were 82,000 on Oahu alone. It was widely assumed that "they" had known in advance of the attack, and had provided intelligence to the enemy or committed acts of sabotage. Navy Secretary Knox had said so, and his statements had been quoted as fact. (No evidence has ever emerged to support that thesis.) Mass internment of the Hawaiian Japanese was never seriously considered as an option: there were far too many, and they provided much of the islands' essential labor. Indeed, many of the Hawaiian National Guardsmen, who were posted along the roads and throughout the islands, were of Japanese descent. Shortly after the attack, a newly arrived group of sailors hitched a ride into Honolulu. "I could see the look of consternation on the faces of my passengers," the driver recalled. "The chief petty officer with four gold hash marks had the courage to speak up, 'Gosh, did the Japs win?'" Though the Hawaiian Japanese were never locked up in camps, they lived under a cloud of suspicion. "The Japanese are good, law-abiding citizens," the Honolulu police chief told a reporter, "and in a wrangle between the United States and Japan I wouldn't trust them for twenty-five seconds."

Servicemen's families were ordered to evacuate to the mainland. The high command wanted fewer civilian mouths to feed, and feared for the safety of wives and children should the islands be invaded. Families were told they must be ready to depart by ship with only twenty-four hours notice, so they packed their bags and waited, living "day to day out of suitcases, never sure when our call would come." Pets had to be left behind. Families moved furniture and other belongings out to the sidewalk and offered them for sale, but there were far more sellers than buyers. Men stationed at Pearl Harbor or the island's other bases were often unable to communicate with their families, even if they were only a few miles away. Wives listened to the radio hoping for news of a husband's ship or unit, but under military censorship the radio reported nothing they could use. Instead, there was constant trafficking in rumors. "Those terrible, dreadful rumors affected the women worse than anything else," recalled the wife of a destroyer skipper. "People could scream because of them!" Lieutenant Horace D. Warden, a medical officer on a destroyer, the USS *Breese*, recalled that he and his crewmates were eager to get to sea, "but my family was on the other end of Oahu, so the first thing I wanted to do was get ashore and let them know that I was okay, and find out that they were okay." Not knowing was the worst ordeal of all, said Warden: "That was probably the worst week of the war for me."

Admiral Kimmel, soon to be relieved by Nimitz, had given plenty of thought to Wake Island even before December 7. The previous April he had surmised that the little atoll might serve as bait to bring Japanese naval forces out into the open, "thus offering us an opportunity to get at naval forces with naval forces." On Wednesday, December 10, Kimmel approved an audacious plan to deploy all three of his carrier task forces far to the west, where with a little luck they might ambush the Japanese fleet and troopships he expected to converge on Wake. *Saratoga*, en route from California, would be placed under the command of Rear Admiral Frank Jack Fletcher. She would be the nucleus of a task force (No. 14) that would reinforce Wake, while evacuating the wounded and civilian workers. A detachment of the 4th Marine Defense Battalion, with ammunition, weapons, and supplies, would embark in the seaplane tender *Tangier*. (Though the initial plan did not call for the abandonment of Wake to the enemy, the option was there; Captain Charles H. McMorris, Kimmel's chief war planning officer, had written on December 11 that the *Tangier* could take the island's entire population of 1,500 aboard: "She would be crowded to an extreme degree, but I believe it could be done.") *Lexington* (Task Force 11, Vice Admiral Wilson Brown, Jr.) would conduct a diversionary raid on the enemy airfield on Jaluit in the Marshall Islands, and then head northwest to join Fletcher if needed. *Enterprise* (Task Force 8, still under the command of Admiral Halsey) would cruise west of Johnston Island and be ready to raise steam and support her sisters if the engagement should develop into a major battle. With the various cruisers, destroyers, and auxiliaries attached to the three flattops, the expedition involved substantially all of the naval power (except submarines) available to Kimmel after the calamity of December 7.

From the start, the rescue mission was plagued by an almost unbelievable series of delays, variously blamed on weather, refueling mishaps, and submarine scares. The hard truth was that the American carrier groups were not yet accustomed to operating at sea in wartime conditions, and were climbing a steep learning curve. Heavy seas slowed the progress of the screening destroyers. Refueling while underway in any kind of weather was an art yet to be refined. Bogus submarine contacts were rife. (In one of the *Enterprise's* early war cruises, Halsey had signaled his task force: "We are wasting too many depth charges on neutral fish. Take action accordingly.") Entries in the CINCPAC war diary dwell on those problems throughout December. December 12: "Task Force Twelve was still unable to fuel at sea and it was decided to bring the *Lexington* group into Pearl Harbor to accomplish this." December 12 again: "The *Saratoga* was being delayed by the effect of rough weather on her escort of three 1200-ton destroyers." December 13: "The arrival of *Saratoga* was still further delayed by weather." She was four hours from Pearl when a faulty report of a Japanese midget submarine skulking in the harbor forced her to hang back: she did not put in until the morning of December 15.

Fletcher sent the *Tangier*, an oil tanker, *Neches*, and a division of destroyers on ahead, with the intention of overtaking them when *Saratoga* was fueled up. The carrier put to sea on December 16 and raised steam for the northwest, overtaking her companions the next afternoon. The task force crept along at the regal pace of 13 knots, the maximum speed of the *Neches*. The weather had been fair for days, but on December 22, when the task force was still 600 miles from Wake, the wind rose to 20 knots and a white-capped cross swell kicked up. Fletcher had received orders from Pearl to refuel at specified coordinates, so that the *Lexington* group could rendezvous if necessary. The underway fueling process was long and painstaking, with all the usual profanity-laced pratfalls of near collisions and broken fuel lines, particularly when the destroyers came alongside the heaving deck of the *Neches*. Ten hours passed and the task force made barely any westward progress at all, and by that time the battle for Wake Island was near its end.

In a sense, the entire world was watching. The stubborn defense of Wake Island had been a balm to the wounded spirits of the American people, who seized upon every new shred of censor-approved news from the embattled atoll. President Roosevelt had hailed their actions. The newspapers and radio networks had relished reporting (and embellishing) the gallant stand of the "Pacific Alamo." "Wake Island's indomitable little garrison of United States Marines still clung tenaciously to the scarred and battered atoll Friday night after beating off two more Japanese onslaughts," the Associated Press reported on December 19. Asked by Pearl Harbor for a list of needed supplies, Commander Cunningham was said to have replied: "Send us more Japs!" He had said nothing of the kind: the quote was a misreading (possibly deliberate) of the meaningless verbal "padding" used in radio communications to throw enemy codebreakers off the scent. When the report was picked up by a shortwave radio on Wake, the defenders were not amused. "More Japanese were absolutely the last thing we needed," Lieutenant Kinney observed. Cunningham thought the tone taken at home was all wrong; it adopted a Hollywood swagger that belied the atoll's dire predicament. "The picture conjured up by the radio reports was as far removed from reality as Wake was from Pearl Harbor," the commander later wrote. "We were doing our best, and we were proud of it, but our best seldom included that disregard for sanity that marks so many romantic visions of the thin red lines of heroes. . . . We wanted to live."

Kimmel had been formally relieved of command on December 17, the same day Nimitz was named as his successor. But Nimitz was not due in Hawaii for another week. During the brief interregnum, the caretaker CINCPAC would be Vice Admiral William S. Pye, commander of the Battle Force (that is, the battleships, now largely out of action). Pye was less confident than Kimmel in the prospect of success of the Wake relief mission, and far more chary of the Japanese. The command situation at Pacific Fleet headquarters was now very confused. Pye listened with one ear to Kimmel's former staff, but he also continued to rely on his old Battle Force staff, made homeless by the heavy damage to his flagship *California*. Pye recruited Rear Admiral Milo S. Draemel, chief of the destroyer flotilla, to serve as his temporary chief of staff—and Draemel, in turn, brought several of *his* destroyermen into the headquarters. The result, in the words of a radio intelligence officer, "was confusion superimposed upon disaster." The fate of Wake (and the carriers converging on Wake) was Pye's most pressing business; but he was mindful that he was only keeping the seat warm for Nimitz, and seems to have felt a heavy obligation to deliver the carriers safely into the hands of the new boss.

Moreover, Pye was being urgently reminded by Washington that Hawaii itself was exposed, and what business did the fleet have in supporting a distant outpost with little military value, when the main American stronghold was thought to be vulnerable? The cruel reality, as Pye, Kimmel, and the Washington admirals all understood and had conceded, was that Wake was a "liability." Sooner or later, Japan would seize it. Though the ostensible aim of the expedition was still to reinforce the garrison and air group on Wake, the fallback plan was to evacuate the atoll completely and perhaps inflict punishment from the air on the Japanese invasion forces. Most important of all was not to lose any of the precious remaining aircraft carriers, even if the 1,500 men on Wake had to be abandoned to the enemy. That was Pye's bottom line, as he would soon reveal.

Pye felt blind. He had no way of knowing the location of the big Japanese carrier force that had hit Pearl on December 7, and feared it might be lying in wait for the American carriers. In attempting to ambush the Japanese, the Americans might themselves be steaming into an ambush. Pye's intelligence staff estimated that most of the force, perhaps four out of six carriers, had returned to Japan for refueling and replenishment, but that was little more than conjecture. There was also the danger posed by land-based bombers operating from bases in the Marshall Islands. There were concerns about the battle readiness of the carriers: antiaircraft drills on the *Lexington* had been alarmingly bad. Could the carriers defend themselves against air attack, even with sufficient notice? On the 20th, Pye and Draemel gave serious consideration to ordering Task Force 14 back to Pearl, but relented in the face of hot-blooded dissent from the CINCPAC war planning chief, Captain McMorris. In notes recorded that day, however, Pye laid the groundwork for his pending decision to abandon Wake. He also radioed Admiral Brown and the *Lexington* group, directing him to abandon the raid on the Marshall Islands and divert north to rendezvous with Fletcher. Brown's staff was incensed, and there was mutinous talk on the bridge about tearing up the orders and throwing them into the sea; but Brown obeyed. On the 21st, Pye informed Admiral Stark, the chief of naval operations, that the Wake operation was continuing but that American carriers would not approach closer to the island than 200 miles.

Pye's doubts seeped into his radio transmissions to Task Force 14. The CINCPAC's instructions were vacillating and irresolute, and tended to eat away at Fletcher's confidence. On December 21, Fletcher was ordered to steam with full speed for Wake, and launch planes at a range of 200 miles. That order was quickly countermanded, and he was told instead to send the *Tangier* at peak speed to embark the garrison and bring them to safety. Not an hour had passed before that order was also revoked.

Conditions on Wake were growing desperate. On December 20 (the 19th in Hawaii), Cunningham reported that his remaining fighter planes were "full of bullet holes," and it could only be described as a "miracle" that they had not been shot down in air-to-air combat. The island was short of critical equipment and supplies, from radar sets to fire control instruments to provisions to ammunition of every caliber. The 3-inch antiaircraft batteries were no good against high-altitude attacks, and in any case the 3-inch ammunition would last only another day, maybe two. Airstrikes continued almost daily. Intra-island telephone communications were a mess, the cables having been shredded by bomb damage. Crews worked dawn to dusk each day improving the island's defenses—digging foxholes and bunkers, filling sandbags, distributing ammunition, throwing branches over gun emplacements—but the casualty list was long and growing longer, and long rows of cots were crowded into makeshift hospitals in empty magazines. Even the "healthy" men were exhausted and sleep-deprived, and there were increasing signs of dysentery. Morale was not enhanced by a ludicrous message from Pearl Harbor, received on the 17th, asking how long it would take to finish dredging the lagoon. Were the admirals totally ignorant of the situation on Wake?

Keeping the marine fighters in the air had required heroic efforts, but without replacement planes or at least additional parts, it was inevitable that Wake would soon have no air defense left at all. On December 14, a bomb struck a Wildcat in its revetment, destroying the tail section but sparing the engine. Lieutenant John Kinney decided to attempt an engine transplant from the destroyed plane to another in which the engine was running very rough. Without a proper engine hoist or maintenance hangar, the operation took nine hours of backbreaking effort. But that same night another plane crash-landed after veering off the runway to avoid a gaggle of civilian onlookers. That left three airworthy planes. By the second week of the war, the shortages became critical, and the flying aircraft had become Frankenstein's monsters—rattling, bullet-ridden, patched-over amalgamations of parts scavenged from the wrecks scattered over the airfield. On December 20, two planes were capable of getting off the ground.

That day and again on the 21st, the island was attacked by single-engine Aichi Type 99 "Val" dive-bombers, which were known to be a carrier-type plane. On the second day, the Vals were accompanied by Zeros. In the aerial melee, one of the Wildcats was shot down and the other crash-landed and was judged a loss. The island now had no air defenses at all.

When Cunningham reported the appearance of the carrier planes, Pye worried that a Japanese carrier task force was covering the approach of a new invasion flotilla. In fact, the dive-bombers had flown from two of the six carriers that had hit Pearl Harbor and were now retiring toward Japan; it had been an opportunistic, hit-and-run raid, and would not be repeated. But a second invasion force *was* en route, this time covered by four heavy cruisers. The warships remained carefully out of range of the shore guns, while sending a force of about 1,000 Japanese marines in on landing barges. The landings began at 2:35 a.m. on December 23 local time (December 22 in Pearl Harbor). That night the invading force quickly swept through the islands, cutting the defenders off into isolated pockets. The marines put up a gallant defense, and claimed the lives of 700 to 900 attackers, but their positions were gradually overrun. At 2:50 a.m. on December 23 local time, Commander Cunningham notified Pye: "Enemy apparently landing." With superior numbers, the invaders gradually advanced across the islands, and at five in the morning Cunningham signaled: "The enemy is on the island. The issue is in doubt."

With those dispatches in hand, Pye huddled with his staff. He asked the war plans chief, Captain McMorris, and his acting chief of staff, Admiral Draemel, to put their recommendations into writing. Both agreed that it was too late to save Wake, either by reinforcement or evacuation. But they differed sharply on the question of whether to send the American carriers to attack the enemy fleet. Fletcher's *Saratoga* group was still 425 miles from Wake, with the destroyers still struggling to refuel in a bumpy cross-swell, but it was still possible for the *Sara* to make a high-speed run toward Wake and launch her attack planes the following morning. Brown's *Lexington* group was near enough to join the fray from the south, and Halsey's *Enterprise* group could have been placed in position to cover the subsequent withdrawal.

In a strongly worded memo, McMorris counseled Pye to push on with the attack. American forces in the vicinity were probably stronger than the enemy's, and to withdraw without offering battle would be "unduly cautious." While it was true that the exact composition of the Japanese forces (the carriers, especially) was unknown, it is often necessary to accept odds in battle, and "The enemy cannot have superior forces in all directions." To retreat would also "tend to destroy service and public confidence." He concluded: "It is an opportunity unlikely to come again soon. We are in great need of a victory."

Draemel's assessment endorsed Pye's more cautious mind-set. The *Saratoga* force's fueling situation was a major problem, and would risk putting American ships within striking range of superior forces without means of escape. "Are we willing to accept a major engagement, at this distance from our base, with an uncertainty in the fuel situation?" His answer was no:

"There are no reserves—*all* our forces are in the area of possible operations. . . . The general situation dictates caution—extreme caution."

Pye had heard enough. At 9:11 a.m. on December 22, he called all three carrier groups back to Pearl Harbor. The order was received with heavy resentment. Men in the task forces sobbed openly. Commander George C. Dyer, executive officer of Admiral Brown's flagship, later charged that "Admiral Pye had had a scare, apparently visualizing the Japanese fleet all over the Pacific Ocean." Commander Edwin Layton, the Pacific Fleet intelligence officer, echoed the point: "To lose to an enemy that fought you, and fought you well, was one thing. But to lose because your own admiral was a 'nervous Nellie' was another." On the *Saratoga's* flag bridge there was loose talk of ignoring the withdrawal order, and some thought Fletcher should have imitated Horatio Nelson's famous gesture at Copenhagen, when he raised his scope to his blind eye and exclaimed that he could not read the signal ordering him to disengage the enemy fleet. The marine airmen on *Saratoga*, who had been ready to fly to Wake to relieve their colleagues, threatened to climb into their planes and go. Rear Admiral Aubrey "Jake" Fitch, whose flag flew on the *Saratoga*, was forced to withdraw to his cabin so that he would not overhear any of the mutinous talk on his bridge. Admiral Joseph M. Reeves, in Pearl Harbor, exclaimed: "By Gad! They used to say a man had to be both a fighter and know how to fight. Now all I want is a man who fights."

For many in Hawaii, both military and civilians, that was the single worst day of the war. The cancellation of the Wake relief operation coincided with ominous news from the Philippines: Japanese transports were pouring troops onto the beaches of Luzon and Leyte without opposition, and MacArthur had fled Manila. The United States had no realistic hope of sending reinforcements or supplies to the Philippines; they would probably be abandoned and conceded to the enemy, as Wake had been.

In Hawaii, the specter of invasion seemed very real to civilians and servicemen alike. Carroll Robbins Jones, age seven, who lived in Honolulu, overheard her mother crying that the island was going to be "taken over." Carroll got on her knees and "confessed to God all my sins and prayed for Him to make me good, thinking somehow my confession and promise of goodness would help end the war." Robert Casey, a *Chicago Daily News* correspondent who had been in Paris during the Nazi *Blitzkrieg* eighteen months earlier, studied the faces of the civilian residents of Honolulu, and was reminded of the expressions he had seen in France in May 1940. "The

Alfred Thayer Mahan (1840–1914). *Getty Images.*

The USS *Arizona* shortly after the
detonation of her forward magazine.
Official U.S. Navy photograph.

Battleship Row, Pearl Harbor, December 7, 1941. From left to right, the stricken battleships *West Virginia*, *Tennessee*, and *Arizona*. *FDR Library.*

A crowd gathers outside the White House, December 7, 1941. *Getty Images*.

FDR asks for war, December 8, 1941. *Getty Images.*

Isoroku Yamamoto in diplomat's attire, 1934. *Getty Images.*

Admiral Yamamoto in the early 1940s, as commander in chief of the Combined Fleet. *U.S. Naval History and Heritage Command photograph.*

Admiral Yamamoto, official portrait taken in 1940 or 1941.

Zeros prepare to launch from a Japanese carrier, 1942. Official U.S. Navy photograph.

parallel was sickening," he wrote. The trauma of defeat had left many officers, even those with sterling records, in a dazed torpor. It was a poorly kept secret that the fleet surgeon, beset by men verging on psychological collapse, had dosed them "with whatever they used for tranquilizers in those days."

Nimitz's plane arrived over Pearl Harbor at seven o'clock on a wet, gray, gloomy Christmas morning. The flight from San Diego had taken seventeen hours. Accompanied by a fighter escort, the big Coronado entered the landing circle over East Loch. From the air, sitting in the left-side pilot's seat, Nimitz got his first direct glimpse of the carnage along Battleship Row. The pilot recalled that the admiral "just kept shaking his head and clucking his tongue." The plane touched down on the oily surface of the harbor and taxied past the immense gray hull of the upturned *Oklahoma*. As the door was flung open, Nimitz caught his first whiff of fuel oil and burning ships, a stench so all-pervading that men stationed at Pearl had ceased to notice it.

A motor whaleboat came alongside, carrying a welcoming committee of staff officers. Nimitz, still dressed in a civilian business suit, bade goodbye to the aircrew and stepped into it. The boat was filthy with fuel oil, and the passengers stood balanced on their feet, not deigning to touch the gunwales or take the handholds for fear of soiling their clothing. The first question on Nimitz's lips was: "What news of the relief of Wake?" Informed that the island had fallen and the relief expedition was called off, he fell silent. The boat bucked along toward the pier through water still smothered in oil and littered with debris. Other boats were at work around the harbor, and one of the officers told him they were recovering bodies that were still bobbing up to the surface two and a half weeks after the raid. "This is a terrible sight," Nimitz said, "seeing all these ships down."

On the pier he was greeted by Admirals Pye and Kimmel. "You have my sympathy," Nimitz said to Kimmel, with whom he was personally close. "The same thing could have happened to anybody." A car took the three admirals to Nimitz's quarters, a rambling four-bedroom house perched on Makalapa Hill, the cone of an ancient and extinct volcano, with a sweeping view of the harbor. Oahu's lodging shortage having reached all the way to the top of the command chain, Kimmel had moved in with Admiral and Mrs. Pye in a slightly smaller but still grand white house across the street. Nimitz invited them in for breakfast, saying, "I won't eat alone after what I've seen." In the week to follow, the Pyes and Kimmel spent every evening at Nimitz's house, and took most of their meals there. After dinner each night they listened to classical music broadcasts or played cribbage. Oddly, the foursome's cordiality did not seem strained by the circumstances. Unspoken tensions must have lurked beneath the surface: Kimmel was already running the gauntlet of post–Pearl Harbor investigations, and Pye had ruined Kimmel's well-laid plans to ambush the Japanese navy off Wake Island. But for men who had served in the navy for forty years or more, or women married to such men, the service was not unlike a small private club. Politics and professional discord were put to one side. They were the brass, and there was a war to win. They were expected to show a united front.

Nimitz did not take command of the fleet immediately. He spent his first week getting to know the lay of the land, with Pye often at his side. Rising each day at 6:30 a.m., he did some exercises, dressed, had breakfast, and arrived at the fleet headquarters before eight. He was briefed by all the department chiefs and subordinate commands. The admiral had a phenomenally good memory for faces, and surprised old colleagues and subordinates by remembering their names. Lieutenant Commander Jasper Holmes had once served as an obscure junior engineering officer in a submarine division commanded by Nimitz. "He had little reason to remember me," wrote Holmes, but when the two men came face to face in a corridor, the new C-in-C not only greeted the younger man by name but evidently knew details of his subsequent service record.

William Ewing, a reporter with the *Honolulu Star-Bulletin*, thought Nimitz seemed too "kindly," too "fatherly," and his khaki uniform seemed at least one size too large. "I thought Admiral Nimitz looked more like a retired banker than the kind of hell-for-leather leader we needed to pull us out of the worst hole the country had ever been in." The remark anticipated Samuel Eliot Morison's observation that "war correspondents who expected admirals to pound the table and bellow as in the movies, were apt to wonder 'Is this the man?'" It was true that Nimitz was not a cinematic naval hero in the mold of Nelson, Decatur, or Jones. Like most American officers of his vintage, he had no experience of combat. He had never even seen a shot fired in anger. But the fleet did not need a show of blood and thunder after the beating it had suffered; there was plenty of the real stuff to go around. Nimitz was an executive, a strategist, and a leader. He was a gentleman of the old school. It was not in him to shout or abuse the furniture or let a word of profanity fall from his lips. Holmes took comfort in the admiral's "aura of calm confidence," while Edwin Layton thought "the incisive thrust of his questions . . . made it clear that he was steeled for the tremendous task he was to assume."

As he toured the stricken ships and shore facilities, Nimitz concluded that the Japanese attack, spectacular as it was, "could have been devastatingly worse." True, the navy had lost 1,999 killed and 710 wounded, three times its combined losses in the Spanish-American War and First World War. (Including all services and civilians, the attack had left 2,403 dead and 1,178 injured.) True, some 300,000 tons of shipping had been knocked out of action, including eight battleships (six would be repaired and returned to service). True, 188 planes had been wiped out, mostly on the ground, representing about two-thirds of total American military aircraft in the Pacific theater. But the Japanese had failed to hit the repair shops along the piers, and especially the fuel tank farms, where the fleet's 4.5 million barrels of fuel oil were stored. "That was a most serious error," Nimitz later said. "These tanks could have been destroyed by machine-gunning them with 50-caliber incendiary machine gun bullets. . . . Had our oil supply been destroyed, and considering the tremendous shortage of fuel and petroleum production, generally, in Europe, it would have taken years to re-establish that supply and would have delayed our Pacific war accordingly." By a stroke of luck, the Japanese had caught the American battleships in port, rather than at sea. "Imagine, if you can," said Nimitz after the war, "what would have happened to our slower battleships in such an action with the aircraft of six carriers working on them and with our fleet having no air cover at all . . . we would have lost by drowning or capture almost 20,000 men had our fleet been in deep water." Finally, the submarine fleet had been entirely spared, and the undersea campaign could begin immediately.

Perhaps Mahan would have turned over in his grave to hear it said, but the loss of the American battleships was no catastrophe. It might have even been entered on the ledger as a net gain, because their crews—thousands of the best trained and most experienced men in the service—were released to serve in other capacities. The battleships were too slow to operate with the carriers, and incapable of defending themselves against air attack. As one officer put it, the Japanese had converted the American fleet from "a seventeen knot fleet to a twenty-five knot fleet." Losing them on the opening day of the war forced the American naval high command to acknowledge the ascendancy of aviation and submarines. The Japanese navy, with its magnificent line of battleships intact, would be slow to make the same adjustment.

On New Year's Eve, in a brief, self-effacing ceremony, Nimitz relieved Pye and assumed command of the fleet. Naval custom required the new C-in-C to unfurl his four-star flag on a flagship, but since Nimitz's command would be shorebound throughout the war, the act was merely ceremonial, a nod to tradition. The ship chosen was a submarine, the *Grayling*, moored at a pier off the CINCPAC headquarters. The choice was fitting. Nimitz had been a submariner in the primitive, pre–First World War days, and had always been proud to wear the dolphin insignia. (He later quipped, in black jest, that nothing else was left.) A small coterie of journalists and photographers were permitted to attend, and at the end Nimitz paused to speak to them. Pressed with questions about how the war would unfold, Nimitz was vague—Casey of the *Chicago Daily News* wrote that he was "reasonably frank about saying nothing." The admiral did forecast that enemy submarines would probably shell the west coast (as indeed they did), but the navy censors later changed "probably" to "possibly."

Afterward, Nimitz crossed the dock to the headquarters and climbed the stairs to his office. He called the senior staff into the room. Having been stationed at Pearl Harbor before the Japanese attack, and having witnessed the craven recall of the Wake relief force, many of those officers carried an enervating burden of guilt, akin to a feeling of personal disgrace. They expected to be shunted off into dead-end billets for the remainder of the war, and many hoped only to be sent to sea, with a chance to redeem themselves in combat. Nimitz saw the problem clearly and understood what had to be done. "These were all fine men," he later said, "but they had just undergone a terrible shock, and it was my first duty to restore morale and to salvage these fine officers for future use, and this I proceeded to do." He spoke briefly, in a low tone. "I know most of you here," he said, "and I have complete confidence in your ability and judgment. We've taken a whale of a wallop, but I have no doubt of the ultimate outcome." December 7 would not be held against them; they could forget the disaster and get on with the war. They were needed, and must remain, at their posts. He would listen to requests for seagoing assignments, but "certain key members of the staff I insist I want to keep."

"In a very few minutes, speaking softly," one such officer recalled, "Admiral Nimitz convinced all hands of his ability to lead us out of this."

Chapter Five

ADMIRAL ERNEST J. KING, COMMANDER IN CHIEF OF THE U.S. FLEET and chief of naval operations, was a hard man with a hard, disapproving mouth. He frequently wore a scowl. He was tall, very slim, and always physically fit. When Teddy Roosevelt handed him his Naval Academy diploma in 1901, King stood six feet tall and weighed 165 pounds. In 1941, at age sixty-three, he was the same height and just 10 pounds heavier. He rarely smiled, and if (for the sake of photographers) he tried to soften the edges of his mouth, he succeeded only in appearing pained. Official navy portraits emphasized his long, narrow face, his sharply cleft chin, his dark, close-cropped hair, and his small, gleaming, close-set eyes. He was said to be a bit vain about his appearance, and sensitive about the expanding bald spot on the top of his head. He was always immaculately turned out, with uniforms purchased from Brooks Brothers in New York, and tailored to fit his slim frame; in his official photographs a white handkerchief was neatly tucked into the breast pocket of his uniform jacket, below a formidable row of ribbons and medals.

Among the principal American military leaders of the Second World War, King has always been the most neglected and least understood. In that he would have taken deep satisfaction. He did not want or seek a public profile, though one was eventually thrust upon him. He thought reporters a nuisance and at first refused to deal with them at all. It was said, half-jokingly, that King would have liked to say nothing until the end of the war, and then release a two-word communiqué: "We won." (When he realized that the army was getting better press than the navy, he did begin speaking to reporters, but off the record.) He was an immensely powerful adviser to President Roosevelt, with whom he met privately at the White House almost every day, and who sought his advice and backing for every significant military decision of the war. But King did not flaunt his influence with the president; indeed, he sometimes seemed intent on disguising it. When he spoke strongly or emphatically to Roosevelt, he did so one on one, or with no one other than Harry Hopkins in the room—in larger White House meetings he kept a still tongue, or spoke only briefly. On such occasions Roosevelt, seeking guidance, sometimes threw a quizzical glance at King. The admiral replied by nodding or shaking his head almost imperceptibly, so that the president and no one else would see the signal.

After the war, King made no effort to secure his place in history. He wrote an unrevealing memoir, concealing his role behind the stilted prose of an after-action report. Only one book-length biography of King has ever been published. His army counterpart, General George Catlett Marshall, went on to serve as President Truman's secretary of state (a role for which King would have been comically unsuited). Marshall gave his name to the reconstruction of postwar Europe; King gave his name to a public high school in his hometown of Lorain, Ohio. Unlike Douglas A. MacArthur, King's erstwhile nemesis, who invented the famous maxim about old soldiers, the old admiral really did just fade away.

History, like nature, abhors a vacuum. Who was this five-star admiral of the Second World War, who left barely a trace of himself in the historical record? In the literature he is usually painted with a few broad strokes of the brush, and the overall effect is unflattering. Four charges have been laid against King, growing simultaneously louder and less coherent as they have reverberated through the historical echo chamber. First, that he was a foul-tempered martinet who was utterly ruthless and as mean as a snake. Second, that he was a narrow-minded navy partisan, who cared only for the parochial interests of his service. Third, that he did not support the "Europe-first" policy, and campaigned to make the Pacific the main theater of the war. Fourth, that he harbored an obsessive animosity against the British, and did his best to undermine the alliance. There was some truth in the first of those four charges, though King's abrasiveness and ruthlessness have been exaggerated, and were facets of a more complex personality. As for the second, third, and fourth, they do not stick.

HE WAS BORN IN 1878, in a workman's cottage in Lorain, Ohio, an industrial town on the southern shore of Lake Erie. His father was a railroad repair shop foreman. As a boy, King passed long hours in the shop, and for the rest of his life took naturally to machines and engineering. He was brilliant—that much was evident even in early childhood—and despite his humble origins he had no trouble winning admission to the Naval Academy in 1897. There he excelled in his academic coursework, and in his senior year attained the rank of battalion commander, the highest leadership position in the student body, allowing him to wear the stripes of a cadet lieutenant commander. At graduation in 1901, he was ranked fourth in his class.

King was always supremely ambitious. From early in his career, he openly avowed his intention to rise to the top of the navy. Someday, he declared to his colleagues, he would be the chief of naval operations. "He told me he was going to the top," recalled an officer who served under him. "No braggadocio, just extreme confidence." He plotted his ascent shrewdly, seizing the coattails of admirals who seemed destined for important commands. He perfected the art of "writing his own ticket"—arranging through backchannels to be assigned billets likely to advance his career, and did not hesitate to lobby for the jobs he wanted. He served at sea on cruisers, destroyers, battleships, aircraft carriers, and submarines. He held a series of prestigious staff and administrative jobs. He was conspicuously good at everything he did. Shiphandling and navigation came naturally to him, but he was also an efficient administrator, handling paperwork fearlessly and efficiently, and communicating in succinct, lucid prose. He was astute enough to understand that he would have to populate his résumé with less glamorous jobs, to do the "drudgery" of the navy, to suffer the "hard knocks of the service." He descended into the hot, dark, cramped, dangerous engine rooms and wrestled with engines, letting his finely tailored uniforms be stained with grease and splattered with oil. He threw himself body and soul into every job, always making a point to work harder than anyone else, until the navy doctors ordered him to ease up.

As ambitious as he was, King did not fit the pattern of a single-minded careerist. In his dealings with others, even superior officers who could have damaged his career prospects, King was inclined to behave with haughtiness and contempt. He did not pay court to officers he did not respect; he did not strive to be liked by anyone, even for tactical reasons. He went through life with the attitude of a man beleaguered on every side by dunces. In his insistence on high standards, even from men above him in the chain of command, he sometimes walked up to the edge of insolence or insubordination. He revealed his integrity through his supercilious refusal to play politics when a principle was at stake. As a lowly ensign he had argued relentlessly with superiors when he believed he was right. "King justified himself by citing regulations, chapter and verse," wrote his biographer. "It was a typical King sea-lawyer tactic. He delighted in compelling flag officers to concede that they were wrong by quoting a regulation in King's favor." Not surprisingly, some of King's early fitness reports suffered as a result, though they never seemed to slow his rate of promotion.

King had a keen interest in military history, and was an insatiable reader. He devoured all the works of Mahan, of course; but he also read deeply into the Napoleonic Wars and the American Civil War. In the early years of his career King caught the reformist spirit, and in 1909 he published a controversial piece in the *Naval Institute Proceedings* entitled "Some Ideas About Organization Aboard Ship." In that prize-winning article, a sharp critique of conservatism in the navy, the thirty-one-year-old lieutenant censured the navy's "inertia to change" and its culture of "clinging to things that are old because they are old. It must be admitted that this characteristic has been in many things a safeguard; it is also true that in quite as many it has been a drag to progress." While running the submarine base at New London, King took the War College correspondence course and passed all twelve installments in just three months, an unprecedented achievement. He was a champion of postgraduate education, and served, as a forty-year-old captain, in command of the Naval Postgraduate School in Annapolis. He pushed to expand the Naval War College and to require all officers headed toward higher rank to pass through it.

In 1928, now a fifty-year-old captain, King threw his lot in with naval aviation. He entered pilot training and earned his wings, a step that qualified him for carrier command. He did the minimum required to win his wings, and never attained more than rudimentary flying skills—but his seniority ensured that King was one of the first qualified naval aviators to reach flag rank, a major advantage in his subsequent career. He held a series of important aviation jobs, ashore and at sea. He was named assistant chief of the Bureau of Aeronautics, then given command of the Naval Air Station at Hampton Roads, Virginia, then (in 1930) named captain of the carrier *Lexington*. Promoted to rear admiral in 1933, he returned to the Bureau of Aeronautics in Washington, this time as chief. King was deeply involved in the development of the navy's reconnaissance seaplanes. He pushed the pilots to fly long hours and in dangerous conditions; when they quit, King bade them good riddance, declaring that he was doing the vital work of weeding the weaker men out of the service.

As captain of the *Lexington*, King consolidated his reputation as an imperious and hard-driving martinet. He hovered on the bridge, glowering down at the men on the flight deck, watching over their every move. If a pilot made a clumsy approach or put his bird down too hard, he could expect to be summoned to the bridge, his name blared humiliatingly through the loudspeakers for the entire crew to hear. As King dressed a man down, he gesticulated wildly, hands waving over his head, and poured out a long tirade laced with sarcasm. When a *Lexington* pilot ran out of fuel and ditched in the carrier's wake, King summoned the pilot to the bridge and told him: "The next time you decide to land in the water, do it ahead of the ship so I won't have to turn around to pick you up." Frequently, he did not even bother bringing offenders up to the bridge to receive their rebukes. "He didn't need a megaphone," said an officer who served under King on the *Lexington*. "He'd just stand on the edge of that bridge, and they could hear him from one end to the other of the flight deck, even in a high wind, because he could really bellow when he was mad." It was not always clear *why* King was angry; he was given to fits of seemingly irrational rage. Suddenly, with no apparent reason and no explanation, he might shove a stack of papers off a desk onto the floor, and then storm off the bridge without saying a word.

King worked harder than the men under his command and faulted them for not keeping to his pace. He declared that he needed only five hours of sleep per night, and often took those five hours without returning to his cabin, but rather "jackknifing his long frame on a short transom in flag plot." He was a stickler for the prerogatives and trappings of his rank, and was not collegial with subordinates. On a cramped bridge he might brusquely order a junior officer to "Get out of my way." When another man was climbing up a ladder and nearing the top, and King wanted to climb down, he did not wait for the climber to reach the top; he simply mounted the rungs, forcing the junior officer to descend to the deck and step out of his way. In the ship's barbershop, an officer recalled, "You could be halfway through a haircut and [King] decided that he wanted a shave. You got out of the barber chair and waited until he was shaved." When a film was screened for the crew in the hangar deck, it did not begin until King had arrived and taken his seat.

King's reputation for personal toughness, for ruthlessness, for wielding the power of his rank with a heavy hand, had probably done his career more good than harm. Roosevelt himself enjoyed trafficking in stories about the admiral's legendary toughness, telling his guests that he "shaved with a blowtorch" and "cut his toenails with a torpedo net cutter." Whether or not King really enjoyed yelling at his subordinates is open to debate, but there is no doubt that he believed in yelling as a matter of principle. King *chose* to be feared rather than loved. "I don't care how good they are," he once said. "Unless they get a kick in the ass every six weeks, they slack off." He did not believe in the culture of collegiality that bound Annapolis graduates to one another, because he understood that it had too often allowed indolent or incompetent officers to survive and thrive. King made it his personal business to rid the navy of such men, and earned many enemies along the way. But he was also fair—he respected men who did their jobs well, whether or not he liked them personally. He praised them in fitness reports and used his influence to see that they were promoted. "If a man knew his business," said Admiral J. J. Clark, "it was easy enough to get on with Ernie King. But God help him if he was wrong; King would crucify him."

Humorless and overbearing while at work or at sea, King also had a hearty appetite for carousing, gambling, dancing, and philandering. He called it his "play time." At nights on shore he was often seen in the officers' club, draining one glass after another, speaking in a loud, raucous voice, roaring with laughter, buying rounds for the bar, playing poker late into the night, and dancing unsteadily with much younger women. He developed his own cocktail, mixing brandy with champagne in tall glasses over ice, which he called "the King's peg." The junior officers found, to their surprise, that he was approachable and even playful on those occasions. They sometimes worked up the courage to call him "Uncle Ernie." He liked women, and was serially unfaithful to his wife. King seemed to take the view, shared widely among his colleagues, that heavy drinking and womanizing were natural outlets for pent-up energy or anxiety. They should not only be tolerated but actually encouraged. "You ought to be very suspicious," he said, "of anyone who will not take a drink or doesn't like women." But King was always up early the next morning, as sharp as a tack, clean-shaven and turned out in a freshly pressed uniform, showing not the slightest sign of a hangover. He demanded no less of the officers with whom he had shut down the bar.

His family life was strained. He shared little in common with his wife, Martha ("Mattie"): they had developed separate lives during his long absences from home, and remained together, it seems, out of a mutual sense of duty. Theirs was a house full of women. The Kings had six daughters—Claire, Elizabeth, Florence, Martha, Eleanor, and Mildred—and finally one son, born in 1922, Ernest Joseph King, Jr. Every one of his children was beautiful, and when King was stationed in Annapolis as a captain, he found to his dismay that he could do nothing to prevent his teenaged daughters from fraternizing with the midshipmen. As a father, King seems to have been fairly aloof, but was surprisingly capable (on occasions) of tenderness. One of his daughters famously called him "the most even-tempered man in the Navy. He is always in a rage." The quip has often been cited as evidence that King was a natural-born bully, but it could just as well be interpreted as the sort of teasing family banter that was rooted in affection. King was capable of warmth and kindness, but seems to have believed it was best to keep that element of his personality mostly bottled up. Now and again he let a bit of it out. In January 1943, at the height of the war, King sent a letter to an eighth-grader in Brooklyn who had written in connection with a class project. Did Admiral King drink or smoke? Who was his favorite movie star? What were his favorite hobbies and sports?

"Dear Harriet," he replied:

> I have your letter of January 6th—and am interested to learn that you have to do my biography as part of your English work.
>
> As to your questions:
>
> I drink a little wine, now and then.
>
> I smoke about one pack of cigarettes a day.
>
> I think I like Spencer Tracy as well as any of the movie stars.
>
> My hobby is cross-word puzzles—when they are difficult.
>
> My favorite sport is golf—when I get to play it—otherwise, I am fond of walking.
>
> Hoping that all will go well with your English work, I am
>
> Very truly yours,
> E. J. King
> Admiral, U.S. Navy

In 1938, VICE ADMIRAL KING did not disguise his ambition. He openly campaigned for the jobs he had always wanted—either commander in chief of the U.S. Fleet or chief of naval operations (CNO). He believed that his service record entitled him to those exalted commands, and he was not wrong. He was eminently qualified. His experience was broad and deep, and his performance had been consistently outstanding. King had served in all the right jobs, in every domain of the service: he had gone to sea in surface ships, submarines, and aircraft carriers; he had excelled in a rich array of staff and planning jobs; he had served as a naval bureau chief; he had dealt with foreign governments and with Congress. His personnel file bulged with letters of commendation.

But in 1939, the courtly, miniature Admiral Harold "Betty" Stark was appointed CNO, and King was placed on the navy's General Board, an advisory panel that was traditionally the last stop before mandatory retirement for senior admirals who had been passed over for the navy's top jobs. He would revert to his permanent rank of rear admiral. It was an overwhelming disappointment—a friend said that King actually cried when he received the news. It was not clear why he had been passed over: no explanation was ever provided. It appears that Navy Secretary Claude A. Swanson and the outgoing CNO, Admiral William D. Leahy, backed Stark. King was one of only three aviators among the navy's seventy-four flag officers, and the "big gun club" may have wanted to keep the job in the hands of a battleship admiral. King was not yet intimate with President Roosevelt, and Roosevelt, an old navy man, preferred to deal with admirals he knew and liked. Finally, there were the darker corners of King's personality—his abrasive style, which had earned him many enemies in the navy; his heavy drinking, which might yet get the better of him; and his reputation for making advances on other men's wives.

But the looming war would soon retrieve King's hopes. He did not treat his appointment to the General Board as a restful transition to retired life—he used it as a megaphone to condemn what he thought to be a criminal lack of naval readiness. He supervised efforts to upgrade the navy's antiaircraft systems, and shoved a $300 million appropriation through Congress. In late 1940, Navy Secretary Charles Edison (Swanson's successor) put King up for the job of commander in chief of the Atlantic Fleet. President Roosevelt, who was also getting to know King better, readily agreed. King helped

Navy Secretary Frank Knox "learn the ropes," after the latter was appointed to that post (succeeding Edison) in July 1940. The admiral handled the arrangements to transport Roosevelt and his entourage to Placentia Bay, Newfoundland, in August 1941, for the first wartime summit with Winston Churchill. He gained a public profile as the German U-boat offensive heated up—in November, his stern face appeared in *Life* magazine, with the headline: "King of the Atlantic." His flagship was based in Newport, Rhode Island, but he found it necessary to take the overnight train to Washington every two weeks. "Well," he would tell his staff officers, "I've got to go down to Washington again, to straighten out those dumb bastards once more."

"We're living in a fool's paradise," King declared on December 7, 1941, when news arrived of the attack on Pearl Harbor. Ten days later, Secretary Knox and the president huddled in the White House. Concurrently with their decision to replace Kimmel with Nimitz, they agreed to bring King to Washington as commander in chief of the U.S. Fleet, or CINCUS. For the time being, Stark would remain as CNO, with a portfolio of duties that included long-range war planning and the overall administrative management of the navy. But by the following March, Stark would be edged out and King would hold both of the navy's two top jobs, making him the most powerful admiral in American history.

King's first act as C-in-C of the fleet was to get rid of the acronym denoting his command, which would appear under his name on all his outgoing orders and communications. "CINCUS" looked fine on the page, but when pronounced out loud—"Sink us"—it sounded too much like the punch line in a Bob Hope routine. King would not stand for it, not after Pearl Harbor. He ordered it changed to "COMINCH." After he absorbed Stark's command, he would be designated as "COMINCH-CNO."

In the past, CINCUS (or COMINCH) had been a seagoing billet in a battleship, but King moved his headquarters to a suite of offices in the Navy Department building on Constitution Avenue in Washington. He preferred to be close to the White House, to the secretary of the navy, to General Marshall and the other military chiefs, and to Congress. "Where the power is," he said, "that is where the headquarters have to be." There was no existing COMINCH staff—the position had most recently been held by Admiral Kimmel, concurrently with his command as CINCPAC in Pearl Harbor. "Nothing was ready," King later recalled. "I had to start with nothing."

He assembled a rudimentary staff by bringing a handful of members of his Atlantic Fleet staff down from Newport. He also plucked several key officers from Stark's staff—including the latter's war planning chief, Admiral Richmond K. "Kelly" Turner, who would serve as King's assistant chief of staff. He summoned a dozen more officers from seagoing billets in the Atlantic and Pacific, though none came with much enthusiasm. As a rule, naval officers in staff jobs clamored to be sent to sea, and those at sea bitterly remonstrated against being recalled to Washington. All wanted a chance at combat. Captain Charles M. "Savvy" Cooke, Jr., who commanded the battleship *Pennsylvania* at Pearl Harbor, wanted no part of the job offered him by King, that of the navy's chief planning officer. King replied baldly that the needs of the navy would come before the preferences of the individual. "I am fully in sympathy with your wish to stay at sea," he wrote Cooke, "but have also to remark that you must expect to be placed where others consider that you can do the most good to the general cause—in which I am sure you will agree." King's policy throughout the war would be to rotate officers in and out of Washington; he insisted on "continuous turnover," sending staff officers out to the theaters of war, and bringing others in from sea duty to headquarters. He argued, persuasively, that the experience and perspective thus disseminated would improve the performance of the entire service.

When King arrived in Washington to set up shop the week before Christmas, pandemonium reigned. "I found Admiral King enthroned in the most disreputable office I have ever seen," an incoming staff officer recalled. "Someone had moved out in a hurry, taking the furniture with him, but not the dirt. The admiral had liberated a flat top desk from somewhere and a couple of chairs. . . . That was all there was. I recall thinking that as the headquarters of the greatest navy in the world it fell somewhat short of being impressive." King and his clerical staff inhabited two rooms on the third deck (floor) of the Navy Department building. The decor was spartan and utilitarian: white plaster walls left blank with the exception of a single analog clock, windows blocked by white Venetian blinds, nondescript wooden desks and chairs, green steel filing cabinets, a linoleum floor. When King needed a member of his staff, he pressed a button in his office. A buzzer sounded harshly in the adjoining room, sending a team of yeomen and secretaries into action.

The job came with lavish perks. King would have at his beck and call a Cadillac and driver, a twin-engine Lockheed Lodestar with aircrew, and a flagship. As his flagship he chose a 1,200-ton, 257-foot private yacht, the *Dauntless*, formerly owned by the Dodge family. She would remain at a berth in the Washington Navy Yard for most of the war. After assuming the duties of CNO, King would also have an official residence in the Naval Observatory on Massachusetts Avenue in northwest Washington (since 1974 the official residence of the vice president of the United States). Throughout the war, King's wife, Mattie, would live at the Naval Observatory, and King would spend most nights aboard the *Dauntless*. There was some grumbling in Congress about the cost of maintaining two residences for one man, and whispers that King was using his yacht as a private refuge for his trysts—but the expense was trivial in the general mobilization for war, and no one chose to make an issue of it.

THE MORNING AFTER PEARL HARBOR, Winston Churchill had told his cabinet he intended to visit Washington as soon as Roosevelt would have him. He needed to be sure that Britain's new ally did not go about fighting the war the wrong way. Above all he feared that the Americans, boiling over in righteous fury at Japan, might divert the better part of their strength from Europe to the Pacific. In prompt reply to Roosevelt's cable of the previous evening, in which the president assured Churchill that the United States was now "in the same boat with you and the people of the Empire and it is a ship which will not and cannot be sunk," the prime minister asked, "Now that we are, as you say, 'in the same boat,' would it not be wise for us to have another conference? We could review the whole war plan in the light of reality and new facts, as well as the problems of production and distribution. I feel that all these matters, some of which are causing me concern, can best be settled on the highest executive level. It would also be a very great pleasure to me to meet you again, and the sooner the better."

Roosevelt stalled for time, referring to the press of business in Washington and his concern for the perils Churchill would face in crossing an ocean infested with German U-boats. His real concern, however, was how Churchill's presence in Washington would play politically. The United States and Britain were Allies in the war against Japan, but not (until Thursday) against Germany or Italy. It was well understood that Churchill would do everything in his power to correct the discrepancy. Replying to Roosevelt's stated concerns for his safety, Churchill cabled on December

10: "We do not think there is any serious danger about return journey. There is, however, great danger in our not having a full discussion on the highest level about the extreme gravity of the naval position as well as upon all the production and allocation issues involved . . . particularly in Pacific." Roosevelt acquiesced. "Delighted to have you here at White House," he replied. Referring to the dismal news of the sinking of the *Prince of Wales* and *Repulse* off Malaya, he added, "The news is bad but will be better. Warm regards."

In a meeting of the British war cabinet that week, someone expressed surprise at the prime minister's newfound assertiveness. Churchill had taken care to use a deferential tone in his earlier dealings with the Americans. According to General Sir Alan Brooke, chief of the Imperial General Staff, there was a "wicked leer" in the prime minister's eye as he replied: "Oh! That is the way we talked to her while we were wooing her; now that she is in the harem, we talk to her quite differently!"

He and a grand entourage of advisers and staff, including all the military chiefs of staff except Brooke (who would mind the store in London), embarked on the battleship *Duke of York* on December 12 for the Arcadia Conference. During the eight-day passage, Churchill drafted three major papers outlining the British view of the war in preparation. When not working he slept, lay awake in bed with a novel, or watched movies. It was a tumultuous winter crossing, with hatches battened down and passengers barred from walking on deck. Churchill told his wife it was "the longest week I have lived since the war began. We have had almost unceasing gales." Paraphrasing Samuel Johnson, he remarked: "Being in a ship in such weather as this is like being in a prison, with the extra chance of being drowned. . . . No one is allowed on deck, and we have two men with broken arms and legs."

The ship anchored in Hampton Roads, off Norfolk, Virginia, on the evening of December 22. The *Duke of York* was to have continued up the Potomac River to Washington, but Churchill was anxious to arrive, and asked to be flown to National Airport. From the air at night the city made a majestic sight, spread out and ablaze with lights. Two weeks after Pearl Harbor, the blackout was only sporadically enforced. Churchill's aide-de-camp, Commander Tommy Thompson, was moved. "Washington represented something immensely precious," he wrote. "Freedom, hope, strength. We had not seen an illuminated city for five years. My heart filled."

On the tarmac they found the president waiting, leaning against his limousine. "I clasped his strong hand with comfort and pleasure," recalled Churchill in his memoirs. Lord Moran (Sir Charles Wilson), the prime minister's personal physician, was impressed by the size of Roosevelt's head. "I suppose that is why Winston thinks of him as majestic and statuesque, for he has no legs to speak of." The president remembered the faces and names of many members of the Churchill party, whom he had met briefly the previous August at the shipboard summit in Placentia Bay. Diplomatic protocol had not required that he drive to the airfield to welcome his visitors, and the gesture was not overlooked by the British. It was a good start.

Churchill had planned to stay at the British Embassy, but when Roosevelt invited him to be a guest at the White House, the British leader accepted at once. Five aides would accompany him, and the rest of his party would lodge at the nearby Mayflower Hotel. The invitation had apparently been extended without fair warning to the first lady—the White House staff would have to scramble to prepare the rooms. Though she was (as always) a warm and graceful hostess, Eleanor later took the unusual step of venting her irritation in her national newspaper column. "It had not occurred to him," she wrote of the president, "that this might require certain moving of furniture to adapt rooms to the purposes for which the Prime Minister wished to use them."

Churchill was moved into the Rose Suite on the second floor of the White House, with an adjoining room for his valet. The Lincoln Study, across the hall, accommodated his two secretaries. Harry Hopkins's bedroom was just down the hall; next to that was the Monroe Room, where Churchill's staff set up his map room. A gloomy hallway, cluttered with Christmas presents for the extended Roosevelt family, connected them all.

At dinner that first night, the conversation ranged widely across the war. Roosevelt had not had time to read the papers prepared by Churchill, so the prime minister did what he did best of all. He talked, and talked, and talked, about every aspect of the conflict: the situation in French North Africa, the battles raging in Libya, the Russian front, the war at sea, the Japanese onslaught in the Pacific. Roosevelt offered a toast, that first night: "I have a toast to offer—it has been in my head and on my heart for a long time—now it is on the tip of my tongue—'To the Common Cause.'"

"My report home shows that we cut deeply into business on the night of our arrival," wrote Churchill after the war. To the prime minister's great relief, Roosevelt quickly allayed any concern that the main thrust of the American war would be diverted away from Europe. Not only would munitions and supplies continue to flow to Britain and Russia, he declared, but such shipments would be increased, notwithstanding the emergency in the Pacific. In his first cable to Brooke and the war cabinet in London, Churchill wrote that the question "was not whether but how" the Europe-first principle would be carried out.

During his long stay, Churchill made himself very much at home. Like Mae West he did much of his best work in bed, though in Churchill's case this involved reading reports and dictating letters or speeches to his secretaries. Until midday he remained propped up against a bank of pillows, reading glasses perched on his nose, clad in bedclothes or a flamboyant knee-length robe, with memoranda, newspapers, and articles of clothing strewn across his bed and the floor. On his first morning in Washington, Churchill accosted the president's butler, Alonzo Fields, and made a short speech that was a model of clarity. "Now, Fields," he intoned, "we had a lovely dinner last night but I have a few orders for you. We want to leave here as friends, right? So I need you to listen. One, I don't like talking outside my quarters; two, I hate whistling in the corridors; and three, I must have a tumbler of sherry in my room before breakfast, a couple glasses of scotch and soda before lunch and French champagne and ninety-year-old brandy before I go to sleep at night." Fields, unfazed, replied: "Yes, sir," and did his part for the Anglo-American alliance by seeing that the requirements were met.

When he did rise and dress for the day, Churchill's outfits stirred lively commentary among the White House staff. The British leader often wore a knee-length double-breasted coat, buttoned to the neck. He carried a wooden walking stick rigged with a flashlight. (It had been a wedding gift from King Edward VII.) Roosevelt's secretary, Grace Tully, first saw Churchill the morning after his arrival, when he appeared as a "chubby, florid, bald-headed gentleman dressed in one-piece, blue denim coveralls and with a big cigar in his mouth shambling toward my office."

For the next three weeks, Roosevelt and Churchill, with Hopkins often in their company, lived together almost as members of an extended family. They dined together, drank together, and smoked together. They invaded one another's private bedrooms for late night discussions; they sat together for a private screening of the Humphrey Bogart film *The Maltese Falcon*;

they ate lunch from plates balanced on the president's desk in his study. Roosevelt was several times wheeled into Churchill's bedroom, while the prime minister remained unashamedly in bed—and Churchill felt no qualms in knocking on Hopkins's bedroom door at all hours of the day and night. (The two men had become close confidantes in January 1941, when Hopkins traveled to London as Roosevelt's personal emissary.) One time, at two in the morning, the British prime minister and the president's *consigliere* engaged in fierce debate while Churchill sat on the edge of Hopkins's bed, their voices hushed so as not to awaken the rest of the household.

Roosevelt, according to a story told by Hopkins, was once wheeled into Churchill's bedroom just as the prime minister was emerging from his bath, stark naked. The president, flustered, told his attendant to back him out of the room, but Churchill theatrically declared, "The Prime Minister of Great Britain has nothing to conceal from the President of the United States." The story was probably embellished for dramatic effect—Churchill later told Robert Sherwood that "he never received the President without at least a bath towel wrapped around him," and added that he would never claim to have nothing to hide from Roosevelt, as "The President himself would have been well aware that it was not strictly true."

Even so, a week after his arrival Churchill was as comfortable in the White House as if he had lived there for years. To the Labour Party leader Clement Attlee, he wrote, on January 3, 1942: "We live here as a big family, in the greatest intimacy and informality, and I have formed the very highest regard and admiration for the President. His breadth of view, resolution, and loyalty to the common cause are beyond all praise."

The two leaders often appeared together in public. On his first day in Washington, Churchill joined Roosevelt at a regularly scheduled press conference in the Oval Office. After brief opening remarks, Roosevelt introduced the prime minister, and invited the reporters, who were crowded in a semicircle around the president's desk, to put questions to him. Churchill was dressed in a dark civilian suit with a blue and white polka-dot bow tie, and was smoking one of his oversized Cuban cigars. Even standing, he could not be seen by the reporters standing in the back of the crowded room, so he climbed onto his chair, an act that drew a round of cheers and applause from the assembled newsmen. Churchill performed masterfully, sparring with good humor, and venturing to say that while the war would be long and hard, "We may wake up and find we ran short of Huns." Asked whether Singapore was "the key to the whole situation" in Asia, Churchill, without a pause, shot back, "The key to the whole situation is the resolute manner in which the British and American Democracies are going to throw themselves into the conflict." How long might it take to win the war? "If we manage it well," the prime minister replied, "it will only take half as long as if we manage it badly." Asked whether he had any doubts about the ultimate victory of the Allies, he replied, "I have no doubt whatever." The *Washington Star* pronounced that the performance had been "electric," a "sparkling and unique scene." *Newsweek* reported that Roosevelt "looked like an old trouper who, on turning impresario, had produced a smash hit, and some thought they detected in his face admiration for a man who had at least equaled him in the part in which he himself was a star."

On Christmas Eve, Churchill participated in the tree-lighting ceremony on the White House lawn. It was a dark night, lit by a crescent moon that hung low on the horizon. Roosevelt, standing with the British leader on the South Portico, pressed a button that illuminated the colored lights of the tree. When the crowd's applause had died down, the president introduced his guest as "my associate, my old and good friend." Churchill spoke to a radio audience numbering in the millions on both sides of the Atlantic. For reasons of blood, or common cause, or a common language, he said, "I can not feel myself a stranger here in the center and at the summit of the United States." He continued, "Let the children have their night of fun and laughter . . . before we turn again to the stern tasks and formidable years that lie before us, resolved that, by our sacrifice and daring, these same children shall not be robbed of their inheritance or denied their right to live in a free and decent world." The night was bitter cold, and Eleanor recalled, "there was little joy in our hearts. The cold gripped us all so intensely that we were glad of a cup of tea on our return to the house."

The day after Christmas, Winston Churchill was driven to Capitol Hill to address a joint session of Congress. He addressed the House chamber through a dense thicket of microphones, looking over his glasses, a conspicuous gold watch chain hanging from the pocket of his trousers, his hands tucked under the lapels of his coat. He spoke for thirty-five minutes, with the audience hanging on his every word. It was a great speech, a classic Churchillian stemwinder; he had sweated blood over it all through Christmas Day and night. He knew there remained considerable anti-British sentiment in Congress, and that the American people were more aroused against Japan than Germany. "I cannot help reflecting," he began, "that if my father had been American and my mother British, instead of the other way round, I might have got here on my own."

The observation received a hearty laugh, and established a friendly tone for a speech that would range across some sensitive territory. The British leader served up some roundabout criticism for the isolationists, hinting at the policy errors that had allowed Germany to rearm, and driven the United States and Britain apart in the 1930s. The room fell very silent during those passages. But when Churchill turned to the Japanese, the legislators were quickly on their feet. He thundered: "What sort of people do they think we are? Is it possible they do not realize that we shall never cease to persevere against them, until they have been taught a lesson which they and the world will never forget?" The congressmen and senators responded with a mighty guttural eruption of savage joy, and Churchill thought to himself, "Who could doubt that all would be well?" As he left the podium he made his signature gesture, his right index and middle fingers held up in a "V" for victory. *The Washington Post* reported that the effect was "instantaneous, electric. . . . The cheers swelled into a roar."

Back at the White House, Roosevelt (who had listened on the radio) told him that he had done extremely well. The prime minister was elated—his powers had not failed him. "I hit the target all the time," he declared in triumph to Moran.

Before dinner each night the two leaders, Hopkins, and various other members of the president's official family gathered for cocktails in the Red Room. Roosevelt sat by a tray of bottles and mixed the cocktails himself. This was a cherished part of the president's daily routine, his "children's hour," as he sometimes called it, when he let the day's tensions and stresses slip away. "He loved the ceremony of making the drinks," said Churchill's daughter Mary Soames; "it was rather like, 'Look, I can do it.' It was formidable. And you knew you were supposed to just hand him your glass, and not reach for anything else. It was a lovely performance." Roosevelt did not take drink orders, but improvised new and eccentric concoctions, variations on the whiskey sour, Tom Collins, or old-fashioned. The drinks he identified as "martinis" were mixed with too much vermouth, and sometimes contaminated with foreign ingredients such as fruit juice or rum. Churchill, who preferred straight whiskey or brandy, accepted Roosevelt's mysterious potions gracefully and usually drank them without complaint, though Alistair Cooke reported that the prime minister sometimes took them into the bathroom and poured them down the sink.

The British leader slept late, napped in the afternoons (sometimes creeping into a random bedroom if his own was too far away), and liked to talk late into the evenings. He imbibed throughout the day, remaining razor-sharp and supremely articulate like the high-functioning alcoholic that he was—he drank sherry in the morning, whiskey at midday, wine with dinner, and smoked Cuban cigars and nursed glasses of brandy well into the small hours of the morning. Roosevelt's aides were amazed. Mike Reilly, chief of the president's Secret Service detail, said that Churchill "ate, and thoroughly enjoyed, more food than any two men or three diplomats; and he consumed brandy and scotch with a grace and enthusiasm that left us all openmouthed in awe." He added: "It was not the amount that impressed us, although that was quite impressive, but the complete sobriety that went hand in hand with his drinking."

During the several weeks that Churchill spent in the White House, Roosevelt stayed up later than was his custom, and drank more heavily, but without the benefit of the afternoon naps. Once, a few days after Christmas, the president smoked and drank and talked with Churchill until three in the morning. Dr. Ross T. McIntire, who was responsible for looking after the president's health, regarded the British leader as "Public Enemy Number One." He tried to impose a bedtime for the president of 11 p.m., but noted, "it was rarely observed." Eleanor was appalled. "There is no question," she said, "when you are deeply interested it is possible to go on working 'til all hours of the night. But for the people who have to wait up 'til you are through, it is a deadly performance." As the daughter of an alcoholic, she was put off by excessive drinking, and did not like the influence that Churchill seemed to exert on both her husband and her sons. She grew increasingly concerned about the effect of late nights and brandy and cigars on Roosevelt's fragile health. "Mother would just fume," Elliott Roosevelt remembered, "and go in and out of the room making hints about bed, and still Churchill would sit there." When she shared her concerns with her husband, he retorted that she "needn't worry because it wasn't his side of the family that had a drinking problem."

Roosevelt had genuine and heartfelt respect for Churchill. After dining with the president that January, Sam Rosenman recalled that "the conversation was mostly about Churchill—Roosevelt was most enthusiastic about him and praised his rugged, bold approach to the problems of the war." Their personal friendship was at the heart of the alliance. The bond was abetted by their shared language, naturally—but also by their patrician upbringings, their elite schooling, their common interests in history and literature, and their self-identification as old lions of the sea, having both held civilian cabinet or subcabinet positions in their respective navies. Hopkins believed that during the long visit, Roosevelt "grew genuinely to like Churchill and I am sure Churchill equally liked the President."

Churchill had originally intended to stay only a week, but once comfortably nested at the White House he accepted Roosevelt's invitation to extend his stay. His visit, interrupted by brief jaunts to Canada and Florida, lasted three weeks, until his departure on January 15, 1942.

NEITHER THE AMERICAN nor the British military staffs were entirely pleased that the two leaders were cocooned together in the White House. They were vexed by the thought that the president and prime minister were cooking up schemes behind their backs, and would settle major issues over their late night libations, without letting their military advisers into the discussions. Each side suspected that his principal was pitted against a master confidence man, and would give away too much in one-on-one negotiations. Their intimacy might fortify the alliance, but it might also short-circuit the rightful function of the cabinets and the military chiefs of staff. Alexander Cadogan, a British diplomat, wrote in his diary that he feared Churchill "hero-worshipped" the American president. American general Joseph W. "Vinegar Joe" Stilwell vented that "The Limeys have [Roosevelt's] ear, while we have the hind tit."

The military leaders met for the conference dubbed "Arcadia" in the opulent boardroom of the Federal Reserve Building, a four-year-old marble edifice that sat directly opposite navy headquarters on Constitution Avenue. Their first meeting convened on the morning of Christmas Eve, under an agenda titled: "Fundamental basis of joint strategy." Eleven more such meetings would follow in the weeks to come. The British were represented by Admiral of the Fleet Sir Dudley Pound, Field Marshal Sir John Dill (recently supplanted by Brooke as chief of the Imperial General Staff), and Air Chief Marshal Sir Charles Portal. General George C. Marshall, U.S. Army chief of staff, was informally acknowledged as head of the American team. He was joined by Admirals King and Stark and General Henry H. "Hap" Arnold, chief of the Army Air Forces.

The British service chiefs, tempered by nearly two and a half years of war, were well accustomed to working together. They came to the meetings well prepared, with well-crafted arguments supported by crackerjack staff work. "They knew their stuff," said Captain John L. McCrea of the American naval staff. "They all talked exceedingly well and made much sense. The staff organization was superb, as well. Three brigadiers did the bulk of the work, and their reports of the meetings were masterpieces."

In contrast to the well-oiled machinery of the British high command, the American chiefs were really nothing more than an ad hoc committee. The army and navy had always been institutionally separate and co-equal, with two cabinet-rank civilian secretaries sitting atop their respective departments, and efforts to blend the military planning process had been halting and unsuccessful. Therefore, the American military chiefs had to learn to deal with one another at the same time they were learning to deal with the British. General Arnold was subordinate to Marshall and tended to defer to him. Both King and Stark represented the U.S. Navy, and to the British it was not immediately clear which admiral was dominant. Having run on fumes for the two weeks since December 7, the Americans had not found much time to prepare for the conference. They spoke off the cuff, throwing their ideas out without having vetted them through an internal process of planning and analysis. Inevitably, they could not avoid seeming confused and amateurish. They were at the base of a steep learning curve.

Marshall, speaking for the Americans, opened with a strong and unequivocal reaffirmation of the Europe-first principle. That policy, spelled out in a secret memorandum to Roosevelt (and signed by Admiral King with the other service chiefs), recognized that "Germany is the predominant member of the Axis Powers." Even with the entry of Japan into the war, "our view remains that Germany is still the prime enemy and her defeat is the key to victory. Once Germany is defeated the collapse of Italy and the defeat of Japan must follow. In our considered opinion, therefore, it should be a cardinal principle . . . that only the minimum of force necessary for the safeguarding of vital interests in other theatres should be diverted from operations against Germany."

The merit of the Europe-first principle was never doubted by King or any other member of the Allied high command. Of the Axis partners, only

Germany could be attacked simultaneously by the United States, Britain, and Russia. Germany possessed greater scientific and industrial resources than Japan, and given enough time might develop new and fearsome weapons of mass destruction. Should Russia fall, Hitler's juggernaut could be concentrated on a single front. But should Germany and Italy fall, the great bulk of Allied naval and military power would be liberated for use in the Pacific. "As far as I know," wrote Dwight D. Eisenhower, the recently promoted brigadier general who was serving as the army's war planning chief, "the wisdom of the plan to turn the weight of our power against the European enemy before attempting an all-out campaign against Japan has never been questioned by any real student of strategy." Even Admiral Nimitz, who had his hands full with the Japanese, said the logic of the Germany-first principle "was well understood by all of us who had to carry on the war in the Pacific."

And yet the strategy, stated in the abstract, left plenty of room for interpretation and debate. Exactly what proportion of available troops, ships, and war matériel would be sent to the Pacific? Ten percent? Twenty? Thirty? If the situation in the Pacific was unstable (as indeed it was), should that theater receive a larger share of resources on a short-term, emergency basis? How much territory should be conceded to the rampaging Japanese? Were Australia and New Zealand to be sacrificed? How much offensive capability should the Allies build up in the Pacific, if only to keep pressure on the enemy's perimeter? Could a Pacific counteroffensive be launched even before Germany was defeated? On those questions, the joint memorandum of the service chiefs to the president was silent. Under the heading "The Safeguarding of Vital Interests in the Eastern Theatre," it stated only that "The minimum forces required to hold the above will have to be a matter of mutual discussion." As Eisenhower observed, there was nothing controversial in Germany-first as a rule, "but it was to prove difficult indeed to develop a feasible plan to implement the idea and to secure its approval by the military staffs of the two nations."

Even as they mulled over the high points of their strategy, the chiefs were forced to reckon with the bad news coming out of the Pacific and East Asia. Japanese sea-air-land forces were threatening to overrun American, British, Dutch, and Australian positions in a theater that spanned Burma to western New Guinea on an east-west axis and the Philippines through Australia on a north-south axis. On December 24, the day of their first meeting, the world learned of the fall of both Hong Kong and Wake Island. There was more bad news from Malaya, where defenses on the mid-peninsula were caving in and British troops were fleeing toward Singapore. The Japanese seemed likely to seize control of the oil fields of Borneo and Sumatra. In Europe, by contrast, there was reassuring news from Africa, where British forces had pushed General Erwin Rommel back from Tobruk, and from Russia, where German forces had been stopped at the gates of Moscow and had suffered heavy losses just as the Russian winter was settling in. The situation in Europe, for the moment, was at least stable; that in the Pacific, not at all.

Admiral King's mind was clear. The entire Allied strategy in the Pacific depended on two cardinal points: Hawaii must not fall, and Australia must not fall. To those ends, King (upon assuming command as COMINCH) ordered the new Pacific Fleet chief, Admiral Nimitz, to secure the seaways between Midway, Hawaii, and the North American mainland. That was to be his first priority. His second priority, in only a "small degree less important," was to protect the lifeline between North America and Australia, chiefly by "covering, securing, and holding the Hawaii-Samoa line, which should be extended to include Fiji at the earliest practicable date." Farther south (where Nimitz's command did not yet extend), it would include several more "strong points" in New Caledonia, New Hebrides, and the Tonga Islands. That long supply line must safely accommodate a large and growing volume of shipping. By those means the Allied war machine would be built up in "Australasia" (which King defined to include New Zealand), and from which a counteroffensive would eventually drive northwest through the Solomons, the Bismarck archipelago, New Guinea, Borneo, and the Philippines.

Every other concern was to be ruthlessly subordinated to what King called those "two vital Pacific tasks." Though it had not yet been acknowledged in Washington, the Philippines would fall. Though it had not yet been acknowledged in London, Malaya and Singapore would fall. Burma would fall; the Dutch East Indies would fall; the remaining British, Dutch, and American forces in the southeast Pacific would disintegrate. The U.S. Asiatic Fleet—a ramshackle array of old cruisers and destroyers—would probably be annihilated by the enemy's ships and planes. Its main contribution to the war effort would be to slow the rate of the Japanese advance and buy a few precious weeks to secure the seaways linking San Francisco, San Diego, and Panama to Brisbane, Auckland, and Sydney.

U.S. – Australian Lifeline, 1942

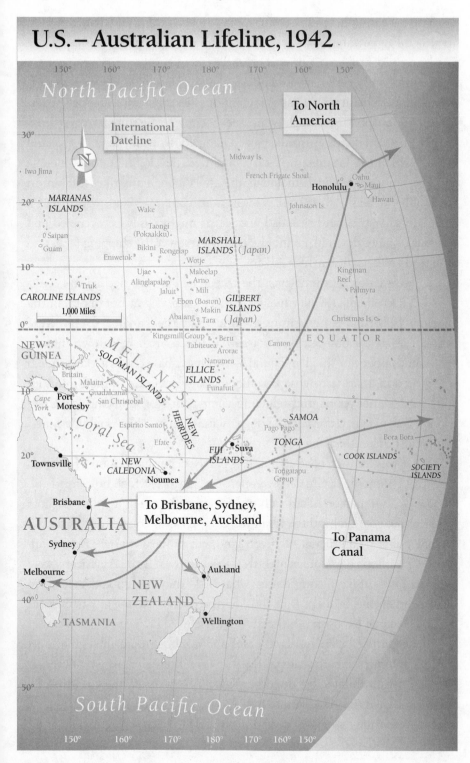

At this early phase of the war, it was thought that the Japanese would try to take advantage of the Allies' temporary weaknesses to sever the American-Australian lifeline. The Allies could only guess at Japanese intentions, and every new development might be a prelude to a new eastward thrust. Shelling by Japanese submarines in the Samoa area seemed to presage an amphibious attack (which never came). The shipping route linking North America to Australia passed dangerously near the Gilbert Island group, which the Japanese had seized and were developing into formidable air bases, and from which they had already launched airstrikes. Makin, in the Gilberts, was just 960 miles away from Canton Island, which had a 5,000-foot airstrip but no Allied aircraft. It might easily be occupied and Japanese planes flown in, giving the enemy eyes over the shipping lanes and the ready means to slaughter Allied convoys from the air.

Those were urgent problems: the threatened islands needed to be garrisoned immediately. A new fueling station was set up at Bora Bora, in the Society Islands, for shipping westbound from the Panama Canal. King asked President Roosevelt that scarce Allied resources be thrown into an emergency policy of "hold and build"—involving base construction, airfield construction, marine defense battalions, army garrisons, aircraft and supporting facilities, ports and refueling equipment—on Samoa, New Caledonia, Suva (Fiji), Tongatapu (Tonga Islands), Efate (New Hebrides), and Funafuti (Ellice Islands).

But King did not have in mind a purely defensive posture. He often spoke of the merits of a "defensive-offensive" posture, which he defined colloquially (in a memorandum to Navy Secretary Knox) as a policy of "hold what you've got and hit them when you can." Digging in and waiting for the enemy might be a prudent tactic on land, but in naval warfare the advantage more often than not lay with the attacker. Even if the Americans were starved of offensive hitting power, what little they had should be used to strike the enemy, to make him consider the cost of leaving any part of his outer perimeter exposed. An effective defense would have to include carrier airstrikes on the Japanese island bases and a submarine campaign against Japan's interior seaborne supply lines. "No fighter ever won by covering up—by merely fending off the other fellow's blows," said the COMINCH, by way of analogy. "The winner hits and keeps on hitting even though he has to take some stiff blows in order to be able to keep on hitting."

In light of this rapidly developing situation, King pushed hard for a larger near-term allocation of scarce military resources to the Pacific theater. He argued as he always did—forcefully and without tact, not troubling to disguise his contempt for those who opposed him. The British, mistakenly assuming that an officer who had risen to the top of the U.S. Navy must be more charming when dealing with his fellow countrymen, marked King as a hard-bitten Anglophobe. But there is no evidence that King was innately prejudiced against the British, nor that he wanted to sabotage the Europe-first principle. Rather, it seems that he deliberately chose to assume the role of special advocate for the Pacific, because he perceived that for various reasons none of the other military service chiefs, American or British, was giving enough thought to the needs of that theater.

Outside the small circle of the military chiefs, there were many others who shared King's point of view. No less a figure than Eisenhower, who would later act as supreme Allied commander in the liberation of Europe, was concerned that the chiefs were neglecting the need to stem the Japanese tide. "I've been insisting that the Far East is critical," Eisenhower noted on his desk memorandum pad on January 1, 1942. He was concerned that "no sideshows should be undertaken until air and ground there are in satisfactory state. Instead we are taking on MAGNET [U.S. forces to Northern Ireland], GYMNAST [invasion of North Africa], etc." There was the wrenching question of the fate of the Philippines: General MacArthur, who had already been hailed as a superstar in the American press, had demanded relief for his beleaguered American and Filipino forces, and in a public proclamation Roosevelt had reflexively promised it: "I renew my solemn pledge to you that your freedom will be redeemed and your independence established and protected." The president wrote Secretary Stimson, on December 30, "I wish that War Plans would explore every possible means of relieving the Philippines. I realize great risks are involved but the objective is important." The Allied nations of Asia and the Pacific Rim had kept faith with their American and British allies, and expected to be shielded against the onslaught. Australia and New Zealand, having dispatched many of their best troops to fight the Germans half a world away, were understandably frantic to protect their homes and hearths. Australian prime minister John Curtain wrote, in a Melbourne newspaper, "Without any inhibitions of any kind, I make it quite clear that Australia looks to America, free of any pangs as to our traditional links or kinship with the United Kingdom. We know the dangers of dispersal of strength, but we know, too, that Australia can go and Britain can still hold on. We are, therefore, determined that Australia shall not go."

Moreover, it was feared that a total collapse of Allied defenses in the Pacific would prompt a Japanese invasion of Siberia, which might in turn knock Russia out of the war. Powerful figures in the Japanese army were known to be eager to attack Russia, and it was assumed Hitler must be pressuring his Japanese allies for such a move. Lieutenant General Stanley Dunbar Embick told the army War Plans Division, in late January, that a "greater degree of immediate aid" to the Pacific would act as a "deterrent to a Japanese attack on Siberia," and a planning document published in March 1942 argued that the "most valuable assistance which can be rendered to Russia is to contain Japanese forces . . . in the South Pacific and the sooner our action clearly indicates to Russia that we shall do this the greater the advantage she can gain from that assistance."

In the ninth meeting of the chiefs, on January 11, 1942, King demanded that a strong force be dispatched to garrison the French colonial islands of New Caledonia, which lay astride the route of communications between Hawaii and Australia, and were the site of productive nickel mines that the Japanese were believed to covet. Should New Caledonia be seized by the enemy, American convoys would have to be rerouted south of New Zealand. King insisted that the islands be taken immediately, by a garrison force of 10,000 troops, even at the cost of diverting forces bound for Europe. That brought the competing demands of the two theaters down from the empyrean realm of high theory to the status of immediate decision.

It appeared that King's plan could be carried out only by diverting troops scheduled to be sent to Iceland and Northern Ireland, and the British stiffly resisted such a change. Nor did King receive much support from the other American service chiefs. General Arnold remarked, somewhat unhelpfully, that his army bombers could simply fly over the islands, drawing King's well-aimed retort that ships were needed to build up forces in the South Pacific, and ships could not fly. The army instinctively resisted placing troops in a theater dominated by the navy. Eisenhower, when he learned of the proposal, noted acerbically, "The Navy wants to take all the islands in the Pacific—have them held by Army troops, to become bases for Army pursuit and bombers. Then the Navy will have a safe place to sail its vessels." (King has been charged with carrying water for the navy, but were the leaders of the other services any less blinkered?)

Churchill had himself asked the president for "three or four" American infantry divisions to be sent to Northern Ireland, both to relieve British troops stationed there and because of the political effect such a development would have in Irish politics. It would be, Churchill wrote, an "assertion of the United States' resolve to intervene directly in Europe." Confronted with King's reasoning, the prime minister seemed willing to accept a delay in the delivery of troops to Northern Ireland. Some 8,000 troops that had been slated for Iceland would be reduced to 2,500; and 16,000 that were slated for Northern Ireland would be reduced to 4,000. But the needed troops could not be sent to the Pacific unless ships could be found to carry them, and ships were scarce. Could a convoy be diverted from Russian Lend-Lease shipments to the northern Russian port of Archangel? King said that he believed that the port of Archangel was already closed for the winter, or that even if it was not, the Russian port facilities would not be able to handle the offloading of those ships. Roosevelt contradicted him, saying that the Russians had said the port was open and had demanded the supplies. The president, clearly hoping to duck an awkward decision, asked whether it would be difficult to reconquer New Caledonia after a Japanese invasion of the islands. King replied that it would be very difficult.

Harry Hopkins spoke up. By his calculations, only seven ships were needed to fill the shortfall in the promised deliveries to Russia. That put the question in a different light. Even in the face of a severe shipping shortage, the government of the United States should be able to lay its hands on seven additional ships. Hopkins offered to find them himself. That broke the logjam. (Hopkins's contribution was characteristic: he often managed to shed light on a subject with a well-timed insight, or steer a debate toward a practical solution. Churchill bestowed a nickname on the gaunt *consigliere*: "Lord Root of the Matter.") It was agreed that 21,800 American troops would embark upon ships from the east coast, pass through the Panama Canal, and reach the South Pacific in mid-February. A portion would be sent to New Caledonia, along with Australian troops—altogether the Allied garrison would amount to about one division. Furthermore, in response to King's urgent entreaties, it was agreed that 20 cargo ships would carry 250 fighters, 143 bombers, 220 tons of cargo, and 4.5 million gallons of gasoline to the South Pacific in the early months of 1942.

CHURCHILL CLAIMED TO HAVE KNOWN even in those first weeks of the war that a "cataract of ruin" would fall upon the Allies in Asia. In his memoir, the prime minister made the point with photorealistic flair: "Even while I spoke in confident tones I could feel in anticipation the lashes which were soon to score our naked flesh. Fearful forfeits had to be paid not only by Britain and Holland but by the United States, in the Pacific and Indian Oceans, and in all the Asiatic lands and islands they lap with their waves. An indefinite period of military disaster lay certainly before us. Many dark and weary months of defeat and loss must be endured before the light would come again."

The unremitting flow of bad news shined a spotlight on the problem of the Allies' fragmented command. The Japanese were encountering feeble, uncoordinated, and chaotic opposition by the ground, air, and naval forces of five different countries: Britain, the United States, the Dutch-in-exile, Australia, and New Zealand. Each of the Allies had its own goals, interests, and constraints. Shipping was a critical bottleneck, but there was little or no coordination of shipping resources. General Marshall believed the situation called for a single Allied commander, with authority over all forces in the theater. He brought the issue up at the second meeting of the chiefs, on Christmas morning, 1941. "I am convinced that there must be one man in command of the entire theater—air, ground, and ships," he said. "We can not manage by cooperation. Human frailties are such that there would be emphatic unwillingness to place portions of troops under another service. If we make a plan for unified command now, it will solve nine-tenths of our troubles." He spoke of his experiences in the First World War, experience that all of the men at that table had shared. "There are difficulties in arriving at a single command, but they are much less than the hazards that must be faced if we do not achieve this. We never think alike—there are the opinions of those on this side of the table and of the people on the other side; but as for myself, I am willing to go the limit to accomplish this."

In facing up to the knotty problem so early in the conflict, Marshall began to reveal why he would prove the one really indispensable American military leader of the Second World War. Command unity was a challenging and sensitive subject, cutting to the heart of the Anglo-American alliance while also laying bare the interservice rivalries on both sides. As much as Marshall might have liked to depict command unity as a purely military problem, it raised thorny issues of diplomacy and politics—and those issues would have to be confronted by the civilian leaders of all the Allied nations. Marshall seemed to understand that if the issue of command unity was not dealt with at the very outset of the conflict, it might never be dealt with at all.

The proposal came as a bombshell: Marshall had not forewarned King or the other American or British service chiefs that it was coming. At first, it met with strong resistance. The British, having been at war for nearly two and a half years, were loathe to place their troops under a nation that had just entered the conflict and seemed to have much to learn. The RAF chief, Charles Portal, argued that the Allies should first decide on overall deployment of forces to the theater before confronting the question of a unified command. King was cautious at first. One of the other officers at the meeting regarded him as "lukewarm." He knew that the rank and file of the American navy would blanch at the prospect of placing ships under the command either of American generals or foreign admirals. King's assistant chief of staff, Admiral Richmond Turner, vehemently opposed placing U.S. Navy units outside the navy command hierarchy, and was not afraid to say so to King or to anyone else. But over the next two days King was brought along by Marshall's reasoning, and in subsequent meetings declared that he supported the proposal. Stark, Turner, and the other admirals fell reluctantly into line. It was a surprising and fortunate development. It cemented the partnership between Marshall and King, and signaled that service coordination and coalition warfare were going to be embraced by the U.S. Navy.

British opposition was more adamant. When the subject was raised in a White House meeting on December 26, Churchill spoke out against it. He seems to have been warned by his chiefs, and prepared his arguments with care. He acknowledged that unity of command had been an important principle in the First World War, but in that conflict there had been a "continuous line of battle" along a long front. In Asia, there was a large and far-flung theater, with islands and landmasses separated by sea, encompassing forces of many different nations, fighting on their own soil or on colonial soil that they had controlled. In such a case, he said, a unified command would only confuse the picture. The greatest problem, he said, was to ensure that adequate military assets were being sent to the theater. The war could be carried on more effectively with the forces of each nation fighting under their own officers, but accountable directly to the chiefs of staff in Washington or London. During these deliberations, Lord Beaverbrook, the British production chief, passed a note to Hopkins: "You should work on Churchill. He is being advised. He is open-minded and needs discussion."

In his memoirs, Churchill recalled that Hopkins said to him: "Don't be in a hurry to turn down the proposal the President is going to make to you before you know who is the man we have in mind." Marshall then nominated a British general, Field Marshal Sir Archibald P. Wavell, as the first supreme Allied commander of "ABDACOM," an acronym denoting the "American-British-Dutch-Australian Command." The ABDACOM theater would embrace Burma, Malaya, the Dutch East Indies, western New Guinea, the northwest quadrant of Australia, and the Philippines, including all the adjacent seas. Wavell would command all forces "afloat, ashore, and in the air."

Churchill recalled, "I was complimented by the choice of a British commander, but it seemed to me that the theatre in which he would act would soon be overrun and the forces which would be placed at his disposal would be destroyed by the Japanese onslaught." The prime minister revealed himself as a dyed-in-the-wool navalist by declaring that he would rather see British ships commanded by an American admiral than by a British general. He counterproposed that Admiral Thomas Hart, commander of the U.S. Asiatic Fleet, should retain command of all ABDA naval forces and merely "conform" to the plans and polices of Field Marshal Wavell. The Americans rejected that as ambiguous. King himself took up a pen and rewrote the order to specify that naval forces would fall under Wavell's command.

Churchill's resistance broke down under the combined heavy pressure of Roosevelt, Marshall, and Hopkins, particularly when King's obstinate backing was thrown on the scale. The British leader might have hoped he could count on Admiral King to oppose the idea of putting his ships under the command of a foreign general—but King, once he had made up his mind, supported Wavell unequivocally. Churchill, in the face of this united front, concluded that "it was evident that we must meet the American view." He did not ask the British war cabinet in London for its approval, but sent a telegram announcing that the decision had been made. The U.S. Navy would "remain responsible for the whole Pacific Ocean east of Philippine Islands and Australasia, including United States approaches to Australasia." He concluded, "I have not attempted to argue case for and against our accepting this broadminded and selfless American proposal, of merits of which as a war-winner I have become convinced."

Receiving the news by cable to London, General Brooke was dismayed. In his diary he wrote: "The whole scheme [is] wild and half baked and only catering for one area of action, namely western Pacific, one enemy Japan, and no central control." However, "cabinet was forced to accept the PM's new scheme owing to the fact that it was almost a fait accompli!" By December 29, only four days after Marshall had first broached the subject, the other ABDA powers had agreed to Wavell's appointment and the unlucky general had received his orders. Despite initial resistance from King, and heavier and more sustained resistance from the British, Marshall had gotten his way in remarkably short order. Wavell arrived at Batavia, on the island of Java, on January 10, 1942. By that time, the Japanese onslaught in that theater was nearing its successful climax.

The ABDA command would be short-lived, but it forced the Allies to confront fundamental questions about how their coalition would be run. From whom would Field Marshal Wavell receive his orders? How would the American and British high commands be blended? Most crucially, where was the high command to be located, Washington or London? Or would it somehow straddle the Atlantic? And what of the smaller nations of the coalition—would they also have a seat at the table? Could the Second World War be waged by a multinational committee? Those questions were painful and difficult, and could not be resolved without spreading dissent and rancor within the Allied camp, but King insisted that they be decided immediately.

Wavell's orders had stated that he would receive his instructions from an "appropriate joint body," accountable to the president and prime minister. Admiral Pound, the British first sea lord, proposed that the Allies should "utilize existing machinery." In other words, the Allied high command would simply be represented by the Anglo-American service chiefs—the men sitting around that table in the Federal Reserve boardroom, plus General Alan Brooke, who had remained in London. Together, they would form a Combined Chiefs of Staff (CCOS) committee, accountable directly to the president and prime minister. They would guide the overall strategic direction of the war, set production goals, allocate military resources, distribute orders to all Allied commands worldwide, and (crucially) control all Allied shipping. In a private lunch at the White House on December 29, Roosevelt told Admiral King that he did not believe the high command could be expanded beyond the United States and Britain without losing coherence. The Australians, New Zealanders, Dutch, Chinese, Free French, and all the other lesser Allies would have to be excluded from those deliberations—they would receive orders from the CCOS and be expected to carry them out. King recognized that these nations would be severely disappointed, but agreed with Roosevelt that it was a price that must be paid for a functioning command structure. The president authorized King to convey his view to the CCOS in the next day's meeting of the chiefs, and he did. "It was obvious that with so many participants in the war, decisions could not be made by a show of hands," King later told a group of war correspondents. "This is a hard-boiled method bound to cause friction and unhappiness among the smaller nations . . . but it is the only way to function effectively."

Where was this "machinery" to be located? The Americans insisted that it should be in Washington, with a British representative acting as a liaison to London. That was a bitter pill for the British to swallow, having run their war from London for nearly two and a half years. They held out for two committees, one in London, the other in Washington—and proposed a system in which major decisions could be formulated through telegraph communications between the two capitals. Roosevelt, King, Marshall, and the Americans replied that this would be impractical, and would represent a fatal weakening in the principle of a single command organization to fight a global war. That was the single most controversial issue of the conference. The Americans pointed out that the United States would produce the great majority of munitions and other war matériel, and that North America was geographically more central to the European and Pacific theaters. Roosevelt primly anticipated that "There will possibly be quite a time over this," while Hopkins noted that "The suggestion of an 'appropriate joint body' has kicked up a hell of a row."

The British angled to retain some power in London by proposing two "coequal" munitions allocation subcommittees, one in London and one in Washington, to be headed by Beaverbrook and Hopkins respectively. The idea was quashed when Marshall heatedly threatened to tender his resignation rather than accept it. It was a bitter point. Bob Sherwood judged that the issue "provoked more heated argument than any other topic considered at the Arcadia Conference. . . . This was one of the few subjects on which a division appeared on nationalistic lines as between British and Americans, and it was never completely closed." Churchill did not accept defeat easily; he persisted in arguing his case robustly and at length. But when it became clear that Roosevelt was going to stand behind Marshall, and that the British must acquiesce or risk an open break, Churchill surrendered with the face-saving suggestion that "the system be set up and tried for one month." Roosevelt gratefully agreed: "We shall call it a preliminary agreement and try it out that way." The arrangement would continue through the end of the war.

Receiving reports by cable in London, General Brooke was appalled: "I could see no reason why at this stage, with American forces totally unprepared to play a major part, we should agree to a central control in Washington." Later, when the British service chiefs had returned to England, Brooke rebuked Portal and Pound for having "sold the birthright for a plate of porridge." But Churchill had not been swindled. He had given in reluctantly, but with his eyes open. Lord Moran, as the prime minister's doctor, observed that he was "possessed with one idea to the exclusion of all others"—to "bring the President into the War with his heart set on victory. If that can be done, nothing else matters." Before December 7, Britain had been in the position of a suitor; afterward, as the prime minister put it to King George VI, "Britain and America were now married after many months of walking out."

There was some consolation in the appointment of Field Marshal Sir John Dill to head the Washington-based British Joint Staff Mission. Dill had been removed by Churchill as chief of the Imperial General Staff and replaced by Brooke. He had come to Washington to assist in the transition; the decision to leave him in Washington came as an afterthought. Dill had an excellent rapport with all the American military leaders, and would remain a vital intermediary between the British and Americans until his death in 1944. The American chiefs traveled to wartime conferences in London and several other places around the world. The CCOS met a total of eighty-nine times between 1941 and 1945, and those summits produced many of the substantive decisions and compromises of the war. Of the CCOS apparatus Churchill later wrote, "There was never a failure to reach effective agreement for action, or to send clear instructions to the commanders in every theatre. Every executive officer knew that the orders he received bore with them the combined conception and expert authority of both Governments."

Lord Beaverbrook, the British production chief, believed the American production targets were "utterly inadequate," and made his case directly to the president on December 29. He urged that U.S. production goals for 1942 should be revised upward to 45,000 tanks, 17,700 antiaircraft guns, and 24,000 fighter planes. As for the navy, Admiral Stark had already proposed to increase the existing building program (based on the 1940 expansion bill) to build an additional 8 aircraft carriers, 24 cruisers, 102 destroyers, and 54 submarines—a total of 900,000 tons. The keels would all be laid by 1944. But even those plans were not grand enough. In January 1942, the General Board of the navy envisioned a fleet composed of 34 battleships, 24 carriers, 12 battle cruisers, 104 other cruisers, 379 destroyers, and 207 submarines. Those figures represented a significant shift in favor of aircraft carriers. There were also calls for more escort vessels, and that would lead eventually to the construction of many destroyer escorts, vessels specially designed for convoy work. The necessary directives enforcing those colossal goals on every agency of the government were distributed widely to all concerned.

The president's State of the Union address, delivered to the Congress on January 6, showcased the president's titanic production targets. "We must raise our sights all along the production line. Let no man say it cannot be done." In 1942, the nation would manufacture 45,000 tanks, 20,000 antiaircraft weapons, 60,000 aircraft, and 6 million deadweight tons of cargo shipping. Those targets, Roosevelt added, "will give the Japanese and the Nazis a little idea of just what they accomplished in the attack at Pearl Harbor." The numbers had been revised by Roosevelt himself, apparently with no actual basis in the estimates that had been given to him—he simply crossed out the estimates he had received and rewrote them with his own hand on the night before the speech. When Hopkins worried that these arbitrary, back-of-the-envelope figures might not be feasible, the president serenely replied: "Oh—the production people can do it, if they really try." Roosevelt, Bob Sherwood observed, "was never afraid of big, round numbers."

The numbers were stunning. Lord Moran wrote that Churchill, more than any of his colleagues, understood what production on that scale would mean for the course of the war: "He is drunk with the figures."

Many thought the targets unrealistic. In the War Department, an officer was said to have remarked that Roosevelt had "gone in for the 'numbers racket'!" Industry leaders, having operated for years at partial capacity during the Great Depression, were skeptical—many suggested that the president had been misled by Harry Hopkins. On January 13, the president responded to those criticisms by summoning a Sears, Roebuck executive, Donald Nelson, and creating a new agency to coordinate a complete mobilization of industry: the War Production Board (WPB). Nelson was appointed on the strong recommendation of Hopkins, who argued that he alone should be given the job rather than a three-man board. The president accepted Hopkins's view that Nelson "was the best of the lot." He would be the "war czar." Under his supervision, the nation's industrial base would be retooled and ramped up to round-the-clock production, seven days a week. Assembly lines would run in three-shift rotations. Vast industries devoted to such peacetime pursuits as building automobiles would be shut down by government decree. No further sales of cars or light trucks to civilians were permitted. All cars that were already in the retail pipeline, sitting on dealer lots, would be subject to a rationing system. Most went to the government, and a few more to professionals whose work was considered essential.

SINCE 1775, ANGLO-AMERICAN RELATIONS had been haunted by a spirit of antagonism, distrust, and jealousy. Even after Pearl Harbor, many Americans suspected that the British had somehow duped a second consecutive generation of their countrymen into pouring their blood and treasure into the European swamp. They feared the British would harness the power of American democracy to save their global empire, and in doing so plant the seeds of future wars.

With those hoary grievances forming the backdrop to the Allies' negotiations, the Arcadia Conference was a triumph of wartime diplomacy. The Allies had reaffirmed the "Europe-first" policy. They had agreed that the major issues of the war would be decided by a Washington-based Anglo-American Combined Chiefs of Staff (CCOS) committee. They had created the ABDA command with Field Marshal Wavell as its C-in-C. In writing Wavell's charter, the Allies were reacting to an immediate crisis in the Pacific—but their ad hoc efforts had established the precedent for unified multinational and interservice theater commanders, and even created the institutional machinery of a blended high command. They had written the Charter of the United Nations, a joint statement of purpose that evolved into the New York–based multilateral organization that still exists today.

They had set extravagant targets for war production, and would achieve them. They had created a true Allied coalition, an achievement that contrasted sharply with the Axis nations, which were never more than allies in name.

Roosevelt and Churchill (with Hopkins in a vital supporting role) had cemented their personal understanding, which was based on genuine mutual fondness. Together, they would sit atop the whole structure, and make the major decisions that could not be resolved by their military chiefs. (Admiral Leahy, who served as Roosevelt's military chief of staff after mid-1942, said flatly that the two leaders "really ran the war.") Britain would work its influence gently, so as not to chafe the fragile American ego—Churchill informed his war cabinet that the Americans "were not above learning from us, provided that we did not set out to teach them."

George Marshall's leadership has been forcefully stressed by historians of the Second World War. King, by contrast, has often been cast in the role of Marshall's antagonist, rival, or spoiler. That there were substantive disagreements between them cannot be denied, but it is all too easy to blow those differences out of proportion. At Arcadia, King backed Marshall on unity of command. He agreed to place the U.S. Asiatic Fleet under the command of a British general. He argued for a larger allocation of scarce military resources to shore up the U.S.-Australia lifeline, a view that was controversial at the time but was largely vindicated by subsequent events. In negotiations concerning the creation of the supreme Allied command, he asked tough, penetrating questions that forced the participants to clarify their thinking. But at the conclusion of the discussion, he and Marshall held the same view.

Above all, Marshall and King were partners. They were the two dominant members of the Joint Chiefs, and as such they always understood that their partnership was at the heart of the American war effort. If they failed to reach agreement on any substantive issue of the war, the dispute would have to be adjudicated by Roosevelt himself. Deadlocks would diminish their credibility and threaten the cohesiveness of the high command. In that spirit, Marshall and King almost always found a way to work out their differences. "King knew he had to get along," one of his staff subordinates recalled. "That was the compelling influence on all of them. They knew they had to get along."

But there was one issue on which King would never yield. "I have no intention whatever of acceding to any unity of command proposals that are not premised on a particular situation in a particular area at a particular time for a more or less particular period," King wrote a colleague during the conference. "I have found it necessary to find time to point out to some 'amateur strategists' in high places that unity of command is not a panacea for all military difficulties—and I shall continue to do so." More directly to the point, King would never consent to place the Pacific Fleet under the command of the messianic, fame-seeking General MacArthur.

JANUARY 13 WAS CHURCHILL'S PENULTIMATE NIGHT in Washington. The president, prime minister, first lady, and various other guests and staffers gathered in the Oval Study for cocktails before dinner. Louis Adamic, an author who had been invited to dinner that night, recalled that Churchill arrived late. He entered the room wearing a "semi-scowl on his big, chubby, pink-and-white face with its light-blue eyes," and "moved as though he were without joints, all of a piece: solidly, unhurriedly, impervious to obstacles, like a tank or a bulldozer. . . . His large, round mug was perfectly smooth, blandly innocent—except for the eyes and mouth, which were shrewd, ruthless, unscrupulous." Adamic had recently published a book advocating a leading role for the United States in promoting democracy in Europe after the war; Eleanor Roosevelt had read it and given copies to the president, the prime minister, and many others. Adamic, a liberal anti-imperialist, was not exactly an impartial observer—he freely confessed that he distrusted Churchill and the British Tories—but his eyewitness account of that evening's dinner was nonetheless vivid and convincing. Watching the interplay between the two Allied leaders, he saw that they were genuine friends, familiar and affectionate toward one another; but he also noted a strained undertone, as if they had recently quarreled. "Gazing at each other, smiling yet not smiling, they seemed to be feeling out each other's measure, speculating, challenging. . . . Each seemed to be saying inaudibly to the other: Now how am I going to handle you tonight? How will you react to my tactics?"

On the morning of the 15th, Roosevelt and Harry Hopkins drove with the prime minister to his private train, which he boarded from a private siding on Sixth Street. The president bid his goodbyes from the car; Hopkins walked with Churchill and his entourage to the train. Hopkins handed Churchill a note and present for Mrs. Churchill ("Clemmie"), in which he had written: "You would have been quite proud of your husband on this trip. . . ."

After a marathon flight across the Atlantic by flying boat, with a refueling stop in Bermuda, Churchill returned to London to find a very difficult political situation. The news had been very bad, both in East Asia and in North Africa. Parliament was threatening a revolt; the criticism of his leadership had grown very pointed. The prime minister might have taken some solace from a warm note from Roosevelt, who had turned sixty on January 30. The president had written, "It is fun to be in the same decade with you." Churchill made a masterful defense in the House of Commons, and demanded a vote of confidence, which he received, on January 27, by a vote of 464 to 1.

Chapter Six

I N THE U.S. NAVY OF 1942, EVERY ADMIRAL KNEW EVERY OTHER ADMIRAL, at least by name and face. But King and Nimitz had never been close, either personally or professionally. King's overbearing domination drew a sharp contrast to Nimitz's soft-spoken collegiality, and if it had been up to the new COMINCH to name Kimmel's replacement, it is safe to assume he would have chosen someone else. Nimitz understood that his tenure was probationary. In letters to his wife, the Texan confided that he and King had not yet established trust or rapport. He would have to tread carefully, for when the COMINCH lost confidence in a man, the consequences were felt immediately.

In a secure cable dated January 2, 1942, King let it be known that he was not pleased with the dilatory and halfhearted deployment of the American aircraft carriers since December 7. He wanted hit-and-run raids on Japan's "fixed aircraft carriers"—Makin in the Gilberts and a constellation of island air bases in the Marshalls. He urged Nimitz to send the carriers steaming at high speed into enemy waters, to launch bombing raids with total surprise on enemy islands, to catch the Japanese in their beds, knock out their planes on the ground, crater their airstrips, level their hangars, machine shops, and barracks, kill their pilots and maintenance crews, blow up their fuel tanks, and torpedo the ships anchored in their lagoons.

Nimitz mulled it over with his staff. There were sensible and well-reasoned objections, not the sort that could be dismissed as timorous or craven. Admiral Claude C. Bloch, chief of the Fourteenth Naval District, who was directly responsible for the defense of Hawaii, baldly stated that the loss of the carriers would leave Hawaii exposed to invasion. As a matter of well-established doctrine, sending carriers into the range of land-based bombers was thought to be a tactical loser, unless the attackers were certain of achieving total surprise. The Japanese had done it successfully on December 7—but now, with the war on, wouldn't they anticipate such attacks along the eastern perimeter of their empire? If so, there was a grave risk of devastating counterstrikes against the American flattops by Japanese twin-engine land bombers that had longer legs than the American carrier planes.

Moreover, was it even worth the risk? Planning documents produced by the CINCPAC staff during that period reveal that very little was known about those secluded atolls of the Marshalls and Gilberts: they were largely shrouded in mystery. But it seemed likely that they offered little in the way of high-value targets. What good was punching craters in a coral airstrip when the damage could be so readily repaired? None of the enemy's major capital ships was likely to be found anchored in those remote islands, and the shore installations were not particularly important or valuable. Why take a gamble and lose more ships so early in the war, when the prudent course was to buy time to rebuild? Risky operations could wait until 1943, when the American economy had been fully mobilized and a new fleet delivered into Nimitz's hands. The danger to the carriers was vividly illustrated on January 11, when the *Saratoga* was struck by a Japanese torpedo about 500 miles south of Oahu. She returned to Pearl under her own power, but the damage required that she return to Puget Sound for repairs. *Saratoga* was one of four American carriers in the Pacific; her loss, wrote Edwin Layton, "cut our offensive strength by 25 percent."

On January 7, Task Force 8, built around the carrier *Enterprise*, entered Pearl Harbor for her periodic refueling and reprovisioning. Vice Admiral Halsey, who had commanded the task force with *Enterprise* as his flagship since before the war began, planted himself at Nimitz's conference table for the regular morning meeting at 8 a.m. on the 8th. With him was his cruiser commander, Rear Admiral Raymond A. Spruance, the trusty understudy who would eventually eclipse Halsey as a superior fleet commander. A week earlier, Halsey had been summoned to testify before the Roberts Commission (the first of several Pearl Harbor investigations), and the questioning had turned to his opinion on the proper use of carriers. Halsey replied that they were tantamount to a naval cavalry, and quoted the Confederate cavalry general Nathan Bedford Forrest: "I think General Forrest's description is the best thing I know, to get to the other fellow with everything you have and as fast as you can and to dump it on him. You have to scout out and find it, and as soon as you find it, send everything you can at him and hit him with it."

Halsey was all for the proposed raid on the Marshalls. It might divert Japanese forces from their southern drive, where they were threatening the Coral Sea area and even Australia itself. Landing a heavy punch on those outer perimeter outposts of the Japanese Empire would protect Samoa and other positions on the Australia lifeline by degrading the effectiveness of their air bases. Halsey theatrically declared that he would take the *Enterprise* into the Marshalls and do it himself. He argued with spirit and conviction. It was important to strike the enemy somewhere, if only to retrieve the navy's self-respect. Certainly there were risks, he acknowledged—but what battle was ever fought without risks? In contrast to the skeptics, he seemed not to have been shaken by the failures and setbacks of the first month of the war.

Halsey had not yet tasted fame, and possibly did not yet realize that he would become the public face of the U.S. Navy, but in pointed contrast to King or Nimitz he was willing to play the part of the salt-stained sea gladiator. Samuel Eliot Morison would observe that the press "expected admirals to pound the table and bellow as in the movies." Halsey pounded and bellowed. He had just the right look for the role. His square face was battered by wind, sun, and salt; his thinning hair was combed straight back from his spacious forehead; his wide-set eyes were crowned by a regal pair of undomesticated Scottish eyebrows. When he smiled, he seemed to leer. Like General George S. Patton (to whom he is inevitably compared), he appeared to love war. He was a sailor's sailor, and popular on the lower deck. "As the general rule," he avowed, "I never trust a sailorman who doesn't smoke or drink." In January 1942, he was eager to get the show on the road. An ordnanceman on the *Enterprise* recalled passing near his quarters and overhearing the admiral "thundering away, cursing Washington and the shore-based admirals for their cowardice."

In a sense, Halsey had lived his entire life in the navy. His father had been a naval officer before him, and as a child he had lived all around the world. At age fifteen he had written directly to President McKinley, asking for a Naval Academy appointment. The letter contained numerous errors of spelling and fact, and was addressed (contrary to protocol) to "Major William McKinley," the president's old army rank. It was never answered. But his mother bent the ears of the right people, and Halsey was admitted as a naval cadet in July 1900. At the academy he ran up a precariously high tally of demerits, but he was always well-liked among his peers. With appealing self-deprecation, he would later brag of being a star fullback on the worst football team in the history of the navy. (In 1903, the team fell to Army by a score of 40–5.) He graduated with the class of 1904, one year before Nimitz, ranked forty-third in his class of sixty-two. The *Lucky Bag* called him "everyone's friend" and "A real old salt. Looks like a figurehead of Neptune."

Halsey's early years in the service were largely in destroyers. He took his first command in 1909 (USS *DuPont*) and by 1920 had commanded a destroyer division. He did tours in the Office of Naval Intelligence in Washington, and as naval attaché in U.S. embassies in Germany, Norway, Denmark, and Sweden. He served (as required for all those officers climbing into the higher ranks) in battleships, and completed the course at the Naval War College in the early years of the Depression. In 1934, as a fifty-two-year-old captain, he took the lateral route into the field of naval aviation by reporting to Pensacola for flight training. It was late in life to learn how to fly, and he was not a naturally gifted flyer, but he earned his wings the following year, qualifying him for carrier command. He had the *Saratoga* for two years, and then returned to Pensacola as commander of the Naval Air Station. He was promoted rear admiral in 1938. By the outbreak of the Second World War he was one of the navy's most seasoned carrier task force commanders.

Nimitz was relieved to have the vigorous support of the man who would lead the operation. Moreover, he was receiving radio intelligence that seemed to improve the risk assessment. Enemy radio traffic had risen sharply in Truk in the Carolines but remained steady in the Marshalls, suggesting the pattern of a southward fleet movement. More concretely, fragmentary radio decrypts referred to a *Koryaku Butai*, or "occupation force," aimed at Rabaul on New Britain. If the Japanese fleet was moving toward Rabaul, there was no danger that the American carrier task forces would blunder into it thousands of miles north, in the central Pacific. Air and submarine reconnaissance also tended to confirm that there would be no unpleasant surprises in the Marshalls.

On January 9, Nimitz assented to the raid and put Halsey in command of it. It would be folded into another, primarily defensive mission. Samoa was to be reinforced by a marine brigade, which had sailed two days earlier from San Diego in a slow convoy of four transports. The convoy was accompanied by Task Force 17, built around the carrier *Yorktown*, recently arrived from the Atlantic and under the command of Admiral Fletcher. Halsey and Task Force 8 would go south to provide air cover and an anti-submarine screen until the convoy arrived safely at its destination. *Enterprise* would join up with the *Yorktown* and then sail northwest for the Marshalls. They would sneak across the International Date Line and race toward the Japanese bases. *Enterprise* would hit Kwajalein, Maloelap, and Wotje in the heart of the Marshall Islands, while *Yorktown* peeled off to the south and hit Makin, Mili, and Jaluit in the Gilberts and southern Marshalls.

As ENTERPRISE LAY AT HER BERTH in Pearl Harbor, her crew worked around the clock, taking aboard fuel, fresh water, provisions, and ammunition. As usual, the rumor mill spun without interruption, and although the crew had been left in the dark, no one doubted that the *Enterprise's* war was about to begin in earnest. The massive loading, on an urgent timetable, could mean only one thing: "Are loading for bear," read a notation in one of the air group diaries.

On the morning of January 11, Nimitz and Halsey walked together from the headquarters to the pier and shook hands at the foot of the gangway. "All sorts of luck to you, Bill!" called Nimitz. At noon, the carrier with her screening cruisers and destroyers took in their lines and got underway. By mid-afternoon they had left the dry, dusty foliage of Barbers Point astern and were steaming into the offing at better than 25 knots. Once they were safely at sea, Halsey briefed his air groups, letting them know that after the rendezvous off Samoa they would turn north and "raise a little hell up in the Gilberts or Marshalls." There was no general announcement as yet, but among the men, who could sense what was coming, there was a discernable lift in morale.

Southward, toward the equator, each day was a little hotter than the last, and soon it was downright uncomfortable belowdecks. Sea level is sea level anywhere, but sea level bulges outward slightly at the equator, so crossing the line from north to south involves climbing over a hill of water. The interior of the *Enterprise* was a warren of metallic corridors connected by hatches, lit with harsh electric overhead lights and lined with cables, air ducts, and piping. Before December 7, most of those internal spaces had

been painted white or gray, but now that the Japanese attack had drama-
tized the flammability of paint, working parties were put to the tedious work
of chipping it all away, inch by square inch, with iron scrapers. They tore up
the linoleum tiles and scraped smooth the steel underneath. They worked
in the sweltering, airless heat—exacerbated by the wartime requirement of
keeping the watertight doors and hatches dogged down—and found that
they sweated through their uniforms so quickly they might as well strip
them off and work in their underwear. It was brutal, hateful, thankless
work—"a labor of the damned," one wrote. The pilots, on their daylight
patrols, kept their canopies open to cool themselves, but even the wind was
sultry and oppressive. When they could fly through a rain squall they did so
gratefully, craning their necks around their windshields, letting the blessed
cool water run all over them and their planes—but such adventures also
raised the risk of getting lost.

Accidents and navigational errors took a heavy toll. One of the SBDs
of Scouting Six came within a whisker of shooting down a four-engine
flying boat that proved to belong to New Zealand. On January 13, a pilot
attached to the same squadron broke radio silence, a violation of orders
and an act that put the entire task force in jeopardy. On January 16, a dive-
bomber landing on the *Enterprise* tore clear of an arresting wire and ran off
the deck onto the catwalk, where it mortally wounded a chief petty officer.
Later that day, one of the bombers of Torpedo Six ditched at sea and its
crew was set adrift in a lifeboat, where they would drift for twenty-four days
and wash up on an island 750 miles away, sun-baked and starving. Pilots
flying search patrols sometimes got lost in the overcast, and drifted far off
course; and on one occasion the *Enterprise* had to break radio silence to
bring a lost bird home, a breach of security that put Halsey and his staff
officers in a bad temper.

Pilots were in short supply; more were due to arrive from the States, but
not until April or May. In the rapid fleet expansion of 1940–41, many new
aviators had entered the air groups. Some of the *Enterprise* pilots would
make their very first carrier landing on this cruise. The rookies were still
learning how to make attack runs. Everything was being learned, practiced,
and improvised. Standards were improving with practice, but this was war,
and war was an unforgiving school. The green pilots were making too many
mistakes. They would have to lift their game, and do it fast.

The screening ships were also were plagued with accidents and bad luck.

A sailor was lost overboard from the destroyer *Blue*. A man on the cruiser *Salt Lake City* was crushed in one of her turrets. Throughout the task force, the results of antiaircraft gunnery practice gave little encouragement. Even after the heavy training schedules in the lead-up to the war, the carrier groups had much to learn about operating at sea in war conditions. They were learning that they needed more of everything: more training, more gunnery practice, more antiaircraft guns of every caliber, more ammunition, more supplies, more spare parts. The .50-caliber ammunition was dangerously scarce, and certain categories of airplane-mounted ordnance were running low. There was a real danger of running out of torpedoes on this cruise. There were not enough floatplanes to carry out reconnaissance flights, either operating from the islands or from the heavy cruisers. For the moment, there were a sufficient number of planes on the carriers but precious few in reserve, and losses would be difficult to replace. There was an urgent need for better communications technology: better radios, better radar, new beacons and homing equipment, and all agreed they urgently needed the emerging technology known as identification-friend-or-foe (IFF) systems, to help gunners distinguish American planes and thus avoid shooting at their friends.

North of Samoa, the *Enterprise* launched heavy air searches to the northwest while 5,000 marines got safely ashore at Pago Pago. Men on the flight deck could see the green hills of the British Samoa Islands. The carrier stood east and then west for five days, waiting to rendezvous with her sister, the *Yorktown*. They met on January 23, and two days later the fleet hauled off to the northwest, toward the Marshalls, which lay some 1,600 miles away, on the far side of the International Date Line. The *Yorktown* group sailed about 150 miles astern of Halsey and the *Enterprise* group, with plans to peel off to the south to hit Jaluit and Mili in the southern part of the Marshalls and Makin in the Gilberts.

The last days of January were fine, and the task force advanced through a gently rolling sea under a pastel blue sky. But as they approached the date line the wind picked up, and as reporter Robert Casey stood on the deck of the *Salt Lake City* he took in an "intensely dramatic" setting—"a gray-blue sea laced with white-gray wave-tops—a cloudy gray sky that was almost black at the zenith and lightened to a sort of mauve by reflected sunset at the horizon." The task force advanced in a circular formation with the carrier always at the center. From the flight deck of the *Enterprise*, men could see the screening vessels spread out around the horizon in every direction. The heavy cruisers bucked along, two on each side of the ship; and the destroyers in the outer ring, riding up and down the waves, throwing up seas on either side, labored mightily. To Casey, the ships on the horizon appeared like "silhouettes"—"motionless, deep cuttings of gray matt pasted against the sky. Only the tremendous white waves looping their bows showed that they were moving. All about us was a high, hissing spume as we drove into the rollers."

They advanced on a zigzagging track as a measure against enemy submarines, but that required mass-choreographed maneuvers that could easily go awry. When one of the cruisers missed a turn and dropped out of position, her captain received a sarcastic message by blinker light from Admiral Halsey: "May I suggest that if at all convenient you get where you belong?" Shortly afterward, he received another: "Have you any officer aboard able to judge distance accurately within 6,000 yards?"

On January 28, the task force refueled from the tanker *Platte*. The cruisers and destroyers completed their refueling during the day, but the *Enterprise* could not maneuver alongside the tanker until 8 p.m., as night was falling fast. Refueling at sea had been the bane of early carrier operations, and Halsey was determined that the *Enterprise* would get it right. Refueling was difficult even in daylight, especially in heavy seas, when there was a constant danger of collision. This was the first time a carrier would refuel at night. It was a supreme test of seamanship for both ships. No light could be shown on either vessel, so the work had to be done in the dark.

Carrier and tanker approached one another on near-parallel courses and closed to within about 70 feet. Each remained underway at a precisely identical speed of 10 knots. Steering and throttle control had to be maintained with perfect conformity to the captain's orders. Heaving lines were thrown across, caught, and made fast. The crew had to work quickly and in perfect unison. Men handling the hoses were in constant danger of falling into the sea between the two vessels; destroyers stood astern to rescue them. Lines or hoses had to be dropped immediately upon the orders of the boatswain's mates, and others stood by with axes, ready to cut them away and get free of the tanker on a moment's notice, if that should be necessary. For obvious reasons it was very important not to be caught at sea, refueling, with large quantities of combustible fuel on deck, if an enemy bomber should appear overhead. The *Enterprise* completed the difficult operation at 1:30 a.m. The operation seemed to take forever, and Casey expressed frustration with the long delay. "Somebody observed last night that it takes just about as long to get into battle now as it did in 1812," he wrote ruefully.

Coded radio messages from Pearl Harbor were plucked out of the air. Nimitz, fortified with new radio intelligence, urged Halsey to hit the Marshalls quickly. On January 27, the C-in-C sent new orders to Halsey, authorizing the latter to expand and extend his strikes on the islands. Nimitz ordered that the raids be "driven home," with several airstrikes on the prime targets, and return strikes if necessary. Halsey's chief of staff, Miles Browning, argued for a new plan of attack that would up the ante, to take the entire carrier group farther west into the heart of the islands and hit Kwajalein, the largest base in the Marshalls. It was risky: the American ships would be well within range of counterattacks by air. By approving the plan, Halsey was gambling that the initial wave of American bombers achieved total surprise over the enemy airfields. Halsey gave his go-ahead and remarked, "It was one of those plans which are called 'brilliant' if they succeed and 'foolhardy' if they fail." The *Enterprise* pilots were thrilled. "Instead of just a hit and run raid we were going to make an all-day long attack," wrote one. "Admiral Halsey had decided to put the carrier within twenty or thirty miles of two big Jap air bases. So, close in, the attack would be launched and we would get to work with plenty of gas. This suited us fine."

On January 31, west of the date line, the *Enterprise* radar picked up a blip. It was a Japanese patrol plane, which apparently flew no more than thirty-four miles west (astern) of the American ships, but it did not make contact and sent no radio message. Halsey watched the blip move across the screen. He was deeply concerned that the enemy airmen would notice the trail of the task force's wakes, even if they did not see the ships themselves. But no radio report was detected on the Japanese frequencies. The blip crept across the radar screen and trailed off to the south. As the range grew, it become evident that the task force had been lucky. Marine Captain Bankson T. Holcomb, Jr., a Japanese-language officer detached from Pearl Harbor's codebreaking unit, picked up a transmission by a Japanese patrol pilot (probably the same one that had been picked up by the carrier's radar). The aircraft had reached the end of its patrol route and the pilot had "nothing to report."

Halsey remarked, "That yellow belly is just thinking about his fish and rice." He had Holcomb prepare a leaflet in Japanese to be dropped on the islands the next day: "It is a pleasure to thank you for having your patrol plane not sight my force."

At 6:30 p.m. on the 31st, the task force parted ways—Spruance's cruiser force to bombard Wotje and Taroa to the south, the *Enterprise* and three destroyers to take a position to the north to launch strikes against Kwajalein atoll as well as Wotje and Taroa. A radio message came in from Nimitz: "It is essential that the attacks be driven home. Exploit this situation by expanding operations, utilizing both task forces in such repeated air attacks and ship bombardments as developments and logistics make feasible. If practicable, extend offensive action beyond one day."

The final night's run-in to battle was done at a breakneck speed of 30 knots. The engines roared and the hull throbbed. The *Enterprise's* four huge propellers bit into the sea, turning 275 times a minute. There were precombat fears and jitters throughout the fleet. Sleeping was nearly impossible—the heat was intense belowdecks, and they all sweated through their sheets, and tossed and turned fitfully until before dawn. The captain of the *Salt Lake City* called the officers to the wardroom and went over the next day's chronology, starting with reveille at 3:45 a.m., breakfast at 4:15, General Quarters at 5:15, and combat at 6:15 to coincide with the dawn. On the subject of combat, the captain and his officers were sober and determined, paying great attention to detail—"the disposition of the ships, the nature of targets, the rate of fire, the spotting process, the frequency to be used by spotting planes in reports, food, water, access to latrines, powder lot, ventilation, bombs, depth charges, airplane fuel." Robert Casey was impressed by their poise, especially since not a man on the ship had any combat experience. "The captain was cheerful and businesslike," he wrote; "the officers grave and interested but no more excited than they might have been over a prospective target competition."

The *Enterprise* pilots were game, but they were also acutely aware that they knew little or nothing about the islands they were to bomb. They were Japan's "mystery islands," and the American fleet did not even possess accurate maps for them. They were relying upon crudely enlarged photostatic prints of old charts, many dating back to Lieutenant Charles Wilkes's "U.S. Exploring Expedition" ("Ex-Ex") survey cruise of 1838–42. It was with a distinct sense of foreboding that they prepared for their mission.

Balanced against that unease, that gnawing fear, was their thirst for vengeance. The pilots wanted to hit back for Pearl Harbor and Wake Island;

Casey observed that they "seem to feel as if they are personally responsible for the vindication of their service." They passed the hours talking about flying and fighting, about the strengths and vulnerabilities of the Japanese planes, filing those morsels of potentially useful knowledge away in their minds so that they would be there when the moment of combat arrived. They had underestimated the Japanese pilots before December 7; but now, scarcely six weeks later, that was all part of the past. The prewar era seemed long ago. Hard as it was for the proud officers and men of the navy, recalled Alvin Kernan, they were now coming around to understand that "theirs was a better navy than ours: better aircraft, better trained personnel, better night training, better torpedoes by far." It was a bitter pill to swallow, but it was also strangely invigorating, because it left every man in the fleet with the bracing realization that he would have to do his part to lift the navy's game.

It was only on the eve of the battle that the pilots and crew of the *Enterprise* were informed that the attack on Kwajalein would not include fighters. At that early stage of the war there were simply not enough fighters on the carriers to fly combat air patrol (CAP) and provide escort for the bombers. When the bomber pilots got the word, they were appalled. "No fighters!" wrote bomber pilot Clarence Dickinson. "On a raid you want fighter escort. Whether they do much good or not, it is a psychological factor of tremendous importance to know they are with you. You fly towards your objective a lot more eagerly if you know you have fighter protection. After all, the thing of first importance is to drop the bombs, not dogfight with Zeros." That night, the deck and hatches were lit up by small blue lights that threw just enough light to guide the footsteps of men whose eyes had adjusted to the darkness. It was in this moment, with danger imminent, that the men felt most deeply bonded to the ship. "However ghostly it seems, you sense solidity through the soles of your shoes and know yourself to be a part of something big and strong," wrote Dickinson; "a thousand other men and more, great guns, a powder magazine, an electric power plant that could run a city, a machine shop, beds and kitchens; all of this is compactly organized inside a vast steel hull, your planet."

This was Halsey's moment. The first weeks of the war, beginning with the fruitless searches for Nagumo's *Kido Butai* (carrier striking force) in the first forty-eight hours of the war, had been profoundly frustrating for him. He could not sleep. He chain-smoked, drank coffee, and read paperback novels. He lay awake in his bunk. Intermittently, he arose and returned

to flag plot. Out on the flag bridge, at two-twenty in the morning, he felt
sand blowing in his face. That could indicate the proximity of islands, so he
called for an immediate position check. The waters were poorly charted and
there was a real danger of running aground. It turned out the admiral had
felt not sand but sugar dropped from the radar platform, where a sailor was
pouring it into his coffee. Halsey retreated to his cabin. There was little he
could do. The die was cast. By the end of the day they might be celebrating
the first significant victory of the war, or the *Enterprise* might be resting on
the ocean floor. Below, on the hangar deck, the ordnance gangs were loading bombs onto the wings and bellies of the attack planes. Their labor was
edgy and intricate. The weapons were hoisted gingerly from the magazines
below, pushed across the deck in carts, and locked into the bomb rack at the
underside of the planes. The fuses were inserted into the bombs and wired
into the arming socket. No mistakes were tolerated. All had to be checked
and checked again.

Reveille came at 3 a.m., long before the first glow rose above the horizon
astern. The pilots made their way to the big wardroom for breakfast. They
sat at long tables, shoulder to shoulder in identical khaki uniforms, eating a hearty breakfast of eggs, bacon, toast, and canned juice. Most were
between the ages of twenty-one and twenty-four. Dickinson observed their
different temperaments: "Many were silent, gone deep inside themselves; a
few were chattering with excitement yet saying very little about what was
ahead of us. I heard scarcely any reference to what actually occupied our
minds. These young aviators behaved as if it would be indelicate to speak of
what we had to do." Afterward they gravitated to the ready rooms, divided
by squadron. There they listened to briefings and spoke freely among themselves. Most had slept little, if at all; they were running on adrenaline and
coffee. But their minds were focused, and they paid great attention to detail.
A yeoman in each ready room listened to reports over a telephone and
then relayed them to the group. The aviators tinkered with their navigation
plots, correcting for the carrier's position, course, and speed, and adding further tweaks for the direction and force of the wind. Not all of them would
be coming back, and they knew it. "Each man was challenging his own soul
to tell him how he would measure up in battle," Dickinson wrote. "No man
ever lived who got the answer in advance."

At the moment of truth the yeoman passed on the order that had come
down from above: "Pilots, man your planes!" They walked out onto the

flight deck, flight goggles pushed up on their foreheads, belts and shoulder straps festooned with gear, parachutes bumping against their rumps. It was a mild night. A radiant trail pointed across the sea to the west, where a full moon hung over the horizon. Deck crews guided each pilot through a maze of planes parked near the stern to his waiting aircraft, and stood by as he climbed onto the wing and slid down into the cockpit, buckled into his shoulder straps, and found the pedals with his feet. From the loudspeaker on deck came the order: "Start engines!"

The cartridge fired; the engine coughed, sputtered, and roared to life; the exhaust belched blue smoke that was quickly caught by the wind and carried away astern; the propeller spun, stopped, and spun again, then quickly dissolved into a blurred disk. The plane captain listened with cocked head to the engine, and when satisfied gave a signal; the pilot shoved his throttle all the way forward, with feet mashed down on the brakes. When given the all-clear (at 4:43 a.m.), the first pilot released his brakes and felt his aircraft lurch forward and clatter down the teak-planked deck. Accelerating into the teeth of the headwind, he balanced the rudder pedals to stay centered in his takeoff lane, demarcated by two parallel rows of hooded yellow lights. The moonlit shape of the carrier's island superstructure flashed by on his right. At the last moment before plummeting into the rapidly onrushing sea, his nose tilted up and his wheels lifted free of the deck. He was airborne.

First into the air were six F4F Wildcats to fly combat air patrol. They were followed immediately by the planes forming two airstrikes headed for the giant atoll of Kwajalein, the furthest target at some 155 miles away to the west. Thirty-seven Dauntless SBD dive-bombers would hit Roi, the island air base at the northern end of the atoll, while nine Devastator TBD torpedo bombers would go after ships anchored in the lagoon near Kwajalein, at the southern end. Once in the air, the SBDs and TBDs flew a circular rendezvous pattern, trying to join up in an orderly formation for their outbound flights. Getting the planes into the air was no great problem (heavily laden though they were with bombs and fuel), but the night rendezvous was unfamiliar and dangerous. The planes lifted into the sky at the rate of one every fifteen seconds. Each pilot was to follow the plane ahead of him by keeping his eyes fixed on a white taillight that was easily lost in the stars. If his eyes were good and he was lucky, he might also make out the two faint blue exhaust flames on either side of the fuselage. At the same time he had to maintain steady speed to allow the pilot behind him to follow.

At altitude, the entire group circled and groped for their assigned places in the formation; the SBDs and TBDs ran afoul of one another and were lucky to avoid collisions. The two Kwajalein-bound strikes managed to form up and fly toward their targets without losses. But an hour later, when a group of Wildcats armed with 100-pound bombs took off for the closer targets at Maloelap atoll, one plane spun into the sea and the pilot went down with it.

The Kwajalein Attack Group climbed into the west, the full moon hanging over their engine cowlings, nearly centered in their windshields. Leveling out at 14,000 feet, the airplanes flew in formation—V's interlocked with V's, stepped down slightly in altitude—and the moon threw so much light that the pilots and aircrews could make eye contact and exchange hand signals. Spread out beneath them was a downy blanket of cumulus clouds; through intermittent gaps they spied moonlit sea and occasional stretches of surf-lined beaches. They were well into the heart of the Marshalls now, and islands were plentiful. The flight leaders studied those shorelines and tried to match them up to the crude nineteenth-century charts they held on their laps. Guesswork and dead reckoning put them over the northern part of the atoll fifteen minutes early, just as dawn was breaking—but morning mists obscured the island of Roi, and at first the SBD flyers could not pick out their assigned targets. They circled, craning their necks as they peered below and looked for anything resembling a coral airstrip, and the drone of their engines alerted the Japanese defenders, who rushed to man the antiaircraft batteries and scramble the fighters. There would be no surprise.

When at last the airfield and hangars of Roi came into focus, Lieutenant Commander Halstead L. Hopping of Scouting Six pushed his nose down and began his approach. The others of his First Division followed close behind. They had intended a glide-bombing attack, with an attack angle of just 45 degrees, because such an attack would leave them with some altitude when they arrived over the target, so they could push their noses down and pick up speed to fly through hostile antiaircraft fire. Hopping apparently gave up too much altitude before arriving over the field, and therefore came in low and slow, his airspeed probably less than 200 knots. He dropped his 500-pound bomb, the first American bomb of the war to be dropped on Japanese territory, but a Nakajima Type 97 fighter locked in on his tail and hit him with tracer fire; simultaneously, his plane was struck by a very close burst of antiaircraft flak. His plane blew apart and spun into the lagoon. Three more First Division SBDs were lost to flak or fighters, but they also scored several well-aimed hits on the ground. Several buildings were destroyed, and two or three Japanese fighters were shot down.

The planes of the Second Division saw the bombs fall and explode among the hangars and along the airstrip. They came in with considerably more speed than Hopping's division, about 300 knots—and although the Japanese gunners were now fully awake and waiting for them, they were able to fly right through the flak, rocking back and forth as the black bursts appeared on either side. Looking down, they saw Japanese fighters racing down the airstrip and leaving the ground. Lieutenant Dickinson dived low over the field and dropped two 100-pound bombs on a complex of buildings adjacent to the airstrip. A bomb dropped by his wingman, Lieutenant Norman West, hit an ammunition dump and touched off a secondary explosion that flattened every building in the vicinity. A tremendous, churning fireball rose thousands of feet into the sky. Dickinson kicked his rudder to yaw his aircraft, and peered back to observe the results. He called it "one of the most glorious fireworks shows I had ever seen. . . . All over the island there was an extravagant flowering of flame. Great white and pinkish streaked fire shapes bloomed profusely, each for just an instant. But these became unimportant as the bombs went off, in big bluish flashes two and two and two each time another plane glided in."

After dropping their bombs, the Dauntlesses swung around and flew back over the field for low-altitude strafing runs. "An eccentric rain of dark red slanting lines" shredded a row of parked planes and cut down men running across the airfield. Dickinson saw a man on a bicycle pedaling across a causeway connecting Namur Island to Roi Island: he may have been a pilot trying to get to one of the Japanese planes. One of the American SBDs dived over the causeway and strafed him. "Probably in the history of wheeling no bicycle has ever been pedaled more furiously than that one, crossing the trestle ahead of the red-hot whip lashes of U.S. bullets," wrote Dickinson. "But with a froglike jump for the water the Jap defaulted the race."

Those Dauntlesses that had dropped their entire payload turned away to make good their escape. They were chased by flak bursts and by the Japanese fighters, mostly now above them and looking for an opportunity to make high side runs. The pilots poured on all the throttle their engines would take. The rear-seat gunners fired their tracers at the pursuing Japanese fighters and beat them off. These fighters were not the feared Zeros but the older, slower, less maneuverable Nakajima Ki-27 Type 97s (Allied code name "Nate"). At least one was shot out of the sky by a rear gunner.

The American pilots would report a smashing success over Roi, with three enemy fighters shot down, seven bombers shot up on the ground, two aircraft hangars leveled, a fuel tank destroyed, an ammunition storage unit blown to kingdom come, and a radio station flattened. Four American SBDs had been lost with the death of all their crews.

The torpedo planes meanwhile flew on to attack the ships anchored off Kwajalein atoll, forty-four miles to the south. Arriving over the anchorage, Lieutenant Commander Eugene Lindsey radioed that there were "suitable objectives" at Kwajalein. Air Group Commander Howard L. Young, circling high over Roi, relayed the report to several SBDs that had dropped only their smaller wing-mounted bombs, preserving their 500-pound bombs, and ordered them south to join the Devastators over the anchorage. Young's message was picked up on the Enterprise, and Halsey ordered aloft nine more torpedo planes that had been held in reserve.

The southward flight of the Dauntlesses over the huge lagoon was slow, because they had dived low over Roi and would have to climb back to altitude to regain proper attacking position. They soon caught sight of the big anchorage inside the atoll, which resolved as "a vast ruffle of beach sand embroidered with lacy surf and touched here and there with green." There were about twenty Japanese ships moored there, including a pair of heavy cruisers and three or four submarines. The work done by the torpedo bombers was evident, as several ships were emitting columns of heavy black smoke, and others were listing visibly. All of the ships were firing their anti-aircraft weapons, and a complex geometry of tracer lines reached up for the American aircraft. But there were no enemy fighters at that end of the atoll, and the accuracy of the antiaircraft guns was very poor.

The SBDs made proper dive-bombing attacks, at a 70-degree dive angle, with lots of flak bursts blossoming in the air around them, but none was shot down. Bombs struck around the ships, sending up tall geysers near the decks. About an hour later, the reserve strike of nine torpedo planes arrived and made a low run, flying directly through the largely ineffective flak, and sent torpedoes into two oil tankers and a 17,000-ton converted ocean liner that had been hit once earlier. One of the cruisers made a run for the sea but was stopped dead by two torpedoes. Several other ships were torpedoed. The dive-bombers and torpedo planes would grossly overestimate the damage they had done to the ships in the lagoon at Kwajalein, but the score was still good. The attackers had sunk a 6,500-ton transport and a subchaser, and had damaged nine other ships, including the light cruiser *Katori*. The local shore support facilities were very limited and the damage would not be easily repaired. Eighteen planes had been damaged or destroyed. The attack had also killed about ninety Japanese, including the Marshall Islands commander, Rear Admiral Yukichi Yashiro.

Shorn of their bombs and torpedoes, the Dauntlesses and Devastators banked east for the long flight back to the carrier. They had ample fuel and were not pursued by enemy planes. The sun was well above the horizon and the overcast had started to break up. When their navigation boards indicated that they were almost home, they peered down at the sea and immediately spotted the flat, rectangular deck of the *Enterprise*. They entered the approach circle in an orderly procession and landed without difficulty shortly after 9 a.m.

As each aviator stepped down off his wing, he demanded to know the status of his squadron mates. What planes had failed to return? Which chairs in the squadron ready rooms would be empty? Famished and tired, hair matted, flight suits stained with sweat, they descended to the wardroom and took sandwiches from trays. The pilots ate quickly, knowing they might be ordered back into the sky at any moment. The deck crews and ordnance gangs were busy refueling and rearming their airplanes. The day's action was far from finished—there were more strikes to be flown, and there was the constant danger that Japanese planes not yet destroyed on the ground would find the *Enterprise* and pounce on her. "These young pilots acted as if they were playing football," Admiral Halsey later said. "They'd fight like the devil, then take a short time-out, and get back into the fight again."

Live radio transmissions from the American fighters engaged over Wotje and Taroa on the nearby Maloelap atoll were piped into the squadron ready rooms, and the aviators listened to that chatter intently, with expert ears. "I could hear voices from the planes making the attacks," recalled Lieutenant Dickinson; "just the voices lifted out of the whole concert of battle noise. You could recognize the voice of the group commander as he portioned out the field, then recognize the voices of the squadron commanders assigning objectives. . . . Now and then we heard an exultant voice and even whoops as somebody hit his target." It was more than the adrenaline-fueled excitement of air combat. It was a dam burst of pent-up anxiety, a flood of relief to be finally engaged with the enemy almost two months after Pearl Harbor. "Bingo! Bingo! I got one! . . . Ease off to the right. . . . That big one's mine. . . . Get that cruiser heading off to the right! . . . Take 'em home, boys, take 'em home! . . . I'm all out of ammunition. . . . Who has lots of gas and ammo left? . . . Affirmative from Blue. . . . OK, I will go along. . . . I will pick up that guy yet. . . . We sure got that big bastard, didn't we, sir?"

Those attacks were being carried out by the twelve F4F Wildcats of Fighting Six, which had been pressed into service as short-range bombers, with 100-pound bombs tucked under each wing. Six planes under the command of the VF-6 skipper, Lieutenant Commander Wade McClusky, had been sent to attack Wotje; six more under Lieutenant James S. Gray had been dispatched to attack Taroa, farther to the south. Wotje was no more than thirty miles south of the *Enterprise*, close enough that men on the carrier's deck could actually see columns of smoke rising from the stricken airfield, the black antiaircraft bursts, and even the tiny silver glints of the airplanes.

McClusky's group, flying the short hop to the target, had climbed to 10,000 feet and then descended over Wotje at high speed in a dive-bombing attack. They had aimed their first set of 100-pound bombs at a cluster of support buildings alongside the small coral airstrip. The base below was quiescent during their first run, but when they turned back for a strafing run, the antiaircraft guns soon blazed from the island batteries and the ships in the lagoon. There was no fighter opposition and none of the Wildcats was lost. McClusky circled to assess damage, counted several burning buildings, and then hauled off to return to the carrier.

On schedule, racing in at flank speed from the east, were Admiral Spruance's cruisers *Northampton* and *Salt Lake City* and the destroyer *Dunlap*. The three ships formed a line of battle, and at 7:15 a.m. they opened fire on a pair of merchant ships anchored in the lagoon at Wotje. That promising bombardment was broken up by a periscope sighting, which prompted Spruance to order an abrupt change of course. During the ensuing lull, the Japanese ships in the lagoon weighed anchor and ran for safety. "Then we reversed course and stood along the atoll looking for targets and for the airfield," Spruance later wrote. Japanese shore guns opened up and sent towers of water around the hulls of the American ships. "Pretty soon the splashes came closer to us, and we were straddled by splashes." During that artillery duel, Spruance's first experience of combat, the unflappable admiral stood erect on his bridge, observing the fall of the enemy's salvos, and did not flinch when members of his staff ducked for cover. His cruisers scored some productive hits on shore targets, leaving some of the buildings on Wotje in flames, but lookouts continued to see periscopes on every side (all of those sightings were probably in error) and emergency course adjustments interfered with the accuracy of the gunners. Spruance remained engaged for almost three hours, suffering no hits to his ships. Shortly before 10 a.m., he ordered his little squadron away to the east for his scheduled rendezvous with the *Enterprise*.

Lieutenant Gray's group, sent farther south to seek out the mysterious island of Taroa at the southern end of Maloelap atoll, at first attacked the wrong target. From 15,000 feet, they mistook the uninhabited island of Tjan for Taroa. Lieutenant Gray and his wingman, Lieutenant (jg) Wilmer Rawie, dived low and dropped one each of their wing-mounted bombs on the unoffending little wisp of beach and palms. Grasping their error, they climbed back to 5,000 feet and led the sextet of Wildcats farther southeast. When Taroa came into view, there was no mistaking it: it was a much more substantial air base than the intelligence reports had led them to expect. There were two long coral runways, one more than a mile in length. There were half a dozen large hangars and support buildings. Several twin-engine Mitsubishi G3M medium bombers (Allied code name "Nell") were parked along the runway. Captain Thomas M. Shock's ships, sent in to bombard the island from the sea, had already been sighted by coastal lookouts, and the base was a hornet's nest.

Three Japanese fighters managed to get into the air right ahead of the arrival of the Wildcats, and they rose to intercept the intruders. Gray pushed down his nose and led his little squadron of makeshift bombers in to attack the parked G3M bombers. Those bombers, he knew, represented an existential threat to the *Enterprise*, just 100 miles north—should they be armed, fueled, and launched, they could easily overtake the carrier and send her to the bottom. Better to wipe them out while they were still on the ground. The Wildcats dived low and strafed the bombers, but they had not been armed with the incendiary rounds best suited to that kind of work, and in many cases their .50-caliber machine guns jammed. Half a dozen 100-pound bombs were dropped on the airfield, punching craters in the coral.

The fighters—not Zeros but the previous-generation A5M4 Type 96 ("Claudes")—gave heated pursuit. Lieutenant Rawie maneuvered beneath

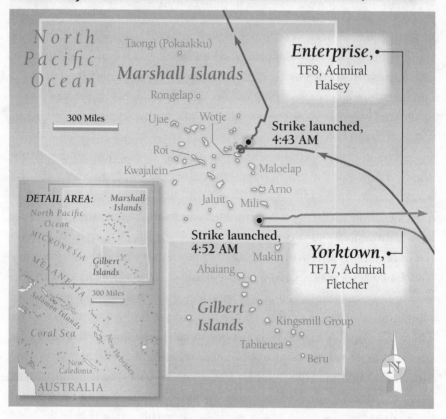

Halsey's Raid in the Marshalls February 1, 1942

one of those planes and fired a close-range burst that tore the fighter's bowels out. Witnesses on the *Chester* were cheered to see the Japanese fighter go down: "One specklike plane expanded magically into a ball of flame and plunged into the palms, leaving a hot red streak above it." That was the first recorded kill of the war by an American navy fighter pilot. Rawie continued on, banked sharply left, and headed back to make a head-on pass at another Japanese plane. Both pilots now held course into the oncoming propeller of his adversary: neither betrayed any inclination to turn away. "This being my first head-on approach," Rawie wrote in his diary, "I muffed it & pressed home too far & hit the Jap's wing with my underside." Both planes suffered in the glancing collision, but the sturdy Grumman remained in the air while the lighter and more fragile Mitsubishi was forced to circle back to the airstrip for an emergency landing. Rawie was then chased by a third Japanese fighter, and saw tracer bullets reaching out for him across his peripheral vision, so he gunned the throttle and banked out over the lagoon and into the clouds. He returned safely to the *Enterprise*.

All that time, the Japanese ground crews bravely soldiered on, pushing their fighters and bombers into takeoff position; and several more enemy planes rose from the airstrip while the aerial melee raged over their heads. Several Japanese aircraft flew out to attack the *Chester* and her two accompanying destroyers offshore, which had kept up a steady fire on the air base for about twenty-five minutes, blowing big craters in the airstrip and setting some of the buildings on fire. The *Chester* maneuvered violently to avoid the air attacks, but she could not manage to escape one of the Type 96s that made a steep diving run from 8,000 feet and planted a 30-kilogram bomb on her stern, blowing a hole in her deck and killing eight of her crew. She was able to proceed under her own power at normal speed, however, and Captain Shock signaled a withdrawal to the east.

The Wildcat pilots, frustrated nearly to the point of tears by the recurring problem of jamming guns, all got away cleanly. Gray's was the last American plane in the vicinity, and he had to twist and dive to escape a horde of vengeful Japanese fighters. His airplane was badly shot up, but he managed to shake free of his pursuers by flying into a bank of low-lying cloud. When he landed on the *Enterprise*, the deck crew was amazed that the bullet-ridden plane had managed the return journey. The *Enterprise* supply officer thought it "looked like the moths had been at it in the attic all summer." The jury-rigged armor plating, installed the day before, was thoroughly nicked and scarred, and had probably saved Gray's life. Here was dramatic proof that the F4F Wildcat, for all the criticism of its sluggish performance, could stand up to heavy punishment.

The American pilots reported that only one of Taroa's twin-engine G3M bombers (out of nine) had been set afire on the ground. Halsey wanted the bombers knocked out: the base would have to be attacked again. The admiral ordered a second strike by Dauntlesses returned from Kwajalein. This strike was led by Lieutenant Commander Bill Hollingsworth, skipper of Bombing Six. The 500-pound bombs carried on the bellies of the SBDs did not have to score direct hits on the parked bombers: a near miss was enough to wreck those planes. The Japanese fighters were all on the ground, apparently to be refueled and rearmed. "This attack encountered no aerial opposition but there was heavy AA fire," the *Enterprise's* after-action report read. "A fuel tank, two hangars, and a radio station, four or five two-engine bombers, and several fighters are known to have been destroyed on this attack." None of the American planes was lost. A third strike of SBDs, led by Lieutenant Richard Best, poured on more destruction. A radio installation and several fuel tanks were set on fire, and a new stone administration building was reduced to rubble. A fourth strike left the *Enterprise* at 11:22 a.m., this one aimed at Wotje, and comprising eight Dauntlesses and nine Devastators under Commander Howard Young. Shortly after noon they arrived over Wotje, found no fighter opposition, and took their time hitting the airfield installations, buildings, and the ships in the anchorage.

The *Enterprise* had been a hive of activity since long before dawn, her flight deck constantly engaged in recovering and launching airplanes. Conceived as a quick hit-and-run raid, the attack had instead developed into a nine-hour shuttle-bombing operation in which returning planes landed, refueled, rearmed, and then headed back into the sky to revisit the enemy bases. She had also kept a combat air patrol of F4F fighters orbiting protectively overhead. At one point during the morning, she briefly had every aircraft in her inventory aloft. For all those hours she remained in a five- by twenty-five-mile rectangle north of Maloelap atoll. She had thrown heavy punches at Japanese air bases all up and down the Marshalls, and done plenty of damage.

The deck crews were hot and tired, their blue chambray shirts stained with sweat and grease; they listened with burning interest to the radioed voices of the pilots piped through the ship's loudspeakers. Men on the carrier kept their eyes peeled for incoming planes, and the antiaircraft gun crews remained alert at their weapons. When green blips appeared on the *Enterprise's* primitive radar screens, the fighter director officer (FDO) classed them as "bogeys," or unidentified incoming planes. He radioed the patrolling fighters and vectored them out on a course to intercept. The Wildcats raced out toward each new constellation of specks on the southern or western horizons, gave them a long hard look, and confirmed that they were the carrier's own airplanes. The *Enterprise* prepared to receive them by swinging her bow into the wind, gunning her engines, raising her speed to near maximum; on the flight deck, the arresting cables were tensioned and the crash barriers were raised. All men on the deck retreated to safety.

As the planes entered the landing circle they passed close to starboard, circled across the bow, flew downwind to port, and then made a final turn aft, directly above the wake. A spotter confirmed that landing gear, flaps, and tailhook were all down. The landing signal officer (LSO) stood prominently on the port quarter and held his two yellow paddles high over his head. At the moment of truth he either waved both paddles above his head—the "wave-off," requiring the pilot to pour on throttle, pass over the deck, and return to the landing circle for a fresh approach—or drew his right-hand paddle across his throat—the "cut," telling the pilot to chop his throttle and let his aircraft fall to the deck, where the tailhook seized one of the cables and brought the plane to an abrupt, jarring halt. The deck crews sprinted out to release the cable from the hook; the hydraulic crash barriers retracted into the deck; and the pilot abruptly gunned his engine to taxi his aircraft forward of the barrier. The barrier shot back up, the arresting wires were tensioned, and the deck was made clear for the next plane in the landing circle. "A tricky and a dangerous business," wrote Ordnanceman Kernan, "and everything depended on doing it fast and doing it well."

Admiral Halsey watched from his flag bridge, dressed in a leather jacket and an oversized white sun helmet. He listened eagerly to the radio chatter of the American pilots, which revealed a fair picture of the action: "Get away from that cruiser, Jack! She's mine! . . . Bingo! . . . Look at that big bastard burn!" He often summoned the squadron leaders to report to him in person. During lulls in the action he sometimes retired to his cabin, where he smoked a cigarette, or tried to lose himself in a paperback novel, or just lay in his bunk and started at the ceiling. By remaining so long in the theater of operations, within easy reach of half a dozen Japanese air bases in broad daylight, he was pushing his luck, and he knew it. Though the destroyer screen was hyper-alert, the danger of submarine attacks grew more critical the longer the *Enterprise* lingered in the neighborhood. The task force was on Wotje's doorstep, sometimes even close enough to see the air action over the island. It was surprising that no enemy planes had approached.

Had the American airstrikes been so effective that the Japanese could not mount a counterattack? Or did they simply have no idea that the *Enterprise* was there? At one o'clock in the afternoon, Lieutenant Commander Hollingsworth of Bombing Six, having made three separate strikes that day, asked: "Admiral, don't you think it's time we got the hell out of here?" Halsey replied: "I've been thinking the same thing myself." The last of the group were taken aboard at 1:22 p.m., and the entire task force turned northeast and poured on steam.

The Japanese had indeed been caught largely by surprise, and would engage in bitter self-criticism after the day's raid. In retrospect, they would realize that the signs had been there. Submarine *I-23* had sighted Halsey's task force at sea at the beginning of January, and as a result alerts had been sent to all the bases in the Marshalls. After the *Saratoga* was torpedoed on January 11, they concluded that the Americans would keep their remaining carriers out of harm's way; when there were no further radio intercepts or sightings in the vicinity, they relaxed their guard a bit. The Marshalls' air defenses had been entrusted to the 24th Air Flotilla (*kohi sentai*), under the command of Rear Admiral Eiji Gota. The local air forces amounted to thirty-three carrier fighters, nine G3M medium bombers, and nine seaplanes. He did not have enough airplanes or pilots to maintain constant air search patterns around the islands. Rear Admiral Sukeyoshi Yatsushiro, who ran the Marshalls Defense Force from a stone headquarters on Kwajalein, had hosted his staff officers at a dinner party the night before the raid, and the sake had no doubt flowed freely. The next morning he was buried under the rubble of his headquarters when it was flattened by a 500-pound bomb. Yatsushiro was the first Japanese admiral killed in the war.

As Taroa licked its wounds, five undamaged G3M bombers lifted off from its pockmarked airstrip and streaked north in search of the American intruders. This strike, which got aloft at about noon, was led by Lieutenant Kazuo Nakai. They searched fruitlessly above the cloud cover for ninety minutes, but at 1:30 p.m. caught sight of the fleeing *Enterprise* through a gap in the cumulus clouds. Nakai pushed his airplane's nose down in a shallow dive, picking up speed; his four companions followed in a loose "V" formation. They appeared as a cluster of blips on the *Enterprise* radar plot, and the FDO ordered the orbiting Wildcats to intercept. This time no one doubted that they were enemy, as the American attack planes were all aboard. Four Wildcats made visual contact with the enemy at 10,000 feet. By that time, the incoming Japanese bombers were a mere fifteen miles away from the *Enterprise*, and doing their best to remain hidden in the clouds. Before the American fighters could get into proper attacking position, the Japanese planes entered the range of the screening ships' antiaircraft fire, and the F4Fs were forced (according to doctrine) to sheer away.

The five intruders dropped through the cloud ceiling at an altitude of 6,000 feet and sped directly toward the starboard bow of the *Enterprise* at a speed of about 250 knots. The piercing, importunate *beep-beep-beep-beep* of

the general alarm sounded on every ship in the task force. "It is a continuous ringing," Dickinson recalled, "a series of dashes made with an electric
bell. A deaf man could hear that clangor." The *Enterprise*'s antiaircraft guns
opened up and "the noise sounded terrific in the steel walls of the ready
room, as it might on the inside of a thunderbolt. The ship shook each time
a bigger gun was fired. We had smaller guns that went off with a crack and
plenty of machine guns to fill any chinks in the tumult." On deck below,
Alvin Kernan and his mates were working to attach a torpedo to the belly
of one of the TBD Devastators when they heard the big 5-inch antiaircraft
guns open up above their heads, and a voice over the loudspeaker cried:
"Stand by to repel enemy air attack." The ship, maneuvering to spoil the
aim of the enemy bombers, turned violently to starboard, causing the deck
to heel sharply to port—and the torpedo they were handling skittered away
across the oily steel deck. The ordnancemen scrambled after it, pounced on
it, and lashed it down to a ring bolt. "I wanted to get the hell out of there,"
Kernan said, "but we couldn't leave the torpedo with its unarmed but still
dangerous charge for fear it would break loose and smash into a bulkhead
and explode."

The carrier and her escorts threw up an impressive volume of antiaircraft
fire, but it was largely futile: the flak bursts tended to appear well behind the
rapidly oncoming planes. Halsey lamented, "Our AA guns might as well
have been water pistols," and Captain George D. Murray of the *Enterprise*
judged that the ineffectiveness of the AA gunners was "a matter of grave
concern." As the enemy planes drew closer the 1.1-inch gun mounts on the
catwalk opened up, and Kernan, unable to see the Japanese planes from his
station in the hangar deck, knew that "when the small-caliber guns cut in,
it was time to put your head down."

All five Japanese planes continued charging along their fixed bombing
track. At an altitude of 3,000 feet, their bomb bay doors opened and sticks
of 100-kilogram bombs fell in a diagonal line behind them. Captain Murray, watching those well-aimed bombs grow larger, called for full power
to 30 knots and a hard turn to port. But now he ordered an ingenious
maneuver, calling for full reverse rudder to starboard: "The effect on the
ship was that its forward speed was checked and at the same time, the ship
was suddenly moved sideways out of its own track." The *Enterprise* neatly
"crabbed" or "sidestepped" the bombs, which fell in a tight pattern off her
starboard bow, some as close as 30 feet away. Those near misses sent up

towers of water to a height of 200 feet. Robert Casey, watching from the deck of the nearby *Salt Lake City*, thought the *Enterprise* had been blown out of the water—the geysers thrown up by the bombs completely obscured her from his view. "But the water comes down and the mist disperses and we see that the carrier has spun about," he wrote. "The bombs fell precisely where she was when the planes came out of the cloud. But by the time they hit she was somewhere else."

One of those near misses had sent fragments into the carrier's port side, which cut a gasoline line and started a fire on the flight deck. Through the loudspeaker a voice cried: "Fire! On the flight deck, aft." An antiaircraft gunner was hit in the leg, so badly that the limb was nearly severed at the upper thigh. He remained at his post, but soon died from loss of blood.

As the bombers pulled out of their dives, scarcely 1,500 feet above the sea, one banked left and came roaring back toward the *Enterprise*. That was the flight leader, Lieutenant Nakai, whose plane had been hit (probably by a flak burst, possibly by one of the fighters). Smoke trailed aft from both engines, and Nakai may have judged that his plane had been mortally wounded and could not make the flight back to Taroa. He seemed determined to make a suicide crash attack on the carrier. He approached from astern, in much the same way that a friendly plane would approach for a normal landing. Bruno P. Gaido, an aviation machinist's mate second class, left his action station in the port catwalk and slid into the rear seat of a parked dive-bomber. He seized the gun and began firing at the incoming G3M. Captain Murray, understanding Nakai's intentions, ordered a hard turn to starboard. Gaido kept firing steadily, standing up to depress his gun; a stream of tracers went into the nose and cockpit of the big bomber at point-blank range. Lieutenant Nakai may have been killed by that determined fire, as his plane seemed not to maneuver at all in the last stage of his attack. His drifting G3M's wing struck a glancing blow off the port side of the flight deck and ripped a parked SBD in half, spilling debris and gasoline across the deck. Nakai's plane splashed into the sea: Gaido continued firing down at the sinking aircraft until the sea closed over it.

Lieutenant Dickinson and several fellow members of his squadron left their ready room to observe the results. The first thing they noticed was an overpowering, cloying odor of gasoline, copiously splashed across the flight deck. Fire control teams, dressed in padded suits with square hoods and rectangular visors, were spraying the deck down with foamite, a "frothy egg-white stuff." Halsey, watching from the flag bridge, was nervy—he told his staff that "my knees are crackin' together." The bombing attack had been deadly accurate, and the misses uncomfortably close. The admiral would no doubt have agreed with Captain Murray's judgment (expressed in the after-action report) that the *Enterprise*'s escape "can only be described as miraculous."

The *Enterprise* and her task force resumed their high-speed withdrawal. The ships tore through the sea at 30 knots, leaving long, plunging wakes behind them. Casey, on the *Salt Lake City*, was repeatedly sent sprawling to the cruiser's deck. "I had trouble getting to my feet with the shock and plunge of the ship," he wrote. "I smashed my head against the bell and battered my bones on the rails and skinned my knees. . . . We are sticking our nose into it and flinging spray up over the bridge. Our wake looks like a waving green stair carpet with white fringe and no particular pattern on a blue floor." Someone coined the phrase "Haul Ass with Halsey." The men of the task force would claim charter membership in the "Haul Ass with Halsey" club.

The *Enterprise* kept up a larger than usual fighter patrol and all of the antiaircraft guns were manned and armed. The carrier remained on high alert for air attacks, and her crew assumed that more enemy bombers would be coming. They were not wrong. At 4 p.m. the radar plots recorded two more incoming G3Ms, this time from an altitude of about 14,000 feet. They were quickly pounced upon by the nine Wildcats flying CAP. As the enemy aircraft came into range of the ships' 5-inch guns, the American fighters veered off to avoid friendly fire. The CAP leader, Lieutenant Commander McClusky, acted as a spotter for the antiaircraft gun crews. "Your bursts are low," he said over the radio. "Get them up. That's better. Now you're little high. Just a little lower now. Now you're on! You're on! You've got him!" One of the bombers rocked and trailed smoke. Both planes released 500-kilogram bombs from high altitude, but the *Enterprise* evaded with a hard turn to port and the bombs dropped harmlessly into the sea off the starboard bow. McClusky radioed, "Knock off AA fire. We'll take 'em." The fighters again bored in and registered several hits. One of the G3Ms burst into fire and glided into the sea. The other escaped with smoke trailing from its engine.

Now the sun lay low in the west, and the enveloping shelter of darkness was little more than two hours away. The task force continued to be haunted by radar contacts, and the Wildcats chased and shot down a Japanese floatplane (Aichi E13A1 Type 0, Allied code name "Jake") as evening approached. The sun set at 6:35 p.m, and a yellow moon rose ten minutes later. By seven, the *Enterprise* had landed all of her fighters and steamed away at high speed, engines roaring, to the northeast. The moon, one day past full, was bright enough that men on deck could read by it, and the ships trailed long, luminescent wakes that could have been seen from the sky, but no more strange planes approached that night. Halsey ordered a turn back to the northwest, hoping that this odd course would throw off any pursuers. At dawn, the Americans were relieved to find that they had sailed into a wet cold front, and were shrouded in rain and fog. The task force turned back to the northeast, toward Oahu. Dickinson called the weather a "nice air raid shelter," and Casey agreed that "Under the circumstances the fog is very acceptable." No flights were attempted in those conditions, and the aviators enjoyed a well-earned day of rest. Task Force 8's passage home was pleasingly uneventful.

The *Yorktown* and Task Force 17 had meanwhile attacked the islands of Jaluit and Mili in the southern Marshalls, and Makin in the Gilberts. The carrier had launched coordinated airstrikes at dawn on all three islands. Flight operations had been hindered by heavy overcast and intermittent squalls of rain; but the raids had not encountered anything like the determined opposition the *Enterprise* air group had found in the islands to the north. Results were meager. At Jaluit, eleven torpedo planes and seventeen dive-bombers dived through layers of wet murk and attacked auxiliary ships anchored in the lagoon. Two were hit, neither sunk. The wretched weather, rather than enemy resistance, claimed six American planes from that flight, lost at sea on the return. At Makin, nine dive-bombers attacked over the lagoon at dawn, possibly hitting an anchored minelayer (but failing to sink it), and lighting up two big Kawanishi Type 97 flying boats, also at anchor. The attack on Mili was a wasted effort, because the SBDs found no targets worth attacking.

The weather grew steadily worse as the morning wore on. The wind rose, the *Yorktown* was tossed in heavy seas, and visibility dropped to little more than zero. Flight operations were suspended for a time. But there were persistent radar contacts indicating the possible presence of Japanese planes, and shortly after 11 a.m. one of the destroyers sighted a strange aircraft west of the *Yorktown*. Conditions having abated enough to launch planes, Captain Elliott Buckmaster sent a division of Wildcats aloft to chase down the intruder. They searched fruitlessly amid rain and heavy overcast and returned empty-handed to the ship. Shortly after one that afternoon, the carrier's radar plot detected another snooper just thirty-four miles away. Wildcats were vectored out to intercept, and after a long game of cat and mouse through the cloud cover, two F4Fs trapped the enemy aircraft in a patch of clear sky. It was a big four-engine Kawanishi Type 97 flying boat, the same type as the two destroyed at anchor that morning at Makin. It was hit several times and exploded; flaming debris fell into the sea within sight of the *Yorktown*. Buckmaster's colorful second-in-command, the recently promoted Captain J. J. "Jocko" Clark (who would soon command his own ship), offered a play-by-play summary over the *Yorktown*'s public address system. "Burn, you son of a bitch, burn!" he exulted.

Admiral Fletcher had planned another round of strikes in the afternoon, but the weather did not improve. Further operations risked losing more American airplanes without promising much in the way of results. Fletcher's run of bad luck seemed endless. Early that evening, Halsey radioed him with orders to disengage and return to Pearl.

AT DAWN ON FEBRUARY 5, the *Enterprise* lookouts glimpsed the green mountains of Oahu through a thick haze. She and the other ships of Task Force 8 approached Pearl Harbor on a tortuous zigzagging track—a measure against enemy submarines—and then raced in toward the entrance channel through two protective lanes of destroyers. For their arrival, Halsey had ordered that all hands dress in white uniforms and man their battle quarters. The *Enterprise* flew her huge battle flags. The ships in the harbor greeted them with a blare of whistles and sirens; sailors on their decks, also dressed in whites for the occasion, shouted and waved. Throngs of sailors and civilian workers stopped working and pressed down to the docks on Ford Island and the Navy Yard. Halsey stood on his flag bridge, high in the *Enterprise* superstructure; even from a great distance his white-clad head and shoulders could be seen above the rail as he saluted and waved. Admiral Nimitz, waiting with an entourage of staff officers on the docks, consented to be hoisted to the hangar deck in a bosun's chair. When he met Halsey on the flight deck, he seized his hand and said, "Bill, it was wonderful, a great job." Halsey, overcome, broke down in tears.

A message was read aloud over the public address system of each ship in the task force: "Commander Task Force 8 to Task Force 8: Well done! You have made history in the Marshalls. I am proud to have the honor to command you. God bless you! Halsey."

Never again in the entire course of the war would Halsey be more closely bonded to the men under his command. They gave him a nickname: "Bull" Halsey. For good measure, they gave him another: "Wild Bill." Rumors circulated that the next mission of the "Haul Ass with Halsey" club would take them deep into the heart of the western Pacific, to relieve MacArthur's beleaguered forces in the Philippines. Or possibly even to Tokyo itself, because "Wild Bill will try anything once."

Newspaper and radio correspondents, having been treated with barely concealed contempt by King and held at arm's length by Nimitz, had almost despaired of finding a star personality in the upper ranks of the navy. Now they had their man. The carrier raids would receive headline treatment in the American newspapers, alongside photos of a beaming Admiral Halsey. The significance of the raids would be exaggerated for effect, even equated with December 7—Pearl Harbor, it was said, had been "avenged." They provided a badly needed respite from the relentless onslaught of bad news emerging from the Pacific theater. They offset (in a small way) the dismal news that Singapore, Britain's main Pacific stronghold, had surrendered to the Japanese.

The estimates made by the *Enterprise* pilots of enemy ships and aircraft destroyed in the Marshalls proved grossly inflated. In all, Task Force 8 had sunk two transports and one smaller craft and damaged another transport and one smaller craft. Nine enemy bombers and three fighters had been destroyed on the ground or in the air. Several buildings had been damaged or destroyed. The Japanese had lost ninety men, including Admiral Yatsushiro. The Americans had degraded the immediate usefulness of Japan's Marshall Islands bases without putting them out of action. The damaged airstrips could be repaired, the installations rebuilt, the men replaced, and the air groups reinforced by the Fourth Fleet, based to the west in Truk. In that sense, the raids had provided a glimpse of the long air war of attrition that would have to be waged across a vast sea frontier. To destroy those outer perimeter bases permanently would not be possible for another two years.

But it was the first offensive operation mounted by the Pacific Fleet, and for that reason alone it was an important boost to morale and self-confidence at a time when those considerations had grown very important. It had provided valuable practice—the navy was learning how to fight by fighting. Seventy-seven pilots of the *Enterprise* air group had flown a total of 158 flights, a few logging five flights and ten hours of cockpit time in a single day. The ship had consumed 148,043 gallons of fuel; in the twenty-four-hour period prior to the raid, she had steamed more than 560 miles, a record for an aircraft carrier. Alvin Kernan wrote that the early carrier raids taught the men of the fleet the skills they needed to win the Battle of Midway. "It was amazing how long it took to get the hang of it and to react instantly in the right way," he observed. "War, we gradually learned, is a state of mind before it can be anything else."

As the officers huddled and debriefed, all agreed that there was plenty of room for improvement. The mission had exposed serious defects in maintaining a task force formation at high speed, in underway refueling, in the use of radar and communications to direct fighters over carriers. The F4F Wildcat's lack of maneuverability and speed in a climb were again noted, and the chronic jamming of its .50-caliber guns was deemed a disgrace. The TBD Devastator was dangerously slow, and it seemed a miracle that none of the *Enterprise*'s torpedo bombers was lost. The ineptitude of antiaircraft gunnery was lamented by everyone, including the gunners themselves—better weapons and more training (especially target practice conducted from ships traveling at speeds of more than 25 knots) were urgently needed. Defense against air attack was hampered by the impossibility of distinguishing between friendly and hostile aircraft on the radar screen. Lookouts had been too quick to imagine submarine contacts. As for the cruisers and destroyers, their gunnery had been poor, and it would have to improve if the surface navy hoped to make a decent showing in the war. More fighters were needed on the carriers—there should be enough to provide ample escorts for outgoing airstrikes while also leaving some behind to protect the carrier. Robert Casey was amused by the earnest self-flagellation, which left the impression "that a great deed which yesterday had seemed like one of the most brilliant, audacious and effective naval performances of modern times was really something we ought to be ashamed of."

February and March would bring new hit-and-run raids on Japanese outposts. On February 20, the *Lexington* and a task force made a bold foray into the heart of the new Japanese empire in the south to hit the big Japanese base (wrested from the Australians) at Rabaul on New Britain. (The *Lex-*

ington was detected on approach by enemy reconnaissance planes and had to hightail it to the east.) Halsey and the Enterprise visited Wake Island on February 24, and then turned north to hit Marcus Island on March 4. The latter was not a terribly significant outpost, but it lay only 1,000 miles away from Tokyo. On March 10, a task force built around Lexington and Yorktown, under Vice Admiral Wilson Brown, Jr., sent carrier bombers to raid primitive Japanese airfields at Salamaua and Lae on the north coast of New Guinea.

The value of those early American carrier raids has often been denigrated by historians. Even during the war, many Americans apparently held the same view; Morison quotes an officer who remarked that "The Japs didn't mind them any more than a dog minds a flea." For the men who went along on them, the impression was of a lot of high-speed steaming across interminable Pacific distances, culminating in a few hours of largely uncontested airstrikes. Casey, who was along for several of them, remarked that "we travel something like 20,000 miles in two months for a total of about five hours of tense action." When Halsey's February 1 attacks were reported in Tokyo, the radio and newspapers reacted with a snore. Moreover, the Japanese, no less prone than the Americans to over-reporting of results, believed they had inflicted heavy damage on the attacking forces. The fighters of the Chitose Air Group made wildly overoptimistic claims of their destruction of American planes—seventeen American aircraft were said to be shot down over Taroa, and the fighters on Roi claimed they had flamed five American bombers.

But a closer look at the private reactions of Japanese naval leaders leaves a sharply different impression. Halsey's raid arrived as a very nasty surprise. Admiral Matome Ugaki, chief of staff to Yamamoto, recorded his impressions in his diary. "They have come after all," he wrote. "They are some guys!" The raids were "a reproach that went to the heart"—they had "made us look ridiculous." Ugaki was disgusted that the Americans had not been detected on approach, and noted that the Marshall Islands should have been better prepared for such an attack than the Americans had been two months earlier, when the two nations were not yet at war. "After experiencing defensive weakness ourselves, we cannot laugh at the enemy's confusion at the time of the surprise attack on Pearl Harbor." He mourned the death of Admiral Yatsushiro, who had been a classmate at the Japanese Naval Academy at Etajima. Captain Yoshitake Miwa, Combined Fleet's chief of operations, reported that Yamamoto's entire staff was infuriated, but "could only grit their teeth and jump up and down in frustration."

As the first reports of the raids came in, the Japanese navy sent bombers based in Truk to chase to the east; several Truk-based submarines were also sent out to take up positions in case the American task forces came farther west. Japanese radio intelligence stations listened carefully for any violation of radio silence that would allow them to home in on Halsey's location, but received nothing except commercial broadcasts from Hawaii reporting the victory of the American task forces. Additional forces were sent out to sea to intercept any remaining U.S. ships. Ugaki lamented that the American raids had been well timed to coincide with the Japanese activity in the south. They had hit on a weak flank when the major Japanese forces were engaged elsewhere. "The enemy's attempt was most timely because our operations were focused in the southwest Pacific and the defensive strength in the Marshalls was thin," he wrote. "In addition to a fairly big result, they achieved their purpose of diverting our strength. Carriers closed in and heavy cruisers' bombardment was also most daring. It seems we have been somewhat fooled. . . . There is little chance of the enemy coming up again tomorrow morning. Anyway, we have missed the game." Dispatching so much naval force on a wild goose chase across the Pacific was "futile" and "impulsive," according to air officer Mitsuo Fuchida. Twelve hundred miles lay between Truk and the Marshalls: in the time it would take the Japanese force to cover that distance, the American task force would surely be safe in port. Even after it was clear the Americans had escaped, two of the six carriers in Nagumo's force, *Shokaku* and *Zuikaku*, were detached to patrol the waters off Japan. That reduced the striking power of the fearsome *Kido Butai*.

Perhaps the most far-reaching consequence of Halsey's raids was that they brought home to the Japanese admirals the vulnerability of their capital. Even if such a raid could not do great damage, the navy's "face" was very much at stake. Ugaki correctly predicted that the Americans would soon attempt to land a direct punch on Tokyo itself. "They will adopt this kind of method in the future," he wrote on February 2. "And the most probable move they would make would be an air raid on our capital. . . . It was fortunate for us that the enemy only scratched us on this occasion and gave us a good lesson instead of directly attacking Tokyo." "Whatever happens," Captain Miwa agreed, "we must absolutely prevent any air attack on Tokyo." And since there was no foolproof defense against carrier raids, a conviction grew within their minds that they must find a way to get rid of the American carriers. Thus were sown the seeds of Yamamoto's plan to hurl the entire strength of the Imperial Japanese Navy against Midway, in hopes of forcing the American carriers out of Pearl Harbor to fight and lose the decisive battle of the war.

Chapter Seven

S AMUEL ELIOT MORISON, THE FIRST AND GREATEST HISTORIAN OF American naval operations in the Second World War, compared Japan's southward offensive to "the insidious yet irresistible clutching of multiple tentacles." It was a wide-ranging sea-air-land *Blitzkrieg*, as precisely choreographed as a ballet. The attacks fell upon one Allied target after another, with staccato rapidity, across a 6,000-mile front. "Like some vast octopus," wrote Morison, the Japanese advance "relied on strangling many small points rather than concentrating on a vital organ. No one arm attempted to meet the entire strength of the ABDA ["American-British-Dutch-Australian"] fleet. Each fastened on a small portion of the enemy and, by crippling him locally, finished by killing the entire animal."

The tip of the Japanese spear was the land-based medium bomber, often accompanied by the ubiquitous Zero. The long range of those aircraft allowed leapfrogging advances of 500 miles or more. Troop convoys approached soon thereafter, protected by cruisers and destroyers. Small parties of resourceful Japanese soldiers were put ashore on lush jungle islands where the Allies had little or no interior communications. They advanced quickly against weak local defenses. Again and again, they captured Allied airfields intact, or with slight damage. Japanese aircraft flew in and began staging for the next series of attacks farther south. When Japanese amphibious forces took control of the air base at Jolo Island, twenty-four Zeros of the Tainan Air Corps flew 1,200 nautical miles to land at the new field. That was an extraordinarily long flight for those single-engine, one-seat aircraft, but all arrived safely.

Two weeks after Pearl Harbor, Allied resistance was crumbling so quickly that planners at the Imperial General Headquarters in Tokyo brought forward their plans for the next phase of the war. That was the invasion of the Dutch East Indies and seizure of its coveted oil fields, the primary war aim of Japan's entire southern offensive. Those assets offered the prospect of self-sufficiency for a Japanese war economy that had until now relied overwhelmingly on imported American oil. The Dutch fields needed to be taken sooner rather than later, as Japan was even then eating into its limited oil reserves. The Japanese would not wait to finish off the beleaguered Allied armies in the Philippines and Malaya—using the airfields wrested from the Americans and British, they would strike south into the heart of Field Marshal Sir Archibald Wavell's newly constituted ABDA command before his forces could dig in.

The rapid advance of Japanese forces on the main Philippine island of Luzon opened the way to an early invasion of the southern island of Mindanao and the capture of the American seaplane base at Davao, which provided a fine staging base for operations in the shallow waters of the Makassar Strait, the Molucca Sea, and the complex island geography of southern Oceania. Landing parties were put ashore on the thinly populated islands against little or no Allied ground resistance. With the Makassar Strait in the hands of the Japanese, the route to Sumatra and Java was suddenly unguarded and exposed.

In late December 1941, Japanese forces landed at Kuching on Sarawak, and on Jolo, between Mindanao and Borneo in the Sulu Sea. Landings continued at Malaya, staged from Indochina through the Kra Isthmus of Siam, or across the Gulf of Siam. The great British naval base at Singapore, celebrated as the "Gibraltar of the East," was supposed to have stood as a bulwark against Japanese advances on the islands south of Malaya. But with command of the sea and air yielded to the Japanese, Singapore was isolated and neutralized, its still considerable defending forces in no position to harass the Japanese troop convoys bypassing its eastern flank. In January 1942, a convoy advanced through the South China Sea on eastern Sumatra, from the Makassar Strait on Dutch Borneo, and established new beachheads at Brunei (January 6) and Jesselton (January 11). Forces sailing from Davao landed at Tarakan Island (January 12) and Balikpapan (January 24) on eastern Borneo, and the Menado Peninsula (January 11) and Kendari (January 24) on Celebes. The little island of Amboina, with its fine airfield, was seized on January 31. Timor, a Portuguese colony, now lay within easy grasp to the south, and from there the long, defenseless north coast of Australia would lie exposed to the conquerors.

Borneo had been shared by the British and Dutch, neither of whom had adequate defensive forces in place. With the island's colonial masters spread too thin, the Japanese forces rapidly gained the upper hand. The Dutch had blown up or set fire to the oil rigs to prevent their use by the Japanese. Between eighty and a hundred Dutch civilians were murdered in reprisal for that application of the "scorched earth" principle. In any case, Japanese engineers got the oil flowing again soon enough. Resistance on the island would be snuffed out by mid-February.

On January 10, the newly appointed Marshal Wavell, supreme commander of ABDACOM, arrived in Java and set up his headquarters in Lembang, seventy-five miles southeast of Batavia. His large staff did not lack for talent—he had under his command a retinue of high-ranking generals and admirals of four nations—but it was all too clear that General Marshall's experiment in command unity would be futile and short-lived. Admiral Hart, commander in chief of the U.S. Asiatic Fleet, had arrived by submarine in Surabaya Harbor on January 1. He would command the ABDA naval forces, officially designated as "ABDAFLOAT" (in those dire conditions the acronym was perhaps too clever). Hart had ordered the remaining surface units of the Asiatic Fleet out of the Philippines after its main base at Cavite had been left in smoking ruins by Japanese bombers three days after Pearl Harbor. The largest ship in the fleet, formerly Hart's flagship, was a heavy cruiser, the USS *Houston*. She had once served as President Roosevelt's yacht. She was accompanied by two other cruisers and thirteen ancient four-stack destroyers.

Thomas Hart had been the first major military commander to voice the unpopular view that the Philippines were indefensible and therefore doomed. His early withdrawal had not endeared him to General MacArthur, who faulted the navy for failing to provide adequate support against the Japanese invasion convoys landing troops on Luzon. But the decision to pull the fleet out of the Philippines was the correct one. Without air cover, the fleet was defenseless, and its withdrawal to the south was necessary if it was to have any effect at all in the war.

Even as the rapid Japanese advance seemed to throw the Allies' basic prewar assumptions into doubt, several of the ABDA commanders were upbeat about their chances. As is usual in such cases, the commanders were expected to buck up the morale of their subordinates, and their bravado may have been calculated. But Wavell seemed adamant when he predicted that the Japanese tide sweeping down the Malay Peninsula would be stopped dead at Singapore, even after learning that the island's northern, land-facing defense works were inadequate. As late as January 31, two weeks before the surrender of more than 60,000 British and empire troops to a much smaller Japanese army, Wavell was expressing confidence that the island would stand. British commanders in Burma likewise thought they could hold the line. The Dutch vice admiral Conrad E. H. Helfrich pledged that his forces would thwart Japanese troop landings in the East Indies. None of those optimistic forecasts would be borne out.

The Japanese clearly intended to take Java, the richest island in the East Indies. They prepared two large invasion forces to advance down the east and west coasts of Borneo to close on opposite sides of the island in a pincer movement. It appeared that the best hope of the ABDA naval forces was to try to intercept and destroy (or at least whittle down) those fleets, perhaps sinking troopships and killing a large number of Japanese soldiers before they could get ashore. In January, however, the ABDA naval forces were busily employed in convoying Allied freighters south, and could not mount effective resistance.

As their transnational crews by now suspected, the ships of the ABDA fleet were pitifully unprepared to meet the onslaught. Nor did they have the option to flee to safer waters and fight another day. It was their duty to face probable annihilation. Their mission was to buy time, to stall the onrushing Japanese while the Allies brought reinforcements into the theater. The fleet itself was inherently weak, a four-nation flotilla of mostly obsolete cruisers and First World War–vintage destroyers. It was a second-rate force even by the assessment of its own commanders. The ongoing decimation of Allied airpower in the theater meant that they would fight, for the most part, without air cover.

Hart organized his surface warships into a "Striking Force" based at Surabaya, under the command of Rear Admiral W. A. Glassford. Glass-ford's ships sortied several times in mid-January, but were stymied by a lack of air reconnaissance and often failed to discover incoming enemy convoys. He withdrew to Kupang Bay in eastern Timor to refuel, and was still there on the morning of January 20 when he received a PBY Catalina's sighting report of an enemy invasion force off Balikpapan, a major Dutch oil-producing complex on the eastern coast of Borneo. He dispatched four old "four-piper" destroyers to foil the landing. They sailed into Makassar Strait, zigzagging to throw enemy air patrols off the scent. Shortly after midnight on January 24, they reached Balikpapan Bay. Admiral Hart sent a one-word command by encrypted radio signal: "Attack!" Commodore Paul Talbot, in the *John D. Ford*, instructed the other captains: "Torpedo attack; hold gunfire until the fish are gone; use initiative and prosecute the strike to your utmost."

The destroyers approached at 27 knots. Fortunately for them, the Japanese fleet was anchored close inshore, and the oil facilities had been set ablaze by the retreating Dutch. That provided a fine backlight. The torpedomen picked out the anchored transports as clear silhouettes. In an action lasting over three hours, Talbot's destroyers made several close approaches and fired all of their torpedoes, sinking three enemy troop transports and a torpedo boat.

That action off Balikpapan was a tactical victory for the Allies, but also a disappointment inasmuch as nine of twelve Japanese transports survived the attack. Having achieved complete surprise, the attackers could have done better. Many of the American torpedoes missed their targets and many more likely hit but failed to explode. The attack did not prevent the important port and oil fields at Balikpapan from falling into the enemy's hands. The victory provided a welcome interruption to the deluge of bad news, but it did nothing to check the speed of the Japanese offensive into the Dutch East Indies, and it was the last significant accomplishment of the ABDA fleet.

IN THE PHILIPPINES, General MacArthur's Manila headquarters had recovered its equilibrium after the chaotic first days of the war, when Luzon's sea and air bases had been pulverized by Japanese airstrikes. The imperious general hoped to rally his combined American and Filipino army to meet the Japanese invasion forces advancing on Manila from their beachheads.

Forty years of war planning had envisioned that the defenders would pull back behind fortified lines bisecting the neck of the Bataan Peninsula, which commanded the sea approaches to Manila Bay. There they would dig in and await rescue by a seaborne convoy to be brought across the Pacific under the wing of the U.S. Navy. But MacArthur, charged with preparing the Filipino army to assume full responsibility for the nation's defense after 1946, could not stomach a plan that yielded the country to a foreign invader. He hoped instead to meet and annihilate the Japanese forces at their beachheads. Such a strategy would have required (at a minimum) superior airpower, highly mobile infantry divisions, and a Pacific fleet that was both intact and committed to sail to the aid of the Philippines. In fact, none of those conditions existed. After the third day of the war, an American airplane was not often seen in the skies above Luzon. Even if the American-Filipino forces had been trained and equipped to move quickly to contest enemy beachheads (which they were not), the primitive condition of Luzon's roads made such operations impracticable. Most of the Pacific Fleet had been knocked out of action on December 7—but even if it had not been, the Europe-first strategy ruled out a large-scale rescue of the Philippines until 1943 at the earliest. Pulling the army back to Bataan was the only move that made any sense, and MacArthur should have done it the first week of the war.

The first Japanese troop landings had come ashore in northern Luzon on December 10. A much larger invasion force—some 50,000 troops with weapons, light tanks, and artillery—sailed from Formosa in a huge fleet of some eighty-four freighters and camouflaged troopships, landing at Lingayen Gulf, north of Manila, on December 22. Reiji Masuda, a merchant marine officer on the freighter *Arizona-maru*, recalled that the invasion convoy sailed "in two long lines extending beyond the horizon in both directions." The American submarine force, which had survived the early airstrikes, was expected to mete out heavy punishment on any enemy invasion convoys that approached the Philippines, but their performance was disappointing. A late sighting report did not give the boats sufficient time to move into position, and they could not maneuver freely in the shallow inland waters of the Lingayen Gulf.

A few U.S. Army B-17s and Navy PBYs appeared and managed to get some licks in on the convoy as it disgorged its troops, but casualties were minimal. Greater Japanese losses were sustained as a result of choppy seas and high winds, as several boats were overturned by breaking waves near the beach. "The swells were high," Masuda recalled. "It was terribly difficult to load soldiers and supplies on the bobbing boats. Enemy planes struck us at dawn, aiming primarily at the beachhead. Bullets from strafing planes chased our boats to the shore. *Arizona-maru* poured fire into the sky. We saw enemy planes spiraling down, trailing smoke. Our ship was rocked by the concussions of exploding bombs and the force of walls of water striking our sides. Most of the ships, however, unloaded successfully and the landing force began its drive on Manila."

It was the largest and most successful amphibious troop landing up to that point in history. The force got ashore with most of its artillery and supplies and about half of its tanks. The way to Manila now was open along Route 3, a paved road, one of the best in the country. The Japanese army advanced rapidly, brushing aside the green, poorly equipped conscripts of the Philippine army, who broke ranks and ran for their lives with distressing regularity. Artillery units manned by American troops were left exposed to withering frontal attacks by the Japanese banzai charges. MacArthur was besieged with requests from his commanders in the field for permission to withdraw.

On the 24th, a second Japanese force came ashore at Lamon Bay, sixty miles southeast of Manila on the east coast of Luzon. That came as a cruel surprise. Now two Japanese armies were advancing on the capital in a great pincer movement from two directions. General MacArthur, at his headquarters in Manila, saw the writing on the wall. He cabled a series of anxious missives to Washington. Could he be reinforced? He urgently needed more airpower. Could planes be ferried up from Australia? Could aircraft carriers get within range of the islands? General Marshall replied that assistance of any kind was unlikely. MacArthur was forced to fall back on War Plan Orange (WPO), the decades-old plan of abandoning Manila and staging a fighting retreat to Bataan, where the army would dig in for a long siege behind fortified lines. He declared the capital an "open city" and issued the order: "Put WPO-3 into effect." MacArthur told his air chief, General Lewis H. Brereton, to send the remaining B-17s out of harm's way. "You go on south. You can do me more good with the bombers you have left and those you should be receiving soon than you can here."

MacArthur and his staff folded up shop and sailed in an old coal steamer across the bay to Corregidor Island off Bataan. Filipino president Manuel Quezon, who was suffering from tuberculosis, made the agonizing decision to go with MacArthur—he feared for the fate of the Filipino people but was unwilling to act as a collaborator. The troops traveled north on Route 3 in long disorderly convoys of trucks, buses, jeeps, and even oxcarts. Horses and donkeys were enlisted to haul artillery pieces. The army shared the road with tens of thousands of civilian refugees on foot. Smoke rose above the dying capital, the work of looters and perhaps fifth columnists. It was Christmas Eve. At St. Fernando, the flow of civilians, troops, and vehicles out of the city met the southward torrent of retreating troops and civilian refugees who were scrambling to get out of the way of the advancing Japanese armies. Those two groups met and turned south together, like tributaries of a river, to the peninsula. The defensive lines held long enough to allow most of the forces engaged to move back through them before drawing back into Bataan.

The Japanese appear to have been caught by surprise by the retreat, and their air forces were strangely quiescent. Strafing attacks on the densely packed road to Bataan could have taken a devastating toll, but for once in the campaign no enemy planes appeared. Had the Japanese even knocked out a few key bridges, a large portion of MacArthur's forces might never have reached the relative safety of the peninsula. Many Filipinos had deserted the army, but those who remained fought with courage and fortitude, so the loss of their less determined comrades had the effect of raising the overall quality of the troops that got to Bataan.

The first Japanese troops entered Manila unopposed on January 2, 1942. Storefronts were boarded up; gangs of native looters were at work in some of the deserted storehouses; crowds of civilians stood and watched in stunned silence. At the house of the American high commissioner, the Japanese lowered the American flag in a military ceremony, and a Japanese sailor ground his feet into it. The Rising Sun was raised in its place, as a band played *Kimigayo*. General Masaharu Homma, the Japanese army commander, had made the mistake of believing that should his forces occupy Manila, the battle for the Philippines would be as good as won. He was slow to realize that the big fight was going to take place across the bay.

MacArthur's forces dug in behind the Abucay-Mauban line, which cut across the northern end of the peninsula and across the flank of an extinct volcano known as Mount Natib. Many of the front-line troops were elite Filipino units, determined to redeem the poor performance of their countrymen in the fight for Lingayen Gulf. MacArthur, who had received clear signals from Washington that he should not expect much in the way of timely aid, nonetheless told his troops on January 15, "Help is on the way from the United States. Thousands of troops and hundreds of planes are being dispatched. . . . No further retreat is possible. We have more troops in

Bataan than the Japanese have thrown against us; our supplies are ample; a determined defense will defeat the enemy's attack. I call upon every soldier in Bataan to fight in his assigned position, resisting every attack. This is the only road to salvation. If we fight, we will win; if we retreat, we will be destroyed."

Probing Japanese attacks on the eastern end of the line brought heavy fighting on January 9. The defenders fought tenaciously and repulsed those first attacks, and in those actions some of the Filipino troops fought with remarkable valor. In the ensuing days, however, Japanese attacks on the western end of the line, followed by ferocious counterattacks by the 51st Philippine Army Division, opened a breach in the defensive positions. Troops under Colonel Susumu Takechi punched a hole in the Abucay line and drove deep into the Abo-Abo river valley. Spirited counterattacks could not dislodge the Japanese. After observing conditions on the line, Lieutenant General Richard Sutherland recommended that troops should withdraw to the Bagoc-Orion line, which ran between two towns of those names, and MacArthur quickly ordered the pullback.

On January 24, the Allied forces poured southward. It was a chaotic retreat, as thousands of soldiers were separated from their units and arrived haphazardly behind the lines. But there was little sign of enemy bombers or fighters, which could have done grievous harm to the troops exposed en masse on the roads. By January 26, the men were securely positioned behind the pillboxes, trenches, and bunkers of the Bagoc-Orion line, and resupplied effectively from the rear by footpaths through the jungle. The American-Filipino forces were well aware that they had been driven back into a peninsula that might be their death trap. By insisting on stopping the invasion at the beaches MacArthur had lost valuable time, and in the overdue rush to effect WPO-3, the army had not managed to transfer all available ammunition, food, and medical supplies to the peninsula. Almost immediately the troops were put on half-rations. But they were secure for the moment—more so than at the northern line—and so long as they held out, big shore guns commanded the entrance to Manila Bay, denying its use to the ships of the enemy.

In late January and February, repeated frontal attacks on the American-Filipino lines led to heavy losses for the Japanese, and amphibious landings on the west coast of the peninsula also resulted in bloody repulses. The Japanese initially underestimated the number of American-Filipino troops on Bataan at no more than 25,000, but there were more than three times that many. And they fought hard. They did not break and run as they had in earlier skirmishes on Luzon—they remained hunkered down behind their lines, and met the Japanese infantry attacks with heavy artillery barrages. By mid-February, General Homma had lost 7,000 troops in the battle for Bataan, and his requests to Tokyo for reinforcements had been spurned. Homma was under pressure to extinguish resistance and declare the entire nation pacified. The army's "face" was at stake, and no less a figure than Hirohito was demanding quick action to snuff out resistance. Those considerations would grow more acute with the conquest of Singapore in mid-February. Homma's chief of staff, Lieutenant General Masami Maeda, argued that the correct strategy was to lay siege to the peninsula and wait for the tens of thousands of men trapped there to eat through their provisions, at which point they would probably surrender without a fight. But a long siege was not acceptable to General Tojo, whose cables made clear that Homma must either attack or be relieved.

President Quezon was incensed by the evidence, readily garnered from reports picked up by shortwave radio in his Corregidor bunker, that the Allies were committed to a Europe-first strategy. "*Que demonio!*" he cried, after listening to such a broadcast in early February. "How typical of America to writhe in anguish at the fate of a distant cousin while a daughter is being raped in the back room!" He was further enraged by reports, denied by MacArthur, that Filipino troops on Bataan were receiving lesser rations than their American counterparts. Quezon, with the unanimous support of his cabinet, proposed giving himself up to the Japanese as a prisoner of war and declaring the Philippines neutral and independent. In that position, he might bargain for the welfare of his people under a prolonged Japanese occupation. MacArthur, who was personally close to Quezon, forwarded the proposal (dated February 8, 1942) to Washington with his qualified endorsement, observing that it "might offer the best possible solution of what is about to be a disastrous debacle."

When the cable was received at the White House, however, President Roosevelt did not give it a moment's consideration. "We can't do this at all," he told Marshall and Stimson. There could be no separate peace with the Japanese. The president was adamant that Bataan must be defended to the last man, and the Philippines must suffer under occupation until they could be liberated by force. Before that day, Marshall had privately doubted whether the amiable New Dealer in a wheelchair was up to the task of waging a world war, but now he grasped that Roosevelt was capable of utter ruthlessness. "I immediately discarded everything I had held in my mind to his discredit," he said. "I decided he was a great man."

In reply to Quezon, Roosevelt evaded the question of reinforcements for the Philippines, but instead emphasized that the great bulk of American aircraft, troops, and other war assets were being sent to the Pacific in the early months of the war. That was true enough. By mid-March, 79,000 troops were scheduled to sail for the Pacific, more than four times the number scheduled for Europe. Though offering no specific commitments for the reinforcement of Bataan, Roosevelt gave Quezon his unequivocal pledge to liberate the Philippines. "So long as the flag of the U. S. flies on Filipino soil . . . it will be defended by our own men to the death. Whatever happens to the present American garrison we shall not relax our efforts until the forces which are now marshalling outside the Philippines return to the Philippines and drive out the last remnant of the invaders from your soil." This message apparently had the desired effect on Quezon, who swore that he would stand by America until the war was won.

The Philippines were done for, but no one was willing to say it out loud. MacArthur's forces on Bataan were expected to hold out as long as they could, perhaps to be annihilated. Their sacrifice would buy time for the stabilization of theaters in the south and east. MacArthur himself would lead the eventual counteroffensive from Australia. On March 11, by order of the president, MacArthur left Corregidor with his senior staff, his wife, and his four-year-old son. They fled under cover of darkness in a PT boat to Mindanao, and there boarded a dilapidated B-17 for the long flight to Australia.

MacArthur was considerably less popular among his own beleaguered forces on Bataan and Corregidor than he was among the American press and public, who had lapped up every word of his grandiloquent press communiqués. Before his departure his men had taken to calling him "Dugout Doug," a reference to his practice of remaining holed up in a bunker on Corregidor and never showing himself among them. After he left for Australia, rumors circulated that MacArthur had taken a large amount of luggage crammed with money, food, and superfluous luxury items, rather than make more room on the plane for others to escape. Those rumors were greatly embellished and largely unfair. However, it is a fact that MacArthur received, by order of President Quezon on January 3, 1942, a payment of $500,000 from the Philippine treasury. Three of his senior staff officers accepted smaller gratuities, amounting in total to $140,000. There is evidence that Roosevelt and Stimson knew of the transactions and did not object to them.

General Jonathan Wainwright, who remained on Corregidor, was promptly promoted to lieutenant general and given nominal command of all Allied forces in the Philippines. But Wainwright was not confident about the prospects of holding out for long—he cabled the War Department to say that if the forces on Bataan did not receive relief supplies by mid-April, they would be verging on starvation and probably would have little choice but to surrender. Conditions among the men on Bataan grew steadily worse throughout February and March. Rations were reduced from one half to one third. Cavalry horses and mules were slaughtered and devoured. Not only malnutrition but illness sapped the men's strength: Bataan was rife with malarial swamps, and dysentery spread widely among their numbers. Supplies of quinine dwindled and then ran out entirely by the end of March. Sick men died in their hospital beds, untreated for lack of medicines. The journalist Frank Hewlett penned a verse that was soon taken up throughout the ranks as a sardonic anthem:

We're the battling bastards of Bataan:
No mama, no papa, no Uncle Sam,
No aunts, no uncles, no cousins, no nieces,
No pills, no planes or artillery pieces,
And nobody gives a damn.

IN MALAYA, the British had been far too confident. The first weeks of the war brought a sequence of sudden, catastrophic defeats on land, on sea, and in the air. To say that morale was poor among the British Commonwealth forces does not quite do the theme justice; between the outset of war and the surrender of Singapore ten weeks later, they suffered something akin to a mass psychological collapse. One can speculate that time, leadership, and a timely victory or two might have retrieved the ugly situation. But time was scarce, leadership was lacking, and all the victories belonged to the invaders.

"Well, I suppose you'll shove the little men off," the civilian colonial governor said to General Arthur E. Percival, upon learning that the Japanese had attacked Kota Bahru in northeast Malaya on the first day of the war. No blackout regulations were decreed in Singapore, and the city lights provided good targets for the Japanese bombers that struck later that night. The sudden reduction of British airpower forced the RAF to concede the skies above northern Malaya, allowing the Japanese amphibious landings to proceed unmolested. Having secured their beachheads, the Japanese forces moved with remarkable speed. Infantrymen traveled on bicycles. They quickly routed the 11th Indian Division, which met them in the west, and forced the 10th Indian Division on the eastern side of the Malay Peninsula into a headlong southward retreat. The Japanese followed close on their heels. When the invaders met resistance, they combined flanking movements with ferocious frontal banzai charges that drove the defenders from their positions and sent them running for their lives. The Japanese navy worked effectively with the army in covering landings and in moving troops down the peninsula with well-coordinated coastal sea lifts. The retreating British blew hundreds of bridges behind them, but the Japanese army engineers quickly rebuilt them using native timbers hewn from the surrounding forest.

It was only now, in the crucible of battle, that the British recognized how feeble the local RAF presence really was. Their best aircraft and pilots had been pulled back to Europe to deal with the Luftwaffe's air assault on England. It was a policy born of the deep institutionalized contempt for the Japanese air forces, a syndrome shared with the Americans. The loss of so many aircraft to combat, mechanical failures, and accidents in the first two weeks of the war was a disaster compounded by the capture of several British airfields by the invasion forces. In some cases, the fields were yielded to the Japanese without a fight. The British Far East commander in chief, General Robert Brooke-Popham, lamented that there were "instances where aerodromes appear to have been abandoned in a state approaching panic. Stores have been left behind, material that is urgently required has been abandoned and a general state of chaos has been evident. . . . In the majority of cases the bombing of aerodromes has been on a smaller scale than that suffered calmly by women and children in London and other towns in England, and aerodromes have usually been vacated whilst still well out of range of enemy land forces."

The RAF commanders pulled their remaining aircraft back to Singapore, where they would be held in reserve for the defense of the city.

But the nightly air raids continued with little or no opposition. On January 13, 1942, a local headline proudly trumpeted: "Singapore Beats Off 125 Raiders." CBS war correspondent Cecil Brown wryly noted in his diary, "What actually happened is that the Japs dropped their bombs and went home." More critically, the near-total absence of friendly planes in the skies above northern Malaya could not be disguised from the British Commonwealth troops fighting on the ground, who were continuously dive-bombed and strafed by Japanese planes. They had counted on total air superiority, but now the enemy aircraft were free to operate with impunity over their heads.

The British commanders had concentrated their defenses on the main roads. They had largely neglected the peninsula's jungles and mangrove swamps, assuming them to be impenetrable. But the Japanese soldier proved a cunning and dexterous jungle fighter. Unlike his British counterpart, who wore boots and carried 40-pound packs, the Japanese infantryman wore light cotton clothing and soft-soled shoes, and carried only a rifle, an ammunition belt, and a bag of rice. In some cases he also carried a light infantry mortar on his shoulders. Small units of five to ten men advanced swiftly and quietly, in single file, along primitive jungle trails. They passed through swamps by hopping lightly from root to root. They crept around the British positions and opened fire with rifles and mortar fire from the flanks and the rear. They blended into the jungle with camouflage facepaint and stems of grass passed through a mesh covering on their helmets. They hid in the underbrush or in the branches of trees, and waited there for days, if necessary, until enemy soldiers wandered into their killing range. They disguised themselves as native workers and infiltrated the British camps, then assassinated their enemies one by one with knives or bayonets. They lay in leech-infested swamps with branches covering their heads, and remained there, motionless, for hours. If and when an enemy soldier advanced into range, they rose suddenly and opened fire. The British deplored those "shrewd oriental tricks" but were slow to amend their tactics to deal with them.

General Brooke-Popham, after observing Japanese troops on the Hong Kong–China border a year before the war, had described them as "various sub-human specimens dressed in dirty grey uniforms, which I was informed were Japanese soldiers. . . . If these represent the average of the Japanese army, the problems of their food and accommodation would be simple, but

I cannot believe they would form an intelligent fighting force." Now, in the jungles of Malaya, the Philippines, Burma, and the East Indies, a different myth was gaining currency. The Japanese infantryman was a "superwarrior," to be feared and respected as a creature uniquely adapted to jungle warfare. When asked to explain why the British forces were faring so badly in northern Malaya, Brooke-Popham now repeated the same observation he had made a year earlier, but with a very different emphasis. "The Japanese have a capacity to live on the country," he said. "They require very, very little and what they do find to eat is what they are used to. The British can't do that."

The subhumans of 1941 had mutated into the superhumans of 1942. Many Allied soldiers apparently believed that the Japanese possessed preternatural senses and abilities. Like bats, they could see in the darkness. Like panthers, they could move soundlessly through the underbrush. Like ants, they could communicate with their own kind by some unspoken brainwave. Unlike men, they had no fear of death. "The Japanese trooper was supposed to be fearless, scornful of U.S. soldiers, invisible, a superb sniper, and willing to fight to the death rather than give up a position," wrote Floyd W. Radike, a junior U.S. Army officer who fought in the South Pacific. "Of course, some of this was sheer nonsense, but unfortunately it took U.S. generals and colonels a long time to figure out how to counter such a creature." The new myth, like those it displaced, was founded on absurd racial canards. But it struck fear into the men who had to face those reputed superwarriors on the ground, and for that reason it threatened to turn self-fulfilling.

Again and again, the pattern was repeated. The British lines quickly crumbled in the face of flank attacks or frontal attacks. The officers tried and failed to rally their fleeing men, then gave up and followed on their heels. The island-city of Penang, off the west coast of Malaya, was evacuated in great haste on December 17. British troops were ordered to demolish military assets and stores, but they had little time to complete the work, and much useful weaponry, supplies, and shipping was left to the enemy. The army evacuated only white civilians from Penang, a practice bitterly resented by the native Malays and Chinese, many of whom had offered to fight alongside the British troops. The British commanders had decreed a "scorched earth" policy, but more often than not the retreating forces could not bring themselves to carry it out, perhaps because they clung to the hope that they would soon recapture the surrendered territory. As a result, the Japanese gained control of Malaya's vital rubber plantations and tin mines with most of the buildings, equipment, and supporting infrastructure intact.

In Singapore, Cecil Brown confided in his diary, "You can almost see morale collapsing like a punctured tire." No one knew the truth, and few trusted the reports of the local civilian or military officials. "People are believing the worst. For all they know the Japs are right outside Singapore." The official communiqués were full of hollow bravado and clumsy euphemisms. After British forces had been driven into retreat near the Krian River, it was reported that they had "successfully disengaged the enemy." Censors attempted to suppress bad news even when it was widely known. Air raids over the city were a nightly trial, and the inhabitants could see the Japanese bombers picked out in the searchlights, flying in perfect formation, seemingly indifferent to the antiaircrafts bursts. Often they attacked in broad daylight, and no RAF fighters rose to engage them. Propaganda leaflets were dropped, sometimes written in Malay or Mandarin Chinese—for example: "Burn all white devils in the sacred white flame of victory."

The native workers did not want to work, and the soldiers did not want to fight. Brown recorded a conversation with a British major who confessed that he could not "work up any venom" against the Japanese because they were (in contrast to the Germans) "unimportant blighters." The journalist was flabbergasted by this case of cognitive dissonance: "The British are getting the pants beat off them and the major doesn't think the Japs are worth bothering about." The local civilian grandees vacillated between dread and denial. Lady Brooke-Popham later said, "It was just parties, bridge and dancing to the very last. . . . They simply refused to believe that war could come to Singapore. . . . I asked a certain lady to help me [with civil defense measures] two hours a day. She said it would interfere with her tennis."

On January 17, it was announced that the Japanese were in the state of Johore, only 110 miles north of the city. British troops retreating from the north brought the incubus of their defeatism with them. It spread. The navy had let them down, the air force had let them down, and the leaders had proved incompetent. In the city, the inhabitants began their unseemly scramble to escape. Ship fares were hiked. Favors were called in to gain seats on outgoing commercial flights. Staff officers arranged to be reassigned to Field Marshal Wavell's new ABDA headquarters on Java. Native Malays, Chinese, Indians, and other Asian ethnic groups knew that they would be left behind, and demonstrated their resentment by refusing to work. In districts bombed out in the Japanese air raids, the dead were left in the streets; work parties could not be raised to cart them away for burial. By late January, the stench of the dead had settled like a pall over the city.

The island-fortress prepared to be laid under siege. On January 31, all remaining British troops retreated across the strait of Johore and dynamited the causeway behind them. But in making Singapore impregnable against attack by sea, the British had neglected to plan adequately for invasion across the strait. Landward defenses were in a shambles. No staff plan even existed to repel the attack that now loomed. The heavy artillery emplacements guarding Singapore harbor could not be moved or even turned to fire in the direction of the forthcoming onslaught. Singapore was virtually naked, with no naval power, no air cover, and diminishing hopes of reinforcement. Food stocks would not feed the population for long. More than 60,000 troops were now in the city, but the best among them were acutely demoralized and the worst were refusing to fight.

Churchill was outraged. He had been led to believe that Singapore Island was a fortress, and now he began to distrust the competence of his military commanders. In meetings with his war cabinet, the prime minister grew uncharacteristically snappish. According to General Brooke, Churchill often burst out with remarks like: "Have you not got a single general in that army who can win battles, have none of them any ideas, must we continually lose battles in this way?" To Admiral Pound he complained that enemy small craft were operating freely off the west coast of the Malay Peninsula, a condition that "must be reckoned as one of the most astonishing British lapses recorded in naval history." After receiving a pessimistic report from Wavell concerning Singapore's landward defenses, he flew into a towering rage. "I must confess to being staggered by Wavell's telegram," he wrote the British military chiefs on January 19. "It never occurred to me for a moment . . . that the gorge of the fortress of Singapore, with its splendid moat half a mile to a mile wide, was not entirely fortified against an attack from the northward. What is the use of having an island for a fortress if it is not to be made into a citadel? . . . How is it that not one of you pointed this out to me at any time when these matters have been under discussion? . . . I warn you that this will be one of the greatest scandals that could possibly be exposed." He ordered that the island-city be "converted into a citadel and defended to the death. No surrender can be contemplated."

General Tomoyuki Yamashita, commander of Japanese forces, prepared his main assault. Troops, landing craft, and heavy artillery were moved into position on the northern side of the strait. On the night of February 7, a diversionary attack was launched to the left of the site of the recently destroyed main causeway, but the main attack fell on the western side of the island the following night, when units of the Japanese 5th and 18th divisions crossed the strait in small boats. They stormed ashore under heavy fire by the Australian 24th Machine Gun Battalion. The Australians fought hard but could not deny the invaders their foothold, and by morning the defenders were falling back. Johore Strait was very shallow; at low tide there were points at which the Japanese soldiers could simply wade across it, holding their rifles above their heads. Small parties of Japanese infantrymen came ashore at several places on the western side of the island and pushed into the city against light and disintegrating opposition. The British Commonwealth troops they encountered broke ranks and ran with distressing regularity. Meanwhile, the crackerjack Japanese army engineers rebuilt the causeway across Johore Strait, and within a matter of hours columns of tanks, trucks, and heavy artillery were rolling across it.

Wavell flew into Singapore on the 9th and toured the defensive lines with General Percival, the local commander. He reminded his commanders on the spot that the British troops in the city heavily outnumbered the enemy. "We must defeat them," he wrote on February 10. "Our whole fighting reputation is at stake and the honour of the British Empire. The Americans have held out on the Bataan Peninsula against far greater odds, the Russians are turning back the picked strength of the Germans, the Chinese with almost complete lack of modern equipment have held the Japanese for four years. It will be disgraceful if we yield our boasted fortress of Singapore to inferior enemy forces." He ordered total ruthlessness, even if it meant the mass slaughter of both the military forces and the civil population. He flew back to Java on February 11 and reported to Churchill that night: "Battle for Singapore is not going well. . . . Morale of some troops is not good, and none is as high as I should like to see." He referred to an "inferiority complex" among the defenders, "which bold and skilful Japanese tactics and their command of the air have caused."

Defeatism was endemic. Australian diggers were overheard to say, "Chum, to hell with Malaya and Singapore. Navy let us down, air force let us down. If the bungs [natives] won't fight for their bloody country, why pick on me?" It was an attitude widely shared by the front-line fightingmen. Amidst such rank ineptitude, in a land so far from home, when the cause was so clearly doomed, why throw their lives away?

As the Japanese swept toward the urban center of Singapore, they gained control of the freshwater reservoirs that provided its drinking supply. That extinguished any remaining hope of a long siege—in a day or two the great city would die of thirst, if nothing else. The ominous thump of Japanese artillery and the whistling of shells could be heard throughout the city. Columns of oily black smoke rose from the blackened shells of bombed-out fuel storage tanks. Panicked throngs pressed down toward the wharves and bid or begged to be taken aboard one of the last departing ships. "There was a lot of chaos and people killed on the docks during these bombardments," recalled an American sailor on a ship in the harbor. "Everywhere you looked there was death. Even in the water there were dead sharks and people floating all around."

Yamashita was shocked and even shaken to learn that British troop strength in the city was twice what he had been led to believe by his intelligence sources. But he resolved to bluff his way through to a negotiated surrender. On the 14th, an ultimatum from Yamashita, addressed to Percival, was dropped from an airplane behind the British lines. "In the spirit of chivalry we have the honour of advising your surrender. . . . From now on resistance is futile and merely increases the danger to the million civilian inhabitants without good reason, exposing them to infliction of pain by fire and sword." On the same day, Percival was forbidden to consider such an offer by Wavell, who urged that "You must continue to inflict maximum damage on enemy for as long as possible by house-to-house fighting if necessary. Your action in tying down enemy and inflicting casualties may have vital influence in other theaters." At the same time, however, Wavell cabled Churchill to report that Singapore was done for, and after consulting with the British military chiefs that night, the prime minister agreed to allow a surrender.

The next morning, Sunday, February 15, Percival traveled under a flag of truce with a Japanese colonel to meet Yamashita. The meeting was lavishly documented by a crowd of Japanese reporters, photographers, and camera crews. Yamashita demanded an unconditional surrender and refused to order a cease-fire until such a surrender document had been signed. The Japanese general pledged to treat the civilian population properly and to observe the rights of prisoners of war. (Neither pledge would be honored.) Percival signed the instrument of surrender, with hostilities to cease at 8:30 p.m. that night.

The "Gibraltar of the East" had fallen. The army charged with its defense had surrendered to an enemy force less than half its size, after a battle lasting less than a week. Even at the time, it was recognized as the most ignominious episode in the annals of British military history. An editorial in the *Daily Mirror* summed up the feelings of the British people: "The Japanese have wrenched out this cornerstone of the greatest Empire in history, and have propped it up as a jeering monument to brave men who are dying for the folly of others who have much on their conscience."

HAVING BET THE POT ON SINGAPORE, and having seen the great pile of chips swept from the table, Field Marshal Wavell did not pretend that the East Indies could be saved. Indeed, he did not even want them reinforced, lest the reinforcements be delivered straight into the hands of the enemy. Java, the only major island in the group still in possession of the Allies, was 500 miles long and threatened with invasion on both its eastern and western flanks. The day after Percival's surrender, Wavell told Churchill: "Landings on Java in near future can only be prevented by local naval and air superiority. Facts given show that it is most unlikely that this superiority can be obtained." On February 21, 1942, he amplified the point:

> I am afraid that the defence of A.B.D.A. area has broken down and
> that defence of Java cannot now last long. . . . It always hinged on the
> air battle. . . . I see little further usefulness for this H.Q. . . . I hate the
> idea of leaving these stout-hearted Dutchmen, and will remain here
> and fight it out with them as long as possible if you consider this would
> help at all.

Picking up the cue, the U.S.-British combined chiefs dissolved the ABDA command. American, British, and Australian ground and air forces were evacuated south to Australia or west to Burma, where they would live to fight another day. Wavell was ordered to fly to India, where he would resume his old post as commander in chief of British forces in that country.

The decision to pull out of the beleaguered Indies was hardhearted but

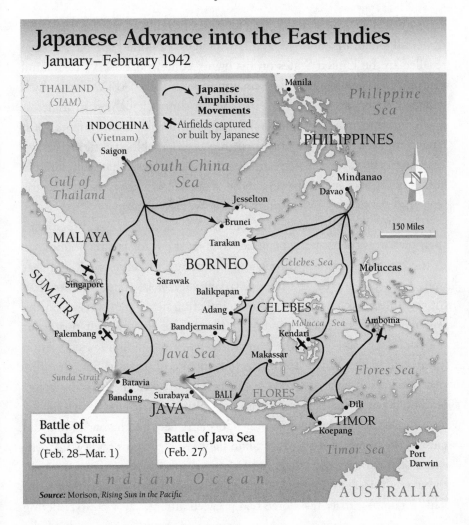

Japanese Advance into the East Indies
January–February 1942

Japanese Amphibious Movements

Airfields captured or built by Japanese

THAILAND (SIAM)

INDOCHINA (Vietnam)

Saigon

Manila

Philippine Sea

PHILIPPINES

South China Sea

Gulf of Thailand

Mindanao

Davao

Jesselton

Brunei

Tarakan

MALAYA

BORNEO

Celebes Sea

Moluccas

150 Miles

SUMATRA

Singapore

Sarawak

Balikpapan

Adang

CELEBES

Amboina

Palembang

Bandjermasin

Kendari

Molucca Sea

Java Sea

Makassar

Flores Sea

Sunda Strait

Batavia

Bandung Surabaya

BALI

FLORES

Dili

JAVA

TIMOR

Koepang

Battle of Sunda Strait (Feb. 28–Mar. 1)

Battle of Java Sea (Feb. 27)

Timor Sea

Port Darwin

Indian Ocean

AUSTRALIA

Source: Morison, *Rising Sun in the Pacific*

logical—in the Philippines and Malaya, the Allies had lost large numbers of men with little to show for it. But the Dutch, still vexed by the Anglo-American decision to freeze them out of the Allied high command, had no intention of joining in the general retreat. In Europe, their home country had long since been broken to the Nazi yoke, and the Netherlands government-in-exile clung tenaciously to its remaining overseas territories. The Dutch presence in those hot, fecund islands dated back more than three centuries. Many of the Dutch officers had spent the better part of their lives living in the East Indies. Whatever the feelings of the natives, the Dutch were inclined to fight for Java as they would fight to defend their own soil.

As Wavell and his staff departed for India, Dutch commanders took control of all remaining land, air, and naval forces. Admiral Hart having been recalled to the United States on his own recommendation, Vice Admiral Helfrich took command of the remaining units of the ABDA fleet, which included American, Australian, and British ships left behind to inflict as much punishment as they could on the approaching invasion convoys. Most remaining fleet units were organized into the "Combined Striking Force," based at Surabaya, on the northern coast of eastern Java. That multinational flotilla of cruisers and destroyers, most of ancient vintage, sailed under the seagoing command of Rear Admiral Karel W. F. M. Doorman.

The officers and men of the Combined Striking Force had seen with their own eyes the extreme penalties they must pay for Japan's dominance in the air. Several times, throughout the month of February, Allied fleet units had been hit by airstrikes. On February 4, Japanese bombers had hit an Allied task force north of Bali, inflicting heavy punishment on the American cruisers *Houston* and *Marblehead*. The *Houston's* aft turret was knocked out of action and the *Marblehead* was sent limping toward Ceylon for an overhaul. On the 15th, near Palembang on eastern Sumatra, successive waves of Japanese G3M bombers had attacked the Striking Force, sending down a rain of bombs from high altitude. With aggressive helmsmanship and violent maneuvering, Doorman's fleet had managed to avoid most of the bombs, but the Australian light cruiser *Hobart* and two American destroyers were damaged, and Doorman was forced to signal a retreat to Batavia through the Gaspar Strait. In mid-February, Vice Admiral Chuichi Nagumo's carrier task force had prowled around the vicinity, offering the unnerving specter of a sudden, overpowering carrier air attack on the Allied fleet at any time or place. That carrier group, *Kido Butai*, was far more powerful than anything the Allies had in the Pacific, let alone in the embattled islands of the East Indies. On February 19, an armada of carrier bombers (joined by land bombers from Kendari and Ambon) had laid waste to the northern Australian seaport of Darwin, sending the residents fleeing into the great red interior. Later that day, a swarm of Zeros had appeared over Surabaya, and in a massive aerial dogfight sent forty Allied fighters down in flames.

The swift reduction of Allied airpower left Doorman feeling blind, while the Japanese naval forces enjoyed steadily improving air reconnaissance. The little Allied fleet was constantly on the move, wrenched here and there by conflicting and often mistaken contact reports. They rarely saw a friendly plane in the skies above their heads. By the end of February, the officers and crews were exhausted and on edge—one of the American skippers referred to his crew's "considerable psychological tension." They were plagued by poor communications, failing equipment, retrograde technology, and inadequate port facilities. Refueling was a recurring headache—storage tanks in Surabaya and Batavia were always on the verge of running dry, and the oil workers who might have helped had fled the scene. Often the ships were obliged to put to sea with half-empty fuel tanks or with a partial supply of ammunition and torpedoes. An insidious female voice, carried over the airwaves by Radio Tokyo, taunted the Americans in California-accented English. "Poor American boys," she mock-lamented. "Your ships are swiftly being sunk. You haven't a chance. Why die to defend foreign soil which never belonged to the Dutch or British in the first place?"

The Japanese drive into the East Indies did not let up for a moment, even at the height of the battle for Singapore. Admiral Yamamoto, directing the campaign from his flagship *Nagato* in her Hashirajima anchorage, was determined to give the Allies no rest and no space to breathe. He insisted on an early seizure of Java, the richest and most populous island in the region. In the last week of February, two invasion convoys converged on Java in a huge pincer movement, the largest amphibious invasion yet mounted in the Second World War. The Eastern Attack Convoy had sailed on the 19th from Jolo in the Sulu Sea: it included forty-one transports and cargo ships with a screening force of one cruiser and ten destroyers. The Western Attack Convoy was made up of fifty-six transports and cargo vessels accompanied by three cruisers, a light carrier, and no fewer than twenty-five destroyers. It had weighed anchor on February 18 from Cam Ranh Bay, Indochina. Those two long columns of ships would pass to the east and west of Borneo, respectively, and disgorge their troops on opposite ends of the 500-mile-long island. Three additional "supporting" groups of cruisers and destroyers were sent into the vicinity, to be summoned into action if needed. Yamamoto correctly inferred that the remaining Allied sea and air forces were too feeble to endanger this mammoth operation, so he ordered Nagumo's carrier force away to the Indian Ocean, where it could intercept and finish off any Allied ships fleeing to the west.

The eastern convoy sailed in two columns a mile apart, each about twenty miles long. The freighters were sluggish and handled poorly by their civilian crews—destroyer skipper Tameichi Hara of the *Amatsukaze* was exasperated by their "obvious laxity," their tendency to break radio silence or allow lights to show from their vessels at night. The convoy advanced at no better than 10 knots. The danger posed by both air and submarine attack seemed ominous. But what few Allied bombers did appear over the convoy did not score any hits, and the American submarines, staging out of Surabaya, made no impression at all. The Japanese freighter *Arizona-maru* was struck by a dud torpedo in early February. "It seemed to pass along the hull, scraping the keel," one of her officers recalled, "and continued on the other side, emitting great clouds of bubbles before finally sinking to port." It was a problem that would continue to plague the American submarine campaign throughout the first year of the war.

Aerial and submarine sighting reports tipped off the Allies to the approach of the eastern convoy, and on February 24, Vice Admiral Helfrich ordered several British cruisers and destroyers to sail from Tandjong Priok in western Java to Surabaya, where they would join up with Doorman's ships. On the evening of the 26th, the Combined Striking Force sortied from Surabaya and steamed north through a typically majestic South Pacific sunset. Despite putting out extra lookouts, Doorman's ships found no sign of the enemy. As dawn rose, Doorman decided to head back into port to top off fuel. While retiring he received terse messages from Helfrich, ordering him back out to sea. He replied: "This day the personnel reached the limit of endurance. Tomorrow the limit will be exceeded." But at 2:27 p.m. on February 27, as the fleet entered the outer roads of Surabaya, a new contact report put the Japanese convoy just ninety miles north. Doorman's flagship put about and signaled his British, American, and Australian companions in a plain English semaphore: "Am proceeding to intercept enemy unit, follow me, details later."

The Striking Force now included two heavy cruisers, three light cruisers, and nine destroyers. It departed Surabaya in a column led by Doorman's flagship, the cruiser *De Ruyter*. The crews had operated at sea in perilous conditions for weeks on end, without much respite, and physical exhaustion was beginning to take a toll on their performance. But now they rallied. They sailed in three columns, with *De Ruyter* leading four other cruisers of three other nations—*Exeter, Houston, Perth,* and *Java.* It was a fine day, with good visibility, light breezes, and moderate swells. The British destroyers sailed ahead as a screening force, while the American and Dutch destroyers followed the cruisers on their rear and port quarter. The antique four-stack destroyers coughed up billows of black smoke as they churned along in the wakes of the larger ships. One of the Dutch destroyers had engine trouble that limited the speed of the entire force to 26 knots.

The multinational character of the force, and its makeshift efforts to coalesce under one command, were highlighted by the difficulty Doorman had in making himself understood to his English-speaking charges. One of the American destroyer skippers described the communication problems as "farcical." The Striking Force had been issued no signal books and no common codes. Doorman's flagship communicated by blinker light in plain English, but in the smoke and confusion of a naval melee that would prove impractical. In some cases, the admiral's orders were transmitted on a Dutch-type high-frequency radio to the *Houston*, which then relayed them to the other ships by TBS ("talk-between-ships," a short-range voice circuit used on the American vessels). In the forthcoming action, Doorman's orders would sometimes arrive at the other ships in the wrong sequence, leaving their skippers flummoxed.

Japanese patrol planes tracked Doorman's column and radioed contact reports to Vice Admiral Takeo "King Kong" Takagi, commander of the eastern convoy covering force. Well before he made direct visual contact, Takagi knew Doorman's speed and course, and he had a good idea of the composition of Doorman's force. He sent the troopships north, out of danger, and took his cruisers and destroyers south toward the enemy at high speed. At 4 p.m., lookouts on the Japanese cruiser *Jintsu* reported several ships hull-down to the southeast. A small forest of mastheads peeked over the horizon, indicating the presence of a large Allied fleet. Dutch, British, and American flags could be seen fluttering in the breeze. Lieutenant Commander Hara of the destroyer *Amatsukaze*, studying the scene through his binoculars and comparing it to what he saw in his ship-recognition diagrams, correctly identified the flagship *De Ruyter* before her hull had risen into his line of sight.

The two columns closed at an oblique angle. At a range of 28,000 yards, the Japanese heavy cruisers *Haguro* and *Nachi* opened fire with their 8-inch guns. Columns of brightly colored water rose on either side of the Allied line—the shells were injected with colored dye markers for shot-spotting—but the range was too great for accuracy, and none fell close. As the range closed, Japanese floatplanes circled overhead and radioed ranging informa-

tion to Takagi's cruisers, and the salvos began creeping steadily closer. To
avoid being raked fore-and-aft, Doorman ordered a 20-degree port turn, a
maneuver that would put him more nearly on a parallel course and bring
the full broadsides of his cruisers to bear on the enemy. A few minutes
after the course change, *Houston* and *Exeter* opened fire. Red-dyed spouts
straddled the Japanese column, but no hits were scored.

A few minutes after five o'clock, the *Exeter* was struck amidships by
an armor-piercing shell fired by the *Haguro*. It penetrated into the boiler
room and exploded, destroying several of the British cruiser's boilers. She
immediately lost about half her power, and turned out of the line to limp
back toward Surabaya at reduced speed. *Houston*, following in her wake,
also turned to avoid a collision, and as a result the Allied column was now
thrown into confusion. The TBS radio on the *Houston* was knocked out of
action by a dud shell, cutting the radio relay link with Doorman's flagship.
"From then on," wrote Commander H. E. Eccles, skipper of the destroyer
USS *John D. Edwards*, "all communication was by flashing lights obscured
by gun smoke, smoke screens, and hampered by rapid maneuver." It seemed
that no one was receiving or understanding Doorman's orders.

At 5:15 p.m., a Japanese torpedo that had been fired at long range some
minutes earlier struck the Dutch destroyer *Kortenaer*, which went up in a
great flash of light and a thunderclap. She broke in two, jackknifed, and
sank. The American destroyers counterattacked with a spread of forty torpedoes, but all either missed their targets or struck an enemy hull and did
not explode. Now Japanese Type 93 torpedoes were slicing through the sea
all around the American ships, and several exploded automatically upon
reaching the ends of their runs. Lookouts on the American ships, ignorant of the great range of the enemy's torpedoes, wrongly assumed that the
Striking Force must be under submarine attack. The situation was mas-
sively confused. "The crystal ball was our only method of anticipating the
intention of Commander Combined Striking Force," wrote Commander
Eccles in his action report. "Then came the orders 'Counter-attack,' 'Cancel
Counter-attack,' 'Make smoke,' 'Cover my retirement.'" At about 5:25 p.m.,
the smoke screen ordered by Doorman allowed the cruisers to break off the
engagement and escape to the southeast, toward the Javanese coast. The
Dutchman hoped to get free of the Japanese cruisers and destroyers, which
had thus far got the better of him. His prime objective was to surprise and
sink the Japanese troopships, later that night or the following dawn.

For the next several hours, the Striking Force ran south, but then doubled back in the enveloping darkness and ran at high speed toward the northwest. Doorman hoped to evade Takagi's warships and get directly at the transports, but without air reconnaissance he would need a stroke of luck to do so. The Japanese cruiser scout planes could be heard droning overhead—they dropped flares in hopes of illuminating the Allied fleet for the guns of their ships. The Japanese cruisers fired star shells and shined their searchlights across the horizon, but could not bring the enemy into effective range for a night action. Shortly before eight, Doorman again changed course and ran south until the moonlit coast of Java came into view. The American destroyers, running low on fuel and having fired all their torpedoes, were dispatched to return to Surabaya for replenishment. At 9:25 p.m. a British destroyer, the *Jupiter*, struck a Dutch mine, exploded, and sank in minutes. Doorman now hoped against the odds that he might circumvent the Japanese screening force and attack the troopships. The four remaining Allied cruisers turned north. They sailed alone, their destroyer brethren having been whittled away by low fuel, expended torpedoes, or the fortunes of war.

Japanese cruiser spotting planes continued to stalk them. At 9:50 p.m., a parachute flare floated down over the Allied ships. The crews felt exposed, with good reason—flares continued falling from the sky, indicating that they had been spotted. Admiral Takagi moved his ships in for the kill. A lookout on the cruiser *Nachi*, scanning the horizon with one of the Japanese navy's excellent night vision glasses, reported a visual contact on Doorman's ships at 11 p.m. Both lines opened fire and the night sky was flashed with heavy naval gunfire and star shells. Reiji Masuda, the merchant marine officer on the *Arizona-maru*, had never seen anything like it: he spoke of the "thunder of big guns, flashes of light, flares in the dark sky, columns of fire." Two cruisers, *Haguro* and *Nachi*, swung northward and closed the range. At 11:53 p.m., when they had closed to 8,000 yards, the two cruisers launched a spread of twelve torpedoes. Thirteen minutes later, the *De Ruyter* exploded with a mighty thunderclap of sound and broke in two. The fires quickly reached her magazine and set off a secondary explosion that briefly lit up the entire seascape for miles around. The two separated sections of her hull slipped quickly beneath the waves, taking 367 men, including Admiral Doorman, to the bottom. Almost immediately thereafter the *Java* also exploded and went down quickly by the bow. A few of her crew managed to leap into the sea, but the British cruiser also went down with the loss of

most of her hands. The sailors on the decks of the Japanese cruisers leaped
and danced and shouted, "Banzai!"

Doorman's final order to the surviving ships was to break off the engagement and withdraw to Tandjong Priok (the harbor of Batavia). *Perth* and
Houston broke away in the darkness. The Java Sea was now a Japanese lake,
and further Allied resistance could only end in total annihilation. All that
remained was for the scattered remnants of the ABDA fleet to escape before
they were hunted down and destroyed, in hopes of living to fight another
day. Exits were few. To the north, the Japanese reigned supreme at sea and
in the air. Bali Strait, east of Java, offered the quickest route south from
Surabaya, but those waters were too shallow to accommodate the cruisers.
The four American four-pipers that had retired to Surabaya managed to
sneak through that strait on the last night of February. They exchanged
long-range gunfire with a Japanese task force dispatched to intercept them,
but managed to break away in the darkness. They reached Fremantle, on
the western coast of Australia, a week later.

The wounded British cruiser *Exeter*, accompanied by the destroyers
HMS *Encounter* and USS *Pope*, crept north out of Surabaya that night.
They hoped against the odds to evade detection the next day, hug the south
coast of Borneo, and then make a high-speed run for Sunda Strait, to the
west of Java, the following night. At first the battle-damaged *Exeter* could
make only 16 knots, though the engine crews eventually coaxed her to
about 23 knots. March 1 dawned with alarmingly good visibility. The three
ships were quickly spotted, both from the air and by patrolling Japanese
ships. Admiral Takagi moved his ships in for an easy kill. Two separate Japanese task forces, including four heavy cruisers and several destroyers, closed
from two directions. A heavy gun duel began at long range at 9:40 a.m., and
several hits were soon taken by all three Allied vessels. At about 11 a.m.,
the Japanese torpedomen launched an effective spread, and one of their
fish hit the crippled *Exeter*. She rolled over and went down at eleven-thirty.
The *Encounter* succumbed to several hits and sank five minutes later. The
Pope, last remaining Allied warship afloat in the Java Sea, was methodically
bombed by planes from the light carrier *Ryujo* and sank shortly after noon.
Her survivors were picked up by a Japanese destroyer; they would spend the
next three and a half years in hell.

The *Houston* and *Perth*, having put the previous night's debacle well
behind them, put into Tandjong Priok at midday on February 28. The two

cruisers refueled in haste and sortied at 7 p.m. that night, with hopes of slipping through the Sunda Strait. At 10:15 p.m., near Bantam Bay, at the western extremity of Java, they stumbled on a group of anchored Japanese transports. They were elements of the Western Attack Convoy, sent to land on the western end of the island. A full moon lit the scene. It was a good opportunity to attack those transports while they were in the vulnerable position of landing troops and supplies on the beach. The Japanese had overwhelming naval forces in the vicinity—seven cruisers, ten destroyers, and a light aircraft carrier, the *Ryujo*, though most of those units were off some distance to the north. *Houston* and *Perth* opened fire on the transports, and at first only one of the Japanese destroyers could return fire. But the other Japanese surface ships rushed into the fray at flank speed and quickly overpowered the two Allied cruisers. Three Japanese cruisers and nine destroyers got into the action, and fired no fewer than eighty-seven torpedoes at them. The battle developed into a general melee, all the more confused because of smoke screens laid by the Japanese destroyers and the geometry of the action, which involved a dozen Japanese ships converging from several directions simultaneously.

Several torpedoes overshot the two Allied ships and struck the defenseless transports in the background. Against such overwhelming force, the *Houston* and *Perth* were not going to last long. They were surrounded by enemy ships in every offshore direction, all pouring shells into them. Japanese planes circled overhead. The last moments were confused and utterly hopeless. Commander A. L. Maher of the *Houston* later wrote: "All communication systems which were still operative were hopelessly overloaded with reports of damage received, of approaching torpedoes, of new enemy attacks begun, or changes in targets engaged." The American and Australian ships gave some punishment back to their tormentors, but took much the worse of the exchange.

In the general melee, five Japanese ships were hit by friendly fire. Two, a minesweeper and a transport, were sunk. With such a great number of torpedoes launched at the two Allied cruisers in a relatively small area, it was perhaps inevitable that some would strike the anchored transports. As the ships were so close inshore, a large percentage of the crews aboard got ashore safely. General Hitoshi Imamura, commander in chief of the 16th Army, swam to shore and staggered onto the beach soaked head to foot in fuel oil.

At midnight the *Perth* took a direct hit from an 8-inch shell. Shortly afterward she was struck by a torpedo under the waterline, and that was too much for her—she sank quickly. The *Houston* was also pummeled by heavy shellfire and three torpedoes. A few minutes after midnight, a shell penetrated the engine room and broke a steam main, scalding the engine-room crew to death. Steam ruptured through the deck and she listed heavily to starboard. At 12:25 a.m., Captain Rooks ordered abandon ship. Shortly after that, the *Houston* was struck directly in the bridge, killing her captain. She rolled onto her side, and at twelve-forty-five that morning she went under. Only about half of her crew survived. Of the crews of the two cruisers, 307 of the *Perth* and 368 from the *Houston* were picked up by Japanese ships, and would languish in prison camps as forced laborers for the remainder of the war.

Those Allied ships remaining on the south coast of Java at Tjilatjap were sent away by Admiral Helfrich on March 1. Some escaped, while others were caught by Nagumo's carrier planes and sunk. A destroyer, the *Edsall*, and an oiler, the *Pecos*, were sunk south of Java the next day.

As a result of those battles, the ABDA fleet was largely annihilated, with losses of ten ships and about 2,173 sailors. Not a single Japanese warship had been sunk in the defense of the Malay barrier, which was now decisively broken. In the immediate aftermath of the battle there was some criticism of the Dutch commanders, though always tempered with admiration for their courage. The skipper of one of the American destroyers that escaped to Australia believed that Admiral Doorman lacked a firm grasp of tactics and communications, but added, "The Dutch fought with unfaltering courage and dogged determination" and "went to their deaths with grim foreknowledge." Admiral King echoed those points, calling the naval campaign in the Java Sea "a magnificent display of very bad strategy," but the judgment is probably a little unfair. The Allied forces in the theater were totally overmatched, both in quantitative and qualitative terms. The U.S. Asiatic Fleet was antiquated and decrepit. Mahanian orthodoxy actually accounted for those deficiencies: Mahan had decreed that the battle fleet must remain as a unit, and if that principle was to be observed unfailingly, the Asiatic Fleet could never be treated as more than an afterthought. The single most important factor in the Japanese victory was their mastery in the air; there was little the ships of the ABDA fleet could expect to do with such weak support from above.

A few ships escaped to Australia, but the Japanese were only briefly delayed in carrying out their invasion of Java on February 28. From widely dispersed beachheads, the invasion forces pushed into the island. Helfrich was informed by subordinate admirals that they judged the attempt to save Java to be a lost cause and had received orders from their countries to withdraw. Helfrich at first demanded that the few remaining ships of the ABDA fleet should continue to resist, but in the face of opposition from his British subordinate officers, he bowed to the inevitable and agreed that the remaining British ships should be withdrawn. The remaining Allied planes took off, jammed with passengers, and completed the hasty evacuation of the island. The main western centers of Batavia and Bandoeng were in Japanese hands by March 5. The remaining Dutch and British troops on Java fought bravely, but all remaining resistance was stamped out within a week. Many of the Javanese natives seemed glad to be rid of their Dutch masters. By March 9, Japan had established complete mastery over the island, and the remaining Allied forces surrendered.

THE HEAVY DEFEATS SUFFERED BY THE ALLIES that winter and spring of 1942 reverberated harshly in their halls of power. The Japanese offensive had made a mockery of their predictions, deranged their plans, sapped their morale, undercut their leaders' reputations, and torn at the seams of their global coalition. Churchill had been among those British leaders who had vehemently maintained that Singapore was impregnable—that it was "vain" and a "bugbear" to suppose that the great "citadel" could ever fall to the Japanese. Now his rivals in Parliament and the British press threw those imprudent oaths back in his face. In his memoirs, Churchill wryly noted that the ABDA charter had been created in painstaking negotiations between half a dozen governments, eating up the scarce time and attention of hundreds of civil and military officials, requiring "scores of thousands of words" to be cabled around the world by the "surest codes," and had been "staffed in strict proportion to the claims of the different powers, all in triplicate for the army, navy, and air." No sooner was the Sisyphean work completed than the Japanese onslaught put the entire enterprise out of business. ABDACOM was stillborn.

With the Malay barrier smashed to pieces, there was nothing left to check the Japanese juggernaut, whether it went east, west, or south. It might even advance in all those directions at once, as the Japanese had given abundant proof of their power and readiness to attack across widely separated fronts. On March 8, the date of the surrender of Allied forces on Java, Japan's 15th Army marched into Rangoon, the capital city of Burma. The demoralized British troops, cut off from the seaport that had been their main source of supply, fell back to the north and west. The British now had to ask themselves whether the population of India would regard the approaching Japanese as invaders or liberators. The Japanese gained control of the Burma Road, the Allies' major route of overland supply for the Nationalist Chinese. Chiang Kai-shek warned of a collapse of Chinese resistance, and threatened to open truce talks with the Japanese.

Also on March 8, Japanese invasion forces went ashore on the coast of New Guinea, at Lae and Salamaua, and began clearing land for new airfields. That pointed toward a further advance along the axis of South Pacific islands lying to the east of the Dutch East Indies—the Admiralties, the Bismarcks, and the northern Solomons—and a direct threat to the line of sea communications between North America and Australia. Australian prime minister John Curtain, in a strident exchange with Churchill, had demanded the return of several Australian divisions from the Middle East, refusing the latter's entreaties that they be diverted for the defense of Burma—he had even broached the term "inexcusable betrayal" in his comments on the defense of Singapore. The vast southern landmass, with its largely unpopulated 16,000-mile coastline, lay totally exposed—its only real defense was its physical remoteness and the red desert wastes of its interior.

Kido Butai, Admiral Nagumo's feared carrier striking force, continued to swallow up enormous swaths of ocean. In the first week of April it was afoot in the Indian Ocean. On the morning of April 5, when many servicemen and civilians were at religious services to celebrate Easter Sunday, Japanese carrier aircraft descended suddenly on the port of Colombo, on the west coast of Ceylon. They sank only one destroyer and a merchantman, but they inflicted heavy damage on the wharves and port installations, and shot down twenty-four British planes that scrambled to intercept them. Later the same day, more of Nagumo's planes found and sank two British cruisers, *Dorsetshire* and *Cornwall*. On the morning of April 9, a wave of Japanese carrier planes appeared over Ceylon's second important base, Trincomalee. As at Colombo, the attackers took a heavy toll on shore-support facilities. A counterattack by nine RAF Blenheim bombers fell on the retreating *Akagi*, but they scored no hits. Five Blenheims were shot down and the others damaged. Later that day, Nagumo's planes found the British aircraft carrier *Hermes* at sea, and sent her to the bottom along with an escorting destroyer. Running low on fuel, *Kido Butai* exited the Indian Ocean through the Strait of Malacca and turned north for home.

Altogether, in carrier and submarine attacks, the Japanese had destroyed twenty-three merchant vessels and five Royal Navy warships including the *Hermes*. That was a heavy blow, and left Burma more isolated than ever, but worse from the British point of view was the prospect that the Japanese might return with troopships, and stage an invasion of Ceylon or even India. In the geopolitics of the Second World War, the Indian Ocean was the crux of the issue. It was a main artery of global Allied supply lines, critical to China, North Africa, and even Russia. It held the key to control of the Persian Gulf, recognized even then as home to the largest oil reserves in the world. In early April, the British asked the Americans to send naval reinforcements to the Indian Ocean, a request that Admiral King refused. By late April, American communications intelligence units had confirmed that the Japanese had no further operations brewing in the Indian Ocean, but the Allies continued to wring their hands over the vision of a German-Japanese linkup in the Persian Gulf, and an Axis chokehold on the greatest oil-producing region in the world.

Nor was there much good cheer radiating from the other theaters of the war. In North Africa, Rommel's Afrika Korps had seized the port of Benghazi, driving the British back toward Tobruk. General Rommel seemed poised to launch a punishing tank offensive against Egypt and the Suez Canal, a campaign that might sever a principal artery of the British Empire. In the Mediterranean, British efforts to resupply the besieged and starving island of Malta had been thwarted by enemy air and submarine attacks. On February 11 and 12, two German battle cruisers and one heavy cruiser broke out of the French port of Brest, eluded a British blockade, darted up the English Channel, ran the big shore batteries at Dover, and reached Germany intact. The "Channel Dash," as the British press acerbically called it, was a thumb in the eye of the Royal Navy. In the United States, German U-boats were sinking merchantmen and oil tankers just off the east coast, often within sight of land, and the U.S. Navy was apparently powerless to stop them. In California, invasion fears were revived by an incident north of Santa Barbara on the night of February 23, when a Japanese submarine surfaced off the beach and shelled an oil refinery. The next night, Los Angeles succumbed to mass panic as the city's antiaircraft batteries let loose at an imaginary Japanese air raid.

Most tormenting of all in those ominous weeks was the prospect of a Russian collapse. Hitler was known to be preparing a huge spring offensive in the Caucasus. Could the Red Army withstand it? And would Japan attack in Siberia, forcing Joseph Stalin to fight on two fronts?

In his correspondence with Roosevelt, Churchill did not conceal his private anguish. He was candid and open-hearted to a remarkable degree, even hinting that the pressure was getting to him. He confided on February 19, 1942: "I do not like these days of personal stress and I have found it difficult to keep my eye on the ball." On March 7: "The weight of the war is very heavy now and I must expect it to get steadily worse for some time to come." Roosevelt's inborn optimism was valuable in those dark days of the war. He acknowledged that the fall of Singapore would give "the well-known back-seat drivers a field day," but urged the British leader to "be of good heart" and to "keep up your optimism and your grand driving force." He encouraged Churchill to take time away from his duties to relax: "Once a month I go to Hyde Park for four days, crawl into a hole, and pull the hole in after me. I am called on the telephone only if something of really great importance occurs. I wish you would try it, and I wish you would lay a few bricks or paint another picture."

But the president also emphasized that the Allies had better "constantly look forward to the next moves that need to be made to hit the enemy." Yes, the defeats in the Pacific were disastrous and shocking, but there was nothing to be gained in agonizing over them. "Here is a thought from this amateur strategist," he wrote Churchill on March 18. "There is no use giving a single further thought to Singapore or the Dutch Indies. They are gone." The immediate concern was to set up a new theater command system to replace the disbanded ABDACOM. Australia must be defended at all costs, as the launching pad for an eventual Allied counteroffensive. The British could do little to protect Australia; on the other hand, the Americans could do little to check Japanese aggression in the Indian Ocean or against the Indian subcontinent. Therefore, asked the president, why not simply divide command responsibility between the eastern and western flanks of the Japanese Empire, with the Americans to be predominant in the Pacific, and the British in the Indian Ocean and Southeast Asia? He made the offer explicit in two long cables of March 7 and 9, 1942. General Brooke was at first suspicious, noting in his diary that the proposal was "good in places but calculated to drive Australia, NZ, and Canada into USA arms, and help to bust up empire!" But no viable alternative lay on the table, and the strain on British military resources ruled out any new force commitments to the Pacific or Australasia. So what reasonable objection could they offer? After a brief, irritable debate, Churchill and his cabinet acquiesced.

Observing the rapid deterioration of Allied fortunes in the Pacific, Admiral King pushed to reinforce the theater even if it meant drawing forces away from pending operations in Europe. President Roosevelt backed him. The president put the point directly to Churchill on March 7: "The energy of the Japanese attack is still very powerful . . . the Pacific situation is now very grave and, if it is to be stabilized, requires an immediate, concerted, and vigorous effort by the United States, Australia, and New Zealand." Shipping was the bottleneck. Troop transports previously intended to sail for Britain would have to be redeployed to the Pacific. That left no option other than to postpone implementation of the buildup of U.S. troops in Britain, the operation code-named BOLERO. It also meant, the president wrote, that the "American contribution to an air offensive against Germany in 1942 would be somewhat curtailed." By agreeing to those revisions, Churchill acknowledged the limits of a Europe-first policy at a time when the Japanese were rampaging across Asia and the Pacific.

The United States had assumed sole Allied command responsibility in the Pacific, including the big southern island groups of Oceania and Australasia. In Washington, it was naturally assumed that General MacArthur would be named supreme commander of the entire theater. He was already on the scene in Australia, and no one else in the American military command even approached his stature or popularity. But Admiral King was implacably opposed to giving MacArthur command of the Pacific Fleet, and if the deadlock could not be resolved, he would appeal his case to the president. King and Marshall apparently thrashed the issue out in private, meeting alone or with a handful of aides behind closed doors. No detailed account of those sessions entered the historical record, but there is reason to believe that hard words were exchanged.

In the end, they emulated the wisdom of King Solomon, and divided the theater between the army and navy. MacArthur was named commander in chief of the "Southwest Pacific Area," which included Australia, the Philippines, the former Dutch East Indies, the Bismarcks, and the Solomons. Admiral Nimitz retained his title of CINCPAC while adding that of commander in chief of the "Pacific Ocean Areas," which included the entire North and central Pacific, and the South Pacific island groups east of the 160th meridian. (Nimitz's new call sign, which he would lug around with him for the rest of the war, was "CINCPAC-CINCPOA.") Within their prescribed theaters, MacArthur and Nimitz would command all Allied forces, on the ground, on the sea, and in the air. The settlement resolved the standoff in Washington, but led to army-navy friction whenever an operation straddled the two spheres, as did the Guadalcanal Campaign in the latter half of 1942. Naturally, the boundaries drawn in Washington would not be respected by the Japanese.

Chapter Eight

To Koichi Shimada, a staff officer with the Eleventh Air Fleet, the plans drawn up before the war for Japan's southern offensive had resembled a "railroad timetable." They were thousands of pages long, meticulous in detail, and scheduled down to the hour. Was it possible, he had wondered, to run a war in such an orderly fashion, "completely at the will of the one side?"

By April 1942, it appeared that Shimada had his answer. Not only had the southern offensive been run like a railroad, but the trains were arriving at the stations ahead of schedule. In four months, Japan had conquered one of the greatest empires ever to be brought under one flag. Its vast perimeter now stretched from the Kurile Islands in the north to Timor in the south, and from the Gilbert Islands in the east to the frontiers of India in the west. Pockets of Allied resistance remained, notably on Bataan and Corregidor in the Philippines, but they could not hold out much longer. Japan, poor in natural resources, had secured bountiful sources of oil, rubber, tin, and bauxite, and could feed those vital inputs into its war machine ad infinitum. Most extraordinarily, the new empire had been won at a negligible cost. Casualties had run to only about 10,000 men. Total merchant shipping losses had amounted to just 25,000 tons. The Imperial Japanese Navy remained virtually unscathed, having lost nothing larger than a destroyer.

In Japan, elation gave way to ecstasy. Three days after the fall of Singapore, the emperor appeared before a rapturous throng outside the walls of the Imperial Palace. Dressed in military uniform and mounted on a white horse, he rode out across one of the bridges spanning his moat, and sat impassively as the thousands below shouted: "Banzai!" In Hibiya Park later that day, Tojo announced that Singapore had been renamed Shonan Island, while a crowd of some 30,000 shouted their acclamations and waved hats and flags in the air. The patriotic fever expressed itself in music, which was blared to distortion on loudspeakers turned out toward the streets. The war songs were numerous, and they were virtually all one ever heard: "Annihilating the Enemy," "Until the Enemy Raises the White Flag," "The Divine Soldiers of the Sky," "Companion Cherry Blossoms," "If You're a Man," and above all, the "Battleship March." In the navy town of Kure, all the restaurants and teahouses had been reserved for celebratory parties and dinners, and the geishas were working overtime. Destroyer skipper Tameichi Hara, whose ship and crew had returned in triumph from the Java Sea, recalled that no geishas were available to perform at his ship's banquet, so several of the enlisted men performed their own drunken singing and dancing routines. "I don't know how much sake I consumed in the process," he wrote. "Nothing but my rugged physique pulled me through the chain drinking that lasted until the banquet ended around midnight."

With very few exceptions, the Japanese people now embraced the war wholeheartedly. Whatever doubts and fears they might have privately entertained before Pearl Harbor had been utterly refuted by subsequent events. Evidently it was true that Japan was a nation of destiny, chosen by heaven to rule over Asia. At home, the tyranny of the militarist regime was unbridled. Elections were not yet abandoned, but political parties were dissolved and replaced with an über-party known as the Imperial Rule Assistance Association, which vetted and approved all candidates for elective office. The lives of ordinary Japanese were intricately controlled through the *tonarigumi*, or "neighborhood associations," which were supervised by the Home Ministry and largely staffed by women. The *tonarigumi* distributed rations, promulgated slogans, organized air-raid drills, stood fire watches, and reported unorthodox behavior or opinions to the police. Rationing of basic goods grew steadily more stringent. Rice had been rationed in the cities since 1940, but now soy sauce and miso were added to the list, followed soon afterward by eggs, fish, tofu, and other grains.

For all outward appearances, the Japanese people seemed perfectly willing to endure those privations. They hulled their own rice using beer bottles, a difficult and dirty job that tore their clothing and blistered their hands; they foraged for food to supplement their meager rations; they cheerfully recited the slogans, sang the songs, and marched in the festive lantern parades that commemorated each new triumph overseas. Departing recruits were lavishly fêted by their families and neighbors. They wore white sashes with red suns across their chests, and marched in procession to a Shinto shrine to be ritually purified. Afterward they were toasted and exhorted in speeches and songs. "When my eldest brother went," recalled a schoolgirl in Numazu, "the block association marched to the station waving rising-sun flags and wearing white sashes boldly inscribed with the message 'Congratulations on Being Called to Service.' . . . When other men in the neighborhood had been called, we all went waving our flags. Now, it was brother's turn and I was bursting with pride." Tears were strictly taboo, and no one was allowed to voice the fear that a departing recruit might never be seen again. Parents, wives, and siblings were expected to appear overjoyed. "No one could reveal their deepest emotions," said a military clerk who distributed call-up notices in Tonami during the war. "The public sent them off with cheers. 'Banzai! Banzai!' You had to say it."

The Japanese people were rapidly succumbing to what would later be called *shoribyo*, or "victory disease"—a faith that Japan was invincible, and could afford to treat its enemies with contempt. Its symptoms were overconfidence, a failure to weigh risks properly, and a basic misunderstanding of the enemy. The syndrome was fanned by an inflammatory state-controlled news media. But the boasts and taunts were unassailable: the facts spoke for themselves, and required no embellishment. The Japanese people could see, with their own eyes, the photographs of American battleships burning at Pearl Harbor, or those of British battleships sinking off the coast of Malaya. They watched newsreel footage of the surrender of Singapore, where a British general had supplicated before his Japanese counterpart and a sea of British prisoners had marched under the guns of their Japanese conquerors. When the editors of the *New Order in Greater East Asia* predicted that the "disgrace" of Pearl Harbor would "long be remembered by the world," who could deny it?

The Japanese had tested Allied strength in the Pacific and found it surprisingly feeble—so feeble that it seemed the deficiency could only be explained by some inherent flaw in the enemy's fighting spirit. Allied soldiers and sailors were dismissed as weak, craven, and interested only in saving their own lives. "Many United States troops suffer from bombphobia," reported the *Japan Times & Advertiser* on April 17, 1942. "They are astounded at the iron nerves of the Japanese soldiers." Back in January, the editors had judged that Britain was a "parasite prolonging her precarious existence by sucking the life-blood of others. But there is a question as to how long these others will consent to remain the meek victims of an ailing vampire." Speeches and editorials declared that the war was as good as won, that a strong perimeter had been captured and fortified, and that no major counteroffensive was to be expected. The journal *Kokusai Shashin Joho* assured its readers in February that bombing attacks on Tokyo were no longer a danger, because any air bases within a threatening radius were now in Japanese hands. Perhaps the Allies were even ready to throw in the towel, General Hatta had mused in a radio lecture, "now that they have seen a sample of what the Imperial forces can do." Whether they sued for peace or not, the editors of the *New Order in Greater East Asia* added, the United States and Britain were in a state of decline "to second-rate or third-rate powers, or even to total disintegration and collapse."

On February 12, 1942, Admiral Yamamoto had transferred his flag from the battleship *Nagato* to the newly commissioned superbattleship *Yamato*. His new quarters were perhaps the largest and most sumptuous to be inhabited by any naval officer in the world—the C-in-C lived like a prince in a suite of huge, air-conditioned cabins on the starboard side of the *Yamato's* upper deck, amidships. He took his meals in an airy wardroom, at a long polished wooden table, under the expressionless royal gaze of Hirohito, whose portrait was prominently mounted on a bulkhead. Yamamoto seemed to have plenty of spare time on his hands, even in wartime—he passed most of each day comfortably settled in his day cabin, a handsomely furnished living space adjoining his sleeping quarters. As always, he was diligent in reading and answering letters, not only those from friends and colleagues but also those written by strangers to congratulate and encourage him. The yeomen who handled his mail had been instructed to place letters from Chiyoko Kawai, the admiral's geisha lover, on the top of the pile. (In late December, Yamamoto had told Chiyoko that he was receiving a flood of letters, "but the only ones I'm always eagerly waiting for are from you.") He spent long hours hunched over a *shogi* board, playing against members of his staff, often for money. He entertained visitors, including naval subcommanders and members of the royal family. Often he hosted sukiyaki dinners. When he showed himself on deck, he was always turned out in a finely tailored white uniform, starched and pressed. His dark complexion contrasted sharply with his very white teeth and the pristine white expanse of his uniform coat. His brass buttons had been polished by his stewards until they shined like mirrors, and his chrysanthemum-crested gold epaulettes gleamed brilliantly in the sun. Admiral Yamamoto always looked the part.

The Japanese press and public were acclaiming Yamamoto as a national hero, but he shrank from their adulation. He felt "intolerably embarrassed at the way the achievements in battle of those under me . . . have made me a star overnight." When the Navy Ministry awarded him two new decorations, he said he would be "ashamed" to wear them. He had not yet laid eyes on an enemy ship or plane, he said, while other men were fighting and dying and had received no medals. He declined an invitation to have his portrait painted, confiding to a friend that "portraits are vulgarities to be shunned only less vigorously than bronze statues."

Yamamoto was troubled by the bombast and braggadocio of the official communiqués. He thought the euphoria infantile and shortsighted, and warned that Japanese forces had not yet encountered the enemy at his best. The Japanese navy, traditionally unwilling to trumpet its accomplishments, had once been nicknamed the "silent navy." Now the term "invincible navy" was often thrown around, even within the ranks of the service. Navy headquarters in Tokyo issued victory bulletins over the radio, always to the accompaniment of stirring orchestral music such as the "Battleship March." Yamamoto winced at these broadcasts. What had happened to the navy's modesty, a trait that had so starkly distinguished it from the army in the past? "All they need do really is quietly let people know the truth," he told a group of officers, as they listened to one such announcement. "There's no need to bang the big drum. Official reports should stick to the absolute truth—once you start lying, the war's as good as lost."

That Japan had scored so many easy victories in the war's early stages came as no surprise to Yamamoto. In a typical passage in one of his prewar letters, the C-in-C had predicted: "For a while we'll have everything our own way, stretching out in every direction like an octopus spreading its tentacles. But it'll last for a year and a half at the most." The war could only end with an armistice, followed by negotiations and concessions. The fall of Singapore, an event he had expected to occur about six months into the war, would present the ideal moment to open truce talks. Britain, he believed, would cut a deal to keep India, a colony it would hate to lose as much as an "old man" would hate "being deprived of his foot warmer." The United States would also have to be appeased, probably through a restora-

tion of conquered territories. Perhaps the Western powers would acknowledge Japan's preeminence in China, as they had once acknowledged Japan's
preeminence in Korea. Fight, conquer, bargain, concede—Yamamoto had
repeatedly urged that formula upon the Tojo-led cabinet, but his ideas had
been ignored.

Yamamoto detested the triumphant propaganda—"all the public hullabaloo"—because it seemed to foreclose the possibility of an armistice. Public
opinion, he believed, should be prepared for a return to diplomacy. Instead,
the Japanese people had been encouraged to believe that Japan was invincible, that its enemies were contemptible, and that its domination of Asia
was preordained. "To end a war while it's going favorably for one's own side
requires a special, different kind of effort," he said. Among the tens of thousands of officers and sailors of the Combined Fleet, Yamamoto was now the
sole remaining combat veteran of the Russo-Japanese War. In that conflict,
he recalled, Japan had agreed to a truce after destroying the Russian navy,
and had entered peace talks in a position of strength. Even so, the treaty
ending that war (the Treaty of Portsmouth in 1905) had been obtained only
with deeply unpopular concessions, including the ceding of territory on
Sakhalin Island. In the heady days of early 1942, the Japanese people were
prouder and more bellicose than ever before. They had been told that they
were a divine race, chosen by providence to drive the Western interlopers
out of Asia. They were evidently succeeding. Nothing less than total victory
would satiate them. But what if the alternative was total defeat?

THE SPEED WITH WHICH JAPANESE FORCES had achieved their assigned
tasks had caught the Imperial General Headquarters by surprise. When
Java was overrun in early March, the southern invasions were running
at least three months ahead of the prewar timetable. Perhaps it was the
sort of problem that any conqueror would be happy to have, but it put the
strategic planning staffs of both the army and navy in a quandary. What
to do next? No detailed operational plans existed for the next phase of
the war. If truth be told, Japanese military leaders had not yet agreed on
their most basic strategic direction, beyond the conquests they had already
achieved. In many cases, the army and navy held sharply divergent views,
and the Japanese regime lacked mechanisms to resolve those differences.
There was further discord within the navy, notably between the Tokyo-

based Naval General Staff (NGS), which held formal responsibility for war planning, and Yamamoto's Combined Fleet staff, which did not. Groping toward a consensus was a muddled and cumbersome process, and it tended to produce decisions that were finessed to give all parties at least part of what they wanted.

One line of thinking held that Japan should dig in and assume a largely defensive posture. Rear Admiral Ryunosuke Kusaka, Nagumo's chief of staff, was a leading proponent of that strategy. He argued that the nation should husband its resources, shore up its interior supply lines, and concentrate its efforts on training and production. On its eastern, Pacific flank, Japan had amassed a network of far-flung islands, many of which were primitive and unfortified. Prewar planning had envisioned feeding matériel and men into those frontier islands, erecting strong defensive works on their beaches, and developing their airfields. Air superiority could be maintained all along that outer perimeter through a network of interlocking, mutually supporting air bases, so that reinforcements could be flown in quickly to repel any new Allied counteroffensive at the point of attack.

But the purely defensive strategy never won much standing in the high command. Cultural factors may have been at work: the samurai tradition favored initiative and aggression over defensive tactics. A preference for offensive warfare permeated the culture of both the army and navy, and was ingrained in their tactical doctrines, weapons systems, and training programs. "It's annoying to be passive," noted Admiral Ugaki (Yamamoto's chief of staff) in his diary on March 11. "Warfare is easier, with less trouble, indeed, when we hold the initiative." Having taken the initiative on December 7, 1941, the Japanese were loathe to yield it to the enemy. Naval planners were also steeped in the Mahanian principle of the "decisive battle," and shared a bedrock belief that the war could only be won by crushing the American fleet at one blow, as the Russian fleet had been crushed at Tsushima. In any case, the concept of the strong "defensive perimeter" had been shown up by the American carrier raids. With their flattops intact, the Americans could penetrate deep into the heart of Japan's oceanic empire, strike without warning, and escape unmolested.

In April 1942, Japan was the dominant military and naval power in Asia and in the Pacific, but it could not hope to maintain that status for long. The titanic warmaking capabilities of the United States had not been destroyed, nor even seriously impaired. It was only a matter of time—perhaps a year, perhaps less—before the enemy's freshly constituted sea, air, and land forces would launch heavy and sustained attacks along the Japanese perimeter. There was no hope in waging a prolonged war of attrition against a nation with ten times Japan's latent military-industrial strength. Japan must therefore try to run out the clock. It must find a way to inflict such devastating punishment on the Allies that they would be forced to sue for peace before the end of 1942.

As a solution to the problem, a group of officers within the NGS proposed an invasion of Australia. Five divisions of the Japanese army could easily be landed on the island-continent's undefended northern coast. Such an invasion might or might not force the British to ask for terms, but at the very least it would deny the Americans their great southern springboard for an eventual counteroffensive. A second proposal was to strike at India by landing troops on Ceylon or possibly even on the subcontinent itself, in hopes of prompting a nationalist uprising that would drive the British out. The Axis partners might then join forces in the Middle East.

But the Japanese army stalwartly opposed all new operations requiring troop commitments on such a large scale. Invading Australia or Ceylon would require transferring part of the Kwantung Army from Manchuria, and army leaders preferred to keep those troops in place with an eye toward invading Siberia, especially if Hitler's spring offensive pushed the Soviet Union to the brink of collapse. In an army-navy liaison conference on March 7, the army representatives urged the navy to curb its ambitions. Admiral Ugaki griped in his diary that when the navy had presented its view, "The army took its usual attitude of refusing it . . . when they had no opinion of their own." The Japanese army had a million troops in Manchuria and another 400,000 in China, but could not spare two divisions for operations in the Pacific or Indian oceans. Captain Yoshitake Miwa, the Combined Fleet's air officer, vented his frustration: "We want to invade Ceylon; we are not allowed to! We want to invade Australia; we cannot! We want to attack Hawaii; we cannot do that either! All because the army will not give us the necessary forces."

The proper focus of future operations in the South Pacific, the army negotiators maintained, was to fortify the existing perimeter and sever enemy sea communications. To that end, they offered a plan to capture Port Moresby, on the southern coast of New Guinea. That Australian-held port was only 300 miles from the Cape York Peninsula, the northeast extremity of Australia, and would provide a fine base from which to menace Allied shipping in the Coral Sea. The beginnings of that offensive had already been set into motion with the capture of Lae and Salamaua, on the northeast coast of New Guinea, in early March. The navy agreed that Australia should be isolated from the United States, but proposed to do so by pushing farther east through the axis of the Admiralties, the Bismarcks, and the Solomons, eventually to capture New Caledonia, Samoa, and Fiji. (That was precisely the line of attack that Admiral King had most feared.) The two alternatives were not mutually exclusive. Both were aimed at interdicting sea communications between the United States and Australia, and both could be staged from Rabaul, the major Japanese sea and air base on the island of New Britain. The path of least resistance was to do both, in two stages—first seize Port Moresby, then New Caledonia, perhaps followed by Samoa and Fiji.

These talks seemed to point toward a rough-and-ready army-navy consensus, but in mid-March, Admiral Yamamoto threw a wrench in the works. He insisted that the full strength of the Combined Fleet should be committed to a major offensive in the central Pacific, aimed at capturing the tiny American atoll of Midway.

The proposal was a scaled-down version of the grander ambition of capturing Hawaii, a scheme that had long been championed by Japanese imperialists. In March 1942, the military and logistical barriers to a Japanese amphibious attack on Hawaii were insurmountable. Oahu was simply too strong and too far away from Japan—the constraints on available shipping and troop transportation alone ruled out such a massive operation. Moreover, the army flatly refused to supply the needed troops. But Midway, near the northwestern extremity of the Hawaiian archipelago, was a much easier nut to crack, and would provide a sea and air base from which to menace the sea routes into Pearl Harbor, which lay 1,149 miles to the southeast. It might even function as a springboard for a future invasion of Oahu.

Combined Fleet staff planners, supervised by Admiral Ugaki, had been analyzing and refining the plan since the first week of 1942. The planning process had included extensive tabletop war gaming exercises in the *Yamato*'s cavernous wardroom. Yamamoto had certainly been kept apprised of these studies, which had been carried out right under his nose. But it was not until mid-March, after the army had quashed the proposed invasions of Australia and Ceylon, that the C-in-C threw the full weight of his considerable prestige and power behind the Midway plan. When he did so, his real objective was not the island itself, which was of dubious value, but the hope of flushing the Pacific Fleet out of Pearl Harbor and destroying it in a pitched naval battle. Above all, Yamamoto wanted to burn, sink, or capture the American aircraft carriers, which had been a thorn in the side of Japan's new Pacific empire ever since they had escaped destruction on December 7, 1941. Enemy carrier planes had struck north and south of the equator—in the Marshalls (February 1, 1942), at Wake Island (February 24), in the waters east of Rabaul (February 20), at Marcus Island (March 4), at Lae and Salamaua on New Guinea (March 10). None of these raids had done a great deal of damage, and they had certainly done nothing to slow the pace of the Japanese advance. But there was no denying that the American flattops posed an ever-present threat. Halsey's March 4 raid on lonely little Marcus Island, a mere 600 miles from the homeland, brought home the naval leadership's most terrible fear—that the Americans might stage an attack on Tokyo itself.

It would be no exaggeration to say that Yamamoto and his navy colleagues were obsessed with the specter of enemy bombers appearing suddenly over the capital. Since time immemorial, the Japanese people had regarded their homeland as inviolate, but their densely built wooden cities were extraordinarily vulnerable to air attack. Japanese middle-aged or older could remember the Great Kanto earthquake and fire of 1923, which had leveled huge swaths of Tokyo and Yokohama and left about 140,000 dead. A few incendiary bombs on a dry, windy day might bring a repetition of the horror. Above all, Tokyo was the imperial seat, and if the city could be hit from the air, then so could the Imperial Palace itself. Fear for the emperor's life, wrote navy airman Mitsuo Fuchida, was an "ever-present and highly disturbing worry. . . . The fighting services, especially, were imbued with the idea that their foremost duty was to protect the Emperor from danger. Naturally, they felt that it would be a grave dereliction of this duty if the Emperor's safety were jeopardized by even a single enemy raid on Tokyo."

In his private correspondence, Admiral Yamamoto returned again and again to the subject. He advised a Shinbashi geisha to move some of her property out of Tokyo, because the navy had no reliable means to deter an enemy air attack on the city. He complained bitterly of radio and press reports assuring the Japanese people that air raids were not to be feared. His staff recalled that the C-in-C asked for daily reports of the weather in Tokyo, and was always relieved to learn that the skies above the city were overcast. He directed Ugaki to arrange for long-range reconnaissance flights to be made over the eastern sea approaches, and to conscript a fleet of fishing sampans to be deployed in a picket line some 600–700 miles off the coast. In February and March, when most of the Japanese navy was engaged in conquest far to the south, erroneous reports of enemy ships or aircraft east of Japan prompted many sensational "scares." On three separate occasions, the Combined Fleet's main division of battleships, which had remained in the Inland Sea, was sent racing into the offing to chase those phantoms. On March 12, as Japanese cities held rallies to celebrate the surrender of the Dutch East Indies, Admiral Ugaki confided in his diary: "If real enemy planes raided amidst the festivities, the mere thought of the result makes me shudder. A great air raid over the heads of the rejoicing multitude! I think it is better to stop such celebrations."

Working around the clock for several days and nights in late March, Combined Fleet staff completed a preliminary draft plan for the Midway operation. It received Yamamoto's endorsement on March 30. The operation would require the approval of the Imperial General Headquarters in Tokyo, but as in the earlier case of the Pearl Harbor raid, the headquarters was loathe to give it. For the second time in six months, Admiral Yamamoto deliberately sought to usurp the rightful planning and policy-making function of the Naval General Staff. In doing so, he seems to have been motivated (at least in part) by a desire to settle some old scores. In the 1930s, his efforts to advance the cause of naval aviation had often run into resistance from conservative battleship officers on the NGS. In the fall of 1941, the NGS had opposed his plan to attack Pearl Harbor, and backed down only when he had come to the brink of tendering his resignation. After the attack had knocked the American battleships out of action, leading officers of the NGS tried to share in the glory by concealing their attempt to obstruct the operation. Yamamoto was an old hand in the politics of the navy, and was not above making a ruthless power play against the headquarters. He was at the height of his power and influence, and seemed determined not to let the moment pass—if possible he would arrogate the planning and strategy-making functions of the NGS to his own staff.

The issue was settled in a planning conference at the Imperial General Headquarters between April 2 and 5. Yamamoto sent an emissary to Tokyo to represent the view of the Combined Fleet: Commander Yasuji Watanabe, a staff gunnery officer and one of the admiral's regular *shogi* opponents. With the boss's half-shaped plan under his arm, Watanabe went into conference with a group of NGS planners. He encountered hard-hitting, tenacious opposition. Those on the staff were irked by the prospect of any diversion or delay of their preferred thrust toward New Caledonia, which they had embraced as a fallback to an invasion of Australia after that operation had been deep-sixed by the army.

Commander Tatsukichi Miyo, First Section Air Officer of the NGS, laid out the case against the Midway operation with clarity and passion. His objections were similar to those raised against the more ambitious plan to invade Hawaii. To mount an operation so far across the central Pacific, said Miyo, required logistical support on a scale that would strain Japan's shipping resources. The carrier force was worn out and could likely not undertake both the northern and southern offensives within the fleet's aggressive timetable. Japanese naval forces would have no land-based air cover or reconnaissance, while the enemy would have it in abundance—the Japanese fleet would be entirely dependent on carrier airpower. The value of Midway, even if occupied successfully, was dubious. An air counterattack from the main Hawaiian Islands would be violent and sustained, and Pearl Harbor's submarine fleet would raise havoc with the shipping link to Japan. Midway would provide little value to reconnaissance, as U.S. task forces could easily skirt the 600- or 700-mile flight radius from the island. As for the hope that the offensive would draw the remnants of the Pacific Fleet out of Pearl Harbor for a decisive battle, Miyo raised the disturbing possibility that the Americans might not cooperate. What if they did not contest the landings, but merely conceded Midway to the invaders? The NGS compared Yamamoto's plan with their preferred attack in the south, and argued that it was inferior in every respect.

After the war, Miyo wrote that he and his colleagues were appalled by the hamhanded way in which the C-in-C had gone about planning his attack on Midway. "One wonders whether C. in C. Yamamoto appreciated just how ineffective aerial reconnaissance using Midway as a base would be," wrote Miyo. "Had he really taken into thorough account the enormous drain on resources and difficulty in maintaining supplies on such an isolated island, or the reduction in air strength necessary in other areas in order to keep it up, and the influence on the fleet's operational activities?"

But Commander Watanabe had not been sent to Tokyo to answer the staff's cogent criticisms. He had been sent to impose Yamamoto's will. After three days of ineffectual haggling, Watanabe called the *Yamato* on a secure telephone line and reported that the discussions were deadlocked. Now it remained only for Yamamoto to play his trump card, the same one he had played several months earlier to force the NGS to approve his raid on Pearl Harbor. Yamamoto told Watanabe to say that the best way to isolate Australia was to destroy the American flattops, and that if the Pacific Fleet did not contest the landing, then the Japanese would be left in possession of a strategically located territory in the central Pacific. The C-in-C's mind was "firmly made up." That was a coded threat to resign his command if the plan was not approved, and the NGS cried uncle. "Come, come," Admiral Shigeru Fukudome told Miyo, when the latter grew heated in reiterating his arguments. "Don't get too excited. Since the Combined Fleet's so set on the plan, why don't we study it to see if we can't accept it?"

On April 5, the NGS gave its tentative approval to Yamamoto's Midway offensive. But critical details remained unresolved, including (most importantly) the date of the operation. Opponents still held some hope of killing the operation through the shrewd use of delaying tactics. Typically in such matters, the sketchy consensus had involved face-saving compromises. Rather than simply choosing one course of action and ruling decisively against the others, the regime gave all parties, including the NGS and the army, part of what they wanted. At the insistence of the NGS, a second operation in the Aleutians was tacked onto the Midway plan, involving the capture of two islands and a raid on Dutch Harbor, on Unalaska Island.

On April 16, the General Headquarters issued Directive No. 86, which laid out the sequence of objectives for the next three months. In May, the capture of Port Moresby; in June, the capture of Midway and the Aleutians; in July, the seizure of New Caledonia and Fiji. Critical details remained to be filled in, but the next phase of the naval war had been decided and decreed.

ON THE FIRST DAY OF APRIL, at the Alameda Naval Air Station in San Francisco Bay, sixteen B-25 Mitchell bombers taxied from the hangars to a pier. Each aircraft was coaxed to a spot directly beneath the crane of the USS *Hornet*, a new *Yorktown*-class aircraft carrier painted in a distinctive blue-gray camouflage pattern. At a ground crewman's signal, the engines were cut and the twin propellers spun to rest. A hook descended and was fastened to a ring bolt on the top of the fuselage. Each aircraft was hoisted with loving care to the *Hornet's* flight deck, where it was let down gingerly, pushed to an assigned mark, and made fast to the deck by sturdy hemp lines. Sixteen times that process was repeated, until the entire after section of the flight deck was crowded with B-25s in a staggered double file.

The next day, April 2, the *Hornet* put to sea with her escorts: two heavy cruisers, four destroyers and a fuel tanker. They had been designated Task Force 18. The morning fog was lifting as the task force passed under the long red span of the Golden Gate Bridge, and the carrier was plainly visible to anyone watching from the hills of San Francisco or Marin. Every day of the war, warships of every size and description passed through that channel for undisclosed Pacific destinations. But in April 1942, an aircraft carrier was still a relatively rare sight, and it would have been natural for honest citizens to stop and stare. Rarer still was a flattop loaded with twin-engine army bombers, because (as anyone familiar with aviation knew) such airplanes did not operate from carriers. The B-25s were much larger than the Dauntlesses, Devastators, and Wildcats that were the standard carrier aircraft of the day. They had two engines and two tails, stood almost 18 feet high, and had a wingspan of 67 feet 6 inches, so that their wingtips protruded over the edges of the flight deck and hung over the sea like diving boards. Among the *Hornet's* crew, who had been told nothing of their mission or destination, it was rumored that the carrier would ferry the B-25s to Pearl Harbor, where they would be lifted off the deck by cranes. That offered the most plausible solution to the mystery, because every man aboard knew that twin-engine army bombers did not, under any circumstances, fly from aircraft carriers.

At Alameda, the *Hornet* had also embarked a large contingent of airmen and ground personnel of the Army Air Forces, 70 officers and 130 enlisted men. The officers shared the staterooms of the *Hornet's* pilots, with cots brought in to provide additional bunks. The two groups of aviators, though they had been conditioned to regard each other as aliens and rivals, got along well. They showed one another around their respective airplanes— the B-25s on the flight deck, the carrier planes crammed below, with wings folded erect, on the hangar deck. Lieutenant Commander Stephen Jurika, Jr., the ship's intelligence and operations officer, thought the army flyboys were laid-back to the point of being "undisciplined." They were careless in their uniforms, with crushed hats, open collars, and "worn-out, scuffed-type shoes." When quizzed by their navy hosts about their mission, they simply shrugged and looked away. They had been ordered not to talk. During the *Hornet's* westward voyage, they often slept in, skipped breakfast, and turned up late to the morning briefing at 0830. They spent most of their days and nights at the poker table. Whatever their mission, they did not seem terribly concerned.

HOURS AFTER THE RAID on Pearl Harbor, President Roosevelt had asked his military chiefs to find a way to hit back at Japan. He had returned to the point many times in the first three months of the war, as American morale descended to its nadir. The commander in chief asked, and asked again—was there any chance of bombing the Japanese home islands?

Admiral King had assigned two senior members of his staff, Captain F. S. "Frog" Low and Captain Donald B. Duncan, to investigate the possibilities. There were no ready options. The greatest obstacle was the great distances lying between Japan and any of the terrestrial airfields from which a long-range bombing attack might be launched. China, the Soviet Union, and the Aleutians were each considered and discarded. A carrier task force might creep within striking range of Japan, but the aircraft would have to be launched from a point no farther than 200 miles off the Japanese coast. In that vulnerable position, like a worm writhing on a hook, the carrier would have to await the return of her planes. The risk of losing one or more of America's precious flattops to a Japanese counter-strike was unacceptably high.

Frog Low, on a trip to Norfolk to inspect the newly commissioned USS *Hornet*, noticed a painted outline of a flight deck on a Naval Station runway. An idea entered his mind. That outline, used by pilots to hone their skills in carrier flight operations, was slightly elongated to reflect the benefit of the "apparent" wind. In actual carrier flight operations at sea, a flattop turned into the wind and used her engines to augment the speed of that wind across her flight deck. Even in a rare dead calm, a carrier could generate an apparent headwind equivalent to her maximum speed (32 knots in the case of the *Hornet*). In the North Pacific, there was normally at least a 10-knot breeze, which would allow for more than 40 knots of apparent wind in flight operations. No one in his right mind would try to land a twin-engine medium bomber on an aircraft carrier. But such an airplane might manage to *take off* from a carrier into the teeth of a gale-force headwind. If configured to fly at an extremely long range, a bomber squadron could be launched 500 miles off the Japanese coast, drop its payload on assigned targets in Japan, and continue across the East China Sea to secret airfields in coastal China. The operation would be risky for the carriers and extremely hazardous for the bomber crews, but it would not be expected by the Japanese. With luck and surprise it might succeed.

Admiral King described the concept to "Hap" Arnold, chief of the Army Air Forces, who was willing and even eager to try it. General Arnold chose as mission commander Lieutenant Colonel James H. Doolittle, one of the most famous aviators in the country, a stunt flyer who had (among other feats) been the first aviator in history to fly an "outside loop." Planning progressed behind a heavy veil of secrecy. Doolittle identified the B-25 Mitchell bomber as the airplane best suited to the job. With some ingenious modifications, the B-25 could be configured to carry a 1-ton bomb payload for an effective range of 2,400 nautical miles. Supplementary fuel tanks in the bomb compartment, crew corridor, and ventral turret would double the fuel capacity of a normally configured B-25. Weight would be saved by stripping the aircraft of all equipment that was not critical to the mission, including the radio, the bottom gun turret, and the Norden bombsight.

Doolittle recruited all-volunteer aircrews from the 17th Bombardment Group, USAAF. A navy flight instructor, Lieutenant Henry F. Miller, was assigned to train the B-25 crews in short-takeoff techniques at Eglin Field, Florida. Upon his arrival, Lieutenant Miller was asked if he had ever flown a B-25. "No," he replied; "I've never even seen one." The army pilots told him that the aircraft needed 110 miles per hour of airspeed to get off the ground, but on the first day of training Miller established that a B-25 could take off at just 65 to 70 miles per hour with full flaps, a speed that would easily be achieved on a carrier deck run.

Miller taught the army pilots to keep their feet mashed down on the brake pedals while the engines were throttled up to full bore. With the engines screaming, manifold pressure set properly, and the stabilizer back three fourths, they were to release the brakes abruptly and let the aircraft accelerate toward the (imaginary) edge of the flight deck. White flags planted along the edge of the runway marked the distances at 200, 300, and 500 feet. As the plane reached liftoff speed, the pilot eased back on the yoke, the nose went up, and the wheels left the deck.

"The man with the blue eyes." Admiral Chester W. Nimitz in a photograph taken c. 1940. *Getty Images.*

Nimitz with his son, Chet Junior. Photo taken in Texas, c. early 1920s, with unidentified man to right. *Getty Images.*

Official portrait of Admiral Nimitz, probably taken in 1940 or 1941, when he was Chief of the Bureau of Navigation. *Official U.S. Navy photograph.*

Admiral Ernest J. King. Official portrait, taken in 1945. *Official U.S. Navy photograph.*

The internationalist. Photo taken in the White House, early 1942. *FDR Library.*

Roosevelt and Churchill face the press, early 1942. *Getty Images.*

The Doolittle Raid, April 18, 1942. An army B-25 claws its way into the sky from the USS *Hornet*. *Official U.S. Navy photograph.*

USS *Hornet* (CV-8), photographed in late 1941.
U.S. Naval History and Heritage Command photograph.

USS *Yorktown* (CV-5) in the South Pacific, c. April 1942. Photo
taken by the crew of one of her own planes shortly after takeoff.
Official U.S. Navy photograph.

Douglas SBD Dauntless dive-bombers. In 1942, this aircraft was the most potent weapon in the U.S. Navy's arsenal. *Gamma-Keystone via Getty Images.*

The USS *Neosho*, a fuel tanker. Fueling at sea was the bane of early American carrier operations in the Pacific War. *Official U.S. Navy photograph.*

Vice Admiral Chuichi Nagumo, commander of *Kido Butai*, Japan's carrier striking force. Portrait photograph, taken c. 1941–42. *U.S. Naval History and Heritage Command photograph.*

It was a simple technique, really. The most difficult and dangerous aspect of carrier flight operations was not the takeoff but the landing. But these army pilots had never set foot on an aircraft carrier. How would their nerves hold up when they were staring down that short, wet, pitching deck into the oncoming seas? Even Colonel Doolittle, when he climbed into the cockpit of his B-25 after it had been parked on the *Hornet*, was surprised at how short the flight deck looked. Lieutenant Miller, who was sitting in the cockpit beside him, assured the colonel that he had taken off with much less deck to spare. "Henry," Doolittle replied, "what name do they use in the Navy for bullshit?"

Eleven days out of San Francisco Bay, the *Hornet* was at latitude 38° north, longitude 180°—directly on top of the International Date Line, about 1,700 miles northeast of Oahu. Dawn broke over a green, rolling sea flecked with whitecaps. There was a low, thick cloud ceiling. The sixteen B-25s heaved and strained at their tie-downs, like butterflies clinging to a windblown leaf.

As the light came up, it revealed the presence of a second aircraft carrier on the *Hornet*'s port beam. She was the *Enterprise*. She had sailed from Pearl Harbor on April 8 with orders to rendezvous with the *Hornet* at these coordinates. *Enterprise* and her screening vessels (the heavy cruisers *Northampton* and *Salt Lake City*, with four destroyers and a fuel tanker) were designated Task Force 16, under the command of Vice Admiral Bill Halsey. The *Hornet*'s Task Force 18 was now subsumed into Task Force 16, and Admiral Halsey assumed command of the combined force. The *Enterprise* air group would provide protection and reconnaissance, since the *Hornet*'s own planes were trapped in the hangar deck until the flight deck had been cleared of Doolittle's bombers.

The crew of the *Enterprise*, who knew nothing of their mission, studied the *Hornet* with intense curiosity. The B-25, with its squarish nose and dual rudders, was an easily recognizable aircraft. Several *Enterprise* fighters had been launched at dawn and were orbiting overhead. "As I flew over the *Hornet*, I looked down and saw those B-25s packed on the flight deck," recalled machinist Tom F. Cheek. "Needless to say, I spent the next three and a half hours wondering about our destination. Tokyo wasn't even considered." According to the most plausible scuttlebutt, they were to ferry the bombers to the Aleutian Islands, or possibly to a Russian base on the Kamchatka Peninsula.

Later that morning, Halsey authorized an electrifying public announcement, which was delivered over the *Enterprise*'s loudspeakers: "This force is
bound for Tokyo." The crew cheered, shouted, applauded, and backslapped
their mates in exultation.

The now-enlarged Task Force 16 set a course of 265 degrees, almost
due west, at speed 16 knots. For the next several days, the two carriers
and their escorts forged across the same desolate ocean expanses that
Nagumo's carriers had traversed four months earlier, in the opposite direction, to attack Pearl Harbor. In those high latitudes, at that season of the
year, the sea and sky were the same tint of gunmetal gray. From the *Salt
Lake City*, war reporter Robert Casey looked out at a line of ships leading
ahead. In the "misty grey" light, he wrote, they looked like "a procession
of Gothic cathedrals." A bitter cold wind sliced into the men stationed
on deck. They wore their heavy winter uniforms with watch coats, wool
gloves, and hats—any exposed skin quickly turned red and raw. "God
damnest weather I've ever seen," said Lieutenant Robin Lindsey, an *Enterprise* landing signal officer. "For three days the waves were so high the
deck was pitching so much that I had to have a person stand behind me
to hold me on the landing signal platform so I wouldn't fall down. Several
times I did, and you can imagine the amazement of the pilot's face as he
passed over with no signal officer there."

On the *Hornet*, the B-25 airmen were briefed by Lieutenant Commander
Jurika, who had once served as a naval attaché in Tokyo and knew the
country well. They pored over maps and intelligence reports, identifying
major landmarks that could be used in navigating to targets at low altitude.
Jurika told them everything he knew about Japanese antiaircraft defenses.
Colonel Doolittle was still refining his plans and assigning targets in Japan.
The colonel's plane would be the first to launch. He would lead the others to Japan, arriving at nightfall. There the sixteen B-25s would fan out
and hit military and industrial targets in Tokyo, Yokohama, Nagoya, Kobe,
and Osaka. They would continue over the Japanese islands and the South
China Sea to newly constructed special airfields along the Chinese coast.
There they would land, refuel laboriously from fuel drums rigged with hand
pumps, and then take off again to fly to safer airfields deep in the interior
of China. The B-25s would be turned over to Chiang Kai-shek's Nationalist
forces, and the aircrews would be smuggled back to the United States by

other means. "If we all get to Chungking," Doolittle told his aircrews, "I'll throw us the biggest Goddamn party you ever saw."

Jurika briefed the aircrews on how to avoid capture by the Japanese army once they had landed in China. If they were forced to crash-land or bail out, he said, they should seek help from Chinese civilians, who might contact local guerrillas who could smuggle them out of the country. They practiced the phrase *Lusau hoo metwa fugi* ("I am an American"). When it seemed to Jurika that the army airmen were not taking his advice seriously, he warned them that they were likely to be beheaded if taken prisoner. "This seemed to settle them down quite a bit."

Four days later, when the task force was about 1,000 miles east of Tokyo, the weather turned. A gale-force wind blew out of the southwest, visibility fell to about one mile, and blasts of cold spray gusted over the flight decks of the *Enterprise* and *Hornet*. The *Enterprise* cancelled flight operations. One of the B-25 pilots noted that the rise and fall of the *Hornet* was caus-ing his cockpit altimeter to fluctuate by as much as 200 feet. The two car-riers and four cruisers refueled from the tankers, a difficult and dangerous procedure that saw two men swept overboard (both were rescued). The destroyers and tankers, which labored mightily in those heavy seas, were ordered to remain behind. The carriers and cruisers continued westward at a speed of 20–22 knots, shuddering with the effort of their engines, climb-ing up the waves and plunging into the troughs, hurling enormous sheets of spray over their decks. In that violent manner they pushed another 400 miles into enemy waters.

On April 18, the day the *Hornet* was scheduled to launch Doolittle's bombers, the task force breached Yamamoto's small craft picket line. At 3:10 a.m., the *Enterprise* radar picked up two blips on the screen, about four miles away to the southwest. Halsey ordered a turn to the northwest to avoid the strange vessels. An hour later, the task force resumed its westerly course. Shortly after first light, the *Enterprise* launched a search flight and combat air patrol. At 7:15 a.m., when the sun was well above the horizon, one of the search planes, an SBD, returned to the carrier and dropped a beanbag message which was taken immediately to Halsey. "Enemy surface ship— latitude 36-04N, Long. L53-10E, bearing 276° true—42 miles. Believed seen by enemy."

The task force continued west. Halsey wanted to get Doolittle as close to his target as possible. At 7:44 a.m., the *Enterprise* lookouts made direct visual contact with a small vessel, about two miles away to the southwest. From the carrier flight deck she seemed to vanish and then reappear as she rose and fell in the heavy seas. The sky was overcast, but below the cloud ceiling visibility was excellent. Halsey ordered the cruiser *Nashville* to destroy the vessel. But there was little hope of blowing her out of the water before she could radio a contact report back to the mainland.

She was the *Nitta Maru*—a steel-hull fishing sampan, about 90 feet long, taken into the Japanese navy to guard the sea approaches to Japan. A Japanese crewman told the skipper that there were "two beautiful Japanese carriers passing by." The skipper, studying the strange ships on the horizon, replied: "Yes, they are beautiful, but they are not ours." He radioed the contact report immediately. His transmission was intercepted by the American ships, and Halsey was notified that the contact report had gone out. Task Force 16's cover was blown. He had hoped to take Doolittle 150 miles farther west, but now he believed he had no choice but to order an immediate launch. To the *Hornet* he flashed the order: "Launch planes. To Col. Doolittle and his gallant command, good luck and God bless you. Halsey."

While the *Hornet* turned into the wind and made ready to get the B-25s aloft, the *Nashville* raced toward the *Nitta Maru* at 35 knots, made a smart turn to port, and opened fire with her main 6-inch battery. The shells fell all around the vessel, throwing up huge geysers on every side—but each time the curtain of spray was torn away to leeward, the little *Nitta Maru* remained afloat and unharmed. She was a daunting target, bobbing on the swells like a cork, and sliding entirely out of view every time she pitched into a trough. The *Nashville* gunners timed their salvos to coincide with the rise and fall of the sea, but try as they might they could not score a hit. "Shells are tossed like machine gun bullets," wrote Casey, who watched from the deck of the *Salt Lake City*. "Flashes run around the ship like lights on a electric sign." The plucky little sampan actually fired back at the *Nashville* with her small-caliber deck guns, but the rounds did not even reach half the distance to the cruiser.

The *Enterprise* VF-6 fighters, guided to the spot by the fall of the *Nashville*'s shells, tried to lend a hand. They flew low over the *Nitta Maru*, intending to strafe the vessel with their 50-caliber machine guns, but they also found it surprisingly tough to hit the little sea-tossed target, which was rising and falling, Warrant Officer Cheek recalled, "like a yoyo." The columns of water thrown up by the *Nashville's* shells actually rose above the height of the planes as they made their strafing runs. After several passes, the Wildcat pilots reported that the vessel was badly shot up and that it was doubtful any of her crew was still alive. Shortly thereafter she sank.

The entire engagement had been watched with great interest (and not without sarcastic commentary) by the crew of the *Enterprise*, who rarely had the opportunity to witness a naval surface action. Neither the *Nashville* nor the *Enterprise* air group could take much pride in the action. The *Nashville* had fired no fewer than 928 6-inch rounds at the little sampan, an expenditure of ammunition that her captain described as "ridiculous" and "excessive." (It is possible that some of those shells struck the vessel but did not detonate, passing cleanly "through and through.") One of the F4F Wildcats fired a full 1,200 rounds of .50-caliber ammunition at the vessel. In his after-action report to Nimitz, Halsey wrote that the performance of the planes had been "disappointing." He added: "It is again indicated that more time must be available for training when air groups are at shore bases. This need is becoming more emphatic as time goes on." The *Nitta Maru's* small machine guns had even managed to take down an *Enterprise* SBD. The pilot was forced to ditch the aircraft in the sea; he and his backseat man got out before it sank and were safely recovered.

Meanwhile, the *Hornet* hurried to get Doolittle's bombers aloft. As the big loudspeakers on the island (superstructure) blared commands, deck crews respotted the B-25s to their launch positions. "In about half an hour," Lieutenant Ted W. Lawson recalled, "the Navy had us crisscrossed along the back end of the flight deck, two abreast, the big double-rudder tail assemblies of the sixteen planes sticking out of the edges of the rear of the ship at an angle." The main 500-gallon wing tanks had previously been filled, but now they were topped off to restore the few pints that had evaporated. The deck crews rocked the planes to break any fuel bubbles that may have formed in the lines or tanks. The jury-rigged reserve tanks, including the bulletproof tank installed in the bottom turret and a metal tank in the top of the bomb bay, were filled to capacity. The ordnance crews brought the bomb carts up in the forward elevator and rolled them back along the heaving deck to the underside of the planes. Into the bay of each airplane were lifted three 500-pound conventional bombs and one 500-pound incendiary bomb. Some were affixed with medals that had been bestowed upon American officers by the Japanese government before the war; others were scrawled with messages such as "I don't want to set the world on fire, just Tokyo," and "You'll get a BANG out of this."

The *Hornet*'s captain, Marc Mitscher, descended to the flight deck to see his guests off. He and Doolittle shook hands as a photographer snapped a photo. Then the colonel poked his head into the *Hornet*'s ready room, where his aircrews were assembled, and said, "Come on, fellas. Let's go." The loudspeaker blared: "Army pilots, man your planes!" The aviators weaved through the parked planes, each to his own, and climbed aboard.

The engines fired to life and began warming at low rpm. The deck crews circled each plane and began removing the tie-downs, one by one. Other navy crewmen walked across the flight deck with large white boards held over their heads, so that they could be read in the cockpits—they were marked with compass readings and notations on the strength and direction of the wind. Fuel hoses continued to feed the tanks, topping off the small quantities consumed as the engines were warmed. At the last minute before the doors were sealed, several additional 5-gallon fuel cans were handed up to the crew, who stowed them at their feet. No B-25 had ever flown a mission with even half the amount of fuel that Doolittle's bombers would carry that day.

The voice on the loudspeaker cried, "Prepare to launch aircraft." The *Hornet* turned into the wind and throttled up to nearly 30 knots. The apparent wind over the deck now rose to some 75 knots, and the deck crews had to drop to their bellies and hang on to the tie-down fittings to avoid being blown into the blurred disks of the propellers. Ordnanceman Alvin Kernan, watching the scene from the nearby *Enterprise*, recalled "high green foam-flecked waves and the taste and smell of the northern ocean." The *Hornet*'s bow climbed and then plunged; climbed and then plunged again. Heavy spray was thrown into the faces of the men stationed on the flight deck. "As the old salts would say," SBD pilot Clayton Fisher recalled, "we took some 'green water' over the flight deck when the bow pitched down. I was watching from the forward starboard catwalk along the flight deck and got rather wet from the spray."

The B-25 pilots had trained for a carrier takeoff, and they had been briefed exhaustively in the theory and practice of a carrier takeoff—but none had ever attempted such a thing even in calm conditions, and these were not calm conditions. As Lawson looked down from his cockpit at the "wet, rolling deck," his heart sank into his stomach. It was a harrowing sight. "The *Hornet* bit into the rough-house waves, dipping and rising until the flat deck was a crazy seesaw," he wrote later. "Some of the waves actually were breaking over the deck. The deck seemed to grow smaller by the minute, and I had a brief fear of being hit by a wave on the take-off and of crashing at the end of the deck and falling off into the path of the careening carrier." The violent pitching of the *Hornet* would require flawless timing. The flight deck control officer would have to give the "Go" signal to each aircraft while the bow was falling, Lieutenant Commander Jurika observed, so that "you would actually launch them into the air at least horizontal but on the upswing, in fact, giving them a boost up into the air." Each heavily laden B-25 would have to begin its full-throttle run "downhill," apparently rushing headlong into the next oncoming wave. That was old hat to the carrier pilots, but it would be a harrowing experience for any aviator who had never done it before. He would have to repress his instinct to pull back too soon, which might stall his airplane at the moment of liftoff.

Every catwalk, every gun gallery, every bridge wing on the *Hornet* was crowded with sailors and officers who stood watching with white knuckles and clenched jaws. A camera crew headed by the Hollywood director John Ford recorded the scene from a post high on the *Hornet*'s island. On the *Enterprise*, half a mile away, many of the observers remained skeptical, and a few insisted that the planned takeoff was impossible. It would be cancelled at the last moment, they said, or else end in disaster. Kernan wrote that a betting pool rode on the outcome, and "there was soon heavy money down on both sides: would they make it, would they not?" Finding himself among the pessimists, Kernan wagered ten hard-earned dollars that fewer than half of Doolittle's planes would get into the air.

The navy control officer stood near the *Hornet*'s bow, leaning back against the gusts, and waved a checkered flag in a circular motion. That signaled the first B-25 in the queue, the aircraft piloted by Colonel Doolittle, to pour on throttle while standing on the brakes. With the twin engines screaming so loudly that onlookers feared they might burn themselves out, and the entire body of the airplane quaking against the wooden wheel chocks, the checkered flag came down in the "Go" signal. The chocks were pulled away in unison and Doolittle released the brakes. His plane lurched forward and hurtled down the port side of the flight deck, the left wing hanging well over the port side of the ship. As the *Hornet*'s bow came up, the 75-knot headwind applied its powerful lift and Doolittle's wheels left the deck.

"I would say he was 50 feet in the air within 50 feet of the bow," said Jurika, watching from the bridge. "He went off with the least run and hopped right into the air." At first, the plane was only moving about 30 knots faster than the carrier, so it appeared to be hovering, edging forward only gradually, like a tremendous kite rising on a string. Lieutenant Lawson wrote that Doolittle "hung his ship almost straight up on its props, until we could see the whole top of his B-25." On the brink of a stall, he forced his nose down, banked left, and flew back along the port side of the carrier, then banked left again to circle across the *Hornet*'s wake. He was on his way to Tokyo.

Doolittle's successful takeoff fortified the morale of the fifteen other pilots, as it had been intended to do. Now they prepared to follow him, one by one, with renewed confidence. But the second B-25, piloted by Lieutenant Travis Hoover, careened off the bow without gaining altitude. From the perspective of men standing on the *Hornet*'s stern, it seemed to drop into the sea. Hoover nosed up and poured on throttle, trying to claw his way into the air, and very nearly stalled. "The pilot held the nose up so high that he was dragging his tail skid," recalled Fisher. "He ballooned up, almost stalled out, cleared the flight deck, and then we lost sight of him as the bow pitched up. I thought he'd crashed, but we finally saw him very low over the water. His props were blowing salt spray off the surface!" He staggered into the air and banked left, following Doolittle.

Each time a B-25 lurched forward to begin its takeoff run, its prop wash added to the cumulative strength of the actual wind and the apparent wind generated by the *Hornet*'s speed through the water. "It sure was windy!" recalled George Bernstein, a plane-pusher normally assigned to Torpedo Squadron Eight (VT-8). "We had to literally drop to the deck and hang on with our fingers in the tie-down fittings when the B-25s revved up. I had a line attached to myself and to other men on the team to keep us from blowing in towards the props." One crewman, aviation machinist's mate Robert W. Wall, lost his grip. He was wafted into the air and thrown into the spinning propeller of another plane. His arm was severed at the shoulder. Lieutenant Bill Farrow, pilot of the plane that had taken Wall's arm, was badly shaken by the accident, and nearly crashed on takeoff, but managed to claw his way into the sky as Hoover had done.

By hook or by crook, all fifteen planes got airborne and fell in behind Doolittle. Without fuel to spare for a rendezvous, they flew away one by one, in a long, irregular procession stretching away toward the gray western horizon. The sailors shouted in exultation, and even Lieutenant Miller, who was exasperated by the army pilots' failure to keep their stabilizers in neutral position as they took off, was moved by their courage: "I think without a doubt every officer and man aboard the *Hornet* would have pinned every medal in the world on those people who went off that deck in those airplanes." On the *Enterprise*, wrote Kernan, "we all cheered loudly and choked down a few patriotic tears. I thought my ten dollars well lost in a good cause, as if I had actually contributed the money to success in the war."

THE *NITTO MARU'S* CONTACT REPORT was received aboard the *Yamato* shortly after breakfast. The little sampan had reported sighting not two but three American aircraft carriers, a detail that must have seemed fantastic to the Combined Fleet staff. The Americans were thought to have only three carriers in the entire Pacific Ocean. Were they all now charging toward Tokyo, and from only a few hundred miles away? The absence of any follow-up transmissions from the *Nitto Maru* only seemed to confirm the report. Admiral Ugaki recorded that the fleet staff "plunged into activities at once." From *Yamato* flashed the signal: "Enemy task force containing three aircraft carriers as main strength sighted 0630 this morning 730 miles east of Tokyo. . . . Operate against American fleet." Yamamoto ordered Tactical Method No. 3, which involved sending units of both the First and the Second Fleet to sea to intercept the intruders. Admiral Nagumo, whose carrier force, *Kido Butai*, was off Formosa, on its way home from the Indian Ocean, was ordered to proceed at speed to the waters east of Japan.

Critically, however, the *Nitto Maru's* crew had failed to note that one of the carriers was carrying twin-engine bombers. If they had, the fleet staff might have put one and one together, and concluded that an enemy airstrike was already en route to Tokyo. An ordinary carrier bombing raid could not be launched outside a radius of about 200 miles, so if the American carriers had just breached the outer picket line, it was safe to assume they were still

400 or 500 miles away from launch position. That meant the capital could not be threatened until the following morning. At 9:45 a.m., a Japanese patrol plane flying along the east coast of Japan reported the appearance of a strange twin-engine bomber. The report was not taken seriously, because (as everyone knew) such airplanes could not operate from carriers. Another Japanese picket vessel spotted incoming B-25s and radioed, "Three enemy planes, course southwest," but that report was also shrugged off as an obvious error.

The first bombers arrived over Tokyo Bay shortly before noon on April 18. They had approached the coast at very low altitude, a measure to avoid detection from the air or ground, and to avoid the effective "cones" of the antiaircraft batteries. In an eerie reenactment of Pearl Harbor, Japanese observers on boats and on the ground assumed the intruders were friendly planes, and waved merrily at them. "You see," Lawson wrote, "the emblems on our plane were the old style: blue circle with white star and a red ball in the middle of the white star. Maybe that's what confused them. I'm sure we weren't being hailed as liberators." The B-25s passed near several Japanese military aircraft which made no attempt to engage or pursue them. Prime Minister Tojo himself was flying over the bay in a Japanese army plane that passed so near one of the incoming bombers that a fellow passenger could identify the pilot as a Caucasian.

A witness at a navy airfield on the bay realized belatedly that enemy planes were directly overhead. "Everyone at our airfield was in a state of shock," he said, "but there was nothing we could do about it. All of our airplanes were lined up on the airfield. But the enemy aircraft didn't even take a look at them. Instead the attackers disappeared and flew towards the Yokohama area."

Koiwa Kazuei was a civilian employee of the Yokosuka navy arsenal. He was on the telephone when an air-raid alert sounded, followed closely by the sound of large explosions outside his window. Looking out, he recalled, "The sky was full of the unfamiliar low-flying squat black American military aircraft. Antiaircraft fire exploded in the sky high above them." In a dry dock in front of his office, the warship *Daiho* had been hit, and was emitting "a ferocious cloud of black smoke. . . . Large numbers of wounded were being carried on stretchers to the infirmary next to the docks." As he watched, he was joined by the commanding officer of the facility, Vice

Admiral Ishichi Tsuzuki, who remarked, with a rueful smile, "The enemy is quite something."

The first group of B-25s, including the airplane piloted by Colonel Doolittle, climbed from the deck to about 1,500 feet as they flew over Tokyo. They hit several targets in Tokyo, including an oil tank, a steel mill, and a power plant. Some of the B-25s passed directly over the Imperial Palace, but Doolittle had issued explicit orders not to drop any bombs on the complex, though it could easily have been done. The next wave of planes remained at treetop altitude, the better to avoid the now-alerted fighter patrols and antiaircraft batteries. Lawson wrote that he flew up a valley toward Tokyo, so low that his aircraft was "lower than the hills on either side." One of the B-25 pilots reported that he flew under a power line to throw off pursuing fighters.

When Admiral Yamamoto was told that Tokyo had been bombed from the air, he became physically ill. His chief steward, Heijiro Omi, attested that he had never seen the admiral look so depressed. He retreated to his stateroom, shut the door behind him, and did not emerge for several hours, during which time Ugaki took effective command of the fleet. Thirty-two medium bombers with fighter escort took off from Yokosuka Naval Base to fly search and destroy missions to the east. A squadron of submarines that had been dispatched to Truk was radioed instructions to sweep back to the north. Three of Nagumo's fleet carriers—*Akagi*, *Hiryu*, and *Soryu*—were ordered to work up to full speed and track down and destroy the unknown intruders that had approached the Japanese homeland. (The carriers, returning via the Bashi Channel from their raids in the Indian Ocean, were in desperate need of repair and recuperation. They had been at sea a long time, having traveled some 50,000 miles since December 7; the accumulated wear and tear to equipment was beginning to tell, and their crews were nearing exhaustion. Even then, four months into the war, the Japanese were beginning to suffer from their blithe unconcern for the effects of fatigue on crew effectiveness.) But no Japanese ship or aircraft had the range or speed to catch the American carriers as they raced away at near-peak speed, dead east on the compass. By nightfall they had safely vanished into the cold, interminable wastes of the North Pacific.

Immediately after the last B-25 had gone aloft, the task force had turned eastward. With the *Hornet*'s flight deck clear for the first time since leaving San Francisco, the plane-pushers hurriedly brought the fighters up on the elevators. Later that morning, several were launched to fly combat air patrol, and to join the *Enterprise* air group in flying a wide air search pattern. The task force ran across several more picket boats during its retreat, which were sunk (with difficulty) by the orbiting American airplanes.

Task force radio operators picked up Japanese naval transmissions sent out in plain language, a clear sign that the enemy was flustered and in disarray. The messages themselves were so confused that they only confirmed that the Japanese had no idea how they had been attacked. Long-range radio bearings suggested that ships were operating at high speeds throughout the seas east of Japan. But no land-based aircraft could possibly reach the retreating task force. Unless enemy submarines happened to be in the vicinity, the American carriers had made a clean escape, and they knew it.

Every ship in the task force tuned in to Radio Tokyo, hoping to learn from the Japanese themselves that Doolittle's bombers had reached the target. At about 2 p.m. local time (noon in Tokyo), the English-language broadcaster suddenly cut short his script. There were a few seconds of confused mumbling in Japanese, and then the channel fell abruptly silent. The first B-25s had apparently arrived over the city. The news was announced over the *Hornet's* loudspeakers, prompting a new round of celebrations among the crew. After about thirty minutes of silence, the announcer came back on the air, this time speaking in shrill, rapid-fire Japanese. Throughout the task force, officers and sailors pressed into the radio rooms to listen. Though few could decipher a single word of Japanese, the howl of air-raid sirens could actually be heard in the background, and anyone could detect the panic in the announcer's voice. Those who understood Japanese translated for those who could not.

Atrocities had been committed, the announcer reported—bombs had fallen on temples, schools, train stations, and hospitals; thirty schoolchildren lay dead, having been strafed from the air. Apparently, rumors were being reported as fact. A woman's voice broke in several times, pleading for blood donors. "Give your blood as the men at the front are giving theirs," she shrieked. "Your lives are in danger. Your country is in danger. Tomorrow—even tonight—your children may be blown to bits. Give your blood. Save them. Save yourselves. Save Japan." Robert Casey, listening in the *Salt Lake City's* radio room, remarked: "We should have thought the whole of Japan in ashes."

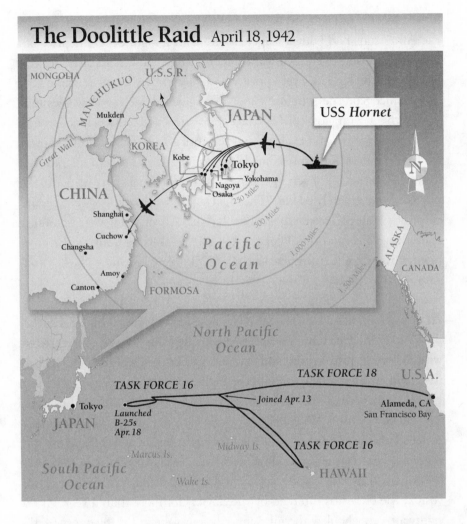

The Doolittle Raid April 18, 1942

It was only after several hours that the quavering radio voices began to subside. They had apparently been handed new scripts. They now calmly declared that military and civil defense officials had the situation well in hand. The air raid had done little damage, and the enemy planes had all been shot down or chased away. At one point it was said that nine bombers had been shot down, though it was not known what kind of planes they were or to what nation they belonged. Another report asserted that the capital had been attacked by an "armada of Chinese, American and Russian planes." Departing from the script, the broadcasters debated whether the airplanes had come from the south (China or the Philippines), from the north (the Aleutians or Soviet Siberia), or perhaps even from some secret airfield hidden in Japan itself. Then a fourth possibility was raised: perhaps the Americans had built a "supercarrier" with a flight deck a quarter of a mile long, capable of launching and landing large bombers. "You notice that nobody on the Jap radio yet knows whose planes they were," remarked one of the officers on the *Salt Lake City*. "They give themselves away guessing."

On the morning of April 19, the U.S. carriers and cruisers rendezvoused with the destroyers and tankers, and the entire Task Force 16 turned south for Pearl Harbor. Rough seas made for accidents, and several planes were lost. The *Hornet* had been operating at sea for so long that the perishable provisions were barely edible. "They had stocked the fantail with cases and cases of potatoes," recalled Stephen Jurika. "All of them were sprouting. Everything was sprouting." For the last half week before raising the green mountains of Oahu, the crew ate their fill of canned Spam.

ALL OF DOOLITTLE'S B-25S escaped Japanese territory unscathed. But as they passed over the East China Sea, the sixteen airplanes were widely scattered, with fuel tanks running dry and darkness gathering. Doolittle climbed over the cloud cover and flew through the night, navigating by dead reckoning. He could not pick up the radio beacon intended to guide him to the airfield in Chuchow, China. With his engines running on fumes, he and his crew strapped on their parachutes, opened the main hatch, and stepped out into the void. Fourteen other aircrews also bailed out over China. One of the B-25s turned north, toward Russia, and landed at an airstrip near Vladivostok; the crew was interned by the Soviets for more than a year. Of the eighty airmen who flew the mission, only four were killed in action. Of the remaining seventy-six, eight were captured by the Japanese.

In the United States, the press was cleared to report that bombs had fallen on Japanese soil. No details were released until months later, but the headline was enough to prompt a round of public rejoicing. Ten-year-old James Covert of Portland, Oregon, recalled wrapping a bedsheet around his torso and holding a flashlight above his head, like a torch—"I was the Statue of Liberty, and all the family danced around me." In Washington, a reporter asked Roosevelt for the location of the airfield from which the mysterious American bombers had taken off. The president's deadpan reply: "They came from our new secret base at Shangri-la."

The news was especially significant because it came little over a week after the surrender of 78,000 American and Filipino troops at Bataan. The "battling bastards" had held out for well over three months, but their strength and morale were sapped by malnutrition and various illnesses that could not be treated for lack of medicines. They had given up hope of seeing the promised "mile-long" convoy of ships bringing food, ammunition, and supplies from the United States. With the surrender of Bataan on April 9, the Japanese had apparently made little or no preparations to handle such a large number of prisoners, and the result was the Bataan "Death March," in which some 10,000 Allied prisoners were murdered, one of the most infamous atrocities of the Second World War. Though the details would not be publicized until much later, those searing events of April 1942—the murder of surrendered prisoners on the road out of Bataan, the bombing of a Japanese city by Doolittle's B-25s, and the subsequent execution of three captured American airmen—did much to embitter both sides and brutalize the war.

By the morning after the Doolittle raid, Japan's state-controlled media had recovered its composure. The new official line emphasized that the bombing attack had been ludicrously ineffective, a mere pinprick. In a pun that must have perplexed its audience, a radio announcer suggested that it was not a "do-little" but a "do-nothing" raid. In fact, as Mitsuo Fuchida later remarked, it would have been more accurate to call it a "do-much" raid. Though it had been brief and relatively benign, the attack was interpreted by many Japanese as a dark portent of the future. In their living memories, and even in their written history, the Japanese had no experience of foreign incursions; they had never dared to imagine that their homeland could be violated in such a manner. The navy fighter pilot Saburo Sakai, stationed in the South Pacific, received a letter from a female cousin who lived in Tokyo. The raid, she told him, "has brought about a tremendous change in the attitude of our people toward the war. Now things are different; the bombs have dropped here on our homes. It does not seem any more that there is such a great difference between the battlefront and the home front." Sakai added that the news "unnerved" his fellow airmen: "The knowledge that the enemy was strong enough to smash at our homeland, even in what might be a punitive raid, was cause for serious apprehension of future and heavier attacks."

The Japanese army, and especially the Japanese navy, had suffered a calamitous loss of face. American warplanes had been permitted to defile the divine skies above the emperor's palace, and not a single intruder had been shot down. "Our homeland has been air raided and we missed the enemy without firing a shot at him," Admiral Ugaki noted in his diary on April 20. "This is exceedingly regrettable." A chagrined Yamamoto remarked that the raid "provides a regrettable graphic illustration of the saying that a bungling attack is better than the most skillful defense." The C-in-C had ordered all available naval forces to sea in a wild goose chase that had only burned fuel and exhausted their crews, while underscoring Japan's vulnerability to future raids of the same sort. Not until the 20th did Yamamoto acknowledge that the American squadron was long gone. An order flashed out to all units by radio: "Cease operations against American fleet."

Overcoming their initial confusion, the Japanese military leaders soon reconstructed what had happened. Signal Corps photographs, developed and studied the afternoon of the raid, confirmed that the bombers had been B-25s. By midnight on the 18th, the Japanese army in China reported crash landings in Chekiang (now Zhejiang) and Kiangsu (now Jiangsu) provinces. The first American pilots to be captured gave false answers, claiming either that they had flown from the Aleutian Islands or from a mythological super-carrier. "They never told the truth," wrote Ugaki on April 19. "We must investigate further promptly so that we can take proper measures for the future." Two days later he noted, with a chilling subtext, "American war prisoners captured at Nanchang have been sent to Nanking, where they told the truth at last." And on April 22, "More truth has been added to the statements of the POWs . . ." Now the Japanese knew that Doolittle's B-25s had been launched from the deck of one of the accursed American carriers.

In China, the Japanese army launched an operation called "Sei-Go," with the goal of capturing the airfields that had been constructed to receive Doolittle's planes. The Japanese were well aware that B-25 airmen had been sheltered by local civilians or guerrillas, and the offensive seems to have degenerated into a mass reprisal against the population of Chekiang and Kiangsu provinces. Japanese troops laid waste to the region, routinely slaughtering the inhabitants of entire towns suspected of aiding the American aviators. Biological warfare units spread cholera, typhoid, and dysentery pathogens. Chiang Kai-shek cabled FDR: "The Japanese troops slaughtered every man, woman, and child in those areas—let me repeat—these Japanese troops slaughtered every man, woman, and child in those areas." It is impossible to know precisely how many were murdered, but the toll certainly ran into the tens of thousands.

Admiral Yamamoto took a newly high tone with the panjandrums of Tokyo. He said that Midway Island had probably been the base of the attack (it had not). Midway was the lynchpin of the American threat to the homeland, he said, and if it was not taken quickly, forces committed to homeland defense would have to be greatly expanded at the expense of further offensives in the south. He would brook no further delay.

Opponents on the Naval General Staff and in the army had hoped to kill the Midway operation by a series of delaying tactics. Now their resistance crumbled. On April 20, at a meeting of army and navy planners, it was agreed to postpone attacks on New Caledonia, Samoa, and Fiji until after the Midway operation. Admiral Nagano of the Naval General Staff threw his support behind Yamamoto. General Tanaka of the army, receiving assurances that the Midway operation would not be the first step in a planned invasion of Hawaii, consented to provide an infantry regiment. Vital details that had been previously withheld—dates, orders, the fleet units to be dispatched—were now forthcoming. The Midway offensive was to take place the first week of June, immediately after the return of major fleet units from "Operation MO," the sea-air-land offensive aimed at capturing Port Moresby, the Australian base on southeastern New Guinea.

Chapter Nine

AT THE FOURTEENTH NAVAL DISTRICT HEADQUARTERS, NEAR TEN-TEN Dock in the Pearl Harbor Navy Yard, a single inconspicuous door opened from the palm-lined sidewalk onto the top of a stairwell. The entrant descended to the basement and encountered a heavy steel gate guarded by a marine. If he showed the right credentials, he was admitted to a large, windowless space bathed in white fluorescent light and furnished with rows of identical desks. A team of yeomen fed punch cards into two car-sized machines known as "tabulators," primitive IBM computers that collated and analyzed alphanumeric data. Day and night, punch cards raced through the machines, filling the subterranean space with a harsh metallic clatter.

This enigmatic bunker was Hawaii's codebreaking unit, charged with peeling back the layers of encryption that cloaked Japanese radio communications. Although no sign was posted outside the door, it was formally called the Combat Intelligence Unit, or CIU. Among the staff it was nicknamed "the dungeon." After a reorganization later in the war it was renamed Fleet Radio Unit, Pacific, abbreviated as FRUPAC. Most commonly (then and in the historical literature) it was known as "Station Hypo"—phonetic code for the letter H, designating the Hawaiian intercept station.

Hypo's chief was Joseph Rochefort, a forty-one-year-old navy commander. He was a tall, aristocratic man, with dark hair and a keen, friendly face. He had learned to speak and read Japanese while stationed in Tokyo as a language officer in the 1920s, and subsequently joined that small, compulsively secretive coterie of officers who worked in the emerging field of communications intelligence. Rochefort did not much like cryptanalysis, finding that the work impaired his personal life, stunted his career prospects, and gave him ulcers. "I considered myself a naval officer," he later said, and he had done his best to avoid communications intelligence assignments. Some of the early histories of the war depicted Rochefort as a brilliant oddball, who paraded around in a flamboyant red smoking jacket and slippers. In his oral history for the Naval Institute, recorded in 1983, Rochefort owned up to the jacket and slippers, but sharply denied that he or they were eccentric. Yes, he wore a smoking jacket over his khaki uniform shirt, but only because it had pockets for his pipe and tobacco pouch. Yes, he padded around the office in slippers, but only because his feet were sore from pacing the concrete floor. He did not wear them outside the closely guarded sanctum of his basement lair, and "it wasn't that I was eccentric or anything."

Perhaps not, but there was no doubt that the dungeon was a zone in which the usual standards of conduct did not apply. It was an organization of freethinkers, in which a spirit of teamwork blended with an ethic of informality and an *esprit de corps*. It was built around a handful of talented codebreakers and language officers who felt free to play their hunches. Rank and hierarchy were of little importance. "Not much attention was paid to uniforms or to military punctilio of any kind," wrote Jasper Holmes, a Hypo veteran. "Although there was never any doubt as to who was boss, a man's status depended on factors other than rank." Freewheeling intuition was respected, but so was the plodding line of attack they called "siege tactics." One man's desk might be orderly and uncluttered, while he pondered one message intercept at a time. His neighbor's might be littered with candy wrappers, decorated with pinup girls, and buried under piles of old intercepts. Rochefort would put up with any method or style so long as it got results.

Throughout the era before the Second World War, the field of cryptanalysis was unproven, little understood, and shrouded in secrecy. It had even been condemned as unethical, most famously in 1929 by Henry Stimson, who was secretary of state at the time and refused to read decrypted foreign communications because "gentlemen don't read each other's mail." (Lieutenant Commander Thomas Dyer, perhaps the most naturally gifted member of Rochefort's team, joked that Stimson's view did not apply to cryptanalysts "because no one could accuse us of being gentlemen.") Rochefort observed that many of the best and most experienced codebreakers were slow to climb the promotion ladder because their classified assignments left black holes in their service résumés: "Every time he goes to Washington and goes in this particular division, nobody knows what he does or anything else, so he becomes known as somewhat of a nut. And some of them were." Men who got the best results were obsessive, preoccupied, and single-minded—"on the verge between brilliance and being crazy." Dyer kept a sign above his desk: "You don't have to be crazy to work here, but it helps a hell of a lot!"

After Pearl Harbor, Rochefort and his key lieutenants worked around the clock. Rochefort went home once every third or fourth night. Most nights he slept on a cot in his office, fueled by coffee and sandwiches. Twenty- or twenty-two-hour days were routine. Dyer sometimes worked two or three days straight, keeping his eyes open by swallowing handfuls of benzedrine tablets that he kept in a bucket on his desk and offered freely to his colleagues. (Asked about this later, Dyer explained: "I figured there were people out there getting shot at. If it should happen that it turned out to inflict some injury on my health in the long run, so what?") Most of the enlisted men and clerks worked in twelve-hour shifts, seven days a week, or what Holmes called a "normal" eighty-four-hour week.

The unit's headcount would expand fourfold in the first six months of the war. When he took over the unit in May 1941, Rochefort was promised that he could pick his own men, and the base's chief personnel officer had honored the agreement. As each new draft of recruits arrived in Pearl Harbor, a chief petty officer lined them up, studied their faces, and chose the candidates who looked bright enough for codebreaking work. The entire military band from the battleship *California*, knocked out of action on December 7, was selected and assigned the task of transferring the code groups from the raw radio intercepts onto the IBM punch cards. They were soon producing millions of these cards every week, and running the big IBM machines without supervision. The musicians took to the work so readily, said Holmes, that "a theory was advanced that there must be a psychological connection between music and cryptanalysis."

Before the war, Station Hypo had been assigned by Washington to focus on secondary tasks such as the Japanese diplomatic code, the flag officers' code, and weather codes. "JN-25," the main Japanese navy operational code, which held the enemy's most important secrets, had been reserved for analysts at Naval Headquarters in Washington. It had been in service for a year, and fragments of it were readable by December 1941. But a new edition of the code, which the Americans called "JN-25-B," had come into use on December 4, 1941. This meant that the second layer of encryption, the "cipher additives," were all entirely new. All the accumulated work on the old cipher was wiped out, and not a word of the new messages could be read. They were, said Rochefort, "in the black."

Rochefort received permission to go to work on the new code. A week after Pearl Harbor, Hypo launched the mind-numbing, Sisyphean campaign to decipher 50,000 five-digit numeral groups. As they began the work, it seemed overwhelming, perhaps even impossible. Every significant code-breaking success before the Second World War had been child's play by comparison; and such breakthroughs (wrote Holmes) "had never occurred except by a combination of lucky accidents relentlessly followed up by men of rare genius." When Holmes looked around at his colleagues, none struck him as a genius: they seemed like a fairly ordinary group of men. The most difficult stage of such an undertaking is the very start, when not a single code group in any intercepted message can be deciphered. Those are the long, painstaking hours, said Rochefort, when "you see a whole lot of letters and a whole lot of numerals, perhaps in the thousands or millions, and you know that there is a system in there, and there's a little key to the system that's something real simple." A Japanese transmission error in mid-December confirmed that the cipher—the five-digit additives—had been changed, but not the underlying code.

By year's end, when Nimitz took command of the fleet, Rochefort and his team had made halting progress. It was not much, but it was something, and it would grow. Dyer, who had an uncanny ability to see patterns in the interminable mass of letters and digits, noted that "if you observe something long enough, you'll see something peculiar. If you can't see something peculiar, if you stare long enough, then that in itself is peculiar. And then you try to explain the peculiarity." So he stared, and he stared, and he stared, until an idea took shape in his mind. If the idea was a testable hypothesis, he tested it. If it failed, he went back to staring. Dyer continued:

> A lot of it is, I'm convinced, done by the subconscious. Sometimes when people ask me how I can solve messages, I say, "Well, you sit there and stare at it until you see what it says, and then you put it down." You look—it depends on what kind of a thing you're dealing

with—but you look at it until you see something that attracts your
attention, your curiosity. Maybe it doesn't suggest anything at all.
You go on to something else. The next day you come back and look
at it again.

Rochefort agreed that it is a matter above all of "persistence, just sticking
with this thing day after day after day."

Readable code groups were few and far between at this early stage of
the war, but much could be gleaned from the raw radio intercepts. "Traffic
analysis" was the name given to the art of drawing useful intelligence out of
nothing more than the rise and fall of enemy radio traffic volume in given
locations. Rochefort said it was "common sense, actually. It's not real intelligence; it's common sense." For instance, a spike in radio traffic emanating
from Truk, the Japanese-held stronghold in the Caroline Islands, combined
with a fall in traffic in the Inland Sea of Japan, might suggest a major fleet
movement to the south. Traffic analysis grew more powerful when combined with the first fruits of cryptanalysis, typically the "message externals"
or headings—geographic designators (to where, from where) or the identity
of sender and addressee (from whom, to whom). Radio call signs for ships,
units, and commanders appeared frequently, in predictable parts of a message, and could sometimes be corroborated by sighting reports and radio
direction-finding (D/F) data, which provided an enemy transmission's point
of origin. Eavesdroppers recognized the personal quirks of an individual
operator—his "fist," they called it—and by tracking that man's movements
could guess the location of a particular ship. For these reasons, the "externals" fell relatively easy prey to cryptanalysis.

Jasper Holmes wrote that in the months preceding the war, he was not
entirely convinced of the value of traffic analysis, finding the reports a "mixture of gobbledygook and vague innuendoes, with very little solid information." But the war itself brought a satisfying surge in traffic from enemy
positions throughout the Pacific, supplying plenty of grist for the mill. In
early January 1942, the daily intelligence bulletin reported a sharp increase
in radio traffic in the Truk area. This pointed south, and when combined
with a few fragments of legible decrypts and a heavy dose of educated guesswork, Rochefort correctly predicted that the Japanese would seize Rabaul,
on New Britain, in the South Pacific. Whether or not the Allies could do
anything to defend Rabaul was an open question, but if the main body of the

Japanese fleet was moving south, that left plenty of other vulnerable points on the long and expanding perimeter of the Japanese Empire, where the Americans might stage carrier raids with little fear of walking into a trap.

None of this information would matter unless it was read and relied upon by decision makers at the highest level of the navy. The admirals of the Second World War had begun their careers at about the same time the first primitive radio communications were used at sea. Cryptanalysis was a black box that few understood and many distrusted. If the codebreakers had already burrowed into the heart of the Japanese code, and were supplying fully decrypted enemy radio communications, no naval commander could afford to ignore them. But Hypo was still months away from producing such airtight intelligence. Traffic analysis was indicative, but could prove nothing. It rested, as Jasper Holmes put it, on "a concatenation of deductions." It would have been within the rights of any admiral to refuse to place his faith in it.

Fortunately for Hypo, and the navy, and the United States, Chester Nimitz was not such an admiral. He was briefed each morning at eight o'clock by his fleet intelligence officer, Lieutenant Commander Edwin Layton. Layton also had a standing invitation to walk into Nimitz's office at any hour of any day if he believed he had important information for the C-in-C. (No one else on the staff, except perhaps the chief of staff, had this privilege.) Hypo provided a daily briefing to Layton, who in turn drew on other sources and briefed Nimitz. Layton and Rochefort had known one another when both men were stationed in Tokyo as language officers in the 1920s. They had shared in the long trial of learning Japanese. They counted one another as friends, and this tended to smooth the contours of their professional partnership, which might otherwise had been complicated by the organizational rivalry between the Fourteenth Naval District (of which Hypo was a part) and the Pacific Fleet staff. Nimitz paid close attention to all the intelligence products that crossed his desk. On his first day as CINCPAC, he told Layton, "I want you to be the Admiral Nagumo of my staff. I want your every thought, every instinct as you believe Admiral Nagumo might have them. You are to see the war, their operations, their aims, from the Japanese viewpoint and keep me advised what you are thinking about, what you are doing, and what purpose, what strategy, motivates your operations. If you can do this, you will give me the kind of information needed to win this war."

BASED ON THE EARLY INTELLIGENCE READINGS, Nimitz had gained the confidence to send Admiral Halsey and the aircraft carriers into the Marshalls on February 1. As predicted, there had been no major enemy fleet units in the vicinity. It was Hypo's first major achievement of the war. But the greatest benefit of Halsey's raid, from the cryptanalysts' standpoint, was the accompanying outpouring of fresh Japanese radio traffic. Hundreds of messages were intercepted by Allied listening posts throughout the Pacific, and rushed to Hypo for decryption. Raw intercepts of any kind were potentially useful to the codebreakers, but transmissions linked to known events in a known geographic location were invaluable. In such messages one found the same recurring externals: geographic designators obviously pointing to the Marshall Islands; radio call signs for Japanese ships, units, and commanders known to be present at the time of the raid; and code groups referring to enemy aircraft carriers.

Hypo had entered a virtuous circle. Nimitz, emboldened by intelligence reports that grew ever more tangible, authorized riskier and more ambitious carrier raids into Japanese waters. Each new raid prompted the Japanese to spew forth an immense volume of raw radio traffic, which in turn accelerated Hypo's progress. By the end of February, the codebreakers were fully in the game. Rochefort's team had correctly determined that all two-letter geographic designators beginning with "A" referred to American (or formerly American) islands in the central Pacific. "P" stood for the Japanese mandated islands of the central Pacific; "R" were British-held islands in the South Pacific; "M" was the Philippines. The second letter identified specific places within these spheres. In March, a message to "AA" requested reconnaissance on ships currently in the harbor of "AK." The string of intercepts, linked to corroborating data, left little doubt that these referred to Wake Island and Pearl Harbor.

On March 9, Japanese air group commanders in the central Pacific were radioed a routine forecast of wind force and direction at "AF." Based on weather patterns, Rochefort surmised that "AF" might be Midway.

Intelligence, as Layton observed, was "a perishable commodity," and Rochefort agreed: "It is useless to obtain intelligence . . . unless you use it." Their field was yet unproven, and the debacle of Pearl Harbor had not enhanced its reputation in the eyes of the fleet. Communications intelligence was a new and untried field, and it was simply unfamiliar to many officers. Acting upon predictions derived from intelligence sources even seemed to contradict Mahan's dictum that a commander should arrange his forces according to the enemy's capabilities, and not his inferred intentions. These were formidable barriers to the proper use of intelligence. Both Layton and Rochefort were aware of the need to "market" their product to policy makers and senior commanders who could act on it in a timely fashion. But how to disseminate their findings without alerting the Japanese that the codes had been breached?

A bedrock tenet of communications intelligence was that the enemy must always be encouraged to "feel safe," and never given cause to suspect that his radio transmissions were less than impenetrable. That the Americans were tunneling into the Japanese naval code was one of the most closely guarded secrets of the war. "Ultra" was the name given to intelligence based on decrypted Japanese messages, and only a small, lofty circle of officers were "cleared for Ultra." When information derived from Ultra had to be distributed outside the privileged circle, it was sanitized. For example, a predicted Japanese fleet movement derived from radio decrypts might be described as a submarine or aircraft scouting report. The trick was to protect the vital secret while also ensuring that fresh intelligence was finding its way to commanders who had the power to act upon it. "This business of secrecy, you see, is a sort of self-defeating thing," Rochefort later said. "If you don't tell anyone about this, how can it be used?"

The shroud of mystery surrounding Hypo aroused enmity throughout the Navy Yard. Whenever Rochefort needed more men, supplies, or square footage, he was inevitably told to explain his need in greater detail. This he could not do. Instead, he appealed directly to Admiral Bloch, commander of the Fourteenth Naval District; and Bloch always decreed that Rochefort should get whatever he wanted, and with no questions asked. Supply officers were not accustomed to being manhandled by a mere commander who headed a shadowy unit that they were not even permitted to ask questions about, but they quickly learned not to deny Rochefort's requests.

Hypo was one unit within a widely dispersed radio intelligence sector that was managed from Naval Headquarters in Washington. The largest unit in the system was "OP-20-G," the Washington-based Navy Radio Intelligence Section. Before the war, there had been additional intercept stations on Corregidor in the Philippines (Station "Cast"), on Guam, and on Bainbridge Island in Puget Sound. The British had an excellent cryptanalytic team at Singapore. (The Japanese onslaught swallowed up the unit at Guam. Later, the Singapore unit evacuated to Ceylon, and Station Cast absconded in a submarine to Melbourne.) Throughout the Pacific, smaller subsidiary D/F stations measured radio direction-finding data on enemy transmissions. When the system functioned properly, information flowed more or less freely between them. Freewheeling collaboration was vital, as breaks made by one unit could lead directly to breaks made by another. All built on the collective effort.

But competition and dissention were in the wind. The surprise attack on Pearl Harbor had been a cataclysmic failure of communications intelligence. The debacle had cast a long shadow over the entire intelligence-gathering branch of the military. Being located on the spot at Pearl Harbor, Hypo was the target of much innuendo, though history would eventually show that the most damaging failures had occurred in Washington, as a result of a hard-fought bureaucratic turf battle between the offices of Naval Intelligence (ONI) and Naval Communications (ONC). In any case, the high priests of the navy agreed that a shakeup was in order. Admiral King and several of his chief subordinates, including war planning chief Admiral Richmond Turner, believed that radio intelligence should be streamlined and centralized in Washington, and that the satellite units of Hawaii and the Pacific should be brought under the firm control of the commander in chief of the U.S. Fleet (COMINCH).

In February 1942, the prewar chief of OP-20-G, Commander Laurence Safford, was removed from his post and replaced by Captain John R. Redman, Naval Academy class of 1919, who had no experience in codebreaking or communications intelligence. The captain's elder brother, Rear Admiral Joseph R. Redman, was named director of naval communications that same month. The brothers, along with Admiral Redman's deputy, Commander Joseph N. Wenger, would form a powerful axis in Washington. Safford and Rochefort had enjoyed a relationship based on personal trust, with the understanding that the different units in the system would not vie for credit. With Safford purged, the trust and rapport were gone, and relations between Hypo and Washington quickly turned sour. Wenger argued that Washington should "assume active coordinating control . . . of all intercept stations, DF nets, and decrypting units," and set up at the headquarters "a central coordinating authority for all communications intelligence activities."

Admiral King, who was favorably inclined to consolidating power and authority in his own headquarters, gave this plan his peremptory approval on February 6. With a stroke of his pen, King had relegated the team at Hypo to a subsidiary role. But the prickly Rochefort was determined to preserve the independence of his unit, which he correctly identified as the best codebreaking outfit in the service. (Indeed, he went further: "I would say with all modesty that this was the best communications intelligence organization that this world has ever seen.") Rochefort and the Redmans were rivals from the start, then enemies—and their feud would very nearly spoil the American victory at the Battle of Midway.

In February, as the Redmans took the reins in Washington, tension was already building between Rochefort and his new bosses. Everyone in the system had access to the same message decrypts and radio traffic reports, but they were seeing different patterns and drawing different conclusions. Even as JN-25 began yielding up its secrets, the decrypts were mostly a series of blanks interspersed with a few tantalizing fragments of broken code. Radio traffic readings were subject to conflicting interpretations. Rarely did all the available evidence point in one direction. More often there were red herrings, and the analysts had to sift through huge amounts of data and develop theories based on deduction and inference. Often their predictions were little more than sophisticated guesses, which for the sake of decorum they called "estimates." In Rochefort's view, Washington's analytic work was shoddy and its conclusions too often flew in the face of common sense. Nor did he trouble to disguise his contempt for the Redmans. In his eyes, they were empire builders, in the game for their "own personal purposes, not for what they could offer." They had foreseen that communications intelligence was a burgeoning field, and hoped to ride its coattails to higher rank, pay, and "personal glory."

Repeatedly throughout February and March, Admiral King predicted Japanese carrier attacks on Hawaii, Midway, the west coast, the Panama Canal, and Allied-held islands on the Hawaii-Australia line. On February 6, in a dispatch to Nimitz and several other Pacific subcommanders, he reported that the Japanese operations in the ABDA theater "may well be accompanied by strong raids against Midway, Oahu, New Hebrides, Northeast Australia, and possibly west coast or Canal." Later the same day, again, King predicted carrier strikes against New Hebrides and New Caledonia. Where else? A skeptical Rochefort replied that the offensives were aimed at Java and Sumatra (they were). On March 11, the COMINCH warned that "recent enemy air and submarine activities may well indicate another full-scale effort against the Hawaii-Midway line with the likely principal objective of crippling or destroying our vital base at Pearl Harbor." Hypo countered that the Japanese were pushing south, and lacked the means to mount simultaneous large-scale operations in the central Pacific. On March 18, Nimitz gave his positive endorsement to Layton's reply, stating, "No indication of immediate major offensive action except in Malaya area."

It appeared that OP-20-G analysts were nourishing King's anxieties by sending him cherry-picked data that could be interpreted as pointing to such attacks. The men who had King's ear were unduly alarmist, and their impulsive theories might incite the fleet to chase its own tail. In the best case, this would waste time and fuel; in the worst, it would leave the fleet out of position to repel a concerted enemy thrust. Rochefort and his team, having lived through the rumor-plagued aftermath of the raid on Pearl Harbor, had learned to filter the evidence with hearty skepticism. Rochefort concluded that Washington was lost in the fog of war, and he was not afraid to say so. That he was often vindicated after the fact did not endear him to Wenger or the Redman brothers.

HYPO EXPANDED STEADILY, and by April, the basement was overcrowded. Rows of desks stretched from wall to wall, occupied by men wearing green eyeshades to protect their eyes from the overhead fluorescent lights. They hunched over their notes and decrypts in an attitude of intense concentration. Several of the key cryptanalysts rarely left the basement, sleeping on field cots shoved up against the walls, or in their chairs with their heads laid down on their desks. Rochefort grew concerned that Thomas Dyer, perhaps the only other indispensable man on his team, would buckle under the strain. In March, he began pushing Dyer out the door every few days, with orders to catch a night of sleep in his own bed. Rochefort himself was usually found at his desk chair, behind a barricade of stacked decrypts, wreathed in a haze of blue smoke from his pipe. One officer estimated that Hypo did a full year's worth of peacetime work in the first three months of the war, and the pace did not slacken in the least until after the Battle of Midway in June 1942.

Jasper Holmes updated the position of all known ships—American,

Allied, and Japanese, including warships, merchant ships, and submarines—on a big plotting board on one of the basement's walls. Stacks of
decrypts and cardboard boxes of IBM punch cards covered all the horizontal surfaces, until finally the yeomen began stacking them on the floor, all
around the desks and along the walls. Paperwork management was provi-
sional and makeshift. Rochefort and his principal analysts knew they ought
to devise a proper filing system, with cross-indexing of archived messages,
but they never found the time for that. Somehow, through the blizzard of
decrypts and IBM cards, order prevailed over chaos. "This is one reason
why these people are mostly crazy," Rochefort later recalled. "We'd have no
problem at all."

> You'd mention something and you'd say, "Now wait a minute. Back
> here when they were around Halmahera on their way down to a land-
> ing at Port Something-or-other, there was a message like this. Let's
> have it." And they'd look in this pile of junk and they were able to
> locate it. . . . And then of course, you'd get a new one here and this
> leads to another thing over here and this leads to another thing and
> this is how you fill the whole works up. One letter leads to another and
> that leads to a third one and so on. Then that's when your memory
> comes in very handy.

Holmes added that a cryptanalyst "needs only time, patience, an infinite
capacity for work, a mind that can focus on one problem to the exclusion of
everything else, a photographic memory, the inability to drop an unsolved
problem, and a large volume of traffic."

At first, decrypted externals were like plaintext islands in a sea of indecipherable code, but even a small island supplied a foothold for logical
deduction. With time, the sea fell and the islands began to merge with
their neighbors. Theories were checked against traffic analysis and sighting
reports. There were fewer blanks and more comprehensible phrases. Then
there were near-complete messages with a few mulishly indecipherable fragments embedded in them. When a newly decrypted code group confirmed
the deductions they had made earlier, the codebreakers rejoiced. Each new
triumph bolstered their conviction in the deductions they could not yet
prove. Dyer compared the sensation of cracking one of the Japanese code
groups, after many weeks of frustration, to a sexual orgasm. "Physiologically,

it's not the same," he added quickly, "but the emotional feeling is pretty much the same."

Not every break brought instant enlightenment. Japanese is a language rich in nuance and subtext. Not infrequently, a fully decrypted plaintext message made no sense to the analysts because they could not properly translate the Japanese words. Even the most competent and seasoned Japanese-language officers might disagree with a colleague's translation. Japanese naval idiom was particularly multifarious, and it seemed to have evolved rapidly even since the late 1930s. Moreover, Pacific place names gave the Hypo analysts a lot of trouble. Over the centuries, the theater's innumerable islands, towns, bays, and shoals had accumulated native names, European names, and Japanese names. Many places were known by multiple names, and even the same name might have various spellings. Analysts could tap into a large in-house library of charts, piloting guides, and gazetteers that had been published in various languages and eras. They spread old charts out on tables and bent over them with magnifying glasses. Even when the Japanese used a Western name that could be found on an old chart, that name was rendered in *kana* (Japanese syllabary)—and the Japanese sequence of syllables might sound very different from the original. It took Jasper Holmes some time to recognize "WO-DO-RA-KU" as "Woodlark Island."

The first inklings of the impending Japanese offensive against Port Moresby in the south Pacific came in the last week of March, when intercepted messages revealed that Japanese naval air units had received orders to attack a target identified as "RZP." At first the geographic designator remained a mystery, but the volume of traffic and the repeated appearance of the term left no doubt that a major push was in the works. Further parsing of related messages from all stations revealed that the operation, whatever it was, was code-named "MO." The drive to break these identifiers was lifted to highest-priority status.

Intelligence culled from many different sources pointed toward the Coral Sea. In early April, Japanese air units based in the Solomons were heavily reinforced. Australian coast-watchers confirmed that enemy air patrols in the region were being extended by length and density. Movement of forces through Truk suggested a shift of forces into the South Pacific. British code-breakers confirmed Rochefort's hunch that Nagumo's foray into the Indian Oceans was merely a raid, and not the beginning of a sustained operation.

The Japanese carriers were heading back to Truk, from whence they would depart for the South Pacific. Rochefort informed Nimitz that "an offensive in the southwest Pacific is shaping up." On April 3, he forecast that the offensive would stage out of Rabaul and would be aimed at the southeastern end of New Guinea. But when? Station Belconnen in Melbourne (the group that had evacuated from Corregidor) forecast April 21, but Rochefort believed that was too early. The first week of May seemed more likely.

At about this time, Admiral King reached down from on high and tapped Joe Rochefort on the shoulder. In a message addressed to the Hypo unit commander, the COMINCH asked for an overall assessment of Japanese intentions. The query short-circuited the chain of command, and came as a bit of a shock. "We were a little surprised that he would ask us what our views were," Rochefort said. "I personally felt that he was not even aware of our existence." Rochefort and his lieutenants dropped everything else and focused on their response, which was on its way back to King in less than six hours. It contained four substantive points. First, the Japanese had completed their current operations in the Indian Ocean, and the carrier groups were on their way home. Second, an offensive into the Coral Sea area was imminent, and would be aimed at securing the southeastern end of New Guinea. Third, there was no evidence that the Japanese intended an invasion of Australia. Fourth, another major operation was in the planning stages, to take place not long after the Coral Sea offensive. Details of time and place had not yet come into focus, but it would be a very large operation, involving "most of the units of the Japanese fleet." The response was a fine balance of logical deduction and acknowledged uncertainty. Even then, Rochefort suspected the as-yet-undetermined offensive was aimed at Midway, but he lacked sufficient evidence to back up his hunch with a concrete forecast.

On April 18, the Doolittle raid brought another dam burst of Japanese radio traffic, the largest and most profitable yet. New details soon emerged about the pending operation in the South Pacific. MO was identified as a designator for Port Moresby. By April 24, Nimitz and King had in hand an intercept that referred to an "MO Fleet," an "MO Occupation Force," and an "MO Attack Force." A large Japanese force comprising air groups and carriers would steam into the Coral Sea, covering the approach of a separate amphibious group, which would land troops at Port Moresby. Working from intercepted and decrypted messages revealing ship departure times, the intelligence analysts estimated the operation's scheduled date as the first week of May.

Nimitz came to realize that Hypo was producing most of the key breaks in JN-25, and that he had better take action to ensure that Rochefort was not hamstrung by the bureaucrats in Washington. In mid-April, he asked King to realign the division of responsibility between Washington and Pearl Harbor. Hypo should be assigned to "reading today's traffic today while it is of value to forces afloat," while the OP-20-G cryptanalysts should focus on back traffic. King endorsed the request with a peremptory flick of his pen, apparently without even asking his subordinates their opinion. Not surprisingly, they took personal umbrage at this maneuver, and the quarrel between Rochefort and the Redmans escalated into a blood feud. Rochefort had the upper hand for the time being, but his higher-ups would take advantage of any stumble. From that point on, freewheeling speculation was not to be shared between units. Meticulous scorekeeping was the new order of the day, and any mistaken estimates would be held against the party who had been so bold as to put them into play.

ON THE MORNING OF APRIL 22, Layton sat down with Nimitz and provided a wide-ranging intelligence review, including the best and most current evidence concerning the pending Coral Sea operation. His major point: "There are many indications that the enemy will launch an offensive in the New Guinea–New Britain–Solomon area . . . [the offensive would] start very soon." But two weeks before battle, there was still a dangerous array of unknowns. He estimated that the enemy force might include "5 carriers, 1 battleship, 5 heavy cruisers, at least 4 light cruisers, 12 destroyers, and more than a dozen submarines," as well as perhaps 135 land-based naval bombers, more than 100 Zeros and a similar number of reconnaissance planes. More than 20,000 troops might be brought into the theater in army transports. Yet there remained major uncertainties. Washington continued to warn of a diversionary raid against Hawaii. No less a figure than Army Chief of Staff George Marshall warned the local army commander of pending air attacks on the Hawaiian Islands. Layton judged that "there were no signs of Japanese movements toward the Hawaiian Islands," and that a lack of any evidence of a buildup of bombers in the nearby Mandates made such an attack highly improbable.

Nimitz was feeling the strain. No matter how well his intelligence advisers did their jobs, the responsibility to act upon their estimates was his alone. They did not disguise from him the gaps in their knowledge. There was the unpleasant possibility that the Japanese were practicing radio deception on a grand scale, hoping to lure the American fleet south, which would leave the great fortress of Oahu vulnerable to another enemy air raid or worse. It was not enough for Nimitz to listen. He had to test his advisers' degree of conviction, to probe for flaws in their logic, and to reconstruct their process of assembling a mosaic from many disparate bits of evidence. After all of that, he had to believe in his gut that they were right. He did. At this precarious juncture, with the war hanging in the balance, Nimitz chose to bet his command on the accuracy of the intelligence. A study produced by his staff in late April 1942 identified intelligence as the most important advantage possessed by the Americans at that stage of the war. The Japanese were superior in carrier, battleship, and shore-based air strength, the study asserted, but the Americans could overcome these deficiencies with "Fairly accurate knowledge of direction of enemy advance" and "probability of being able to detect change in enemy deployment." Nimitz decided (as he put it) to "accept odds in battle if necessary"—to throw his two available carriers against the Japanese fleet and hope that they prevailed. But he would have to sell the plan to King, who remained concerned about the safety of both the carriers and Pearl Harbor.

On April 24, Nimitz boarded his big Coronado flying boat and flew to San Francisco for a face-to-face summit with the COMINCH. The city by the bay was at about the midpoint between Washington and Hawaii, and so offered a convenient rendezvous. (It was the first of eighteen meetings between King and Nimitz during the war; most of these would be held in San Francisco.) Nimitz and his staff checked into a top-floor suite in the St. Francis Hotel on Union Square. For the next three days they held day-long meetings with King and his staff at the main conference room of the San Francisco Federal Building.

Their most pressing business was to settle their strategy to deal with the pending MO offensive, but there were other items on the agenda. King enlightened Nimitz on the larger context of the war—the production ramp-up, haggling with the British and Soviets, prospects for an invasion of Europe, and how the Pacific fit into the Allies' global strategy. King suspected that Nimitz had been too gentle with his subcommanders and staff.

He wanted the Pacific Fleet purged of "pessimists and defeatists," and the ousted men banished to peripheral billets. Navy Secretary Knox had advocated retiring many of the more senior admirals and placing junior admirals into seagoing commands, and King supported the policy. Nimitz did not object, but he recommended that assignments be made through the established channel of his old bureau in Washington. He believed in the navy's personnel system and was willing to let it function without interference.

King was specifically after Vice Admiral Frank Jack Fletcher. This "black shoe" (surface navy) admiral had accumulated a mixed record in the early months of the war. He had seemed to demonstrate a lack of aggressiveness, and his task forces had been embarrassed by unreasonably long fueling delays. King's faith in Fletcher was hanging by a thread, but Nimitz maintained that all the American carrier task forces were climbing a steep learning curve, and Fletcher had done about as well as could be expected in the circumstances. King conceded the point, and granted Fletcher a stay of execution. The best American carrier task force commander was Bill Halsey, but Halsey was on his way back to Pearl Harbor from the Doolittle raid, and would not be able to get the *Enterprise* to the South Pacific in time for the pending confrontation. King grasped that he had perhaps overreached in committing two of four available carriers to the Tokyo raid at a time when they might all be needed to deter a concerted enemy offensive in the south, but now it was too late to do anything about it.

A third important question was a subtheater commander for the South Pacific. On April 14, Nimitz had assumed direct command of this area, but the great distances involved required a commander on the spot. This would be Vice Admiral Robert L. Ghormley, who had served until now as the navy's liaison in London. King considered him a "very able man," and Nimitz concurred. Ghormley would establish his headquarters in New Zealand. Rear Admiral J. S. McCain, an officer who had earned his wings at age fifty-one, was named commander of air forces in the South Pacific.

Though Nimitz had explained his decision to contest the Japanese advance on Moresby as a willingness to "accept odds in battle if necessary," the truth is that the CINCPAC was spoiling for a fight in the Coral Sea. Port Moresby was simply too important to yield to the enemy. It would give the Japanese a launching platform for new attacks on air bases and port facilities in Queensland, Australia; it would extend Japanese air search patterns over the Coral Sea; it would allow for a buildup of forces for the planned offensive farther east against New Caledonia, Fiji, and Samoa. Though the Japanese army had definitely ruled out an invasion of Australia, possession of Moresby might accomplish much the same thing—to cut the great island-continent off, to draw the noose around its neck. On the other hand, Port Moresby was far enough east that the Japanese supply lines into the area would be stretched very thin. It was at the outer range of airstrikes from Rabaul and other bases. Contesting its occupation would not expose Allied forces to the brand of overpowering Japanese sea and air attacks they had suffered in and around Malaya and the Dutch East Indies. For the first time since Pearl Harbor, a pitched sea battle with the Japanese fleet was deemed an acceptable risk.

With King's go-ahead, Nimitz returned to Pearl on April 28 and issued plans and orders for the approaching Battle of the Coral Sea. Carrier groups built around Fletcher's *Yorktown* group (Task Force 17), and Rear Admiral Aubrey "Jake" Fitch's *Lexington* group (Task Force 11), would arrive in the Coral Sea in time to attack the Japanese invasion fleet. They would rendezvous off the New Hebrides with an ANZAC (Australia–New Zealand) force of cruisers, under the command of Rear Admiral John C. Crace. Fletcher would assume command of all local Allied naval forces. His orders, which he received on April 29, were to "check further advance of the enemy in the New Guinea–Solomon area by destroying enemy ships, shipping and aircraft."

The *Enterprise* and *Hornet*, returning from the Doolittle raid, would put into Pearl Harbor for fuel and provisions. Then they would hurry south, to reach the Coral Sea by mid-May. They would not arrive in time to meet the initial thrusts of the Japanese fleet—that was the price paid by the Americans for bombing Tokyo—but they could at least be in a position to reinforce their sisters if the battle should expand into a protracted campaign.

The Japanese had been building up their strength in the region for ten weeks, since their shockingly early invasion (January 23) of Rabaul. From that major staging base, they had spread out like the spokes of a wheel to seize satellite positions in adjacent island groups. Small amphibious landing parties went ashore, usually unopposed, and secured a flat stretch of ground that would accommodate an airfield. Work parties cleared trees and brush and leveled a primitive dirt landing strip. Mechanics, spare parts, fuel drums, and ammunition were brought in by freighters. The planes flew in with their aircrews. By May 1, Japan had established a large and growing network of these little satellite airfields—Kavieng, on New Ireland; Salamaua and Lae on the north coast of New Guinea; Buin on Bougainville Island; Buka Island. None was terribly important in its own right, but together they were mutually supporting and backed by the power of Rabaul. And all signs indicated that the buildup was ongoing. The Japanese submarine presence in local waters was expanding. Convoys from the west brought freighters, minelayers, gunboats, submarine and seaplane tenders, and troopships. The enormous four-engine Kawanishi Type 97 flying boats, with ranges approaching 3,000 miles, patrolled far and wide. The eye of Tokyo was over the Solomons, New Guinea, and a large and growing swath of the Coral Sea.

Operation MO involved a tortuous amalgamation of naval surface forces, carrier task forces, amphibious landing parties, and various landbased air units amounting to about 150 aircraft. Vice Admiral Shigeyoshi Inoue, commander of the Fourth Fleet, retained command of the operation from his headquarters in Rabaul, but no fewer than six other admirals sailed with fleet elements at sea. Vice Admiral Takeo "King Kong" Takagi, victor of the Java Sea, commanded the Carrier Strike Force, built around the big fleet carriers *Shokaku* and *Zuikaku* with their screening vessels of cruisers and destroyers—but a subordinate, Rear Admiral Tadaichi Hara, commander of Carrier Division 5, would exert tactical control of the two carriers during the battle. The invasion itself would be brought to the beaches by the Port Moresby Invasion Force, including about 10,000 army and navy troops in twelve lumbering transports. Several other surface naval units and one light carrier group (built around the 12,000-ton baby flattop *Shoho*) were dispatched to cover the landings. Though Port Moresby was the main objective, the Japanese also intended to take the little tropical island of Tulagi—in the waters that would later be made famous during the Guadalcanal Campaign as "Ironbottom Sound"—with the idea of building a small seaplane base for reconnaissance flights to the south and east. Tulagi would be taken on May 3, Port Moresby on May 10.

Admiral Inoue was unpleasantly conscious that everything was being rushed, that nothing was being done with the care or attention it deserved. He had been forced into a schedule that was compressed and inflexible. The planned incursion into the Coral Sea had already been twice delayed, because of the proven presence of American carrier forces in the vicinity. Now that the Midway sortie had been definitely scheduled for the last

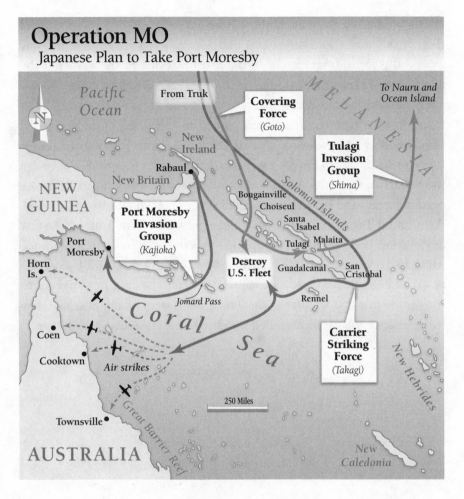

Operation MO
Japanese Plan to Take Port Moresby

week of May, there could be no further slips. The Japanese carriers had just returned from their foray into the Indian Ocean, but they were once again racing out to a distant theater. The MO plan, like so many Japanese naval campaigns, seemed unnecessarily complex. Forces were divided in such a way as to flout Mahanian doctrine. Japanese strategists justified these deployments by pointing to airpower and radio communications, two elements that had been unknown in Mahan's day. Nevertheless, a complex arrangement of forces relied upon close coordination and timing, and was more prone to unravel in the face of determined enemy counterstrikes.

Thus far in the war, Minoru Genda's concept of massed carrier airpower, embodied in the six-carrier task force of *Kido Butai*, had been brilliantly vindicated. In four months, Nagumo's carriers had traveled more than 50,000 miles, spreading terror and devastation a full third of the way around the earth, from Hawaii in the east to Ceylon in the west. But the mileage was beginning to wear. The ships and crews had been sent on too many missions in too many directions; they had traveled too many miles with too little rest; they had been pushed to the limits of endurance by commanders who were loathe to accept that such limits even existed. Three carriers—half of *Kido Butai*—had been slated for Operation MO, but *Kaga* was scratched from the mission at the last minute. She was in desperate need of repairs and refitting, and would stay in port to prepare for Midway. As Admiral Takagi's Carrier Strike Force put to sea from Truk on the first day of May 1942, it included only the *Shokaku* and *Zuikaku*. *Kido Butai*, which had operated as a unified striking force since December 7, had for the first time been cleaved into its component parts. The curtain was about to rise on the first duel of aircraft carriers in the history of war at sea, and by happenstance the two fleets sailed into battle with near-equivalent force.

Chapter Ten

T HE *LEXINGTON*, TENDERLY KNOWN BY HER CREW AS "*LADY LEX*," WAS one of the oldest and largest aircraft carriers in the world. She had been launched in 1925, when carrier aviation was still in its infancy. Like her twin sister, the *Saratoga*, she had been originally intended as a battlecruiser, but converted to a carrier once the great hull had been finished. The *Lexington's* 36,000-ton displacement dwarfed that of the *Enterprise, Yorktown,* or *Hornet,* each of which displaced less than 20,000 tons. She was 60 to 70 feet longer than her younger sisters, and her island was smaller, leaving her with a long, sweeping parade ground of a flight deck.

Even in the mid-twentieth century, when most seafaring superstitions were a thing of the past, sailors held idiosyncratic feelings about the various ships of the fleet. The *Lex* was always held especially dear. "The *Lexington* was a 'good ship' as was said in the navy," recalled Alvin Kernan, who served on the *Enterprise,* "while her sister ship the *Saratoga* was not, for unknown reasons."

Zigzagging out of Pearl Harbor on April 15, she and her escorts (heavy cruisers *Minneapolis* and *New Orleans* and seven destroyers) steamed away to the southwest toward Palmyra Island, where the *Lexington* had been ordered to ferry fourteen Brewster Buffalos of Marine Fighting Squadron 211. Every morning at dawn, the ship launched half a dozen F4F Wildcats to fly combat air patrol over the task force. Shortly afterward, several SBD scout bombers took off and flew air search patterns to the south and west, to a range of 200–250 miles. During her sojourn in Pearl Harbor, where the *Lex* had spent more than a week in dry dock and another week moored in the repair basin, the carrier had been fitted out with the latest radar technology. A big new "bedspring" antenna rotated atop her foremast. Radar gave the crew a shared feeling of security, a sense of being less vulnerable to nasty surprises, and therefore boosted morale. "We knew radar could see things we couldn't see," wrote Signalman Floyd Beaver, who served on Rear Admiral Aubrey Fitch's flag allowance. "It is scary even now to think about what the carrier war would have been like without radar."

Farther south, in the equatorial doldrums, the sea was as warm as a bath and the sun radiated its stultifying heat into the ship. Belowdecks, the temperature held above 100° Fahrenheit throughout the day, and never fell below 90° even at night. The *Lexington's* colossal power plant, deep in the bowels of the ship, included sixteen huge steam boilers and four 33,200-kilowatt turbine engines. Scorching heat was an inevitable byproduct of those great machines, and much of it remained trapped in the steel envelope of the carrier's interior. On the flight deck at midday, where the ambient heat from below merged with the overbearing rays of the equatorial sun, the steel deck plates were like skillets. They would burn exposed flesh or melt rubber soles, and sailors sometimes amused themselves by frying eggs on them. On the saunalike lower decks, where condensation collected on every surface, *Chicago Tribune* reporter Stanley Johnston observed that the ship appeared to sweat like a human being: "Beads of moisture combined to form rivulets which forever coursed down floors, walls and roofs, the bulkheads, decks and side plates of this great floating city." No place was hotter than the engine room itself, in which the "black gang" (the engineers) toiled in a harshly lit subterranean cavity where the temperature never fell below 110° and sometimes approached 130°, about the upper limit of human endurance. Sailors who grumbled of the heat in the mess hall or hangar deck were sent to pay a courtesy call on the engineers, an experience that put their complaints into perspective. When Robert Casey visited the black gang on another ship, he felt his "eyeballs hardening like over-boiled eggs." After a few hideous minutes he escaped to the "chilly upper world," where a temperature of 100° felt mild by contrast.

While at Pearl, the *Lex* had been shorn of her 8-inch guns, relics of an era when it was thought that an aircraft carrier should be capable of exchanging fire with enemy surface ships. The two heavy mounts had been located fore and aft of the island, and could be fired only to starboard—had they been turned and fired to port, their muzzle blasts would have smashed the flight deck. Even now, at that early stage of the war, it was evident that what every carrier needed more of—what every ship of every class needed more of—was "ack-ack," or antiaircraft weaponry. The Navy Yard had installed several new batteries of 5-inch/38-caliber dual-purpose guns on the bow and stern. These powerful weapons, when handled skillfully, could knock down a heavy bomber passing over the ship at an altitude of 10,000 feet. More than a hundred shorter-range guns—1.1-inch and 20mm Oerlikons—were mounted on the galleries around the perimeter of the flight deck. They were ineffective at long range, but could be fired rapidly and aimed by a single man strapped into shoulder braces, making them handy for last-ditch defense against incoming aircraft.

In the *Lexington's* combat experience to date, the performance of her gunners had not been at all encouraging, and Captain Frederick C. Sherman ordered an intensive training regimen. The guns were manned every hour of every day and night, in two twelve-hour watches; the gunners stood or sat by their weapons with steel helmets pushed back on their foreheads and kapok life vests drawn tight around their chins. When the carrier's own airplanes were aloft, the 5-inch gun crews swung their muzzles to follow them in a pantomime of ranging and sighting. The off-duty crews spent an additional hour each day with a "dummy loader" on the machine deck, mastering the steps of manhandling the 60-pound shell into the breech, setting the fuse, pointing the weapon, and mock-firing. The crews learned to work together, to anticipate one another, to function as a creature with one mind and eight sweaty hands; with constant repetition their error rates fell and their rate of fire rose. On the *Lex*, some of the 5-inch batteries were manned by sailors, others by marines; and as Johnston observed, "the healthy rivalry between the two units in practice shoots sure was something to behold."

Most days at sea, the *Lexington* held live-firing drills. One of the 5-inchers threw up a time-fused target shell, which ejected a magnesium flare attached to a parachute. The other guns opened fire, their incandescent red tracers stretching up toward the target in intersecting lines. The trick was to estimate height properly and to fire quickly, before the target was destroyed by one of the competing batteries. "Inside of two weeks after leaving Pearl Harbor," Johnston wrote, "these gunners were able to tear the small parachute to shreds, or shoot the flare to bits in a few rounds." Hitting a fast-moving target proved more difficult. In one of Sherman's drills, a cruiser scout plane passed over the carrier, towing a brightly colored target sleeve from a 4,000-foot cable. The 5-inchers blasted away on the first pass, at high altitude; then the plane returned at lower altitude to let the Oerlikons have at it. The recurring problem with antiaircraft fire, both in combat and in live-firing exercises, was that the gunners tended to aim too low and did not "lead" the target sufficiently. Their bursts, it seemed, were always low and behind, never high and ahead. On the *Lexington*, the gun crews took turns skeet-shooting at clay pigeons with shotguns off the carrier's stern, to inculcate a better instinct for leading their targets. With time and practice, results improved. The ship's crew watched these drills with curiosity, aware that their collective safety depended on how well the gunners mastered their craft.

As the *Lex* approached the equator, her crew prepared for the traditional "crossing the line" rites, which divided the ship's company into the "shellbacks"—those old salts who had crossed the line before—and the "pollywogs," who had not. For twenty-four hours, the shellbacks would impose a reign of terror over the pollywogs, initiating them by various hazing rituals into the domain of *Neptunus Rex*, sovereign ruler of the Raging Main. An academic dissertation will someday be written about that peculiar seafaring custom, with its centuries-old lineage and its overtones of ancient pagan idolatry. "Neptune's Court" allowed distinctions of rank to be put to one side, and military authority to be briefly subverted—only on a ship at the equator, for example, might one see a navy commander crawling on his hands and knees before an enlisted man. It was a period of high hilarity, when tension was released and the veterans flexed their muscles against the *Lexington*'s fresh recruits, about 500 of whom had never been to sea. The ship's combat readiness was never relaxed; the air patrols took off and landed as before, and half the crew always remained at their duty stations. Indeed, several of the leading officers of the ship were actively involved in the ceremonies, including several of the air squadron skippers and even Commander Mort Seligman, the ship's executive officer, who headed the court that determined each man's status and passed "sentences." Not coincidentally, the officers saw to it that the shellbacks were assigned to their posts while newcomers were left idle, and could not therefore plead that duty ought to release them from the looming ordeal.

The court and jury convened in the mess hall, two decks below the flight deck. A "Grand Inquisitor" interrogated the pollywogs with the help of "scribes" and "kibitzers." The accused were asked preposterous and insulting questions, and no matter how they answered, they were likely to be held in "contempt of court." Some pollywogs were defiant, others submissive; all were bullied equally, though leniency could be bought by bribing the court with Coca-Cola, ice cream, or cigarettes. An officer who testified that he had served in naval intelligence was convicted of perjury, on the grounds that no such thing had ever existed. Rookie pilots were required to spend the day in fur-lined winter flight suits with helmets and gloves, scanning the horizon for icebergs using "binoculars" fashioned from a pair of Coke bottles.

The ceremony closed in the afternoon on the forward end of the flight deck, where King Neptune (usually a long-serving chief petty officer) wore a crown, held a trident, and sat on a throne, flanked by his "queen" and the "royal baby." Each pollywog was stripped to his underwear and painted ("anointed") with a concoction blended from egg yolks, banana oil, torpedo grease, and whatever else might have been scrounged in the galley or machine shops. After receiving the sea-king's benediction, each painted victim was forced to "run the gauntlet" down an 800-foot lane flanked by several hundred shellbacks who smashed him on the buttocks with canvas tubes. Staggering to the end, he was awarded a certificate stating that he had entered King Neptune's domain, and could call himself a genuine shellback. Johnston, watching the scene from the *Lexington's* bridge, looked out at the cruisers and destroyers of the task force and noted that the same ritual was being played out on every other deck.

The *Lexington's* sailors forgot how it felt not to sweat, and found it difficult even to imagine cool weather. Their blue shirts and dungarees were soaked through within minutes of putting them on. They were plagued not only by the debilitating heat and incessant sweat but by the odor of their own bodies—for as one carrier sailor from that period observed, "This was before the popularity of deodorants." They could shower as often as they liked, but they took saltwater showers with a brief freshwater rinse. Signalman Beaver recorded that the *Lexington's* washrooms collected 3 or 4 inches of "soapy oil-and-dirt streaked water that rushed from side to side with the rolling of the ship and sometimes slopped over into the passageways outside." They shaved with salt water and endured the toll it took on their faces. The salt also aggravated their heat rash, a condition apparently suffered by almost every man aboard. It was worst around the waistline, where sweat-soaked underwear and clothing chafed at the skin, and the raw red welts rose to a height of a quarter of an inch. Belowdecks, powerful fans circulated air through the passageways and berthing compartments, but the wind from the ducts was as hot as a hairdryer. Few men could sleep in that heat; Kernan recalled "endless nervous shifting in the bunks and constant movement back and forth to the heads in the red glare of the night-lights." Some sought refuge above, in the bomb nets off the flight deck, with a blanket thrown across the metal mesh for padding. With the breeze generated by the forward progress of the ship, the air was actually pleasant after midnight.

New orders arrived from Nimitz on April 19. The *Lexington* and her screening ships were to proceed at "economical speed to point ACORN," about 300 nautical miles northwest of New Caledonia, where they would fall in with *Yorktown*, Task Force 17, and a force of Allied cruisers and destroyers under Rear Admiral Crace of the Royal Navy (Task Force 44). They continued on their southerly course, their long foaming wakes tailing off toward the northern horizon; they climbed up and over the equatorial bulge, toward the familiar waters of the South Pacific. Everywhere the sea looked the same: a rich deep blue, "the blue of vast deeps." The mid-Pacific was one of the most remote and inaccessible regions in the world. The *Lex* might have been cruising on some sweltering ocean-planet, where the occasional low-lying palm-crowned atolls were prizes to be studied through binoculars but never approached. Each day merged into the next, and only the night sky betrayed their progress. Polaris, the North Star, edged closer to the northern horizon each night; Crux, the Southern Cross, rose in the south. The night that *Lexington* crossed the equator, sailors on deck could see both on opposite horizons.

It was a region of glorious sunsets, painted on a broad western palette with mauve, lavender, turquoise, and rose—"flaming skies with cloud embers strewn about them," as Casey remembered them, with "bands of weird luminous green at the horizon." Southward, toward the southern edge of the doldrums, each passing day seemed faintly cooler, if only (as Casey remarked) "as much as melted lead may be cooler than melted brass." Soon they picked up the southern trade wind, a fine steady breeze that blew out of the southwest instead of the northeast, as it did north of the line. On April 29, under overcast skies with frequent rain squalls, they passed between New Hebrides and the Solomons and entered the northern Coral Sea, where (wrote Navy Lieutenant James Michener, stationed on the nearby island of Efate) "the waves of this great ocean formed and fled in golden sunlight. There was a fair breeze from Australia, as if that mighty island were restless, and from the Tasman sea gaunt waves, riding clear from the polar ice cap, came north and made the sea choppy."

As THE LIGHT CAME UP on May 1, at latitude 16° 16' south and longitude 162° 20' east, the *Yorktown* was visible in the distance. Admiral Fletcher, a frosty Iowan who had graduated from the Naval Academy in 1906, assumed overall command of both task forces. His first concern was fuel; he wanted every fighting ship's tanks near full when the main action commenced. But the task force was supported by fleet oilers that had made the long run from Pearl Harbor, and underway fueling was still a slow, painstaking process. The *Lex* and her escorts, freshly arrived from a long voyage, needed more fuel and thus more time to refuel. By visual signals, Fletcher ordered Task Force 11 south to meet the heavy cruiser *Chicago* and refuel from the oil tanker *Tippecanoe*. *Yorktown* and her charges refueled from another tanker, the *Neosho*, and then turned north toward the Louisiade Archipelago. All crews were placed on twenty-four-hour alert. Fletcher concealed his presence by maintaining absolute radio silence and by hanging back beyond the outer range of Japanese patrol flights.

Army air patrols operating from Townsville, Australia, had reported that Japanese units were moving down from the Bismarcks into the eastern Solomons, and those reports were corroborated by fresh intelligence breaks at Hypo, which had revealed that the Japanese intended to take the little tropical island of Tulagi, just off the south coast of Florida Island. Fletcher hoped to catch the invasion force on the beach, when it would be most vulnerable. On May 3, the Tulagi Invasion Force landed unopposed, the Australian garrison having been withdrawn a week earlier. Construction teams got to work on a seaplane ramp right away, and most of the Japanese naval forces that had escorted the invasion convoy withdrew to the north. At 7 p.m. that evening, Fletcher received confirmation, also from Australian-based army air patrols, that the landing had occurred and Japanese ships were anchored off the island. Under cover of darkness, the *Yorktown* and her escorts dialed up 27 knots and raced north to launch a strike at dawn on the 4th. The *Lexington*, still fueling and more than 100 miles south, was left behind. Strict radio silence was the order of the day, and Fletcher had not a moment to lose—in that first skirmish of the unfolding battle, *Yorktown* would go it alone. He sent off the *Neosho* in company with a destroyer, the *Russell*, to find Fitch and instruct him to rendezvous at a point 300 miles south of Guadalcanal, the following morning.

That night, as the *Yorktown's* engines raced at near-peak speed, the carrier's air groups gathered in their ready rooms and studied maps and photographs of the intended target. The entire region was obscure, and the only maps that were available were rough photographic copies with little detail. After taking off from the *Yorktown* the next morning, they would fly directly over the 70-mile-long island of Guadalcanal (a name that did not yet hold any special significance for them). The long east-west axis of Guadalcanal was a spine of sharp-toothed mountain peaks reaching as high as 6,000 feet. They would conceal the approach of the American carrier planes and improve the likelihood of total surprise. Passing over that hump, the planes would be a mere twelve miles from Tulagi—they would trade altitude for speed, passing across the body of water that had not yet been named Ironbottom Sound, and lay waste to the Japanese ships off Tulagi and in the adjacent Gavutu harbor.

At first light on May 4, the *Yorktown* was about 100 miles south of Guadalcanal. A cold front had overtaken them, and the weather had turned nasty, with heavy overcast, winds gusting to 35 knots, and sporadic rain showers. That was fine with the officers and crew: a carrier's most desirable situation was often to remain concealed in murk, thus protected against counter-air attack, while her planes flew out of the front into clear weather. They were awakened well before dawn by the bugle call—"boots and saddles"—pumped through the loudspeakers. The strike package included twenty-eight dive-bombers and twelve torpedo bombers. Six F4F fighters were first off the deck, at 6:31 a.m.; they would fly CAP over the task force. The first bomber was airborne by 7:01 a.m. Each of the dive-bombers was armed with a big 1,000-pound bomb; the torpedo planes carried Mark 13 torpedoes.

The bombers ascended quickly toward Guadalcanal, soaring well above the island's central peaks in the hazy morning light. As the verdant northern slopes fell steeply away, they flew into fine clear weather. The cobalt panorama of Ironbottom Sound unfolded ahead, with Florida and Tulagi islands clearly laid out in front of them, their contours matching up to the maps they had scrutinized. They pushed their noses down and picked up speed. Lieutenant Commander William O. Burch, Jr., leader of Scouting

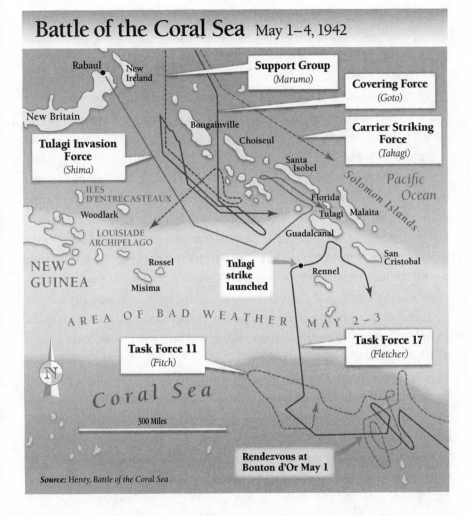

Battle of the Coral Sea May 1–4, 1942

Rabaul
New Ireland
New Britain
Support Group (*Marumo*)
Covering Force (*Goto*)
Bougainville
Choiseul
Carrier Striking Force (*Takagi*)
Tulagi Invasion Force (*Shima*)
Santa Isobel
ILES D'ENTRECASTEAUX
Florida
Pacific Ocean
Solomon Islands
Woodlark
Tulagi   Malaita
LOUISIADE ARCHIPELAGO
Guadalcanal
NEW GUINEA
Rossel
Tulagi strike launched
Rennel
San Cristobal
Misima
AREA OF BAD WEATHER   MAY 2–3
Task Force 11 (*Fitch*)
Task Force 17 (*Fletcher*)
N
Coral Sea
300 Miles
Rendezvous at Bouton d'Or May 1
Source: Henry, *Battle of the Coral Sea*

Five, was the first over Gavutu harbor, at a little after 8 a.m. He and his pilots, at altitude 19,000 feet, thought they saw a powerful Japanese fleet spread out beneath them, but their ship-recognition training failed them. They believed they saw a light cruiser, two destroyers, a seaplane tender, five troopships, and sundry gunboats and small craft. What was actually there, as it was later revealed, was a minelayer, two small minesweepers, a small transport, two destroyers, and a few landing barges.

Most historians of the war have explained such errors as the result of poor visibility or pilot inexperience, but the curmudgeonly Samuel Eliot Morison was not so accommodating. He noted that the aviators' tendency to overestimate the size and class of enemy ships was endemic, and did not diminish over time: "As usual throughout the war, the pilots overestimated what they saw; all their swans were geese, and all their geese, ducks or goslings."

The raid came as a complete surprise to the Japanese, who had no air cover and were virtually defenseless. Their ships threw up some antiaircraft fire, but their unpracticed gunnery was very poor, and no American planes were lost in that first wave. The torpedo planes followed sometime later and attacked without scoring a hit, but were equally untroubled by the flak. Their bombs and torpedoes expended, all of the *Yorktown*'s planes turned south and flew back to the waiting carrier, which had in the meantime drawn twenty miles closer. They rearmed and refueled so quickly, Lieutenant Commander Burch quipped, that the aircrews did not have time to get a cup of coffee before being ordered back into their cockpits. By 11 a.m. they were back into the air to give Tulagi and Gavutu another working over. So close was the *Yorktown*—the hop over Guadalcanal required little more than half an hour of flying time—that the carrier managed to launch three separate attacks before the day was done, sending more than sixty planes into battle and losing only three.

The triumphant aircrews believed (and reported to Admiral Fletcher in rich, convincing detail) that they had wiped out an entire Japanese surface fleet. After interviewing the *Yorktown* pilots, journalist Stanley Johnston concluded that they had sunk or heavily damaged fourteen of fifteen Japanese ships in the harbor, including three cruisers—and added that "our fliers again demonstrated that combined dive-bombing and torpedo-plane attack is the most certain, destructive and deadly method yet devised for attacking ships."

Not until later was it revealed that the claims had been enormously exaggerated. No Japanese cruisers had been in the vicinity, and the raid's complete tally had been one destroyer, the *Kikuzuki*, one small transport from which troops had already disembarked, and two patrol boats. The torpedo attacks had been almost embarrassingly unproductive. The dive- and torpedo-bombing attacks had not been well coordinated because the squadrons had not arrived at the target simultaneously. The SBD pilots complained that their bombsights and windshields had fogged over as they dived through 7,000 feet, limiting their visibility and spoiling their drops. (A lower altitude approach provided part of the solution; eventually the sights and shields were redesigned to eliminate the issue altogether.) An immense amount of ordnance and ammunition had been flung at the little Japanese fleet: 22 torpedoes, 76 1,000-pound bombs, and 12,570 rounds of .50-caliber and 7,095 rounds of .30-caliber ammunition. Nimitz later told King: "Considering that there was practically no air opposition and very little antiaircraft fire, the ammunition expenditure required to disable the number of enemy ships involved is disappointing." The action, he added, had emphasized the "necessity for target practices at every opportunity in order to keep pilots completely trained in all phases of aerial warfare."

Had Fletcher believed his pilots' story of a naval Armageddon, he might have gambled on staying through the night to finish off the cripples in the morning. Instead, he chose the more prudent course of withdrawing at high speed under cover of darkness to the southeast, safely beyond the range of Japanese land-based planes operating from the north coast of New Guinea. It was a fortunate decision. Perhaps the most important result of the *Yorktown*'s raid was that it alerted the Japanese to the presence of at least one American carrier in the neighborhood, since the single-engine bombers and torpedo planes that had screamed out of the skies over Tulagi were correctly identified as carrier-type aircraft. Immediately after the arrival of the first strike, several of the Japanese ships had heaved up their anchors and raced north, toward the safety of Rabaul. They had delivered their troops to the island, and the seaplane base would be up and running two days later, so there was no reason to hang around and be attacked repeatedly from the air.

Admiral Hara's two big fleet carriers had been fueling north of Bougainville, 350 miles north. When he learned of the raid over Tulagi, he ordered the fuel hoses disconnected and thrown over the side, and the *Shokaku* and *Zuikaku* came charging down into the eastern Solomons. Admiral Aritomo Goto, whose Port Moresby invasion force had sailed that day from Rabaul, ordered the 12,000-ton escort carrier *Shoho* to part ways with the Port Moresby invasion force and go in hunt of the enemy. But none arrived in time to catch the lucky *Yorktown* before darkness fell the night of the 4th, and she made good her retreat into the pall of bad weather to the south.

She fell in with the *Lexington* at 8:16 the next morning, about 320 nautical miles south of Guadalcanal. Both carriers immediately began the dull and potentially dangerous business of topping off their fuel tanks from the tanker *Neosho*, while proceeding at moderate speed on a southwesterly course. The *Lexington* had already sucked the last gallon of fuel out of the *Tippecanoe*. Now some of her escorting destroyers came alongside and drank from the carrier's gigantic tanks. By Fletcher's operations order 242, Task Force 11 was subsumed into Task Force 17, and the entire fleet, spread out over a wide ocean path, joined in a circular formation with the carriers in the center and the cruisers and destroyers arrayed in inner and outer defensive rings. Though Fletcher remained in overall command, he signaled his intention to place Admiral Fitch, an aviator and veteran carrier officer, in tactical control of the two flattops during air operations. Fletcher's orders, which took effect on the 6th, echoed those he had received from Nimitz— all units were directed to "destroy enemy ships, shipping, and aircraft at favorable opportunities in order to assist in checking further advances by enemy in the New Guinea–Solomon area."

Each side was now tipped off to the presence of the other. But neither had a reliable notion of exactly where the enemy was to be found. May 5, 6, and 7 were a confused interlude in which the opposing carrier groups groped for one another in vain. The weather was variable—sometimes clear and fair, sometimes overcast and squally, with winds building to gale force and heavy seas on the make. Chance, baffling and imprecise intelligence, contradictory and erroneous scouting reports, and inept or misdirected attacks were the overriding themes. For most of the five-day battle, the American forces fumbled around in confusion, and were saved only by the fact that the Japanese forces were equally bewildered. Commander Layton called it a "deadly round of blind man's buff." It was almost as if some providential will had chosen to keep them apart.

The aircraft carrier, as they all knew, was a weapon suited to hit-and-run warfare. The ships themselves were extremely vulnerable, but they could inflict heavy punishment on an enemy from long range, if they could find him and strike him first. The tactical imperatives were to keep moving; to keep your scouts in the air, flying wide search patterns; and to hide your flight decks in weather fronts while pinning your enemy down in zones of clear visibility. "If they can't find you they can't hit you," said Captain Sherman of the *Lexington*. "The carrier is a weapon that can dash in, hit hard and disappear."

The carrier scouts flew wedge-shaped sectors out to a range of 175 or 200 miles. "We simply drew a limiting circle in the direction of the area of interest and assigned planes to go out on radii so that at the outer end of their search they would be twice visual distance apart," explained Lieutenant Commander Paul D. Stroop, flag secretary to Admiral Fitch. "In other words, the objective was to cover the outer limits of your search sector completely." Theoretically, the aircrews should be able to see every inch of sea in their assigned sectors. In practice, however, they rarely did. Even when the weather was mostly clear, as it was on the morning of May 5, the floating cumulus clouds tended to thicken and spread into solid blankets of overcast by the afternoon. The tremendous efforts required to stage aerial search flights in many directions at once depleted the American carriers of their aircraft and overtaxed the pilots, who flew long flights in the blazing heat, their canopies open to circulate air through the cockpit. They returned with necks and cheeks bronzed from long exposure to the sun, and when they removed their flight goggles or aviator glasses, they revealed "raccoon" tan lines. Part of the air reconnaissance load was shared by a seaplane base in Nouméa, the French colonial capital of New Caledonia, but it had only twelve PBY Catalinas in service and was too distant to search effectively in the Solomons. The army bombers operating out of Townsville flew the sectors between Rabaul and the Coral Sea, but they provided little in the way of reliable reconnaissance. Acknowledging that the army planes were dogged by bad weather, Captain Sherman lamented: "Whatever they saw, whether a transport, tug, or destroyer, was apt to be reported as either a battleship or a carrier." Furthermore, the army pilots' position reports were often far off the mark because their own navigation was faulty.

The Japanese relied heavily on their seaplanes, which staged out of several bases in New Guinea and the eastern Solomons. The Americans were quick to praise the superior qualities of the four-engine Type 97 Kawanishi flying boat, whose breathtaking range extended to as far as 3,000 miles, giving it an effective search radius of more than 1,000 miles. Commander Mort Seligman, the *Lexington* XO, judged that the more modest range of the SBD scout bombers put the Americans "under a handicap out here. . . . If we want to find out what the enemy is doing we've got to move up to within easy range of his land-based aircraft to find out. . . . That limits our attacks almost to early morning only after an all-night fast approach. And it makes it very difficult for us to gain the advantage of the element of surprise which is a much more important factor in war than most people realize."

It was a reasonable point, but the Japanese had scouting problems of their own. Even when the ubiquitous snoopers did spot American fleet units, they were usually preoccupied with finding cloud cover to avoid being shot out of the sky by the American Wildcats, and tended to misidentify

the types of ships they had seen. Due to persistent technical problems in
their radio communications, the sighting reports often failed to get through
to Admirals Takagi or Hara. Contacts at long range, even when reliable,
might not be actionable—if the American carriers lay beyond air-striking
range, a few hours of high-speed zigzagging might take them somewhere else
entirely. Though Seligman could not know it until later, the Japanese felt as
blind as the Americans during the five-day battle.

The American carrier aircraft, both the scouts and the fighters orbiting the task force, were constantly running into enemy air patrols. On the
Lexington, staff officers crowded into the radio control room to listen to the
live pilot transmissions: "Agnes to Lilly. A plane at 17,000, bearing 130, five
miles. Having a look." "Lilly acknowledged. Will be around."

Late on the afternoon of May 5, Lieutenant Commander James H. Flatley, Jr., executive officer of the *Yorktown*'s "Fighting 42" and one of the most
famed American fighter pilots of the war, radioed that he had spotted a
Kawanishi above the cloud ceiling, about twenty-seven miles from the *Yorktown* and fifteen miles from the *Lexington*. The *Yorktown*'s fighter director
radioed back: "Where is the Kawanishi?" Flatley replied in the distinctively
cocky-laconic drawl of the fighter jock: "Wait a minute, and I'll show him
to you." Perhaps a minute passed, and the blazing remains of a seaplane fell
spinning out of the cloud cover to the northeast, trailing a ribbon of black
smoke behind it. It hit the sea and exploded, plainly visible from the deck
of the *Lexington*.

Flatley was on the radio again, this time addressing the *Lexington* combat
air patrol: "A fine thing when we have to come over here and shoot these
fellows down from on top of you. Why don't you keep your own nose clean?"

Lieutenant Noel A. M. Gayler, one of the *Lexington*'s F4F pilots, came
on the circuit: "That one nearly fell on top of me, Jimmy. I was climbing
up through those clouds and when that ball of fire swept past me I couldn't
make out for a minute what it was."

"That'll teach you not to fly underneath me," said Flatley.

The carrier pilots had plenty of good reasons to be apprehensive of a
showdown with their Japanese counterparts. In the first five months of the
war, the Japanese carrier forces had struck many hard blows against the
Americans, receiving none in return. Through May 4, 1942, U.S. Navy
pilots could claim a cumulative score of twenty-four Japanese aircraft shot
down. There was just one navy ace—Butch O'Hare, who would give his

name to the busiest commercial airport in the world. Nonetheless, the American flyboys were restless, tense, but surprisingly upbeat. They were spoiling for a fight. They gathered in their smoke-filled wardroom lounges each night after dinner, when darkness had fallen and their airplanes had been put to bed, and pored over maps of the theater. They talked endlessly about flying and fighting, illustrating maneuvers with their hands, chalking diagrams on a blackboard—and in those exchanges much useful work was done, because it was the aviator's way to share his knowledge with his colleagues, and glean all of theirs in return.

Recent encounters with the quick and maneuverable Zero had revealed its weaknesses; months of experience with the clumsier but sturdier F4F Wildcat had enhanced their pilots' respect for its virtues. "Don't forget now, no dogfighting with these babies," one of the *Lexington*'s fighter pilots said. Another replied, "I think if we stick to our pair combinations we should be able to handle 'em."

There was a steady flow of new communications intelligence each day, from Rochefort's basement to Layton to Nimitz to Fletcher via long-range coded radio transmissions, which were received in the *Yorktown* radio shack, decrypted, and delivered to the admiral on the flag bridge. But until May 6, the specific timing and direction of Japanese fleet movements remained ambiguous. Captain Sherman of the *Lexington* would later reflect that intelligence on the position of the Japanese fleet was so "sketchy" as to be almost worthless. Reports from Pearl Harbor indicated the presence and direction of many Japanese units between New Guinea and the Solomon Islands, but those reports were multifarious and confused. Radio intercepts from the fleet were of very little use in the early days of the battle, either because the Japanese adhered to radio silence or because their forces were too distant to allow for good intercepts. Fletcher was an old school officer who, not having much experience in dealing with the world of communications intelligence, could not bring himself to trust it. Lieutenant Forrest R. Biard had been detached from Hypo to sail with the *Yorktown*, but he ran afoul of the admiral when he declined Fletcher's invitation to brief the entire flag staff on the nature of his work. To do so would have been a clear violation of security measures designed to protect Ultra. Though Biard was clearly in the right, Fletcher did not relish being defied by a lowly lieutenant, and the exchange appears to have poisoned the relationship before it ever had a chance to develop.

But Hypo still managed to provide Fletcher and Fitch with a vital advantage in the battle. The Allied force was less powerful than the combined Japanese forces that were being brought into the area (albeit in several task groups, complicating the need for coordination). But whatever the disparity in force, the Allies had the advantage of knowing in advance that the Japanese intended to take Port Moresby, and must send vulnerable troopships in that direction from Rabaul. On May 3, Station Hypo broke and distributed to key parties the substance of the orders relayed to Admiral Takagi. Four days later, the codebreakers intercepted and decoded several messages sent from the MO Occupation Force which revealed its position and plans. On May 5, Fletcher learned from radio intelligence that the big Japanese carriers would move into the position they were to assume for the Moresby landings by 10 a.m. that day. That gave him the warning he needed to run south, out of the way of Takagi's air search patterns.

By the end of the day on May 6, it was clear that the Port Moresby Invasion Force would advance around the eastern end of New Guinea via the Jomard Passage, in the Louisiades Archipelago, on either May 7 or 8. With that hard information in hand, Fletcher put the task force on a northwesterly course, topping off fuel tanks from the *Neosho* as they steamed at moderate speed, hoping to gain a position from which to attack the Japanese carriers, which he presumed to be covering the invasion convoy's progress toward Moresby. Fletcher kept his carriers "cocked"—geared up to launch an all-out airstrike upon receiving the anticipated contact report. He cut the *Neosho* loose and sent her south with a destroyer, the *Sims*; the trusty oil tanker held his only remaining fuel reserve, and he needed her well out of harm's way. He also took the curious decision to detach three cruisers and three destroyers, designated as Task Group 17.3 under the command of Admiral Crace, to oppose the invasion force as it entered the Jomard Passage. The decision was controversial even at the time, as the Allies had learned the hard way that unprotected surface units should not be sent into waters dominated by enemy aircraft. It also stripped the American carriers of a large part of their antiaircraft screening defense. Apparently, Fletcher was willing to run those risks rather than allow Japanese troops to land at Moresby unopposed while Task Force 17 was pinned down in battle.

Assuming the Japanese carriers were still several hundred miles north, Fletcher would have been appalled to know that they were actually to the east, on his starboard flank, well into the Coral Sea. On the basis of a contact report received earlier that day, Admiral Takagi had ordered Hara to make an end run around the southern Solomon Islands and advance south to find and destroy the American carriers. At that moment, Task Force 17 was totally exposed and in mortal peril. If the Japanese had been luckier, they might have won the battle outright, perhaps sinking both *Yorktown* and *Lexington* while they were refueling. (Such a blow might then have altered the outcome at Midway, and therefore changed the entire course of the war.) But the Japanese scout's report had been mistaken in putting the American carriers on a bearing of 190 degrees, nearly due south. Takagi interpreted the report in a way that was consistent with what he already believed—that the American carriers were deep in the Coral Sea, nowhere near the invasion force's route of advance. On the night of May 6–7, the two mutually oblivious fleets passed within seventy nautical miles of one another, each giving chase to the other but in the wrong direction.

DAWN REVEALED A LEADEN CEILING of cumulus clouds. A southern cold front had overtaken Task Force 17, bringing cool, gusty winds, choppy seas, and intermittent rain squalls. Visibility was limited to ten or fifteen miles. The *Lexington's* meteorological officer, Lieutenant G. L. Raring, estimated that the frontal area extended only a few miles north of the American carriers. North of the island of Tagula, where the enemy was thought to lurk, the skies should be clear and visibility excellent. That was reassuring, as the conditions provided good cover for the task force, while perhaps leaving the enemy exposed to a knockout air attack.

Crace's Task Group 17.3, having separated from the main Allied fleet the previous afternoon, found itself under clear skies, 115 miles south of the eastern Louisiade Archipelago. As it happened, the combined Australian and American cruiser and destroyer force would not meet the invasion flotilla, which turned back toward Rabaul the next day; but it was subjected to multiple high-level bombing attacks and an aerial torpedo attack on the afternoon of May 7. The Japanese pilots apparently believed they had won a major victory, claiming one *California*-class battleship sunk, one British *Warspite*-class battleship damaged, and one cruiser damaged. Those claims were subsequently reported as fact in the Japanese press. In truth, Crace's ships had dodged perhaps a hundred bombs and torpedoes with adept use of their helms, and had come through the barrage without taking a single direct hit. (The U.S. cruiser *Chicago* suffered seven casualties by enemy strafing.) Before the day was done, the squadron endured the added indignity of being bombed by three of MacArthur's B-26s, whose aircrews apparently mistook them for enemy ships. "Fortunately," Crace remarked, "their bombing, in comparison with that of the Japanese a few minutes earlier, was disgraceful."

The SBD scout bombers were off the *Yorktown* and *Lexington* shortly after first light, and it was not long before a contact report came back. At 8:15 a.m., Lieutenant John Nielsen of VB-5 reported "two carriers and four heavy cruisers" near the Jomard Passage, northeast of Misima Island in the northern Louisiades. A glance at the charts showed that the reported position was about 175 miles to the west-northwest, within air-striking range. Assuming Nielson had found the main Japanese carrier force, Fletcher did not hesitate. He ordered the full Monty—a combined strike package of eight fighters, fifty-three dive-bombers, and twenty-two torpedo bombers—launched from both flight decks. The *Lexington*'s group began roaring into the sky at 9:25 a.m., the *Yorktown*'s about twenty minutes later. The airborne armada climbed to altitude and soon flew out of the frontal zone into clear, sunny skies, with magnificent visibility all around the compass. Spread out below them were the Louisiades, an archipelago of green tropical islets surrounded by coral reefs. Rows of breakers advanced upon the beaches at uniform intervals. The aircrews could look straight down through the clear, cerulean water to the shallow, sandy bottom.

With the strike in the air and on its way to the target, Lieutenant Nielsen returned to land on the *Yorktown*. No sooner was he out of his cockpit when he denied that he had seen any such thing as an aircraft carrier—he had spotted only two cruisers and two destroyers. Confronted with his contact report, the red-faced pilot realized that he had made a coding error in his transmission. It was an innocent mistake, but potentially a very costly one—the *Yorktown* and the *Lexington* had shot their bolt against a quartet of mere surface ships, when the big Japanese carriers were still in the vicinity, exact whereabouts unknown. Fletcher blew his fuse. "Young man, do you know what you have done?" he cried. "You have just cost the United States two carriers!" Nielsen deserved the rebuke, as his error could easily have led to the result Fletcher foretold; but it did nothing to inspire confidence in the assembled staff to see their chief lose his composure at such a moment, to cry out in despair (as Lieutenant Biard put it) that "we had already lost a battle we were yet to fight."

Fletcher briefly considered recalling the strike, but elected to allow it to press on in hopes of destroying the invasion force itself, which might be in the same area. That aggressive decision was soon vindicated. At 10:22 a.m., a new sighting report was received from MacArthur's headquarters—an army B-17 had spotted a carrier and several escorts, only thirty-five miles southeast of the first contact. The *Yorktown* radioed a course correction to the flight leaders. As it happened, however, Lieutenant Commander Weldon L. Hamilton, commander of the *Lexington*'s Bombing Squadron Two, had already spotted the only Japanese carrier in the vicinity. A few miles north of Tagula Island, cruising at 15,000 feet, he had scanned the horizon with his binoculars and spied white filaments laid across the blue surface of the sea, about forty miles east. Those were wakes, and if there were wakes there must be ships. He radioed the other skippers and they banked to starboard. As they drew nearer, Hamilton made out the unmistakable flat rectangular shape of a flight deck. He got back on the circuit: "I see one flattop bastard."

She was the 12,000-ton escort carrier *Shoho*, accompanied by four cruisers and one destroyer. This was Admiral Goto's Covering Group, vanguard of the Port Moresby Invasion Force, which was not far behind. Goto's lookouts saw the American planes approaching on the starboard bow, and the *Shoho*'s Captain Ishinosuke Izawa ordered a hard turn to port at 11:07 a.m. The carrier had only three fighter planes aloft, a pittance when compared to the huge air armada that was preparing to ruin the *Shoho*'s day; what was more, two of those were not even Zeros, but the previous-generation A5M Type 96 fighters ("Claude"), which were not nearly as dangerous.

Commander William B. Ault, commanding the *Lexington*'s air group, was the first to attack. He and his command group of two wingmen, each in a Dauntless SBD armed with a 500-pound bomb, pushed over and dived on the carrier at 11 a.m. Her hard port turn spoiled their aim, and all three bombs fell in the sea, missing narrowly, though one near miss apparently blew five of *Shoho*'s planes over the side. A few minutes later, the ten SBDs of Lieutenant Commander Robert E. Dixon's Scouting Two dove from 12,500 feet; they were pursued by two Type 96s, which followed the dive-bombers down but overran them when the Americans popped their airbrakes. The *Shoho* continued her hard port turn, coming full circle; the one Zero in the air attacked on the tails of the SBDs and threw off their approach; and all ten 500-pound bombs dropped by the squadron missed. Thus far the *Shoho* had been extraordinarily lucky. Her violently evasive maneuvers had helped her dodge thirteen bombs, and her game little threesome of fighters had done well against heavy odds to frustrate the attacks. Now Captain Izawa seized the moment to quick-launch three more Zeros.

Lieutenant Commander Hamilton of Bombing Two had been maneuvering his squadron at high altitude to set up a coordinated attack with the *Lexington*'s torpedo planes. Just as Dixon's SBDs released their bombs, the fifteen dive-bombers of his squadron, each armed with a 1,000-pound bomb, rolled into their dives. "The Jap was exactly downwind as I nosed down, simplifying my problem tremendously," said Hamilton. "My bomb, which was the first 1,000 pounder to hit, struck in the middle of the flight deck's width, just abaft amidships. As I looked back the entire after-portion of the flight deck was ablaze and pouring forth heavy black smoke." Dixon, recovering from his dive, saw a thunderclap of an explosion and a ball of fire mushrooming to a height of 400 feet. He congratulated Hamilton over the radio: "Mighty fine, mighty fine." A second bomb struck centerline-aft, near *Shoho*'s elevator, touching off secondary explosions on the hangar deck. As his SBD pulled away from the scene, Hamilton turned back to have a look. "The ship was a flaming wreckage, rent by tremendous explosions, slowed to nearly stopping—a spectacular and convincing pageant of destruction."

The *Shoho*'s fate was probably sealed by those two hits, but the Americans were not yet finished with her. *Lexington*'s Torpedo Squadron Two, led by Lieutenant Commander James H. Brett, Jr., was approaching from the southwest, broad on the burning carrier's beam; they had found a path through the screening vessels where the antiaircraft fire was relatively thin. The lumbering TBDs spread out to set up an "anvil" attack, in which torpedoes would be dropped on both bows simultaneously, so that the *Shoho* could not maneuver to avoid them both. The attackers were concealed behind the curtain of smoke and the geysers of water sent up by the dive-bombers' near misses, and though they were dogged by fighters they made excellent drops. The "fish" separated from the aircrafts' bellies at an altitude of 100 feet and dived nose-first into the sea, then recovered and ran true into the *Shoho*, where they detonated and tore great holes in her hull beneath the waterline. Five torpedoes apparently struck the carrier, two on the starboard side and three on the port. As the torpedo planes retreated, it was obvious that the *Shoho* was dead in the water. Despite the notoriously low airspeed of the Devastators, none was lost in the attack or the withdrawal.

The *Yorktown's* air group arrived over the carrier at 11:25, and from his altitude of 18,000 feet, Lieutenant Commander William Burch, Jr., did not realize that the *Shoho* was crippled. He led his seventeen SBDs into a dive-bombing attack that probably added another five or six 1,000-pound bombs to her tally of misery. Five minutes later, the *Yorktown's* torpedo planes arrived and put another two to five torpedoes into her hull. That coup de grâce was entirely superfluous. With too many bombs to count raining down along her whole length, and too many torpedoes to count tearing out her bowels, the *Shoho* simply blew apart and sank. Burch recalled that she "just ploughed herself under." Wildcat pilot Jimmy Flatley, orbiting at 5,000 feet, was moved by the spectacle. "The sight of those heavy dive bombers smashing that carrier was so awful I was physically ill," he said. "They followed each other at three or four-second intervals, and those powerful explosions were literally tearing the big ship apart."

Flatley was disappointed that the Dauntlesses and Devastators had wasted bombs and torpedoes on a target that was done for, while four enemy cruisers and a destroyer were allowed to escape unmolested. There should have been a tactical coordinator to observe the action from altitude and divert attacks to other targets. Lieutenant Commander Stroop, flag secretary to Admiral Fitch, agreed that the Yorktowners had flogged a dead horse. "It was a very successful attack," he said, "except that we had an overkill on the carrier. . . . Looking back on this, it was too bad that the attack hadn't been better coordinated and some of the force spread around on other ships. But this being our first battle of that kind, everybody went after the big prize, and they sank this rather soft carrier very quickly."

Captain Izawa ordered abandon ship at 11:31 a.m., and in the last moments before she sank, a quarter of her crew leapt into the sea. Two hundred and three men survived; 631 were killed in the explosions or were trapped in the ship when she went down. All twenty-one of the *Shoho's* airplanes were lost. Though she was only a baby flattop, far less valuable or dangerous than the *Shokaku* or *Zuikaku*, she was the first major Japanese ship destroyed in the war. Dixon prompted a round of applause on the *Yorktown* and *Lexington* when he radioed back the prearranged message: "Scratch one flattop! Dixon to Carrier, Scratch one flattop!"

The immediate significance of the sinking of the *Shoho* was that it prompted Admiral Inoue, monitoring events from his headquarters at Rabaul, to fear for the safety of the Port Moresby invasion convoy. He ordered the flotilla to turn around and beat a hasty northward retreat, thus abandoning (at least for the moment) the objective of the entire MO operation. Until the American carriers were caught and killed, he was not willing to risk the safety of his troops and other surface units. As it turned out, they would not return. The attempt to take Moresby by sea would be given up for good, delivering a strategic victory to the Allies and placing Australia forever beyond the threat of invasion.

TWO HUNDRED MILES TO THE EAST, the two big Japanese fleet carriers had duplicated Fletcher's error of launching an all-out attack on a secondary target based on a flawed sighting report. At 7:22 a.m. that morning, a cruiser-based floatplane pilot radioed that he had spotted one carrier and one escorting cruiser 163 miles due south of the *Shokaku* and *Zuikaku*. The scout confirmed his report at 7:45 a.m., and a second Japanese patrol plane corroborated the sighting. Takagi and Hara took the bait. Assuming they had found the *Saratoga*, which they thought to be the only American flattop in the theater, the Japanese commanders ordered a massive air attack from both flight decks. At 8 a.m. the airplanes began roaring into the sky, and thirty minutes later a formidable air armada was southbound. It included seventy-eight planes in all: thirty-six D3A2 dive-bombers ("Vals"), twenty-four torpedo-armed B5N2 Nakajimas ("Kates"), and a fighter escort of eighteen Zeros.

But the Japanese scouts had botched the job. They had come across the tanker *Neosho* and the destroyer *Sims*, which Fletcher had sent away the previous day. After the Japanese airstrike had departed, new contact reports arrived on the bridge of the *Shokaku*—two American carriers, Hara realized with a shock, were 288 miles to the northwest, almost in the opposite direction of the first reported contact. Japanese ship-to-air radio technology being unreliable, Hara was concerned that he could not reroute his outbound strike—the risk of a garbled transmission was too great. So he allowed it to continue on its way, but the Japanese carriers meanwhile turned northwest in the hope of getting to within striking range when their planes returned: "We will join battle with the enemy in the west after we have attacked to the south." Upon learning that the "carrier" to the south was nothing more than an oiler and destroyer, however, he radioed an urgent recall order. Perhaps, Hara hoped, there would be time enough to recover the planes, refuel them, and send them after the big game in the northwest.

The *Neosho*, 25,000 tons, and the little *Sims*, 1,570 tons, were marked ships. Their officers and crews apparently did not realize how dire the situation was until the huge enemy airstrike came over the horizon at 10:38 a.m. The oiler and destroyer were entirely without air cover, and their antiaircraft defenses were pitiful in comparison to the number of enemy planes circling overhead. But the Japanese did not attack immediately. Visibility having improved significantly since that morning's flyover, the strike leaders knew at once that they had been led astray. To send the whole strike down on those two puny ships would be a waste, and the squadron leaders directed some of the airplanes to disperse in a search pattern to look for any other good targets. Finding none, the torpedo planes and Zeros broke away without attacking, and returned to the carriers. The dive-bombers remained to take care of the *Neosho* and *Sims*.

They attacked at their leisure, rolling into their dives as if they were performing at an air show, and sent a rain of bombs down on the two star-crossed ships. The *Neosho* was pulverized with seven 250-kilogram bomb hits; the *Sims*, hit with three bombs, broke in half and went down, taking 178 of her 192-man crew with her. The burning, crippled *Neosho* appeared to be finished, and the Japanese planes flew away to the north. Some of her crew panicked and leapt into the water though no abandon ship order had been given; the captain sent whaleboats to fetch them back on board; and the remaining crew went through the requisite steps of destroying classified documents and codebooks. But the *Neosho* would not founder—she drifted, ablaze, with only weak auxiliary radio communications. All of her whaleboats were lowered into the sea and kept station with the mother ship as she battled for survival.

The *Neosho* would wage a four-day struggle for survival against rising winds and heavy seas. She had no power, a severe starboard list, and two thirds of her crew were missing and presumed dead. On May 11, her ordeal was brought to an end by the destroyer *Henley*, which removed the survivors and sent her to the bottom with two torpedoes.

Receiving the urgent distress signal from the *Neosho*, Fletcher was taken aback. The nervous tension on the *Yorktown*'s flag bridge was palpable. The *Yorktown* and *Lexington*'s planes were already en route to the northwest, where Fletcher had believed they would find the two big Japanese flattops. The *Neosho*'s report, if true, could only mean that the enemy carriers were in the opposite direction, or perhaps (even more unnerving) he might be bracketed by enemy carrier task forces on two flanks. On the other hand, the report also suggested that the two big Japanese carriers had shot their bolt in the wrong direction, and could not attack the *Lexington* and *Yorktown* until late in the day, at the earliest. Both sides had committed to attacking the wrong target, and the two errors had effectively cancelled one another out. By sinking the *Shoho*, in fact, the Americans had come away with the better consolation prize. In any case, it was now clear to both sides that their big carriers were finally on the verge of coming to grips—if not later that afternoon, then the next morning without fail.

Between 12:45 and 1:15 p.m., the American strike returned and landed aboard the carriers, having lost only three Dauntless SBDs. The aircrews filed into the wardrooms for lunch, their merriment at having sunk an enemy carrier intermixed with sorrow for fallen comrades. Several of the aircraft had been badly shot up, and the *Lexington*'s deck hands clustered around the machines and gaped at the damage. Here was dramatic proof of the value of sturdy construction. Stanley Johnston wrote that one of the Dauntlesses reminded him of a "colander." Wings, fuselage, tail, and Plexiglas windshield were riddled with bullet holes.

By 2:20 p.m. the air groups were refueled and rearmed, and might have made another sortie against the Port Moresby Invasion Force, which was still within range. But the conservative Fletcher elected not to launch a second strike, as he did not yet know precisely where the big Japanese carriers were and did not want to be caught shorn of his planes. Postwar analysis would show that his onboard radio intelligence specialist, Lieutenant Forrest Biard, had picked up an enemy homing beacon giving a course and speed of the Japanese carriers: "280 degrees speed 20 knots." With this partial information Fletcher might have made sound deductions about their location, but a language officer initially mistranslated the signal as a Japanese patrol plane's report of the heading and speed of the American carriers. The confusion was soon cleared up, but Fletcher lacked confidence in the intelligence and was unwilling to gamble on it. Later in the war, it would become a court-martial offense to refuse to act on good intelligence, but for now it was Fletcher's privilege to ignore his intelligence officer if he so chose, and he did. Task Force 17 would lie doggo for the remainder of the afternoon.

It was late in the day, and the weather was turning for the worse: a low-ering cloud ceiling, southeasterly winds gusting to 30 knots, and frequent rain squalls. The American aviators had not been trained in night opera-tions, and it was sensible to worry that some might not be able to navigate back to the carriers on their return leg. Fletcher turned the task force to the southwest, better to slip under the protecting veil of the weather front and await the morning to launch his next attack. He would later explain that he had judged there was "insufficient daylight for an attack following an extensive search." The *Yorktown* and *Lexington* would keep a strong force of fighters flying CAP, but the bombers and torpedo planes would remain deck-bound until morning.

The Japanese were bolder. At 4:15 that afternoon, with a new contact report in hand, Hara chose to roll the dice on a late-day strike. His pilots would have to land after nightfall, in conditions of dubious visibility, and he must have known the risk of losses was high. The aircrews were handpicked; the most seasoned and skillful among them were chosen for the mission. Several had already made the long round-trip flight to the *Neosho* and *Sims*, and they were fatigued, but still game as always. Hara launched twelve dive-bombers and fifteen torpedo planes from *Shokaku*, with orders to fly 277 degrees to a range of 280 nautical miles. They were to search for and attack the American carriers. If they were successful, the Japanese might win the Battle of the Coral Sea outright in time for a late celebratory dinner.

The American task force was only about 170 miles west, and the out-bound planes apparently flew over the American carriers and their escorts, failing to spot them through the heavy overcast. At six, the strike leaders, talking by radio, decided to turn back. They jettisoned their bombs and torpedoes and reversed course, hoping to pick up their carriers' homing signals. The Americans' newly installed radar sets tracked the bombers fly-ing above the cloud cover, and a group of F4F fighters were vectored out to intercept them on their return flight. They closed at 6:15 p.m., right as the sunlight faded out of a gunmetal gray sky. The American fighters emerged out of cloud cover on the tails of several of the Japanese planes. In the ensuing aerial melee, the Japanese got the worst of it, losing nine aircraft (eight Kates, one Val), against three American Wildcats. That was one of the war's earliest demonstrations of the game-changing potential of radar.

After nightfall, when most of the American planes had been taken aboard, a new formation of planes arrived over the task force. First, the

drone of their engines could be heard above the cloud cover; then they
slipped into view, at about the height of the *Lexington*'s masts. "These
planes were in very good formation," recalled Lieutenant Commander
Stroop. They had their navigation lights on, indicating that they intended
to land. But many observers on both carriers and several of the screening
vessels noted that something was awry. Captain Sherman of the *Lexington*
counted nine planes, more than could be accounted for among the American planes that were still aloft. They were flying down the *Yorktown*'s port
side, a counterclockwise approach, the reverse of the American landing
routine. They were flashing their blinker lights, but none of the Americans
could decipher the signal. Electrician's mate Peter Newberg, stationed on
the *Yorktown*'s flight deck, noticed that the aircraft exhausts were a strange
shape and color, and Stroop noted that the running lights were a peculiar
shade of red and blue.

The TBS (short-range radio circuit) came alive with chatter. One of the
nearby destroyers asked, "Have any of our planes got rounded wingtips?"
Another voice said, "Damned if those are our planes." When the first of
the strangers made his final turn, he was too low, and the *Yorktown*'s landing signal officer frantically signaled him to throttle up. "In the last few
seconds," Newberg recalled, "when the pilot was about to plow into the
stern under the flight deck, he poured the coal to his engine and pulled
up and off to port. The signal light flicked briefly on red circles painted on
his wings."

One of the screening destroyers opened fire, and red tracers reached up
toward the leading plane. A voice on the *Lexington* radioed to all ships in
the task force, ordering them to hold fire, but the captain of the destroyer
replied, "I know Japanese planes when I see them." Antiaircraft gunners on
ships throughout the task force opened fire, and suddenly the night sky lit
up as if it was the Fourth of July. But there were friendly planes in the air as
well; one of the *Yorktown* fighter pilots complained: "What are you shooting at me for? What have I done now?" On the *Yorktown*, SBD pilot Harold
Buell scrambled out to the port-side catwalk to see what was happening. "In
the frenzy of the moment, with gunners firing at both friend and foe, some
of us got caught up in the excitement and drew our .45 Colt automatics
to join in, blasting away at the red meatballs as they flew past the ship—
an offensive gesture about as effective as throwing rocks." The intruders
and the Americans all doused their lights and zoomed back into the cloud

cover; none was shot down. It was not the last time in the war that confused Japanese pilots would attempt to land on an American carrier.

Later that night, fascinated radar operators on the *Lexington* tracked the enemy planes on their flight to the east and reported that they were circling only thirty miles away. Could the Japanese carriers be that close? So it seemed. When the intelligence unit tuned in to the Japanese flight frequency, they could overhear the carriers communicating with the pilots in plain Japanese, trying to talk them in. (After the war it was determined that they had been farther east, perhaps sixty to a hundred miles.) There was some discussion of dispatching the task force's destroyers to stage a night torpedo attack, but Fletcher chose not to risk it.

Hara's gambit had been a debacle. The Japanese carriers lit up their searchlights to guide their planes back in, but twenty-one of the twenty-seven planes launched that late afternoon failed to return to their carriers. Nine had been shot down in aerial combat, twelve more lost at sea, and none of the lost aircrews were rescued. The pilots who did return reported having sighted the American carriers fifty to sixty miles to the east. As night set in, the opposing commanders prepared for the battle that would follow the next day. Fletcher turned southwest and prepared a large search pattern to be flown at dawn. Admiral Takagi accepted Hara's proposal that the Japanese task force should head north, so they could concentrate their morning search flights toward the south.

THE AMERICAN AVIATORS ATE AN EARLY DINNER and debriefed in their ready rooms. Each side was now perfectly aware of the other's presence, so neither could count on surprise. The big Japanese carriers might even be visible on the horizon at daybreak. "In our enemy we recognized a tough, fanatical foe whose courage and cunning could not be discounted," wrote Johnston. "Our forces appeared about equal. It seemed to be a question of who would get the first blow home. We had seen on the previous day what aircraft could do to a carrier and so we knew the consequences that day might bring." On the *Yorktown*, mimeographed copies of the following day's "ops plan" were posted in the ready rooms. At 5:40 a.m., the aircrews would go to flight quarters. At 6:20 a.m., the scout bomber aircrews would man their planes. They would sit in their cockpits as their engines warmed, awaiting the flight officer's signal. They would launch at first light and fly their assigned reconnaissance patterns. The fighters would launch immediately afterward, and then the SBDs and TBDs of the airstrike would be brought up from the hangar deck, ready to get aloft upon the first contact report.

The flyboys slipped back to their cabins and fell into deep, insensible sleep, their nervous tension overridden by physical and mental exhaustion. (Flying, though essentially sedentary, was much more taxing than driving a car, especially under the strain of combat). Crewmen crept down corridors dimly lit by the blue battle lamps, taking care not to wake the aviators as they passed the propped-open doors of their cabins. Except for the whirring fans and the steady throbbing of the engines, the ship was quiet. The task force steamed out of the frontal area into a clear, still night lit by a half moon in the west. On deck, the gunners stood alert by their batteries, wearing steel helmets and cumbersome kapok life vests that smelled strongly of the flame-retardant chemicals with which they had been treated. The screening ships drew in close, advancing at exactly the same speed and heading as the carriers. Their white bow waves—"bone in teeth," as the sailors called them—stood out in stark relief against their darkened hulls. As always, the fleet zigzagged to thwart enemy submarines, turning often and in perfectly timed unison, as if connected by an unseen thread. They did not seem to communicate at all, except by the occasional dim flashing of blinker lamps. The phosphorescence whipped up by the mighty screws could be seen in every direction, and if a man leaned over his ship's stern and looked down into the wake, the blue-green glow appeared to descend to a depth of 30 or 40 feet.

A blazing sunrise revealed a nearly cloudless sky. It was a beautiful morning, with no sign of the fog, scud, or squalls that had provided cover for the task force in recent days. The Americans would have gladly done without the change, as it left them feeling naked and vulnerable—"with no place to hide," as Signalman Beaver put it. Worse, the frontal zone had passed over them and swept north, where the enemy now lay at a distance of about 175 miles; the *Shokaku* and *Zuikaku* would have the advantage of dirty weather in which to conceal themselves against airborne scouts and attackers. It would be a vital factor in the action to come.

As soon as light was sufficient for flight operations, the *Lex* launched eighteen scouts to fly search patterns all the way around the compass, spreading out from the task force like spokes radiating from the hub of a wheel. Those flying the northern semicircle were directed to fly to a distance of 200 miles, about the limit of the SBD's radius. Shortly thereafter, the F4F fighters went aloft to fly CAP. The Japanese search planes would no doubt appear overhead soon.

The expected sighting report did not come until 8:20 a.m. Lieutenant (jg) Joseph Smith—who had flown his northeast segment to the end of its outbound leg, completed his cross-leg, and flown fifty miles of his return leg—radioed that he had spotted the Japanese fleet: "Two carriers, four heavy cruisers, many destroyers, steering 120 degrees, 20 knots." The position was 175 miles from the American task force, bearing 028 degrees. "It was thrilling news," wrote Captain Sherman, "the first sighting of the large Japanese carriers by either land-based or carrier planes."

Aubrey Fitch, who now took over tactical command of both American carriers, decided to steam north for an hour to close the range. The distance to the reported contact was about as far as the short-legged Devastators could fly with enough fuel to return safely. The admiral was also painfully aware, based on recent experience, that the first sighting report was not always to be trusted. The aircrews copied down all last-minute navigational data off the chalkboards and filed out of their ready rooms. Festooned with gear, flight goggles pushed up on their foreheads, they ducked and weaved through the maze of parked planes, guided by the plane crews with their multicolored hoods. Both carriers went into "condition Zed," when interior doors and hatches were slammed closed and dogged down, a measure to seal the hull off into watertight compartments. Unneeded gear was stowed out of the way, the fuel hoses were drained, and the firefighting equipment brought out and readied. The crew on deck put on their life vests and helmets and went to their battle stations. On the bridge, the glass plate windows enclosing the crowded wheelhouse were retracted into their sills, leaving the interior exposed to the open air.

The two carriers turned into the wind, and the first airplanes left the flight decks at 9:07 a.m. Half an hour later, a massive seventy-five-plane strike was on its way toward the Japanese fleet: thirty-nine dive-bombers (all armed with 1,000-pound bombs), twenty-one torpedo planes, and fifteen fighters.

Lieutenant Commander Dixon, the skipper of Scouting Two, had been flying the segment adjacent to that of Lieutenant Smith, who radioed the contact report. Upon intercepting the contact, Dixon abandoned his own segment and made a beeline for the reported location. He circled above a heavy squall, failing to see the enemy fleet at first; but he kept at it until he spotted several ships through a gap in the overcast. He stalked the enemy for more than two hours, radioing more than a dozen position corrections and guiding the incoming strike into the target. That was a very dangerous move, as the Zeros were aloft and determined to shoot him down. He slipped in and out of the clouds in a deadly game of cat and mouse, and shot back at them with his aircraft's powerful .50- and .30-caliber Browning machine guns. The Zeros made feinting runs at him, apparently trying to tempt Dixon and his rear gunner to throw away ammunition, but the Americans did not take the bait. "If they came in too close," Dixon recounted, "I would make a steep turn and head toward them with one wing low. This allowed me to be in shooting position with my front guns and also permitted my gunner to fire forward over the wing with his twin flexible mounted guns."

The air armada flew north, but not in good order. The *Yorktown* and *Lexington* groups drew apart, eventually losing sight of one another. The different plane types—dive-bombers, torpedo planes, fighters—flew at different speeds and altitudes, and drifted further apart as they put the miles behind them. The dive-bombers had to climb to high altitude, above 15,000 feet, to be in position for their diving attacks; the torpedo planes, lugging their heavy fish, could not spare the fuel to climb so high, and had no need to do so as they would approach the enemy at low altitude. The fighters had to throttle back to maximize fuel economy, which left them vulnerable to sudden diving air attacks. Flying into the frontal area, the pilots craned their necks to find gaps in the wet, white murk; often they lost sight of their own wingmen.

The *Yorktown* SBDs and fighter escorts were the first to spot the Japanese carriers, at 10:32 a.m. The carriers were about five miles apart, heading due south at 25 knots. Lieutenant Commander William Burch, Jr., who had tactical command of the *Yorktown*'s two SBD squadrons, held the dive-bombers in a circling pattern while awaiting the arrival of the torpedo planes, so they could make a coordinated attack. The decision was consistent with tactical doctrine, but the twenty-minute delay was not worth it. The Japanese carriers took the opportunity to launch more Zeros for air defense, and the *Zuikaku* slipped away to the south and found cover behind a black squall line. One of the *Yorktown*'s SBD pilots judged that "This loss of initiative was more costly than any advantage gained by a coordinated attack." When the *Yorktown's* torpedo planes came lumbering onto the scene at 10:57 a.m., they fanned out to make an "anvil" approach on the *Shokaku*.

Lacking any fighter escort, they made awkward torpedo drops at ranges of a quarter to a third of a mile, and scored no hits. High above, Burch and his seven-plane squadron (VS-5) rolled into their dives. As they hurtled through 8,000 feet, their bombsights and windshields became fogged over (as they had done over Tulagi four days earlier), and the problem was so severe that they were nearly blinded. Burch estimated that the fogging prob-lem reduced the accuracy of their drops by 75 percent, and remarked that they had been obliged to "bomb from memory." All seven of their bombs went into the sea.

The seventeen Dauntlesses of Lieutenant Wally Short's Bombing Five, which had circled around to take up a better initial diving position, followed about three minutes later. Plummeting toward the *Shokaku* at a 70-degree angle, they were harassed by Zeros and their windshields fogged over. Yet they somehow managed to plant two 1,000-pound bombs on the flight deck, one fore and one aft. The second was dropped by Lieutenant John J. Pow-ers, who held his dive to below 1,000 feet before releasing. The low drop guaranteed that he would not survive—the explosion of his own bomb, on the starboard side abaft of the *Shokaku's* island, engulfed his aircraft. It was virtually a suicide attack; Powers traded his life (and that of his rear-seat man) to remove the possibility of missing the target. He was awarded a posthumous Medal of Honor.

Maintenance officer Hachiro Miyashita of the *Shokaku* was below, in one of the machine shops on the hangar deck. The first blast ignited sec-ondary explosions that wiped out the machine and maintenance facilities. Several dozen men were killed outright, and many more succumbed to smoke inhalation as they tried to escape. Miyashita climbed a ladder to the flight deck, which he reached just in time to see Power's bomb hit that deck. Those two bombs tore gaping holes in *Shokaku's* flight deck and left her burning furiously for several hours. She had suffered casualties of 108 men killed and 40 wounded. She was not fit to conduct flight operations until she could be repaired in port, and her air group was obliged to land on the *Zuikaku*. But the *Shokaku's* wounds were not mortal. Her damage control teams eventually managed to subdue the fires. Having taken no torpedo hits, her hull was intact and she could make way under her own power at 30 knots. Her captain requested permission to withdraw from the battle, and was granted it. At 12:10 p.m., the *Shokaku* retreated toward Truk with an escort of two destroyers.

The *Lexington* air group had a frustrating day. The outbound flight had been confused and disjointed, and most of the *Lexington* planes arrived in small formations, separated by intervals of five to ten minutes. Three Wildcats and nine SBDs failed to find the enemy fleet at all, and turned back. The *Lexington* air group commander, Commander Bill Ault, caught sight of both Japanese carriers through a break in the fog and rain, but he could muster only four dive-bombers, eleven torpedo planes, and six fighters. "You couldn't see much," recalled Lieutenant Gayler, one of the *Lexington's* fighter pilots. "Big towering columns of rain clouds, sort of like pillars. You'd go around them and all of a sudden you'd see the carrier. Here he is, and there he's gone. . . . It was just such an incredibly confusing, mixed-up, screwed-up situation. Poor visibility and people yelling on the radio." The ubiquitous Zeros seemed to attack from every direction. The Wildcats fought them off, while the sluggish torpedo planes sought cover in the mists. "There was always one of them making a run at me," said Gayler. "Early in the scrap I evaded the attack of one and then jumped his tail. He immediately resorted to the old Zero trick of zooming for altitude. Remember those babies will climb 4,000 feet a minute. They just love to have you on their tail trying to follow them up. If you do, they climb out of your range, flop over backward at the top of their zoom and you suddenly find them diving back at you when you are almost stalled and easy meat."

Before the Lexingtonians could organize themselves, the overcast moved back in and hid the enemy fleet from view. Ault began a quartering "box" search and soon found the wounded *Shokaku* about twenty miles west. He attacked immediately with three wingmen. The four SBDs dived and scored one additional hit on the starboard side of the flight deck. All twelve of *Lexington's* torpedo planes also attacked the carrier, and came away with the optimistic belief that five of their fish had scored. But it is a confirmed fact that no torpedoes struck the *Shokaku* that day—or if any did, they must have failed to detonate.

SPREAD OUT ON A SPARKLING BLUE SEA under a fair sky, Task Force 17 was like a worm writhing on a hook. The officers and crew of the American flattops knew they would come under heavy air attack that day, probably before noon. So it came as no surprise when the *Yorktown's* radio room intercepted a contact report transmitted by Warrant Officer Kenzo Kanno in a Nakajima Type 97 at 8:28 a.m., just a few minutes after Lieutenant Smith had found the Japanese carriers. "Have sighted enemy carriers. Location of enemy carriers 205 degrees and 235 miles from your position, course 170 degrees, speed 16 knots."

"This was a beautiful report," remarked Ensign Kenji Hori, a dive-bomber pilot based on the *Zuikaku*. It was clear, unequivocal, and perfectly correct, a refreshing contrast to the previous day's deadly pandemonium. Admiral Hara sent off his sixty-nine-plane "air shot" quickly, with orders to stay together in formation and follow the strike leader, Lieutenant Commander Kakuichi Takahashi.

The American task force sailed in a circular formation with the two carriers at the hub. Periodically both carriers turned port, into the wind, to launch or recover aircraft—but the destroyer and cruiser escorts continued to make way at 20 knots to the northeast, toward the direction of the enemy. Captain Sherman, bronzed by long exposure to the sun, spent the morning on his signal bridge on the island, twenty-five feet above the flight deck. He was dressed for battle in a khaki uniform, a canvas windbreaker, and a steel helmet secured with a chin strap. Although this was the first exchange of carrier airstrikes in naval history, the skipper had an intuitive sense of how the battle would unfold. He deduced that the Japanese carriers had launched their planes at about the same time as the Americans (they had); that the two air groups had passed one another en route (they had); and that the enemy planes would attack Task Force 17 at approximately 11 a.m. (they would). He thought it possible that both airstrikes would sink the other's carriers, leaving all surviving planes marooned in the air. Speaking briefly to Stanley Johnston, who was permitted to observe the action from the bridge, he explained his reasoning by way of a boxing metaphor. The aircraft carrier was a fighter with a long reach, a strong punch, and a glass chin. "I feel that at the present time an air attack group cannot be stopped," he remarked. "It's likely that the position will be similar to that of two boxers, both swinging a knockout punch at the same time, and both connecting."

Returning SBD scout bombers were quickly refueled and sent back up to fly low-level "antisubmarine" patrols, which would also put them in the path of the incoming torpedo planes. The engine room raised steam so that the *Lexington* could quickly accelerate to 30 knots. High-speed evasive maneuvering—the helm—was still a ship's best defense against air attack.

American radar screens picked up the incoming enemy planes at 10:55 a.m., when they were sixty-eight miles away, but the primeval system in use at that time could not accurately measure altitude. The *Lexington's* fighter director officer (who had control of all seventeen fighters in the air, including the *Yorktown's*) estimated that they would be above 10,000 feet. Fitch's air staff was reluctant to vector the Wildcats out to intercept at long distance, lest they miss the incoming planes and leave the carriers unshielded. The fighters were kept close, altitude 10,000 feet. Several SBD Dauntless dive-bombers were assigned to fly a low-altitude patrol, at 2,000 feet, to watch for submarines and intercept the enemy torpedo planes. This use of dive-bombers as makeshift fighters was resented by their aircrews, who believed they were utterly disadvantaged in such a role and were being served up to the Zeros as cold meat. It was the most significant controversy to emerge from the battle, and contributed to the growing feeling in navy air circles that all the American carriers needed many more fighters.

Five *Lexington* fighters made contact with the enemy air armada at a distance of twenty miles, and found them in layered formations from 10,000 to 13,000 feet. They climbed to altitude, but lost speed in the effort, and had to turn onto the Japanese tails in chase. The *Lexington's* loudspeakers broadcast the radio communications between the FDO and the aircraft: "*Norma* to carrier. Enemy torpedo planes, Nakajima 97s, spilling out of a cloud eight miles out. They are at 6,000 feet in a steep glide. We're intercepting now." Takahashi's attack was finely choreographed, and the contrast with the discombobulated American air groups was stark. With fifteen miles to go, they fanned out into two groups of torpedo planes and one large group of dive-bombers. Lieutenant Willard Eder, of the *Lexington's* squadron VF-2, was one of those who intercepted: "My wingman and I headed for two Jap planes, which ducked into a cloud. We lost them in the clouds. Then he and I became separated and I turned out and saw below me this fighter. He turned up toward me. I headed down toward him and we met head-on. I was firing four .50-calibers in a down slant and he was firing in an up slant. I could see his 20-mms were falling quite short of me. His 7.7-mms were doing better when my .50-caliber began hitting him. Almost immediately his plane sort of snap-rolled, then spiraled downward, uncontrolled."

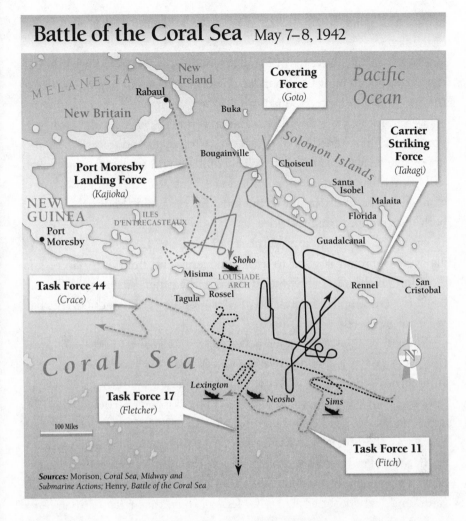

Battle of the Coral Sea May 7–8, 1942

Sources: Morison, *Coral Sea, Midway and Submarine Actions*; Henry, *Battle of the Coral Sea*

The *Lexington's* lookouts first saw the enemy planes at 11:13 a.m. They appeared as "clusters of black dots" on the northeast horizon, hardly moving at all. Gradually each dot resolved into a recognizable shape—a fuselage, a horizontal wing-line, a propeller-disk, a bomb or torpedo attached underneath. The torpedo planes fanned out and approached from two directions, while the dive-bombers soared overhead and rolled into their dives. "Here they come!" cried the lookouts on the catwalk around the stack. The *Lexington's* engines surged as the ship accelerated, and her deck sloped steeply to port as Sherman ordered the first evasive turn to starboard. Antiaircraft guns on the carrier and the nearby cruisers and destroyers opened fire, and the sky filled with dirty gray-black flak bursts. Vertical plumes of smoke marked the spots where American or Japanese aircraft had been shot out of the sky.

"Never in all my years in combat have I even imagined a battle like that!" said Lieutenant Commander Shigekazu Shimazaki, group leader of the two Japanese torpedo squadrons. "When we attacked the enemy carriers we ran into a virtual wall of antiaircraft fire; the carriers and their supporting ships blackened the sky with exploding shells and tracers. It seemed impossible that we could survive our bombing and torpedo runs through such incredible defenses. Our Zeros and enemy Wildcats spun, dove, and climbed in the midst of our formations. Burning and shattered planes of both sides plunged from the skies."

From the perspective of witnesses aboard the *Lexington*, a swarm of malevolent aircraft seemed to attack suddenly and from every angle and direction. In the adrenaline-fueled chaos of the general melee, no one man could form a complete impression of what was happening—the events had to be pieced together after the fact.

Shimazaki's Nakajimas approached on the *Lexington*'s port beam, traveling very fast in a shallow dive from 4,000 feet. Six broke away to circle around the carrier's starboard bow in a classic "anvil" pattern, leaving Captain Sherman with few viable options. (The skipper later wrote that the attack had been "beautifully coordinated.") To port, Shimazaki's planes flew low across the bow of the *Minneapolis*, and the cruiser's fusillade of antiaircraft fire blew the first out of the sky, but the others flew on toward the *Lexington*, seemingly unfazed. When they had drawn to within about 1,000 yards, and leveled out at about 100-feet altitude, they released their Type 91 800-kilogram aerial torpedoes. Each weapon dived nose-first into the sea with a splash, then recovered and streaked toward the *Lexington* under its own internal propulsion, just beneath the surface, running straight and true at 50 knots.

The Japanese planes continued on the same track, descending to the height of the *Lexington*'s flight deck or even lower, nearly grazing her bow as they passed. Antiaircraft gunners claimed one at point-blank range—the explosion was so close aboard that fragments of flaming aluminum skittered across her flight deck. "I had to fly directly above the waves to escape the enemy's shells and tracers," said Shimazaki. "In fact, when I turned away from the carrier, I was so low that I almost struck the bow of the ship, for I was flying below the level of the flight deck. I could see the crewman on the ship staring at my plane as it rushed by. I don't know that I could ever go through such horrible moments again."

Torpedoes were in the water to port and starboard, and dive-bombers were hurtling down from overhead, but Captain Sherman appeared completely unperturbed, as if the *Lexington* fought off such an attack every day of the week. "From my bridge I saw bombers roaring down in steep dives from many points in the sky, and torpedo planes coming in on both bows almost simultaneously," he later wrote. "There was nothing I could do about the bombers, but I could do something to avoid the torpedoes." In an even tone, he told the helmsman, "Hard astarboard." The long axis of the *Lexington's* hull was agonizingly slow to respond, even with more than 30 knots of speed. The captain recalled that she turned "majestically and ponderously," and that those moments "seemed an eternity."

A trail of foam marked the track of each torpedo as it closed the range toward the ship. Some were "porpoising"—alternately breaking the surface and then diving. Johnston watched the submerged missiles with dismay, and realized that the *Lex* was not going to dodge them all. "Their wicked noses look to me like death incarnate. I have the illusion they are alive, and breaking water to peek at us, only to dive again after having made sure of their courses."

The ascending shriek of the dive-bombers served notice that bombs were about to fall from above. The Aichi D3A1 Type 99s, with their distinctive fixed landing gear, were streaking down in near-vertical dives, spaced out at regular intervals. They released one by one, at about 1,500 feet. Each bomb, a sinister black dot, separated from the fuselage and took a divergent trajectory as the aircraft began to pull out of its dive. The first several fell astern, into the *Lexington's* wake, and several more fell close abeam. Each near miss was marked by a deep, rippling explosion that seemed to come from within the hull itself; each blast threw up a white waterspout to the height of the carrier's highest masts, and soaked men stationed on the catwalks. One 242-kilogram high-explosive bomb struck forward, near the port forward 5-inch gun gallery. A blinding reddish flash reached to a height of 50 feet. The entire marine gun crew was wiped out, and firefighting teams hurried over to extinguish the flames. Another projectile came within a few feet of hitting the island itself, but missed and fell into the sea. A third hit the *Lexington's* big smoke funnel, high on its port side, killing several of the gunners stationed on the catwalks around the rim. A near miss had cut a rod that operated the ship's steam siren, jamming it open so that it screamed without interruption for the next several minutes while the battle continued.

A second wave of torpedo planes approached in a shallow glide on the *Lexington*'s port quarter, through an intense barrage of antiaircraft fire. They dropped their fish at a range of 1,000 yards and continued over the ship, strafing the carrier's deck as they flew over her. The *Lexington* twisted and turned on a violent serpentine path. Her screening destroyers and cruisers, which the enemy planes had completely ignored, were unable to remain in their circular formation.

With a dozen Japanese torpedoes converging on his carrier, Captain Sherman realized he was powerless to avoid them all. But not all of the weapons were functioning correctly—two that had seemed sure to hit the *Lexington* apparently dove right under her keel, and were seen to emerge on the opposite side. Another pair ran parallel, one on either side of the ship about 50 yards away, and an officer on the navigation bridge shouted: "Don't change course, Captain! There's a torpedo on each side of us running parallel!" Sherman held course until they passed ahead and disappeared. But at 11:20 a.m., the *Lexington*'s luck ran out. She was struck by two torpedoes in quick succession, on her port side, forward and amidships. Unlike the bomb blasts, these submerged explosions were muffled, but the great carrier's entire hull lurched and shuddered with enough violence to throw men from their feet. Beaver recorded that the two blasts "seemed to lift the ship's entire bulk right out of the water and let it fall back into the sea in a series of up-and-down bounces that had the masts staggering and the rigging jingling. Bits of old paint and the dust of fourteen years was jarred from the ship's secret cracks and crannies." The first blast punctured the port aviation gasoline tanks and released gasoline vapors that would later ignite a crippling internal explosion. The second severed a water main, which had the doubly destructive effect of cutting water to the firehoses and to several of the engine boilers. The ship listed 7 degrees to port, and a heavy oil slick trailed in her wake.

The last of the Japanese planes were escaping low over the carrier's bow, chased by mostly ineffective antiaircraft fire. "They were curious and sort of thumbed their noses at us," said Stroop of the Japanese aircrews. "We were shooting at them with our new 20-mm and not hitting them at all. The tracers of the 20-mm were falling astern of the torpedo planes." Several Japanese aircraft raked the ship with their machine guns as they flew over. Then they were gone, shrinking into black specks on the horizon, and the antiaircraft guns fell silent. The entire action had lasted less than twelve minutes.

The sea around the ship was littered with burning debris and downed airplanes. Two miles away, a plume of black smoke could be seen rising from the *Yorktown*. She had apparently taken a hit on her flight deck, amidships.

The *Lex*'s damage control teams appeared to have the situation well in hand. Between 11:45 a.m. and noon, Captain Sherman received a series of upbeat reports from Commander H. R. "Pop" Healy, the chief damage control officer, who was supervising the coordinated efforts of several hundred men from his command center below the hangar deck. Two Japanese torpedoes had struck the *Lexington* below the waterline, and thousands of tons of water had entered the hull, causing her 7-degree list—but Healy's men were isolating the damage by sealing off flooded compartments and shoring up bulkheads, and the list was soon corrected by pumping fuel and fresh water from port tanks into empty starboard tanks. Medical corpsmen were collecting the wounded and transferring them down to the hospital on stretchers. Firefighting crews were smothering the fires with foamite, and by 11:45 a.m., no more smoke could be seen emerging through the flight deck. Men were patching over the damage inflicted near the port forward gun gallery with fresh steel plates. Both the fore and aft elevators were jammed in the up position, rendering it impossible to transfer aircraft to or from the hangar deck, but the flight deck was still able to launch and recover planes. The *Lexington*'s engines were in good working condition, and even with the wounds in her hull, she could do 25 knots and maneuver briskly.

To aircrews of returning airplanes, looking down at the ship from above, nothing seemed amiss. "She looked okay from the air," Lieutenant Gayler later recalled. "It was only when I landed . . . I looked around and some of the faces were looking sort of strange. Then I saw flecks of firefighting foam all over the deck and I knew she had been hit."

Admiral Fitch and Captain Sherman had good reason to believe that the *Lexington* could stand up to two torpedo hits and two topside bomb hits. She had been designed to absorb that much punishment and more. The damage control squads had trained long and hard, and they were well equipped and well led. An hour after the action, it appeared that the *Lexington* was nearly squared away. She seemed capable of fighting off another enemy air attack, should one come. "We felt like throwing out our chests at our condition after the attack," wrote Sherman. "But our satisfaction was soon to be changed to apprehension."

The carrier's aviation gasoline storage tanks, installed on her port side against the inner hull, had been ruptured by the two torpedo blasts. There was no visible fuel leak, but the odor of gas fumes was unmistakable throughout the compartments adjoining the IC motor generator room. Highly combustible vapors were spreading through the lower regions of the ship like a malignant virus, and because the exact location of the leak could not be pinpointed, there was no obvious way to contain the problem.

At 12:47 p.m., a tremendous explosion rocked the ship. From his post on the bridge, the captain thought the blast had seemed to come from the "bottom" of the carrier, just above her keel. Almost at once, oily black smoke boiled up around the edges of the elevators on the flight deck. Internal telephone connections had cut out, so runners were sent below to receive Commander Pop Healy's verbal report. They descended the steel ladders into a Stygian warren lit by battle lanterns, choked with smoke, and crowded with grievously wounded men who were crying out for help. Central Station, Healy's damage control command post, had been completely wiped out with the loss of twenty-five lives, and the compartments around it were a raging inferno. Steel doors had been ripped from their hinges all along a 300-foot length of corridor leading to the hospital in the bow. A lieutenant described having been lifted up and thrown against a bulkhead by "a gale of wind with the force of a hurricane. . . . The wind seemed to be made up of streams of flame and myriads of sparks. . . . The flames were between a cherry red and white, and the sparks were crimson. The gale lasted for only a few seconds and left nothing but heavy choking fumes. There were cries from the surrounding rooms, so I shouted at the top of my voice: 'Take it easy and hold your breath, and we'll all get out.'"

Firefighting gangs descended into that hellish world, dragging long hoses behind them. They wore masks against the smoke, breathed from portable oxygen tanks, carried flashlights to light the way, and when the water pressure in their hoses failed, they turned handheld chemical extinguishers on the advancing flames. The sweat ran into their eyes and they became light in the head—but they fought on, enduring the ovenlike heat, the choking smoke, and the constant threat of new explosions. They dragged the burned and wounded men to the ladders and carried them up to the hangar deck, where medical corpsmen had commandeered plane-handling dollies to transport the stretchers aft.

Though Sherman and Fitch did not yet know it, the *Lexington* had entered a vicious spiral that would end in her total loss. By tearing open watertight doors and bulkheads, the first internal gasoline explosion had allowed volatile fumes to circulate more widely through the ship, and the damage control teams could no longer seal off and isolate the critical areas. New explosions rippled through the ship every ten to fifteen minutes. Fuel tanks were further damaged, bleeding their combustible fluids into the inferno. Water mains were crushed or cracked, causing the pressure in the firehoses to diminish and then fail entirely. Electrical mains fell to the advancing flames, cutting out power and leaving the lower decks in darkness. The chemical extinguishers and oxygen tanks began to run low. Firefighters fell wounded and had to be evacuated by their mates. Even in areas where the watertight doors were shut and sealed, the fire heated the bulkheads to such a degree that the paint on the opposite sides ignited, allowing the flames to penetrate through the steel walls. There was a second devastating explosion at 2:42 p.m. and a third at 3:25 p.m., and by that time it was clear that the fires were unmanageable.

From the bridge, the captain looked down on a flight deck that was showing increasing signs of the trauma below. Even after the first big explosion, the carrier had continued to launch and recover aircraft, but the explosion at 2:42 p.m. had shut her flight operations down for good. The forward elevator was glowing red-orange, with tongues of flame licking around its perimeter. Wounded men were brought up from the hangar deck, now rendered uninhabitable by smoke and flames. Stroop recalled explosions "that sounded like a freight train rumbling up the hangar deck. Actually, it was a rushing wall of flame which would erupt around the perimeter of the elevator. These flames would shoot up two or three feet, and these were occurring with increasing frequency." As dense smoke and searing heat drove the damage control parties farther aft, they took increasingly desperate actions to get hoses on the fire. A hose was snaked down one of the ammunition hoists in hopes of dousing the fires below by flooding the burning compartments. But nothing could arrest the advancing conflagration. "The forward part of the ship was ablaze, both above and below the armored deck with absolutely no means left to fight the fire, which was now spreading aft on the flight deck," wrote Commander Seligman, the executive officer. "It was inevitable that the 20-odd torpedo warheads on the mezzanine of the hangar deck must eventually detonate."

The ship's internal communications were failing fast, and Sherman and Fitch found it increasingly difficult to get accurate reports of the situation in the lower regions of their crippled ship. The main telephone to the bridge had failed hours earlier, and much of the communications between the captain and the damage control teams had been done by runner. The power cables to the helm cut out, and steering was reduced to an emergency system that required course changes to be relayed by word of mouth. As water pumps failed, her port list returned and she settled lower into the water. Fitch ordered the screening vessels to keep clear, as the *Lexington* was becoming considerably more difficult to handle. A sound tube to the engine room (requiring no electricity) continued to function for some time, but the sound quality deteriorated steadily. Captain Sherman realized that if he did not order the engineers to evacuate, and the last remaining communications link cut out entirely, the men stationed there would remain at their posts until consumed by the flames. At 4 p.m. he ordered them to douse the engines, blow off the steam from the boilers, and evacuate to the flight deck. The excess steam rushed up the funnel with a throaty *whoosh*, the engines felt silent, the four big propellers came to rest, and the *Lexington* lay dead in the water. The carrier's loyal escorts, the destroyers *Anderson, Hammann,* and *Morris,* and the cruisers *Minneapolis* and *New Orleans,* drew in close to the dying ship and awaited instructions.

At 4:30 p.m., Sherman sent a messenger to find Commander Seligman, who had taken over the remaining damage control efforts, to bring all remaining crewmen up to the flight deck. The hunt through the lower decks was a dangerous job, but it had to be done—the loudspeaker system was long gone, and every man needed to know that he had been ordered away from his station. Injured men were being brought up to the flight deck in a steady stream, many suffering from severe burns or smoke inhalation, but there was never a shortage of volunteers who were willing to go below and help retrieve other members of the crew. Lifeboats and other flotation devices were made ready in anticipation of the abandonment. Destroyers nosed up close under the port quarter and stretchers were lowered onto their decks.

Time was short. Every man aboard knew that the bombs and torpedoes on the hangar deck were slow-roasting as the fires proceeded. The temperature of the metal casings surrounding the torpedo warheads had been measured at 140° Fahrenheit. Eventually, they would reach detonation point and blow the ship to kingdom come. But by five o'clock, when it was clear that no hope remained, and preparations to abandon the ship were well underway, the captain still had yet to give the order. Sherman may have waited a bit longer than Fitch thought prudent, because at 5:07 p.m. the admiral leaned over the balcony, looked at the skipper on the signal bridge, and said: "Let's get the boys off the ship."

Knotted lines were secured to the net railing along both sides of the ship, and several dozen circular "doughnut rafts" were lowered into the sea. Men began going down the lines, some descending directly into the rafts, some onto the decks of the faithful destroyers, some into whaleboats, and some directly into the water, 50 feet beneath their feet. It was a calm night, and the sun went down in a typically spectacular blaze of tropical glory. The abandonment was oddly leisurely. There was no rush, no panic, and many seemed in no hurry to leave. A tub of ice cream was brought up from the ship's service store and served out in paper cups. Antiaircraft crews lowered 20mm gun barrels and ammunition clips to the decks of the destroyers, to save them going to waste when the carrier went down. Men stood in orderly lines behind each rope, and left their shoes in neat rows on the edge of the flight deck. They gave three cheers for the captain. Lieutenant Gayler dived from the flight deck and swam out about 100 yards, then swam back and climbed back up one of the ropes to the flight deck. When asked why he had returned, he replied: "Oh, I got a bit lonely out there. I didn't know any of those guys. When are you fellows going to come?"

Admiral Fitch left the island, now deserted, trailing a small entourage of staff officers. A marine orderly continued to observe correct punctilio, following one step behind Fitch with the admiral's coat folded neatly over his arm. "I remember going across the flight deck and realizing it was pretty hot and pretty soon the whole thing was going to be in flames," Stroop recalled. "Port side, forward, we had what little breeze there was that made that the coolest part of the ship." Stroop, as Fitch's flag secretary, used his arms to make a semaphore signal to one of the cruisers: "Send a boat for admiral." A motor launch pulled up directly under the spot, and Fitch lowered himself down the line and stepped swiftly into the launch.

By six o'clock, only a handful of men remained on the *Lexington*. The flight deck was painfully hot underfoot. "Little licking tongues of flame

raced in erratic patterns across the wooden expanse, only to die out and
to be replaced moments later by others," recalled Signalman Beaver, one
of the last men to leave the ship. "We could see nothing aft but fire and
smoke. The bow was still clear, but the tar caulking between deck planks
was beginning to bubble up. We could feel the heat on our faces."

The captain and executive officer were the last to go. They had paced
the flight deck one last time, looking for stragglers. Finding none, they stood
above one of the knotted lines on the *Lexington's* stern for a moment, both
apparently unwilling to take the final step. Sherman ordered Seligman to
go down ahead of him, as it was the captain's "duty and privilege" to be
the last man to leave the ship. As Seligman lowered away, an explosion
went up amidships, throwing flames and airplanes high into the air, and
Sherman ducked under the edge of the flight deck to get cover from falling debris. Seligman shouted at the skipper to come down the line. "I was
just thinking," Sherman replied: "wouldn't I look silly if I left this ship and
the fires went out?" The captain later wrote that abandoning the *Lexington* was "heartbreaking," and "the hardest thing I have ever done." But the
venerable old carrier had run her race, and it was Sherman's duty to deliver
himself, physically intact, into the continuing service of the U.S. Navy. He
went down the line and dropped into the warm dark water of the Coral Sea.

The sea around the burning carrier was dotted with the heads of hundreds of swimmers awaiting rescue. Many later remembered that the sea felt
pleasant, neither too warm nor too cold, and a welcome respite from the
heat of the *Lexington's* fires. Their life jackets kept them afloat. They could
hang onto a line from one of the rafts and drift comfortably while awaiting their turn to be hauled into one of the whaleboats or destroyers. Some
men held packets of cigarettes aloft. The healthy swimmers took their time,
allowing their mates who were weakened or dog-tired to be taken on board
first. The destroyers *Morris* and *Hammann* picked their way through the
swimmers with extreme care, and men climbed into their cargo nets. Those
too weak to climb were winched up on cranes.

Twilight having fallen, the burning carrier made a beautiful and terrible
sight. Lit up against the night sky, she looked even more enormous than
usual. Every aperture in her hangar deck revealed the maelstrom of red
and orange flames within, and parts of her hull glowed like molten lead.
Beaver recalled: "She listed heavily and burned with dirty red flames that
blossomed from time to time as bombs in the parked airplanes—and the

airplanes themselves—exploded on her flight deck. The darkening waters reflected the fire's light in a way that made the scene seem even more terrible than it was."

By this time the torpedo warheads and bombs on the hangar deck were nearing ignition temperature, and at 6:30 p.m. they went up in a vast, rippling explosion. A dozen aircraft on the flight deck were blown overboard like a child's toys. The No. 2 elevator, amidships, popped off the flight deck like a bottle cap, and from the breach rose a solid sheet of flames. From a nearby cruiser, Stanley Johnston saw "bits and particles, airplanes, plates, planks, pieces large and small all going up into the air in the midst of a blinding white flame and smoke. We pressed lovingly against the heaving steel sides of that cruiser, hugging her for seconds while the debris splashed into the sea for hundreds of feet around."

Admiral Fletcher had already decided against making another attack that day, and ordered the entire task force to make way to the south to draw off from the enemy. He had considered but rejected a proposal to send the cruisers and destroyers after the Japanese task force to draw them into a surface action, as they would probably meet with heavy air attack. That decision probably saved most of the *Lexington*'s crew by ensuring there were enough ships to take the survivors aboard. The men were picked up and distributed to the cruisers and destroyers of the task force, which were heavily overpopulated as a result. But the crews went out of their way to offer hospitality to the now-shipless men of the *Lexington*, sharing their extra clothes and yielding up their bunks so that all could sleep in shifts.

Fletcher ordered the *Lexington* sunk, both to prevent her falling into enemy hands and to eliminate the danger that she might serve as a signal beacon for enemy planes. The destroyer *Phelps* moved in to a range of 1,500 yards to carry out the dreadful task. Captain Sherman, choked up, watched from the cruiser *Minneapolis*. The *Phelps* fired a spread of eight torpedoes into the carrier's starboard side; it appeared that four detonated. Sherman recalled: "The stricken vessel started getting deeper in the water, slowly going down, as if she too were reluctant to give up the battle. With her colors proudly flying and the last signal flags, reading 'I am abandoning ship,' still waving at the yardarm, she went under on an even keel, like the lady she always was." At 7:52 p.m., the *Lexington* went down in a cloud of hissing steam, taking the bodies of more than a hundred of her crew with her. About a minute later, a tremendous underwater explosion was felt and heard for miles around, even on the other ships of the American task force a full ten miles away. It was "Lady Lex's" last defiant roar. She was on her way into the abyss.

THE YORKTOWN, smaller and more maneuverable than the Lexington, had dodged eight torpedoes and perhaps a dozen bombs. Captain Elliott Buckmaster had conned the ship from the signal bridge, shouting, "hard to starboard!" and "hard to port!" Taking advantage of his ship's tight turning radius, Buckmaster had dealt with the torpedoes by taking them "bow on"—that is, he turned the Yorktown directly toward the incoming tracks and neatly threaded them, missing the nearest by less than 50 feet. "The ship's wake was boiling into a large, white curve as she turned," recalled William G. Roy, a photographer stationed near Buckmaster on the bridge. Those violent turns at more than 30 knots had caused the ship to roll steeply, obliging crewmen to seize hold of whatever handholds they could find to avoid sliding across the deck.

The Yorktown took one hit from the dive-bombers, a 500-pound bomb that struck near the island and went right through the flight deck, leaving a 14-inch hole in the steel plate; it passed through a ready room, the hangar deck, the second deck, and the third deck, and finally detonated deep in the ship, in an aviation storeroom on the fourth deck. For a bomb to puncture six decks without exploding gives some idea of the force with which it was delivered—it was traveling perhaps 500 miles per hour. A sailor stationed aft on the hangar deck judged that the blast "raised the whole stern of the ship at least ten feet"—high enough to lift the carrier's propellers clear out of the water, and the sound of the racing engine was heard over the din of battle. The internal bulkheads and deck were buckled visibly by the blast. Thirty-seven men were killed outright, and many more injured. Seaman Otis Kight was assigned to the cleanup detail, and recorded his recollections years later: "There were parts and particles: some ship, some shipmate. . . . We sorted out the pieces of the ship, put pieces of the crew in the body bags, and put the other trash in garbage bags until the compartment was clear enough to use shovels, then fire hoses, then disinfectant and swabs. And always, 'the sweet smell of death.' And the thought crossed my mind then and many times later, where is my number?"

Surprisingly, perhaps, the ship did not suffer much beyond that initial damage; the fires were brought under control, the flight deck operations continued, and she was able to maintain 24 knots. The chief engineer, asked by the captain whether the engines should be throttled down, replied, "Hell, no. We'll make it!"

While the *Lex* burned, the *Yorktown* kept constantly on the move, both to avoid making herself an easy target for Japanese submarines and to collect her airplanes. When it became clear that the *Lexington* would not survive, Admiral Fitch had had the foresight to send off as many as possible of the *Lexington*'s undamaged planes to land on her sister ship while flight operations remained possible. Reinforced with more than a quarter of the *Lex*'s aircraft, *Yorktown*'s air strength was better than it had been at the start of the battle. Yet Fletcher's range of options was limited. The American aviators had claimed hits on both Japanese carriers and were confident that one must have sunk. But afternoon sighting reports confirmed that two Japanese carriers were afloat and did not appear to be on fire or otherwise crippled. With *Lexington* gone, the Americans could not afford to lose the *Yorktown*. Moreover, fuel reserves were worryingly low, and the screening vessels of the task force were heavily encumbered with more than 2,700 *Lexington* survivors. Fletcher first intended remaining in the Coral Sea, but late in the afternoon of May 8 he heard from Nimitz. Fletcher was to withdraw out of attack range. Task Force 17 turned south.

On the destroyers, the *Lexington* sailors took up every spare patch of deck space, and it was difficult to move around the ships. No meals were served in the mess hall: sandwiches and black coffee were passed out to the men where they sat. Hundreds of men slept on the deck that night, their exhaustion overcoming the uncomfortable conditions, and not even the sheets of salt spray thrown back from the bow were enough to awaken them. The doctors and corpsmen worked around the clock to treat the wounded. Burn cases were numerous, and they were treated with tannic acid, applied directly to the burns, and copious injections of morphine. Bandages were wrapped and rewrapped; plaster casts were set on broken bones. The worst of the burn cases were given plasma transfusions. Several of the destroyers were laboring and rolling heavily as they charged southward: those ships were small enough that the weight of extra passengers diminished their seaworthiness. The problem grew more acute as fuel levels fell, which raised each destroyer's center of gravity. Fletcher ordered that *Lexington* survivors be redistributed onto the cruisers.

The *Yorktown* made good speed, but her internal damage was severe, and she was bleeding oil into a long slick that trailed behind her for miles. That was a dangerous state of affairs, as a slick could be tracked by hostile airplanes. Fletcher ordered one of the destroyers to follow close behind in the carrier's wake in hopes of breaking up the slick. The passengers and crew, being told nothing of the enemy's whereabouts, tended to assume that the Japanese were in hot pursuit. Lieutenant Wally Short confessed: "We were running scared, if the truth were told."

Task Force 17 turned east in the early hours of May 9, and snuck out of the Coral Sea by a route south of New Caledonia. Low on fuel, the *Yorktown* paused in port at Tongatapu in the Tonga Islands, awaiting the arrival of another oiler. Several of the surface ships put in at Nouméa, capital of New Caledonia. The fleet buzzed with rumors about a forthcoming operation in the North Pacific.

THE JAPANESE WERE ALSO IN HEADLONG RETREAT. On the afternoon of May 8, Admiral Shigeyoshi Inoue concluded that he had no other choice but to call off the Port Moresby landing and send both aircraft carriers back toward Truk. "Port Moresby attack will be postponed to a later date," he radioed Yamamoto. "Your approval is requested." He had several respectable motives for his decision, including a low fuel state and the risk that the invasion force would come under devastating air attack if sent back toward Moresby. Even if both American carriers had been sunk, as the Japanese airmen would have him believe, the heavy presence of Australia-based army bombers had been noted. The *Shoho*, which was to have provided air cover for the troopships, was gone; and although the *Zuikaku* was in one piece, the Japanese carrier air groups had been decimated in the air battles of May 7 and 8. At the end of the second day, total carrier air strength had been reduced to thirty-nine planes—twenty-four Zeros, nine dive-bombers, and six torpedo planes. Many of the best and most seasoned aircrews had been shot down or lost at sea.

Inoue's request exasperated Admiral Yamamoto, who thought him craven and passive. At midnight, the commander in chief peremptorily denied permission to pull back and directed Takagi to hunt down and annihilate all Allied naval forces left in the vicinity. Takagi did not have the fuel to go after the Americans—some of his destroyers were at 20 percent fuel, his cruisers at about 50 percent—but for appearance's sake he launched some searches in the direction of the retiring American fleet. May 9 and 10 were occupied in refueling his ships from a tanker, and by that time it was clear that Fletcher's forces had fled the scene.

The Japanese could have pushed on and taken Moresby with little opposition, and many have wondered why they did not. It was a strange failure of nerve for a nation that had shown such consistent boldness in the war to date. It ensured that the Battle of the Coral Sea would go into the history books as a strategic victory for the Allies.

On May 11, Yamamoto countermanded his earlier order and told Takagi to bring *Zuikaku* home. She was needed for the Midway offensive.

LEST ANYONE FORGET THE COST OF WAR, both the *Shokaku* and the *Yorktown*, as they retreated from the scene of battle, buried large numbers of their fallen crewmen in their wakes. Maintenance officer Hachiro Miyashita of the *Shokaku* said that his ship rang out with the cries of the wounded, but many of those plaintive voices fell silent as the men succumbed to their wounds. He was moved by the plight of his lieutenant, whose body was so thoroughly riddled with shrapnel that the doctor was reminded of "picking potatoes from the soil." On May 9, *Shokaku* committed 107 bodies to the deep. "We covered their faces with gauze and wrapped their bodies in blankets," Miyashita said. "Then we placed a practice non-explosive 30 kilogram bomb between their legs in the crotch area in order to weigh down the body for burial at sea. However, after being put in the water, the caskets later broke up due to water pressure, and the dead bodies floated back up to the surface."

Chief Warrant Officer Frank Boo of the *Yorktown* would never forget seeing "bloody handprints" on white sea bags, where men stricken by the bomb blast had tried to raise themselves to their feet. The corpsmen laid the dead on wire-mesh stretchers and pulled sheets over their faces. On the night of May 8, many of those stretchers were left in officers' staterooms (near the ship's hospital) until a sea burial could be arranged. Ensign Buell, the *Yorktown* SBD pilot, was so exhausted that he crawled into a bunk in a room full of dead shipmates. He was awakened in the small hours of the morning by "hands grasping me and lifting me from the bunk. It was still dark, and I had no idea what was happening so I asked in a rather loud voice what the hell was going on. At the sound of my voice I was immediately dropped halfway out of the cubicle, and a rather startled voice said: 'My God, Doc, this one ain't dead!'"

Chapter Eleven

A DMIRAL FLETCHER'S FIRST BUOYANT REPORTS TO PEARL HARBOR AND Washington had been transmitted when the *Lexington* was still fighting for her life and seemed likely to survive. "First enemy attack completed, no vital damage our force," he radioed Nimitz, and a relieved CINCPAC replied, "Congratulations on your glorious accomplishments." Fletcher's subsequent updates described the deteriorating conditions aboard the *Lex*. Finally came the abysmal news that she was gone. Commander Layton recorded that Nimitz was "visibly jolted and muttered several times that they should have saved her."

Now there were only three American carriers left in the Pacific, and one (*Yorktown*) had suffered battle damage that might or might not require her to return to the mainland for repairs. Later that evening, Nimitz did his best to buck up his staff's morale, reminding them that the Japanese were undoubtedly bleeding too. "We don't know how badly he's hurt," he told them. "You can bet your boots he's hurt too! Remember this—the enemy has got to be hurt, and his situation is not all a bed of roses." But on May 10, he wrote Admiral King privately in a very different tone: "At present stage of our carrier building program, we cannot afford to swap losses with this ratio."

King had followed the progress of the battle closely from his office in Washington, but resisted the temptation to interject himself into the flow of radio communications between Nimitz and Fletcher, reasoning that "they need all the communications they can use in order to coordinate their work effectively." When he learned that the *Lexington* was no more, however, the COMINCH was badly shaken. As one of her former skippers, King knew the ship as well as any man in the service. He ordered that her loss be concealed from the press. He told Admiral Sir Dudley Pound, the British first sea lord, that the battle had been "merely the first round of an engagement that will continue, with increasing strength on the part of the enemy, which we shall have difficulty in matching."

Coral Sea, it is often said, was something new under the sun—the first naval battle in which the opposing ships never came into direct sight of one another. It was also one of the most confused and confusing battles in the history of war at sea, characterized on both sides by an almost incredible series of miscues, miscommunications, misidentifications, misinterpretations, and miscalculations. In immediate material terms it was a victory for the Japanese, though not by so great a margin as they claimed and apparently believed. In addition to the *Lexington*, they had done away with the valuable oil tanker *Neosho* and the destroyer *Sims*; they had damaged the *Yorktown*; they had destroyed fifty *Lexington* planes (including those that went down with the ship) and sixteen *Yorktown* planes. The Allies had sunk the light carrier *Shoho*, one light cruiser, two destroyers, a transport, and four gunboats. They had damaged the *Shokaku* and one aircraft tender. Though the Japanese had come out ahead in the tally of ships sunk, however, they had lost twice as many aircraft as the Americans, and suffered twice as many casualties. In aerial combat, the Japanese had lost thirty-three fighters, three four-engine patrol bombers, five floatplanes, sixteen dive-bombers, and seventeen torpedo planes. An additional thirty planes had gone down with *Shoho*. They had suffered ninety aircrew killed, compared to only thirty-five Americans, because the latter had done a much better job at recovering their downed aviators.

A tactical victory for the Japanese; a strategic victory for the Allies. That is the time-honored and often-repeated verdict on the Battle of the Coral Sea. Certainly it was the latter. The objective of the Japanese operation had been the capture of Port Moresby, and their failure to achieve it was the first major reversal in their five-month Pacific offensive. If Admiral Inoue had been bolder, the Japanese could have taken the port with little effort or risk. After the battle of May 8, there was nothing to stop a successful troop landing at Moresby except the Allies' land-based bombers, which had never posed much of a threat to ships underway at sea. Captain Sherman judged that Moresby would have fallen within forty-eight hours.

As important as the Battle of the Coral Sea was to the United States, the battle was of supreme importance to Australia. Japanese possession of Moresby would have posed a serious threat to northern Australia's cities and military bases. General MacArthur, who did not often praise the navy, said that the battle had been "the real safeguard of Australian independence." It was, in a sense, Australia's Trafalgar—a naval victory that shattered the hopes of a formidable would-be invader. For years after the war, the anniversary of the battle was celebrated by Australians as a quasi-national holiday.

But was Coral Sea really a tactical victory for the Japanese? *Shokaku* was damaged and later repaired; *Zuikaku* was unscathed, but suffered heavy losses to her air group. Most crucially, neither flattop was back in action in time for the Battle of Midway, where their presence might well have altered the outcome. The *Yorktown*, though damaged, was the only aircraft carrier on either side to make an appearance at both Coral Sea and Midway, and her air group would play a decisive role in the second battle. At the risk of engaging in semantics, Webster's defines tactics as "the science of arranging and maneuvering military and naval forces in action, especially (as distinguished from strategy) with reference to short-range objectives." Less than one month elapsed between Coral Sea and Midway. Taking them together, did not the Allies score a tactical victory on May 8 by knocking the two big Japanese flattops out of the action to come on June 4?

Combat was a hard and unforgiving school, but the U.S. Navy was taking its lessons to heart. If the navy did one thing right after the debacle of December 7, it was to become collectively obsessed with learning and improving. Each new encounter with the enemy was mined for all the wisdom and insights it had to offer. Every after-action report included a section of analysis and recommendations, and those nuggets of hard-won knowledge were absorbed into future command decisions, doctrine, planning, and training throughout the service. The insights offered by the Battle of the Coral Sea were many. The battle had exposed the problem of fogging bombsights in the SBD Dauntless dive-bombers, which Nimitz judged to be the "outstanding material defect of the 3-day action." The battle had revealed the need for more and better antiaircraft gunnery training. Plainly, the number of F4F fighters embarked on the carriers should be increased significantly, both to accompany and protect outbound airstrikes and to fly combat air patrol over the task forces. The CAP should be stationed at a greater distance from the carriers, to give them time to intercept incoming bogeys, and at much higher altitude, so they could trade some of that altitude for speed when engaging incoming enemy attack planes. The Douglas TBD Devastator was disastrously obsolete and must be replaced as quickly as possible. The American air groups must learn how to keep an outbound air group together, so that dive-bombing and aerial torpedo attacks could be coordinated. In that the Japanese excelled, as the officers and crew of the *Lexington* had learned to their distress.

Perhaps the greatest significance of the battle was that the American aviators had fought their enemies to a draw. The Japanese flyers and aircraft were losing their mystique. The F4F pilots were learning how to use the greater diving speed and structural resilience of their machine to advantage against the lighter and more vulnerable Zero. These improved tactics, pioneered by aviation leaders like Lieutenant Commander Jimmy Flatley, accounted to a large degree for the heavy air losses suffered by the Japanese. Squadron leaders set pen to paper and distributed their conclusions. Flatley advised his fellow Wildcat pilots:

> Gain plenty of altitude before contact with enemy VF [fighters]. You can lose altitude fast but you can't gain it fast enough when up against enemy VF. Use hit and run attacks diving in and pulling out and up. If your target maneuvers out of your sight during your approach, pull out and let one of the following planes get him. If you attempt to twist and turn you will end up at his level or below and will be unable to regain an altitude advantage. If you get in a tough spot, dive away, maneuver violently, find a cloud. Stay together. The Japs' air discipline is excellent and if you get separated you will have at least three of them on you at once. You have the better plane if you handle it properly, and in spite of their advantage of maneuverability you can and should shoot them down with few losses to yourselves.

IMPERIAL HEADQUARTERS IN TOKYO announced that two American carriers, identified as the *Saratoga* and *Yorktown*, had been sent to the bottom. The claimed sinking of the *Yorktown* was based on the aviators' optimistic impression that they had hit her with three torpedoes and eight to ten 550-pound bombs, presumably enough punishment to sink any carrier in the world. Rear Admiral Hara, in his after-action report, had surmised that the *Yorktown* was probably sunk, but acknowledged that he could not confirm it. Tokyo also announced that Japanese forces had sunk an American battleship, disabled a British heavy cruiser, and badly damaged a British battleship of the *Warspite* class. Those latter claims were a flight of fantasy—no Allied battleships had been in the area, and no cruisers had been hit.

Emperor Hirohito published a rescript lauding the fleet for its latest splendid victory. Even Adolf Hitler joined in the chorus. "After this new defeat," the Führer predicted, "the United States warships will hardly dare to face the Japanese fleet again, since any United States warship which accepts action with the Japanese naval forces is as good as lost."

Among the officers of the Combined Fleet staff, however, there was little joy. Even if it proved true that two enemy carriers were on the floor of the Coral Sea, the price had been heavy: the *Shoho* was the first major Japanese ship destroyed in the war, and the loss of so many aircraft and veteran aircrews came as a nasty shock. Moreover, the senior officers of the Japanese navy knew what the public bulletins did not disclose—that the main objective of Operation MO, Port Moresby, remained in Allied hands. Combined Fleet staff faulted Takagi and Hara for having been insufficiently aggressive in hunting down the American fleet, and condemned Inoue for timidity in withdrawing his forces prematurely.

Air staff officer Masatake Okumiya summed up the feelings of the staff: "The truth of the matter was that our senior naval commanders in the Coral Sea area lacked the fighting spirit necessary to engage the enemy." In his private diary, Admiral Ugaki confided: "A dream of great success has been shattered. There is an opponent in a war, so one cannot progress just as one wishes. When we expect enemy raids, can't we employ the forces in a little more unified way?"

The battle confirmed a feeling, widely shared by Japan's naval airmen, that the two carriers of Hara's Division 5 were the "little brothers" of *Kido Butai*. They were regarded as the "B" team, whose aviators were less experienced and less skilled than the "A" team, represented by Carrier Divisions 1 (*Akagi*, *Kaga*) and 2 (*Soryu*, *Hiryu*). Yet even the B team was believed to have sunk two American carriers at Coral Sea—and if the B team could deal so punishing a blow to an evenly matched enemy, then the A team should have nothing to fear at Midway. The sentiment was summed up in an epigram that made the rounds through the ranks of *Kido Butai*: "If the sons of the concubine [*Shokaku* and *Zuikaku*] could win the victory, the sons of legal wives should find no rivals in the world."

There may have been merit in those criticisms of the Japanese commanders and the aviators of Carrier Division 5, but they also tended to deflect attention away from a more urgent question. Had the Japanese underestimated their adversaries? Whatever the material outcome of the battle in the south, it had revealed that the American pilots were not pushovers; that the F4F Wildcat, handled properly, was a match for the Zero; and that the American dive-bombers posed a dangerous threat to ships. The enemy had appeared suddenly, at a very inconvenient moment, well within striking range of Japanese fleet units. The Americans were not incompetent and demoralized. They were evidently willing and able to give a good account of themselves in battle. But Yamamoto and his key subordinates were unwilling to interpret the result at Coral Sea for what it was—an ill omen, signifying that the Midway plan carried much graver risks than they had allowed themselves to believe.

On May 5, two days before the big fight in the Coral Sea, orders for the Midway and Aleutians operations had been disseminated throughout the Japanese fleet. Navy Order No. 18, under the signature of Admiral Osami Nagano, had instructed Yamamoto to "carry out the occupation of Midway Island and key points in the western Aleutians in co-operation with the Army." It would be the largest naval-amphibious operation ever attempted in the history of naval warfare. It would split the Japanese forces into five largely independent tactical groups, operating throughout a vast North Pacific battle zone, from the icy outer islands of the Aleutian archipelago to the atoll of Midway, 2,000 miles south. Nearly 200 Japanese ships would participate in the offensive, and more than 700 planes. "Taken together, Operations AL and MI represented the commitment of almost the entirety of the Imperial Japanese Navy," write Jon Parshall and Tony Tully in *Shattered Sword* (2005), their groundbreaking study of the Japanese experience at Midway; "all of its carriers, all of its battleships, all but four of its heavy cruisers, and the bulk of its lesser combatants. Twenty-eight admirals would lead those forces into battle, and they would log more miles and consume more fuel in this single operation than was normally used in an entire year."

The plan involved a complex, highly choreographed series of attacks which would have to unfold with exquisite timing and in strict radio silence.

On June 3, a northern force would launch an air raid on the American base at Dutch Harbor on Unalaska Island—the chief American air base in the Aleutians—followed by attack and seizure of three outer Aleutian Islands. At dawn on June 4, the Japanese carriers would launch airstrikes on Midway from the northwest, with the aim of destroying its aircraft on the ground and clearing the beaches for the invasion forces, which would land on the atoll the night of June 5. Once the atoll was secured, two construction battalions would land and begin upgrading and expanding its air facilities. Any American naval forces sallying out of Pearl Harbor to oppose the invasion would be set upon and destroyed.

The Midway operation was not a product of sound military planning. It was a farrago of compromises struck to quell internal dissent and to balance the demands of rivals in the Combined Fleet and the Naval General Staff. Not surprisingly, it was shot through with contradictions, flaws, and unnecessary risks. It exposed a fatal hubris and an unwarranted contempt for the enemy. The plan spread Japanese forces too thinly over a huge expanse of the North Pacific, and relied on dubious conjectures about how the Americans would react. It asked too much of a few elite aviators who had been flying and fighting almost without respite since December 7. Though the Japanese were loathe to admit it, the most experienced of their carrier aircrews were bone-weary, while the newcomers lacked the training and seasoning to equal the skill of the veterans. In his subsequent report on the battle, Admiral Nagumo would observe that there had been "considerable turnover in personnel. . . . Inexperienced flyers barely got to the point where they could make daytime landings on carriers. It was found that even some of the more seasoned flyers had lost some of their skill."

The Aleutians operation, which had been tacked on at the insistence of the Naval General Staff, bore no clear strategic relationship to the attack on Midway. The forces there engaged, at such a great distance north of Midway, would be incapable of coming to the timely support of the main fleet in the south. The Japanese could take the islands of Attu and Kiska with little opposition, but their possession was meaningless. They were of little value to either the Japanese or the Americans. Lacking any nearby bases of support, the occupiers would be left powerless to beat back a determined counterattack.

The Midway offensive seemed motivated, at least in part, by a desire to make work for the main Japanese surface fleet of battleships, which had spent most of the war swinging peaceably at their anchors at Hashirajima anchorage in Hiroshima Bay. The disparaging term "Hashirajima fleet" had been making the rounds among the Japanese carrier task forces. Moreover, the crews of the anchored ships were growing more restless as the weeks wore on. Admiral Ugaki fretted that "the morale of the Main Body is stale after a long stay in home waters. I have encouraged them, but we must study methods of training afresh and at the same time engage in some operational action."

With such a formidable armada, possessing a clear margin of superiority in both carrier and surface naval strength, why didn't Yamamoto just concentrate his forces and overwhelm the Americans? Why not just fight and win the battle "by the numbers"? Apart from the Aleutians misadventure, a face-saving concession to the Naval General Staff, it appears that the Midway plan was an attempt to balance the Mahanian rule of concentration with the need to disguise the true scale of the Japanese offensive from the Americans. Yamamoto's main purpose in attacking Midway was to lure the American carriers into battle. If Nimitz should discover that nearly the entire Japanese navy was hovering off Midway, he would likely keep his ships safe in port, even if to do so meant conceding the atoll to the enemy. Yamamoto's intention was to keep the bulk of his forces safely beyond range of Midway-based reconnaissance flights, so that an unsuspecting Nimitz would send the Pacific Fleet out to give battle. But in that case, could the widely dispersed Japanese forces get into action in time to make a difference?

The dilemma, write Parshall and Tully, was never satisfactorily resolved. "If the premise is accepted that the Americans would have to be lured from Pearl Harbor in order to create the needed battle, there was no way to construct an operational plan whose distribution of warships was both deceptive and mutually supporting. The two goals were antithetical. Yamamoto knew he couldn't have it both ways, and he willingly sacrificed mutual support to the perceived need for stealth."

Underlying the planned Midway offensive was a casual and yet insidious assumption that Japan was fated to continue its run of victories, an affliction of mind that the Japanese later called, with the benefit of grim hindsight, shoribyo, or "victory disease."

During the first week of May, Yamamoto and ranking officers from throughout the fleet gathered on the battleship Yamato for a multi-day planning conference. "The whole ship was aglitter with brass," writes

Yamamoto's Japanese biographer; "at mealtimes, everywhere was jammed with distinguished officers; the most junior among the vice admirals were turned out of the C. in C.'s wardroom and obliged to dine in the ordinary wardroom, while rear admirals went to the gun room, and mere captains and the like were reduced to eating standing on the deck." Conference tables and folding chairs were set up in the forward mess halls for the larger meetings. Tabletop war-gaming exercises were held in the *Yamato*'s spacious staterooms and wardrooms, with model ships placed on maps of the North Pacific and throws of the dice to signify the omnipresent role of chance. These exercises were putatively intended to scrutinize the plan and shed light on its weaknesses, but it was soon made clear that Yamamoto and his key staff officers had no interest in scrutiny, much less criticism. The games' purpose, put simply, was to certify and validate Yamamoto's plan. He was a gambler, and he had decided that he liked the odds.

During one tabletop exercise on the second day of the conference, carriers of the "red team" (representing the U.S. Navy) appeared on *Kido Butai*'s port flank and dealt it a sudden, crippling air attack. The table judge, acting in his godlike capacity as umpire, ruled that the scenario was unbelievable, and expunged the results. With self-satisfied assurance, the judge declared that if the games had yielded such a result, the games must be flawed—for it was clear that the American carriers could not get into battle until they had been alerted to Nagumo's presence by the first Japanese airstrikes on Midway.

In a second episode, Midway-based land bombers counterattacked *Kido Butai*. The dice determined that the attacking planes had scored nine hits on the Japanese carrier group, sending two—*Akagi* and *Kaga*—to the bottom. Admiral Ugaki, Yamamoto's despotic chief of staff, was acting in the role of supervisor and chief judge. "Wait," he said; "we'll reduce the number of hits to three." With that arbitrary revision, it was determined that only *Kaga* was sunk, and *Akagi* lightly damaged. Later, Ugaki arranged to resurrect the *Kaga* for the next stage of operations, involving attacks against New Caledonia and Fiji.* These were only the most egregious of several other

---

* While reviewing this manuscript, Alan Zimm pointed out that the subsequent resurrection of the *Kaga* may not have been blameworthy, if the war-gaming exercises were being conducted as discrete events. He will address this subject in a forthcoming book, *Attack on Pearl Harbor: Strategy, Combat, Myths, Deceptions.*

rulings in favor of the Japanese side. "This kind of supervision," said Mit-suo Fuchida, "was enough to disgust even the most hardened flying officers among us."

When Yamamoto himself asked the very salient question at the heart of the problem—what would happen if American carriers suddenly appeared within striking range of *Kido Butai*?—Lieutenant Commander Minoru Genda simply dismissed the threat, exclaiming: "*Gaishu Isshoku!*" ("One touch of the armored gauntlet!"), an idiomatic expression translated as "We'll wipe them out!" Yamamoto's one concession to the games was to instruct Nagumo to maintain a reserve strike on board the carriers after the Midway attack had been launched, in case the American carriers should appear.

By revealing the weaknesses of the plan and demonstrating the threat to Japanese forces, the tabletop games had done what they were designed to do. But they had been sloppy and halfhearted from the outset, and in the end they were little more than a charade. They had been necessary for appearance's sake, but any flaws they revealed were swept under the rug. Among the officers of the fleet, there was whispered criticism, but few dared voice open opposition. According to Fuchida, who was present at the planning sessions, overconfidence was endemic. He and his fellow carrier aviators "were so sure of our own strength that we thought we could smash the enemy fleet single-handed, even if the battleship groups did nothing to support us."

The plan's most eminent critic was Vice Admiral Nobutake Kondo, commander in chief of the Second Fleet, who met privately with Yamamoto on May 1 and laid out his objections. Kondo urged that Midway be post-poned in favor of a renewed westward push through the Solomons to New Caledonia. There, in the south, the fleet could count on shore-based air support. None was available in the attack on Midway. And even if Midway were successfully occupied, the Japanese would face daunting logistical and military challenges in keeping the atoll supplied. Kondo later wrote that he thought Midway a dead end, because it would "not be easy for Japan to maintain a powerful air force there because of a too-long supporting route."

Yamamoto was unyielding. He brushed off Kondo's suggestion that the operation be delayed a month, to allow for further study and preparation. There were important meteorological factors favoring early June. Only then (it was believed) would high tide arrive at the right moment, shortly after dawn, to allow the amphibious boats carrying the invasion force to clear the reef fringing Midway. By July, the Aleutians would be shrouded in fog. Moreover, it was too late to postpone the operation—the resources of virtually the entire Japanese navy had already been set in motion.

Six months earlier, Yamamoto had demanded the surprise strike on Pearl Harbor over the objections of more prudent critics, and achieved a tactically spectacular victory. He had predicted that Japanese airpower would prevail over Allied surface naval strength, and he had been proved right. Having never failed and often succeeded, he enjoyed an aura of infallibility. He was a national figure, who had won the adulation and trust of the Japanese people. He had twice used the threat of his resignation to cow his critics. He would not hesitate to do so again.

In his diary, Ugaki confided: "I could not help being a bit tired after a week of continuous conferences starting with the war lessons, table maneuvers, and briefings." On the other hand, spring had arrived, the weather was fair, and the flowers along the shores of the Inland Sea were in full bloom. May 5 was the Japanese holiday known as Boys' Day, and though Ugaki could not see any of the carp-shaped *koinobori* banners on shore, he was moved by the "fresh green" foliage on the steeply ascending slopes of the islands around the fleet anchorage. He added a few lines of verse to his entry for that day:

> *All day long, verdant isles fresh to see,*
> *Around us, floating on the sea.*

HIGH UP IN THE HILLY BACKCOUNTRY of central Oahu, amongst cane fields and lush flora, a U.S. Navy radio-monitoring station plucked coded Japanese transmissions out of the atmosphere. No secure communications link then existed between the station and the Navy Yard at Pearl Harbor, so the raw coded intercepts were typewritten and entrusted to the care of a courier, who drove them down the hill in a jeep and delivered them by hand to the basement of the Fourteenth Naval District Headquarters, home of Joe Rochefort's cryptanalysis unit.

Operation MO and the big clash in the Coral Sea, like every other large-scale Japanese naval operation, had released a flood of radio messages that could be linked to known locations, events, and fleet units. It was, in other words, a codebreaker's bonanza. In May 1942, the Allies were intercepting about 60 percent of Japanese naval radio traffic, attempting to decrypt about 40 percent of the intercepts, and managing to break about 10 to 15 percent of the code groups in those messages.

Except in rare instances, however, they could not read complete messages, but only a few phrases in messages that were otherwise gibberish. Rochefort spent his eighteen-hour days hunched over messages in which fragmentary phrases appeared alongside blanks. "My job was to fill it in," he said, and for that he relied on his encyclopedic memory. "I could remember back three or four months when that command had sent a similar message." The previously deciphered phrases shed light on the blanks, especially when the same phrase appeared repeatedly alongside the same blank. With the help of the IBM machines, a working hypothesis was tested against every other message in which a given code group had occurred. In this manner, the breakdown of JN-25 (the main Japanese naval code in use at that time) proceeded geometrically—as the staff recovered more code groups, they gained more leverage over the remaining blanks.

Even before the Battle of the Coral Sea, Rochefort had suspected that the Japanese were planning another major operation in the central Pacific possibly aimed at Midway or even Hawaii itself. In early May, Allied listening posts noted a surge in radio traffic emanating from Saipan, in the Marianas, but no corresponding rise from Truk, Japan's principal naval base in the South Pacific. That pointed to a new offensive aimed directly across the Pacific, north of the equator, rather than a renewed offensive thrust in the south. A request for a large quantity of fueling hoses to be sent to Saipan seemed to indicate a fleet operation ranging far from Japanese bases. Reconnaissance flights from Kwajalein, in the Marshall Islands, were growing in length and frequency. Traffic patterns gave the impression that the "pending operations" would be large in scale, probably involving the First, Second, and Fifth fleets. Evidently, something big was about to happen in the central Pacific.

On May 12, Rochefort called Layton. "I've got something so hot here it's burning the top of my desk," he said. "You'll have to come over and see it. It's not cut and dried, but it's hot! The man with the blue eyes will want to know your opinion of it." The message included a recovered code group for *Koryaku Butai*, or "invasion force." Another phrase, tentatively identified as "forthcoming campaign," was linked to the geographic designator "AF." On the following day, May 13, two significant messages were intercepted and partially decrypted. In one, a Japanese vessel submitted a request for charts covering the Hawaiian Islands area. In the second, a forecast of movements by a supply ship indicated that the future base of the Third Air Group would be "AF," and discussed logistics of moving base equipment, ammunition, spare parts, and ground crews to that location.

As early as March, Rochefort had postulated that "AF" was Midway. All geographic designators beginning with A had been shown to be in the Hawaiian Islands and other American-held islands in the central Pacific. But Rochefort did not believe the Japanese possessed the military forces or (especially) the shipping to mount an invasion of Oahu or any of the other main islands of the Hawaiian group. What else in the region would be a likely target? Midway was the only atoll large enough to support an air group; the others, such as Palmyra or Johnston Island, were thought too small to be worth a major effort. A simple process of elimination, therefore, pointed to Midway. By May 12, there was no doubt in Rochefort's mind that Midway was the target of the pending attack. Layton agreed: "We knew that AH was Oahu and that AK was probably the French Frigate Shoals. Now that the base supplies for an air unit were being readied for shipment into 'AF' with the occupation forces, it had to be one of our island bases within striking distance of Pearl Harbor. Midway was the obvious target, since it was nearly 150 miles nearer the Japanese on Wake than the alternative, Johnston Island."

The deduction was sound, and the conclusion correct—but none of that would matter unless Admiral Nimitz could be convinced. There was no ironclad proof that "AF" was Midway. It was a supposition, relying on a mosaic picture made up of many disparate bits of evidence. But Layton and Rochefort, having correctly foretold the Japanese move against Moresby, now enjoyed the CINCPAC's full attention. In the month between Coral Sea and Midway, Nimitz would be called upon to make the most high-stakes decisions of his forty-year naval career, and he was willing to risk everything, based on the best estimates of his intelligence advisers.

But Nimitz, in this instance, was not the ultimate authority. Behind Nimitz, in Washington, loomed the imperious figure of Admiral King, who was anxious not to lose any more of the navy's few remaining aircraft carriers and was taking an active hand in choosing where and how to deploy them. In the period immediately after the Battle of the Coral Sea, King remained uneasy about New Caledonia, Fiji, and the other island groups straddling the U.S.-Australia sea link. Analysts at OP-20-G, the communications intelligence unit in Washington, fed King estimates that reinforced his preexisting belief that the Japanese would aim their heaviest blows in the South Pacific. They were fixated on a series of decrypts referring to a fleet rendezvous at Truk, and argued that enemy naval forces were moving south. Rochefort agreed that a Truk rendezvous was in the cards, but believed it would not occur until after the capture of Midway. "The amazing part of the whole thing was that many people could not accept this line of reasoning," said Rochefort later. "We were quite impatient at Station Hypo that people in Washington could not agree with our rationale, because they had the same information and should, without any particular stress on their brains, have come up with the same answer."

Some even suspected that the cryptanalysts were being conned—that Japanese radio dispatches pointing toward Midway might be an elaborate hoax. One of Rochefort's strongest pieces of evidence was the May 13 intercept in which the Third Air Group had announced its future base as "AF." To critics, that seemed too good to be true. No less a figure than General Marshall, the army chief of staff, remarked that "one Japanese unit gave Midway as its post office address, and that seemed a little bit too thick." Army commanders were concerned about the safety of Oahu, and feared that Nimitz's deployments would denude the island of its air defenses. When asked to send B-17s to reinforce Midway, General Delos C. Emmons, the local commander of Army Air Forces, was reluctant to comply. "Japs may be practicing deception with radio orders intercepted by us," he warned Nimitz. "Estimates should be directed at capabilities rather than probable intentions. [Enemy forces] have sufficient strength to make damaging raid on Oahu with view to wrecking facilities [in] Pearl Harbor and Honolulu."

As these conflicting points of view came to a head, the feud between Washington and Hypo became bitter, ugly, and personal. In secure radio transmissions between the units, insults were even woven into the message "padding"—the random phrases placed before and after message texts for security. Layton suspected that someone in Redman's camp even took steps to destroy records of internal communications that would have exposed OP-20-G's errors to scrutiny. "It was a mess," recalled Lieutenant Commander Ham Wright, one of Hypo's senior codebreakers. "We would fight with OP-20-G all the time; we could not get together." The Hawaiians charged that the Washingtonians were too apt to jump at shadows—that they made too much of stray, fragmentary decrypts, often failing to apply basic common sense to their own predictions. Having worked through the immediate aftermath of the raid on Pearl Harbor, when an almost unbelievable array of lurid rumors had circulated, the Hypo team had learned the importance of skepticism. They did not believe their counterparts in Washington had absorbed the same lesson. As Jasper Holmes put it, "No one who has not experienced it can realize how difficult it is to track the shadow of truth through the fog of war."

Rochefort and his team were certain that "AF" was Midway, and that the attack would come in the first week of June. They had convinced Nimitz of their reasoning. But they lacked enough evidence to overcome Washington's obstinate claims to the contrary. To that end, Rochefort had a timely brainstorm. He proposed a ruse. The local commander on Midway would be told to transmit a plain-language radio broadcast back to Pearl Harbor, reporting that Midway's desalination plant had broken down, and that as a result the atoll was short of fresh water. This was done. A Japanese monitoring station on Wake intercepted the broadcast and immediately passed it on to Imperial General Headquarters in Tokyo, which in turn alerted the Combined Fleet to a freshwater shortage on "AF." The latter message was intercepted and broken by Hypo and by the cryptanalyst unit in Melbourne.

The ploy had succeeded brilliantly, providing outright confirmation that "AF" was indeed Midway. But OP-20-G, incredibly, did not relent. Perhaps, they suggested, the Japanese were trying to mislead the Allies with radio deception? Or, as a fallback, perhaps the Japanese were planning an operation against Midway, but it would not take place until the second half of June, after another major offensive in the South Pacific?

Nimitz was under intense strain. Admiral Halsey's Task Force 16, built around the *Enterprise* and *Hornet*, had been sent south across the equator to provide support to their sisters *Lexington* and *Yorktown* in the Battle of the Coral Sea. They had reached the waters east of Efate, in the New Hebrides. If Rochefort and Layton were right, and the Japanese were planning a huge offensive against Midway in the first week of June, Nimitz needed to summon Halsey back from the South Pacific right away. But he did not have an entirely free hand to recall the carriers, because Admiral King, who was not yet convinced of the Midway theory, was looking over his shoulder. How directly could the CINCPAC afford to defy the autocratic COMINCH?

On May 16, Nimitz threw down the gauntlet. He radioed Halsey: "Desire you proceed to Hawaiian area." He laid out his reasons in a cable to King the same day. The Japanese would mount an attack "against Midway-Oahu line, probably involving initially a major landing attack against Midway, for which it is believed the enemy's main striking force will be employed." Further, the CINCPAC diary noted: "Unless the enemy is using radio deception on a grand scale, we have a fairly good idea of his intentions."

The order prompted Admiral King to call his advisers into his office for a thorough evaluation of the latest intelligence. By the end of the day, he concluded that Nimitz was right. In an "urgent and confidential" cable the next morning, he wrote: "I have somewhat revised my estimate and now generally agree with you." The new offensive would be aimed at capturing Midway, and in the course of the campaign, the Japanese navy would attempt to "trap and destroy a substantial portion of the Pacific Fleet." King agreed that the American carriers should be positioned to give battle, but added that Nimitz must "not repeat not allow our forces to accept such decisive action as would be likely to incur heavy losses."

Even now, however, critical details were missing. When would the attack come? What forces would be involved? What was the exact sequence of attacks? On May 18, Nimitz turned up pressure on Layton and Rochefort to provide answers. Communications intelligence was now more important to the Americans than it had ever been before: at that moment, the entire fleet was being staked on a series of intercepts and a complex matrix of deductions.

On May 20, Hypo received a long radio intercept—its length gave away its importance—and the cryptanalysts turned their full attention to breaking it. The IBM tabulators stripped the additives and converted more than 80 percent of the transmission to plaintext. It provided complete orders for the Midway operation, including a detailed description of the forces to be employed. But the super-enciphered poly-alphabetic time-date codes in the message remained impenetrable, so the Hawaiians could not yet prove that the attack would come the first week of June. Rochefort and Layton closed in on the date gradually, marshalling the evidence point by point. Stray decrypts referred to a May 27 sailing date from Saipan, and a June 6 arrival date for a division of destroyers that were to protect invasion transports. Layton recalled that he had worked "by applying the rule that when you don't know things, you had to try to see them as if you were a Jap. Working backward from the sailing dates, and the decrypted orders for the 6 June arrival of the invasion force transports, I reconstructed a tentative plot that was accurate enough to predict when and where the transports carrying the assault troops should be sighted by search planes from Midway."

On the morning of May 27, Rochefort and Layton met with Nimitz and several senior members of his staff in a conference room at the fleet headquarters. Rear Admiral Raymond Ames Spruance, soon to be appointed commander of Task Force 16, was present, as was General Emmons, the local army commander, and Lieutenant General Robert C. Richardson, who had been sent to Hawaii as a personal emissary of General Marshall. Rochefort, who was pulling together briefing materials at the last minute, turned up half an hour late. (He was perhaps the only naval officer in the Pacific who could get away with that.) Layton recalled that Rochefort appeared "disheveled and bleary-eyed from lack of sleep," and that his apology was met by Nimitz's "icy gaze."

Rochefort's forecasts—a carrier air attack on Dutch Harbor at dawn on June 3, followed by another on Midway the next morning—were so specific that several members of Nimitz's staff found them difficult to believe. Was it really possible that the Americans were reading the enemy's entire playbook? Some continued to suspect that the Japanese had cooked up an elaborate ruse: an entry in the CINCPAC diary that day reads: "Of course it may turn out that the Japanese are pulling our leg and using radio deception on a grand scale." Others asked why the Japanese would hurl their entire fleet against Midway, when the atoll's capture made so little strategic sense. (Their objections were essentially the same as those put to Yamamoto by Admiral Kondo and the Japanese Naval General Staff.) Rochefort was surprised at the degree of skepticism—to his mind, the case was, if not exactly airtight, at least proven beyond a reasonable doubt. "Of course," he later said, "as somebody who had been living this development over two months to the exclusion of everything else. . . . I just could not understand why there should be any doubt in anyone's mind."

As Nimitz probed for flaws in Rochefort's reasoning, the latter freely admitted that there were gaps in his knowledge, and that those gaps had been filled with inferences and deductions. "All I can do in a situation like this is to explain my position and hope that the admiral accepts it," Rochefort said. Nimitz alone bore the "horrible" burden of command: "It stops right there, and no one else can take it away from him, and no one else can help him."

The admiral turned to Layton and asked him to predict exactly how he believed the coming battle would unfold.

"I have a difficult time being specific," replied Layton.

Nimitz held his gaze. "I want you to be specific," he said. "After all, this is the job I have given you—to be the admiral commanding the Japanese forces, and tell me what is going on."

"All right then, Admiral," Layton said. "I've previously given you the intelligence that the carriers will probably attack Midway on the morning of the 4th of June, so we'll pick the 4th of June for the day. They'll come in from the northwest on bearing 325 degrees and they will be sighted at about 175 miles from Midway, and the time will be about 0600 Midway time."

That afternoon, Nimitz issued Operation Plan 29-42, which stated that the Japanese would "attempt the capture of Midway in the near future." The *Enterprise-Hornet* Task Force (16) would proceed to the suitably code-named Point LUCK, about 350 miles northeast of Midway. There they would rendezvous with Admiral Fletcher and Task Force 17, comprising the newly repaired *Yorktown* and her eight screening vessels. The three American flattops would lie in wait until the Japanese carriers were spotted by air reconnaissance, and then launch a surprise attack on Nagumo's flank. The commanders were to "inflict maximum damage on enemy by employing strong attrition tactics," but they should not "accept such decisive action as would be likely to incur heavy losses in our carriers and cruisers."

Nimitz, wrote Layton, had "crossed his Rubicon." The entire war now hung in the balance, and Layton could not sleep at all that night.

The Hypo staff was aware that the entire war had been staked on their forecast. The week before the Battle of Midway was a breathless interlude. Had they got it right? Rochefort urged his colleagues not to worry. The die was cast—the Japanese fleet had presumably sailed, and Nimitz had moved his forces into position. Even if the attack did not come on June 3 or 4, it would come in mid-June without fail. "If we get ready for this attack on June 3 and it does not come off, we may look silly, but there will be time for our ships to refuel and get back on station," Rochefort told Layton. "If we are not prepared and the Japs strike, it will be a case of Pearl Harbor all over again—and the navy will have no excuse."

But Hypo had one more crowning victory to add to its record. The Japanese had used a super-enciphered time-date code in many of its communications, including Yamamoto's long battle plan, which had been sent out to the fleet on May 20. Rochefort's unit had been so engrossed in breaking new messages that it had not found the time to focus on the problem. On the night of May 26, Ham Wright had just completed a twelve-hour shift and was about to walk out the door when Lieutenant Joseph Finnegan accosted him and said, "Ham, we're stuck on the date and time." Wright went back to his desk, cleared off the clutter, and concentrated on the problem. He collected and collated every message intercept in which the code had appeared. He began working through the possibilities, linking old codes to dates that were known after the operations in question had been completed. One by one, with painstaking care, he constructed hypotheses, tested them, and discarded them. Later that night, Wright and Finnegan drew the dungeon's other veteran cryptanalysts into the effort, including Tom Dyer and Rochefort himself.

By mid-morning on the 27th, they had it. The time-date cipher was a simple substitution code, using a table of *kana* twelve rows down (months) and thirty-one columns across (days). It confirmed that the Japanese attacks on the Aleutians would commence on June 3, and the attack on Midway a day later. It was exactly as Hypo had forecast, and exactly as Nimitz had spelled it out in his orders to the fleet.

With this victory in hand, Jasper Holmes went upstairs to absorb some sunshine and breathe some fresh air. While standing on the Administration Building's lanai, he ran into an old friend, an officer now serving on the *Yorktown*. As they chatted, Dyer emerged from the dungeon, on his way home, with his battered lunchbox under his arm. He had been working around the clock for several days. Holmes wrote:

His uniform looked as though he had slept in it for three days. He had. He was unshaven and his hair looked as though it had not been cut for a month. It had not. His eyes were bloodshot from lack of sleep, and his gait betrayed how close he was to utter exhaustion. With a seaman's contempt for a landlubber, my carrier friend remarked, "Now there goes a bird who should be sent to sea to get straightened out." For an instant my blood pressure soared to the bursting point and I nearly blurted out the truth. Dyer was one of the kingpins of the little band of officers whose genius and devotion to duty, over many years, had given us an opportunity to win a victory at last. If he wasted his time on spit, polish, and punctilio, the war would be much longer and cost many more lives. Fortunately, I regained control of myself in time and mumbled something like, "Oh, he's all right," feeling like Peter when he betrayed the Lord. Dyer would have been the first to condemn me if I had broken the secrecy that we all prized much more than any credit or the hope of reward.

ADMIRAL HALSEY'S TASK FORCE 16 had arrived in the South Seas too late for the Battle of the Coral Sea. The radio operators of the two carriers (*Enterprise* and *Hornet*) had followed the progress of the battle by eavesdropping at long distance on the transmissions of Fletcher's ships and pilots. News of the *Lexington*'s loss came as a cruel shock. She was the first American carrier ever destroyed in naval combat. Alvin Kernan wrote that many of the *Enterprise*'s veteran carrier sailors had served on the *Lexington* in the past—to them, in particular, her sinking "was felt as a personal blow."

The officers and men craved revenge, and at first there was some hope of hunting down the Japanese naval forces as they withdrew from the Coral Sea. Having delivered a marine fighter squadron to Efate on May 11, Task Force 16 was free to engage the enemy, who was believed to be aiming a new attack against islands east of the Solomons. The carriers cruised north along the 170th meridian and conducted long-range searches to the west, with some hope of pinning down the retreating Japanese forces.

Nimitz's May 16 recall order had included an unusual proviso. In an "eyes-only" message to Halsey, the CINCPAC had instructed that the task force should allow itself to be sighted by a Japanese patrol plane before turning north for Pearl Harbor. That bit of subterfuge was intended to lull the Japanese into believing that the road to Midway was clear, and to deter any further near-term aggression in the South Pacific. Halsey pointed the task force west, knowing full well that the heading would take them under the search umbrella of the ubiquitous Kawanishis. A Tulagi-based long-range patrol spotted the task force several hundred miles east of the Solomons Islands, prompting Admiral Inouye to rule out any renewed effort against Moresby before July. Then Halsey turned north and began a high-speed run toward Oahu.

Only Halsey and a few other senior officers knew what was up. Down the ranks, these quixotic maneuvers were interpreted with a combination of bafflement and disgust. Robert Casey, aboard the *Salt Lake City*, thought it strange that the force had been sighted, when it could easily have concealed its presence by hanging back to the east, and noted: "There's something fishy about this." With the task force racing north at 20 knots, it was obvious that they were hurrying home to Pearl Harbor, and it felt uncomfortably like a retreat. "It seemed to us like craven cowardice," Kernan recalled; ". . . and there was a good deal of muttering."

On May 26, under a sweltering tropical sun, the twenty-one ships of Task Force 16 crawled into Pearl Harbor. Though the *Yorktown* and her screening vessels had not yet even arrived, the East Loch was crammed full of ships, and maneuvering among them was difficult, delicate work. Minutes after the *Enterprise* was safely in her berth, Halsey and his flag lieutenant descended into the admiral's barge to be taken across to the Pacific Fleet headquarters.

When Nimitz and Halsey came face to face, the CINCPAC was taken aback. The task force commander was not well. He was gaunt; his eyes were sunken; he had lost 20 pounds. His skin had erupted in scaly patches of red and white, later diagnosed as "general dermatitis," a condition that was undeniably stress-related. During his last days at sea, he had tried to soothe the spreading rash by standing on the bridge, exposed to the sun and air, dressed in nothing but his "skivvies," but to no avail. The painful condition had made it increasingly difficult for him to sleep, and a sleep-deprived admiral was not the man to lead the navy's few remaining carriers into the most important battle of the war. Halsey had carried the burden of seagoing command too long without a break, and Nimitz ordered him to the naval hospital. He would miss the Battle of Midway while confined to a hospital bed, his body smeared with a medicinal ointment. It was, he would later remember, "the most grievous disappointment of my career."

Nimitz downplayed Halsey's condition in his report to the COMINCH. "He is in the best of spirits, full of vim and vigor, and anxious to get going," he wrote King on May 29. "But he does need a short period of rest. He is neither ill nor on the sick list."

On May 28, Admiral Frank Jack Fletcher was notified that he would retain command of Task Force 17. With Halsey laid up, he would be the ranking admiral afloat. But another flag officer would have to step into Halsey's shoes as commander of Task Force 16. Halsey recommended Rear Admiral Spruance, commander of the task force's cruiser division. Nimitz, who shared Halsey's high opinion of Spruance, agreed without hesitation. Spruance was a "black shoe" admiral, but he would retain Halsey's first-rate staff, and he was well practiced in carrier operations. Indeed, Nimitz had already tapped Spruance as his next chief of staff, and planned to bring him on in that capacity immediately after the forthcoming battle.

Spruance and Halsey were as different as it was possible for two career naval officers to be. Spruance was soft-spoken, prudent, a listener who distrusted rhetoric and never strived for dramatic effect. He led through example and through the quiet projection of confidence and competence, never allowing excitement or emotion to influence his decisions. He tried to avoid reporters, and when he could not avoid them he gave them nothing remotely interesting or quotable. Halsey was gruff, blunt-spoken, and swaggering, and when addressing the press or the men under his command he could not resist colorful bombast. Yet Halsey and Spruance had been personally close since the early 1920s, when they had served together in the Pacific Destroyer Force. Their wives, Fanny and Margaret, had become good friends during that period, when both families were stationed in San Diego. Their sons, Billy and Edward, were the same age and had been inseparable childhood playmates.

Spruance had been born into a wealthy Baltimore family, and had lived the first years of his life in a mansion. But his family was bankrupted while he was still a boy, and he was packed off to Indianapolis to live with two aunts. He applied to the Naval Academy because his family could not afford to send him to college. He had not liked the academy at all, regarding it as a hidebound, narrow-minded institution in which poorly qualified instructors emphasized rote memorization of technical details, and in which barbaric hazing rituals were tolerated as character-building exercises. He graduated in 1906, ranked 26th in a class of 209. The *Lucky Bag* called him a "shy young thing with a rather sober, earnest face and the innocent disposition of an ingénue. . . . Would never hurt anything or anybody except in the line of duty."

The young Spruance had been doe-eyed and slightly built, but with age he developed a more formidable bearing. He was a reserved man who smiled little, but he did not (like Ernest King) come across as cold or arrogant. He kept himself fit with long daily hikes, holding a fast, steady pace. He did so even while at sea, by walking endless circuits of the deck of his flagship. Spruance has often been described as "cerebral," and the adjective is fitting—he was a naval intellectual who had read deeply into the art of war at sea in all its aspects. He communicated with penetrating clarity, both verbally and in writing; he asked questions and absorbed the full meaning of the answers he received; he was quick to grasp all the elements of any assignment given him. A navy doctor, upon first meeting Spruance, "saluted a trim, perhaps underweight, average-height officer . . . his face deeply tanned, strikingly calm, almost a poker face. He had extraordinary piercing blue eyes that seemed to see and read your very thoughts." He was, added the doctor, "a true Spartan in every sense."

Like many of history's great sea warriors, Spruance was prone to seasickness. But he never regarded the ailment as more than a nuisance. Standing on his bridge, his ship laboring in heavy seas, he might suddenly approach the rail and launch the contents of his stomach over the side, and then go on about his business as if nothing had happened. He had a valuable quality of endurance and durability while serving at sea, never succumbing to the sort of physical or nervous exhaustion that claimed so many other commanders (and that had just landed Halsey in the hospital). Like every career officer of his vintage, Spruance had rotated through seagoing assignments and shore billets, but he much preferred to serve at sea. He would accept the burden of coming ashore, as Nimitz's chief of staff, without enthusiasm but also without complaint.

Later in the war, Spruance and Halsey's careers would remain closely intertwined. In 1944 and 1945, the two admirals would alternate in the Pacific's top seagoing command—that of commander of the Third Fleet, which was designated the Fifth Fleet whenever Spruance held the post. Halsey would be far better known to the American public, and he would attain the exalted five-star rank of "Fleet Admiral," an honor Spruance equally deserved but never received. But the officers and men of the fleet would rate Spruance as the more reliable and effective of the two leaders, a judgment that has been largely ratified by historians of the Pacific War.

In May 1942, however, Spruance was still a wild card. The crew of the *Enterprise* regarded the loss of their beloved Admiral Halsey not only as sad but disconcerting. Who was this slim cruiser commander, this junior admiral who had never flown an airplane or skippered a carrier? Naturally, wrote dive-bomber pilot Clarence Dickinson, "the men in the ship were piecing together their various scraps of information about this man with two stars on his collar. Would he be as ready as Admiral Halsey to put us into battle?" Spruance was seen out on the flight deck for hours each day, pacing for exercise. As he walked, he beckoned other officers to walk alongside him. Though Spruance could certainly "walk the legs off any man on the ship," he used those long miles of walking and talking to educate himself. "We saw with satisfaction," wrote Dickinson, "that this man whose flag flew overhead asked questions and listened."

The *Yorktown*, having been ordered to make her way back to Pearl Harbor as quickly as her condition would allow, crept into the ship channel on the afternoon of May 27. She had made 20 knots of sustained speed, and could dial up 30 knots to launch and recover planes. Her elevators were working normally, and her flight operations were unimpeded. The hole in her flight deck had been patched over so neatly that no one could have guessed, by looking down on the ship from above, that she had been hit by a Japanese bomb. The only sign of her suffering was a long oil slick trailing in her wake, the result of the fuel tank ruptured by the blast force of one of the Japanese dive-bombers' near misses. As she limped into the crowded harbor, the fleet welcomed her home with an ovation of steam whistles and sirens.

The *Yorktown* had been ordered directly into Drydock No. 1. The huge caissons (gates) closed behind her, and the pumps began expelling water into the harbor. The carrier settled onto the concrete blocks, and the lowering waterline gradually revealed the gaps in her hull plates where rivets had been torn out. Nimitz pulled on a pair of waders and descended to the dry-dock floor, a long entourage of officers following behind him. Slogging through water knee-deep, the great gray, oil-streaked shape of the hull looming above him, he scrutinized the damage and listened to the engineers.

According to one of the many myths of the Battle of Midway, the engineers asked Nimitz for three months to repair the *Yorktown*, and Nimitz grandly replied that they must finish the job in three days. The truth is more nuanced and less cinematic. It was not Nimitz's style to demand the impossible of men who had been working to the utmost limit of their physical and mental capacities since the first day of the war. It was enough to make his priorities understood. When the CINCPAC told the repair party, "We must have this ship back in three days," he had already been advised that he could have her. The repair superintendent and a small team of engineers had been flown out to the carrier the day before her arrival, and had already made their assessment. No, the *Yorktown* did not require three months of work (as Admiral Fitch had apparently predicted). She would not even need to return stateside to have the repairs done. Pearl Harbor could have her as good as new in a month—and in a pinch, she could be patched up and sent back to sea in three days. They would meet the deadline not by completing the needed repairs quickly, but by not doing them at all. Rather than repairing each ruptured seam, the yard would simply weld a single enormous steel plate over her wounds. As for the internal bulkheads which had buckled, they would be reinforced with heavy wooden beams. It was an interim patch-up job rather than a proper restoration of the ship, but the *Yorktown* would be battleworthy for the coming campaign.

The yard put 1,400 men on the job. They worked in shifts, night and day, with floodlights rigged at night in defiance of the blackout. Some went sleepless for forty-eight hours. Hundreds of the ship's crew were pressed into service, going without relief or liberty. At the same time that she was repaired, the carrier had to be reprovisioned, having consumed all her victuals with the exception of a few powdered eggs, powdered milk, and pasta. In those three days, Otis Kight recalled, the *Yorktown* "did a humongous amount of resupplying." Early on the morning of May 29, water began surging back into Drydock No. 1, and the patched-up carrier was lifted off the blocks and floated free. At 11 a.m. the gates opened and she was towed to her berth, no longer leaking oil.

The crew of the *Enterprise* was denied liberty during the carrier's brief stay in her berth. All hands worked at provisioning the ship. Food and provisions were lifted aboard from lighters. Ammunition was hoisted onto the ship and secured in her magazines. Fueling lines filled her tanks. Teams of men unpacked machine-gun rounds from their crates and inserted them into ammunition belts. The work went on all night, with the ship illuminated by floodlights. On the 27th, Admiral Nimitz came aboard and presented medals to several white-clad aviators and sailors, while the ship's company stood to attention and the Marine Guard presented arms.

Though all the carriers and their escort ships had been long at sea, few officers or men were granted liberty during their brief stopover at Pearl. Even those who were allowed to leave their ships were largely confined to base, and many of the aviators were sequestered at other bases on Oahu. The *Hornet*'s dive-bomber squadrons flew into Ewa Field. Upon descending from their planes, the airmen were told that they would be confined to base for the duration of their stay. Other members of the *Hornet*'s crew were let loose in Honolulu the day they flew in, but the following night they were all recalled: "All liberty cancelled. Report at once to the ship." The *Enterprise* pilots moved into the Royal Hawaiian Hotel on Waikiki and devoted their liberty to a bout of hard drinking, but they too were summoned back to base early.

Fear of leaks undoubtedly explained those curious restrictions. The fleet was pulsating with rumors about the pending operation, and much of the scuttlebutt was apparently on the mark. It was obvious from the hurried provisioning and loading of the ships that something big was about to happen. Ordnanceman Kernan recalled that the entire crew of the *Enterprise* knew in advance that a large Japanese fleet was to attack Midway, that "the strategy and tactics for the coming battle were learnedly discussed by the admirals of the lower deck, who were, on the whole, as always, of the opinion that the officers would screw it up." Robert Casey, being a civilian, was permitted to leave his ship and hitchhike into Honolulu. While there he spoke to an army colonel who informed him that army pilots had been standing watches in their cockpits, and that an air attack on Oahu was expected at any time. The colonel "had it on good authority that an advance detachment of the Japanese navy, complete with carriers, battleships and transports, had been sighted off Midway." Casey correctly dismissed the report as "cockeyed"—the Japanese fleet would not be sighted for several more days—but the focus on Midway was dead to rights.

As the rumors circulated, a pervasive sense of foreboding settled over the American fleet. Without knowing all the particulars of the coming battle, many assumed that they would be heavily outnumbered by the enemy. "As usual we seem to be holding the short end of the stick, this time shorter than usual," wrote Casey in his diary. "We muster carriers, cruisers, and about half a dozen destroyers to face one of the biggest fleets ever turned loose on the Pacific. An armada that rates as a good half of the Jap fleet and we're meeting it as usual with a fly swatter and a prayer."

The *Yorktown* air group, having suffered heavy losses in Coral Sea, was largely reorganized and rebuilt in the week before battle. Squadrons were cobbled together with sundry planes and newly trained pilots who happened to be on hand at Pearl. *Saratoga*'s Bombing Three (VB-3) replaced *Yorktown*'s Scouting Five (VS-5), which had lost too many planes and aircrew to remain viable. A new fighter squadron, Fighting Three (VF-3), absorbed several of the planes, pilots, and mechanics of VF-42, which had served on the *Yorktown* since late 1941. A newly constituted Torpedo Three

(VT-3) replaced Torpedo Five (VT-5), which also went ashore for a period of rest and training.

Jimmy Thach, skipper of the new Fighting Three, had become a lonely evangelist for the F4F Wildcat. He was one of the few American fighter pilots (Jimmy Flatley was another) to say outright that the F4F, if handled properly, was superior to the Zero. The key was to match the Wildcat's strengths against the Zero's weaknesses. He believed that the Americans were better gunners, and were armed with better guns. To ensure that the guns could be brought to bear on a Zero in aerial combat, it was essential that the American pilots conserve altitude before engaging the enemy, and they must fight as a team, relying on wingmen to shoot pursuers off their flanks. His formation maneuver, the "Thach weave," would prove highly effective in aerial combat.

Thach's squadron was being equipped with a new version of the Wildcat, the F4F-4, which had folding wings. Because it occupied less space on the hangar deck, each carrier could accommodate twenty-seven fighters, nine more than before. But there was a cost—the F4F-4's .50-caliber machine guns fired only for twenty-two seconds before ammunition was expended, down from forty seconds on the earlier version of the plane. The sacrifice of precious firepower on the eve of the big showdown was considered an ominous development.

Lieutenant E. Scott McCuskey, a veteran fighter pilot of VF-42, remembered "a profound feeling of doom. This whole situation looked desperate. Admiral Nimitz was throwing everything he had against the superior Japanese force approaching Midway Island—including the battle-damaged *Yorktown*." McCuskey expected to be ordered to cover the low-altitude approach of the obsolete Devastators, and he did not like the Wildcats' chances against the Zeros at low altitude. "I had been shocked by the performance of the Zeros in the Coral Sea," said McCuskey. "They had flown around me like a swarm of bees."

Some of the rookies were barely out of flight training and had only a few hours of flight time in the planes to which they would be assigned. Clayton Fisher, a dive-bomber pilot on the *Hornet*'s Bombing Squadron Eight, had flown the SBD Dauntless for the first time in late March, just two months earlier. He was twenty-two years old. "It's hard to describe the mental pressure we were all under at that time," he said. "You know you were going into a battle completely outnumbered. . . . How many of us would survive?" Sequestered at Ewa, Bombing Eight's airmen finagled a few bottles of whiskey, and a drunken wrestling match turned ugly when punches were thrown. Fisher wrote home, as they all did. He mulled over the prospect that it was the last letter he would ever write, as they all did. "I was worried and just plain scared," he confessed. "Nobody wants to die."

But it was the torpedo squadrons who had the most to fear in the looming struggle. They knew perfectly well that their lumbering TBD Devastators were overdue for retirement. Flying into the heart of an enemy task force at a little over 100 knots, a few hundred feet above the sea, they would be cold meat for the Zeros. The Devastator's successor, the Grumman TBF Avenger, was just then entering the fleet—a few would actually operate from Midway in the upcoming battle. But the carriers would sail with the older aircraft. A strong fighter escort might provide some hope, but the Battle of the Coral Sea had revealed that the Americans had much to learn about keeping air groups together while outbound to an enemy target.

The *Hornet's* Torpedo Eight was skippered by Lieutenant Commander John C. Waldron, a lean, hatchet-faced South Dakotan, bronzed by long exposure to the tropical sun. At forty-one years old, he was one of the older flyboys in the carrier squadrons, but he kept himself in superb physical shape with vigorous daily calisthenics routines. Waldron often led his airmen in group exercises on the flight deck while at sea, to the amusement of the *Hornet's* crew. Many of Torpedo Eight's pilots were raw ensigns, barely out of flight school. When Ensign George Gay and his fellow newcomers joined the squadron shortly before the Battle of Midway, none had ever carried a torpedo on a plane before, let alone dropped one on a target. They were ludicrously unprepared, and they knew it. "Quite a few of us were a little bit skeptical and leery," Gay later said, "but we'd seen Doolittle and his boys, when they hadn't even seen a carrier before, and they took the B-25s off, [and] we figured by golly if they could do it, well we could too."

With so many inexperienced men in the squadron, and so little opportunity for training flights in the rushed prelude to the battle, Waldron conveyed as much knowledge as he could in daily classroom sessions. He chalked out diagrams on a blackboard, and then posed questions. "After asking a question," wrote Ensign Fred Mears, another of Torpedo Eight's rookies, "the skipper had a characteristic way of leering out of the corner of his eyes at the squadron, his head cocked, his mouth open in a silly, almost idiotic, fashion. Suddenly he would snap his mouth shut like a trout after a fly, straighten his head, and begin to stroke his chin, staring at them from under his bushy eyebrows and beseeching the answer." The aircrews discussed the finer points of target leads, angles of attack, fighter evasion tactics, antiaircraft defense, and how to escape an enemy task force after dropping a torpedo. Waldron invited them to play the devil's advocate, to probe for flaws in his reasoning. "Then," wrote Mears, "in a few masterful sentences he proves definitely that his theory is the only one which could be correct. This process keeps the pilots on the alert and rivets in their minds the point he is trying to get across."

Waldron took care to convey confidence, to assure his men that they were the best torpedo squadron in the fleet, and even to guarantee that the squadron would score hits on the Japanese carriers in the coming battle. But he also emphasized that they should arrange their personal affairs and write letters to their families, "just in case some of us don't get back."

Nimitz's orders to his task force commanders began famously: "In carrying out the tasks assigned . . . you will be governed by the principle of calculated risk, which you shall interpret to mean the avoidance of exposure to attack by superior enemy forces without good prospect of inflicting, as a result of such exposure, greater damage to the enemy." The orders included very specific information about the Japanese plan, and as officers throughout the fleet perused them, there was much speculation about the source of the intelligence. Some assumed that the Americans must have a "mole" in Japan. "That man of ours in Tokyo is worth every cent we pay him," remarked an *Enterprise* officer to Layton.

Late on the morning of May 28, Task Force 16 put to sea. The antisubmarine nets at the harbor entrance opened, and the long line of ships began filing down the "slot." The destroyers went first, then the cruisers, finally the *Enterprise* and *Hornet*. The gunners at Fort Weaver were practicing antiaircraft drill, and the angry black bursts hung in the air as the task force steamed past. Admiral Halsey watched the scene from his hospital window, as the ships passed one by one off Hospital Point. Mears recalled watching from the flight deck of the *Hornet* and feeling "amazed at the size of our force and at the way the cruisers and destroyers were boiling around the sea in all directions about us. The *Hornet* itself wheeled sharply once or twice, and the flat surface of the flight deck made a crazy angle with the horizon." When the planes flew out from Oahu, Mears noted that they were so numerous "the sky seemed to be filled with them."

The task force turned northwest, and on each ship an announcement was made to the crew. On the *Hornet*, a voice on the loudspeaker said only, "We are going out to intercept a Jap attack on Midway." The task forces would rendezvous at "Point LUCK," 32 north by 173 west, about 300 miles northeast of Nagumo's expected position at daylight on June 4. Spruance's message, as usual, eschewed any effort at memorable oratory; he stuck to the cold hard facts:

> An attack for the purpose of capturing Midway is expected. The attacking force may be composed of all combatant types, including four or five carriers plus transports and train vessels. If the presence of [Task Forces 16 and 17] remains unknown to the enemy, we should be able to make surprise flank attacks on the enemy carriers from a position northeast of Midway. Further operations will be based on the result of these attacks, damage inflicted by Midway forces, and information of enemy movements.

Almost as an afterthought, he added the obvious: "The successful conclusion of the operation now commencing will be of great value to our country."

Chapter Twelve

IN THE SECOND WEEK OF MAY, DURING THE FINAL, HARRIED PREPARATIONS
for the Midway offensive, the *Yamato* put into the naval base at Kure
to load provisions and undergo minor repairs. Shrugging off the risk of a
public scandal, Yamamoto invited Chiyoko Kawai, the famed geisha who
had become his surrogate wife, to take the train down from Tokyo. They
checked into a small inn in the city under false names. Returning to the
flagship four days later, the admiral wrote her: "I myself will devote all my
energy to fulfill my duty to my country to the very end—and then I want
us to abandon everything and escape from the world to be really alone
together." He closed with a few lines of verse:

> *Today too I ache for you,*
> *Calling your name*
> *Again and again*
> *And pressing kisses*
> *Upon your picture.*

Kure harbor was bustling with activity. Ships came and went; warships
embarked crates and casks from lighters; yellow tugs plied to and fro, trailing thick black smoke from their stacks. It seemed that the entire civil population of Kure, and perhaps all of coastal Japan, knew of the upcoming
operation. One officer was quizzed about it by his barber. "I personally felt
angry," recounted Ensign Takeshi Maeda of the *Kaga*, because senior naval
officers "talked about our secret plans for the upcoming Midway operation
to the prostitutes in the red-light district. Prior to our departure everyone

was talking about our Midway plans, so it wasn't a secretive mission like the Pearl Harbor attack . . . this was a bad omen." As the *Kaga* prepared to sail, women pressed against the fence at the entrance to the base, calling out to the men they knew and wishing them farewell.

On the 21st, major fleet units put to sea for two days of fleet maneuvers, and then returned to Hashirajima anchorage on May 25. Final details of the grand sortie were disseminated to the fleet. Tactical groups would depart independently, according to a meticulous timetable, from three different staging points—Hashirajima; Ominato harbor in northern Honshu; and Saipan, in the Marianas. Nagumo was forced to tell Yamamoto that *Kido Butai*, the carrier striking force, would not be prepared to sortie on May 26 as ordered. The crews were working at a breakneck pace to embark provisions and other supplies, but needed an extra day to complete the work. Yamamoto consented, but would not alter the operation's timetable—if the carriers had to leave a day late, so be it; they could make up the lost time by fast steaming. Commanders and staff officers gathered for a party and toasted the emperor with cups of hot sake.

Many in the fleet felt that they were being forced into a rushed, inflexible schedule. Maintenance and repairs were neglected; training exercises were cut short; the distribution of final orders was chaotic and slipshod. A destroyer captain assigned to escort the Midway invasion force later wrote: "Instinctively, I felt that something was wrong with this operation, and my heart was not buoyant." Flight training was badly needed, and not only for the recently commissioned aviators. In aerial torpedo exercises held on May 18, even the veteran Nakajima Type 97 aircrews turned in disgracefully bad results. Dive-bombing drills held in the western Inland Sea had to be drastically curtailed because of the time spent by the airmen in flying to and from the remote site. Aerial gunnery, formation flying, and carrier takeoff and landing exercises were similarly neglected for lack of time. "Since the carriers were undergoing repair and maintenance operations," Nagumo later observed in his post-battle report, "the only available ship for take-off and landing drills was the *Kaga*. She was kept busy from early morning to nightfall but even at that the young fliers barely were able to learn the rudiments of carrier landings. The more seasoned fliers were given about one chance each to make dusk landings."

On the morning of May 27, Nagumo's flagship *Akagi* raised a signal to her signal yard: "Sortie as scheduled!" The carriers and their screening vessels heaved their anchors out of the Hashirajima mud and steamed out toward the Bungo Strait. Crews of moored ships lined the rails and waved their caps in the air, and Ensign Maeda of the *Kaga* recalls being sent off by "military marching songs" blared from the loudspeakers. Anti-submarine seaplanes of the Kure Naval Air Corps circled protectively overhead, but despite several false alarms, no enemy submarines were sighted. "Through scattered clouds the sun shone brightly upon the calm blue sea," Fuchida wrote. "For several days the weather had been cloudy but hot in the western Inland Sea, and it was pleasant now to feel the gentle breeze which swept across *Akagi*'s flight deck." By noon, *Kido Butai* had emerged from Bungo Strait into the open ocean, and the *Akagi* signaled the destroyers and cruisers to assume their normal circular cruising disposition, spaced at intervals of 1,000 yards. The carriers sailed in two columns at the center of the ring.

Night passed uneventfully, and on the morning of the 28th, the sun revealed a clear blue sky. The carrier crews were relaxed and in good spirits. In port they had bent might and main to get their ships to sea, and now, in these tedious days of open-ocean cruising, they were grateful for the chance to catch their breath. Men sunned themselves, played cards, smoked, read, and wrote letters. They assembled on deck each afternoon to sing patriotic and sentimental songs at the top of their lungs. They ate better than usual, having recently laid fresh victuals into the galleys; by tradition, on the eve of an expected battle, they were served *shiruko* (red-bean soup with rice cake). The officers enjoyed other, more sumptuous delicacies such as broiled sea bream served in miso. *Kido Butai* churned through the gray waters of the North Pacific at 14 knots, the better to conserve fuel. Refueling from tankers continued en route, almost constantly: most ships in the force refueled at least twice during the passage. Search patrols were sent out from the cruisers and carriers; a combat air patrol orbited ahead throughout the long daylight hours. "White clouds drifted lazily across the sky," recalled Yeoman Mitsuharu Noda. "The thin smoke which poured out of the stacks hung in the air like summer clouds over a field in May."

On June 1, *Kido Butai* left the clear weather behind and sailed into a zone of heavy overcast, rain showers, and low-lying mists. By early evening, visibility had fallen to a few hundred feet. In such a fog, with a fleet of that size, there was a real and constant danger of collisions, and every ship posted extra lookouts to peer into the obsidian gloom. Searchlights cut through the gray murk, and fog buoys were trailed in the wakes of all ships to give following vessels a proximity warning. Nagumo deemed it safe to discontinue their anti-submarine zigzagging course, and the speed of the striking force was cut to 12 knots.

At dawn the next day, from the Plexiglas windows of *Akagi's* bridge, Nagumo and his officers gazed out at impenetrable whiteness in every direction, as if the ship were enclosed by four plaster walls. Even during intermittent periods of slightly better visibility, the nearest ships in the formation could be discerned only as ghostlike shapes. Operational plans called for a course change on June 2, but *Akagi* was to order the change using blinker lights, and the fog rendered that impossible. Nagumo was under a strict injunction to maintain radio silence. But he decided to transmit the order using a low-powered voice radio, which he hoped would not carry beyond a few miles. At ten-thirty that morning, *Akagi* broadcast the order to the task force: "At 1200 hours, change to course 100 degrees." As noon came, the task force turned and began its final approach toward Midway on a south-southeast heading.

The Japanese had no reliable recent intelligence on the whereabouts of the American carriers, or even on the state of American naval strength at Pearl Harbor. For that information, Yamamoto had counted on long-range reconnaissance flights by Kawanishi flying boats operating out of the Marshalls. But Nimitz had sent a destroyer and seaplane tender to prevent the Kawanishis from refueling at French Frigate Shoals, forcing Yamamoto to cancel those flights on May 31. Yamamoto's second source of intelligence was to have been a picket line of submarines, spread out between Oahu and Midway; but the two American task forces traversed that position before the Japanese submarines reached their assigned stations. Thus the Japanese had no clue that the American carriers were even north of the equator, let alone lying in ambush on Nagumo's eastern flank.

On June 3, more than 1,000 miles to the north of *Kido Butai*, the light carriers *Ryujo* and *Junyo* launched a predawn strike on Dutch Harbor. Though the defenders knew the raid was coming, and met the enemy planes with heavy antiaircraft fire, the bombers inflicted heavy damage on the port facilities, and killed about twenty-five men. Four days later, Japanese forces stormed the beaches of the remote fog-shrouded islands of Kiska and Attu against minimal resistance.

June 3 also marked the first direct encounter between American planes and the Japanese fleet converging on Midway. Rear Admiral Raizo Tanaka's

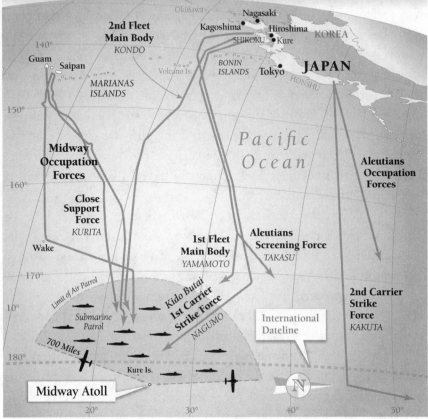

Japanese Naval Forces
Advance on Midway and Aleutians, May 24 – June 3, 1942

troop transportation group, approaching Midway from the southwest, had passed under the shadow of the atoll's far-ranging air search radius. Nine army B-17s under the command of Lieutenant Colonel Walter C. Sweeney took off from Midway at 12:40 p.m., and flew west to attack the group. Locating Tanaka's convoy at 4:23 p.m., they dropped their 600-pound bombs from between 8,000 and 12,000 feet. Six months of war had provided abundant evidence that high-altitude bombing of ships at sea was fruitless, and this case was no different. The Japanese crews watched the bombs fall from high overhead, and steered their ships to avoid them. All of Sweeney's bombs fell into the sea, some missing by more than half a mile. The Japanese destroyers returned fire with their antiaircraft guns, but they could not reach the altitude of Sweeney's planes with any degree of accuracy. Divested of their bombs, the B-17s turned home toward Midway.

The encounter served only to boost the morale of the Japanese. "We were well aware that we were advancing against a fully prepared enemy," wrote Lieutenant Commander Tameichi Hara, skipper of one of the destroyers, "but I was no longer ill at ease. The attempts thus far against our convoy had been furtive and feeble." A group of four American PBY seaplanes armed with torpedoes came upon Tanaka's group and attacked at 1:30 a.m. on the morning of the 4th. One torpedo struck an oil tanker, the *Akebono Maru*, killing a dozen sailors. But the oiler was able to continue east with her speed undiminished. The Japanese now knew that their presence had been revealed, but took comfort in the relative ineffectiveness of the American attacks.

At midday on the 3rd, *Kido Butai* raised speed to 24 knots. A strong combat air patrol circled overhead, as always, and additional Zeros were fueled and spotted for a quick launch in case of a sudden air attack. At first light on the 4th, the force altered its cruising formation for flight operations. The four carriers edged apart into a "box" pattern, each separated from the others by several miles. Extra lookouts were posted, and several false contacts were reported, one of which turned out to be a star.

Reconnaissance floatplanes were launched by catapult from the cruisers *Chikuma* and *Tone*. Though the force had sailed out of the heavy weather front that had dogged it for the past three days, those same murky conditions remained just to the northeast, and the search patterns would have to be flown directly into this zone of poor visibility. Intermittent squalls and cumulus overcast with ceilings of 1,000 to 3,000 feet would make it difficult for the scouts to see anything at all. It was conceivable that they would fly directly over an enemy fleet and fail to see it.

The plane crews had been roused from their bunks at 2:30 a.m., and toiled throughout the predawn hours to arm and fuel the attack planes for launch. Then they pushed the planes into the elevators and spotted them on the flight deck. This was accomplished before the first glow of dawn rose on the eastern horizon. When each machine had been tethered down to its assigned position, its wings were unfolded and locked into position. A crewman climbed into the cockpit to fire the engine, and tongues of blue flame flashed from the exhaust pipes. The engine was run steadily at 1,000 to 1,500 rpm, allowing it to warm; the mechanics watched and listened to confirm that it was turning smoothly. Then the throttle was pushed forward and the engine howled at near-maximum rpm. "The sound of engines alternately hummed and then rose to a whining roar," wrote Fuchida. "The flight deck was soon a hell of ear-shattering noise."

At 4:15 a.m., with the ships still in darkness, the aircrews were summoned from their ready rooms by the loudspeaker: "Airmen line up!" The aviators, bundled in their brown flight suits and helmets, emerged on the flight deck and gathered around the island, where they were briefed by their squadron leaders. Then they spread out among the maze of planes, climbed onto the wings, and slid down into their cockpits. The hooded deck lights at the center and margins of the decks provided a takeoff path in the darkness. On the flight deck of each carrier, the ship's radio antennae were lowered into the horizontal position to allow room for the sweep of the wings as the planes took off. It was a calm night, with an easy breeze from the southeast, and fine visibility over a moonlit sea.

The four carriers of *Kido Butai* turned into the wind, and Nagumo gave the order: "Launch the air attack force." Genda relayed the order via speaker tube, while the flagship's signal lamps began flashing the order to *Akagi's* three sisters. A stream of white vapor was released from a stack at the bow, an indicator of wind direction. An officer on the air platform waved a white flag; a figure standing forward on the flight deck swung a green signal lantern in a wide circle; the deck crewmen pulled away the wheel chocks; the lead pilot pushed his throttle forward and lifted his feet from the brakes. The first plane clattered down the teak decks and lifted into the air, red and green lights on its wingtips. It banked left and began the well-honed rendezvous routines that allowed the air groups of multiple carriers to coalesce into one large flight formation, a trick the Americans had not yet mastered. By 4:45 a.m. the entire force, 108 planes, was aloft—they wheeled around the fleet in a wide counterclockwise corkscrew pattern, and droned away to the southeast at 125 knots.

MIDWAY, A LOW-LYING RING OF SAND AND SCRUB, was armed to the teeth and ready to receive the enemy. Radar discovered the incoming strike at 5:53 a.m. The air-raid alarm rang out, though the atoll's defenders were already wide awake and at their stations. By 6:15 a.m., Midway had managed to get every serviceable aircraft aloft, so none could be caught on the ground. One of the search planes, a Catalina PBY piloted by Lieutenant William A. Chase, caught sight of the incoming armada, and transmitted his report at once, in plain language: "Many planes heading Midway bearing 320 degrees, distance 150."

As the Japanese planes rose over the northern horizon, the marine anti-aircraft gunners were ready and waiting at their gun emplacements, well concealed under camouflage netting. They sent up a wall of flak as the intruders came into range. Several Japanese bombers took heavy damage in the first minutes of the action and went into the sea trailing smoke and flame. The antiaircraft fire was so thick in volume, and so densely distributed around the circumference of the atoll, that it appeared to take the shape of a cylindrical wall. The *Hiryu*'s after-action report noted of these weapons: "the accuracy is excellent, and the anti-aircraft fire is intense."

The same was not true of Midway's fighter defenses. Marine Fighting Squadron 221 was equipped with twenty obsolete Brewster Buffalos, the same aircraft that had been massacred by the Zeros over Malaya. There were only four F4F Wildcats on the atoll. In an aerial melee, the Zeros destroyed virtually every one of Midway's fighter planes, while losing none. With no fighters left to oppose them, the carrier bombers lined up to make their attacking runs. They concentrated their efforts on the buildings, hangars, fuel drums, and ammunition pits, and inflicted heavy damage on the atoll's installations. Power and gas lines to Eastern Island were knocked out. The mess hall, hangars, and oil tanks were left as burning ruins. The Japanese airmen did little damage to the antiaircraft batteries, however, and they avoided the runways, as they would need them in serviceable condition after capturing the islands. Most of the men on the ground survived by taking cover in concrete dugouts and slit trenches. The antiaircraft batteries were almost unscathed, and Midway's air force, with the exception of its ill-fated fighters, was still intact.

The attackers had lost eleven aircraft in the action, and more than twice that number damaged; twenty aviators had been killed or downed in the sea, and several more were injured. Those losses were not devastating, but if the Japanese were ordered to make several more strikes on the atoll, the cumulative losses would multiply. Once rid of their bombs, the Japanese planes rendezvoused west of the islands. At 6:45 a.m., they began their return flights to the carriers, joining up in flight formation as best they could. Lieutenant Joichi Tomonaga, the leader of the attack force, radioed back to Nagumo advising that a second strike was needed.

Akagi began cycling her combat air patrol—landing the defending Zeros for refueling, and launching new ones to take their place. This was a housekeeping task that Nagumo hoped to complete before Tomonaga's reappearance, so that the flight decks would be clear to recover the returning airplanes.

A few minutes after 7 a.m., the first of several small, assorted groups of American airplanes from Midway arrived to attack the Japanese carriers. All of these attacks would be bravely carried out but ineffective, scoring no hits on any Japanese ship. But the continuous pressure of new air attacks, however ineffectual, put the Japanese off balance, and began to deform Yamamoto's painstaking plans. These first air attacks on *Kido Butai* limited Nagumo's flexibility to react to the morning's various twists of fate, and started a chain of events that would climax, three hours later, in the most decisive five minutes of the entire Pacific War.

The first group came in low, from the south, directly onto the Japanese carriers' bows—six new navy TBF Avenger torpedo planes, flying into combat for the first time ever, and four army B-26 medium bombers from Midway. Both flights were armed with torpedoes. On the Japanese ships, trumpets were blown to alert the crews. A swarm of about thirty Zeros came down to intercept, and battered the intruders with their 20mm guns. All but one of the Avengers was sent spinning into the sea. Ensign Albert K. Earnest, the sole survivor, said of the Zeros: "There were so many of them they were getting into each other's way. You couldn't help but be impressed by how maneuverable they were." The B-26s fared only slightly better, because they were brawny enough to absorb more punishment. Three of the six managed to launch their torpedoes, but made poor drops—too far from their targets, with inadequate lead—and the Japanese carriers easily maneuvered to evade the incoming tracks. One of the shot-up B-26s seemed to bore directly in for the *Akagi's* bridge—the pilot apparently knew his plane was finished, and tried to take some of the enemy's reigning brass with him to the afterlife. Nagumo and his staff, astounded by the suicidal blitz, ducked for cover. But at the last second before impact, the big twin-engine bomber veered off, missing the flagship narrowly, and splashed into the sea.

Yamamoto had ordered that a reserve strike be kept on board in case enemy aircraft carriers should suddenly materialize on *Kido Butai's* exposed port flank, but Nagumo had received no sighting reports and expected none. His reconnaissance planes had been aloft for nearly three hours. Radiating north and east like the spokes of a wheel, they had reached the end of their outbound flights, turned on their dog legs, and most were now due to turn back toward home. It was theoretically possible, but not likely, that they would find enemy ships while flying their return legs. Nagumo, therefore, had no reason to believe American ships were in the vicinity. The near miss of the dying B-26, however, seems to have aroused him to the need to put Midway's air force out of action. The Nakajima Type 97 ("Kate") torpedo planes of the second strike were armed with torpedoes for anti-ship operations. If they were to attack Midway instead, they must be rearmed with Type 80 land bombs. At 7:15 a.m., Nagumo gave the order: "Planes in second attack wave stand by to carry out attack today. Reequip yourselves with bombs."

On the hangar decks, the hard-run armorers again sprang into action, and started the intricate process of removing torpedoes and attaching bombs to the bellies of the aircraft. The task would require at least an hour and a half.

No sooner was the order given than one of the search planes reported a contact. The cruiser *Tone*'s No. 4 floatplane, which had flown a heading of 100 degrees from the Japanese force, radioed at 7:28 a.m.: "Sighted what appears to be the enemy composed of 10 (ships), bearing 10 degrees, distance 240 miles from Midway, on course 150 degrees, speed 20 knots." Petty officer Hiroshi Amari, the pilot, had not mentioned carriers, and it was possible he had spotted a surface force which could pose no immediate threat at that range. On the other hand, the possibility that *Tone* No. 4 had stumbled across the outer screening vessels of a carrier task force could not be lightly dismissed. At 7:58, Amari reported that the enemy ships had changed course to 80 degrees, and Nagumo shot back: "Advise ship types."

This initial sighting report was too vague to be of much use to Nagumo, and it was very possibly mistaken. What did "ten enemy surface units" mean? Were there any enemy carriers? The reported location was off Amari's assigned search line. Six months of naval war, and the Battle of the Coral Sea in particular, had given ample reason to distrust initial contact reports. Nonetheless, Nagumo ordered the plane crews to cease rearming the reserve strike. If subsequent contact reports persuaded him that an American car-

USS *Lexington* (CV-2) during the Battle of the Coral Sea, May 1942, seen from the *Yorktown*. *Official U.S. Navy photograph.*

Battle of the Coral Sea: the end of the *Lexington*. Shortly after the last of her crew abandoned ship, an explosion blew an aircraft over her side. *Official U.S. Navy photograph.*

Battle of Midway, June 1942. Torpedo bombers prepare to launch from the deck of the USS *Enterprise*. *Official U.S. Navy Photograph.*

Battle of Midway. A Grumman F4F Wildcat takes off from *Yorktown* on the morning of June 4, 1942. *Official U.S. Navy Photograph.*

Battle of Midway. Japanese aircraft carrier *Hiryu* maneuvers to dodge bombs dropped by USAF B-17s, morning of June 4, 1942. *U.S. Air Force photograph.*

Douglas TBD Devastator torpedo plane. By 1942, this aircraft was disastrously obsolete. *Official U.S. Navy photograph.*

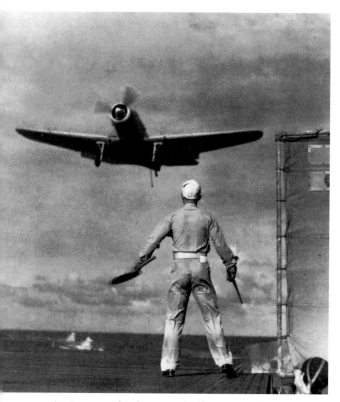

An *Enterprise* landing signal officer (LSO) guides a TBD Devastator in for landing. *Official U.S. Navy photograph.*

Air attack on the *Yorktown*, afternoon of June 4, 1942. Japanese Type 97 torpedo planes fly past the ship after launching their torpedoes. *Official U.S. Navy photograph.*

Yorktown, struck by bombs and torpedoes, lists heavily to port. Late afternoon of June 4, 1942. *Official U.S. Navy photograph.*

SBD Dauntless dive-bombers from *Hornet* prepare to attack the Japanese cruiser *Mikuma*, June 6, 1942. *Official U.S. Navy photograph.*

A generation bred to take the hardships of war in stride. Children at a rehabilitation clinic in Arkansas, c. mid-1930s. *FDR Library.*

rier was within striking range, he needed those planes armed with anti-ship ordnance. So Nagumo hesitated, and awaited further information.

To suspend rearming was one thing; to reverse the rearming and rush the reserve strike up the elevators to be launched against the strange ships in the northeast was another. Nagumo did not choose the latter, more aggressive course of action, and for that he has been pilloried by generations of historians on both sides of the Pacific. Certainly, with the clarity offered by hindsight, Nagumo's best option was to launch an immediate strike, with whatever airplanes he had on hand—even if that meant sending torpedo planes armed with land bombs, and even if Tomonaga's planes returning from Midway found the flight decks congested, and were forced to ditch at sea. But at 7:45 on the morning of June 4, Nagumo did not have the benefit of hindsight. He had to act on the basis of what he knew. He knew that Midway's airfields posed a threat to *Kido Butai*, and would continue to pose a threat until knocked out of action. He knew that Tomonaga's force was inbound, with fuel tanks running dry, and needed clear flight decks on which to land. He knew, as of 7:40 a.m., that the Japanese fleet had a mere fourteen fighters flying combat air patrol, down from thirty-one earlier that morning—the ineffectual but troublesome attack of the Avengers and Marauders had forced the Zeros to consume fuel and expend ammunition, requiring them to land and replenish. On the other side of the ledger, he had a vague contact report from *Tone* No. 4, inconclusive as to ship types and very possibly mistaken. Less than a month earlier, in the Coral Sea, another Japanese carrier task force commander had been misled by a flawed contact report and sent a huge airstrike in the wrong direction. Based on what he knew and did not know, Nagumo could be forgiven for electing to await more definite information before deranging his entire order of operations.

Nagumo's scope of action was sharply limited by time and circumstances. His four flight decks were scarce resources, much in demand, and none could launch and recover airplanes simultaneously. The flight elevators were a bottleneck; the time required to rearm the reserve strike on the hangar decks was a bottleneck; the need to cycle the CAP was a bottleneck. Waves of attacking enemy planes had the effect of shrinking those bottlenecks, because they forced the Japanese carriers to maneuver evasively, closing their decks to flight operations, and because they forced the protecting Zeros to return to the carriers more frequently for fuel and ammunition.

Nagumo's entire naval career had led him to this point—his lofty post as commander of *Kido Butai*, the tepid support he had received from Yamamoto, the criticism he had absorbed for his supposed failures at Pearl Harbor; the delicate balance between the need to attack and the need to preserve his own force; his conviction that further airstrikes on Midway were needed to shut down that atoll's air attacks on the Japanese fleet. Nagumo had many high-stakes decisions to make, and very little time to make them. He and his officers were stationed on *Akagi's* cramped bridge, pressed cheek to jowl around a small chart table, and hemmed in by lockers and pedestal-mounted binoculars. Even when the flagship and her sisters were not maneuvering violently to avoid incoming enemy planes, there was a flood of new sightings of enemy aircraft and periscopes, some accurate and others bogus. In such an environment, without peace or privacy, the admiral must have found it difficult to hear himself think.

At 7:53 a.m., Japanese lookouts spotted a group of sixteen incoming SBD Dauntless dive-bombers. This was a Midway-based U.S. Marine squadron, VMSB-241, led by Major Lofton R. Henderson. Most of Henderson's marine flyboys had not seen the inside of an SBD until a week prior to the battle, and none had trained in dive-bombing tactics, so Henderson brought them down from 9,500 feet in a shallow dive. They pressed in bravely, flying through heavy flak, but the Zeros swooped in behind them and cut them up badly, splashing Henderson's plane first. Several bombs narrowly missed the *Hiryu*, which was obscured by a curtain of high water spouts as the bombs detonated on impact with the sea, but she suffered no damage. The Zeros gave chase to the retreating Dauntlesses and shot down several more.

Just as the surviving marine SBDs left the scene, fourteen B-17s under Lieutenant Colonel Sweeney soared high overhead at 20,000 feet. They had been vectored out to the west to bomb the same transports they had attacked the previous day, but were subsequently instructed to turn east and attack *Kido Butai*. Lieutenant Commander Iyozo Fujita, a Zero pilot, began a steep climb to intercept the high-flying army bombers, but discovered that "their flying altitude was much too high for me." Nor could Japanese anti-aircraft fire reach that lofty height with any degree of success. The B-17s, unmolested, dropped their sticks of bombs on the carrier *Soryu*. Their aim was apparently much better than it had been the previous day, because several fell surprisingly close to the ship, though none hit. "Geysers of water engulfed the *Soryu*," recalled Lieutenant Hiroshi Suzuki of the *Akagi*, "and since I couldn't see the carrier, I thought it must have been hit very badly. However, after the water went back down it looked like the ship was okay."

As the hapless B-17s removed themselves from the picture, eleven SB2U Vindicator scout bombers of VMSB-241 attacked the battleship *Haruna*. No hits were scored, and three of the American planes were shot down. To add to the excitement, at 8:24 a.m., the periscope of an American submarine, the *Nautilus*, peeked up through the waves in the heart of the Japanese fleet. She was sighted by lookouts on several Japanese ships, and the alarm went out in plain language on the short-range radio. A destroyer moved in to depth-charge her, and a Zero swooped low to strafe her. She crash-dived.

Thus far, the Japanese had brushed off every successive wave of attacking planes with seeming ease, and no American bomb or torpedo had so much as scratched any ship in the carrier force. "Frankly," Fuchida said, "it was my judgment that the enemy fliers were not displaying a very high level of ability, and this evaluation was shared by Admiral Nagumo and his staff. It was our general conclusion that we had little to fear from the enemy's offensive tactics." On the other hand, said Takeshi Maeda of the *Kaga*, "We were very impressed by the enemy aviators' sheer determination to fight, as they kept on coming to attack us." No American squadron had yet arrived with a fighter escort. What if one did? Moreover, the Japanese had not yet seen a proper dive-bombing attack, the most dangerous anti-ship tactic in the American arsenal—but such an attack could arrive at any time. Maeda also realized that the relentless pressure was hindering flight operations, and would make it difficult to get the reserve strike off before Tomonaga's return. He said: "To me things looked pretty dim."

Even in the midst of these aerial melees, the Japanese carriers had to cycle the CAP, so as to keep their air defenders fueled up and freshly armed. *Kaga* managed to land some of her planes right as the B-17 attack was beginning, though it required her to hold course into the wind. The first planes of Tomonaga's force began arriving while American planes were still in the area and the carriers were still making evasive turns. They could do nothing but circle at low altitude and wait for the American attacks to disperse. None of the returning planes could stay aloft for long, as all were low on fuel—some were damaged, and some of the aircrews were injured. To allow them to land safely, the carriers would have to steam into the wind for at least fifteen minutes; another thirty minutes would be needed to move the aircraft down to the hangar decks.

Such was the state of play at 8:20 a.m., when *Tone* No. 4 radioed: "The enemy is accompanied by what appears to be a carrier in a position to the rear of the others." The report must have made Nagumo's blood freeze. In the first six months of the war, *Kido Butai* had always dictated events, forced the enemy to react, inflicted heavy punishment, and then withdrawn before any real danger could materialize. There had been tense moments, as in the Indian Ocean, but this was an entirely new and perilous set of circumstances. For the first time in its renowned career, *Kido Butai* was compelled to react to events dictated by a foe.

The cardinal rule of carrier warfare, the rule that ruled over all others, was to strike first. But Tomonaga's planes had been orbiting patiently, their engines running on fumes, and if they were not recovered immediately, they would go into the sea. Japanese carrier doctrine did not allow for one group of airplanes to be warmed up forward of the crash barriers while another group was recovered. Nagumo was now forced to choose between two disagreeable alternatives. The first was to order Tomonaga's entire strike to make a water landing (ditch their planes in the sea and hope to be rescued), in which case the reserve strike might have been ready to launch by about 9:15 a.m. But that would involve the certain loss of all orbiting planes, and the probable death of some portion of the aircrews. Nagumo chose his second option: to recover the morning strike and move them to the hangar decks, in which case the reserve strike would be ready to launch against the American fleet shortly after 10 a.m. With a bit of luck, *Kido Butai* would be left in relative peace for the next hour and a half.

Below, in the hangar decks, the rearming of the reserve strike proceeded. When the exhausted mechanics received Nagumo's order to switch the ordnance back to anti-ship types, maintenance petty officer Kaname Shimoyama recalled, "There was utter confusion on *Akagi*. . . . Inside our hangar there was very little room, and it was very hard to do this job. Our torpedoes also were very heavy and were manually loaded on our aircraft. In general, there were two groups of men; one group worked on the torpedoes, while the other group had the specific job of loading the torpedoes on the aircraft. When I looked at all this confusion, even though I was a low-ranking person, I thought, is it really wise to be doing this?" According to Lieutenant Suzuki, also on the *Akagi*, "It was very difficult to do this job while our ships were under attack, and there was a lot of noise around us." Ensign Maeda recalled that their work was interrupted by the steep heeling of the deck while the *Kaga* was under air attack. Loading torpedoes onto planes was intricate work, and demanded to be done with care, but a voice on the loudspeaker ordered: "Speed up the loading of the torpedoes!" In the rush to complete the job, bombs removed from the airplanes were stored in racks on the hangar deck, rather than lowered back into the magazine on hoists. That oversight would pose a mortal hazard if the ship should be hit by an untimely enemy airstrike.

At 8:45 a.m., *Tone* No. 4 radioed a new contact: "Sight what appears to be two additional enemy cruisers in position bearing 8 degrees, distance 250 miles from Midway." Amari's plane was now emerging over the edges of the second American carrier group, Task Force 16. Though Nagumo did not immediately realize it, these fragmentary reports were pointing to the presence of two separate enemy carrier task forces, both within striking range, offering the specter of a large and coordinated air attack on the Japanese flattops. Though his little floatplane was running low on fuel, Amari was ordered to remain on station above the American fleet and gather additional information about its composition. He was to turn on his radio transmitter and leave it on, so that *Kido Butai*'s radio receivers could use it for direction finding. This left *Tone* No. 4 vulnerable to interception by American planes, but the survival of one cruiser floatplane was not a priority in the big scheme.

Amari did as he was told. At 8:55 a.m., he radioed another update. He had sighted ten American torpedo bombers on a heading that would take them directly to the Japanese fleet.

FOR THE AMERICAN TASK FORCES, pushing north from Oahu through rough seas and biting winds, the first three days of June had brought cold, wet air and a gray, dirty sky. Throughout the long hours of daylight, the ships zigzagged prodigiously, a measure against enemy submarines. They steamed at 20 knots, rising and plunging through white-flecked chop, heeling sharply as they turned in unison every few miles. On Wednesday, June 3, the word was passed that Japanese carrier planes had attacked Dutch Harbor in the Aleutians. Admiral Spruance's dispatch to Task Force 16 had forecast that the battle would pit "four or five" enemy carriers against the *Enterprise*, *Hornet*, and *Yorktown*. Robert Casey, a passenger on one of the task force's faithful cruisers, did not like the odds. "I knew our limitations a couple of days ago," he confided in his journal, "but it didn't look then as if we should be called upon to monkey with more than three carriers. Our present position is what you might call interesting but unpromising."

That night, on the *Hornet*, the aviators of Torpedo Squadron Eight filed into their ready room and sat for Lieutenant Commander Waldron's final briefing. "The approaching battle will be the biggest of the war and may well be the turning point also," he told them. "It is to be known as the Battle of Midway. It will be a historical and, I hope, a glorious event." Waldron projected an air of relaxed confidence, but Ensign Mears detected an undertone of cold realism. The skipper knew that his squadron was unseasoned and undertrained, and would fly into battle in slow, outdated airplanes. In all likelihood, they would arrive over the enemy fleet without a fighter escort, leaving them at the mercy of a swarm of deadly Zeros. Waldron's closing speech sounded unnervingly like a valediction. "We have had a very short time to train," he said, "and we have worked under the most severe difficulties. But we have truly done the best humanly possible. I actually believe that under these conditions, we are the best in the world. My greatest hope is that we encounter a favorable tactical situation, but if we don't and worse comes to worst, I want each one of us to do his utmost to destroy our enemies. If there is only one plane left to make a final run-in, I want that man to go in and get a hit. May God be with us all. Good luck, happy landings, and give 'em hell."

Waldron urged them all to get a good night of sleep, but few aviators of any American squadron slept soundly that night. Ensign Gay recalled feeling "a little bit nervous, kind of like before a football game." Warrant Officer Tom Cheek, one of the *Yorktown*'s fighter pilots, lay awake in his bunk and listened to the "faint vibration of machinery through the hull" and the "swish and hissing surge of water past the skin of the ship." Clayton Fisher, dive-bomber pilot on the *Hornet*, wrote letters to his wife and mother before turning in, privately reflecting that his "odds of survival the next morning were minimal, even if we achieved our planned surprise attack on the Japanese carriers with all their experienced air groups."

The flyboys were shaken awake and sent to flight quarters in the small hours of the morning. Reveille for the torpedo aircrews was at 3 a.m. They pulled on their flight suits and filed down to the mess hall for coffee and breakfast. On the *Yorktown* they were served steak and eggs, much better than the usual fare, and one torpedo airman was overheard joking that it was a "feast for condemned men." After eating they drifted back to their ready rooms, where the flight rosters were "grease-penciled on the Plexiglas schedule board." Each aviator worked on his own navigational plotting board, and entered new data forwarded from AirPlot by teleprinter. He constantly checked and rechecked the position, course, and speed of the enemy fleet and of his own ship. He added corrections for the strength and direction of the wind, and for the magnetic deviations on his compass readings. He reckoned flight times and fuel consumption, and plotted his return course to "Point Option," where he was to find his carrier at the end of his flight.

Hours passed. New data churned out of the teleprinter, including a report of the PBY attack on the troop transportation group southwest of Midway. Clarence Dickinson, executive officer of *Enterprise*'s Scouting Six, recalled that the mood of his fellow aviators varied widely as they prepared to fly into battle: "Some were quiet, replying briefly, even curtly to any questions. Others were chattering. A few behaved, and with no pretense, as if this were just another day at sea." Some dozed in their comfortable leather reclining chairs, while their colleagues sipped coffee and tinkered with their navigational solutions. The waiting seemed endless, and tension rose. "Five o'clock. Six o'clock. Seven o'clock," wrote Dickinson. "Never as during those three hours had the men in those seven rows of chairs been so quiet. Yet the confidence was something one could feel. The squadron believed that when the carriers were found our group was good enough to put them on ice."

Before first light, the F4Fs of the combat air patrols took off, and ten scout bombers were sent off the *Yorktown* to fly search patterns to the north. The main airstrike was kept on deck, however—Fletcher had decided to close the distance on the enemy, and wait for a definite sighting report before sending the attack planes on their way. At 5:45 a.m., the task forces received word that a Midway-based PBY had sighted a small armada of Japanese planes winging in toward Midway from the northeast. "From that moment until they climbed into their cockpits," Mears wrote of Torpedo Eight, "the pilots gobbled every sentence off the teletype." They were on tenterhooks, awaiting a sighting report pinpointing the location of the Japanese carriers. Finally the order came, blared through the *Enterprise* and *Hornet*'s loudspeakers: "Pilots, man your planes!"

The morning was fair, with fresh, cool air and a beautiful blue sky dotted with small, fleecy clouds. Visibility was superb.

Task Force 16 turned southeast into the soft morning breeze and poured on speed to get wind across the deck. The aircrews filed out of their ready rooms in their flight suits—hands gloved, goggles pushed up on their foreheads, parachutes bouncing on their rumps—and made their way through the maze of close-parked gray-blue airplanes, each to his assigned "deck spot." The *Enterprise* plane-pushers had spotted ten F4Fs to fly CAP, and twenty-two SBD dive-bombers to sortie against the enemy. The Wildcat engines were fired with explosive cartridges rammed into the starting system by a mechanic. The pilot hit the starter switch and the cartridge fired, bringing the big Pratt & Whitney radial engine to life. It was allowed to idle for several minutes at 1,000 rpm, warming itself. The pilots put on their oxygen masks and taxied forward in obedience to a hooded figure on deck. Upon receiving the signal for "wind up," each fighter pilot pushed his throttle forward to the limit while holding foot pressure on the brakes to keep the plane rooted to its spot. A haze of blue exhaust fumes wafted toward the stern. A deck officer lowered a flag and the pilot released the brakes: the takeoff run began with a lurch and the plane accelerated toward the bow, its wheels rattling noisily along the teak planks. Its nose lifted, then its tail, and it was airborne.

The screening cruisers and destroyers turned with the carriers and matched their speed, knifing into the oncoming waves, plunging and rolling, dropping their rails into the foam, kicking up spray at their sterns. The intersecting wakes of the fleet left intricate patterns on the sea. "It would seem that the carriers are sending up all they've got," wrote Casey, as he watched from the deck of a nearby cruiser. "The sky over toward the starboard horizon is filling up with little black crosses. . . . It's all spectacular and beginning to be thrilling. Few men, after all, have had a chance to look upon a spectacle like this. In the nature of things, few will look on anything like it again."

The *Enterprise* dive-bombers got aloft quickly, but the carrier's plane-pushers were inexplicably slow to spot the next deckload, which would include the torpedo planes and ten Wildcats to fly with the outbound strike as a fighter escort. During each minute of the ensuing delay, the orbiting SBDs were burning precious fuel and progressively shrinking their flight radius. Meanwhile, the *Enterprise* radio shack intercepted *Tone* No. 4's message to the Japanese fleet, revealing that the enemy was probably now aware of the presence of the American task forces. Spruance wisely chose to throw doctrine to the wind, and send the SBDs off without waiting for the rest of the strike to get aloft. The carrier signaled Lieutenant Commander Clarence "Mac" McClusky, Jr., the air group leader, by blinker light: "Proceed on mission assigned."

The dive-bombers coalesced into a single large formation—Bombing Six and Scouting Six, thirty-three planes in all—and set out on heading 231 degrees, where McClusky expected to find the enemy at distance of 142 miles. They flew in stepped-down, wedge-shaped sections of three planes each, with the sections stacked in a single integrated "Vee-of-vees" formation. Being dive-bombers, they climbed and climbed until they reached their cruising altitude, with the highest planes in the formation at 20,000 feet. "The visibility was excellent that day, as good as I have ever experienced," wrote Lieutenant Dickinson. "Except for big, fleecy clouds there was nothing to mar it. We saw Midway Island while we were a hundred miles away. As we were flying almost four miles high there was a marvelous breadth of ocean within our view, and it was blue, as blue as a dye of indigo."

The *Hornet's* launch went more smoothly, and the entire air group, under the command of Commander Stanhope C. Ring, was aloft by about 7:40 a.m. Traditional accounts held that Ring led the *Hornet's* fifty-nine-plane strike group away on a heading of 240 degrees, the base course of the task force. But a convincing body of evidence suggests that he flew a heading of 265 degrees, almost due west—a course that would take the *Hornet's* strike far north of the last reported position of the Japanese fleet. The issue remains controversial, and perhaps the truth will never be known. However, it is irrefutable that only one of the *Hornet's* squadrons managed to find the enemy that day—and that squadron, Torpedo Eight, was annihilated. No battle report was filed by Ring, in violation of standing regulations. The omission was likely deliberate; Ring did not want to admit he had flown so far north of the last reported position of the enemy fleet.

Earlier that morning, *Yorktown* had parted ways with her two sisters to recover her returning scouts at Point Option, some distance to the northeast. The diversion took her out of striking range of the enemy, and she had to steam southwest at 25 knots to rejoin Task Force 16. As a result, Fletcher did not begin launching his planes until 8:38 a.m., when the *Enterprise* and *Hornet* strikes were well on their way. *Yorktown* launched thirty-five aircraft, including six fighters, seventeen dive-bombers, and twelve torpedo planes. The SBDs of Bombing Three launched first, followed by the Devastators, which needed a full deck run to lift their heavy Mark 13 torpedoes into the air. The torpedo planes had orders to continue immediately on their outbound course toward the enemy, followed by the SBDs, and at last the fighters. The launch went smoothly, and all her planes were in the air by a few minutes after nine. The *Yorktown* air group was ordered to fly a course of 240 degrees to a distance of 150 miles. If they had not located the enemy, they were to turn north and fly the reciprocal of *Kido Butai's* known inbound course toward Midway. If all went well, the faster SBDs and fighters would overtake the torpedo planes and perhaps even arrive over the enemy ships simultaneously, allowing for a coordinated attack.

The American strike, for better or worse, was airborne. By contrast with the Japanese carrier operations of that morning, it had been a chaotic and discombobulated process. Lieutenant Tomonaga's 108-plane Midway attack force had required only fifteen minutes to rise en masse from the four flight decks of *Kido Butai*, and once aloft they had rendezvoused quickly and flown toward Midway in one huge, integrated formation. In June 1942, such a feat was simply beyond American capabilities. The *Hornet* and *Enterprise* had required a full hour to get their strikes in the air. Once aloft, they did not attempt to rendezvous; they did not even fly off in the same direction. Each air group took a different course according to their leaders' independent and sharply varying navigation solutions. To confuse the picture further, none of the outbound groups managed to stay together. Many of the American planes would fail to find the enemy at all, and others would arrive over the Japanese fleet in small, splintered formations, rendering them vulnerable to the concentrated attention of the Zeros and the enemy antiaircraft gunners.

For all of that, the American strike was in the air and on its way to the enemy. The enemy had not yet replied. As it would turn out, that single fact mattered more than any other.

THE *HORNET'S* DAUNTLESSES began a long slow climb to altitude, straining to lift the weight of their 1,000-pound and 500-pound bombs. The SBD aircrews, wearing lightweight summer flight suits, shivered as the temperature in their cockpits dropped. Ice accumulated in their oxygen masks. The fifteen Devastators of Waldron's Torpedo Eight cruised far below, at 1,500 feet—they did not have the fuel to make the climb while carrying their even heavier Mark 13 torpedoes, and at any rate they would attack the enemy fleet at low altitude. The entire air group had left the *Hornet* on an initial course of 265 degrees, but Waldron had disagreed with Ring's navigational solutions, and shortly after departing the carrier he broke radio silence to urge Ring to turn south on heading 240 degrees. Ring either refused the request or did not copy the transmission, and Waldron banked to port to follow his own nose to the enemy fleet. His squadron turned with him. They flew in formation for about 100 miles. Waldron signaled the squadron to spread out in a scouting line, to increase their chances of sighting the enemy fleet. At about 9:15 a.m., several of the pilots saw black smudges against the sky on the horizon. In a few seconds, the gray figures of Japanese ships came into distant view. Waldron altered course and closed the Japanese fleet in a shallow glide.

Ensign Gay recalled that Waldron had urged his men, before they climbed into their cockpits that morning, "not to worry about our navigation but to follow him as he knew where he was going. And it turned out just exactly that way. He went just as straight to the Jap Fleet as if he'd had a string tied to them."

To the Japanese lookouts, the squadron first appeared as a constellation of black specks, low on the northeast horizon, sunlight occasionally glinting off their wings. Their low altitude gave them away as torpedo planes. According to Fuchida, the mood among his shipmates darkened—though the Japanese fleet had thus far brushed off a series of attacks by many different kinds of planes, they had been lucky, and their luck could not last forever. But the carriers had just completed their recovery of the Midway strike, so they were free to maneuver evasively. They turned away from the sluggish TBDs, thus lengthening the time and distance the attackers would have to fly. The Zeros closed in from overhead, on all sides, executing wingovers and half-loops to line up their killing shots on the incoming American planes.

Waldron had demonstrated temerity and skill in leading his squadron directly to the Japanese fleet, when Ring had taken the rest of the *Hornet*'s air group on a fool's errand to the northwest. But Torpedo Eight now found itself in dire circumstances. Obsolete planes flown by unprepared pilots were approaching a powerful enemy fleet, in clear visibility, with no fighter escort and no dive-bombing attack to divert the attention of a swarm of superbly handled Zeros. Inevitably, Torpedo Eight's attack has drawn comparisons to the Charge of the Light Brigade in the Crimean War, described in Alfred,

Lord Tennyson's famous poem. Both would be celebrated as exhibitions of supreme valor against desperate odds. Both were tactically rash, a waste of young lives to no good purpose, and both would be blamed on inept decisions up the chain of command. ("Was there a man dismay'd? / Not tho' the soldier knew / Some one had blunder'd.") Waldron's parting words in the Hornet's ready room the previous evening were still fresh in Ensign Gay's mind: "My greatest hope is that we encounter a favorable tactical situation, but if we don't and worse comes to worst, I want each one of us to do his utmost to destroy our enemies. If there is only one plane left to make a final run-in, I want that man to go in and get a hit." Worse had most definitely come to worst, but like Tennyson's light cavalrymen, it was "Their's not to make reply, / Their's not to reason why, / Their's but to do and die."

The Zeros fired well-aimed salvos with their 20mm cannon, punching holes in the cockpit canopies, fuselages, and wings of the underpowered Devastators. One by one they caught fire, broke in pieces, blew up, or cartwheeled into the sea. "The Zeros that day just caught us off balance," Ensign Gay later said in his debriefing. "We were at a disadvantage all around." Waldron's plane was struck in the fuel tank and burst into flames. Gay glimpsed the skipper as he stood up in his cockpit and tried to climb out, but there was not enough time, and his plane tumbled into the sea. Gay's plane was hit several times, and Gay himself was struck in the arm by machine-gun fire, but he somehow survived the approach long enough to fly into range of the antiaircraft fire, and the Zeros peeled off. On Akagi's flight deck, Fuchida recalled, "all attention was fixed on the dramatic scene unfolding before us, and there was wild cheering and whistling as the raiders went down one after another."

Gay bore in on the Soryu, launched his torpedo from 800 yards, and kept his aircraft headed right toward the fantail of the big carrier, into the teeth of heavy antiaircraft fire. The tracer lines reached up and past him, but his aircraft, he believed, was not hit. He cursed his feeble .30-caliber machine gun—a "pea shooter"—then pulled up and over the ship, narrowly missing the superstructure. He later recounted that as he flashed past the bridge, he "could see the little Jap captain up there, jumping up and down, raising Hell." He dropped down on the other side of the ship and flew low, hoping to beat a lucky retreat, but another group of Zeros pounced on him and "shot my rudder control and ailerons out and I pancaked into the ocean. The hood slammed shut, I couldn't keep the right wing up. It had hit the water first and snapped the plane in, and bent it all up and broke it up and the hood slammed shut and it was in the sprained fuselage. I couldn't hardly get it open. That's when I got scared. I was afraid I was going to drown in the plane." Gay managed to clamber out onto his TBD's one remaining wing, clutching his rubber life raft and seat cushion. He tried but could not pull his rear gunner out of the backseat before the sea closed over his airplane; then he dropped into the water and concealed himself as best he could behind his seat cushion.

Soon the eagle-eyed Japanese lookouts spotted another group of black specks in the south, on *Kido Butai*'s port beam. This was Torpedo Six of the *Enterprise*, led by Lieutenant Commander Eugene Lindsey. As it flew into the outer circumference of the Japanese fleet, the squadron separated into two divisions and advanced on the bows of the nearest flattop, the *Kaga*. The four carriers turned in unison to starboard (north), presenting their sterns to the slow-approaching Devastators.

"A stern chase is a long chase" was a centuries-old naval adage, and in this case it held—for although the slowest airplane could outpace the fastest ship, these particular airplanes were only about four times faster than the Japanese carriers. To execute an "anvil" attack on the fleeing flattops, it was not enough merely to catch them; the torpedo planes had to overtake their prey, to loop around them, and approach on both bows simultaneously. This stern chase would be a long and deadly chase, but the obsolete torpedo planes of VT-6 would have it easier than their colleagues of VT-8, for two reasons. First, the Zeros had bunched up on the northern perimeter of the fleet, where VT-8 had attacked, and had to fly about thirty miles south to intercept VT-6; and second, some of the Japanese fighters had apparently expended most of their 20mm ammunition on Waldron's group, and would have to shoot more deliberately in this round. Even so, few of the hapless Devastators of VT-6 would survive the attack. Two aircraft of the division sent to the *Kaga*'s starboard bow managed to release their torpedoes, but the carrier easily dodged the incoming tracks. The second division, led by Lindsey himself, flew into a group of nine Zeros that swooped down and shot down four planes, including Lindsey's. Five VT-6 planes survived the retreat; four landed safely on the *Enterprise*, while one ditched at sea—the aircrew was rescued some days later by a PBY.

As the lucky few survivors of VT-6 sped away, the Japanese officers and crewmen must have felt relieved and at least relatively confident. Since seven that morning, they had seen a virtual air show of American war-planes—six different kinds of aircraft, including four different single-engine carrier-type planes, a twin-engine medium bomber, and a four-engine heavy bomber. Though the Japanese did not know it at the time, they had been attacked by airmen representing three branches of the American services—army, navy, and marines. They had been level-bombed, glide-bombed, and torpedo-bombed. They had caught their first glimpse of the Grumman TBF Avenger, and although the new torpedo plane's combat debut had been none too impressive, it would inflict plenty of misery on the Imperial Japanese Navy in the three years to come. No Japanese ship had yet been scratched, and the Zeros had brushed off every successive wave of attackers while losing only a few planes.

Even so, by interrupting flight operations and forcing a more rapid cycling of the CAP, the constant pressure of new air attacks had kept *Kido Butai* on its back foot. Within another twenty minutes or so, the first bombers would be lifted up on the elevators and spotted on the flight decks, and if the decks could be kept clear for about forty-five minutes, a powerful counterstrike could be launched against the American fleet, probably before 11 a.m. Until then, the Japanese carriers would remain in the treacherously vulnerable position of having their attack planes fueling and arming in their hangar decks.

Most worrying to Admiral Nagumo and his officers, perhaps, was that *Kido Butai* had not yet been subjected to a proper dive-bombing attack. They knew that the SBD Dauntless dive-bomber was the most lethal carrier aircraft in the American inventory. Less than a month earlier, at Coral Sea, dive-bombing attacks had maimed the *Shokaku* and obliterated the *Shoho*. So the Japanese commanders must have asked themselves, where were the Dauntless squadrons, and what would happen if they appeared suddenly in the skies overhead?

THIRTY-TWO SBDS FROM THE *ENTERPRISE*, the combined force of Scouting Six (under Lieutenant Wilmer Earl Gallaher) and Bombing Six (under Lieutenant Richard Halsey Best), had flown southwest from the task force at 231 degrees. After about a hundred miles, the air group leader, Lieutenant Commander McClusky, concluded he had passed the line of Nagumo's advance on Midway. McClusky surmised that he was most likely to find the enemy to the northwest, and the two squadrons executed a right turn. Half an hour later, there was still no sign of the Japanese fleet. Fuel was low, and the risk was growing that none of the planes would make it back to the American task force. Shortly before 10 a.m., the squadrons turned again, this time to the east. Sharp-eyed pilots and gunners searched through the gaps in the clouds below, looking for ships or wakes—any telltale sign of the Japanese fleet. They were at 19,000 feet. Ensign Fred Mears of the *Hornet* later described the art of stalking an enemy fleet across a vast and unvarying seascape:

> Sometimes the carrier stack will stand out as the tiniest of regular smudges on the horizon. Sometimes the wake of a large vessel or the combination of several wakes forming straight white lines strikes the eye. A flash of sunlight reflection may give the force away, or the ships may suddenly emerge as small gray slivers on the water. Whenever there is a straight line or regular form on the water it can be taken as something more than the sea itself.

At about five minutes to ten, McClusky spied a destroyer, later identified as the *Arashi*. She was south of *Kido Butai*, having chased and depth-charged the U.S. submarine *Nautilus*. She was knifing through the sea on a northward course, throwing mighty waves off her bows and leaving a long, frothing wake astern. Apparently her lookouts did not spot the bombers soaring far above. McClusky turned to follow her line of advance. Five minutes later, several pilots saw wakes in the sea about forty miles ahead—"thin, white lines; mere threads, chalk-white." They flew on above the cumulus ceiling for a few minutes. As they approached a break in the clouds, the entire enemy fleet came into view beneath them, like a collection of toy boats on a pond. "Among those ships, I could see two long, narrow, yellow rectangles, the flight decks of carriers," wrote Clarence Dickinson. "Apparently they leave the decks either the natural wood color or possibly they paint them a light yellow. But that yellow stood out on the dark blue sea like nothing you have ever seen. Then farther off I saw a third carrier." Each of the flight decks was marked with a red *hinomaru* (the red "Rising Sun" disk) and Dickinson made a mental note to use it as a bull's-eye.

McClusky radioed the *Enterprise*: "This is McClusky. Have sighted the enemy." He did not fly directly toward the enemy carriers, but led his thirty-two aircraft on a long detour around the enemy fleet to the northeast. He intended to attack with the sun behind them, hoping that it would conceal their approach and spoil the aim of the antiaircraft gunners. He nosed down slightly to pick up speed, and the rest of the formation followed his lead—the higher their airspeed, the better their chances against the enemy fighters they expected to encounter at any moment. They flew directly over several screening destroyers, but none of the Japanese lookouts raised an alarm, probably due to a combination of scattered cloud cover and the distraction afforded by yet a third wave of incoming torpedo planes boring in toward *Kido Butai* from the southeast, nearly 15,000 feet below.

The new group was Torpedo Three of the *Yorktown*, led by Lieutenant Commander Lance E. Massey. Massey's twelve lumbering airplanes were no better than those of VT-8 or VT-6, but VT-3 had the advantage of a fighter escort—six F4F Wildcats of VF-3 under Lieutenant Commander Jimmy Thach. Thach, one of the best fighter pilots in the U.S. Navy, had developed a group formation that he called the "beam defense" maneuver, which would later take the more popular name "Thach weave." Now it was put into practice for the first time in the war, with results that must have come as a nasty surprise to the veteran Zero pilots who had grown accustomed to having their way with all types of American planes. The technique involved close cooperation between wingmen. When a pilot saw a Zero on his beam, approaching in a typical high side run, he simply banked his plane away from the attacker. His wingman, tipped off by the sight of the neighboring Wildcat turning toward him, turned toward the turning Wildcat and passed it in a weaving pattern. This brought the attacking Zero into his sights, setting up a head-on shot.

Thach's F4Fs were flying about 2,000 feet above and slightly behind Massey's TBDs. Thach's six fighters were beset by about fifteen Zeros, and Thach recalled thinking that not one of his aircraft would survive the fight. But the weave seemed to catch the Japanese pilots off balance, and for the first time in the battle, flaming and spinning Zeros were seen going into the ocean. "A number of them were coming down in a string on our fighters," wrote Thach; "the air was just like a beehive. It didn't look like my weave was working, but then it began to. I got a good shot at two of them and burned them. One had made a pass at my wing man, pulled out to the right and then came back. We were weaving continuously, and I got a head-on shot at him."

Tom Cheek, one of Fighting Three's pilots, recalled his amazement at the Zero's performance. When he fired on two, they rolled out of his sights and began to climb away. "Their climbing ability was stunning to watch, they were out of sight and mind in seconds as I rolled to the right, reversing course. . . . The thought struck home, this was not one to tangle with in a dogfight, at least not with an overweight F4F-4."

Massey's Devastators droned gamely on toward *Hiryu*, the closest of the four carriers and the only one in range. Despite Thach's gallant efforts, he could not draw all the Zeros away from VT-3. Perhaps a dozen swarmed on the torpedo planes and began sending them down into the sea in flames, one by one. No hits were scored by VT-3, while ten of twelve aircraft were shot down. "That first attack on us and the torpedo planes was beautifully coordinated," Thach later said. "It was something I had to admire. It was beautifully executed. This was their first team and they were pros."

Far above, the *Enterprise* dive-bombing squadrons neared their pushover points. McClusky did not yet realize it, but by a lucky accident the seventeen SBDs of *Yorktown's* Bombing Three were arriving on the scene at the same time, and from a different direction: east. The Japanese fleet, caught between two large waves of enemy dive-bombers, was utterly unprepared to repel the attack. No Zeros were at high altitude, having descended to fight off the torpedo planes. The four carriers of *Kido Butai*, in maneuvering to avoid the past hour's successive attacks, had deranged their favored box formation and were now strung out in a ragged line, spreading the defending Zeros over a long axis, and diluting the concentration of the screening ships' antiaircraft fire. In any event, it seems that no one in the Japanese task force even spotted the dive-bombers until they were screaming out of the sky, and by that time it was too late.

McClusky's division leaders signaled the moment by kicking their rudders back and forth, causing each plane's tail to "wag." The lead Dauntlesses in the formation nosed up in a stalled position and opened their flaps, then peeled off to one side and pushed over. They dived steeply, at a 70-degree angle, centering their optical bombsights on the flight decks of their chosen targets. It was 10:20 a.m. The *Enterprise* planes dived on the *Kaga* and the *Akagi*; Lieutenant Commander Maxwell F. Leslie's *Yorktown* planes attacked the *Soryu*. "I was making the best dive I had ever made," recalled Lieutenant Dickinson, who attacked the *Kaga*. "The people who came back said it was the best dive they had ever made. We were coming from all directions on the port side of the carrier, beautifully spaced." The *Kaga* was tearing through the water at 28 knots, but her tormentors were numerous and plummeting down on her at an ideal angle. Thach, still fighting off Zeros while trying to shepherd the two remaining torpedo planes of VT-3 to safety, detected a "glint in the sun, and it just looked like a beautiful silver waterfall, these dive bombers coming down . . . I'd never seen such superb dive-bombing."

On the *Kaga*, crewmen on the flight deck were cheering the Zeros as they cut the torpedo planes to pieces. The antiaircraft gunners had depressed their weapons to the horizontal to fight off the low-altitude attack. One of the carrier's pilots, standing on the catwalk, recalled that "one of our machine gun commanders pointed his baton to the sky and shouted something. When I looked up, several dive-bombers appeared between the clouds and were plunging down on us." Several voices shouted: "Enemy dive-bombers!"

The first group of Dauntlesses descended on her port quarter, and her captain, Jisaku Okada, ordered hard astarboard to send the big carrier into a clockwise turn. But the *Kaga* was slow to respond to her helm, and the SBDs made the needed corrections to keep the flight deck in their sights. The Japanese crew watched in dismay as the bombs separated from the bellies of the diving planes and fell directly toward them. The first three missed narrowly, throwing huge towers of water up on either side of the ship. But the next four hit in quick succession, two amidships and two forward. The results were cataclysmic. The carrier's small superstructure was almost completely destroyed, killing most of the ranking officers, including Captain Okada. The island's windows were blown out, its outer skin was stripped off, and its interior spaces were flooded with so much smoke that the survivors were driven out on deck. No one manned the bridge; no one was left at the helm. The forward elevator took a direct hit and was smashed downward, never to operate again. A bomb pierced the flight deck amidships and exploded in the crew's quarters adjacent to the hangar, killing unknown scores (hundreds?) of men in a few seconds. Fuel tanks and munitions detonated on the hangar deck. Ensign Maeda sought cover under the flight deck near the stern. As the bombs struck, he shouted to some of his fellow pilots in their staterooms—"It is dangerous here, get the hell out!" As he climbed the ladders, he noticed the ship was taking on a dangerous list; then an explosion flung him to the deck and pierced his leg with shrapnel.

Lieutenant Dickinson, whose bomb struck forward near the elevator, saw "the deck rippling and curling back in all directions exposing a great section of the hangar below. I knew the last plane had taken off or landed on that carrier for a long time to come." Thach, still watching the scene from the cockpit of his Wildcat, saw pink and blue flames burst up through the *Kaga's* flight deck: "I remember looking at the height of the flames from the ship and noticing that it was the same as the length of the ship—just solid flame going up, and, of course, there was a lot of smoke on top of that."

Soryu had just begun to turn into the wind to launch Zeros, and most of the crew was still looking in the direction of the still-developing attack of the torpedo planes, when lookouts shouted that *Kaga* was under attack. Heads turned, and stunned crewmen watched in horror as the *Kaga's* flight deck erupted in a chain of massive explosions. Broken cloud cover overhead apparently concealed the final approach of Leslie's *Yorktown* dive-bombers, but now they appeared through a hole in the clouds—one by one, evenly spaced, obviously about to push over. The antiaircraft guns were cranked up quickly and the frantic fire director tried to set up a firing solution, but as on the *Kaga*, there was simply not enough time. The *Soryu* swung hard to port, but the diving planes turned with her, and a moment later they began peeling off the formation, one by one, and pushing over into steep dives.

The first bomb struck on the starboard side, forward, and caused the ship's entire hull to lunge violently to port. Another landed almost dead center amidships on the flight deck and passed right through the wood and steel skin to detonate in the hangar deck. A third struck aft on the flight deck and made a blinding flash. Many of the men on deck were killed outright or blown overboard by the blast. Commander Hisashi Ohara, the ship's executive officer, felt a wave of heat, not particularly painful, but realized that he must have been badly burned when men brought wet towels to press against his face.

The *Soryu's* engines cut out and she went dead in the water. A column of smoke rose from the great wound that had been torn in her flight deck. Burning sections of eviscerated Zeros were strewn across the deck amidst bodies and parts of bodies. To the survivors, these terrible scenes appeared through a shimmering heat haze.

Nagumo's flagship, the *Akagi*, very nearly escaped the unwelcome attentions of the American dive-bombers. This was due to a tactical error committed by McClusky, who was a recent convert to the dive-bombing ranks,

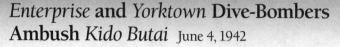

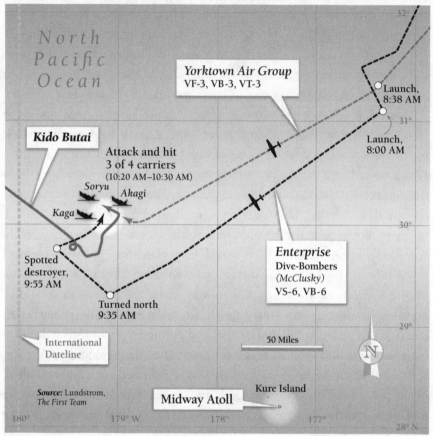

Enterprise and Yorktown Dive-Bombers Ambush Kido Butai June 4, 1942

having switched from fighter planes. Doctrine held that when two divisions of dive-bombers arrived over multiple targets, the lead division should take the farther of the two. But McClusky took his division down on the *Kaga*, the nearer of the two. As a result, the entire thirty-two-plane armada almost concentrated all of their bombs on the *Kaga* while leaving the *Akagi* alone.

Lieutenant Dick Best, commander of VB-6, saw what was happening and led his two wingmen to attack the *Akagi*. Because he had not had time set up the attack properly, Best's dive angle was shallower than that taken by the planes over the *Kaga*, placing his three planes in greater danger as they approached. They did not attack in textbook fashion, by diving in an evenly spaced file of planes, but maintained their "Vee" formation throughout the dive.

On the deck of the *Akagi*, lookouts shouted in alarm and a warning trumpet sounded harshly over the loudspeakers, but the antiaircraft guns were slow to respond, and what little fire they threw up missed widely. A few alert crewmen, with a well-founded sense of self-preservation, managed to fling themselves flat on deck. Captain Taijiro Aoki put the ship into a hard starboard turn, but that merely turned the flagship's port beam toward the attackers, and they were able to make the necessary adjustments to stay on target. The first bomb to drop struck the water close to the hull, sending up a towering geyser that came down near the island and soaked the officers stationed there to the skin. Though it had missed, its blast force was strong enough to throw men to the deck, and its heat sufficient to blacken their skin.

Only one bomb struck the *Akagi*, near the center of the flight deck. That hit, probably the 1,000-pound bomb dropped by Best, hit on the middle elevator. Had it missed, the entire course of the battle might have been turned, because the Japanese might have dealt a more severe retaliatory attack on the American carriers. But not only did Best's bomb hit the target, it penetrated through the *Akagi*'s flight deck to the upper hangar deck, where its destructive force was amplified and multiplied by secondary explosions among the fueled-up strike planes, the fuel in the fuel lines, and the hastily stored bombs and torpedoes. Fuchida saw "a huge hole in the flight deck just behind the amidships elevator. The elevator itself, twisted like molten glass, was drooping into the hangar. Deck plates reeled upward in grotesque configurations. Planes stood tail up, belching livid flame and jet-black smoke."

Kaname Shimoyama, stationed in the *Akagi*'s hangar deck, described the chain of devastating explosions. "It all happened so quickly," he recalled. "The hangar was very dark, but engulfed in a sea of fire . . . I thought that our carrier would sink at any moment. I saw some men who could not keep their composure and they lost all self control. They just went crazy and tried to escape." A few Zeros, spotted on the flight deck, were picked up and flung into the sea. Hiroshi Suzuki remembered that the fire blew the fuel tanks of several of the parked Zeros, and also ignited shells in their 20mm guns, which began to fire. "Due to the intense heat," he recalled, "the rivets from the steel plates started to pop out like they were bullets. One of my classmates was wounded because he was hit by some of these lethal rivets flying through the air." The third bomb, a near miss off the *Akagi*'s stern, detonated close enough aboard to wrench the flight deck up and jam the rudder at 20 degrees port, forcing the stricken flagship to travel helplessly in a wide turn until she came to a dead stop.

Tom Cheek, one of the F4F pilots in Thach's squadron, had dived down to sea level to escape pursuing Zeros. When he leveled off, just above the wavetops, his plane's nose happened to be pointed directly at the carrier force. Spread out across the horizon above his engine cowling, Cheek could see *Kaga*, *Akagi*, and *Soryu*, and was able to confirm that they were traveling at speed by the size of their bow waves. Almost at once, he saw a "brilliant orange flash" on *Akagi*'s deck, followed by water spouts indicating near misses. A few seconds later came a "rolling, greenish-yellow ball of flame" that seemed to "open the bowels of the ship." His peripheral vision registered a series of explosions that seemed to envelop the full length of *Kaga*'s flight deck, which "erupted with bomb bursts and flames." Beyond and to the right of *Akagi*, the *Soryu* was pouring out a column of black, oily smoke. He also noted that all three ships had lost propulsion, as their bow waves had diminished markedly.

By 10:26 a.m., all three carriers had suffered terrible blows. None would land or launch an airplane ever again, and by the following morning all would be abandoned by their surviving crews and sent to rest on the bottom of the sea.

As THE THREE STRICKEN CARRIERS BURNED, the American air groups fled the vengeful Zeros and antiaircraft gunners. All of the retreating aircraft were now at low altitude—the TBDs because they attacked and launched their fish from low altitude, the Wildcats because they had accompanied the torpedo planes, the SBDs because they had pulled out of their dives a few hundred feet above the sea. The dive-bombers and torpedo planes, rid of their bombs and torpedoes, and low on fuel, were lighter, faster, and more maneuverable than they had been. Many escaped safely through gaps in the screening vessels. As Lieutenant Dickinson pulled out of his dive on the *Kaga*, he was less than 100 feet above the sea. Looking back, he saw three Zeros on his tail. A destroyer lay dead ahead, and her antiaircraft batteries opened up on him. Flak bursts blossomed above and below him; he dived or climbed to avoid the anticipated range corrections. Two or three miles far-ther, when he had shaken the Zeros and flown out of range of the gunners, Dickinson looked back and saw three columns of fire and smoke, marking the positions of the *Akagi*, *Kaga*, and *Soryu*.

Tom Cheek of Fighting Three, separated from his wingmen in a wild aerial melee, heard a command shouted through his radio—"Group rendez-vous! Rendezvous!"—but he could see none of his squadron mates through his windshield, nor any friendly planes of any squadron. The prearranged rendezvous point was twenty miles north of the Japanese task force, but in that direction lay more enemy ships, and Cheek was too low on fuel to take any but the most direct route home. He chose a heading that seemed likely to take him back to "Point Option," where he was to find his carrier, the *Yorktown*.

The American air groups were spread out all over the sky, flying alone or in small groups. Some of the flyers had been shot or taken shrapnel, and were bleeding under their flight suits. The environment in the cockpit grew punishing. The men struggled with heat, sweat in their eyes, mental and physical fatigue, improperly functioning gas masks. No airplane had gas to spare, and many did not have enough left in their tanks to reach home. From the time they left the scene of battle, the American aircrews' entire effort was bent to the task of navigating back to their carriers with their limited fuel reserves. Each pilot had to make continuous corrections for a host of variables—his position, airspeed, compass headings, wind direction and velocity, the imputed speed and heading of the carrier. He had to moni-tor perhaps a half a dozen different instrument readings, including fuel, time, rpm, airspeed, manifold pressure, and the "needle and ball." Calculat-ing wind velocity was more art than science—flyers studied the sea beneath them, judging the play of wind on waves, noting whether spray was being blown from the whitecaps.

In theory, the American aircraft could follow a "YE-ZB" radio hom-ing signal, a coded bearing transmitted by each carrier to a receiver in the radioman-gunner's cockpit. If a pilot was receiving a clear signal, he could simply fly the reciprocal heading back to his carrier. But many of the Ameri-can planes were returning at low altitude, beneath the line-of-sight horizon to the antennae atop the carriers. With their fuel tanks running danger-ously low, they could not afford to climb above that horizon in search of the homing signal. They had to find their way home by dead reckoning.

Lacking fuel to search for his squadron mates, Lieutenant Dickinson turned his Dauntless home and flew on alone. Even leaning his fuel mixture to the utmost limit, he would barely make it to Point Option; and even if he reached the task force, he doubted he would have enough fuel to make a carrier landing. Flying his easterly course in fine visibility, he caught sight of a pattern of wakes ahead in the distance. With about twenty miles yet to fly, the arrow on Dickinson's fuel gauge bounced on zero and the engine "began to sputter and miss." He was going down. He unbuckled his parachute and cleared his harness; he disconnected the radio cord from his helmet; he cleared away any gear that would prevent him from exiting the cockpit in seconds. With his last few drops of fuel he turned into the wind, put down his flaps, dropped to a few feet above the wavetops, nosed up, gave the engine a last burst of throttle and then chopped it. With his propeller windmilling, he dead-sticked his SBD into the oncoming waves.

The impact was surprisingly violent, and Dickinson braced his hand against the instrument panel to protect his head. In seconds he had unbuckled his safety belt and climbed out of the cockpit. Standing on the right wing, he pulled the lanyard of his CO_2 cylinder and inflated his life jacket. His radio-gunner climbed onto the other wing. They did not bother with their rubber rafts; the fleet was so close that they could expect to be picked up in short order. They stepped into the sea. Within a minute, the propeller and cowling went under, dragged by the weight of the engine; the dripping tail lifted from the sea; and the entire aircraft dived from view. A friendly destroyer was already bearing down on them, the faces of her crew staring down curiously.

Tom Cheek cruised toward home at 1,500 feet, just beneath the cloud ceiling, hoping to sight the ships of the American task force. He gave up trying to raise his squadron mates on the radio. He could not find the York-town's homing signal. For a long while he could see nothing but the North Pacific wastes stretching away in every direction. At last, off his right wing-tip, he caught sight of a "faint streak of white on the blue-grey water." It was a "genuine made-in-the-USA destroyer." He turned to follow her, dropping to 500 feet, and eventually caught up to the Yorktown. He entered the landing circle, cranked down his landing gear, and got a "cut" from the LSO on his first approach. His tailhook missed the arresting wire, and his plane somersaulted over the barrier and landed upside down on the deck. Cheek had balled himself forward to protect his head from the coming impact, and was unharmed in the crash. To the crewmen who came running to peer under the plane, he shouted: "Get this SOB off of me!" They lifted the tail, giving him enough room to crawl out on deck.

Having seen nothing of the battle, the carrier crews were naturally eager to learn as much as they could from the returning airmen. As the pilots climbed out of their cockpits, curious deckhands, bundled in their bulky canvas life vests, crowded around them and asked questions. In the interest of keeping up crew morale, bridge officers had provided regular updates over the loudspeaker system, and the sailors had given these announcements their full attention. At one point during the battle, Alvin Kernan recalled, "An information officer on the *Enterprise* tried to draw a map with chalk on the huge gray side of the stack, so that all on deck could follow the battle, and we were fascinated at the idea of being given information; but every fifteen minutes the man on the painting scaffold suspended from the top of the stack changed the location and size of the fleets." The truth was that no one, not even Admirals Fletcher or Spruance, knew precisely how the battle was unfolding. It was too big, too spread out; too much was happening at once, and what little data could be pieced together may or may not be reliable. They were all feeling their way through the fog of war.

For the aviators who returned safely, survival was bittersweet. They had lost many friends. Ensign Fisher, after landing on the *Hornet*, was shocked to learn that he was the only pilot of his squadron (VB-8) who had thus far returned, while none of the carrier's fighter or torpedo planes had been accounted for. (Shortly thereafter, Ring and most of the other pilots of VS-8 landed safely.) Another VB-8 pilot who returned safely, Ensign Roy P. Gee, was likewise shocked to learn of the losses suffered by the carrier's air group. "When I entered the VB-8 ready-room," he said, "I was shocked to learn that none of VT-8's fifteen TBDs nor VF-8's ten F4Fs had returned, and that all the crews had been declared MIA. I went to the wardroom to get something to eat and paused to look at the empty chairs that were normally filled by my friends from VF-8 and VT-8." Lieutenant Dickinson, who was aboard the destroyer that had fished him out of the sea, studied the planes landing on the *Enterprise* through binoculars, trying to read the aircraft numbers so that he could know who among his squadron mates had survived. On the *Enterprise*, the fighters returned first, landing entirely unharmed and intact. Shortly afterward came four torpedo planes, all badly shot up. They were the only survivors of their squadron. One of the returning TBD pilots was so incensed at the lack of fighter support provided his squadron that he leapt out of his cockpit, drew his .45 automatic, and threatened to shoot the F4F squadron leader, Lieutenant James Gray. Others physically restrained and disarmed him.

The aviators were hungry, sweaty, and tired. They made their way down to the "admiral's pantry" for coffee and sandwiches. They spoke excitedly about what they had seen and done, and as more and more airmen came aboard, it became increasingly evident that they had dealt the Japanese fleet a devastating blow. When the *Enterprise* SBD squadrons came aboard, the aircrews were jubilant. "They were shouting and laughing as they jumped out of the cockpit, and the ship that had been so somber a moment before when the torpedo planes returned became now hysterically excited," recalled Kernan, who listened to their banter with growing exhilaration. "These were heroes dressed in their khaki and green nylon flight suits, carrying pistols and knives over their yellow Mae Wests, and describing with quick hands and excited voices how they had gone into their dives, released their bombs, and seen the Japanese flight decks open up in flames just below them." As more planes came aboard, eyewitness after eyewitness corroborated the story. "There were three carriers," Cheek told his squadron leader. "I saw bomb hits on all of them and I think one torpedo hit on one. They were all burning like hell when I left."

As the hours dragged on, and none of the *Hornet's* torpedo planes appeared, the mood on the carrier grew darker. Some voiced the hope that Waldron's squadron had landed on Midway, but that seemed unlikely. All were aware of the shortcomings of the TBD Devastator. But what had happened to the *Hornet's* fighters? No one could say, and no one would know for days. As the truth emerged, it became evident that the *Hornet's* air group had had a disastrous morning. Her torpedo planes had been slaughtered; her fighters had lost their way and been forced to ditch at sea; her SBDs failed to find the enemy fleet, though most survived either by landing on Midway or by returning safely to the carrier. In sum, all of the *Hornet's* TBDs had been destroyed; a third of her fighters had been lost; and a third of her dive-bombers had landed on Midway, though they would return to the carrier later that afternoon. With the exception of the fifteen TBDs of Waldron's Torpedo Eight, all of which had been wiped out without scoring a hit on the enemy carriers, no *Hornet* aircraft had engaged the enemy.

THE THREE STRICKEN JAPANESE CARRIERS were engaged in a life-and-death struggle against the fires raging below their decks. Even if their hangars were not crammed wingtip to wingtip with aircraft that had been fueled up and armed with bombs and torpedoes, each ship was filled with other flammable materials to feed and nourish the flames. Their aviation fueling systems offered a network of highly combustible fuel-filled lines that transported the fire throughout the ships—forward and aft, down to the lower decks, down to the main storage tanks. Bombs, torpedoes, and ammunition were stored in racks and storage lockers in the hangars, or even scattered haphazardly along the deck, and many detonated within the hulls of the ships. The Japanese navy, with its overriding emphasis on offensive warfare, had neglected to train and prepare adequately for firefighting and damage control. The interior of the ships offered plenty of sustenance for the conflagration—wood flooring and furniture, internal timber support beams, cotton pipe insulation, cotton bedding. The galleys and ovens were caked with accumulated grease and oils. Firehoses and foam-spraying systems were installed on the hangar decks, but these systems were fed by water mains that were vulnerable to bomb or fire damage.

The *Kaga*, hit by four (possibly five) bombs, was in the worst shape of the three stricken carriers. Her hangar was engulfed by a maelstrom of fire, touching off bombs and torpedoes on the planes and in the storage rooms. Burned, mutilated, and mangled bodies were scattered along the length of the deck. No more than a handful of crewmen stationed there at the time of attack would survive. The fire mains were knocked out, as was the electric generator that powered the fire pumps. Smoke filled the enclosed space, and the lights cut out. The fuel mains were ruptured, pouring aviation gas onto the fires, which erupted in a blazing inferno. A few hideously burned survivors crawled through the wreckage and the scattered remains of their shipmates.

The *Kaga*'s fires spread so rapidly that they simply overwhelmed damage control efforts. Many of the men who had drilled in firefighting were either killed or so severely wounded that they could not function effectively. Lieutenant Takayoshi Morinaga, a Nakajima torpedo plane pilot, recalled that he and other survivors gamely tried to control the fires with old-fashioned bucket relays from the latrines, but "the water evaporated quickly, and it was useless." Two or three minutes after the attack, munitions on the hangar deck detonated, and a rolling ball of fire and a mushroom cloud ascended to a height of several thousand feet above the ship. The sides of the ship were peeled open and thrown outward by the explosion, ejecting bodies, debris, and parts of aircraft into the sea. "Numerous explosions rocked *Kaga* over and over," said another Nakajima pilot, Ensign Haruo Yoshino. "When I came to my senses and looked around, everyone who was there just a moment ago had disappeared."

On the *Soryu*, the situation was much the same. The hangar deck had been penetrated by three bombs, the hangar crews had been decimated, and the secondary explosions of fuel and munitions quickly overwhelmed the efforts of damage control teams. By chance or fate, one bomb had struck in each of three separated compartments on the hangar deck, ensuring the complete devastation of the entire area. In the engine room, deep in the lower reaches of the ship, the men heard the tremendous explosions over their heads and realized that the space between them and the open air above decks was blocked by a sea of fire. Lieutenant Michitaro Naganuma recalled that the explosions caused the deck above their heads to warp downward, and tongues of flame shot out of the ventilation ducts. The temperature climbed quickly, and the supply of breathable air suddenly dropped. Within fifteen minutes of the attack, the *Soryu's* officers had concluded that the ship was probably beyond saving, and Captain Ryusaku Yanagimoto ordered abandon ship. Many of the crew had anticipated the order—or, not receiving it, obeyed it anyway. Men leapt from the deck into the sea, driven overboard by the intolerable heat of the fires. Others were lifted from their feet by explosions and catapulted into the water.

At first, it seemed that the *Akagi*, having taken only one direct hit, was not as badly mauled as her two sisters. But that one bomb, having touched off a chain of powerful secondary explosions on her hangar deck, sealed her fate. Her fires quickly overpowered the firefighting squads by driving the men back, cutting the water mains, and killing the electrical power to the pumps. Captain Aoki ordered the magazines flooded, but water would not flow into the aft magazine, possibly because the valves had been damaged by the near miss off the stern. The conflagration descended into the lower hangar deck and found more fuel to feed upon. The crew, working with hand pumps, could not get enough water on the fire. "Firefighting parties, wearing gas masks, carried cumbersome pieces of equipment and fought the flames courageously," Fuchida recalled. "But every induced explosion overhead penetrated to the deck below, injuring men and interrupting their desperate efforts. Stepping over fallen comrades, another damage-control party would dash in to continue the struggle, only to be mowed down by the next explosion." Lieutenant (jg) Kiyoto Furuta, a Type 99 pilot, recalled that when the ship's power plant was disabled, "our fire extinguishing pump didn't work, and even if it worked, the pump would not have put out this inferno. So we just gave up trying to put out the blaze."

It was clear that the *Akagi* could no longer serve as Nagumo's flagship. The fire emerging from the flight deck threatened to consume the island. Admiral Nagumo was reluctant to leave the ship, insisting, "It is not time yet." But Nagumo's chief of staff, Rear Admiral Kusaka, pressed him to transfer his flag to the light cruiser *Nagara*: "Sir, most of our ships are still intact. You must command them." Captain Aoki added: "Admiral, I will take care of the ship. Please, we all implore you, shift your flag to *Nagara* and resume command of the force." Tearfully, Nagumo assented. The bridge was filling with smoke, and the lower sections were engulfed in flames. The only route of escape was to descend by rope from the forward window of the bridge down to the deck. He and Kusaka did so. At 10:46 a.m., the two admirals went down a rope ladder from the anchor deck into a waiting launch to be taken to *Nagara*.

On the bridge of the *Hiryu*, flagship of Carrier Division 2, Admiral Tamon Yamaguchi and his staff watched the three burning carriers in horror and incredulity. The *Soryu*, second carrier of Carrier Division 2, was nearby, and her death throes were vivid to behold. A witness compared her to "a giant daikon radish that had been sliced in two. Now it was possible to see right through her to the other side." Yamaguchi sent a profoundly unhelpful message: "Try to save your carrier!" (No reply was made, perhaps the most eloquent response possible under the circumstances.) Miles astern, the two carriers of Carrier Division 1 discharged towering columns of dense black smoke. *Hiryu* was the sole remaining carrier of *Kido Butai* capable of conducting flight operations, and the entire hopes of the Japanese navy now rested on her air group.

Showing all the alacrity and resolve that Nagumo had lacked earlier that morning, Yamaguchi elected to throw everything he had at the enemy, as quickly as possible, without waiting for a full deckload of planes or a balanced strike package. Getting the planes aloft was as much a defensive measure as an offensive one—the fate of *Hiryu's* sisters had supplied an awful illustration of the consequences of being caught with fueled and armed planes on board. He had a flight of eighteen Type 99 "Val" dive-bombers fueled up and armed, and he ordered them into the air without delay. When the *Hiryu's* Nakajima Type 97 torpedo planes were ready to launch, they would follow. If they could find and kill all three American carriers, the Midway invasion might go forward. If they could kill two, perhaps *Akagi* could be salvaged and the battle could be fought to a draw. On the other hand, the safe return of *Hiryu's* air group was doubly important now that three Japanese flight decks were ablaze, so Yamaguchi urged his airmen to take no unwarranted risks, and to do their best to bring their planes and themselves back to the carrier.

A few minutes before 11 a.m., eighteen Vals and six Zeros took off and began climbing to attitude. The strike, led by Lieutenant Michio Kobayashi, stayed below the cloud cover to maintain visual contact with the ocean. The American carriers were now less than 100 miles away. Not long after the strike had departed, *Chikuma's* No. 5 floatplane reported: "The enemy is in position bearing 70 degrees, distance 90 miles from our fleet's position." Kobayashi made a slight course correction south. Some of his airmen spotted a group of *Enterprise* dive-bombers at lower altitude, commanded by Lieutenant Charles Ware. The six Zeros peeled off and dived to engage them. Ware's Dauntlesses acquitted themselves well, maintaining tight formation and firing back at the Zeros, damaging two. (Both returned to the *Hiryu,* and one was forced to ditch at sea.) The encounter weakened Kobayashi's strike by depriving it of one third of its fighter protection.

Task Force 17's radar screens picked up the incoming Japanese strike at a range of thirty-two miles, bearing 255 degrees. *Yorktown's* radar set managed to establish that the bogeys were gaining altitude, which seemed to confirm that they were enemy dive-bombers. Lieutenant Commander Oscar Pederson, the *Yorktown* fighter direction officer (FDO), vectored the Wildcats out to intercept at an altitude of "angels 10" (10,000 feet). The radio circuit rang with excited voices speaking in their specialized lingo. Altitude was given in 1,000-foot units—"angels." Bearings were given as "vectors" or "arrows." Unidentified aircraft were "bogeys"; if they were confirmed as enemy, they were "bandits." *Yorktown* was "Red Base." F4F patrol divisions were "Red" (*Yorktown*), "Blue" (*Hornet*), and "Scarlet" (*Enterprise*). A pilot acknowledged the FDO's commands with "Roger" ("I understand") or

"Wilco" ("Will comply"). When an American pilot spotted enemy planes, he cried: "Tally Ho!" Excerpts from the *Yorktown*'s fighter control transcript for June 4 reflect the confusion and false alarms that were endemic at this early stage of the war:

"Red 17, arrow 265 from your present position. Acknowledge."

"Red 17. Wilco."

"Red 17, bandit in your vicinity ahead, keep sharp look."

"Red 17. Roger."

"This is Scarlet 17. One bogey, angel 4, distance 20."

"This is Scarlet 17. Just a minute. Friendly."

"Scarlet 17. Resume patrol overhead, report on station."

"This is Scarlet 17, on station."

"Red 26, Red 23. Arrow 295, 20 miles, 5,000 feet. Acknowledge."

"This is Red 23. Wilco."

"This is Red 26. Wilco."

"Red 26, Red 23. You better make that about 8,000, unidentified bogey."

"This is Red 23. Wilco."

"Red 26, Red 23. Arrow 180. Acknowledge."

"This is Red 23. Wilco."

"This is Red 26. Repeat."

"Red 26, Red 23. Arrow 180. Step on it. Acknowledge."

"This is Red 26. Wilco."

"Red 26, Red 23. Bogey a bandit in cloud. Step on it."

"Red 21. 270. Cloud level acknowledge."

"This is Red 21. Wilco."

"Red 13 and 11. Bandit in your vicinity, keep good lookout above and below."

"This is Red 13. Plane has been identified as friendly."

"Roger. Return to combat station."

"This is 13. Wilco."

"All Scarlet planes keep a sharp lookout for a group of planes coming in at 255 unidentified."

"Scarlet 9, take your group and look for bogeys bearing 255. Appears to be a large group."

"This is Scarlet 9. Roger."

"Scarlet 23 from 19. What is your position?"

"Scarlet 23. Many bogeys, angels 10, arrow 305. Step on it."

"20 bandits approaching 305. 30 miles, large group of bandits."

"Scarlet 19. What information have you on bandits?"

"Bandits above me heading for ship. Appear to be 18."

"About 12 miles away from ship, 255."

"All Scarlet planes, bandits 8 miles, 255, angels 10."

"Bandits bearing 255, distance 8."

"This is Scarlet 19. Formation seems to be breaking up. Planes still same course."

"OK, break 'em up."

"Scarlet 19, going to attack 3 enemy bombers about 5 miles."

"Tally Ho!"

At noon, Lieutenant (jg) Elbert S. McCuskey, flight leader of the *Yorktown* CAP, spotted Kobayashi's incoming strike at 7,000–8,000 feet. He flew directly into the oncoming enemy formation, firing as he passed, forcing the Japanese planes to veer right and left to avoid a collision. "With my six .50-caliber wing guns blazing, I literally sawed my way through the lead division," he said later. "I didn't use my sight; it was all done at point-blank range." Two more planes, right behind him, made good firing passes and scored several hits. In the ensuing aerial melee, the American fighters shot down seven enemy bombers and damaged three others. The four escorting Zeros attacked the Wildcats and got the worst of it—three were splashed; only one of the American fighters was shot down.

From the deck of the *Yorktown*, the crew studied the distant air battle and saw burning airplanes spinning into the sea. Each left an incandescent trail of flaming aviation fuel which turned to black smoke after a few seconds. But from that distance there was no telling which side was prevailing. As the first black puffs of flak blossomed around the incoming planes, Jimmy Thach shouted to his VF-3 pilots: "Get back in the ready room! You cost Uncle Sam too much money to be out here!" The aviators could see nothing of the air battle from inside that sealed, windowless chamber, but they could track the approach of the enemy planes by listening to the anti-aircraft fire. "The bark of the five-inch guns signaled the approach of each attacker," said Tom Cheek, "followed in sequence by the pump-pump of the 1.1-inch mounts, the chattering 20 millimeters, and finally the rattle of the .30 and .50 caliber machine guns as the enemy approached his drop point."

As the enemy planes drew close, the frequency and intensity of the firing rose until "the AA fire became a constant roar."

Only seven dive-bombers got through the American fighters to attack the *Yorktown*, but those seven pilots were among the first team of the Japanese carrier air force, and they knew their business. They came in from several different directions and peeled off to make steep dives, apparently unperturbed by the barrage of antiaircraft fire thrown up by the gunners. In maneuvering to evade the plummeting attackers, the *Yorktown* turned hard to port and heeled sharply to starboard. The first Aichi to dive was hit by flak right as it dropped its bomb—it exploded and broke into three flaming pieces that splashed into the ship's wake. But the pilot's aim was true—the cartwheeling bomb struck the deck just aft of the *Yorktown*'s island structure. The blast decimated the crew of the 1.1-inch antiaircraft mount that had just splashed the same plane that had dropped the bomb. The explosion tore a hole in the flight deck and ignited fires on the hangar deck. The second plane was also hit and torn apart by antiaircraft fire; and its bomb missed narrowly, exploding right at the fantail. The third came roaring down in a 75-degree dive; its drop was another near miss, and a towering water spout erupted just off the *Yorktown*'s stern.

Seconds later the second *chutai* (three-plane formation) came screaming down on the starboard side. The first plane missed again off the stern. The second, piloted by Iwao Nakazawa, parked a 250-kilogram bomb near the center of the ship; the blast punched a broad hole in the flight deck. The third and final blow, delivered by a plane that had dived at a shallower angle off the *Yorktown*'s starboard bow, hit and disabled the forward elevator. Raging fires on the hangar deck threatened to consume the aviation gasoline tanks and perhaps even to spread into the magazine, which would put the *Yorktown* in the same unenviable position as the three Japanese carriers hit that morning. But the *Yorktown*'s hangar deck was better fireproofed than those of her Japanese counterparts. Importantly, the fueling hoses had been drained and filled with CO_2 gas.

The first bomb had penetrated into the ventilation system and flooded the bridge and other island spaces with acrid black smoke and noxious fumes. Admiral Fletcher and his staff were compelled to leave their battle stations and seek fresh air on the deck, and the admiral immediately considered the need to transfer his flag, saying, "I can't fight a war from a dead ship." He made arrangements to transfer with several members of his staff to the cruiser *Astoria*. Tom Cheek and his fellow airmen of VF-3 were forced out of their ready room: "Gasping and teary eyed, we looked around in the fresh air on the open flight deck." The ship's boilers cut out, and she went dead in the water. A heavy plume of jet black smoke spewed from the hole in her flight deck. Sailors—coughing, bleeding, faces blackened—clambered up the steel ladders to reach the open air. The 1.1-inch mount aft of the island, which had been struck directly, was a terrible sight. Cheek saw "a bloody splotch on the gray painted side of the superstructure" and a "mass of bloody flesh encased in shredded denim." On the 20mm battery on the catwalk, the gunner's head had been blown off but his body remained strapped securely into the chair.

YAMAMOTO'S "MAIN BODY" was some 600 miles west, churning through the same heavy fog that the carriers had passed through three days earlier. Operating in fog conditions, with radio silence, required that the ships of his force slow their progress and post sharp-eyed lookouts to guard against collisions. The foghorns sounded constantly. Yamamoto had passed the last few days in his customary stoic silence, standing on the *Yamato's* spacious bridge and gazing out into the wet, gray gloom. He had been suffering a stomach ulcer, and was pale and queasy.

The need for radio silence limited what Yamamoto and his staff officers could know about the progress of the battle, but they monitored the Japanese aviators' radio chatter. Confidence remained high on the *Yamato's* bridge, even after the sighting of the American carriers. But at 10:50 a.m., a signal officer handed the commander in chief a radio message from Rear Admiral Hiroaki Abe, commander of the screening force: "Fires raging aboard *Kaga*, *Soryu*, and *Akagi* resulting from attacks by enemy carrier and land-based planes. We plan to have *Hiryu* engage enemy carriers. We are temporarily withdrawing to the north to assemble our forces." One officer recalled that Yamamoto "groaned" as he read the message, then handed it back without a word. He and the other officers were dumbstruck, and their mood turned to "black despair."

The admiral's yeoman, Mitsuharu Noda, recollected that the officers "bent their heads together in confusion" and stared at one another with "their mouths shut tight. . . . The indescribable emptiness, cheerlessness and chagrin did not bring forth tears." There was no word from Nagumo, who was then shifting his flag from *Akagi* to a cruiser. Was he dead? The staff, reluctant to acknowledge that the battle was already lost, brainstormed. Some of their proposed gambits were far-fetched, others foolhardy; all were desperate.

The Main Body was too far to render direct and timely assistance, and its lack of air cover would have probably rendered it useless in any case. But the force raised its speed to 20 knots and began a high speed run to the east. The *Yamato*'s towering antennae transmitted new orders to the various elements of the Japanese fleet. The smaller force of carriers which had covered the Aleutian landings, far to the north, was ordered to race southward to fall in with *Kido Butai*. The troop transports were ordered to peel off to the north, out of range of Midway's attack planes. The surface fleet accompanying the transports was to make speed for Midway and bombard the atoll. The Main Body and the surface vessels of *Kido Butai* were to seek a surface engagement that night with the American carriers.

Tameichi Hara, skipper of the destroyer *Amatsukaze*, was badly shaken by the news that three carriers were hit. "What was I reading?" he wondered. "Was I dreaming? I shook my head. No, I was wide awake! . . . The horrifying reports continued until there was no room for doubting their accuracy." To Hara, it seemed clear that the invasion could not go forward without the covering airpower provided by the carriers, but without orders to turn around, his column could do nothing but surge onward toward Midway, drawing ever closer to the atoll's air-striking range. "What was our high command doing?" Hara thought. "My grief over our carrier losses abruptly turned into black anger. Were we to fall into the trap as the main task force had done? Damn! Damn!" Not until 9:20 a.m. (on his clock) did they receive Yamamoto's orders for the transports to withdraw to the "northwestward temporarily" and for the destroyers to attack Midway.

Five surviving dive-bombers returned to the *Hiryu*, where the exhausted hangar crews had been racing to prepare the carrier's torpedo planes for another sortie against the American fleet. Admiral Yamaguchi came down to the flight deck and spoke to the pilots before they climbed into their cockpits. By about 1 p.m., scouting reports had confirmed that there were not two but three American carriers, correctly identified as the *Hornet*, *Yorktown*, and *Enterprise*. "There are three enemy carriers; you got that," he told them. "The kanbaku-tai [dive-bombers] hit one of them, so there are two left. Try to hit a new carrier, which was not damaged, if you can, as a priority. If you do that, we can do a one to one fight."

The new strike lifted off the flight deck: ten Nakajima Type 97 *kanko* ("Kate") torpedo planes accompanied by six Zeros, commanded by Joichi Tomonaga, who had led the air attack on Midway that morning. Tomonaga's aircraft had been shot up in the action over Midway, and was leaking fuel from the left wing tank. He knew that his damaged aircraft would probably never return to land on the *Hiryu*, but he gallantly insisted on going nonetheless, and refused offers to exchange planes with his subordinates. The *Akagi*, *Kaga*, and *Soryu* were plainly visible, spread out across the horizon. This was the last opportunity to hit the American carriers, to exact some retribution for the mortal punishment suffered by the *Hiryu's* three burning sisters, and Tomonaga's aviators were conscious that the hopes of the entire Japanese navy now rested on their shoulders. Taisuke Maruyama, an aircrewman in one of the damaged planes, recalled a "sense of desperation."

The sixteen-plane formation made a long slow climb, eventually reaching 13,500 feet. They did not have far to fly—the American fleet had been sighted only ninety miles from the *Hiryu*. At 2:30 p.m., Lieutenant Toshio Hashimoto, who had been scanning the sea through his binoculars, caught sight of a pattern of wakes on the sea ahead. He conveyed a sighting report to Tomonaga with hand signals, cockpit to cockpit, and the flight leader corrected their course southward to take them directly into the heart of the enemy carrier group. Fatefully, they had stumbled on the injured *Yorktown*, rather than the *Enterprise* or *Hornet*. Her fires had been brought under control, and she no longer trailed a telltale column of smoke. She was underway at good speed. Detecting no sign of her injuries, the Japanese flyers assumed she must be one of the two American flattops that had not yet been attacked. As the task force came fully into view, spread out beneath them under scattered clouds, Tomonaga radioed: "*Zengun totsugeki seyo!*"— the order for the two five-aircraft *shutais* of torpedo planes to separate and begin their coordinated runs on *Yorktown's* bows.

The carrier's radar operators picked up the incoming bogeys well before they came into view. Despite the damage she had sustained, the *Yorktown* was still a fighting ship. Her fires had been brought under control, and the holes in her flight deck had been patched. She could still conduct air operations. When Tomonaga's planes were forty-five miles off, the fueling system on the hangar was shut down and the hoses purged with CO_2 gas. Only six Wildcats were aloft over the task force; all were vectored out to intercept the intruders. Lieutenant Scott McCuskey intercepted the incoming planes, but had to turn and dive from altitude. The Nakajimas, rendered sluggish by the 800-kilogram torpedoes fixed to their bellies, pushed their noses down in a shallow dive, trading altitude for speed, and flew through a curtain of antiaircraft fire thrown up by the screening vessels. When they leveled off at 200-feet altitude, they were traveling at 200 knots, almost twice the speed of the American Devastators.

Yorktown launched five more Wildcats into the teeth of this attack. Lieutenant Commander Jimmy Thach, commander of VF-3, banked right and pointed the nose of his Grumman right into the first plane in Tomonaga's incoming *shutai*. He held down his .50-caliber firing button and drove several rounds into the left wing of Tomonaga's plane, setting it ablaze. Thach later said that he could not help admiring Tomonaga's determination:

> The whole left wing was burning, and I could see the ribs showing through the flames, and that devil still stayed in the air until he got close enough and dropped his torpedo, and that one almost hit the *Yorktown*. He was a dedicated Japanese torpedo plane pilot. Even though he was already shot down, he went ahead and dropped his torpedo. By that time, the whole airplane looked like it was on fire, the top surface of both wings was burned away, everything but the ribs. He must have had some wing surface underneath to hold him up, but he was obviously sinking all the time and he fell in the water right after he dropped his torpedo. They were excellent in their tactics and in their determination. . . . Nothing would stop them, if they had anything to say about it.

The second plane in Tomonaga's *shutai*, also on fire, released its fish and then tried to crash into the *Yorktown*, but the tracers continued to slam into the incoming plane and it cartwheeled into the sea just off the port bow.

To observers on the decks of the other ships of the task force, watching the wild aerial melee from a distance, it was difficult to tell what was happening or which side was winning. The sky was mottled with flak bursts; airplanes blew up and fell from the sky; the *Yorktown* turned sharply, first starboard and then port, and her deck heeled sickeningly. "The ack-ack was ragged but the thunderheads of it blackened the horizon," wrote Robert Casey, who studied the scene through a pair of binoculars. Fred Dyer, a floatplane aviator on the cruiser *Portland*, felt a "wave of extreme patriotism." "All the ships flew huge American battle flags from mastheads," he said. "Ships knifing through huge breaking blue swells, boiling wakes from high-speed ships, flags flying. . . . It was a scene I will never forget."

The second *shutai*, winging in on the *Yorktown's* port bow, launched four torpedoes. The planes took heavy fire, both from the Wildcats and the antiaircraft gunners. Lieutenant Hashimoto compared the sound of the flak fragments striking his plane to hail falling on a metal roof. Ensign Maruyama's rear-seat man was hit in the leg and "the tail of our aircraft looked like a honeycomb because it was full of holes." One plane, after releasing its torpedo, flew across the *Yorktown's* bow. It was so low and so close that American crewmen stationed on the flight deck made eye contact with the Japanese airmen. "I could see the pilot hunkered down in front," said aircraft mechanic Bill Surgi. "The fellow in the second seat was holding a camera to take a picture of our ship. The third man, in the rear seat, was not using his gun. He held up his hand and I thought of stories I had read about chivalry. I thought he was saluting us."

Two torpedoes slammed into the *Yorktown* on the port side, amidships. The first, recalled Lieutenant Joseph Pollard, caused "a sickening thud and rumble throughout the ship and the deck rose under me, trembled and fell away. . . . Then another sickening thud and the good ship shuddered and rapidly listed hard to port." Tom Cheek, who had been ordered to take cover in the Fighting Three ready room, was twice lifted out of his seat by the successive blasts. "Although I was separated from the chair a mere fraction of an inch," he wrote, "there was the impression that I'd risen high in the air. The entire ship twisted and whipped in a motion like a terrier shaking a rat." After the second explosion, the lights cut out, the carrier listed heavily, and the ready-room chairs slid down the deck to pin men and chairs against the port-side bulkhead. "The only sounds in the compartment were those of squirming bodies and heavy breathing," said Cheek. "Then, the sound of voices and curses in the dark as those nearest the exits attempted to open the hatches." The hatches were wrenched open and the men exited one by one, quickly but without panic.

Below, the medical corpsmen were overwhelmed with wounded. With the lights cut out, they were forced to work with flashlights; they could do

Carrier Task Forces: Track Charts June 4, 1942

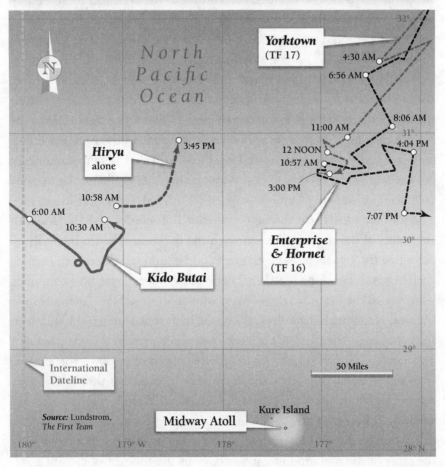

little but cover the suffering men with blankets, inject them with morphine, give them a drink of water, and apply bandages and tourniquets to stem the bleeding. A medical officer recalled: "Some men had one foot or leg off, others had both off; some were dying, some dead." Stretcher bearers kept bringing men into the battle dressing stations and sickbay, which were soon filled to capacity, and stretchers were put down in the adjoining passageways.

The two torpedoes had done serious damage. The first, at frame 90, took three boilers out of commission and killed the engines. The second, at frame 75, flooded the forward generator room and cut electrical power. The emergency diesel generators started up but just as soon short-circuited.

Without power, the pumps could not counterflood to correct the port list, which soon reached 30 degrees. Men on the flight deck had to find hand-holds to avoid sliding into the sea. There seemed a real risk that the ship would capsize and take hundreds of men down with her. At 3 p.m., Captain Buckmaster ordered abandon ship.

For the hundreds of Yorktowners stationed belowdecks, the escape from the crippled carrier was a harrowing ordeal. The electrical generators having failed, much of the ship was left in total darkness, or was lit only by the still-burning fires. The decks were canted as steeply as the roof of a house, and men had to look for hand and footholds, as if they were mountaineers; but the steel surfaces were so hot in places that they could not be touched by bare skin, and the climbers wrapped their hands with clothing or rags. The journey took them through a labyrinth of scuttles and ladders, with the voices of shipmates calling through the darkness to guide them. By all accounts, the crew behaved with great courage and self-possession, keeping their heads and working together. They made way for the medical corpsmen, who carried the wounded men out on wire-mesh stretchers. Emerging onto the steeply sloping hangar deck, they took in a scene through the shimmer-ing heat haze—the twisted, blackened wrecks of aircraft, the grisly remains of slaughtered sailors. Lining up in orderly fashion to go down the knotted lines into the sea, they left their shoes in neat rows, as if they intended to return. The sharp list of the deck was unnerving. "At long intervals the ship would roll slowly to port," said Cheek; "a few degrees at the most, yet each roll to port seemingly increased the angle of list in that direction. Scanning the faces of those around me, it was obvious the thought of capsizing was on everyone's mind."

Hundreds of men needed to go over the side, but there were only half a dozen knotted lines. Some jumped. Many went into cargo nets, which were then lowered gently into the sea. Stretchers were winched down into the whaleboats, to be taken to the supporting ships of the screening force. The torpedoes had punctured the Yorktown's fuel tanks, and the sea around the ship was covered with a 4-inch layer of bunker oil. Swim-mers were pushed back against the Yorktown's hull by wind and waves. "As each wave broke over my head, oil and gas vapors burned my eyes and nose, making it difficult to breathe," photographer's mate Bill Roy recalled. "I was covered with bunker oil. Some sailors swallowed oil and water, then vom-ited trying to hang on. Wind and waves kept all of us against the rough side of the steel hull, which was tearing at our skin. It was difficult to get away. We were all afraid the *Yorktown* would roll over, sink, and take us down."

Whaleboats and destroyers moved in to rescue the swimmers. When the boats were filled to capacity, they towed lines behind them, with life jackets tied to the lines at intervals, and towed dozens of floating men to the ships, where they piled into the cargo nets. As the rescued sailors fell, dripping and exhausted, to the decks of the cruisers and destroyers, each was given a cursory examination. If no medical treatment was needed, he was given a cup of coffee with the order: "Drink this!" Fireman first class Herman A. Kelley was hauled aboard a destroyer, the *Benham*. As he reached the deck, he was handed a bottle of whiskey with instructions to take a swig and pass it on to the next man. It was, he recalled, "just what the doctor ordered."

EVEN WITH *Yorktown* OUT OF ACTION, the Americans now held the high cards. The two *Hiryu* strike groups had each attacked the same target, leaving the *Enterprise* and *Hornet* unscratched and fully functional. The Americans had suffered catastrophic losses among their torpedo squadrons, but their dive-bomber squadrons were largely intact—and it was the dive-bombers that had done in three Japanese flattops, and posed the greatest threat to the fourth. More than five hours of daylight remained. The *Hiryu* was well within range, without means to escape by nightfall, and she had lost all but a few of her planes. If she could be destroyed, every carrier aircraft in the Japanese fleet would be destroyed with her, for as one American officer dryly observed, "If four carriers are smashed, their planes are going to have a hell of a time finding a place to land."

Fletcher had descended into a whaleboat to take him to his new flagship, the cruiser *Astoria*, and for the moment the *Enterprise* and *Hornet* were operating independently. Admiral Spruance and the skipper of the *Hornet*, Marc Mitscher, were preparing two deckload strikes to attack the *Hiryu*, which had been sighted by a *Yorktown* scout bomber at 2:45 p.m., only 110 miles east.

Enterprise began launching her planes—twenty-five Dauntless dive-bombers, escorted by eight F4F Wildcats. The group was led by Lieutenant Gallaher, skipper of Scouting Six. They lifted off, surged 400 yards ahead into the wind, gaining altitude, then banked wide to the left and flew low over the accompanying screening ships. In less than twenty minutes the entire strike was aloft. They did not have far to fly. Forty minutes after leaving the *Enterprise*, droning along at 19,000 feet, Gallaher sighted the Japanese fleet some thirty miles ahead.

The *Hiryu*'s remaining planes—four dive-bombers, five torpedo planes, and an experimental Type 2 dive-bomber from *Soryu*—were refueling in the hangar, which was therefore a tinderbox of fuel and munitions, leaving the ship in much the same vulnerable position as her sisters that morning. The pilots and plane crews had been driven too hard for too long, and were nearing the point of complete physical exhaustion. Yamaguchi ordered that the pilots be fed stimulants and given rice balls, which they devoured wolfishly.

Gallaher led his group in a wide circle off to the north. Peering down through scattered cloud cover, he could see three stricken Japanese flight decks, all still blazing furiously. Finally he spotted the *Hiryu*, his target. He flew farther west to set up an up-sun approach, in hopes of spoiling the aim of the antiaircraft gunners. With so many dive-bombers in his formation, Gallaher judged that he did not need them all to attack the *Hiryu*, and directed the fifteen planes of *Yorktown*'s Bombing Three to attack the battleship *Haruna*. Lookouts on the cruiser *Chikuma* spotted the approaching planes at 5 p.m., right before Gallaher reached his pushover point. The *Hiryu* went into a hard port turn, forcing the first dive-bombers to steepen their dives. Flak bursts mottled the sky, and the Zeros dived with the first SBDs, shooting down several with their 20mm cannon. The combination of fighters, flak, and the carrier's evasive maneuvers spoiled the aim of the first bombers in the dive, and their bombs splashed harmlessly into the sea. Lieutenant Dewitt W. Shumway, who had been detached to attack the *Haruna*, saw that the attack on the *Hiryu* was going awry, and made the quick-headed decision to turn his attack against the carrier.

The *Hiryu* was well defended, but with three groups of bombers attacking her, she was simply overwhelmed. Four 1,000-pound bombs struck the flight deck forward, punching through to the hangar deck and igniting fires below. The forward elevator was blown upward and sent hurtling through the air to hit the side of the carrier's island. The electrical power cut out, and the pilot ready rooms were flooded with smoke, forcing the inhabitants out onto the flight deck. Taisuke Maruyama felt "very strong vibrations, which sounded like the ship was split into two parts. Those intense vibrations continued on and on." The stern, which had remained largely undamaged, was used as a base for the firefighters and damage control teams—but the water mains had ruptured, reducing water pressure to the hoses, and what little water could be brought to bear on the flames tended to evaporate before it could do any good. The *Hiryu* was still able to make 30 knots, but the wind created by her speed through the water fanned the flames and pushed them back toward the stern. "When I saw the sun through the smoke on the deck it looked red, which made me miserable," Maruyama said. "I felt it was like a castle being burned, once the battle was lost, back in the samurai days."

The last few SBDs from *Hornet*, arriving late, realized that the *Hiryu* was done for, and concentrated their attack on two nearby cruisers, *Chikuma* and *Tone*. To make matters even more confused, Lieutenant Colonel Sweeney's B-17s had returned from Midway, refueled and rearmed, and they dropped bombs on the task force from high altitude. As usual, these high-altitude bombs would score no hits on the enemy, but some fell right through the formation of SBDs, giving the navy pilots the strange sensation that they were being bombed from above.

One glance at the *Hiryu* was enough to know that her flight deck had been closed for good, and the Zero pilots who remained aloft now had to reckon with the knowledge that they were marooned in the air, with no friendly airfield within thousands of miles, and would have to fly around until their fuel tanks ran dry, and then execute that oxymoronic trick known as a "water landing."

Yamamoto received Nagumo's unwelcome report at 5:55 p.m.: "*Hiryu* hit by bombs and set afire, 1730." Four out of four of *Kido Butai*'s flight decks were crippled, but the commander in chief and his staff were not yet ready to consider withdrawal; indeed, they seemed to believe the battle could still be retrieved. Admiral Ugaki inquired of Nagumo's staff "whether or not friendly units will be able to use shore bases on Midway tomorrow." As if the invasion of Midway was still a possibility! The very notion, as Parshall and Tully write, "demonstrated just how out of touch Yamamoto and his staff were. . . . Blissfully ignorant, or simply unwilling to admit the true nature of the combat conditions then pertaining, and physically located so as to be of no use whatsoever to the ongoing operation, Yamamoto's staff was clearly having difficulty coming to grips with reality. This trend would only get worse as the evening continued."

At 7:15 p.m., Yamamoto sent an upbeat assessment to his entire command: "The enemy task force has retired to the east. Its carrier strength has practically been destroyed." He ordered his forces to concentrate and finish off the American fleet. The surface ships of Nagumo's Striking Force were to hunt the American carriers down and destroy them in a night action. Other fleet elements were to attack and occupy Midway. The Main Body raised speed to 20 knots and charged east through coagulating fogs, in hopes of bringing their big guns into action.

Fuchida and Okumiya judged the message "so strangely optimistic as to suggest that Commander in Chief Combined Fleet was deliberately trying to prevent the morale of our forces from collapsing." Destroyer skipper Tameichi Hara agreed: "Even with my limited view of events in this battle," he wrote, "I did not understand how Yamamoto could have issued that order. It now appears that he was trying to prevent the morale of his forces from collapsing, but at the time I thought he must have taken leave of his senses." Yamamoto's staff was slightly manic, with "jangled nerves and bloodshot eyes," and apparently no man wanted to be the first to warn that the Americans could use their now absolute air supremacy to wipe out the remnants of the Japanese fleet.

ENSIGN GEORGE GAY, lone survivor of Torpedo Eight, treaded water in the midst of the Japanese task force. He concealed his head under a float cushion whenever a ship came near, and rejoiced as he watched the enemy carriers burn. Gay, a Texan, compared the *Soryu* to "a very large oil field fire, if you've ever seen one. The fire coming out of the forward and aft end of the ship looked like a blow torch, just roaring white flame and the oil burning . . . I don't know how high, and just billowing, big red flames belching out of this black smoke." The stricken carriers would "burn for a while and blow up for a while and I was sitting in the water hollering 'Hooray, Hooray.'"

Firefighting efforts persisted on all four carriers, to varying degrees—but in every case the fires steadily prevailed. Japanese damage control equipment and training was unequal to the task—the navy, with its all-consuming devotion to offensive warfare, simply had not emphasized it. Even when the firefighters could get hoses on the fires, the water pressure was too weak to make much of an impression; in some cases, it actually made matters worse, by spreading spilled aviation fuel to as-yet-undamaged portions of the ships. Fire-suppressing foam would have been better, but the Japanese ships were not equipped with it. Firefighters descended into the lower reaches of the ships, where the passageways were choked with smoke and heated to ovenlike temperatures. Lacking gas masks, they held wet rags to their mouths, or they crawled on all fours, to breathe the slightly better air near the deck, across steel plates that seared their hands and knees. But on all four carriers, no matter how bravely the firefighters persisted in their hellish labors, they could not extinguish the fires. Their only real hope was to outlast them. The conflagrations would persist so long as there was fuel to feed them—and between the aviation gasoline, the bunker oil, and the munitions, there was no shortage of fuel on the burning flattops.

The doctors did their best to cope with the wounded, often without medical supplies because the fires had put them out of their reach. Burn cases were numerous, and not much could be done for them, even to ease their pain. There were reports of dreadfully burned men taking their own lives by staggering into the fires. Toxic fumes emitted by the burning of paint and other materials filled men's lungs, sickening or killing them. On all of the stricken flattops, the sailors were thirsty, but in many cases there was no water to drink; they were exhausted but they could not rest; they were hungry but there was no food. The fires drove them back—pushed them inexorably to the edges of the decks, to the catwalks and anti-torpedo bulges on the hulls.

Soryu was the first of the four to be abandoned. The order was given at 10:45 a.m., just twenty minutes after Bombing Three's devastating attack. Hundreds of her crew had been driven back to the edges of the bow and stern, or to the catwalks—and these extremities became so crowded that men had to hold their arms above their heads to move. When the order came, many were reluctant to comply and had to be urged to go by their officers. Finally, with three cheers of "*Soryu Banzai!*," they began to leap into the sea. It was a long drop, about 35 feet, but they felt the heat radiating from the fires, and their mates pushed from behind. Each man hit the sea hard, feet-first, and was yanked back to the surface by his vest. He then had to swim away from the ship as quickly as he could, to avoid being struck by the jumpers dropping from overhead.

On the *Kaga*, fires raged out of control, and the surviving crew retreated to the edges of the flight deck. The hangar, completely engulfed by flames, was so hot and choked with smoke that not even the firefighters could descend into it. The rungs of the ladders leading up from the hangar deck glowed bright orange, and the steel surface of the flight deck melted the rubber soles of men who walked on it. "The inside of the hangar was bright red," said Haruo Yoshino, the *Kaga* pilot. "The series of explosions were still going on. An extraordinary flame appeared with each explosion." The carrier's last remaining electrical power was lost for good by 1 p.m. At 4:40 p.m., when it was abundantly clear that nothing could be done to save the ship, Commander Takahisa Amagai, the senior surviving officer, ordered all survivors into the sea. Most men leapt 30 feet or more into the oily sea, and clung to oil-soaked debris until they could be picked up by one of the circling destroyers.

Conditions on the *Akagi* were somewhat more manageable, and her crew labored mightily in hopes of saving her. At noon, with her fires still raging, her engines unexpectedly came back to life, and she surged ahead at low speed. But her rudder had been jammed to starboard by a near miss, and she could only travel in a wide clockwise pattern. The damage control parties managed to set up a pump on the bow and get it working, but the water pressure was pitiful and did little good. By 1:50 p.m., the engines had failed again, leaving the ship dead in the water. An hour later, a powerful explosion in the hangar deck caused the entire ship to shudder as if she was trying to tear herself apart. Lieutenant (jg) Kiyoto Furuta recalled that the *Akagi* did not seem to be in her death throes, but her flight deck amidships was glowing bright red. The crew fought on valiantly, but at 6 p.m., with the numbers of dead and wounded multiplying, Captain Aoki concluded that the cause was lost, and ordered abandon ship. Stretchers were winched down into boats sent by the destroyers, and men descended by ropes from both the bow and the stern, where they had retreated to escape the heat and the repeated explosions.

At seven o'clock that evening, in the gathering dusk, the *Enterprise* and *Hornet* tucked themselves into bed. They had already brought their strike aircraft aboard, and began landing their last cycle of CAP. When Spruance radioed Fletcher to ask if he had any further instructions, the latter replied: "Negative. Will conform to your movements." This was, in effect, a generous transfer of tactical command from Fletcher to his subordinate. With *Yorktown* abandoned, Task Force 17 had no air-striking capability, and Fletcher apparently concluded that he had no business directing a carrier duel from a cruiser. Moreover, Spruance could draw on the counsel of Halsey's staff, the most experienced carrier air staff in the American fleet. Relinquishing tactical command mid-battle was an unusual step, but it did Fletcher credit.

Spruance elected to stand off to the east until midnight, so as to keep the Japanese surface units safely at arm's length. In the early morning hours of June 5, they would turn north, and then southwest, to put themselves under Midway's air umbrella by dawn. The decision to pull back was conservative, because there was no great risk that the Japanese battleships and cruisers would find the American carriers in the dead of night. But Spruance's prudence was consistent with Nimitz's desire that he should avoid "exposure to attack by superior enemy forces without good prospect of inflicting, as a result of such exposure, greater damage to the enemy." Retreating to the east would ensure that the American fleet would fight in the daylight, when it was most effective, and prevent the Japanese from bringing their comparative skill in night fighting to bear on the carriers.

It was a controversial decision, even at the time. As a student of military history, Spruance was well aware that he might be committing the classic and recurring tactical error known as the "failure to pursue." Lieutenant Commander Thach, who had fought a magnificent battle on June 4, urged Spruance to chase the Japanese fleet, even if it meant steaming headlong into the west all through the night. He told the admiral, on the flag bridge of the *Enterprise*, "I saw with my own eyes three big carriers burning so furiously they'll never launch another airplane." Spruance replied (in Thach's version of the conversation the admiral wore a slight smile as he spoke): "Well, you know we don't have any battleships. All we have are cruisers, and if we start chasing them, they may be able to chew us up before we can get within gun range at night, and we don't have much of a night attack capability."

It had been a long day, and Spruance was aware that he needed sleep to remain fresh on June 5. At 1 a.m., he ordered a course change to the southwest, with a speed of only 15 knots, and then crawled into his bunk and fell asleep. Later he explained: "I had good officers with me; they knew their jobs; they would carry on. Why should I not sleep soundly? Besides, a mind that suffers from lack of sleep is not likely to be clear and have good judgment. So I had to sleep soundly."

THE FOUR JAPANESE CARRIERS blazed into the night, but none had been struck by a torpedo, leaving their hulls intact beneath their waterlines. If left alone, they would not sink; they would burn until the fires burned themselves out, leaving nothing but four charred, drifting hulks. In that case, they might be seized by the Americans and towed into Pearl Harbor. As military assets they would probably be worthless, apart from their scrap value—but as trophies of war, to be exhibited in newsreels and newspapers, they would make bravura propaganda showpieces. This the Japanese could not abide. Further, destroyers had been left to rescue survivors and to guard each floating inferno, but the fires and smoke might serve as beacons to attract enemy submarines or aircraft, putting the destroyers at serious risk. Moreover, the destroyers were needed for the night surface attack that Yamamoto had ordered. As painful as it was to contemplate, the Japanese now reckoned with the need to scuttle the stricken carriers.

Kaga and *Soryu* were each torpedoed by Japanese destroyers between 7:15 p.m. and 7:30 p.m., though Nagumo's post-action report obscured the fact by referring only to their "sinking." At about the same time, Captain Aoki of the *Akagi* radioed Nagumo to ask permission to scuttle the former flagship, but the transmission was intercepted on the *Yamato*, and Admiral Yamamoto intervened to deny the request. Aoki then returned to the *Akagi* alone and lashed himself to an anchor, resigned to sharing his ship's fate.

Though he had been ordered to chase down and engage the American carriers, Nagumo continued to withdraw to the northwest, the still-burning *Hiryu* in company. Based on a misleading scouting report by a cruiser floatplane, he believed that the Americans had four operational carriers, and that they were headed west, directly toward him. He reported as much to Yamamoto at 9:30 p.m. But Nagumo's transmission was received on the bridge of the *Yamato* with surprise and disgust. Other scouting reports, to which Nagumo was not privy, had correctly reported that the Americans were withdrawing to the east. Yamamoto's staff was quick to blame Nagumo for the loss of the Japanese carriers, though he had acted according to the battle plan. Ugaki thought Nagumo's decision to withdraw was "entirely passive," and should be corrected by a "strong lashing order of the supreme command."

Yamamoto placed Admiral Kondo in tactical command of the pending operation—a humiliation from which Nagumo never recovered. Kondo was directed to rally all available surface forces, form a battle line, and chase the American carriers into the east. With luck, they would meet the enemy in a pitched battle sometime after 1 a.m. Nagumo appears to have simply ignored the order, and kept the remnants of *Kido Butai* on a northwesterly course.

Within two hours, however, doubts crept into Yamamoto's mind. Dawn was drawing steadily closer, and with it the prospect of devastating air attacks on his remaining forces. No new enemy contact reports arrived. Was he sending the fleet into a trap? All the senior staff officers had gone sleepless for the better part of twenty-four hours; fatigue and stress were taking a toll on the decision-making capabilities of the Japanese high command. None wanted to acknowledge defeat, but the danger of further crippling losses weighed more heavily on their minds as the night progressed. Ugaki judged that there was "little prospect of challenging the enemy with a night engagement before dawn," and worried that the continued pursuit with daylight approaching risked "bringing the situation after dawn beyond control." They had ordered Kurita's cruisers to bombard Midway atoll without air cover, but it was clear that the cruisers would have to contend with Midway's still-formidable air forces before coming within 200 miles of the islands. The hunters would become the hunted.

At 12:15 p.m. on June 5, Yamamoto ordered Kurita to turn his cruisers around and retreat to the west; he instructed Kondo and Nagumo to reverse course and fall in with the Main Body. Plainly, these orders amounted to a declaration of defeat, and must be followed by a general retreat back to Japan. But the staff, passing through the stages of grief, could not bring themselves to admit it to themselves or each other. "Everyone inwardly recognized that we were defeated," wrote Fuchida and Okumiya, "yet not a single member of the staff proposed suspension of the operation. Instead, they desperately cast about for a way to salvage something from the defeat. They were like drowning men grabbing at straws." Commander Yasuji Watanabe proposed bringing the light carriers down from the Aleutians and reinforcing their small air groups with cruiser and battleship floatplanes. With luck, he said, they might inflict enough punishment on the American carriers to reduce the risk of a surface engagement. Captain Kuroshima proposed throwing all available surface units against Midway atoll, in hopes of knocking out the runways and destroying the islands' defenses.

Yamamoto and Ugaki listened to these desperate ploys, but rejected them with increasing vehemence. They were likely only to multiply the losses the Combined Fleet had already suffered. Inevitably, the officers turned to *shogi* metaphors. "You ought to know," Yamamoto scolded Watanabe, "that of all naval tactics, firing one's guns at an island is considered the most stupid." He added: "In *shogi* too much fighting causes all-out defeat. One can lose everything." Ugaki agreed, observing that the staff officers "ought to have known the absurdity of attacking a fortress with a fleet!"

Yamamoto sealed his decision to withdraw with a bald statement: "This battle is almost coming to an end."

Watanabe, chastened, left the bridge and returned with a draft order calling for a general retreat. Yamamoto glanced at it and gave his approval. "DesOpOrd #161" was radioed to all commands at 2:55 a.m.:

(1) The Midway Operation is cancelled.

(2) The Main Body will assemble the Midway Invasion Force and the First Carrier Striking Force (less *Hiryu* and her escorts), and the combined forces will carry out refueling during the morning of 6 June at position 33°N, 1700 E.

(3) The Screening Force, *Hiryu* and her escorts and Nisshin will proceed to the above position.

(4) The Transport Group will proceed westward out of range of Midway-based planes.

One of the officers on *Yamato*'s bridge, with tears streaming freely down his face, asked what would become of *Akagi*. She was immobilized and burning. She could not be towed nor travel under her own power. No one on the *Yamato* was yet aware that the *Kaga* and *Soryu* had been scuttled, and the prospect of firing Japanese torpedoes into the flagship of *Kido Butai* was terrible to contemplate. Captain Kuroshima exclaimed, "We cannot sink the Emperor's warships with the Emperor's own torpedoes!" His passionate outcry silenced the bridge, Watanabe recalled, as "virtually all the members of Yamamoto's staff choked and stopped breathing." Yamamoto, a former skipper of the *Akagi*, was not unmoved. But there was no other alternative, he quietly replied; to allow her to fall into enemy hands was unacceptable. He added: "I was once the captain of the *Akagi*, and it is with heartfelt regret that I must order that she be sunk. I will apologize to the Emperor for the sinking of *Akagi* by our own torpedoes."

The message went out to Nagumo at 3:50 a.m.; Nagumo relayed the order to the destroyers standing by the *Akagi*. The torpedo specialists wept at the order, but carried it out. Four destroyers fired on the *Akagi*, tearing out her bowels, while the crews shouted: "*Akagi banzai!*" At 4:55 a.m., just as the sun peeked over the eastern horizon, the former flagship of *Kido Butai* went under. "Gradually, our once magnificent ship began to tilt over and sank very slowly," Lieutenant Hiroshi Suzuki recalled. "After the carrier was completely submerged underwater there was a very big explosion, and *Akagi* was gone."

The *Hiryu* had kept pace with the rest of Nagumo's force until about 10 p.m., when she had gone dead in the water. She continued to burn furiously, surrounded by destroyers that played their hoses over the flames to little apparent effect. At midnight, a powerful explosion rocked the ship and reignited the fires on her hangar deck. "Half of the deck was completely burned away," said Ensign Maruyama, "and because the edges remained, it looked like a huge casket. Also, in the pockets along the flight deck there were charred bodies of the men who had manned the machine guns. They were hit by the blast from the bombs. All around me I could smell burned flesh. However, what surprised me most was a big wall that was standing upright in front of the bridge area. When I looked more carefully at it, I realized this wall was actually part of the front elevator."

Shortly after midnight, Captain Tomeo Kaku ordered abandon ship, but the process unfolded at a stately, ceremonial pace. Eight hundred men assembled amidships, and stood to attention as Admiral Yamaguchi gave an emotional speech. The crew faced west, toward the Imperial Palace, and gave three "Banzais." The battle ensign and admiral's flag were lowered to the sounds of *Kimigayo*. Then the men began dropping down lines into the sea, where they would be picked up by the destroyer *Makigumo*.

Yamaguchi and Kaku resolved to go down with the ship. Several other officers begged to join them, but Yamaguchi ordered them away, declaring, "Young men must leave the ship. This is my order." To Captain Kaku, the admiral said, "There is such a beautiful moon tonight. Shall we watch it as we sink?" As the other men left the ship, they waved farewell with their caps. The destroyer *Makagumo* fired two torpedoes into the ship, and then left the scene.

Incredibly, however, the *Hiryu* refused to go down. On the morning of the 5th, she was still afloat, and still emitting a long column of smoke. She had dozens of survivors aboard, including members of the engine-room gang who had made an improbable escape from the lower reaches of the burning vessel to reach the flight deck. At last, a few minutes after 9 a.m., the ship went down and the sea closed over her. Thirty-four survivors escaped in a cutter and were later picked up by the Americans.

WITH HIS BLEAK PRONOUNCEMENT on the bridge of the *Yamato*—"This battle is almost coming to an end"—Yamamoto had resigned himself to the inevitable. The Combined Fleet, divided into half a dozen tactical groups that were hundreds or even thousands of miles apart, sped westward in headlong retreat.

Dispossessed of air cover, the fleeing Japanese fleet units could expect to be pursued and assailed by enemy aircraft, and their overriding concern was to escape without further losses. The most vulnerable were the four cruisers of Admiral Kurita's Cruiser Division 7, as they had drawn to within fifty nautical miles of Midway before receiving Yamamoto's order to reverse course and make good their escape. At 2:15 a.m. on June 5, they were sighted and tracked by an American submarine, the *Tambor*. Shortly thereafter, the submarine was in turn spotted by lookouts on the cruiser *Kumano*. The reported contact threw the Japanese column into confusion. *Kumano* signaled a starboard turn to avoid a torpedo attack, but the third cruiser in the column, the *Mikuma*, turned too sharply and collided with her sister, the *Mogami*.

Both ships exceeded 13,000 tons, and were traveling at better than 25-knot speed; the forces brought into play by the collision were spectacular and catastrophic. *Mogami's* bow caved in, and was folded over at right angles to the port side, all the way back to the No. 1 turret. The damage shortened the hull by a full 40 feet. Somehow her engineers were able to get her underway at much-reduced speed. *Mikuma* trailed oil from a ruptured fuel tank, but her wounds were far more manageable. Two destroyers, *Arashio* and *Asashio*, were left behind to escort the damaged cruisers while the rest of Kurita's force surged ahead.

At dawn on the 5th, the cripples were still within air-striking range of Midway. A PBY flew overhead and reported the contact as "two battleships" on a heading of 264 degrees. The cruisers were subjected to heavy air attack from the remaining squadrons at Midway, including six SBD Dauntless dive-bombers and six SB2U Vindicators of VMSB-241, and later a squadron of eight army B-17s. None of these attacks scored a hit, but one of the Vindicators, damaged by antiaircraft fire, crash-dived on the *Mikuma* and struck a glancing blow on the ship's rear turret. *Mikuma* survived and limped westward.

Task Force 16 stayed close to Midway on June 5, in case a new Japanese attack on the atoll developed. Spruance did not receive definite confirmation that the Japanese were in general retreat until late morning, and by that time the *Enterprise* and *Hornet* were socked in by fog, and flight operations were suspended. A few minutes after 3 p.m., both flight decks began launching more than fifty SBD dive-bombers to attack the fleeing stragglers at long range—more than 250 miles. They flew over a tremendous oil slick marking the spot of *Hiryu's* sinking, and soon thereafter sighted a lone Japanese destroyer. That ship, the little 2,000-ton *Tanikaze*, had already been attacked by four Midway-based B-17s, whose bombs had (as usual) missed. She now endured the concentrated attentions of four different squadrons of SBDs—VB-3, VB-6, VS-6, and VS-5. With her speed dialed up to 30 knots, the *Tanikaze* went into a "snake dance"—hard astarboard, hard port, hard astarboard—and the whitewater columns of near misses towered over her on either side. Twenty-year-old Signalman Masashi Shibata leaned out of a window on the bridge and watched the Dauntlesses as they rolled into their dives. He shouted: "Enemy bomber right!" or "Enemy bomber left!" The skipper, Commander Motoi Katsumi, relayed instructions to the helmsman. Near misses killed several of her crew, but the *Tanikaze* somehow managed to avoid taking a single direct hit. Later, after sunset, she was attacked by five more B-17s from Midway. Altogether, she dodged some ninety bombs, one of the most extraordinary escapes in the entire war. The *Enterprise* and *Hornet* SBDs turned back in failing light to follow their carriers' "YE" homing beacons home.

On June 6, the third and final day of the Battle of Midway, Spruance resolved to make a last, all-out attempt to finish off the *Mogami* and *Mikuma*. At daybreak, Task Force 16 launched eighteen Dauntlesses to fly long search missions to the west; at 6:45 a.m., one such plane discovered the two damaged cruisers and two accompanying destroyers. The American flight decks began launching a large strike under the command of Stanhope Ring. They overtook the quartet of surface ships at 9:30 a.m. and launched a series of heavy dive-bombing attacks. With no Zeros in the air to oppose them, they took their time, circling and setting up their dives with painstaking care, and descending in small groups. *Mogami* was hit with two 500-pound bombs that caused her main gun turrets to collapse into her scoutplane hangar deck. *Mikuma* was hit at least five times and suffered two near misses, bringing her to a dead stop. She was set afire and devastated by secondary explosions belowdecks. Looking down from overhead, an American TBD radio-gunner compared her to "a huge bathtub, full of scrap iron and junk." *Mogami* parted ways with her doomed sister, and eventually made her way back to Japan. *Mikuma* sank at dusk on the 6th, taking most of her crew of 888 down with her.

With a long return flight ahead of them, many of the American planes would again stagger back to Task Force 16 with night falling and fuel tanks running dry. At Spruance's order, the *Enterprise* and *Hornet* turned on their searchlights to guide the wayward planes home. It was an unusual decision and a controversial one, as the lights could also draw enemy submarines. In his bland, reticent way, the admiral explained his decision thus: "If planes are to be flown so late in the day that a night recovery is likely, and if the tactical situation is such that the commander is unwilling to do what is required to get the planes back safely, then he has no business launching the attack in the first place."

The returning planes arrived in small groups, descending through heavy overcast, and entered the landing circles as the band of orange light across the western horizon faded to darkness. "The scene was reminiscent of a summer storm on a lake," wrote Ensign Mears, "with the warm, buffeting wind, the darkening clouds, and the lightning stabs of light into the night." Ensign Roy Gee of the *Hornet* had never trained for a night landing, and doubted he could do it safely. He spied a carrier's lights in the distance, and followed the taillights of his squadron leader's aircraft into the landing circle. Gee kept his head, mechanically ticking off the items on his check-list: "wheels down and locked, flaps down, tailhook extended." As he flew the downwind leg of his approach, he made out the illuminated tips of the wands held by the landing signal officer, but could not see the LSO himself. Making his final turn, he received a cut and snagged the third arresting wire. Only after climbing out of his cockpit did he realize he had landed on the *Enterprise*, having mistaken her for the *Hornet*.

FOR TWO NIGHTS AND A DAY, the abandoned *Yorktown* drifted and burned. Admiral Fletcher and the remaining units of Task Force 17 had followed Spruance east, then west, leaving a lone destroyer, the *Hughes*, to stand by the crippled flattop. The captain of the *Hughes* had been ordered to torpedo the *Yorktown* if the Japanese fleet should appear on the horizon;

under no circumstances would she be permitted to fall into enemy hands. But Fletcher had not entirely given up on his former flagship. As long as she floated, there was hope of bringing her back into Pearl Harbor, and the admiral had summoned a tug for that purpose. With the Japanese fleet in retreat, there seemed a real possibility that she could be saved.

On the morning of June 6, Captain Buckmaster assembled a 170-man salvage team and reboarded his blacked-out ship. The *Yorktown* was listing heavily to port—so heavily, indeed, that Buckmaster's party could step directly from the gunwales of the motor launches onto the hangar deck, which was normally 25 feet above the sea. One sailor recalled: "It was weird to see all those pairs of shoes lined up around the hangar deck, some with cigarettes and matches, even a wristwatch, as though they were coming back soon." The oil-smeared deck sloped as steeply as the roof of a house. Without electrical power, the lower reaches of the ship were lit only by firelight. The men inched down the ladders, probing ahead with the beams of their flashlights, as if descending into a cave. They shouted, but no one answered; apparently no survivors had been left aboard the *Yorktown* when she was abandoned two days earlier.

The men got to work stamping out the fires and restoring power to the ship. Everything that could be removed from the upper decks was thrown over the side—the 5-inch guns on the flight deck, the spare aircraft stowed overhead on the hangar deck. The destroyer *Hammann* came close alongside to provide water, electrical power, and foamite. At Buckmaster's order, the *Yorktown*'s starboard fuel tanks were counterflooded with water from the *Hammann*'s firehoses. Gradually, the list diminished, until the *Yorktown* was nearly on an even keel. Buckmaster presided over a burial service for thirty-five men who had been killed in the action of June 4, and had been left on the deck, covered with canvas sheets.

By one o'clock in the afternoon, all remaining fires had been extinguished. A minesweeper, the *Vireo*, had managed to secure a towline to the bow and was towing the carrier through the water at about 3 knots. Suddenly there was hope—perhaps she might be brought into Pearl in one piece. Several more screening destroyers circled protectively at a distance of 2,000 yards.

But the column of smoke trailed by the stricken flattop had attracted a stalker—Japanese submarine *I-168*, commanded by Lieutenant Commander

Yahachi Tanabe. Tanabe approached skillfully and with great audacity, slipped beneath the destroyer screen undetected, and raised his periscope to discover that he was ideally positioned for a close-range attack on the *Yorktown's* starboard beam. At 1:36 p.m., *I-168* launched four torpedoes. At that range, fired on a target that was nearly dead in the water, they could hardly miss. One torpedo hit the *Hammann*; two more passed under the *Hammann's* keel and detonated against the hull of the luckless *Yorktown*. The fourth fish narrowly missed both ships, astern.

The *Hammann's* lookouts spotted the incoming torpedo tracks. All at once, the destroyer's 20mm guns opened up, her alarms sounded, and men on her decks rushed to cut away all the lines, cables, and hoses connecting her to the *Yorktown*. Navy chief machinist's mate Dwight G. DeHaven, standing on the stern of the *Yorktown*, recalled that the destroyer's turbines were screaming and her port propeller was clanging against the *Yorktown's* hull, which "rang like a bell" each time the blade struck. But from that range, there was no time to get clear of the incoming fish. The *Hammann* was struck amidships; the impact lifted more than a hundred sailors off her decks and flung them into the sea; the explosion cut the little tin can in half. The bow section sank in seconds. The stern section, DeHaven recalled, "was standing vertically with her screws coasting to a stop. I could see the damaged flukes flashing in the sunlight."

Fatefully, the *Hammann's* depth charges were fully charged and armed—they would detonate when they reached the depths for which they had been set. A quick-thinking sailor rushed to disarm them, but there was no time. The stern sank from sight, and a few seconds later, the entire rack of depth charges detonated with a tremendous underwater blast that threw men on the *Yorktown* off their feet. Many suffered broken bones in their feet and legs. The men thrown into the sea by the initial torpedo strike had been treading water. "Great walls of water and fuel oil rolled over us and about the time you caught your breath and wiped the oil out of your eyes another wave would hit you," recounted Fireman first class Elmer Jones. Clarence C. Ray, a communications officer, remembered seeing "perhaps a hundred heads, floating on the water as she went under." Most of these were *Hammann* sailors who had been catapulted off the destroyer by the initial torpedo strike. "Just then, the depth charges all exploded. All those heads that had been on the water just before the depth charges exploded suddenly disappeared, something like a windshield wiper erases the droplets from your windshield when it's raining. They were all gone." Eighty-one of the *Hammann*'s complement of 251 men were lost in the action.

Two other torpedoes passed under the *Hammann* and detonated against the starboard side of the *Yorktown* at frames 84 and 95. As they hit, said Bill Roy, the carrier "rocked up and rolled hard. Great explosive sheets of fire, oil, water, and metal blew up between the two ships."

The Japanese submarine dived to her maximum depth and passed directly under the *Yorktown*. The vengeful U.S. destroyers hunted her for two hours, depth-charging her so furiously that she was brought to the brink of destruction. Her batteries were nearly exhausted and toxic acid fumes permeated the ship. But she made good her escape, and returned intact to Kure. Hers had been the most devastating torpedo attack up to that point in the war.

At first it seemed that the *Yorktown* might take these fresh wallops in stride. *I-168*'s torpedoes had struck her starboard side, whereas the wounds she had suffered on June 4 were on her port side. The natural counter-flooding effect brought the *Yorktown* back onto an even keel, though she was much lower in the water, and it was no longer possible to tow her. The salvage teams secured every watertight door they could reach, but the flooding continued, and she continued to settle lower into the sea. As dusk approached, Buckmaster prudently ordered every man off the ship. They would pass the night aboard the *Vireo*, with hopes of returning and continuing to fight for the carrier's life the next morning.

But at dawn on the 7th, the *Yorktown* had settled still further in the water, and her port list had returned. Gradually she rolled all the way onto her beam ends, so that her flight deck was vertical. Her surviving crew watched sadly from the circling destroyers. The two huge wounds torn in her hull by *I-168*'s torpedoes were exposed to view. "We could hear the heavy machinery tearing lose and crashing thunderously into the bulkheads, tearing herself apart internally," said DeHaven. At 7 a.m., the great ship began going down by the stern, "and as she did the bow slowly lifted out of the water about one-third of her length and tons of water cascaded out of the flooded compartments on the forecastle deck. The ship rolled back and forth until the bow stem was plumb, and as she rocked back and forth, she looked like she was waving goodbye. I've never seen so many grown men cry; we all had tears in our eyes." For a few moments, her bow stood straight up out of the sea, like a tombstone. Then the sea closed over the *Yorktown* and she set out on her three-mile voyage into the abyss.

Captain Buckmaster, watching silently from one of the destroyers, asked the helmsman to drive the ship through the foam and debris. In silent tribute it was done. Then the destroyers formed up in a column and retired toward Pearl Harbor.

EPILOGUE

TASK FORCE 16 (*Enterprise*, *Hornet*, AND THEIR ACCOMPANYING surface ships) might have chased the retreating Japanese fleet far into the west, but to do so would have entailed various risks. Admiral Spruance was wary of bringing his ships within air-striking range of Wake Island's land-based bombers. Nor did he want to blunder under the 18-inch guns of the *Yamato* or the 16-inch guns of the other mighty Japanese battlewagons. He later wrote that he had "a feeling, an intuition perhaps, that we had pushed our luck as far to the westward as was good for us." The destroyers, having run at high speed for days, were short of fuel. Barring some dramatic and unlikely reversal of fortune, the Battle of Midway had been decisively won. As night fell on June 6, Spruance decided to let well enough alone. The task force turned back toward Oahu.

The remnants of Admiral Fletcher's Task Force 17 were congested with survivors and wounded men of the late *Yorktown* and *Hammann*. These ships retired toward Pearl Harbor at high speed, to foil enemy submarines—but with their engines dialed up to 25 knots, the destroyers shuddered violently and unremittingly, causing the wounded men terrible agony. The worst casualties were those who had been caught in the water when the *Hammann's* depth charges exploded. Many died during the three-day passage back to Oahu, and were buried at sea. "When they were ready to send one over," an injured sailor on the destroyer *Benham* recalled, "they would blow a whistle and everyone was supposed to come to attention. My stretcher bearers set me down right in line with the dead bodies. I let them know I was still alive!" When the doctors cut open some of the dead, "in order to see what they were dealing with," they discovered that the intestines were perforated with tiny holes, as if filled with buckshot.

They had won the battle—that much the American officers and sailors understood. But they did not yet know the dimensions of their victory, and whatever elation they felt was tempered by uncertainty, disorientation, sorrow, and exhaustion. In his journal, Robert Casey observed that the whole story of the Battle of Midway would not be told for some time to come. "This was a cataclysm observed by tens of thousands of eyes and yet a spectacle that no man saw," he wrote. "Hundreds of men brought back their little bits of it—bits that sometimes fitted together and sometimes didn't— to make the mosaic in which we may one day see the picture of what happened at Midway." Ensign Mears, one of the few survivors of Torpedo Eight (he had not been assigned to fly), recalled that the Hornet aviators tried to collate their experiences into a coherent account, but there remained many questions that none could answer. "Bit by bit, as one fits pieces into a jigsaw puzzle, we learned from one individual and another, by rumor and hearsay, what squadrons had attacked what objectives, and the results."

They knew nothing of what had happened to the defenders on Midway itself, or in the Aleutians, or what the army airmen had achieved. What did it all mean? What was the relative significance of these events? No one could say with confidence.

Every carrier aviator knew, as a matter of cold statistical fact, that his profession was among the most dangerous in the navy. From the earliest stages of their flight training, and many times since, they had been warned that they would lose friends and squadron mates. But the "irrevocable finality of death," as one young dive-bomber pilot put it, came as a terrible shock. There was never a body to bury. The slain airmen were simply never seen again. Their deaths were potently symbolized by the rows of empty chairs in the carrier ready rooms. "The reaction of the pilots to the annihilation of their comrades was one of bewilderment," wrote Mears. "There was no evidence that they had been killed. The dead just were not there, and it was hard for the others to realize that they never would be." Ensign Clay Fisher recalled entering the Torpedo Eight ready room and finding it "completely empty except for the pilots' uniforms hanging on the hooks, left there after they had changed into their flight suits." Both young ensigns—Mears and Fisher—were assigned to sort through their fallen colleagues' personal possessions and pack them off to the next of kin. They did the job with heavy hearts. Mears: "Going through every person's private effects—seeing a characteristically battered cap, a girl's picture, an earmarked Prayer Book, or a wallet with various cards in it—made us realize how much each one would be missed at home."

On the other hand, there was no arguing with the fact that the Japanese navy had sent an enormously powerful fleet into battle, and lost four first-line carriers. The American colors still flew over Midway atoll, and the remnants of the enemy fleet were in abject retreat toward Japan. "It turns out that we have fought a major engagement—one of the biggest naval battles of all time," Casey observed. "And miracle of miracles, we have won. It was too stupendous to contemplate as we lolled in a mist of nervous exhaustion, mumbling to one another in senseless monosyllables, falling to sleep over our coffee."

Nimitz had followed the course of the battle from the operation plot room in the CINCPAC headquarters. The room, as Layton described it, was "a rather primitive affair that consisted of a large chart of the Pacific laid over plywood across a pair of sawhorses." Over that chart was placed a large sheet of tracing paper, and a staff officer continually drew, in blue crayon, the known position and tracks of American and Japanese fleet units. Scattered radio intercepts had told the tale of the battle. Nimitz and the staff had alternated between elation and anxiety as the action progressed. On the morning of June 4, Nimitz learned of the massacre of Torpedo Eight. Layton recorded that he was "as frantic as I have ever seen him. He appeared agitated and called for his communications officer, Commander Curtis, to know why we were not getting any messages or hearing something. Although they must have known by now that they could break radio silence, it seemed that our task force commanders were neglecting to keep Nimitz informed of what was going on."

Later that afternoon, Spruance broke radio silence to report that four Japanese carriers were hit and burning. A relieved Nimitz sent a dispatch to all units: "You who have participated in the battle of Midway today have written a glorious page in our history. I am proud to be associated with you. I estimate that another day of all-out effort on your part will complete the defeat of the enemy." On June 6 he issued a communiqué, which appeared the next day in the American newspapers: "Pearl Harbor has now been partially avenged. Vengeance will not be complete until Japanese seapower is reduced to impotence." The CINCPAC allowed himself a bit of uncharacteristic levity. "Perhaps we will be forgiven if we claim we are about midway to our objective."

THE REMNANTS OF *Kido Butai* crawled westward to fall in with the Main Body. Admiral Nagumo, whose flag now flew on the light cruiser *Nagara*, told his staff officers that he was inclined to take his own life, and some vowed to join him. But Admiral Ryunosuke Kusaka, Nagumo's chief of staff, rejected suicide as a coward's exit. "You are just like hysterical women," he told them; "first you get excited over easy victories, and now you are worked up to commit suicide because of a defeat! This is no time for Japan for you to say such a thing. Why not think of turning a misfortune into blessing through your efforts?" Nagumo listened but was not immediately persuaded, replying in low tones, "You must understand that everything a Commander in Chief does cannot be by reason." After further discussion, Nagumo relented. "Very well. I will never commit a rash act."

The surface ships were crowded with survivors of the late carriers, and many slept on cramped decks, exposed to the weather. Miyasato Yoshihito of the *Chitose* recalled burying the ship's dead at sea. The crew stood to attention while the naval anthem *Umi Yukaba*—"Across the Sea"—was played over the loudspeaker. An honor guard fired a salute. A casket was released into the sea. "It didn't sink for quite a while," he recalled, "and we could see it drifting farther and farther away, in and out of the waves."

As dawn broke each day, the cruisers and battleships launched their floatplanes to fly search patterns back toward the east, but those aircraft had little value in aerial combat. The fleet had no fighter protection at all; if caught by the American carrier planes, they would be sitting ducks, and they all knew it. On the other hand, there was some hope that the American flattops could be coaxed into air-striking range of Wake's big land-based bombers, or perhaps even the guns of the Japanese battleships. On the morning of the 8th, it was apparent that the Americans had given up the chase. Ugaki observed, "We had no choice but to give up our intention of launching an all-out counterattack with the whole Combined Fleet." With fuel running low, there was nothing left but a long, melancholy passage to the home islands.

The Combined Fleet staff, in their cavernous quarters on the great flagship *Yamato*, stared out to sea, shocked and depressed. They said little; there was not much that could be usefully said. Yamamoto's yeoman, Mitsuharu Noda, recalled that air officer Sasaki "looked as if he felt he was personally responsible for the defeat, showing it in his growth of beard, his sunken eyes, his unhappy, weary face." Yamamoto himself was sick, sallow, and deflated. He spent most of his days behind the closed door of his stateroom, said Noda, and appeared only briefly to stand on the compass bridge and sip rice gruel. Ugaki noted that the commander in chief "suffered from a stomachache, which did not improve much in spite of treatment by a fleet doctor. This, too, is a source of concern in such a grave moment as this." The ailment was diagnosed as roundworms, and treated with doses of "vermifluge." By June 9 he seemed better, though his officers noted that Yamamoto "had been out of action for rather longer than treatment for worms would normally have required."

As Nagumo's force joined up with the Main Body on June 10, Yamamoto's staff played nice. No blame was shed, for indeed all must have realized that the greatest weight of responsibility for the defeat rested on Yamamoto's shoulders. Yamamoto had acknowledged as much, declaring that the defeat was "all his responsibility, and they were not to criticize the Nagumo force." Genda, Onishi, and Kusaka, appearing haggard and exhausted, went aboard the *Yamato* by breeches buoy. Entering Yamamoto's private cabin, Kusaka said: "Admittedly, we are not in a position to come back alive shamelessly after having made such a blunder, but we have come back only to pay off the score some day, so I beg you from the bottom of my heart to give us such a chance in the future." Yamamoto replied curtly: "All right." Ugaki tried to ease Kusaka's mind, offering him gifts and even money, and listened for the first time to the eyewitness accounts of the demise of the four carriers. The three men returned to the *Nagara* that afternoon.

SINCE DECEMBER 7, the people of Oahu had lived under the constant threat of invasion. Now, as the American fleet returned to Pearl, they breathed easier—for the first time in six months the safety of the Hawaiian Islands seemed assured. Nimitz often went down to the wharves to greet returning ships. As the *Enterprise* and *Hornet* slid into their berths, the carrier aircrews left their ships and checked into the Royal Hawaiian or the Moana Hotel, both on Waikiki Beach, which had been commandeered for officers' R&R. They plunged into their customary all-night bacchanals, but their carousing was more anguished than joyful. Some young men wept drunkenly for their dead friends; others brawled or vandalized hotel property. The MPs, shore patrol, and hotel detectives were harassed at every turn. "The routine of the returning airmen for the next few nights consisted of their tramping from room to room hunting for liquor, talking, arguing, fighting, and breaking the furniture," Mears recalled. "Some few were feeling tender enough to want to find a girl, but for the most part their emotions were released in being just as mean as they could. I saw two boys who were good friends beating each other in the face with their fists, not trying to duck or box, until they both had black eyes and were crimson with blood. Another pilot tried to throw his smaller friend out of a window." The aviators were infuriated by press reports wrongly crediting the Army Air Forces with sinking the Japanese carriers. When airmen of the two services met in Honolulu, hard words were exchanged, and in some cases fisticuffs. Not until after the war would it be conclusively established that navy dive-bombers had done all of the damage to the Japanese fleet.

In Washington, on June 7, reporters filed into a Naval Headquarters conference room to be briefed by Admiral King. It was King's first press conference since the start of the war. "In comparison with the losses of the enemy," he said, "United States losses are inconsiderable." He admitted that it was not yet clear what was happening in the Aleutians, partly because heavy fog had limited contact with enemy forces. A reporter asked if it was true that the Japanese had hurled their entire navy into the conflict. "Perhaps not everything, but the bulk of it. One of their methods of doing things is not to send a boy to do a man's job." Pressed to reveal whether the American fleet would pursue the retreating Japanese forces, King grew touchy. He pointed out that the Japanese had substantial shore-based airpower on Wake Island. "With 130,000,000 amateur strategists in this country, many would undoubtedly advocate some such follow-up action," he said, but "for us to rush in to a mop-up operation might not be well-advised."

Four of Japan's finest fleet carriers and a heavy cruiser sunk; a cruiser and several destroyers damaged; 292 aircraft destroyed; more than 3,000 Japanese killed. The Americans had won their stunning victory at the cost of the *Yorktown* and *Hammann* sunk, 145 planes destroyed, and 307 men killed in action. In Raymond Spruance, Nimitz had discovered the most valuable American seagoing commander of the Second World War (though for the time being he was to be cast ashore as the CINCPAC's chief of staff). Spruance, characteristically, did not even deign to answer his critics, who faulted him for a lack of aggressiveness in not pursuing the enemy fleet on the night of the 4/5th. Though he might have leveled damaging criticism at Captain Mitscher for the poor performance of *Hornet*'s air group, or at Halsey's staff (and his chief of staff, Captain Miles R. Browning, in particular), he held his fire. He was generous in his praise of Fletcher, to whom he wrote on June 8: "If it had not been for what you did and took with the *Yorktown*, I am firmly convinced that we would have been badly defeated and the Japs would be holding Midway today. As it is, I think their ears will be pinned back for some time to come."

Possessing foreknowledge of Japanese intentions, Nimitz had been dealt a very strong hand. It is also true that he played that hand skillfully, indeed flawlessly. In arranging his forces, Nimitz had concentrated on one overriding objective to the exclusion of all others: to ambush and destroy the Japanese carriers. Whereas Yamamoto's plan was vast and fatally complex, Nimitz's was straightforward, and aimed at the enemy's most vulnerable point. He had provided Midway atoll with all the airpower he could scrape together, overruling the local Army Air Forces commanders who wanted to retain more aircraft on Oahu. He had placed his three carriers on Nagumo's port flank, distant enough to avoid early detection, but near enough to launch a punishing attack. Though he knew the Japanese would attack the Aleutians, he had refused to divert the bulk of his forces from the main event north of Midway. He had been content to concede the loss of the westernmost islands in the Aleutians archipelago, knowing they offered little value as military assets and could be recaptured in good time. That attitude was consistent with the teachings of Miyamoto Musashi, the renowned samurai swordsman of the sixteenth century. "As far as attacks made on you are concerned," Musashi had advised, "let opponents go ahead and do anything useless, while stopping them from doing anything useful. This is essential to the art of war."

Fletcher and Spruance had evaded detection until Nagumo's airstrike on Midway was aloft and on its way; they had launched their aircraft before Nagumo could respond; they had maneuvered their ships out of the way of the onrushing guns of the Main Body. Once *Yorktown* was abandoned, Fletcher had generously ceded tactical command of remaining American forces to Spruance. After the decisive first day of the battle, Spruance had resisted the temptation (and the advice of some of the other officers) to chase far to the west, demonstrating a prudence that kept faith with Nimitz's instructions to act according to "calculated risk," and consolidating the American victory.

Even so, the Americans had needed more than a few strokes of good luck. The battle had been a near-run thing, and easily might have gone the other way. The Japanese cruiser scouts might have found the American carriers an hour earlier, giving Nagumo precious time to prepare and launch an effective counterstrike before the dive-bombers hurtled down on *Kido Butai*. Those dive-bombers, the most potent weapon in the American arsenal, arrived over the enemy at just the right time and in the right sequence, when the Zeros had been spread far and wide at low altitude. By lucky happenstance, the *Enterprise* and *Yorktown* Dauntlesses, having launched at different times and flown widely divergent courses to the enemy, converged on the fleet simultaneously from different directions. Luck (and some quick thinking on the part of Lieutenant Dick Best, leader of Bombing Six) ensured that the SBDs attacked and scored fatal hits on three different Japanese carriers, when they easily might have concentrated their attacks on only one or two. Subsequently, *Hiryu's* two strikes each targeted the *Yorktown*, although the *Enterprise* and *Hornet* were well within range, with the result that two of three American flattops survived the battle with no damage at all.

In Spruance's view, he had merely acted out his part in a script written by Nimitz. He had done nothing brilliant; he had been lucky. "We were shot with luck on the morning of June 4, when the fate of the operation was decided," he wrote later. As for his own role in the action: "All that I can claim credit for, myself, is a very keen sense of the urgent need for surprise and a strong desire to hit the enemy carriers with our full strength as early as we could reach them."

As momentous as it was, Midway did not in itself turn the tide of the Pacific War. The American mobilization was proceeding apace, but would require another six months to take effect on the distant frontiers of the Pacific theater. For the Japanese navy, the destruction of four fleet carriers with all their aircraft was obviously a devastating blow, as was the loss of so many trained mechanics and crewmen. But most of the Japanese aircrews had survived the action. By one historian's estimate, 110 Japanese carrier aviators died at Midway—only about one quarter of those who had sailed with *Kido Butai*. Those surviving veterans were, at this stage of the war, the most valuable asset in the Japanese naval air arsenal.

Even so, Midway had blunted the tip of the Japanese spear. Yamamoto had gambled on knocking the U.S. Navy out of the war, and lost. He would never again muster the forces to mount a sustained offensive against any Allied territory. Midway made certain that the Pacific War would be a prolonged war of attrition—precisely the sort of war that Yamamoto had warned against. The Japanese navy retained a cadre of superb pilots, but Japan was not producing enough new flyers to replace those inevitably killed in action. Facing shortages of aircraft, fuel, and ammunition, and with too few seasoned professional instructors, Japan had no obvious means of expanding its flight training pipeline. In 1943, 1944, and 1945, the Japanese navy would speed the flight training process by relaxing its standards—critically, by reducing the number of flying hours each trainee would perform before graduating into front-line service. An increasing proportion of newly minted Japanese aviators would be shipped off to war with no live firing experience. With little hope of relief, Japan's remaining veteran flyers were condemned to keep flying until they died, and they knew it. Many would give their lives in the latter half of 1942, during the long, arduous, and ultimately futile struggle for control of the island of Guadalcanal.

In the American view, Midway eliminated the risk of a Japanese attack on Hawaii or the west coast of North America. As important, it relieved political pressure on FDR to transfer a greater share of forces to the Pacific, freeing him to emphasize his greatest priority, which was to keep the Soviet Union in the war against Germany. In that sense, the Battle of Midway ratified and confirmed the vital "Europe-first" strategy. For that reason, it ranks as one of the most essential events of the Second World War, bearing not only on the conflict in the Pacific but on the fate of Nazi Germany.

Joe Rochefort and his team of cryptanalysts had been brilliantly vindicated, but none found it easy to savor the triumph. A week before the battle, just as the Japanese fleet had put to sea, the Japanese navy had adopted a new cipher book for its main operational code, JN-25. This changeover, from "JN-25-B" to "JN-25-C," wiped out the codebreakers' accumulated efforts of the previous six months. Once again, Japanese radio intercepts were indecipherable. They would remain so until the exhausted cryptanalysts could summon the will and energy to do it all again. According to Jasper Holmes, the mood among his colleagues was gloomy. "Perhaps it was exhaustion, like that of a distance runner collapsing over the tape at the end of a long, hard race, but cryptanalysis was always a manic-depressive business. . . . Each man feared in his bones that we would never again succeed in the long and difficult task of breaking a new code."

Rochefort allowed his team to take a short break, and someone organized a staff party at a private home on Diamond Head. "This thing was a great big drunken brawl," Rochefort later recalled. "That's all it was . . . just a straight out-and-out drunken brawl." But after a day or two, they all drifted back in to the dungeon and resumed their customary round-the-clock routine, "because by this time we had this new edition [of the Japanese code] we had to start reading as of yesterday hopefully."

Admiral Nimitz concluded that the Battle of Midway was "essentially a victory of intelligence." His foreknowledge of the Japanese plan was an asset equivalent in value, perhaps, to two additional carrier groups. Nimitz had known when the Japanese forces would sortie, and from where; he had known where the attacks would fall, and when; he had known that the Japanese would attempt to reconnoiter Pearl Harbor with seaplanes before the battle, and that they would deploy a submarine picket line to observe and intercept the American fleet. He had known when and where the enemy forces would rendezvous after the operation. The success of the American codebreaking campaign was so complete that it consolidated the field of communications intelligence within the U.S. Navy. By making believers out of the key decision makers in the upper ranks, who had entered naval service when radio technology was in its infancy, the victory at Midway ensured that communications intelligence would never again suffer for funding, manpower, or respect.

Many men had contributed bits and pieces to the breaking of the Japanese code, including those stationed in Melbourne and Washington; but it was Joe Rochefort who had taken those bits and pieces and assembled them into an accurate mosaic. Rochefort had a rare genius for the art of sifting through masses of disparate and contradictory data. He drew liberally upon his knowledge and experience as a naval officer who had served long years at sea, and also upon his understanding of the Japanese language and culture. He relied upon logical deduction; he played hunches; he developed theories and tested them repeatedly until he was sure he was right. No less important, he knew how to persuade his superiors (Nimitz, especially) of the soundness of his conclusions even when he lacked absolute proof. Tom

Dyer said that Rochefort's special talent was to "make a silk purse out of a sow's ear." The early intercepts referring to Midway "were perfectly capable of being read in a totally different way than the correct way. Knowledge of the character of the Japanese . . . enabled him to get the right meaning."

However belatedly, Rochefort's historic achievement has won the recognition it deserves. Edward L. Beach, the submarine captain–turned–historian of the U.S. Navy, memorably concluded: "To Commander Joe Rochefort must forever go the acclaim for having made more difference, at a more important time, than any other naval officer in history." In 2003, the Battle of Midway Roundtable, an online community of veterans and historians, was asked to name the single "most important combatant" in the battle. The result of the survey, fittingly, was a tie between Nimitz and Rochefort. Support for Rochefort was particularly strong among the Midway veterans.

But in June 1942, no one outside a privileged circle knew that the Japanese code had been broken—and even within that privileged circle, few were aware that Rochefort had drawn the right conclusions while his superiors in Washington had clung obdurately to the wrong ones. Rochefort may have been vindicated by events, but he was a marked man. For proving his rivals wrong, he would pay with his career. His enemies in Washington—the Redman brothers, Commander Wenger, and unidentified members of Admiral King's staff—apparently conspired to seize credit for the victory while diminishing Hypo's role. The conspirators, perfectly aware that strict wartime secrecy would abet their misconduct, did not merely shade the facts but directly lied. The Redmans falsely maintained that analysts at OP-20-G, rather than Hypo, had identified June 3 as the date of the initial attacks; they argued that Rochefort was unqualified to run Hypo and should be removed from the post, because he was "an ex-Japanese language student" who was "not technically trained in Naval Communications"; and they told everyone who would listen that "Pearl Harbor had missed the boat at the Battle of Midway but the Navy Department had saved the day." When word of the codebreaking success was inadvertently leaked to the *Chicago Tribune*, the Redmans maliciously implied that Rochefort had been the source of the leak.*

---

* It was later discovered that *Lexington* executive officer Mort Seligman had improperly shared a classified dispatch with *Tribune* reporter Stanley Johnston.

The campaign succeeded. Both men were soon promoted, and the elder brother, Rear Admiral Joseph R. Redman, was awarded a Distinguished Service Medal. When Rochefort was put up for the same medal with Nimitz's strong endorsement, the application was denied. Rochefort was recalled to Washington and shunted into jobs in which his talents were wasted. "I have given a great deal of thought to the Rochefort affair," Tom Dyer later wrote, "and I have been unwillingly forced to the conclusion that Rochefort committed the one unforgivable sin. To certain individuals of small mind and overweening ambition, there is no greater insult than to be proved wrong." Jasper Holmes made the same point a bit more poetically: "It was not the individual for whom the bell tolled but the navy [that] died a little."

Years later, after he had retired from the navy, Rochefort was asked to comment on the affair. He steadfastly refused to do so. Whether he deserved a medal for his efforts, he said, was beside the point. "We felt that we had earned our pay, because we felt that we had done the job," he said. "We would have preferred to be on ships, but this was the job to which we had been assigned and the job that we seemed to be best fitted for, so therefore we did the best we could." When the interviewer pressed him to elaborate, he demurred. "This would be a very sad and disappointing story, and I would not think that anything would be gained by going into it now." Pressed further, Rochefort grew testy. "That's history. I'm not going to discuss this matter any longer with you."

NEWS OF THE ABYSMAL DEFEAT filtered into Japan. At the Imperial Headquarters in Tokyo, a witness recalled, the staff officers muttered to one another, "This is terrible. A disaster." At Nagasaki, at the dockyard where the *Musashi* had been built, navy personnel "seemed strangely confused, standing silently with their arms folded." The emperor was informed of the loss of the four carriers by an officer of the Naval General Staff. He was badly shaken, but managed to keep his chin up. "I had presumed the news of the terrible losses sustained by the naval air force would have caused him untold anxiety," wrote Lord Privy Seal Koichi Kido on June 8, "yet when I saw him he was as calm as usual and his countenance showed not the least change. He said he told the navy chief of staff that the loss was regrettable but to take care that the navy not lose its fighting spirit. He ordered him to ensure that future operations continue bold and aggressive."

On June 10, in a meeting of the liaison conference, navy officers discussed the battle but omitted the tally of Japanese losses. Even General Tojo, who as prime minister of Japan might have expected prompt and unadulterated reports from the battle fronts, did not learn of the full extent of the navy's losses until a week after the fact. Hirohito took a direct hand in the cover-up. He named an army general to oversee the process of disseminating the truth to military planners, in hopes of limiting the circle to a bare minimum. The emperor also directed that the returning wounded be sequestered in hospitals and naval bases until they could be reassigned to a departing ship or sent to a forward combat area.

The initial Japanese press reports were risibly exaggerated even when compared to the official results released later by the Imperial General Headquarters. On June 6, the English-language broadcasts of Radio Tokyo announced that "Six carriers of the United States Navy, which is very deficient in carriers, were sunk in a single smashing blow. Our fleet broke down the pitiful opposition of the United States fleet, bombarded the defenses of Midway and captured the islands with insignificant losses on our part. An attack has been started on Pearl Harbor and Honolulu. Honolulu is still holding out."

Subsequent Japanese news reports dwelled on the aerial bombing of Midway and Dutch Harbor, the successful occupation of the two Aleutian islands, and the shelling of Sydney, Australia, by a Japanese submarine (the incident had occurred the same week). Newspapers and magazines published lavish photo spreads that appeared to substantiate the triumphant headlines. Soldiers stood to attention as the Japanese flag was raised over the island of Kiska. In pictures taken from the air over Midway and Dutch Harbor, one could see warehouses, hangars, and oil tanks burning fiercely. A column of soldiers on Attu, grinning broadly for the camera, pulled a machine gun on a bobsled over a snowfield; in an adjoining photo, they slid down an icy hill on their bottoms. They laughed merrily, as if on a winter holiday.

"It is curious that the enemy was unable to prevent the Japanese army and naval units from landing and occupying . . . his own territory," said Captain Hideo Hiraide, an Imperial Headquarters spokesman. "Naval operations have crossed the International dateline and entered the Eastern Pacific area, while the occupation of western Aleutians islands has pointed a sword at the enemy's throat."

Rear Admiral Tanetsugu Sosa, writing in the *Nichi Nichi*, explained that the next stage of the war would take the Japanese navy to California. "Now that America's northern attack route against our country and the most important enemy base in the Pacific Ocean have been crushed by the Imperial Navy in the recent battles of Dutch Harbor and Midway, Japan can now concentrate on attacking the mainland of the United States," he wrote. "With its east coast constantly menaced by German and Italian war-craft and its west coast fully exposed to the possible attack by Japan, the United States has been driven between the devil and the deep sea."

Reported Japanese losses were suspiciously vague and inconsistent. On the 10th, the Navy Ministry notified all commands that the official tally would be cited as one carrier sunk, one carrier and one cruiser damaged, and thirty-five airplanes lost. The next day, a well-known civilian naval expert reported in a radio broadcast that two Japanese carriers had been sunk. Not until June 21 did the navy promulgate its official story about the fate of *Kido Butai*. Two carriers, *Kaga* and *Soryu*, would be "taken off the ship's register when there is suitable opportunity"—i.e., the navy would tacitly admit that they were gone, but quietly and in the most enigmatic manner possible. The *Akagi* and *Hiryu* would remain on the register, "but will not be manned"—in other words, the navy would concede that they had been damaged, but maintain the fiction that they had returned safely to Japan and were undergoing repairs. It was essential that "secrecy will be maintained . . . and discretion manfully exerted."

Had these accounts been intended to mislead the Americans, they might have had a valid military purpose. (Indeed, the Americans had suppressed news of the sinking of the *Lexington* after the Battle of the Coral Sea.) But the Japanese also claimed that the U.S. Navy had lost a *San Francisco*-class cruiser, a submarine, and 150 planes—assertions the enemy could not be expected to believe. Mitsuo Fuchida observed that the Americans had "promptly announced to the whole world the damage inflicted on the Japa-nese, accurately naming the ships damaged and sunk. Thus it was clear that our efforts to conceal the truth were aimed at maintaining morale at home rather than at keeping valuable knowledge from the enemy."

The Japanese fleet put into Hashirajima on June 14, through Bungo Strait waters shrouded in a gray fog. Returning crewmen were shuttled from ships to bases to overseas posts, where their eyewitness accounts of the battle could not seep out into civilian society. Many were confined to base, while others received brief liberty passes but were warned not to travel to Tokyo on penalty of arrest. Wounded men were carried off their ships in the dead of night, sheets drawn up over their faces as if they were dead, and quarantined in isolated medical wards. Though he was not seriously injured, Fuchida was put in a secure ward at the Yokosuka Naval Base. "My room was placed in complete isolation," he recorded. "No nurses or corpsmen were allowed entry, and I could not communicate with the outside. In such manner were those wounded at Midway cut off from the rest of the world. It was really confinement in the guise of medical treatment, and I sometimes had the feeling of being a prisoner of war."

Nagumo and the top surviving officers of the First Air Fleet staff met on the battleship *Kirishima*. There was much discussion of needed changes—better plane-handling, armored flight decks, better damage control and fire-fighting procedures, a larger complement of Zeros to fly combat air patrol over the carriers. Many Japanese officers blamed the defeat on inadequate reconnaissance flights. Air officer Minoru Genda later gave his opinion that a lack of emphasis on patrol flights and reconnaissance was "the vital cause of defeat." The Japanese were "fully aware" of the importance of reconnaissance, and yet, in spite of that, "we esteemed attack forces too highly." Admiral Nobutake Kondo agreed: "We met with fiasco because we did not get any sign of the existence of an American task force near Midway Island. The need of high-speed, long-range reconnaissance planes was badly felt. It was our great regret that we lacked sufficient measures in establishing guard screens by means of submarines both ahead and to the sides of our fleet, as well as the fact that we failed to have some submarines go to Midway Island beforehand to get some information."

Japan's two remaining fleet carriers, *Shokaku* and *Zuikaku*, were organized as Carrier Division 1. They would remain under the command of Admiral Nagumo. (Many in the fleet blamed Nagumo for flaccid decision making in the desperate hours of the morning of June 4, but Yamamoto refused to allow his subordinate to take the blame.) Now, somewhat belatedly, the Japanese navy acknowledged the primacy of carriers over battleships and other surface units. Hulls that had originally been laid down as battleships were converted on the stocks to new carriers.

Reassured that the navy had won another spectacular victory, the Japanese public had no reason to expect heads to roll, and no senior officer lost his post. Yamamoto remained one of the most prominent and beloved figures in Japanese public life. But it was he who bore the greatest share of responsibility for the Japanese defeat. His plan had dispersed the fleet too widely, forfeiting the possibilities of mutual support. It had violated Mahan's most fundamental tenet—concentration of forces—and for no good reason. It allowed the American fleet to isolate and destroy Nagumo's carriers before any support could be rendered by the other elements of the Japanese fleet.

ON JUNE 10, the *New York Times* quoted an unnamed Japanese admiral who had commented in a Tokyo newspaper on the result at Midway. Though the admiral had not revealed details of Japanese losses, he did hint that the Japanese navy now anticipated a prolonged war of attrition in the Pacific. He maintained that Japan's superior endurance and fighting spirit would prevail in such a struggle. "If the war should be protracted, both sides would be greatly exhausted," he said. "Hence, in the long run that side would lose that first tired of the struggle and the losses entailed by it." Two days earlier, the *New York Times* had quoted Admiral King, who emphasized the importance of American material superiority. In a war of attrition, said King, the Japanese would be gravely disadvantaged, because "their capacity to replace their losses is all too obviously not equal to our capacity."

Here, neatly encapsulated in these two remarks, were the two combatants' strategic paradigms for the remaining war. Japan's transcendent "fighting spirit" was to be pitted against America's overwhelming industrial-military might.

For the three years of war to come, the Japanese acclaimed their unique "*Yamato* spirit," and willed themselves to believe that it must deliver ultimate victory. They believed themselves to be a race like no other—a family of 100 million (the figure was about 30 million too high), racially pure and homogenous, descended from the gods, and united under the benevolent guidance of a father-emperor. The ideology was reinforced and disseminated by official slogans: "100 million advancing like a ball of flame"; "Think as one, act as one"; "Extravagance is the enemy." Fired with overriding spirit, the Japanese at home and on the front lines would endure privations and hardships that the enemy could never withstand—they would work harder, eat less, and face death with samurai-like indifference. The new ethic was derived from traditional samurai and Zen ideas; at the same time it was a monstrous perversion of those ideas.

Military production and the relative size of the American and Japanese economies meant nothing, as one commentator said—for "true combat power is arms multiplied by fighting spirit. If one of them is infinitely strong, you will succeed." As a corollary to that equation, it followed that nothing was impossible; every failure was, in essence, a failure of will. The answer to any military problem was to exhort the soldiers, sailors, and airmen to strive harder, to find the motivation to overcome whatever difficulties they encountered. They must abhor retreat or surrender. As the war grew more desperate in 1944 and 1945, many Japanese servicemen resolved to seek death for death's sake, "to die as one of the emperor's limbs"—for death in combat was a kind of ritual purification, and to spill one's own blood was akin to the Shinto "ablution with water."

For all its industrial-military power, the Japanese militarists calmly asserted, the United States lacked the requisite intangible spiritual qualities to prevail over Japan. A mongrel people, hopelessly individualistic and democratic, pitted against one another in bitter capitalist competition, the Americans would soon tire of the fight and go home. American women, whose excessive political influence was symbolized by the prominence of Eleanor Roosevelt, would not tolerate the loss of so many husbands, sons, and brothers. They would demand an end to the bloodshed before the war ever reached Japanese shores. Therefore it followed that the harder and more brutally the Japanese waged the conflict, the more quickly American resolve would wither. So it was said.

If the premise had been correct, Japan's "fighting spirit" paradigm would undoubtedly have won the war. Latent industrial-military strength would count for little if the American people did not consent to fight. But from the day Nagumo's carriers attacked Pearl Harbor, there was never any realistic prospect that the United States would fail to conquer and subjugate Japan. The American conception of "fighting spirit" was very different from that of the Japanese, but once fully aroused it was sufficient to the task, and sufficiently resilient. Bob Sherwood, the playwright–turned–presidential speechwriter, offered a very wise and provocative observation on this topic. Writing shortly after the war, he concluded that the American people's collective morale "did not become a vital consideration. Morale was never particularly good nor alarmingly bad. There was a minimum of flag waving and parades. It was the first war in American history in which the general disillusionment preceded the firing of the first shot. It has been called, from the American point of view, 'the most unpopular war in history'; but that could be taken as proof that the people for once were not misled as to the terrible nature and extent of the task that confronted them."

Broadly united behind the war, the United States nonetheless remained a fractious democracy. There was no sudden scarcity of partisan acrimony, scandalmongering, electioneering, labor strife, violent crime, war profiteering, bid-rigging, ration-dodging, race riots, black marketeering, and bureaucratic turf-skirmishing. The hard-core isolationists had professed to fall in line behind the war, but they generally continued to hate the president and his circle of advisers no less ardently than they had before Pearl Harbor. Influential voices in Congress and the press demanded that the great weight of American power be turned away from Europe toward the Pacific. Roosevelt's critics suggested that the president should relinquish his constitutional powers as commander in chief and confer them upon a properly qualified military authority, perhaps in the person of General MacArthur. CBS broadcaster Elmer Davis famously quipped: "There are some patriotic citizens who sincerely hope that America will win the war—but they also hope that Russia will lose it; and there are some who hope that America will win the war, but that England will lose it; and there are some who hope that America will win the war, but that Roosevelt will lose it!"

Even so, the retooling of the American economy for war was accomplished in remarkably little time. In April 1942, the U.S. War Production Board announced that the United States was already outproducing the Axis. The swift mobilization was overseen by an "alphabet soup" of new federal agencies—OPA, OPM, DPC, WPB, WRB, and SPAB.* It was not enough to write new federal contracts for ships, airplanes, and tanks. To effect an overnight militarization of the American economy, it was thought necessary to control the allocation of vital materials, and even to ban private industry from serving consumer markets. William Knudsen, chief of the Office of Production Management (OPM), refused to allow scarce raw materials to be fed into Detroit's automobile assembly lines. The nation could no longer afford to manufacture automobiles for non-military uses, he said, because there was not enough rubber for the tires. The factories would manufacture weapons of war or they would not manufacture at all. The

---

* Office of Price Administration; Office of Production Management; Defense Plant Corporation; War Production Board; War Resources Board; Supply, Priorities, and Allocations Board.

intrusion of federal power into the private economy was unprecedented in all of American history, up to that time and ever since, but the effort succeeded in spectacular fashion.

Between 1940 and 1943, Britain tripled its war production; Germany and Russia doubled theirs; and Japan increased its war production fourfold. In that three-year period, the United States multiplied its war production by twenty-five times. U.S. aircraft production had stood at 5,856 units in 1939; in 1942, the figure reached 25,436. In the year 1944 alone, the United States would produce 96,318 aircraft, more than Japan's total production between 1939 and 1945. Shortly after Pearl Harbor, Roosevelt approved a proposal to augment the 1940 naval expansion bill to build an additional 8 aircraft carriers, 24 cruisers, 102 destroyers, and 54 submarines—a total of 900,000 tons. The keels would all be laid by 1944. But even these plans were not sufficiently grand. In January 1942, the General Board of the Navy envisioned a fleet composed of 34 battleships, 24 carriers, 12 battle cruisers, 104 other cruisers, 379 destroyers, and 207 submarines. Since the nation's shipyards were already producing at capacity, there were only so many new keels that could be laid right away. By 1945, however, the U.S. Navy would be larger (as measured either by number of ships or tonnage) than the combined fleets of every other navy in the world.

New recruits flooded into navy boot camps, where they had their hair sheared off—"leaving only an inch on top, bare on the sides." They were assigned to two-story barracks where (they were firmly informed) there were no floors, no stairs, no elevators, no walls, no beds, and no bathrooms. (This being the navy, there were decks, ladders, hoists, bulkheads, bunks, and heads.) Dressed in dungaress, leggings, and round white hats, they drilled and marched for hours each day on blacktop parade grounds, "under arms, back and forth, up and down, on the oblique, to the rear rear rear harch." Each crack of dawn they were rudely awakened with the shouted order: "Let go of your cocks and grab your socks." Then they were off on trains and buses to distant regions of the country, and if they were sailors they were probably headed west, to San Diego or San Francisco or Puget Sound, the great staging and transshipment centers of the Pacific War.

The trains were inundated. General Eisenhower recalled of that period: "Guns were loaded on flatcars, if flatcars were available; on gondolas if they could be had; and freight cars if nothing else was at hand. The men traveled in deluxe Pullmans, in troop sleepers, in modern coaches, and in

day cars that had been obsolete and sidetracked in the yards for a generation and were now drafted for emergency troop movements." Nineteenth-
century coal-burning steam engines were hauled out of retirement. Plumes
of dirty black smoke swept back into the old wicker passenger cars and
blackened the servicemen's uniforms. Men played cards, smoked, read,
whistled at women, and watched the country roll by. When the trains ran
out of food, the hungry men jostled and elbowed their way through the
ubiquitous crowds, down the steps onto the platforms, and into the teeming
stations to raid the shops and restaurants.

In 1942, it seemed as if the entire nation was on the move—not only
troops and sailors but civilians seeking after war work. Because military personnel enjoyed priority on all buses and trains, civilians (including entire
families) squatted in the stations, sleeping on benches or floors, waiting
days or weeks to be assigned seats. America's train and bus stations, wrote
marine aviator Samuel Hynes,

> were the sad places of the war, the limbos of lost souls. All those
> troops, far from their hometowns, and miserable-looking in their new
> uniforms, and the sad, young country girls, pregnant or holding babies,
> not looking around much, just standing, waiting. Lines everywhere.
> There was no place you could go that you didn't have to stand in a line
> first. Piles of duffel bags. And MP's with their white leggings and night
> sticks, patrolling, representing discipline, *being* discipline in their stiff
> postures and their sharp uniforms. War could do worse things than
> this to plain people, but for a sense of the ordinary outrages of life in a
> country at war, the stations were the place to go.

Reaching California, many of the Pacific-bound servicemen were caught
in limbo, waiting for a ship, and that suited them fine. No one doubted
that the route to Tokyo would be long and bloody, and they were in no
hurry to travel it. The sweating malarial jungles of the South Pacific, the
infinitesimal atolls of the central Pacific, all those obscure islands with their
alien names—Efate, Espiritu Santo, Malaita, Guadalcanal, Emirau, Tarawa,
Majuro, Kwajalein, Eniwetok, Ulithi, Palau, Saipan, Morotai, Mindanao,
Iwo Jima, Okinawa—they would see them soon enough.

"Golden Gate in '48, bread line in '49." That pessimistic slogan, which
began circulating in 1942, revealed a great deal about the attitudes of the

American servicemen who fought in the Pacific. They fully expected that the war would last twice as long as it eventually did, and they assumed, as a matter of course, that the long effort would exhaust and bankrupt the nation. But the words also indicated a gritty, persevering determination. The Japanese had fatally misjudged them. They were not cowed by the prospect of a long war and a destitute homecoming. They would go on fighting, killing, and dying, overcoming fear, fatigue, and sorrow, until they reached the beaches of the detested empire itself. There, in 1945, the irresistible force of the Yankee war machine would meet the immovable object of the "*Yamato* spirit," until two mushroom clouds and an emperor's decision brought the whole execrable business to an end.

ACKNOWLEDGMENTS

THANKS TO THE STAFFS OF THE NAVAL HISTORY AND HERITAGE Command, the U.S. Naval War College, the FDR Presidential Library, the National Archives, the Independence Seaport Museum, the Wolfsonian-FIU Museum, the San Francisco Public Library, the Japan Center for Asian Historical Records (JACAR), the Japan Maritime Self-Defense Forces (JMSDF) Staff College, and the Japanese National Defense Academy at Yokosuka.

Special thanks to Professors Douglas V. Smith and Timothy H. Jackson of the U.S. Naval War College, and to Evelyn M. Cherpak, chief archivist and special collections curator at the same institution. With each passing week (so it seems) the wealth of online resources available to historians and researchers expands. Among the Web sites I have found most useful are www.history.navy.mil, CombinedFleet.com, and ibiblio.org/hyperwar. The Battle of Midway Roundtable (www.midway42.org) is a fine example of how the Web can expand the frontiers of historical knowledge by providing a virtual discussion forum for veterans and historians. Several of the BOMRT's discussion threads have been published in *No Right to Win*, edited by Ronald Russell.

For reviewing portions of the manuscript and providing expert and/or editorial commentary, thanks to David Howell, Kenneth Pyle, Ronald Russell, Floyd Beaver, Jon Parshall, Vincent Anderson, VADM George Emery (USN, ret.), Yukio Satoh, Yoshihisa Komori, Koji Handa, and Kiyohiko Arafune. Russell and Beaver read the entire manuscript and provided constructive feedback, from typos to grammar to expert historical insights to (in Beaver's case) corrections of the record based on his personal recollections. After reading my chapters on Japan, Ambassador Arafune provided thirty single-spaced pages of erudite commentary, composed in flawless English, drawing upon not only his deep knowledge of the history but also his boyhood memories of the war. As usual, any errors of fact or interpretation in these pages are to be blamed on the author alone.

For providing introductions and other invaluable assistance in Japan: Kiyohiko Arafune, Yukio Satoh, VADM Yoji Koda (JMSDF, ret.), VADM Masanori Yoshida, Hiroshi Takaku, Eiichi Ishii, Yoshie Nakatani, RADM Umio Otsuka, Cdr. Kuniaki Yamanaka, Prof. Naoyuki Agawa, and Prof. Haruo Tohmatsu.

For the maps, thanks to my illustrator, Loren Doppenberg. For tracking down the photographs and obtaining rights to publication, thanks to Susan Buschhorn.

In the spirit of Samuel Johnson's epigram "No man but a blockhead ever wrote, except for money," I remain heartily grateful to my agent, Eric Simonoff.

I am indebted to the entire team at W. W. Norton. My editor, Starling Lawrence, continues to be a valuable advocate, counselor, and friend.

NOTES

Prologue

xiv to "double time down the corridor": Potter, *Halsey*, p. 28.

xv "We do not need": TR's 1906 Annual Message to the Congress; online at www .millercenter.org/scripps/archive/speeches.

xvii "I tackled the job": Mahan, *From Sail to Steam*, pp. 278, 276.

xviii "War, once declared": Asada, *From Mahan to Pearl Harbor*, p. 8.

xviii "From 1892 on": Livezey, *Mahan on Sea Power*, pp. 72, 59.

xviii "We owe to [Captain Mahan] the three million pounds": Beach, *The United States Navy: A 200-Year History*, p. 332.

xviii "I am just now not reading": Asada, *From Mahan to Pearl Harbor*, p. 3.

xix "more of my works": Mahan, *From Sail to Steam*, p. 303.

xix "total absorption": Cleary, *The Japanese Art of War*, p. 79.

xix "Naval strategists of all nations": Tribute reproduced in Taylor, *The Life of Admiral Mahan*, p. 115.

xix "During the last two days": TR to Alfred Thayer Mahan, Washington, May 12, 1890, in Auchincloss, ed., *Theodore Roosevelt: Letters and Speeches*, pp. 45–46.

xix an admiring review: TR's review in *Atlantic Monthly* (October 1890), in *Works*, Vol. 14, pp. 306–16.

xx "only too glad": Mahan to TR, October 24, 1906, quoted in Turk, *The Ambiguous Relationship: Theodore Roosevelt and Alfred Thayer Mahan*, p. 149.

xx "There is a homely old adage": Speech given in Chicago, April 2, 1903, in TR, *Presidential Addresses and State Papers*, Vol. 1, pp. 265–66.

xx "as strong as the United States Navy": TR (1916), *Mem. Ed.* XX, 261; *Nat. Ed.* XVIII, 225, reproduced in *TR Cyclopedia*, p. 352.

xxi "In the century that is opening": TR, "Address at Mechanics' Pavilion," San Francisco, May 13, 1903; "America's Destiny on the Pacific," *New York Times*, May 14, 1903.

xxi "The enemies we may have to face": "Washington's Forgotten Maxim," Address by TR, U.S. Naval War College, June 2, 1897. *Naval Institute Proceedings* 23, p. 456.

xxi "In a dozen years": TR to Cecil Spring-Rice, June 16, 1905, in Auchincloss, ed., *Theodore Roosevelt: Letters and Speeches*, pp. 391–92.

xxii "I greatly admire": TR to Theodore Roosevelt, Jr., October 4, 1903, in ibid., pp. 296–99.

xxii "some exuberance": Brands, *T.R.: The Last Romantic*, p. 554.

xxii "not physical exercise": TR to Charles Joseph Bonaparte, February 17, 1906, in Auchincloss, ed., *Theodore Roosevelt: Letters and Speeches*, pp. 448–49.

xxii Even by 1906: Karsten, *The Naval Aristocracy*, p. 360.

xxiii The British navy: Ibid., p. 13.

xxiii "old-style naval officers": TR to Secretary of the Navy, August 28, 1905, in Auchincloss, ed., *Theodore Roosevelt: Letters and Speeches*, p. 402.

xxiii to "encourage the best among them": Roosevelt, *America and the World War*, p. 167.

xxiii But in Roosevelt's navy: Karsten, *The Naval Aristocracy*, p. 69.

xxiii "They must have skill": "Washington's Forgotten Maxim," Address by TR, U.S. Naval War College, June 2, 1897.

xxvi "If you affect valor": Dower, *War Without Mercy*, p. 61.

xxvi At sea, the Japanese fleet: Edgerton, *Warriors of the Rising Sun*, p. 137.

xxvi "Europe has not recovered": *Illustrated London News*, quoted in ibid., p. 223.

xxvi "The Japs interest me": TR to Cecil Spring-Rice, June 13, 1904, in Auchincloss, ed., *Theodore Roosevelt: Letters and Speeches*, p. 336.

xxvi "I believe in them": TR, *Autobiography*, p. 378.

xxvii "My right ankle": TR to Theodore Roosevelt, Jr., April 9, 1904, in *Letters to His Children*, p. 31.

xxvii "the growth of Japan": TR's 1906 Annual Message to the Congress.

xxvii "fairly startled the world" . . . "as thick almost": Asada, *From Mahan to Pearl Harbor*, pp. 13, 6.

xxviii "cold, wet, and shivering": Mahan, *From Sail to Steam*, pp. 233, 244.

xxviii Japan had financed the war: Edgerton, *Warriors of the Rising Sun*, pp. 215–16.

xxviii the Japanese people exploded: Ibid., p. 219.

xxviii in Hibiya Park: Buruma, *Inventing Japan*, p. 69.

xxviii Armed mobs charged: Wheeler, *Dragon in the Dust*, p. 54.

xxix When the riots came to an end: Edgerton, *Warriors of the Rising Sun*, p. 219.

xxix "should not be placed": Bailey, *Theodore Roosevelt and the Japanese-American Crisis*, p. 14.

xxix "The danger to American institutions": "Japanese a Menace to American Women," "Whole State Stirred by Menace of the Invasion," and "Brown Men an Evil in the Public Schools," *San Francisco Chronicle*, Feb. 27, 1905, March 1, 1905, and March 5, 1905.

xxx thousands of homeless refugees: Bailey, *Theodore Roosevelt and the Japanese-American Crisis*, p. 23.

xxx Japan had donated $246,000: Ibid., p. 17.

xxx "It will be easy work": Ibid., p. 50.

xxx Secretary of State Elihu Root suspected: Neu, *An Uncertain Friendship*, p. 137.

xxxi "but the exclusion of Japanese": Bailey, *Theodore Roosevelt and the Japanese-American Crisis*, p. 54.

xxxi "while at the same time refusing": TR to Henry Cabot Lodge, May 15, 1905, in Morison, *The Letters of Theodore Roosevelt*, Vol. 4, p. 1181.

xxxi published a cartoon: *Harper's Weekly*, Nov. 10, 1906, cover art by William A. Rogers. Captioned: "For Heaven's Sake Do Not Embarrass the Administration."

xxxi "The feeling on the Pacific slope": TR to Henry Cabot Lodge, June 5, 1905, quoted in Neu, *An Uncertain Friendship*, p. 24.

xxxi "wicked absurdity": TR's 1906 Annual Message to the Congress.

xxxi the "Gentlemen's Agreement": Starr, *Embattled Dreams*, p. 44.

xxxi Digging was proceeding: Sprout and Sprout, *The Rise of American Naval Power: 1776–1918*, p. 250.

xxxi Rumors flourished: Starr, *Embattled Dreams*, p. 53.

xxxii "I had been doing my best": TR to Sir George Otto Trevelyan, Oct. 1, 1911, in *TR Cyclopedia*, p. 36.

xxxii "The Philippines form": TR to Taft, August 21, 1907, quoted in Neu, *An Uncertain Friendship*, p. 142.

xxxii "would have a good deal": TR to Henry Cabot Lodge, July 10, 1907, in *TR Cyclopedia*, p. 35.

xxxiii "Did you ever see": Brands, *T.R.: The Last Romantic*, p. 613.

xxxiii In a voyage of fourteen months: Ibid., pp. 636–37.

xxxiii demonstrated that "the Pacific": Zimmermann, *First Great Triumph*, p. 6.

xxxiv "War Plan Orange": Miller, *War Plan Orange*, pp. 43–46, 53–55, and 66–67.

xxxv "one of the cardinal principles": TR, "Japan's Part," Japan Society, New York, 1919, p. 13; *TR Cyclopedia*, p. 275.

xxxv "bent upon establishing": TR to Eugene Hale, October 27, 1906, in Auchincloss, ed., *Theodore Roosevelt: Letters and Speeches*, p. 505.

xxxv "woe to our country": TR, "The Navy as a Peacemaker," *New York Times*, Nov. 22, 1914, Magazine section, p. 5.

xxxv a "bitter awakening": TR, "Problems of Power," *New Outlook* 104, May 31, 1913.

xxxvi "practically memorized": Toland, *The Rising Sun*, p. 53.

xxxvi "I do not anticipate trouble": TR to FDR, May 10, 1913, in Auchincloss, ed., *Theodore Roosevelt: Letters and Speeches*, p. 681.

Chapter One

8 "Wow, spectacular maneuvers": Dan Kong account in Richardson and Stillwell, *Reflections of Pearl Harbor*, p. 46.

8 "I had to admit": Brown, *Hawaii Goes to War*, p. 20.

8 "the best goddamn drill": Marine Major Alan Shapley of the *Arizona*, recalling

an anonymous shipmate's words, quoted in Prange, Goldstein, and Dillon, *At Dawn We Slept*, p. 510.

8 "smoke bombs": Brown, *Hawaii Goes to War*, p. 20.

8 a "practice smoke screen": Petrie quoted in Prange, Goldstein, and Dillon, *December 7, 1941*, p. 121.

8 "We interrupt this broadcast": Gene White account in Richardson, *Reflections of Pearl Harbor*, p. 37.

8 "This is no maneuver": Quoted in Bailey and Farber, *The First Strange Place*, p. 2.

8 "Why are those planes flying": William Duffie Clemons account in McCabe, *Pearl Harbor and the American Spirit*, p. 68.

8 "Why are the boys shooting" . . . "What a stupid, careless pilot": Prange, Goldstein, and Dillon, *At Dawn We Slept*, p. 506.

8 "Somebody goofed big": Leonide (Lee) R. Soucy account in McCabe, *Pearl Harbor and the American Spirit*, p. 136.

8 "My God!": Kenton Nash account in LaForte and Marcello, eds., *Remembering Pearl Harbor*, p. 280.

9 "What kind of a drill": Soucy account in McCabe, *Pearl Harbor and the American Spirit*, p. 137.

9 "a lone, berserk": A. L. Seton account in Stillwell, ed., *Air Raid—Pearl Harbor!*, p. 183.

9 "armed soldiers": Maxwell R. Urata account in McCabe, *Pearl Harbor and the American Spirit*, p. 150.

9 "every conceivable vehicle": Lawson P. Ramage account in Stillwell, ed., *Air Raid—Pearl Harbor!*, p. 198.

9 "We heard what sounded like": Larry Katz account in McCabe, *Pearl Harbor and the American Spirit*, p. 97.

9 Jack Lower, a civilian electrician: Lord, *Day of Infamy*, pp. 139–40.

9 "Suddenly from the shock of bullets": Dickinson, *The Flying Guns*, p. 24.

10 "a mighty thunderclap": Mason, *Battleship Sailor*, p. 221.

10 "There were steel fragments": Martin Matthews account in LaForte and Marcello, eds., *Remembering Pearl Harbor*, p. 30.

10 "These men were zombies": James Cory account in ibid., p. 18.

12 "Hell, I could even see": Col. William J. Flood quoted in Prange, Goldstein, and Dillon, *At Dawn We Slept*, p. 523.

12 "They were so low": Leon Bennett account in LaForte and Marcello, eds., *Remembering Pearl Harbor*, p. 81.

12 "let go the handles": Quoted in Dickinson, *The Flying Guns*, p. 39.

12 "I still expect": Elphege A. M. Gendreau quoted in Prange, Goldstein, and Dillon, *At Dawn We Slept*, p. 567.

12 "The entire scene": Mason, *Battleship Sailor*, p. 219.

12 "It was like being engulfed": CPO Charles A. Russell quoted in Prange, Goldstein, and Dillon, *December 7, 1941*, p. 277.

12 "If you didn't go through it": John H. McGoran account in Nardo, ed., *Pearl Harbor*, p. 106.

13 "about things far removed": Hopkins's notes, Dec. 7, 1941, quoted in Sherwood, *Roosevelt and Hopkins*, p. 430.

14 the president had sent word: Eleanor Roosevelt, *This I Remember*, p. 232.

14 Hopkins was incredulous: Sherwood, *Roosevelt and Hopkins*, p. 431.

14 the president took a call: Tully, *F. D. R.: My Boss*, p. 255.

14 "stood around in stupefied": Mrs. Charles S. Hamlin quoted in Prange, Goldstein, and Dillon, *December 7, 1941*, p. 250.

14 "was concentrating": Eleanor Roosevelt, *This I Remember*, p. 233.

15 "The Boss maintained": Tully, *F. D. R.: My Boss*, p. 255.

16 "a crisis had come": Stimson diary, Dec. 7, 1941, quoted in Goodwin, *No Ordinary Time*, p. 294.

16 "I thought that": Eleanor Roosevelt, *This I Remember*, p. 233.

16 "People who have never seen": Cory account in LaForte and Marcello, eds., *Remembering Pearl Harbor*, pp. 19–20.

16 "gummy black oil": Mason, *Battleship Sailor*, p. 235.

17 "Each time this was done": Ephraim P. Holmes account in Nardo, ed., *Pearl Harbor*, p. 112.

17 "I remember one sailor": Leslie Le Fan account in LaForte and Marcello, eds., *Remembering Pearl Harbor*, p. 162.

17 "was loaded": Ed Johann quoted in Van der Vat, *Pearl Harbor: The Day of Infamy—An Illustrated History*, p. 106.

17 "I was trying": Shipfitter 3rd class Louis Grabinski account in LaForte and Marcello, eds., *Remembering Pearl Harbor*, p. 66.

17 "Some of these men": Victor Kamont quoted in Prange, Goldstein, and Dillon, *December 7, 1941*, p. 230.

18 "laying across from me": Carl Carlson account in Nardo, ed., *Pearl Harbor*, p. 99.

18 "I would run": Seaman 1st class Nick L. Kouretas, USS *Raleigh*, account in LaForte and Marcello, eds., *Remembering Pearl Harbor*, p. 183.

18 "I'll tell you one thing": William W. Fomby account in ibid., p. 46.

19 "There was a lot of us there": Elmo F. Rash account in McCabe, *Pearl Harbor and the American Spirit*, p. 125.

19 "There was mass confusion": Howard C. French quoted in Prange, Goldstein, and Dillon, *December 7, 1941*, p. 278.

19 "You wiped off": James Lawson in Jasper, Delgado, and Adams, *The USS Arizona*, p. 161.

19 The marine quartermaster sergeant issued: Clemons account in Richardson, *Reflections of Pearl Harbor*, p. 70.

20 "dry sandwiches and coffee": Jack Rogo quoted in Prange, Goldstein, and Dillon, *December 7, 1941*, p. 332.

20 "you could walk out": Thomas H. Moorer account in Stillwell, ed., *Air Raid—Pearl Harbor!*, p. 204.

20 "I recall finding": Charles T. Sehe account in McCabe, *Pearl Harbor and the American Spirit*, p. 133.

20 the survivors made a concerted effort: Lord, *Day of Infamy*, p. 176.

20 The crew of the *Nevada*: Lorenzo Sherwood Sabin account in Stillwell, ed., *Air Raid—Pearl Harbor!*, p. 146.

20 "Things were so bad": Mason, *Battleship Sailor*, p. 253.

21 "Kimmel seemed calm": Lt. Cdr. Layton quoted in Prange, Goldstein, and Dillon, *December 7, 1941*, p. 304.

21 As the admiral watched: Brig. Gen. Howard C. Davidson quoted in ibid., p. 370.

21 "people were frightened": Lt. (jg) Walter J. East quoted in ibid., p. 356.

22 "some indication": "Running Summary of the Situation," Dec. 7, 1941; CINCPAC Grey Book, Bk. 1, p. 2.

22 "two enemy carriers": Ibid.

22 "The view was held": Ibid., p. 3.

22 "with the result that": Moorer account in Stillwell, ed., *Air Raid—Pearl Harbor!*, p. 204.

23 "Somebody handed me": Warren G. Harding account in LaForte and Marcello, eds., *Remembering Pearl Harbor*, p. 90.

23 Sailors were seen carrying: Kouretas, USS *Raleigh*, account in ibid., p. 183.

23 "You guys stay right here": Joseph Ryan account in Nardo, ed., *Pearl Harbor*, p. 92.

23 "I had no real sense": Scott Leesberg account in Richardson, *Reflections of Pearl Harbor*, p. 67.

24 James Erickson of Chicago: James Erickson, Iris Bancroft, and Pat Vang accounts in ibid., pp. 55, 96, and 85.

24 Winston Churchill was at Chequers: Churchill, *The Second World War*, Vol. 3: *The Grand Alliance*, p. 605.

25 "So we had won after all!": Ibid., pp. 666–67.

25 "slept the sleep": Ibid., p. 608.

26 "baskets of documents": "Japanese Embassy Burns Papers," *Philadelphia Inquirer*, Dec. 8, 1941, in Caren, ed., *Pearl Harbor Extra*, p. 38.

26 As Kato made his way outside: Kato, *The Lost War*, pp. 61–62.

26 "could hear those unrehearsed songs": Smith, *Thank You, Mr. President*, p. 116.

26 "quiet and serious": Ickes, *The Secret Diary of Harold L. Ickes*, entry dated Dec. 14, 1941, p. 661.

27 "It was very cold": Perry, *"Dear Bart,"* p. 22.

27 Shortly after nightfall: Tully, *F. D. R.: My Boss*, p. 256.

27 "already had that air": Cooke, *The American Home Front*, p. 8.

27 "The press room was a madhouse": Perry, *"Dear Bart,"* p. 21.

28 The president's face . . . was drawn and gray: Frances Perkins account in Stillwell, ed., *Air Raid—Pearl Harbor!*, pp. 117–18.

29 "represented only the just": Stimson quoted in Prange, Goldstein, and Dillon, *December 7, 1941*, p. 387.

29 "pressed his point so hard": Ickes, *The Secret Diary of Harold L. Ickes*, entry dated Dec. 14, 1941, p. 665.

30 "the principal defense": FDR quoted in Prange, Goldstein, and Dillon, *At Dawn We Slept*, p. 558.

30 "The effect on the Congress": Stimson's diary, entry dated Dec. 7, 1941, quoted in Prange, Goldstein, and Dillon, *December 7, 1941*, p. 388.

30 "How did it happen": Goodwin, *No Ordinary Time*, pp. 292–93.

30 "They are doing things": Morgan, *FDR: A Biography*, p. 618.

30 "There is no politics here": "Congress Decided," *New York Times*, Dec. 8, 1941, in Caren, ed., *Pearl Harbor Extra*, p. 22.

30 The lights on the second floor: "F.D.R. Asks War Declaration at Joint Session Today," *Washington Times Herald*, Dec. 8, 1941 in ibid., p. 29.

31 "A laundry cart": Cornelius C. Smith account in Stillwell, ed., *Air Raid—Pearl Harbor!*, p. 221.

31 men fired their weapons: Ada M. Olsson account in LaForte and Marcello, eds., *Remembering Pearl Harbor*, p. 257.

31 "You couldn't go five feet": Joseph Ryan account in Nardo, ed., *Pearl Harbor*, p. 92.

31 At the Navy Yard tank farm: Prange, Goldstein, and Dillon, *December 7, 1941*, p. 365.

32 "a genuine firefight": Army Lt. Charles W. Davis quoted in ibid., p. 354.

32 "all ships present": Ibid., p. 359.

32 "Will anyone smack them?": Allen G. Quynn quoted in ibid.

33 "It looked like the Fourth": Curtis Schulze account in LaForte and Marcello, eds., *Remembering Pearl Harbor*, p. 146.

33 "By God": Mason, *Battleship Sailor*, p. 241.

33 "We had gotten addicted": Fomby account in LaForte and Marcello, eds., *Remembering Pearl Harbor*, p. 46.

33 "My God, what's happened?": Lundstrom, *The First Team*, p. 19.

33 "the sky turned so dark": Carl Schmitz account in Richardson, *Reflections of Pearl Harbor*, p. 21.

Chapter Two

34 Britain had declared war: Craig Thompson, "Britain Joins U.S. against Japanese," *New York Times*, Dec. 9, 1941, p. 14.

34 "a tense, grim throng": "Tense Throng Fills Grounds at Capitol Awaiting President," *Washington Evening Star*, Dec. 8, 1941, in Caren, ed., *Pearl Harbor Extra*, p. 44.

35 "solemn as owls": Frances Perkins account in Stillwell, ed., *Air Raid—Pearl Harbor!*, p. 121.

35 "one arm locked in his son's": Cooke, *The American Home Front*, pp. 13–14.

35 "Now the president of the United States": Eleanor Roosevelt, *This I Remember*, p. 234.

36 "solemn and angered": "Roosevelt Says Date of Attack in Pacific Will Live in Infamy," *Washington Evening Star*, Dec. 8, 1941, in Caren, ed., *Pearl Harbor Extra*, p. 44.

36 "I do not think": Sherwood, *Roosevelt and Hopkins*, p. 437.

36 "their eyes puffy": Cornelius C. Smith, Jr., account in Stillwell, ed., *Air Raid—Pearl Harbor!*, p. 222.

37 "No one could imagine": Lt. Ruth Erickson quoted in Prange, Goldstein, and Dillon, *December 7, 1941*, p. 369.

37 "charred, crisp skin": Smith, Jr., account in Stillwell, ed., *Air Raid—Pearl Harbor!*, p. 222.

37 "I can still smell it": Erickson quoted in Prange, Goldstein, and Dillon, *At Dawn We Slept*, p. 535.

37 "I started to go back and see": Vivian Roberts Hultgren account in McCabe, *Pearl Harbor and the American Spirit*, p. 90.

38 it "got to where": Jack Kelley account in LaForte and Marcello, eds., *Remembering Pearl Harbor*, p. 59.

38 "The worst part was": Cox. Richard L. Frost quoted in Prange, Goldstein, and Dillon, *December 7, 1941*, p. 369.

38 At Aiea Landing: Dan Wentrcek account in LaForte and Marcello, eds., *Remembering Pearl Harbor*, p. 76.

38 "One flatbed truck": Leslie Le Fan account in ibid., p. 165.

38 For weeks after the attack: Brown, *Hawaii Goes to War*, p. 43.

39 "A feeling of elation": Mason, *Battleship Sailor*, p. 237.

39 "Friends back home": Smith, Jr., account in Stillwell, ed., *Air Raid—Pearl Harbor!*, p. 220.

39 "What am I going to say": Seaman 1st class Nick L. Kouretas, USS *Raleigh*, account in LaForte and Marcello, eds., *Remembering Pearl Harbor*, p. 183.

39 "We had been told": George E. Waller account in ibid., p. 50.

40 They had been due back in Pearl Harbor: Richardson, *Reflections of Pearl Harbor*, p. 50.

40 At sunset on Monday: Halsey, *Admiral Halsey's Story*, p. 80.

40 She inched around the stern: Beaver, *Sailor from Oklahoma*, p. 150.

40 In the failing light: Kernan, *Crossing the Line*, pp. 25–26.

40 "in sullen little folds": Beaver, *Sailor from Oklahoma*, p. 151.

40 "Where in hell were *you*?": Kernan, *Crossing the Line*, p. 26.

40 "In a violent way" . . . "there wasn't anything else": Ibid.

41 "Before we're through": Halsey, *Admiral Halsey's Story*, p. 81. Captain Doug Moulton was named as the witness.

41 Halsey descended: Ibid.

41 "What the hell is there": Prange, Goldstein, and Dillon, *December 7, 1941*, p. 372.

41 A long line of sailors: Beaver, *Sailor from Oklahoma*, p. 151.

42 "down the channel": Kernan, *Crossing the Line*, p. 27.

42 "when the resting firemen": Cooke, *The American Home Front*, p. 18.

42 "By nightfall": Brinkley, *Washington Goes to War*, p. 92.

42 quarter of a million government workers: See Cooke, *The American Home Front*, p. 18.

43 A nationwide strike: "Welders Call Off Strike," *Philadelphia Inquirer*, Dec. 8, 1941, in Caren, ed., *Pearl Harbor Extra*, p. 38.

43 "Enemy planes": "N.Y.-Bound Enemy Planes Alarm Entire Northeast," *Brooklyn Eagle*, Dec. 9, 1941, in ibid., p. 55.

43 Numerous reports: "Japs Try to Bomb Coast; Routed Off Golden Gate," *Albany Times Union*, Dec. 9, 1941, in ibid., p. 57.

44 "Death and destruction": *Honolulu Advertiser*, Dec. 10, 1941, in ibid., p. 59.

44 "The atmosphere in the Capitol": Childs, *I Write from Washington*, p. 245.

45 With timing that could not have been: Jackson, *That Man*, p. 104.

45 "Equipped with amazing": Advertisement for *The American Magazine* in the *New York Times*, Dec. 8, 1941, p. 21.

45 Presidential speechwriters: Rosenman, *Working with Roosevelt*, p. 312.

46 "sudden criminal attacks": Buhite and Levy, eds., *FDR's Fireside Chats*, "War with Japan," Dec. 9, 1941, pp. 198, 200, and 204.

47 Sam Rosenman went to see him: Rosenman, *Working with Roosevelt*, p. 312.

47 "There is no such thing": Buhite and Levy, eds., *FDR's Fireside Chats*, "War with Japan," Dec. 9, 1941, p. 204.

48 At dawn on December 7: Peattie, *Sunburst*, pp. 166–67.

49 "the whole area was boiling": Astor, *Crisis in the Pacific*, p. 61.

49 No sooner had the bombers: Morison, *History of United States Naval Operations in World War II*, Vol. 3: *The Rising Sun in the Pacific*, p. 170.

49 The truth about MacArthur's weird malfunctioning: See Burton, *Fortnight of Infamy*, p. 123, and Manchester, *American Caesar*, p. 208.

50 "a lot like the racing planes": Davis, *Sinking the Rising Sun*, p. 75.

50 The underpowered Buffalo: Burton, *Fortnight of Infamy*, pp. 300–301.

50 That impression was nourished: See Stillwell, ed., *Air Raid—Pearl Harbor!*, p. 80.

50 Japanese cultural norms: See Dower, *War Without Mercy*, pp. 100–105.

51 In fact, the Japanese naval aviators: See Burton, *Fortnight of Infamy*, p. xii; Peattie, *Sunburst*, pp. 172 and 174.

51 "She handled like a dream": Sakai, Caidin, and Saito, *Samurai!*, p. 190.

52 One of the Tigers: Charles Bond's diary entry, Nov. 21, 1941, in Bond and Anderson, *A Flying Tiger's Diary*, p. 46.

52 "like a flock of well-disciplined buzzards": Lt. John Buckley quoted in White, *They Were Expendable*, p. 16.

53 "They'd flattened it": Ibid., p. 18.

53 "finish quickly": Quoted in Costello, *The Pacific War, 1941–45*, p. 153.

54 "the main topic of conversation": Bert Wynn account in "The Sinking of the Prince of Wales and Repulse: A series of personal accounts compiled from crew members," comp. Alan Matthews; online at www.microworks.net/pacific/person al/pow_repulse.htm.

54 "Oh, but they are Japanese": Brown, *Suez to Singapore*, p. 304.

54 That night over dinner: Ibid., pp. 307–8.

55 "For me": Ibid., p. 318.

55 "Suddenly there was a massive explosion": Ted Matthews account in "The Sinking of the Prince of Wales and Repulse."

55 "You've put up a good show": Costello, *The Pacific War, 1941–45*, p. 158.

56 "We have finished our task now": Ibid.

56 "After an hour": Flt. Lt. Tim Vigors, DFC, RAAF, quoted in the *London Gazette*.

57 "The enemy attacks": Peattie, *Sunburst*, p. 170.

57 Churchill was awakened: Churchill, *The Grand Alliance*, p. 620.

58 Scenes of chaotic and panicked retreat: Burton, *Fortnight of Infamy*, p. 150.

59 "The turning point!": Hitler quoted in Harvey Asher, "Hitler's Decision to Declare War on the United States Revisited (A Synthesis of the Secondary Literature)," Newsletter of the Society for Historians of American Foreign Relations (SHAFR), September 2000; online at www.shafr.org/publications/newsletter/september-2000.

59 "A complete shift": Goebbels quoted in Black, *Franklin Delano Roosevelt: Champion of Freedom*, p. 697.

60 The Führer's speech: "Hitler Declares War on the United States," recorded by the BBC Monitoring Service, Dec. 11, 1941; online at www.jewishvirtuallibrary.org.

60 When he turned to the United States: Ibid.

60 "The forces endeavoring": Frank L. Kluckhohn, "U.S. Now at War with Germany and Italy," *New York Times*, Dec. 12, 1941, p. 1.

62 "There was just one thing": Sherwood, *Roosevelt and Hopkins*, p. 430.

Chapter Three

63 "News special": Koshu Itabashi account in Cook and Cook, eds., *Japan at War*, p. 77.

63 "as if my blood boiled": Ibid.

63 "I felt like someone": Toshio Yoshida account in ibid., p. 80.

63 "Is it all right": Ei Hirosawa account in ibid., p. 244.

64 "I was thrilled": Ryuichi Yokoyama account in ibid., p. 96.

64 "Never in our history": Quoted in Buruma, *Inventing Japan*, p. 111.

64 "perfectly calm": Diary of Marquis Koichi Kido, entry dated Dec. 8, 1941, in Goldstein and Dillon, eds., *The Pacific War Papers*, p. 135.

64 "imperial rescript": Emperor's rescript printed in Cook and Cook, *Japan at War*, p. 72.

65 "In order to annihilate": Prime Minister Hideki Tojo, in an address in Tokyo carried by radio, trans. in the *Japan Times & Advertiser*, Dec. 8, 1941.

65 "were swaggering up": Yoshida account in Cook and Cook, eds., *Japan at War*, p. 80.

65 A special celebratory sweet: Harumichi Nogi account in ibid., p. 55.

65 "To be perfectly honest": Okumiya, Horikoshi, and Caidin, Zero!, p. 43.

65 Admiral Isoroku Yamamoto: Agawa, The Reluctant Admiral, p. 259.

66 "sneak thievery": Entry dated Dec. 9, 1941, Ugaki, Fading Victory, p. 49.

66 Japanese historians: See Mitsuharu Noda account in Cook and Cook, eds., Japan at War, p. 83; and Agawa, The Reluctant Admiral, pp. 255–57.

66 "Like a once-bitten stray dog": New Order in Greater East Asia (April 1942), cited in Tolischus, Through Japanese Eyes, p. 152.

66 In other publications: Kokusai Shashin Joho (International Graphic Magazine) 21, no. 12, Feb. 1, 1942.

67 "He ordered me": Noda account in Cook and Cook, eds., Japan at War, p. 82.

67 He seemed well aware: Agawa, The Reluctant Admiral, p. 260.

67 "A military man": Ibid., pp. 285–86.

67 "the greatest admiral": Quoted on the jacket of Agawa, The Reluctant Admiral.

68 He was a short man: Ibid., p. 2.

69 Some 120 separate pieces: Ibid., pp. 64–65.

69 Yamamoto's "pronounced individuality": Asada, From Mahan to Pearl Harbor, p. 275.

69 As a captain in the mid-1920s: Agawa, The Reluctant Admiral, p. 76.

69 "white elephants": Ibid., p. 91.

69 He was an internationalist: Asada, From Mahan to Pearl Harbor, p. 183.

70 "Anyone who has seen": Ibid.

71 "taciturn and extremely uncommunicative": Agawa, The Reluctant Admiral, pp. 78, 54, and 5.

71 "Yamamoto was every inch": Quoted in Okumiya, Horikoshi, and Caidin, Zero!, p. 176.

71 "when one was seated": Agawa, The Reluctant Admiral, p. 54.

72 "who would tell you straight out": Ibid., p. 139.

72 "I viewed him": Edwin T. Layton account in Stillwell, ed., Air Raid—Pearl Harbor!, p. 276.

72 "mischievous devil" . . . "Don't be silly": Agawa, The Reluctant Admiral, p. 63.

72 "Hey, that's the C-in-C!": Ibid., p. 207.

73 "sometimes lost his whole uniform": Noda account in Cook and Cook, eds., Japan at War, p. 83.

73 He haunted the casinos: Agawa, The Reluctant Admiral, pp. 151, 54, 164, and 84.

73 "strong as a horse" . . . "Eighty Sen": Ibid., pp. 67, 2.

74 When traveling abroad: Ibid., pp. 53, 147, and 64.

74 Chiyoko Kawai: Ibid., p. 65.

74 "younger sister" and the quotes that follow: Ibid., pp. 63, 161, 242, and 58–59.

75 a party of geishas: Ibid., p. 178.

75 "If the army had ever seen": Noda account in Cook and Cook, eds., Japan at War, p. 83.

75 "If any of you doesn't fart": Agawa, The Reluctant Admiral, pp. 147, 85.

75 "A man of real purpose": Ibid., p. 85.

77 Many Japanese were scandalized: Storry, *The Double Patriots*, p. 24.

77 "Our Imperial Ancestors": "The Rescript on Education of the Meiji Emperor," online at www.danzan.com/HTML/ESSAYS/meiji.html.

77 "Liberalism and individualism": Baron Kichiro Hiranuma, Dec. 28, 1940, cited in Tolischus, *Through Japanese Eyes*, p. 67.

78 all of the "small selves": Ikki Kita quoted in Buruma, *Inventing Japan*, p. 78.

78 "supreme and only God": Goro Sugimoto, "The Emperor," quoted in Victoria, *Zen at War*, p. 117.

78 "The Empire of Japan": The Meiji Constitution (1889) can be found online at the Hanover Historical Texts Project, http://history.hanover.edu/texts/1889con.html.

79 "Specimen collection": Bix, *Hirohito and the Making of Modern Japan*, p. 60.

79 As a young man: Storry, *The Double Patriots*, p. 52.

80 Upon his return: Irokawa, *The Age of Hirohito*, p. 10.

80 "Crown Prince Hirohito": Ibid.

81 "one mind united": Bix, *Hirohito and the Making of Modern Japan*, p. 195.

81 The dreaded *Kempei Tai*: Deacon, *Kempei Tai*, pp. 160–61.

83 Naval spending: See Asada, *From Mahan to Pearl Harbor*, Table 1, for summary of costs, pp. 99–102.

83 Some 1,700 commissioned: Ibid., p. 100.

84 A brand-new 40,000-ton battleship: Yoshimura, *Battleship Musashi*, p. 11; Hara, *Japanese Destroyer Captain*, p. 12.

84 "It is as if Japan": Asada, *From Mahan to Pearl Harbor*, p. 157.

85 "It is a most high-handed": Ibid., p. 143.

86 The cabinet and the *genro*: Bix, *Hirohito and the Making of Modern Japan*, p. 269.

86 "If, as Hirohito later stated": Irokawa, *The Age of Hirohito*, p. 13.

86 In Manchuria, gangs: Storry, *The Double Patriots*, p. 94.

86 Minister Osachi Hamaguchi: Shillony, *Revolt in Japan*, p. 8.

87 spoke of a "Showa Restoration": Storry, *The Double Patriots*, p. 103.

87 Parliamentary party democracy: Irokawa, *The Age of Hirohito*, p. 15.

87 "Such a movement": Storry, *The Double Patriots*, p. 142.

88 "We cannot afford": Quoted in ibid., p. 168.

88 "In Japan there is a tradition": Morita, Reingold, and Shimomura, *Made in Japan*, p. 27.

89 According to statistics: Irokawa, *The Age of Hirohito*, p. 8.

89 Japan was poor in natural resources: Kase, *Journey to the Missouri*, p. 25.

89 The seizure of territory: Benedict, *The Chrysanthemum and the Sword*, p. 256.

89 Millions of Japanese: Irokawa, *The Age of Hirohito*, p. 7.

89 The main building of the *Asahi Shinbun* . . . "Japan now confronts": Storry, *The Double Patriots*, pp. 185–87.

90 There is considerable evidence: Ibid.

90 On February 29: Shillony, *Revolt in Japan*, p. 206.

91 None of the leaders was above: Storry, *The Double Patriots*, pp. 183–84.

91 The conspirators enjoyed broad: See Shillony, *Revolt in Japan*, p. 203.

92 navy built a full-size mock-up: Peattie, *Sunburst*, p. 41.

93 The story of the development: Yoshimura, *Zero Fighter*, p. 47.

93 The Zero's control surfaces: Ibid.

94 "The naval air corps": Agawa, *The Reluctant Admiral*, pp. 109–10.

95 "It was they who did": Tagaya, *Imperial Japanese Naval Aviator, 1937–45*, p. 4.

95 "I guess they did it": Hideo Sato account in Cook and Cook, eds., *Japan at War*, p. 233.

95 A contemporary photograph: Photo reproduced in Tagaya, *Imperial Japanese Naval Aviator, 1937–45*, p. 7.

96 "Because of the friction": Ens. Takeshi Maeda account in Werneth, ed., *Beyond Pearl Harbor*, p. 100.

96 instant retribution: Description of beatings in Kiyosawa, *A Diary of Darkness*, p. 136.

96 dragged out of his hammock: Sakai, Caidin, and Saito, *Samurai!*, p. 18.

96 "How could a human being": Maeda account in Werneth, ed., *Beyond Pearl Harbor*, p. 100.

97 "beatings were a form of education": Quoted in Gibney, ed., *Senso*, p. 28.

97 "human cattle": Sakai, Caidin, and Saito, *Samurai!*, p. 19.

97 the most violent instructors: Maeda account in Werneth, ed., *Beyond Pearl Harbor*, p. 101.

97 Recruits could not fight back: Tetsu Shimojo account in Gibney, ed., *Senso*, p. 31.

97 "was feared far more": Sakai, Caidin, and Saito, *Samurai!*, p. 23.

98 They were required to hang: Ibid., pp. 23–24.

98 "With every pilot-trainee": Ibid., p. 22.

98 "Gradually": Ibid., p. 25.

99 the ancient principles of *kendo*: See Kiyosawa, *A Diary of Darkness*, p. 118.

99 the trainee sat in the front cockpit: Tagaya, *Imperial Japanese Naval Aviator, 1937–45*, p. 11.

99 "You're so stupid!": Maeda account in Werneth, ed., *Beyond Pearl Harbor*, pp. 100–101.

100 Having logged an average: Peattie, *Sunburst*, p. 31.

100 A popular song: Tagaya, *Imperial Japanese Naval Aviator, 1937–45*, p. 45.

101 In mock air battles: Peattie, *Sunburst*, pp. 44, 43.

102 "The main strength": Asada, *From Mahan to Pearl Harbor*, p. 186.

102 "should be either scrapped": Peattie, *Sunburst*, p. 83.

102 "The battleship squadron": Asada, *From Mahan to Pearl Harbor*, p. 163.

102 Genda found a patron: See ibid., pp. 164–66, 182–84.

102 "I don't want to be a wet blanket": Agawa, *The Reluctant Admiral*, p. 93.

103 "We've got to go through with it": Yoshimura, *Battleship Musashi*, p. 33.

103 The ships were to be: Skulski, *The Battleship Yamato*, pp. 10, 17.

103 Shells fired: Yoshimura, *Battleship Musashi*, pp. 18, 77.

104 The launch of the *Musashi*: Ibid., p. 114.

105 Their decks were covered: Skulski, *The Battleship Yamato*, p. 22.

105 "Their superstructures" and the details that follow: Ibid., p. 182.

105 *Yamato*'s first sea trial: Ibid., p. 25.

105 These colossal weapons: See ibid., p. 19, Tables 10 and 12.

106 their "guts had suddenly": Yoshimura, *Battleship Musashi*, p. 127.

107 Correct thoughts and beliefs: Slogans cited in Cook and Cook, eds., *Japan at War*, p. 169; see also Dower, *War Without Mercy*, p. 215; Shigeru Sato letter to *Asahi Shinbun* in Gibney, ed., *Senso*, p. 288.

107 Lachrymose ballads: Irokawa, *The Age of Hirohito*, p. 138.

107 In the cinema: Ei Hirosawa account in Cook and Cook, eds., *Japan at War*, pp. 242–43.

107 "To hell with Babe Ruth!": Wheeler, *Dragon in the Dust*, pp. 210, 140.

107 In a popular newsreel: Atsuo Furusawa letter to *Asahi Shinbun* in Gibney, ed., *Senso*, p. 15.

108 a nationwide anti-luxury campaign: Shigeko Araki account in Cook and Cook, eds., *Japan at War*, p. 320.

108 On the final night: Kiyoshi Hara account in ibid., p. 63.

108 Schoolchildren were taught: Chigaku Tanaka, "What Is Nippon Kokutai?" (1935–36), cited in Tolischus, *Through Japanese Eyes*, p. 14.

108 one of his teachers had explained: Hideo Sato account in Cook and Cook, eds., *Japan at War*, pp. 232, 236.

108 It was Japan's purpose: Bix, *Hirohito and the Making of Modern Japan*, p. 11.

109 "As in the heavens": Storry, *The Double Patriots*, p. 2.

109 "If Japan had declared": Koshu Itabashi account in Cook and Cook, eds., *Japan at War*, p. 78.

109 "Excavations of ancient relics": Chikao Fujisawa, "The Great Shinto Purification Ritual and the Divine Nation of Nippon," February 1942, cited in Tolischus, *Through Japanese Eyes*, p. 17.

109 they had even reached Europe: *Shinajin wa Nipponjin nari* (*The Chinese Are Japanese*), *Asiatic Problems Society* (June 1939), cited in ibid., p. 18.

109 "all mankind became estranged": Fujisawa, "The Great Shinto Purification Ritual," cited in ibid.

109 "The Pacific, Indian": Professor T. Komaki on Japanese radio, Feb. 22–27, 1942, cited in ibid., p. 19.

110 "mutual existence of nations": Matsuo, *How Japan Plans to Win*, p. 13.

110 "the colored races constitute": Hidejiro Nagata, *Nippon no Senshin* (*The Advance of Japan*), Tokyo, 1939, cited in Tolischus, *Through Japanese Eyes*, p. 83.

110 When Japan fought: Daisetz T. Suzuki's principles explained in Victoria, *Zen at War*, p. 30.

110 "its unreasonableness corrected": Hayashiya and Shimakage, *The Buddhist View of War*, quoted in ibid., p. 90.

110 "the gospel of love": Suzuki, *Zen and Japanese Culture*, quoted in ibid., p. 110.

111 "Three-All" policy: Cook and Cook, eds., *Japan at War*, p. 75.

111 "I had already gotten": Yoshiro Tamura account in ibid., p. 164.

112 "When I looked at": Shozo Tominaga account in ibid., pp. 40, 42–43.

112 "commented with deep bitterness": McIntire, *White House Physician*, p. 198.

113 The Foreign Ministry at Kasumigaseki: Storry, *The Double Patriots*, p. 6.

113 "The diplomats in fact": Kase, *Journey to the Missouri*, p. 16.

113 "Events sometimes overwhelm you": Toshikazu Kase account in Cook and Cook, eds., *Japan at War*, p. 95.

113 "What does it all matter?": Agawa, *The Reluctant Admiral*, pp. 10, 125, and 128.

114 "I have serious doubts": Ibid., p. 168.

114 "Orders must naturally come": Asada, *From Mahan to Pearl Harbor*, p. 212.

114 Ensconced in his Navy Ministry office: Agawa, *The Reluctant Admiral*, p. 120.

114 Yamamoto had presented himself: Asada, *From Mahan to Pearl Harbor*, p. 217.

114 In 1939, the conflict: Storry, *The Double Patriots*, p. 246.

115 The ultranationalist right: Asada, *From Mahan to Pearl Harbor*, pp. 162–72.

115 "Japanese youth at that time": Harumichi Nogi account in Cook and Cook, eds., *Japan at War*, p. 51.

115 The military triumphs: Kase account in ibid., p. 92; see also Agawa, *The Reluctant Admiral*, p. 167; Irokawa, *The Age of Hirohito*, p. 28.

115 "given the existing state": Asada, *From Mahan to Pearl Harbor*, p. 217.

115 "I want you to tell us": Ibid., pp. 225–26.

116 "We are prepared": Agawa, *The Reluctant Admiral*, p. 159.

116 "a competition of mediocrities": Quoted in Asada, *From Mahan to Pearl Harbor*, p. 296.

117 "It is too late now": Ibid., p. 276.

118 "It makes me wonder": Agawa, *The Reluctant Admiral*, p. 200.

118 "What a strange position": Asada, *From Mahan to Pearl Harbor*, p. 278.

118 Genda . . . had been studying the possibilities: Minoru Genda account in Stillwell, ed., *Air Raid—Pearl Harbor!*, p. 24.

118 there were two significant problems: Shigeru Fukudome account in ibid., pp. 60–61.

119 "Don't keep saying": Lord, *Day of Infamy*, p. 11.

119 "Unless it is carried out": Fukudome account in Stillwell, ed., *Air Raid—Pearl Harbor!*, p. 63.

119 "It is obvious that": Asada, *From Mahan to Pearl Harbor*, p. 277.

120 "Inwardly we felt": Ibid., pp. 239, 216, and 271.

121 "Will you decide for war": Ibid., p. 273.

122 "do your best": Irokawa, *The Age of Hirohito*, p. 89.

122 "I cannot yield": Storry, *The Double Patriots*, p. 288.

122 At an Imperial Conference: Fukudome account in Stillwell, ed., *Air Raid—Pearl Harbor!*, p. 63.

122 "no compromise": Buruma, *Inventing Japan*, p. 118.

122 "Sometimes people have to shut": Ibid., p. 119.

122 "I did have doubts": Nogi account in Cook and Cook, eds., *Japan at War*, p. 54.

123 "I held the view": Hirohito's postwar "monologue" quoted in Irokawa, *The Age of Hirohito*, p. 89.

123 "straining at the leash": Browne, *Tojo: The Last Banzai*, p. 100.

Chapter Four

124 "Main Navy": *Main Navy Building: Its Construction and Original Occupants.* Washington, DC: A Naval Historical Foundation Publication, series 2, no. 14, Aug. 1, 1970.

124 "unadorned offices": Whitehill, "A Note on the Making of This Book," in King and Whitehill, *Fleet Admiral King*, p. 647.

124 "an ant hill": Buell, *Master of Sea Power*, p. 152.

125 "Rear Admiral John Wainwright": H. Arthur Lamar account in Stillwell, ed., *Air Raid—Pearl Harbor!*, p. 259.

125 "a guard lowered": Cooke, *The American Home Front*, p. 27.

125 "We were busy as bird-dogs": James L. Holloway account in Stillwell, ed., *Air Raid—Pearl Harbor!*, p. 107.

126 "An enormous crowd": Diary entry for Dec. 15, 1941, Perry, *"Dear Bart,"* p. 27.

126 He admitted that: "Heroic Acts Cited," *New York Times*, Dec. 15, 1941.

126 damaged "in varying degrees": "Defense Shake-Up," *New York Times*, Dec. 18, 1941.

126 "very cleverly organized": "Heroic Acts Cited," *New York Times*, Dec. 15, 1941.

127 angry rumblings: Childs, *I Write from Washington*, p. 247.

127 a "formal investigation": Layton, *"And I Was There,"* p. 336.

127 "the land and sea forces": "Defense Shake-Up," *New York Times*, Dec. 18, 1941.

127 "Tell Nimitz": Potter, *Nimitz*, p. 11.

127 "insulted that anyone": Lamar account in Stillwell, ed., *Air Raid—Pearl Harbor!*, p. 259.

128 Like most of his colleagues: Stillwell, ed., *Air Raid—Pearl Harbor!*, p. 259.

128 "We have suffered": Potter, *Nimitz*, p. 8.

128 "From the time the Japanese": Nimitz letter to William H. Ewing, in Ewing, "Nimitz: Reflections on Pearl Harbor," Fredericksburg, TX: Admiral Nimitz Foundation, 1985, p. 11.

129 "You always wanted": Potter, *Nimitz*, p. 12.

129 "a tanned, white-haired": "Careers of Men Shifted in Service," *New York Times*, Dec. 18, 1941.

129 "Washington reaction": Diary entry for Dec. 17, 1941, Perry, *"Dear Bart,"* p. 28.

129 "to catch up on my sleep": Nimitz letter to William H. Ewing, in Ewing, "Nimitz," p. 9.

130 "At no point": Potter, *Nimitz*, p. 14.

130 "two good slugs": Lamar account in Stillwell, ed., *Air Raid—Pearl Harbor!*, p. 259.

130 "really refreshed": Hoyt, *How They Won the War in the Pacific*, p. 46.

132 "A man he seems": *Lucky Bag*, 1905—entry on passed midshipman Chester W. Nimitz, Naval Historical Collection, Washington, DC.

133 "I was asked once": Hoyt, *How They Won the War in the Pacific*, p. 43.

133 "If you love me at all": Chester Nimitz to Mrs. Anna Nimitz, Aug. 18, 1912, in Potter, *Nimitz*, p. 118.

133 "Chester, if there was": Ibid., p. 120.

134 "through lovely rolling country": Ibid., p. 13.

134 "As I get more sleep": Hoyt, *How They Won the War in the Pacific*, p. 47.

134 The admiral spent long hours: Details of Nimitz's rail journey drawn from "Along Your Way: Facts about stations and scenes on the Santa Fe," pamphlet distributed to passengers on the Santa Fe Super Chief, 1946; online at www.titchenal.com/atsf/ayw1946.

134 "Don't let this out": Lamar account in Stillwell, ed., *Air Raid—Pearl Harbor!*, p. 259.

135 "It could have happened": Ibid. See also Lamar, "I Saw Stars," Fredericksburg, TX: Admiral Nimitz Foundation, 1985. Foreword, p. 2.

135 "My life in the Navy": Potter, *Nimitz*, p. 185.

135 In 1915: Ibid., p. 126.

136 "he was convinced": Ibid., pp. 1–2.

136 "working with young": Hoyt, *How They Won the War in the Pacific*, p. 43.

136 the controversial policy: Potter, *Nimitz*, p. 3.

137 "Admiral Nimitz never raised": Lamar, "I Saw Stars," p. 43.

138 "This is one of the responsibilities": Ibid., p. 16.

138 "Had a fine sleep": Potter, *Nimitz*, p. 17.

138 They rolled on: Details of Nimitz's rail journey from "Along Your Way."

139 "I only hope": Hoyt, *How They Won the War in the Pacific*, p. 47.

140 At noon on December 8: Morison, *The Rising Sun in the Pacific*, p. 230.

141 "flames licking over them" . . . "broken bodies": Cunningham, *Wake Island Command*, p. 60.

141 "Our planes on the ground" . . . Seven of the eight Wildcat: Kinney, *Wake Island Pilot*, pp. 57–58.

141 Pilots and mechanics: Commander NAS Wake to Commandant, 14th Naval District, Dec. 20, 1941.

142 The wounded were transported: Cunningham, *Wake Island Command*, p. 63.

142 "The destruction": Kinney, *Wake Island Pilot*, p. 61.

143 "They were like black ghosts": Urwin, *Facing Fearful Odds*, p. 320.

143 Commander Cunningham was alerted: Cunningham, *Wake Island Command*, p. 86.

143 "Stand quiet till I give": Urwin, *Facing Fearful Odds*, p. 316.

143 "We were scared to death": Ibid., p. 320.

145 "Knock it off": Morison, *The Rising Sun in the Pacific*, p. 232.

146 "Nothing could bother": Cunningham, *Wake Island Command*, p. 89.

146 "Their deflection was perfect": Urwin, *Facing Fearful Odds*, p. 330.

146 "Well, it looks as if": Ibid., p. 331.

147 "When the Japanese withdrew": Ibid., p. 334.

147 "I am very certain": Ibid.

147 "They had no illusions": Morison, *The Rising Sun in the Pacific*, p. 235.

147 "instantly and without question": "Martial Law Declared," *Honolulu Star-Bulletin*, 3rd extra, Dec. 7, 1941, p. 1, in Caren, ed., *Pearl Harbor Extra*, p. 17.

147 Curfew violators: Casey, *Torpedo Junction*, p. 41.

148 "No one has much aloha": *Paradise of the Pacific* (November 1942), quoted in Dye, ed., *Hawai'i Chronicles III*, p. 9.

149 "We absolutely refused": Peggy Hughes Ryan account in Stillwell, ed., *Air Raid— Pearl Harbor!*, p. 234.

149 "I could see the look": Evelyn W. Guthrie account in ibid., p. 241.

149 "The Japanese are good": Casey, *Torpedo Junction*, p. 61.

149 living "day to day": Ryan account in Stillwell, ed., *Air Raid—Pearl Harbor!*, p. 235.

149 "Those terrible, dreadful rumors": "Soldier" Burford quoted in Prange, Goldstein, and Dillon, *December 7, 1941*, p. 349.

150 "but my family": Excerpt from Oral History of Lt. Horace D. Warden, MC (Medical Corps), USN, Medical Officer aboard USS *Breese* (DM-18) on Dec. 7, 1941; "Overview of the Pearl Harbor Attack," www.history.navy.mil.

150 "thus offering us": CINCPAC to OPNAV, April 18, 1941, quoted in Morison, *The Rising Sun in the Pacific*, p. 227.

150 "She would be crowded": C. H. McMorris recommendation to CINCPAC for action against Wake, Dec. 11, 1941; CINCPAC Grey Book, Bk. 1, p. 75.

150 *Lexington*: Morison, *The Rising Sun in the Pacific*, pp. 235–37.

151 "We are wasting": Potter, *Bull Halsey*, p. 16.

151 Entries in the CINCPAC war diary: "Running Summary of Situation," Dec. 12 entry; CINCPAC Grey Book, Bk. 1, p. 45.

151 December 13: "Running Summary of Situation," Dec. 13 entry; ibid., p. 46.

151 "Wake Island's indomitable": AP story quoted in Sloan, *Given Up for Dead*, p. 192.

151 "Send us more Japs!": Cunningham, *Wake Island Command*, p. 109.

152 "More Japanese": Kinney, *Wake Island Pilot*, p. 69.

152 "The picture conjured up": Cunningham, *Wake Island Command*, p. 110.

152 "was confusion superimposed": Holmes, *Double-Edged Secrets*, p. 42.

152 what business did the fleet have: "OPNAV to CINCPAC," Dec. 17, 1941; CINCPAC Grey Book, Bk. 1, p. 70.

152 a "liability": "OPNAV to CINCPAC," Dec. 22, 1941; ibid., p. 72.

153 In notes recorded that day: "Estimate by Admiral Pye on 20 December"; ibid., p. 76.

153 On the 21st, Pye informed Admiral Stark: "CINCPAC to OPNAV," Dec. 21, 1941; ibid., p. 72.

153 "full of bullet holes": Commander NAS Wake to Commandant, 14th Naval District, Dec. 20, 1941.

155 "Enemy apparently landing": Morison, *The Rising Sun in the Pacific*, p. 248.

155 "The enemy is on the island": Ibid. (Some sources mistakenly attribute this message to Maj. Devereux.)

155 In a strongly worded memo: "Estimate by Captain McMorris as to action regarding enemy investing Wake 0800 December 22, 1941"; CINCPAC Grey Book, Bk. 1, pp. 80–81.

155 "Are we willing": "Decision by Admiral Draemel as to action regarding enemy investing Wake—0700—22 December"; CINCPAC Grey Book, Bk. 1, p. 82 (italics in the original).

156 At 9:11 a.m. on December 22: Morison, *The Rising Sun in the Pacific*, p. 252.

156 "Admiral Pye had had a scare": George C. Dyer account in Stillwell, ed., *Air Raid—Pearl Harbor!*, p. 46.

156 "To lose to an enemy": Layton account in ibid., p. 283.

156 was forced to withdraw . . . "By Gad!": Morison, *The Rising Sun in the Pacific*, pp. 252, 254.

156 "confessed to God": Jones and Jones, *Hawaii Goes to War*, p. 38.

157 "The parallel was sickening": Casey, *Torpedo Junction*, p. 33.

157 "with whatever they used": Holmes, *Double-Edged Secrets*, p. 42.

157 "just kept shaking his head": Frank L. DeLorenzo account in Russell, ed., *No Right to Win*, p. 10.

157 "What news of the relief": Layton, *"And I Was There,"* p. 353.

157 "This is a terrible sight": Potter, *Nimitz*, p. 20.

157 "You have my sympathy": Ibid., p. 17.

158 "He had little reason": Wilfred Jay Holmes account in Stillwell, ed., *Air Raid—Pearl Harbor!*, p. 255.

158 "I thought Admiral Nimitz": Ewing, "Nimitz," pp. 1–2.

158 "war correspondents": Morison, *The Rising Sun in the Pacific*, p. 256.

159 "aura of calm confidence": Holmes account in Stillwell, ed., *Air Raid—Pearl Harbor!*, p. 255.

159 "the incisive thrust": Layton, *"And I Was There,"* p. 354.

159 "could have been devastatingly": Nimitz, "God's Divine Will," in Stillwell, ed., *Air Raid—Pearl Harbor!*, p. 261.

159 the navy had lost: Prange, Goldstein, and Dillon, *At Dawn We Slept*, p. 539.

159 some 300,000 tons: Lord, *Day of Infamy*, p. 212.

159 "That was a most serious error": Ewing, "Nimitz," p. 11.

159 "a seventeen knot fleet": Casey, *Torpedo Junction*, p. 132.

160 He later quipped: Potter, *Nimitz*, p. 23.

160 "reasonably frank": Casey, *Torpedo Junction*, p. 59.

160 "These were all fine men": Ewing, "Nimitz," p. 5.

160 "I know most of you": William Waldo Drake account in Stillwell, ed., *Air Raid—Pearl Harbor!*, p. 269.

160 "certain key members": Potter, *Nimitz*, p. 25.

160 "In a very few minutes": Drake account in Stillwell, ed., *Air Raid—Pearl Harbor!*, p. 269.

Chapter Five

161   Admiral Ernest J. King: Buell, *Master of Sea Power*, p. 10.

161   always immaculately turned out: Photo in Reynolds, *On the Warpath in the Pacific*, p. 207.

161   "We won": Whitehill, "A Note on the Making of This Book," in King and Whitehill, *Fleet Admiral King*, p. 652.

163   "He told me" . . . "hard knocks": Buell, *Master of Sea Power*, pp. 64, 39, and 71.

164   "King justified himself": Ibid., p. 57.

164   "inertia to change": Quoted in ibid., p. 28.

165   "The next time" . . . "He didn't need": Ibid., pp. 91, 86.

165   "jackknifing his long frame": Ibid., pp. 115, 91, and 111.

166   "shaved with a blowtorch": Tully, *F. D. R.: My Boss*, p. 263.

166   "I don't care": Buell, *Master of Sea Power*, p. 87.

166   "If a man knew": Reynolds, *On the Warpath in the Pacific*, p. 95.

166   "You ought to be very suspicious": Buell, *Master of Sea Power*, p. 89.

167   "the most even-tempered man": Stoler, *Allies and Adversaries*, p. 69.

167   "Dear Harriet": Whitehill, "A Note on the Making of This Book," in King and Whitehill, *Fleet Admiral King*, p. 651.

169   "King of the Atlantic": *Life* magazine, Nov. 24, 1941, p. 92.

169   "Well": Buell, *Master of Sea Power*, p. 150.

169   "We're living in a fool's paradise": Ibid., p. 152.

169   "Where the power is" . . . "Nothing was ready": Ibid., pp. 153–54.

170   "I am fully in sympathy": Ibid., p. 156.

170   "I found Admiral King": Rr. Adm. Richard S. Edwards quoted in ibid., pp. 155–56.

170   The decor was spartan: King and Whitehill, *Fleet Admiral King*, description from photograph; illustrations after p. 368.

171   "in the same boat": FDR to WC, Dec. 8, 1941, in Loewenheim, Langley, and Jonas, eds., *Roosevelt and Churchill: Their Secret Wartime Correspondence*, p. 169.

171   "Now that we are": WC to FDR, Dec. 9, 1941, in ibid.

172   "We do not think": WC to FDR, Dec. 10, 1941, in ibid., p. 170.

172   "Delighted to have you": FDR to WC, Dec. 10, 1941, in ibid., p. 171.

172   a "wicked leer": Alanbrooke, *War Diaries, 1939–1945*, p. 209.

172   "the longest week": Churchill to Clementine Churchill, Dec. 21, 1941, in Soames, ed., *Winston and Clementine: The Personal Letters of the Churchills*, pp. 459–60.

172   "Washington represented": Goodwin, *No Ordinary Time*, p. 301.

173   "I clasped his strong hand": Churchill, *The Grand Alliance*, p. 587.

173   "I suppose that is why": Moran, *Winston Churchill: The Struggle for Survival, 1940–1965*, p. 25.

173   "It had not occurred to him": Chadakoff, ed., *Eleanor Roosevelt's My Day: Her Acclaimed Columns, 1936–1945*, p. 227.

173   "I have a toast": Beard, *President Roosevelt and the Coming of the War, 1941*, p. 555.

173   "My report home": Churchill, *The Grand Alliance*, p. 558.

174 "Now, Fields": Goodwin, *No Ordinary Time*, p. 302.

174 "chubby, florid": Tully, *F. D. R.: My Boss*, p. 300.

175 they ate lunch from plates: Ibid.

175 "The Prime Minister of Great Britain": Sherwood, *Roosevelt and Hopkins*, p. 442.

175 "We live here as": Churchill, *The Grand Alliance*, p. 686.

175 "We may wake up": *The Public Papers and Addresses of Franklin D. Roosevelt* (1941), pp. 588, 589, and 591.

176 The *Washington Star . . . Newsweek*: Meacham, *Franklin and Winston*, pp. 142, 144.

176 "my associate": Black, *Franklin Delano Roosevelt: Champion of Freedom*, p. 705.

176 "I can not feel myself": Churchill, *The Grand Alliance*, p. 594.

176 "there was little joy": Eleanor Roosevelt, *This I Remember*, p. 243.

177 "I cannot help reflecting": "Winston Churchill, Speech to Joint Session of Congress," Dec. 26, 1941, in Gilbert, ed., *The Churchill War Papers: The Ever-Widening War*, Vol. 3: *1941*, p. 1685.

177 "What sort of people": Ibid.

177 "Who could doubt": Churchill, *The Grand Alliance*, p. 595.

177 "instantaneous, electric": Meacham, *Franklin and Winston*, p. 154.

177 "I hit the target": Moran, *Winston Churchill: The Struggle for Survival, 1940–1965*, p. 16.

177 "He loved the ceremony": Meacham, *Franklin and Winston*, p. 144.

178 "ate, and thoroughly enjoyed": Reilly and Slocum, *Reilly of the White House*, p. 125.

178 "it was rarely observed": McIntire, *White House Physician*, p. 132.

178 "There is no question": Goodwin, *No Ordinary Time*, p. 303.

178 "the conversation was mostly": Rosenman, *Working with Roosevelt*, p. 319.

179 "grew genuinely to like": Sherwood, *Roosevelt and Hopkins*, p. 478.

179 "hero-worshipped": Black, *Franklin Delano Roosevelt: Champion of Freedom*, p. 695.

179 "The Limeys have": Stilwell and White, eds., *The Stilwell Papers*, p. 16.

179 "Fundamental basis of joint strategy": Sherwood, *Roosevelt and Hopkins*, p. 445.

180 "They knew their stuff": Buell, *Master of Sea Power*, p. 163.

180 a secret memorandum to Roosevelt: Marshall, Stark, Arnold, and King, "Memorandum for the President," Jan. 14, 1942. Folder: American–British Joint Chiefs of Staff Index; President's Secretary's File (hereafter PSF), Safe Files, Franklin D. Roosevelt Library, Hyde Park, NY.

181 "As far as I know": Eisenhower, *Crusade in Europe*, p. 28.

181 "was well understood": Ewing, "Nimitz," p. 11.

181 "The minimum forces": Marshall, Stark, Arnold, and King, "Memorandum for the President," Jan. 14, 1942.

181 "but it was to prove difficult": Eisenhower, *Crusade in Europe*, p. 28.

182 a "small degree less important": "COMINCH to CINCPAC," Dec. 30, 1941; CINCPAC Grey Book, Bk. 1, p. 121.

182 which King defined: Adm. King, "Memorandum for the President," March 5, 1942, in King and Whitehill, *Fleet Admiral King*, pp. 384–85.

182 "two vital Pacific tasks": Glen Perry to Edmund P. Bartnett, Nov. 7, 1942, regarding King's off-the-record press conference, in Perry, *"Dear Bart,"* pp. 88–89.

184 The Allies could only guess: "COMINCH to CINCAF, INFO CINCPAC," Dec. 31, 1941; CINCPAC Grey Book, Bk. 1, p. 122.

184 policy of "hold and build": See King's "Memorandum for the President," March 5, 1942, in King and Whitehill, *Fleet Admiral King*, pp. 384–85.

184 "hold what you've got": King to Navy Secretary Frank Knox, Feb. 8, 1942, quoted in ibid., p. 373.

184 "No fighter ever won": Buell, *Master of Sea Power*, p. 121.

185 "I've been insisting": Eisenhower, *Crusade in Europe*, p. 22.

185 "I renew my solemn pledge": Sherwood, *Roosevelt and Hopkins*, p. 454.

185 "Without any inhibitions": *Australia and the Pacific*, Australian Institute of International Affairs, p. 15.

186 "deterrent to a Japanese attack": Stoler, *Allies and Adversaries*, pp. 73–74.

186 "The Navy wants to take": Morton, *U.S. Army in World War II*, p. 218.

187 "three or four": Churchill, *The Grand Alliance*, p. 606.

187 Some 8,000 troops: United States–British Chiefs of Staff, "Defense of Island Bases between Hawaii and Australia," Jan. 13, 1942. Folder: Arcadia Index, 1941–42; PSF, Safe Files, FDR Library, Hyde Park, NY.

187 "Lord Root of the Matter": Kimball, ed., *Churchill and Roosevelt: The Complete Correspondence*, Vol. 1, p. 87n.

187 It was agreed that: United States–British Chiefs of Staff, "Defense of Island Bases between Hawaii and Australia," Jan. 13, 1942.

188 "Even while I spoke": Churchill, *The Grand Alliance*, p. 680.

188 "I am convinced": Ambrose, *The Supreme Commander: The War Years of General Dwight D. Eisenhower*, p. 26.

188 "There are difficulties": Hayes, *The History of the Joint Chiefs of Staff in World War II: The War Against Japan*, p. 46.

189 "lukewarm": Buell, *Master of Sea Power*, p. 164.

190 "You should work on Churchill": Sherwood, *Roosevelt and Hopkins*, p. 457.

190 "Don't be in a hurry": Churchill, *The Grand Alliance*, p. 597.

190 The ABDACOM theater: United States–British Chiefs of Staff, "Directive to the Supreme Commander in the ABDA Area," Jan. 2, 1942. Folder: ABCD Powers II Index, 1941–42; PSF, Safe Files, FDR Library, Hyde Park, NY.

190 "I was complimented": Churchill, *The Grand Alliance*, p. 597.

190 He counterproposed: Buell, *Master of Sea Power*, p. 166.

190 "it was evident": Churchill, *The Grand Alliance*, pp. 597, 599.

191 "The whole scheme [is] wild": Entry for Dec. 29, 1941, Alanbrooke, *War Diaries, 1939–1945*, p. 215.

191 "appropriate joint body": "Minutes," United States–British Chiefs of Staff Con-

ference, Dec. 29, 1941. Folder: Arcadia Index, 1941–42; PSF, Safe Files, FDR Library, Hyde Park, NY.

192   "It was obvious": Buell, *Master of Sea Power*, p. 169.

192   "The suggestion of an": Sherwood, *Roosevelt and Hopkins*, p. 469.

192   "provoked more heated argument": Ibid., pp. 470–71, 472.

193   "I could see no reason": Alanbrooke, *War Diaries, 1939–1945*, p. 216.

193   "sold the birthright": Ibid., entry dated Feb. 9, 1942, p. 228.

193   "possessed with one idea": Moran, *Winston Churchill: The Struggle for Survival, 1940–1965*, p. 20.

193   "Britain and America were now": Gilbert, *Churchill and America*, p. 254.

193   "There was never a failure": Churchill, *The Grand Alliance*, p. 609.

194   "utterly inadequate": Letter, Beaverbrook to FDR, Dec. 29, 1941. Folder: Beaverbrook, Lord, Index; PSF, Safe Files, FDR Library, Hyde Park, NY.

194   should be revised upward: "U.S. production goals for 1942" . . . "Memorandum for the President," Lord Beaverbrook, Dec. 29, 1941. Folder: Beaverbrook, Lord, Index.

194   "As for the navy" and the statistics that follow: See Davidson, *The Unsinkable Fleet*, pp. 32–33.

194   "We must raise our sights": State of the Union address, Jan. 6, 1942. *The American Presidency Project*, Santa Barbara, CA, online at www.presidency.ucsb.edu.

194   "Oh—the production people": Sherwood, *Roosevelt and Hopkins*, p. 474.

194   "He is drunk": Moran, *Winston Churchill: The Struggle for Survival, 1940–1965*, p. 22.

194   "gone in for the 'numbers racket'!": Sherwood, *Roosevelt and Hopkins*, p. 473.

195   "was the best of the lot": Ibid., p. 475.

196   "really ran the war": Leahy, *I Was There*, p. 106.

196   "were not above learning": Gelb, *Desperate Venture*, p. 47.

196   "King knew he had to": Spector, *Eagle Against the Sun*, p. 125.

196   "I have no intention whatever": Buell, *Master of Sea Power*, p. 166.

197   wearing a "semi-scowl": Adamic, *Dinner at the White House*, pp. 25–27.

198   "You would have been quite proud": Sherwood, *Roosevelt and Hopkins*, p. 478.

198   "It is fun to be": Ibid., p. 494.

198   demanded a vote of confidence: "I Demand a Vote of Confidence," Jan. 27, 1942, in Churchill, ed., *Never Give In!: The Best of Winston Churchill's Speeches*, pp. 324–25.

Chapter Six

199   secure cable dated January 2, 1942: "COMINCH to CINCPAC," Jan. 2, 1942; CINCPAC Grey Book, Bk. 1, p. 122.

200   "cut our offensive strength": Layton, *"And I Was There,"* p. 356.

200   "I think General Forrest's": Potter, *Bull Halsey*, p. 37.

201 "expected admirals": Morison, *The Rising Sun in the Pacific*, p. 256.

201 "As the general rule": Thomas, *Sea of Thunder*, p. 36.

201 "thundering away": Kernan, *Crossing the Line*, p. 36.

201 Halsey had lived his entire life: Details of Halsey's early career in Potter, *Bull Halsey*, pp. 23–31.

202 "everyone's friend": Ibid., p. 32.

202 Enemy radio traffic had risen: See Layton, *"And I Was There,"* pp. 359–60.

203 "Are loading for bear": Stafford, *The Big E*, p. 41.

203 "All sorts of luck": Potter, *Bull Halsey*, p. 39.

203 "raise a little hell": Lundstrom, *The First Team*, p. 58.

204 "a labor of the damned": Kernan, *Crossing the Line*, p. 38.

204 One of the SBDs: Stafford, *The Big E*, p. 44.

205 They were learning: "Running Summary of Situation," Jan. 2, 1942; CINCPAC Grey Book, Bk. 1, p. 121.

205 "intensely dramatic": Casey, *Torpedo Junction*, p. 104.

206 "May I suggest": Ibid., p. 105.

207 "Somebody observed": Ibid., p. 135.

207 "It was one of those plans": Potter, *Bull Halsey*, p. 41.

207 "Instead of just a hit and run": Dickinson, *The Flying Guns*, p. 70.

207 Bankson T. Holcomb, Jr.: Layton, *"And I Was There,"* pp. 362.

207 "That yellow belly": Potter, *Bull Halsey*, p. 42.

208 "It is essential": Potter, *Nimitz*, p. 37.

208 The captain of the *Salt Lake City*: Casey, *Torpedo Junction*, pp. 141–42.

208 They were relying upon: Jones and Jones, *Hawaii Goes to War*, p. 39.

209 "seem to feel as if": Casey, *Torpedo Junction*, pp. 101–2.

209 "theirs was a better navy": Kernan, *Crossing the Line*, p. 36.

209 "No fighters!": Dickinson, *The Flying Guns*, pp. 69–92, 72.

210 "Many were silent": Ibid., pp. 71–72.

213 "one of the most glorious fireworks": Ibid., p. 87.

213 "An eccentric rain": Ibid.

214 "suitable objectives": CO of USS *Enterprise* to CINCPAC, "Report of action on February 1, 1942 against Marshall Island Group," Feb. 7, 1942; online at www.cv6 .org/ship/logs/action19420201.htm.

214 "a vast ruffle of beach sand": Dickinson, *The Flying Guns*, p. 91.

215 "These young pilots acted": Potter, *Bull Halsey*, p. 47.

215 "I could hear voices": Dickinson, *The Flying Guns*, p. 100.

216 "Bingo! Bingo!": Pilot chatter recorded by Layton, listening from Pearl Harbor, in Layton, *"And I Was There,"* p. 362.

216 Those attacks were being carried out: CO of USS *Enterprise* to CINCPAC, "Report of action on February 1, 1942 against Marshall Island Group," Feb. 7, 1942.

216 "Then we reversed course": Raymond Spruance to Saavy Cooke, Feb. 9, 1963,

Raymond Spruance Papers, MS Collection 12, Box 2, Folder 6, U.S. Naval War College, Newport, RI.

217 Three Japanese fighters: CO of USS *Enterprise* to CINCPAC, "Report of action on February 1, 1942 against Marshall Island Group," Feb. 7, 1942.

218 "One specklike plane": Rawie's account in Lundstrom, *The First Team*, p. 68.

219 "looked like the moths": Potter, *Bull Halsey*, p. 46.

219 The jury-rigged armor: CO of USS *Enterprise* to CINCPAC, "Report of action on February 1, 1942 against Marshall Island Group," Feb. 7, 1942.

219 "This attack encountered": Ibid.

221 "A tricky and a dangerous": Kernan, *Crossing the Line*, p. 41.

221 "Get away from that cruiser": Potter, *Bull Halsey*, p. 44.

221 "Admiral, don't you think": Ibid., p. 47.

222 The five intruders: CO of USS *Enterprise* to CINCPAC, "Report of action on February 1, 1942 against Marshall Island Group," Feb. 7, 1942.

223 "It is a continuous ringing": Dickinson, *The Flying Guns*, p. 101.

223 "Stand by to repel": Kernan, *Crossing the Line*, pp. 41–42.

223 "Our AA guns": Stafford, *The Big E*, p. 57.

223 "a matter of grave concern": CO of USS *Enterprise* to CINCPAC, "Report of action on February 1, 1942 against Marshall Island Group," Feb. 7, 1942.

223 "when the small-caliber guns": Kernan, *Crossing the Line*, p. 42.

223 "The effect on the ship": CO of USS *Enterprise* to CINCPAC, "Report of action on February 1, 1942 against Marshall Island Group," Feb. 7, 1942.

224 "But the water comes down": Casey, *Torpedo Junction*, p. 154.

224 "Fire!": Dickinson, *The Flying Guns*, p. 101.

224 "frothy egg-white stuff": Ibid., p. 103.

225 "my knees are crackin' together": Potter, *Bull Halsey*, p. 48.

225 "can only be described as": CO of USS *Enterprise* to CINCPAC, "Report of action on February 1, 1942 against Marshall Island Group," Feb. 7, 1942.

225 "I had trouble": Casey, *Torpedo Junction*, pp. 154–56.

225 "Your bursts are low": Stafford, *The Big E*, p. 59.

225 The task force continued: CO of USS *Enterprise* to CINCPAC, "Report of action on February 1, 1942 against Marshall Island Group," Feb. 7, 1942.

226 "nice air raid shelter" . . . "Under the circumstances": Dickinson, *The Flying Guns*, p. 103; Casey, *Torpedo Junction*, p. 158.

227 "Burn, you son of a bitch": Lundstrum, *Black Shoe Carrier Admiral*, p. 69.

227 "Bill, it was wonderful": Layton, *"And I Was There,"* p. 364.

228 "Commander Task Force 8": Casey, *Torpedo Junction*, p. 161.

228 "Wild Bill will try anything": Dickinson, *The Flying Guns*, p. 113.

229 Seventy-seven pilots: CO of USS *Enterprise* to CINCPAC, "Report of action on February 1, 1942 against Marshall Island Group," Feb. 7, 1942.

229 "It was amazing how long": Kernan, *The Unknown Battle of Midway*, p. 3.

229 "that a great deed": Casey, *Torpedo Junction*, p. 164.

230 "The Japs didn't mind": Morison, The Rising Sun in the Pacific, p. 268.

230 "we travel something like": Casey, Torpedo Junction, p. 275.

230 wildly overoptimistic claims: See Lundstrom, The First Team, p. 77.

230 "They have come": Entry dated Feb. 1, 1942, Ugaki, Fading Victory, p. 81.

230 "a reproach that went": Entry dated Feb. 2, 1942, ibid., pp. 83–84.

230 "After experiencing": Entry dated Feb. 1, 1942, ibid., p. 81.

231 "could only grit their teeth": Layton, "And I Was There," p. 363.

231 "The enemy's attempt": Entry dated Feb. 1, 1942, Ugaki, Fading Victory, p. 82.

231 "futile" and "impulsive": Fuchida and Okumiya, Midway: The Battle That Doomed Japan, p. 62.

231 "They will adopt": Entry dated Feb. 2, 1942, Ugaki, Fading Victory, pp. 83–84.

231 "Whatever happens": Layton, "And I Was There," p. 363.

Chapter Seven

233 "the insidious yet irresistible clutching": Morison, The Rising Sun in the Pacific, p. 292.

233 When Japanese amphibious forces: Okumiya, Horikoshi, and Caidin, Zero!, p. 60.

235 the "scorched earth" principle: McDonald and Swakk-Goldman, eds., Substantive and Procedural Aspects of International Criminal Law, p. 782.

236 As late as January 31: Morison, The Rising Sun in the Pacific, p. 296.

237 He dispatched four old "four-piper": Ibid., p. 285.

238 sailed "in two long lines": Reiji Masuda account in Cook and Cook, eds., Japan at War, p. 86.

238 "The swells were high": Ibid., p. 87.

239 He cabled a series of anxious missives: Radiogram, MacArthur to the Adj. General, Dec. 23, 1941; PSF, Safe Files, FDR Library, Hyde Park, NY.

239 He declared the capital: Toland, The Rising Sun, p. 287.

239 "You go on south": Burton, Fortnight of Infamy, p. 278.

240 "Help is on the way": MacArthur's "Order of the Day," Jan. 15, 1942, quoted in Costello, The Pacific War, p. 193.

242 "How typical of America": Kratoska, ed., South East Asia: Colonial History, Vol. 5, p. 413.

242 "might offer the best possible solution": Quoted in Stimson, On Active Services in Peace and War, p. 398.

243 "I immediately discarded": Black, Franklin Delano Roosevelt: Champion of Freedom, p. 717.

243 "So long as the flag": Quoted in Stimson, On Active Services in Peace and War, p. 403.

243 it is a fact that MacArthur: Carol M. Petillo, "Douglas MacArthur and Manuel Quezon: A Note on an Imperial Bond," Pacific Historical Review 48, no. 1 (February 1979), pp. 107–17.

244 "We're the battling bastards": Douglas A. MacArthur, "MacArthur's Reminiscences: Part 5," *Life* magazine, July 10, 1964, p. 72.

244 "Well, I suppose": Layton, *"And I Was There,"* p. 311.

245 "instances where aerodromes": Burton, *Fortnight of Infamy*, p. 289.

246 "What actually happened": Brown, *Suez to Singapore*, p. 411.

246 "shrewd oriental tricks": Ibid., p. 365.

246 "various sub-human specimens": Quoted in Allen, *Singapore 1941–1942*, p. 54.

247 "The Japanese have a capacity": Brooke-Popham at a public meeting in Singapore, Dec. 22, 1942, quoted in Brown, *Suez to Singapore*, p. 360.

247 "The Japanese trooper": Radike, *Across the Dark Islands*, p. 132.

248 "You can almost see": Brown, *Suez to Singapore*, pp. 349–50, 378.

248 could not "work up any venom": Ibid., pp. 392, 529.

249 "Have you not got a single": Alanbrooke, *War Diaries, 1939–1945*, p. 226.

249 "must be reckoned as one": "Prime Minister to First Sea Lord," Jan. 22, 1942, quoted in Churchill, *The Second World War*, Vol. 4: *The Hinge of Fate*, pp. 39–40.

249 "I must confess": "Prime Minister to C.O.S. Committee," Jan. 19, 1942, in ibid., p. 44.

250 "We must defeat them": Wigmore, *The Japanese Thrust*, p. 341.

250 "Battle for Singapore": "Wavell to Prime Minister," Feb. 11, 1942, in Churchill, *The Hinge of Fate*, p. 88.

250 an "inferiority complex": Ibid.

250 "Chum": Hack and Blackburn, *Did Singapore Have to Fall?*, p. 263.

251 "There was a lot of chaos": Marshall Ralph Doak, *My Years in the Navy*, online at www.historycentral.com/Navy/Doak.

251 "In the spirit of chivalry": Toland, *The Rising Sun*, p. 274.

251 "You must continue": "Wavell to Percival," Feb. 14, 1942, in Churchill, *The Hinge of Fate*, p. 91.

252 "The Japanese have wrenched": *Daily Mirror* (London) quoted in Brown, *Suez to Singapore*, p. 499.

252 "Landings on Java": "General Wavell to Prime Minister," Feb. 16, 1942, in Churchill, *The Hinge of Fate*, p. 141.

252 "I am afraid that": "General Wavell to Prime Minister," Feb. 21, 1942, in ibid., p. 144.

255 "considerable psychological tension": "Action Report—USS *Pope* (DD-225), 1 March 1942," by Welford C. Blinn, Former Commanding Officer; online at www.ibiblio.org/hyperwar/USN/ships/logs/DD/dd225-Java.html.

255 Radio Tokyo: Radio Tokyo quoted in Thomas, *Sea of Thunder*, p. 58.

256 "It seemed to pass along": Masuda account in Cook and Cook, eds., *Japan at War*, pp. 88–89.

256 "This day the personnel": Hornfischer, *Ship of Ghosts*, p. 70.

256 "Am proceeding to intercept": "Battle of Bawean Islands—Report of action; events prior and subsequent thereto," Commanding Officer, USS *John D. Edwards*

(DD-216) to Commander, U.S. Naval Forces, Southwest Pacific, March 4, 1942; online at www.ibiblio.org/hyperwar/USN/ships/logs/DD/dd216-Bawean.html.

257 "farcical": Ibid.

258 "From then on": Ibid.

258 "The crystal ball": Ibid.

259 "thunder of big guns": Masuda account in Cook and Cook, eds., *Japan at War*, p. 89.

259 Thirteen minutes later: Hara, *Japanese Destroyer Captain*, p. 76.

260 They hoped against the odds: "Action Report—USS *Pope* (DD-225), 1 March 1942," by Welford C. Blinn, Former Commanding Officer.

261 "All communication systems": Cdr. A. L. Maher, Report on loss of *Houston*, Nov. 13, 1945, quoted in Morison, *The Rising Sun in the Pacific*, p. 368.

262 "The Dutch fought": "Battle of Bawean Islands—Report of action; events prior and subsequent thereto."

262 "a magnificent display": Morison, *The Rising Sun in the Pacific*, p. 380.

263 "vain" and a "bugbear": Thorne, *Allies of a Kind*, p. 3.

263 "scores of thousands of words": Churchill, *The Hinge of Fate*, p. 132.

264 Australian prime minister John Curtain: Ibid., pp. 15–19, 57–59, and 155–58.

266 "I do not like these days": "WC to FDR," Doc. 97, Feb. 19, 1942, in Loewenheim, Langley, and Jonas, eds., *Roosevelt and Churchill: Their Secret Wartime Correspondence*, p. 181.

266 "The weight of the war": "WC to FDR," Doc. 103, March 7, 1942, in ibid., pp. 186–87.

266 "the well-known back-seat drivers": "FDR to WC," Doc. 96, Feb. 18, 1942, in ibid., p. 179.

266 "keep up your optimism": "FDR to WC," Doc. 110, March 18, 1942, in ibid., p. 196.

266 "Once a month": Ibid.

266 "constantly look forward": "FDR to WC," Doc. 96, Feb. 18, 1942, in ibid., p. 179.

266 "Here is a thought": "FDR to WC," Doc. 110, March 18, 1942, in ibid., p. 195.

267 "good in places": Entry dated March 10, 1942, Alanbrooke, *War Diaries, 1939–1945*, p. 238.

267 "The energy of the Japanese attack": "FDR to WC," Doc. 104, March 7, 1942, in Loewenheim, Langley, and Jonas, eds., *Roosevelt and Churchill: Their Secret Wartime Correspondence*, pp. 188–89.

Chapter Eight

269 a "railroad timetable": Koichi Shimada, "The Opening Air Offensive Against the Philippines," in Evans, ed., *The Japanese Navy in World War II*, p. 89.

269 the emperor appeared: *Kokusai Shashin Joho* (International Graphic Magazine) 21, no. 12, Feb. 1, 1942.

270 The war songs: Song titles cited in Yamashita, ed., *Leaves from an Autumn of Emergencies*, pp. 231–32.

270 "I don't know": Hara, *Japanese Destroyer Captain*, p. 86.

271 "When my eldest brother went": Wakana Nishihara account in Cook and Cook, eds., *Japan at War*, p. 328.

271 "No one could reveal": Shigenobu Debun account in ibid., p. 124.

271 the "disgrace" of Pearl Harbor: *New Order in Greater East Asia* (April 1942), in Tolischus, *Through Japanese Eyes*, p. 149.

271 "Many United States troops": *Japan Times & Advertiser*, April 17, 1942, in ibid., p. 112.

272 a "parasite prolonging": *Japan Times & Advertiser*, Jan. 2, 1942, in Caren, ed., *Pearl Harbor Extra*, p. 77.

272 bombing attacks on Tokyo: *Kokusai Shashin Joho* (*International Graphic Magazine*) 21, no. 12, Feb. 1, 1942.

272 "now that they have seen": General Hatta over the radio, Jan. 9, 1942, quoted in Tolischus, *Through Japanese Eyes*, p. 147.

272 "to second-rate or third-rate powers": *New Order in Greater East Asia* (April 1942), in ibid., p. 112.

272 "but the only ones": Agawa, *The Reluctant Admiral*, p. 287.

273 "intolerably embarrassed": Ibid., pp. 284, 297, and 287.

273 "All they need do really": Ibid., p. 288.

273 "For a while we'll have everything": Ibid., p. 292.

274 "all the public hullabaloo": Ibid., p. 286.

275 "It's annoying to be passive": Diary entry dated March 11, 1942, Ugaki, *Fading Victory*, p. 103.

276 "The army took its usual attitude": Diary entry dated March 14, 1942, ibid., p. 104.

276 "We want to invade Ceylon": Miwa quoted in Willmott, *The Barrier and the Javelin*, p. 79.

278 an "ever-present and highly disturbing": Fuchida and Okumiya, *Midway: The Battle That Doomed Japan*, p. 91.

279 "If real enemy planes": Diary entry dated March 12, 1942, Ugaki, *Fading Victory*, p. 104.

280 "One wonders whether": Agawa, *The Reluctant Admiral*, p. 296.

281 "firmly made up": Ibid., p. 297.

282 The next day, April 2: Capt. Marc Mitscher to Adm. Nimitz, "Report of Action, April 18, 1942, with notable events prior and subsequent thereto," April 28, 1942.

282 "undisciplined": Stephen Jurika, Jr., account in Wooldridge, ed., *Carrier Warfare in the Pacific*, p. 26.

283 When quizzed: Lawson, *Thirty Seconds Over Tokyo*, p. 35.

283 Admiral King had assigned: King related the details in an off-the-record press interview dated June 8, 1943, in Perry, *"Dear Bart,"* p. 171.

284 an "outside loop": "Doolittle Performs 'Outside Loop' Feat," *New York Times*, May 26, 1927.

284 "No," he replied: "The Reminiscences of Rear Admiral Henry L. Miller, U.S. Navy (Retired)," U.S. Naval Institute, Annapolis, MD, 1973, p. 32.

284 Miller taught the army pilots: Details of training the B-25 aircrews in ibid., p. 33; see also Lawson, *Thirty Seconds Over Tokyo*, p. 26.

285 "Henry," Doolittle replied: "The Reminiscences of Rear Admiral Henry L. Miller, U.S. Navy (Retired)," p. 38.

285 Eleven days out: Capt. Murray, USS *Enterprise*, to CINCPAC, "Report of action in connection with the bombing of Tokyo on April 18, 1942," April 23, 1942, item 1.

285 "As I flew over": Cheek's recollections in Russell, ed., *No Right to Win*, p. 15.

286 "This force is bound": Stafford, *The Big E*, p. 77.

286 The now-enlarged Task Force 16: Capt. Murray, USS *Enterprise*, to CINCPAC, "Report of action in connection with the bombing of Tokyo on April 18, 1942," April 23, 1942, item 2.

286 In the "misty grey" light: Casey, *Torpedo Junction*, p. 300.

286 "God damnest weather": Lundstrom, *The First Team*, p. 148.

287 "If we all get to Chungking": Lawson, *Thirty Seconds Over Tokyo*, p. 37.

287 They practiced the phrase: Jurika account in Wooldridge, ed., *Carrier Warfare in the Pacific*, p. 27.

287 A gale-force wind: Capt. Murray, USS *Enterprise*, to CINCPAC, "Report of action in connection with the bombing of Tokyo on April 18, 1942," April 23, 1942, item 3.

287 One of the B-25 pilots noted: Lawson, *Thirty Seconds Over Tokyo*, p. 42.

287 At 3:10 a.m., the *Enterprise* radar: Capt. Murray, USS *Enterprise*, to CINCPAC, "Report of action in connection with the bombing of Tokyo on April 18, 1942," April 23, 1942, item 5.

287 "Enemy surface ship": Ibid., item 6. See also Toland, *The Rising Sun*, p. 350.

288 "two beautiful Japanese carriers": Thomas, *Sea of Thunder*, p. 63.

288 "Launch planes": Stafford, *The Big E*, p. 78.

288 "Shells are tossed": Casey, *Torpedo Junction*, p. 426.

288 "like a yoyo": Cheek's recollections in Russell, ed., *No Right to Win*, p. 16.

289 "ridiculous" and "excessive": Commanding Officer, USS *Nashville*, to Admiral Nimitz, "Report of sinking of two enemy patrol boats on April 18, 1942," April 21, 1942.

289 "disappointing": Admiral Halsey to Admiral Nimitz, "Report of action in connection with the bombing of Tokyo on April 18, 1942," April 23, 1942, item 2(d).

289 "In about half an hour": Lawson, *Thirty Seconds Over Tokyo*, p. 52.

290 "Come on, fellas": Stafford, *The Big E*, p. 78.

290 large white boards: Lawson, *Thirty Seconds Over Tokyo*, p. 53.

290 "Prepare to launch aircraft": Jurika account in Wooldridge, ed., *Carrier Warfare in the Pacific*, p. 30.

290 "high green foam-flecked waves": Kernan, *Crossing the Line*, p. 39.

290 "As the old salts would say": Fisher's recollections in Russell, ed., *No Right to Win*, p. 14.

291 the "wet, rolling deck": Lawson, *Thirty Seconds Over Tokyo*, pp. 52–53.

291 "you would actually launch": Jurika account in Wooldridge, ed., *Carrier Warfare in the Pacific*, p. 31.

291 "there was soon heavy money": Kernan, *Crossing the Line*, p. 38.

292 "I would say he was 50 feet": Jurika account in Wooldridge, ed., *Carrier Warfare in the Pacific*, p. 31.

292 "hung his ship": Lawson, *Thirty Seconds Over Tokyo*, p. 55.

292 "The pilot held the nose up": Fisher's recollections in Russell, ed., *No Right to Win*, p. 14.

292 "It sure was windy!": Bernstein's recollections in ibid., p. 18.

292 One crewman: Rose, *The Ship That Held the Line*, p. 70.

293 "I think without a doubt": "The Reminiscences of Rear Admiral Henry L. Miller, U.S. Navy (Retired)," p. 44.

293 "we all cheered loudly": Kernan, *Crossing the Line*, p. 40.

293 "plunged into activities": Diary entry dated April 18, 1942, Ugaki, *Fading Victory*, p. 111.

293 "Enemy task force": Layton, "*And I Was There*," p. 386.

294 "You see": Lawson, *Thirty Seconds Over Tokyo*, p. 61.

294 "Everyone at our airfield": Ens. Takeshi Maeda account in Werneth, ed., *Beyond Pearl Harbor*, p. 116.

294 "The sky was full": Koiwa Kazuei letter in Gibney, ed., *Senso*, p. 203.

295 "lower than the hills": Lawson, *Thirty Seconds Over Tokyo*, p. 62.

295 One of the B-25 pilots reported: War Department communiqué, April 20, 1943, in ibid., p. 194.

295 When Admiral Yamamoto was told: Toland, *The Rising Sun*, p. 309.

296 "Give your blood": Casey, *Torpedo Junction*, pp. 308, 307.

297 an "armada of Chinese": Ibid., p. 309.

298 "They had stocked the fantail": Jurika account in Wooldridge, ed., *Carrier Warfare in the Pacific*, p. 34.

298 "I was the Statue of Liberty": Harris, Mitchell, and Schechter, eds., *The Homefront*, p. 73.

298 a reporter asked Roosevelt: Dallek, *Franklin D. Roosevelt and American Foreign Policy, 1932–1945*, p. 334.

299 a "do-much" raid: Fuchida and Okumiya, *Midway: The Battle That Doomed Japan*, p. 97.

299 "has brought about a tremendous change": Sakai, Caidin, and Saito, *Samurai!*, p. 104.

300 "Our homeland has been air raided": Diary entry dated April 20, 1942, Ugaki, *Fading Victory*, p. 115.

300 "provides a regrettable graphic": Agawa, *The Reluctant Admiral*, p. 300.

300 "Cease operations": Layton, "*And I Was There*," p. 387.

300 "They never told the truth": Diary entries dated April 19, 1942, April 21, 1942, and April 22, 1942, Ugaki, *Fading Victory*, pp. 113, 115.

300 "The Japanese troops slaughtered": Chiang Kai-shek to FDR, April 28, 1942, quoted in Gruhl, *Imperial Japan's World War Two, 1931–1945*, p. 79.

Chapter Nine

302 "the dungeon": Layton, *"And I Was There,"* p. 358.

303 "I considered myself": "The Reminiscences of Captain Joseph J. Rochefort, U.S. Navy (Retired)," U.S. Naval Institute, Annapolis, MD, 1983, pp. 45, 125, 126.

303 "Not much attention": Holmes, *Double-Edged Secrets*, p. 16.

303 "gentlemen don't read": Ibid., p. 44.

303 "because no one could accuse": "The Reminiscences of Captain Thomas H. Dyer, U.S. Navy (Retired)," U.S. Naval Institute, Annapolis, MD, 1986, p. 140.

303 "Every time he goes": "The Reminiscences of Captain Joseph J. Rochefort, U.S. Navy (Retired)," pp. 32–33.

304 "You don't have to be crazy": "The Reminiscences of Captain Thomas H. Dyer, U.S. Navy (Retired)," p. 228.

304 Rochefort went home: "The Reminiscences of Captain Joseph J. Rochefort, U.S. Navy (Retired)," p. 124.

304 "I figured there were people": "The Reminiscences of Captain Thomas H. Dyer, U.S. Navy (Retired)," p. 249.

304 As each new draft: Ibid., p. 273.

304 "a theory was advanced": Holmes, *Double-Edged Secrets*, p. 38.

305 "in the black": "The Reminiscences of Captain Joseph J. Rochefort, U.S. Navy (Retired)," p. 113.

305 Hypo launched: "The Reminiscences of Captain Thomas H. Dyer, U.S. Navy (Retired)," p. 234.

305 "had never occurred": Holmes, *Double-Edged Secrets*, p. 21.

305 "you see a whole lot of letters": "The Reminiscences of Captain Joseph J. Rochefort, U.S. Navy (Retired)," p. 34.

305 "if you observe something": "The Reminiscences of Captain Thomas H. Dyer, U.S. Navy (Retired)," pp. 227, 278.

306 "persistence": "The Reminiscences of Captain Joseph J. Rochefort, U.S. Navy (Retired)," p. 35.

306 "common sense, actually": Ibid., p. 190.

306 the "message externals": For a discussion of this issue, see Layton, *"And I Was There,"* p. 27; see also Henry F. Schorreck, "Battle of Midway: 4–7 June 1942: The Role of COMINT in the Battle of Midway" (SRH-230). Department of the Navy monograph, online at NHC Web site; and Holmes, *Double-Edged Secrets*, pp. 18, 59.

306 "mixture of gobbledygook": Holmes, *Double-Edged Secrets*, p. 18.

307 "a concatenation of deductions": Ibid., p. 24.

307 had a standing invitation: Layton, *"And I Was There,"* pp. 356–57.

307 stationed in Tokyo as language officers: "The Reminiscences of Captain Joseph J. Rochefort, U.S. Navy (Retired)," pp. 145–46.

307 "I want you to be the Admiral Nagumo": Layton, *"And I Was There,"* p. 357.

308 a routine forecast: Ibid., p. 373.

308 "It is useless to obtain": "The Reminiscences of Captain Joseph J. Rochefort, U.S. Navy (Retired)," p. 25.

309 Acting upon predictions: Schorreck, "Battle of Midway: 4–7 June 1942: The Role of COMINT in the Battle of Midway" (SRH-230).

309 "cleared for Ultra": Holmes, *Double-Edged Secrets*, pp. 23, 63.

309 "This business of secrecy": "The Reminiscences of Captain Joseph J. Rochefort, U.S. Navy (Retired)," p. 25.

310 Throughout the Pacific: Schorreck, "Battle of Midway: 4–7 June 1942: The Role of COMINT in the Battle of Midway" (SRH-230).

310 hard-fought bureaucratic turf battle: Layton, *"And I Was There,"* p. 20.

310 "assume active coordinating control: Ibid., p. 368.

311 "I would say with all modesty": "The Reminiscences of Captain Joseph J. Rochefort, U.S. Navy (Retired)," p. 105.

311 their feud would very nearly spoil: Holmes, *Double-Edged Secrets*, p. 54.

311 "estimates": "The Reminiscences of Captain Joseph J. Rochefort, U.S. Navy (Retired)," pp. 115, 100.

311 "may well be accompanied": "COMINCH to CINCPAC" and others, Feb. 6, 1942; CINCPAC Grey Book, Bk. 1, p. 220.

312 "recent enemy air and submarine": "COMINCH to CINCPAC," March 11, 1942; CINCPAC Grey Book, Bk. 1, p. 285; and Layton, *"And I Was There,"* p. 378.

312 "No indication": Layton, *"And I Was There,"* p. 380.

312 One officer estimated: Holmes, *Double-Edged Secrets*, p. 59.

313 "This is one reason": "The Reminiscences of Captain Joseph J. Rochefort, U.S. Navy (Retired)," pp. 132–34.

313 "needs only time": Holmes, *Double-Edged Secrets*, pp. 53–54.

313 "Physiologically": Holland, ed., *The Navy*, p. 103.

314 It took Jasper Holmes: Holmes, *Double-Edged Secrets*, pp. 17, 65.

315 "an offensive in the southwest Pacific": Layton, *"And I Was There,"* p. 382.

315 "We were a little surprised": "The Reminiscences of Captain Joseph J. Rochefort, U.S. Navy (Retired)," pp. 177, 174–75.

315 By April 24: Schorreck, "Battle of Midway: 4–7 June 1942: The Role of COMINT in the Battle of Midway" (SRH-230).

316 "reading today's traffic": Layton, *"And I Was There,"* p. 394.

316 "There are many indications": Ibid., p. 390.

316 "5 carriers, 1 battleship": "Running Estimate of the Situation," April 23, 1942; CINCPAC Grey Book, Bk. 1, p. 409.

316 "there were no signs": Layton, *"And I Was There,"* p. 390.

317 "Fairly accurate knowledge": "Estimate of the Situation," April 22, 1942; CINCPAC Grey Book, Bk. 1, p. 384.

317 "accept odds in battle": Layton, *"And I Was There,"* p. 391.

318 a "very able man": Buell, *Master of Sea Power*, p. 198.

319 "check further advance": Schorreck, "Battle of Midway: 4–7 June 1942: The Role of COMINT in the Battle of Midway" (SRH-230).

Chapter Ten

323 "The *Lexington*": Kernan, *Crossing the Line*, p. 43.

324 "We knew radar": Beaver, *Sailor from Oklahoma*, p. 162.

324 "Beads of moisture": Johnston, *Queen of the Flat-Tops*, p. 18.

324 "eyeballs hardening": Casey, *Torpedo Junction*, p. 191.

325 The Navy Yard had installed: Lt. Cdr. Paul D. Stroop account in Wooldridge, ed., *Carrier Warfare in the Pacific*, p. 36.

325 "the healthy rivalry": Johnston, *Queen of the Flat-Tops*, p. 22.

325 held live-firing drills: Casey, *Torpedo Junction*, p. 189.

325 "Inside of two weeks": Johnston, *Queen of the Flat-Tops*, p. 42.

326 "crossing the line" rites: Ibid., pp. 4–9.

326 A "Grand Inquisitor": Ibid., p. 30.

327 "This was before the popularity": Otis Kight account in Russell, ed., *No Right to Win*, p. 70.

327 "soapy oil-and-dirt": Beaver, *Sailor from Oklahoma*, p. 155.

327 They shaved with salt water: Kernan, *Crossing the Line*, pp. 40–41.

327 heat rash . . . "endless nervous shifting": Ibid., and p. 32.

328 The *Lexington* and her screening ships: War Diary, USS *Lexington*, Flagship of Commander, Task Force 11; entry for April 19, 1942.

328 "the blue of vast deeps": Johnston, *Queen of the Flat-Tops*, p. 1.

328 "flaming skies": Casey, *Torpedo Junction*, pp. 328, 331.

328 "the waves of this great ocean": Michener, *Tales of the South Pacific*, p. 27.

329 Fletcher concealed his presence: Lundstrom, *The First Team*, p. 167.

330 That night: Ibid., p. 168.

332 "As usual throughout the war": Morison, *History of United States Naval Operations in World War II*, Vol. 4: *Coral Sea, Midway and Submarine Actions*, p. 26.

332 Johnston concluded: Johnston, *Queen of the Flat-Tops*, p. 123.

332 The SBD pilots complained: On the problem of fogging sights in the SBD, see Buell, *Dauntless Helldivers*, pp. 57–58.

333 "Considering that there was": Nimitz to King, "Naval Action in Coral Sea Area, 4–8 May 1942" (CINCPAC endorsement of Fletcher's after-action report), p. 3.

334 "destroy enemy ships, shipping": U.S. Strategic Bombing Survey (USSBS), "The Campaigns of the Pacific War." Chap. 4, "The Battle of the Coral Sea" (1946); online at www.ibiblio.org/hyperwar/AAF/USSBS.

334 "deadly round": Layton, *"And I Was There,"* p. 398.

334 "If they can't find you": Johnston, *Queen of the Flat-Tops*, p. 153.

334 "We simply drew": Stroop account in Wooldridge, ed., *Carrier Warfare in the Pacific*, p. 37.

335 "Whatever they saw": Sherman, *Combat Command*, p. 98.

335 "under a handicap out here": Johnston, *Queen of the Flat-Tops*, p. 130.

336 On the *Lexington*: Ibid., pp. 110–11.

336 "Where is the Kawanishi?": Ibid., p. 128.

336 "A fine thing": Ibid., p. 129.

337 "Don't forget now": Ibid., p. 135.

338 Assuming the Japanese carriers: Layton, *"And I Was There,"* pp. 389–404.

340 "Fortunately," Crace remarked: Ibid., p. 400.

340 "two carriers and four heavy cruisers": Sherman, *Combat Command*, p. 99.

340 "Young man": Layton, *"And I Was There,"* p. 399.

341 As it happened, however: Johnston, *Queen of the Flat-Tops*, p. 142.

342 "The Jap was exactly downwind": Ibid., p. 143.

342 "The ship was a flaming wreckage": Hamilton quoted in Astor, *Wings of Gold*, p. 65.

343 "just ploughed herself": Buell, *Dauntless Helldivers*, p. 67.

343 "The sight of those heavy": Flatley quoted in Astor, *Wings of Gold*, p. 66.

343 "It was a very successful attack": Stroop account in Wooldridge, ed., *Carrier Warfare in the Pacific*, p. 38.

343 Two hundred and three men: Morison, *Coral Sea, Midway and Submarine Actions*, pp. 41–42.

344 "We will join battle": Layton, *"And I Was There,"* p. 399.

346 a "colander": Johnston, *Queen of the Flat-Tops*, p. 153.

346 "280 degrees speed 20 knots": Layton, *"And I Was There,"* p. 400.

347 "insufficient daylight": Ibid., p. 401.

348 "These planes were in": Stroop account in Wooldridge, ed., *Carrier Warfare in the Pacific*, p. 39.

348 counted nine planes: Sherman, *Combat Command*, p. 102.

348 stationed on the *Yorktown*'s flight deck: Peter Newberg account in Russell, ed., *No Right to Win*, p. 21.

348 "Have any of our planes": Astor, *Wings of Gold*, p. 67.

348 "In the last few seconds": Newberg account in Russell, ed., *No Right to Win*, p. 21.

348 "I know Japanese planes": Stroop account in Wooldridge, ed., *Carrier Warfare in the Pacific*, p. 39.

348 "What are you shooting": Dick Wright quoted in Lundstrom, *The First Team*, p. 216.

348 "In the frenzy": Buell, *Dauntless Helldivers*, p. 69.

349 "In our enemy": Johnston, *Queen of the Flat-Tops*, p. 157.

349 At 5:40 a.m.: Buell, *Dauntless Helldivers*, p. 69.

350 Crewmen crept down corridors: Kernan, *Crossing the Line*, p. 32.

350 "with no place to hide": Beaver, *Sailor from Oklahoma*, p. 164.

351 "Two carriers": War Diary, USS *Lexington*, Flagship of Commander, Task Force 11; entry for May 8, 1942.

351 "It was thrilling news": Sherman, *Combat Command*, p. 103.

351 The aircrews copied down: Ibid., p. 107.

352 "If they came in too close": Johnston, *Queen of the Flat-Tops*, p. 164.

352 The dive-bombers had to climb: Sherman, *Combat Command*, p. 104.

352 "This loss of initiative": Buell, *Dauntless Helldivers*, p. 71.

353 High above: Ibid., and Lundstrom, *The First Team*, p. 230.

353 Miyashita of the *Shokaku* was below: Maintenance Warrant Officer Hachiro Miyashita account in Werneth, ed., *Beyond Pearl Harbor*, p. 81.

354 "You couldn't see much": Gayler quoted in Astor, *Wings of Gold*, p. 69.

354 "There was always one of them": Johnston, *Queen of the Flat-Tops*, p. 166.

355 "Have sighted enemy carriers": Lundstrom, *The First Team*, p. 223.

355 "This was a beautiful report": Ens. Kenji Hori account in Werneth, ed., *Beyond Pearl Harbor*, p. 67.

355 the skipper had an intuitive sense: Sherman's action report, "The Battle of the Coral Sea, 7 and 8 May 1942," item 14.

355 "I feel that at the present time": Johnston, *Queen of the Flat-Tops*, p. 175.

356 The *Lexington's* fighter director officer: Sherman's action report, "The Battle of the Coral Sea, 7 and 8 May 1942," item 16.

356 "*Norma* to carrier": Johnston, *Queen of the Flat-Tops*, p. 180.

356 "My wingman and I": Willard Eder quoted in Astor, *Wings of Gold*, p. 69.

357 The *Lexington's* lookouts: Sherman's action report, "The Battle of the Coral Sea, 7 and 8 May 1942," item 15.

357 "clusters of black dots": Beaver, *Sailor from Oklahoma*, p. 166.

357 "Here they come!": Johnston, *Queen of the Flat-Tops*, p. 182.

358 "Never in all my years": Lt. Cdr. Shigekazu Shimazaki quoted in Okumiya, Horikoshi, and Caidin, *Zero!*, p. 104.

358 "beautifully coordinated": Sherman, *Combat Command*, p. 109.

358 "I had to fly directly": Shimazaki quoted in Okumiya, Horikoshi, and Caidin, *Zero!*, pp. 104–5.

359 "From my bridge": Sherman, *Combat Command*, p. 109.

359 "Hard astarboard": Johnston, *Queen of the Flat-Tops*, p. 182.

359 "majestically and ponderously": Sherman, *Combat Command*, p. 109.

359 "Their wicked noses": Johnston, *Queen of the Flat-Tops*, p. 184.

360 "Don't change course, Captain!": Sherman, *Combat Command*, p. 110.

360 at 11:20 a.m., the *Lexington's* luck: Sherman's action report, "The Battle of the Coral Sea, 7 and 8 May 1942," item 18.

360 "seemed to lift": Beaver, *Sailor from Oklahoma*, p. 167.

360 "They were curious": Stroop account in Wooldridge, ed., *Carrier Warfare in the Pacific*, p. 42.

361 received a series of upbeat reports: Details of damage control efforts drawn from Sherman's action report, "The Battle of the Coral Sea, 7 and 8 May 1942," items 19, 20.

361 "She looked okay": Gayler quoted in Astor, *Wings of Gold*, p. 70.

362 "We felt like throwing out": Sherman, *Combat Command*, p. 112.

362 From his post on the bridge: Ibid.

362 "a gale of wind": Lt. H. E. Williamson quoted in Johnston, *Queen of the Flat-Tops*, p. 203.

363 the fire heated the bulkheads: See Beaver, *Sailor from Oklahoma*, pp. 169–70.

363 "that sounded like a freight train": Stroop account in Wooldridge, ed., *Carrier Warfare in the Pacific*, p. 44.

363 "The forward part": Executive Officer to Commanding Officer, USS *Lexington*, May 14, 1942. "Action in the Coral Sea, May 8, 1942—report of" (A16-3/CV-2), item 27.

365 "Let's get the boys": Sherman, *Combat Command*, p. 114. Also see Johnston and Stroop.

365 "Oh, I got a bit lonely": Johnston, *Queen of the Flat-Tops*, p. 217.

365 "I remember going across": Stroop account in Wooldridge, ed., *Carrier Warfare in the Pacific*, pp. 45–46.

365 "Little licking tongues": Beaver, *Sailor from Oklahoma*, pp. 170–71.

366 "duty and privilege": Sherman, *Combat Command*, p. 115.

366 "I was just thinking": Johnston, *Queen of the Flat-Tops*, p. 220.

366 "heartbreaking": Sherman, *Combat Command*, p. 114.

366 "She listed heavily": Beaver, *Sailor from Oklahoma*, pp. 170–71.

367 "bits and particles": Johnston, *Queen of the Flat-Tops*, p. 224.

367 "The stricken vessel": Sherman, *Combat Command*, p. 116.

368 "hard to starboard!": William G. Roy account in Russell, ed., *No Right to Win*, p. 20.

368 "The ship's wake": Ibid.

368 "raised the whole stern of the ship": Warren Willenburg account in "Veterans' Biographies," published for the Battle of Midway Celebration, Marines Memorial Club, San Francisco, 2009, p. 55.

368 "There were parts and particles": Kight account in Russell, ed., *No Right to Win*, p. 72.

369 "Hell, no. We'll make it!": U.S. Strategic Bombing Survey (USSBS), "The Campaigns of the Pacific War." Chap. 4, "The Battle of the Coral Sea"—"Attack on the *Yorktown*," p. 29. Online at www.ibiblio.org/hyperwar/AAF/USSBS.

370 "We were running scared": Short quoted in Buell, *Dauntless Helldivers*, p. 75.

370 "Port Moresby attack": Layton, *"And I Was There,"* p. 403.

371 "picking potatoes from the soil": Miyashita account in Werneth, ed., *Beyond Pearl Harbor*, p. 81.

371 "bloody handprints": Frank Boo account in "Veterans' Biographies," p. 7.

372 "hands grasping me": Buell, *Dauntless Helldivers*, p. 77.

Chapter Eleven

373 "First enemy attack completed": Layton, *"And I Was There,"* pp. 402–3.

373 "We don't know how badly": Ibid., p. 403.

373 "At present stage of our carrier": "CINCPAC to COMINCH," May 10, 1942; CINCPAC Grey Book, Bk. 1, p. 463.

373 "they need all the communications": Buell, *Master of Sea Power*, p. 199.

374 "merely the first round": King and Whitehill, *Fleet Admiral King*, p. 378.

374 Captain Sherman judged: Sherman, *Combat Command*, p. 387.

375 "the real safeguard": Layton, *"And I Was There,"* p. 404.

375 "outstanding material defect": Nimitz to King, "Naval Action in Coral Sea Area, 4–8 May 1942" (CINCPAC endorsement of Fletcher's after-action report), p. 5.

376 The Douglas TBD Devastator: Though the TBD had fared well at Coral Sea, scoring several hits on the *Shoho*, Nimitz concluded, "Obsolescent torpedo planes reduce effectiveness of VT squadrons"—Ibid., p. 7.

376 "Gain plenty of altitude": Flatley quoted in Astor, *Wings of Gold*, p. 72.

377 Tokyo also announced: *Kokusai Shashin Joho* (*International Graphic Magazine*), June 1, 1942.

377 "After this new defeat": Morison, *Coral Sea, Midway and Submarine Actions*, p. 62.

377 "The truth of the matter": Okumiya, Horikoshi, and Caidin, *Zero!*, p. 148.

377 "A dream of great success": Entry for May 7, 1942, Ugaki, *Fading Victory*, p. 122.

378 "If the sons of the concubine": Parshall and Tully, *Shattered Sword*, p. 64.

378 "carry out the occupation": Fuchida and Okumiya, *Midway: The Battle That Doomed Japan*, p. 98.

378 "Taken together": Parshall and Tully, *Shattered Sword*, p. 51.

379 "considerable turnover in personnel": Nagumo's Midway action report, June 15, 1942. Part II, Sec. 3, "Preparations for the Operation," in "The Japanese Story of the Battle of Midway," OPNAV P32-1002. Office of Naval Intelligence, Washington, DC, June 1947.

380 The disparaging term: Agawa, *The Reluctant Admiral*, p. 301.

380 "the morale of the Main Body": Entry for March 3, 1942, Ugaki, *Fading Victory*, p. 100.

380 "If the premise is accepted": Parshall and Tully, *Shattered Sword*, p. 55.

380 *shoribyo*, or "victory disease": Layton, *"And I Was There,"* p. 406.

380 "The whole ship was aglitter": Agawa, *The Reluctant Admiral*, p. 302.

381 "Wait," he said: Ibid., p. 303.

382 "This kind of supervision": Quoted in ibid.

382 "*Gaishu Isshoku!*": Parshall and Tully, *Shattered Sword*, p. 63.

382 "were so sure": Fuchida and Okumiya, *Midway: The Battle That Doomed Japan*, p. 128.

382 it would "not be easy for Japan": Adm. Nobutake Kondo, "Some Opinions Concerning the War," in Goldstein and Dillon, eds., *The Pacific War Papers*, p. 312.

383 "I could not help being": Entries for May 4 and May 5, 1942, Ugaki, *Fading Victory*, p. 120.

384 "My job was to fill it in": Layton, *"And I Was There,"* p. 423.

384 "I've got something so hot": Ibid., p. 411.

385 "We knew that AH": Ibid., p. 412.

386 "The amazing part": "The Reminiscences of Captain Joseph J. Rochefort, U.S. Navy (Retired)," U.S. Naval Institute, Annapolis, MD, 1983, p. 203.

386 "one Japanese unit": Layton, *"And I Was There,"* p. 426.

386 "Japs may be practicing deception": Ibid.

386 "It was a mess": Ibid., p. 413.

387 "No one who has not experienced it": Holmes, *Double-Edged Secrets*, p. 5.

387 "Desire you proceed": "CINCPAC TO CTF 16 INFO COMINCH," May 16, 1942; CINCPAC Grey Book, Bk. 1, p. 469.

388 "against Midway-Oahu line": "CINCPAC TO COMINCH," May 16, 1942; ibid., p. 471.

388 "Unless the enemy": CINCPAC War Diary, May 16, 1942; ibid., p. 482.

388 "I have somewhat revised": "COMINCH TO CINCPAC," May 17, 1942; ibid., pp. 489–90.

388 "by applying the rule": Layton, *"And I Was There,"* p. 429.

389 "disheveled and bleary-eyed": Ibid.

389 "Of course it may turn out": CINCPAC War Diary, May 27, 1942; CINCPAC Grey Book, Bk. 1, p. 545.

389 "Of course," he later said: "The Reminiscences of Captain Joseph J. Rochefort, U.S. Navy (Retired)," p. 220.

389 "All I can do": Ibid., p. 221.

390 "I have a difficult time": Layton, *"And I Was There,"* p. 430.

390 "All right then, Admiral": Layton quoted in Potter, *Nimitz*, pp. 102–3.

390 "attempt the capture of Midway": "Operation Plan 29-42," U.S. Pacific Fleet, CINCPAC File A16-3/(16); 27 May 1942.

390 "crossed his Rubicon": Layton, *"And I Was There,"* p. 430.

390 "If we get ready": Ibid., p. 431.

390 Hypo had one more crowning victory: Holmes, *Double-Edged Secrets*, pp. 95–96.

392 "was felt as a personal blow": Kernan, *Crossing the Line*, p. 52.

393 "There's something fishy": Casey, *Torpedo Junction*, p. 351.

393 "It seemed to us": Kernan, *Crossing the Line*, p. 52.

393 Halsey and his flag lieutenant: Potter, *Bull Halsey*, p. 77.

393 He was gaunt: Kernan, *Crossing the Line*, p. 55.

393 "the most grievous disappointment": Potter, *Nimitz*, p. 84.

393 "He is in the best of spirits": Hoyt, *How They Won the War in the Pacific*, p. 93.

395 "saluted a trim": "Reminiscences of Admiral Spruance as related by Dr. David Willcutts, Fifth Fleet Medical Officer." MS item 297, U.S. Naval War College Archives, Newport, RI, pp. 3–4.

396 "We saw with satisfaction": Dickinson, *The Flying Guns*, p. 137.

397 "did a humongous amount": Russell, ed., *No Right to Win*, p. 243.

398 "All liberty cancelled": Rose, *The Ship That Held the Line*, p. 109.

398 "the strategy and tactics": Kernan, *Crossing the Line*, p. 53.

398 "had it on good authority": Casey, *Torpedo Junction*, p. 361.

398 "As usual we seem to be holding": Ibid., p. 365.

399 "a profound feeling of doom": Scott McCuskey account in Hammel, *Aces Against Japan*, pp. 38–39.

399 "It's hard to describe": Fisher, *Hooked*, pp. 73, 76.

400 "Quite a few of us": "Narrative by Lt. George Gay," debrief recorded October 12, 1943, at Navy Department; Office of Naval Records and Library, Washington, DC, p. 1.

400 "After asking a question": Mears, *Carrier Combat*, p. 59.

401 "Then," wrote Mears: Ibid., pp. 60–61.

401 "just in case": Ibid., p. 61.

401 "In carrying out the tasks": "Letter of Instructions," covering "Operation Plan 29-42," U.S. Pacific Fleet, CINCPAC File A16-3/(16); 27 May 1942.

401 "That man of ours": Layton, *"And I Was There,"* p. 432.

401 feeling "amazed": Mears, *Carrier Combat*, pp. 54–55.

402 "We are going out": Ibid., p. 54.

402 "An attack for the purpose": Casey, *Torpedo Junction*, p. 369.

Chapter Twelve

403 "I myself will devote": Agawa, *The Reluctant Admiral*, p. 309.

403 "I personally felt angry": Ens. Takeshi Maeda account in Werneth, ed., *Beyond Pearl Harbor*, p. 117.

404 The crews were working: Fuchida and Okumiya, *Midway: The Battle That Doomed Japan*, p. 140.

404 "Instinctively, I felt that": Hara, *Japanese Destroyer Captain*, p. 90.

404 "Since the carriers were undergoing": Nagumo's action report, June 15, 1942. Part II, Sec. 3, "Preparations for the Operation," in "The Japanese Story of the Battle of Midway," OPNAV P32-1002. Office of Naval Intelligence, Washington, DC, June 1947.

404 "Sortie as scheduled!": Fuchida and Okumiya, *Midway: The Battle That Doomed Japan*, p. 25.

405 "military marching songs": Maeda account in Werneth, ed., *Beyond Pearl Harbor*, p. 118.

405 "Through scattered clouds": Fuchida and Okumiya, *Midway: The Battle That Doomed Japan*, p. 26.

405 The officers enjoyed other: Agawa, *The Reluctant Admiral*, p. 310.

405 "White clouds drifted lazily": "Prisoner statement," in NHC, Morison Papers, b. 22, "No. 4, Action at Midway," cited in Prados, *Combined Fleet Decoded*, p. 330.

406 "At 1200 hours, change to course": Parshall and Tully, *Shattered Sword*, p. 106.

407 The Japanese crews watched: Hara, *Japanese Destroyer Captain*, pp. 90–91.

408 "We were well aware": Ibid., p. 91.

409 "The sound of engines": Fuchida and Okumiya, *Midway: The Battle That Doomed Japan*, p. 183.

410 "Many planes heading Midway": Astor, *Wings of Gold*, p. 90.

410 "the accuracy is excellent": Parshall and Tully, *Shattered Sword*, p. 202.

411 radioed back to Nagumo: Nagumo's action report, June 15, 1942. Part III,

"Description of the Operation," in "The Japanese Story of the Battle of Midway."

411 "There were so many of them": Astor, *Wings of Gold*, p. 91.

412 "Planes in second attack wave": Smith, *Carrier Battles*, p. 116.

412 "Sighted what appears to be": Nagumo's action report, June 15, 1942. Part III, "Description of the Operation."

414 "their flying altitude was": Lt. Cdr. Iyozo Fujita account in Werneth, ed., *Beyond Pearl Harbor*, p. 237.

414 "Geysers of water": Hiroshi Suzuki account in ibid., p. 92.

415 "Frankly," Fuchida said: Fuchida and Okumiya, *Midway: The Battle That Doomed Japan*, p. 196.

415 "We were very impressed": Maeda account in Werneth, ed., *Beyond Pearl Harbor*, p. 119.

416 "The enemy is accompanied": Nagumo's action report, June 15, 1942. Part III, "Description of the Operation."

416 "There was utter confusion": Kaname Shimoyama account in Werneth, ed., *Beyond Pearl Harbor*, p. 194.

416 "It was very difficult": Suzuki account in ibid., p. 92.

417 "Speed up the loading": Maeda account in ibid., p. 119.

417 He had sighted: Parshall and Tully, *Shattered Sword*, p. 198.

417 "I knew our limitations": Casey, *Torpedo Junction*, p. 370.

418 "The approaching battle": Gay, *Sole Survivor*, p. 108.

418 "We have had a very short time": Astor, *Wings of Gold*, p. 96.

418 "a little bit nervous": "Narrative by Lt. George Gay," debrief recorded Oct. 12, 1943, at Navy Department; Office of Naval Records and Library, Washington, DC, p. 2.

418 "faint vibration of machinery": Tom Cheek account in Russell, ed., *No Right to Win*, p. 93.

418 his "odds of survival": Clayton Fisher account in Russell, ed., *No Right to Win*, p. 112.

419 "feast for condemned men": Lloyd Childers account in "Veterans' Biographies," published for the Battle of Midway Celebration, Marines Memorial Club, San Francisco, 2009, p. 11.

419 "grease-penciled": Cheek account in Russell, ed., *No Right to Win*, p. 95.

419 "Some were quiet": Dickinson, *The Flying Guns*, pp. 140–41.

419 "From that moment": Mears, *Carrier Combat*, p. 52.

419 "Pilots, man your planes!": Dickinson, *The Flying Guns*, p. 142.

420 "It would seem that": Casey, *Torpedo Junction*, p. 377.

421 "Proceed on mission assigned": Lundstrom, *The First Team*, p. 335.

421 "The visibility was excellent": Dickinson, *The Flying Guns*, p. 145.

423 black smudges against the sky: Mears, *Carrier Combat*, p. 79.

423 "not to worry about our navigation": "Narrative by Lt. George Gay," p. 2.

424 "My greatest hope is that": Astor, *Wings of Gold*, p. 96.

424 "The Zeros that day": "Narrative by Lt. George Gay," p. 3.

424 "all attention was fixed": Fuchida and Okumiya, *Midway: The Battle That Doomed Japan*, p. 209.

424 "pea shooter" . . . "could see the little Jap": "Narrative by Lt. George Gay," pp. 5, 7.

427 Sharp-eyed pilots and gunners: See Dickinson, *The Flying Guns*, pp. 143–46.

427 "Sometimes the carrier stack": Mears, *Carrier Combat*, p. 93.

427 "thin, white lines" . . . "Among those ships": Dickinson, *The Flying Guns*, pp. 148–49.

427 "This is McClusky": Smith, *Midway: Dauntless Victory*, p. 140.

428 "A number of them were coming": John S. Thach account in Wooldridge, ed., *Carrier Warfare in the Pacific*, p. 56.

429 "Their climbing ability": Cheek account in Russell, ed., *No Right to Win*, p. 100.

429 "That first attack on us": Thach quoted in Astor, *Wings of Gold*, p. 97.

429 had deranged their favored box formation: See diagrams and text in Parshall and Tully, *Shattered Sword*, pp. 218–21.

429 "I was making": Dickinson, *The Flying Guns*, p. 153.

430 a "glint in the sun": Thach account in Wooldridge, ed., *Carrier Warfare in the Pacific*, p. 58.

430 "one of our machine gun commanders": Ens. Haruo Yoshino account in Werneth, ed., *Beyond Pearl Harbor*, p. 142.

430 "The results were cataclysmic" and the details that follow: See Parshall and Tully, *Shattered Sword*, pp. 234–36.

430 "It is dangerous here": Maeda account in Werneth, ed., *Beyond Pearl Harbor*, p. 120.

431 "the deck rippling": Dickinson, *The Flying Guns*, p. 155.

431 "I remember looking": Thach account in Wooldridge, ed., *Carrier Warfare in the Pacific*, p. 60.

431 The first bomb struck: For a description of this attack, see Parshall and Tully, *Shattered Sword*, pp. 237–38.

433 "a huge hole in the flight deck": Fuchida and Okumiya, *Midway: The Battle That Doomed Japan*, p. 213.

433 "It all happened so quickly": Shimoyama account in Werneth, ed., *Beyond Pearl Harbor*, p. 194.

433 "Due to the intense heat": Suzuki account in ibid., p. 92.

434 The third bomb: Lt. (jg) Kiyoto Furuta account in ibid., p. 24.

434 a "brilliant orange flash": Cheek account in Russell, ed., *No Right to Win*, p. 102.

435 "Group rendezvous!": Ibid., p. 103.

435 Each pilot had to make: Maeda account in Werneth, ed., *Beyond Pearl Harbor*, p. 118.

436 Dickinson turned his Dauntless home: Dickinson, *The Flying Guns*, pp. 164–66.

436 a "faint streak of white": Cheek account in Russell, ed., *No Right to Win*, pp. 105–6.

437 "An information officer": Kernan, *Crossing the Line*, p. 58.

437 was shocked to learn: Fisher, *Hooked*, p. 81.

437 "When I entered": Roy Gee account in Russell, ed., *No Right to Win*, p. 116.

437 One of the returning TBD pilots: See Kernan, *Crossing the Line*, p. 50.

438 "They were shouting and laughing": Ibid., p. 64.

438 "There were three carriers": Cheek account in Russell, ed., *No Right to Win*, p. 106.

439 vulnerable to bomb or fire damage: For the vulnerability of Japanese carriers to fire, see Parshall and Tully, *Shattered Sword*, pp. 244–47.

439 "the water evaporated quickly": Lt. Takayoshi Morinaga account in Werneth, ed., *Beyond Pearl Harbor*, p. 163.

440 "Numerous explosions": Yoshino account in ibid., p. 142.

440 The temperature climbed quickly: Parshall and Tully, *Shattered Sword*, p. 252.

440 Within fifteen minutes: Nagumo's action report, June 15, 1942. Part III, "Description of the Operation."

440 Her fires quickly overpowered: Ibid.

440 "Firefighting parties": Fuchida and Okumiya, *Midway: The Battle That Doomed Japan*, p. 216.

441 "our fire extinguishing pump": Furuta account in Werneth, ed., *Beyond Pearl Harbor*, p. 24.

441 "It is not time yet": Fuchida and Okumiya, *Midway: The Battle That Doomed Japan*, p. 214.

441 At 10:46 a.m.: Nagumo's action report, June 15, 1942. Part III, "Description of the Operation."

441 "a giant daikon radish": Parshall and Tully, *Shattered Sword*, p. 264.

442 "The enemy is in position": Prange, Goldstein, and Dillon, *Miracle at Midway*, p. 277.

443 "Red 17, arrow 265 from your present position": Commanding Officer, USS *Yorktown*, to CINCPAC. Battle of Midway after-action report, June 18, 1942. Enclosure: fighter control transcript.

444 "With my six .50-caliber wing guns": Scott McCuskey account in Hammel, *Aces Against Japan*, p. 62.

444 "Get back in the ready room!": Cheek account in Russell, ed., *No Right to Win*, pp. 80–81.

445 "I can't fight a war": Chief Radioman Richard Brown account in "Veterans' Biographies," p. 9.

446 "Gasping and teary eyed": Cheek account in Russell, ed., *No Right to Win*, p. 81.

446 "Fires raging aboard": Fuchida and Okumiya, *Midway: The Battle That Doomed Japan*, p. 243.

446 "bent their heads together": Prados, *Combined Fleet Decoded*, p. 331.

447 "What was I reading?": Hara, *Japanese Destroyer Captain*, pp. 91–92.

447 "There are three enemy carriers": Ens. Taisuke Maruyama account in Werneth, ed., *Beyond Pearl Harbor*, p. 182.

448 a "sense of desperation": Ibid.

449 "The whole left wing": Thach account in Wooldridge, ed., *Carrier Warfare in the Pacific*, p. 62.

449 "The ack-ack was ragged": Casey, *Torpedo Junction*, p. 381.

450 "wave of extreme patriotism": Fred Dyer account in "Veterans' Biographies," p. 18.

450 hail falling on a metal roof: Parshall and Tully, *Shattered Sword*, p. 315.

450 "the tail of our aircraft": Maruyama account in Werneth, ed., *Beyond Pearl Harbor*, p. 182.

450 "I could see the pilot": Bill Surgi account in Russell, ed., *No Right to Win*, p. 239.

450 "a sickening thud": Oral history: Lt. Joseph P. Pollard, medical officer; online at www.history.navy.mil/faqs/faq81-8.htm.

450 "Although I was separated": Cheek account in Russell, ed., *No Right to Win*, p. 82.

451 "Some men had one foot": Oral history: Lt. Joseph P. Pollard.

451 The first, at frame 90: Commanding Officer, USS *Yorktown*, to CINCPAC. Battle of Midway after-action report, June 18, 1942. Enclosure C: Engineering.

452 "At long intervals": Cheek account in Russell, ed., *No Right to Win*, p. 83.

452 "As each wave broke": Bill Roy account in ibid., p. 86.

453 Whaleboats and destroyers moved in: Otis G. Kight account in "Veterans' Biographies," p. 33.

453 "Drink this!": Cheek account in Russell, ed., *No Right to Win*, p. 85.

453 hauled aboard a destroyer: Herman A. Kelley account in "Veterans' Biographies," p. 32.

453 "If four carriers are smashed": Casey, *Torpedo Junction*, p. 383.

454 with three groups of bombers attacking her: For a description of this attack, see Parshall and Tully, *Shattered Sword*, pp. 326–27.

454 "very strong vibrations": Maruyama account in Werneth, ed., *Beyond Pearl Harbor*, p. 186.

455 "*Hiryu* hit by bombs": Fuchida and Okumiya, *Midway: The Battle That Doomed Japan*, p. 248.

455 "demonstrated just how out of touch": Parshall and Tully, *Shattered Sword*, p. 320.

455 "The enemy task force": Nagumo's action report, June 15, 1942. Part III, "Description of the Operation."

456 "so strangely optimistic": Fuchida and Okumiya, *Midway: The Battle That Doomed Japan*, p. 248.

456 "Even with my limited view": Hara, *Japanese Destroyer Captain*, p. 92.

456 "jangled nerves and bloodshot eyes": Fuchida and Okumiya, *Midway: The Battle That Doomed Japan*, p. 249.

456 "a very large oil field fire": "Narrative by Lt. George Gay," p. 10.

458 "The inside of the hangar": Yoshino account in Werneth, ed., *Beyond Pearl Harbor*, p. 142.

458 the *Akagi* did not seem to be in her death throes: Furuta account in ibid., p. 24.

458 "Negative": Lundstrom, *The First Team*, p. 417.

459 avoid "exposure to attack": "Letter of Instructions," covering "Operation Plan 29-42," U.S. Pacific Fleet, CINCPAC File A16-3/(16); 27 May 1942.

459 "I saw with my own eyes": Thach account in Wooldridge, ed., *Carrier Warfare in the Pacific*, p. 64.

459 "I had good officers": Prange, Goldstein, and Dillon, *Miracle at Midway*, p. 333.

460 their "sinking": Nagumo's action report, June 15, 1942. Part III, "Description of the Operation." See also Parshall and Tully, *Shattered Sword*, pp. 334–35.

460 lashed himself to an anchor: Fuchida and Okumiya, *Midway: The Battle That Doomed Japan*, p. 217.

460 "entirely passive": Entry for June 5, 1942, Ugaki, *Fading Victory*, pp. 145–46.

461 "little prospect of challenging": Ibid., p. 145.

461 "Everyone inwardly recognized": Fuchida and Okumiya, *Midway: The Battle That Doomed Japan*, p. 250.

461 "You ought to know": Agawa, *The Reluctant Admiral*, p. 320.

461 "In *shogi* too much fighting": Prange, Goldstein, and Dillon, *Miracle at Midway*, p. 319.

462 "ought to have known": Entry for June 5, 1942, Ugaki, *Fading Victory*, p. 147.

462 "This battle is almost": Prange, Goldstein, and Dillon, *Miracle at Midway*, p. 319.

462 "(1) The Midway Operation is cancelled": Fuchida and Okumiya, *Midway: The Battle That Doomed Japan*, p. 253.

462 "We cannot sink": Prange, Goldstein, and Dillon, *Miracle at Midway*, p. 320.

462 The message went out to Nagumo: Ibid., p. 321.

463 "Gradually, our once magnificent ship": Suzuki account in Werneth, ed., *Beyond Pearl Harbor*, p. 92.

463 "Half of the deck": Maruyama account in ibid., p. 186.

463 "Young men must leave": Prange, Goldstein, and Dillon, *Miracle at Midway*, p. 313.

463 "There is such a beautiful moon": Thomas, *Sea of Thunder*, p. 84.

465 That ship, the little 2,000-ton *Tanikaze*: Masashi Shibata's account, "The Destroyer *Tanikaze* Returns from 'The Sea of Death,'" in Fisher, *Hooked*, pp. 95–98.

466 "a huge bathtub": ARM3/c Ronald W. Graetz account in Russell, ed., *No Right to Win*, p. 124.

466 "If planes are to be flown": Buell, *The Quiet Warrior*, p. 158.

466 "The scene was reminiscent": Mears, *Carrier Combat*, p. 73.

466 "wheels down and locked": Gee account in Russell, ed., *No Right to Win*, p. 121.

467 "It was weird to see": Navy chief machinist's mate Dwight G. DeHaven account in "Veterans' Biographies," pp. 15–16.

468 "rang like a bell": Ibid.

468 "perhaps a hundred heads": Nesmith, *No Higher Honor*, p. 253.

469 "rocked up and rolled hard": Roy account in Russell, ed., *No Right to Win*, p. 87.

469 "We could hear the heavy machinery": DeHaven account in "Veterans' Biographies," pp. 15–16.

470 Captain Buckmaster, watching silently: Roy account in Russell, ed., *No Right to Win*, p. 88.

Epilogue

471   "a feeling, an intuition": Spruance's Foreword in Fuchida and Okumiya, *Midway: The Battle That Doomed Japan*, p. 9.

471   "When they were ready": Fireman 1st class Elmer Jones account in Russell, ed., *No Right to Win*, pp. 153–54.

472   "This was a cataclysm": Casey, *Torpedo Junction*, p. 396.

472   "Bit by bit": Mears, *Carrier Combat*, p. 76.

472   "irrevocable finality of death": Buell, *Dauntless Helldivers*, p. 83.

472   "The reaction of the pilots": Mears, *Carrier Combat*, p. 76.

472   "completely empty": Ens. Clay Fisher account in Russell, ed., *No Right to Win*, p. 125.

473   "Going through every person's": Mears, *Carrier Combat*, p. 77.

473   "It turns out that we have fought": Casey, *Torpedo Junction*, p. 395.

473   "a rather primitive affair": Layton, *"And I Was There,"* p. 434.

473   "as frantic as I have ever seen him": Ibid., p. 441.

473   "You who have participated": Potter, *Nimitz*, pp. 99, 107.

474   "Perhaps we will be forgiven": "'Midway' Spurs Pun by Admiral Nimitz," Associated Press, June 7, 1942.

474   "You are just like": Prange, Goldstein, and Dillon, *Miracle at Midway*, p. 328.

474   The surface ships were crowded: Ibid.

474   "It didn't sink": Navy seaman 3rd class Miyasato Yoshihito letter, in Gibney, ed., *Senso*, p. 130.

474   "We had no choice": Entry for June 8, 1942, Ugaki, *Fading Victory*, p. 158.

475   "looked as if he felt": Prados, *Combined Fleet Decoded*, p. 335.

475   "suffered from a stomachache": Entry for June 7, 1942, Ugaki, *Fading Victory*, p. 157.

475   "had been out of action": Agawa, *The Reluctant Admiral*, p. 321.

475   "all his responsibility": Ibid.

475   "Admittedly, we are not in a position": Entry for June 10, 1942, Ugaki, *Fading Victory*, p. 160.

475   Ugaki tried to ease: Ibid., p. 162.

476   "The routine of the returning airmen": Mears, *Carrier Combat*, pp. 77–78.

476   "In comparison with the losses": C. Brooks Peters, "Report by Admiral King," *New York Times*, June 8, 1942, p. 1.

477   "If it had not been for what you did": Spruance to Fletcher, June 8, 1942, Raymond Spruance Papers, U.S. Naval War College (USNWC) Archives.

477   "As far as attacks made on you": Cleary, *The Japanese Art of War*, p. 79.

478   "We were shot with luck": Fragment of undated and unaddressed correspondence, signed by Spruance, in Raymond Spruance Papers, USNWC MS Collection 12, series I, correspondence.

478   "All that I can claim credit for": Spruance's Foreword in Fuchida and Okumiya, *Midway: The Battle That Doomed Japan*, p. 8.

478 By one historian's estimate: Peattie, *Sunburst*, p. 174.

480 "Perhaps it was exhaustion": Holmes, *Double-Edged Secrets*, p. 100.

480 "This thing was a great big": "The Reminiscences of Captain Joseph J. Rochefort, U.S. Navy (Retired)," U.S. Naval Institute, Annapolis, MD, 1983, p. 266.

480 "essentially a victory of intelligence": Kahn, *The Codebreakers*, p. 573.

481 "make a silk purse" . . . "were perfectly capable": "The Reminiscences of Captain Thomas H. Dyer, U.S. Navy (Retired)," U.S. Naval Institute, Annapolis, MD, 1986, p. 247.

481 "To Commander Joe Rochefort": Beach, *The United States Navy: A 200-Year History*, p. 450

481 single "most important combatant": Russell, ed., *No Right to Win*, pp. 170–73.

481 "an ex-Japanese language student": Layton, *"And I Was There,"* p. 451.

481 "Pearl Harbor had missed the boat": Ibid., p. 450.

482 "I have given a great deal of thought": Ibid., p. 452.

482 "It was not the individual": Holmes, *Double-Edged Secrets*, p. 117.

482 "We felt that we had earned": "The Reminiscences of Captain Joseph J. Rochefort, U.S. Navy (Retired)," pp. 238, 254.

482 "This is terrible": Asai Tatsuzo account in Cook and Cook, eds., *Japan at War*, p. 206.

482 "seemed strangely confused": Yoshimura, *Battleship Musashi*, p. 128.

482 "I had presumed the news": Kido's diary quoted in Bix, *Hirohito and the Making of Modern Japan*, p. 450.

483 "Six carriers of the United States Navy": Notes taken by Robert Casey, June 6, 1942, Casey, *Torpedo Junction*, p. 404.

483 pictures taken from the air . . . A column of soldiers: *Kokusai Shashin Joho* (*International Graphic Magazine*), June 1, 1942.

483 "It is curious that the enemy": "Only One Carrier Lost, Says Tokyo," *New York Times*, June 11, 1942, p. 4.

484 "Now that America's northern attack": Rr. Adm. Tanetsugu Sosa, "Plans for Invading America," *Nichi Nichi*, June 11, 1942, cited in Tolischus, *Through Japanese Eyes*, p. 154.

484 "but will not be manned": Parshall and Tully, *Shattered Sword*, p. 388.

484 "promptly announced": Fuchida and Okumiya, *Midway: The Battle That Doomed Japan*, p. 16.

485 "My room was placed": Ibid.

485 "the vital cause of defeat": Minoru Genda account in Stillwell, ed., *Air Raid—Pearl Harbor!*, p. 27.

485 "We met with fiasco": Goldstein and Dillon, eds., *The Pacific War Papers*, p. 313.

486 "If the war should be protracted": "Tokyo Press Hints at Midway Defeat," *New York Times*, June 10, 1942, p. 1.

486 "their capacity to replace": C. Brooks Peters, "Report by Admiral King," *New York Times*, June 8, 1942, p. 1.

486 "100 million advancing": Dower, *War Without Mercy*, p. 215.

487 "true combat power is arms": Hata Shoryu account in Cook and Cook, eds., *Japan at War*, p. 210.

487 "to die as one of the emperor's limbs": Hirosawa Ei account in ibid., p. 247.

487 "did not become a vital consideration": Sherwood, *Roosevelt and Hopkins*, p. 438.

488 "There are some patriotic citizens": Elmer Davis quoted in ibid., p. 437.

488 William Knudsen: Brinkley, *Washington Goes to War*, p. 173.

489 Between 1940 and 1943: Kennedy, *The Rise and Fall of the Great Powers*, p. 354.

489 "leaving only an inch" . . . "under arms": Kernan, *Crossing the Line*, p. 7.

489 "Let go of your cocks": Davis, *Sinking the Rising Sun*, p. 49.

489 "Guns were loaded": Eisenhower, *Crusade in Europe*, p. 14.

490 "were the sad places of the war": Hynes, *Flights of Passage*, pp. 109–10.

BIBLIOGRAPHY

Government Reports, Presidential Papers,
Correspondence, Diaries, and Oral Histories

Alanbrooke, Lord. *War Diaries, 1939–1945*, ed. Alex Danchev and Daniel Todman. Berkeley: University of California Press, 2001.

Auchincloss, Louis, ed. *Theodore Roosevelt: Letters and Speeches*. New York: Library of America, 2004.

Bond, Charles R., and Terry Anderson. *A Flying Tiger's Diary*. College Station: Texas A&M University Press, 2001.

Buhite, Russell D., and David W. Levy, eds. *FDR's Fireside Chats*. New York: Penguin Books, 1992.

Carroll, Andrew, ed. *War Letters: Extraordinary Correspondence from American Wars*. New York: Scribner, 2001.

Carter, Worrall Reed. *Beans, Bullets, and Black Oil: The Story of Fleet Logistics Afloat in the Pacific During World War II*. Washington, DC: Department of the Navy, 1953.

Churchill, Winston S., ed. *Never Give In!: The Best of Winston Churchill's Speeches*. New York: Hyperion, 2003.

Churchill, Winston, and Martin Gilbert, ed. 3 vols. *The Churchill War Papers*. London: William Heinemann, 1993.

Churchill, Winston, Clementine Churchill, and Mary Soames. *Winston and Clementine: The Personal Letters of the Churchills*. Boston: Houghton Mifflin, 1999.

Commander-in-chief, U.S. Pacific Fleet. "CINCPAC Grey Book: Running Estimate of the Situation for the Pacific War." [War diary] Book 1, December 1941 to June 1942. Naval Historical Center, Washington, DC (on CD).

Cook, Haruko Taya, and Theodore F. Cook, eds. *Japan at War: An Oral History*. New York: The New Press, 1992.

Department of the Army, Office of the Chief of Military History. "Japanese Monograph No. 1, Philippine Operation Record, Phase 1, Nov. 1941–Jul. 1942."

———. "Japanese Monograph No. 101, Naval Operations in the Invasion of Nether-lands East Indies, Dec. 1941–Mar. 1942."

———. "Japanese Monograph No. 107, Malaya Invasion Naval Operations (Revised), Dec. 1941–Feb. 1942."

Dyer, George C. *The Amphibians Came to Conquer: The Story of Admiral Richmond Kelly Turner.* Washington, DC: Government Printing Office, 1972.

Evans, David C., ed. *The Japanese Navy in World War II: In the Words of Former Japanese Naval Officers.* Annapolis, MD: Naval Institute Press, 1993.

Fahey, James J. *Pacific War Diary, 1942–1945.* Boston: Houghton Mifflin, 1963.

Forrestal, James. *The Forrestal Diaries,* ed. Walter Millis. New York: Viking Press, 1951.

Gibney, Frank, ed. *Senso: The Japanese Remember the Pacific War.* Armonk, NY: M. E. Sharpe, 1995.

Goldstein, Donald M., and Kathryn V. Dillon, eds. *The Pacific War Papers: Japanese Documents of World War II.* Washington, DC: Potomac Books, 2006.

Hammel, Eric. *Aces Against Japan: The American Aces Speak.* New York: Pocket Books, 1992.

Harris, Mark Jonathan, Franklin D. Mitchell, and Steven J. Schechter, eds. *The Home-front: America During World War II.* New York: G. P. Putnam's Sons, 1984.

Heimdahl, William C., and Edward J. Marolda, eds. *Guide to United States Naval Administrative Histories of World War II.* Washington, DC: Naval History Division, Dept. of the Navy, 1976.

Ickes, Harold. *The Secret Diary of Harold L. Ickes.* New York: Simon & Schuster, 1954.

Kiyosawa, Kiyoshi. *A Diary of Darkness: The Wartime Diary of Kiyosawa Kiyoshi,* trans. Eugene Soviak and Kamiyama Tamie. Princeton, NJ: Princeton University Press, 1999.

LaForte, Robert S., and Ronald E. Marcello, eds. *Remembering Pearl Harbor: Eyewitness Accounts by U.S. Military Men and Women.* New York: Ballantine Books, 2001.

Litoff, Judy Barrett, and David C. Smith, eds. *Since You Went Away: World War II Let-ters from American Women on the Home Front.* New York: Oxford University Press, 1991.

———. *American Women in a World at War: Contemporary Accounts from World War II.* Wilmington, DE: Scholarly Resources, 1997.

Loewenheim, Francis L., Harold D. Langley, and Manfred Jonas, eds. *Roosevelt and Churchill: Their Secret Wartime Correspondence.* New York: Saturday Review Press / E. P. Dutton, 1975.

Matloff, Maurice, and Edwin M. Snell. *Strategic Planning for Coalition Warfare 1941–1942.* Washington, DC: Office of the Chief of Military History, Dept. of the Army, 1953–59.

Moran, Charles. *Winston Churchill: The Struggle for Survival 1940–1965: Taken from the Diaries of Lord Moran.* London: Sphere, 1968.

"Narrative by Lt. George Gay." Debrief recorded October 12, 1943, at U.S. Navy Department; Office of Naval Records and Library, Washington, DC.

Naval Historical Center. *U.S. Naval Administration in World War II* [microfilm]. Washington, DC: Dept. of the Navy, Naval Historical Center, 1976.

Perry, Glen C. H. *"Dear Bart": Washington Views of World War II*. New York: Greenwood Press, 1982.

"Reminiscences of Admiral Spruance as related by Dr. David Willcutts, Fifth Fleet Medical Officer." Ms. Item 297, U.S. Naval War College Archives, Newport, RI.

"The Reminiscences of Captain Thomas H. Dyer, U.S. Navy (Retired)." U.S. Naval Institute, Annapolis, MD, 1986.

"The Reminiscences of Rear Admiral Henry L. Miller, U.S. Navy (Retired)." U.S. Naval Institute, Annapolis, MD, 1973.

"The Reminiscences of Captain Joseph J. Rochefort, U.S. Navy (Retired)." U.S. Naval Institute, Annapolis, MD, 1983.

Richardson, K. D., and Paul Stillwell. *Reflections of Pearl Harbor: An Oral History of December 7, 1941*. New York: Greenwood Press, 2005.

Roosevelt, Eleanor, Rochelle Chadakoff, and Martha Gelhorn. *Eleanor Roosevelt's My Day: Her Acclaimed Columns, 1936–1945*. New York: Pharos, 1989.

Roosevelt, Theodore. *Letters to His Children*. New York: Charles Scribner's Sons, 1919.

———, Albert Bushnell Hart, and Herbert Ronald Ferleger. *Theodore Roosevelt Cyclopedia*. New York: Roosevelt Memorial Association, 1941.

———, and Elting Elmore Morison. *The Letters of Theodore Roosevelt*. 8 vols. Cambridge, MA: Harvard University Press, 1951–54.

Rosenman, Samuel I., ed. *The Public Papers and Addresses of Franklin D. Roosevelt*. 13 vols. New York: Harper & Bros., 1950 (1941–45 vols.).

Russell, Ronald W., ed. *No Right to Win: A Continuing Dialogue with Veterans of the Battle of Midway*. New York: iUniverse, 2006.

Shenk, Robert, ed. *Authors at Sea*. Annapolis, MD: Naval Institute Press, 1997.

Stillwell, Paul, ed. *Air Raid—Pearl Harbor! Recollections of a Day of Infamy*. Annapolis, MD: Naval Institute Press, 1981.

Stimson, Henry L. *Henry Lewis Stimson Diaries*. XV, 20 (microfilm ed., reel 3), Manuscripts and Archives, Yale University Library, New Haven, CT.

U.S. Army. Far East Command. *The Imperial Japanese Navy in World War II: A Graphic Presentation of the Japanese Naval Organization and List of Combatant and Non-Combatant Vessels Lost or Damaged in the War*. Japanese Operational Monograph Series, No. 116. Tokyo: Military History Section, Special Staff, General Headquarters, Far East Command, 1952.

U.S. Civilian Production Administration. *Industrial Mobilization for War: History of the War Production Board and Predecessor Agencies, 1940–1945*. Vol. I: *Program and Administration*.

U.S. Office of Naval Intelligence. *The Japanese Story of the Battle of Midway*. Washington, DC: Government Printing Office, 1947 [Nagumo Report].

U.S. Office of Naval Operations. *U.S. Naval Aviation in the Pacific*. Washington, DC: Government Printing Office, 1947.

U.S. Strategic Bombing Survey. *Air Campaigns of the Pacific War.* Washington, DC: U.S. Strategic Bombing Survey, Military Analysis Division, 1947.

———. *Interrogations of Japanese Officials.* 2 vols. Washington, DC: Government Printing Office, 1947.

———. *Japanese Merchant Shipping.* Washington, DC: Government Printing Office, 1946.

———. *Summary Report (Pacific War).* Washington, DC: Government Printing Office, 1946.

———. *The Campaigns of the Pacific War.* Washington, DC: U.S. Strategic Bombing Survey (Pacific), Naval Analysis Division, 1946 (reprinted 1969 by Greenwood).

Ugaki, Matome. *Fading Victory: The Diary of Admiral Matome Ugaki, 1941–1945,* trans. Masataka Chihaya. Pittsburgh, PA: University of Pittsburgh Press, 1991.

"Veterans' Biographies," published for the Battle of Midway Celebration, Marines Memorial Club, San Francisco, 2009.

The War Reports of General of the Army George C. Marshall, Chief of Staff, General of the Army H. H. Arnold, Commanding General, Army Air Forces [and] Fleet Admiral Ernest J. King, Commander-in-Chief, United States Fleet and Chief of Naval Operations. Philadelphia: Lippincott, 1947.

Werneth, Ron, ed. *Beyond Pearl Harbor: The Untold Stories of Japan's Naval Airmen.* Atglen, PA: Schiffer Publishing, 2008.

Wooldridge, E. T., ed. *Carrier Warfare in the Pacific: An Oral History Collection.* Washington, DC: Smithsonian Institute Press, 1993.

Yamashita, Samuel Hideo, ed. *Leaves from an Autumn of Emergencies: Selections from the Wartime Diaries of Ordinary Japanese.* Honolulu: University of Hawaii Press, 2005.

Books

Adamic, Louis. *Dinner at the White House.* New York: Harper, 1946.

Agawa, Hiroyuki. *The Reluctant Admiral: Yamamoto and the Imperial Navy.* New York: Kodansha International, 1979.

Albion, Robert G. *Makers of Naval Policy, 1798–1947.* Annapolis, MD: Naval Institute Press, 1980.

Allyn, John. *The 47 Ronin Story.* Tokyo: Charles E. Tuttle Co., 1970.

Ambrose, Stephen E. *The Supreme Commander: The War Years of General Dwight D. Eisenhower.* Jackson: University Press of Mississippi, 1999.

Asada, Sadao. *From Mahan to Pearl Harbor: The Imperial Japanese Navy and the United States.* Annapolis, MD: Naval Institute Press, 2006.

Astor, Gerald. *Crisis in the Pacific: The Battles for the Philippine Islands by the Men Who Fought Them.* New York: Donald I. Fine Books, 1996.

———. *Wings of Gold: The U.S. Naval Air Campaign in World War II.* New York: Presidio Press/Ballantine Books, 2004.

Bailey, Beth, and David Farber. *The First Strange Place: Race and Sex in World War II Hawaii.* Baltimore: Johns Hopkins University Press, 1994.

Bailey, Thomas Andrew. *Theodore Roosevelt and the Japanese-American Crisis*. Stanford, CA: Stanford University Press, 1934.

Beach, Edward L. *The United States Navy: A 200-Year History*. Boston: Houghton Mifflin, 1986.

Beard, Charles A. *President Roosevelt and the Coming of the War, 1941: A Study in Appearances and Realities*. New Haven, CT: Yale University Press, 1948.

Beasley, W. G. *Japanese Imperialism, 1894–1945*. New York: Oxford University Press, 1999.

Beaver, Floyd. *Sailor from Oklahoma: One Man's Two-Ocean War*. Annapolis, MD: Naval Institute Press, 2009.

Belote, James H., and William M. *Titans of the Seas: The Development and Operations of Japanese and American Carrier Task Forces During World War II*. New York: Harper & Row, 1975.

Benedict, Ruth. *The Chrysanthemum and the Sword: Patterns of Japanese Culture*. Tokyo: Charles E. Tuttle Co., 1954.

Bercuson, David J., and Holger H. Herwig. *One Christmas in Washington: The Secret Meeting Between Roosevelt and Churchill That Changed the World*. Woodstock, NY: Overlook Press, 2005.

Bergamini, David. *Japan's Imperial Conspiracy*. New York: William Morrow, 1971.

Bix, Herbert P. *Hirohito and the Making of Modern Japan*. New York: HarperCollins, 2000.

Black, Conrad. *Franklin Delano Roosevelt: Champion of Freedom*. New York: Public Affairs, 2003.

Blum, John Morton. *V Was for Victory: Politics and American Culture During World War II*. New York: Harcourt Brace, 1976.

Bradlee, Benjamin C. *A Good Life: Newspapering and Other Adventures*. New York: Simon & Schuster, 1995.

Brands, H. W. *T. R.: The Last Romantic*. New York: Basic Books, 1997.

Brinkley, David. *Washington Goes to War: The Extraordinary Story of the Transformation of a City and a Nation*. New York: Alfred A. Knopf, 1988.

Brown, Cecil B. *Suez to Singapore*. New York: Random House, 1942.

Brown, DeSoto. *Hawaii Goes to War: Life in Hawaii from Pearl Harbor to Peace*. Honolulu, HI: Editions Limited, 1989.

Browne, Courtney. *Tojo: The Last Banzai*. New York: Holt, Rinehart & Winston, 1967.

Budiansky, Stephen. *Battle of Wits: The Complete Story of Codebreaking in World War II*. New York: Free Press, 2000.

Buell, Harold L. *Dauntless Helldivers: A Dive-bomber Pilot's Epic Story of the Carrier Battles*. New York: Orion, 1991.

Buell, Thomas B. *Master of Sea Power: A Biography of Fleet Admiral Ernest J. King*. Boston: Little, Brown, 1980.

———. *The Quiet Warrior: A Biography of Admiral Raymond A. Spruance*. Annapolis, MD: Naval Institute Press, 1987.

Burns, James MacGregor. *Roosevelt: The Soldier of Freedom*. New York: Harcourt Brace Jovanovich, 1970.

Burton, John. *Fortnight of Infamy: The Collapse of Allied Airpower West of Pearl Harbor*. Annapolis, MD: Naval Institute Press, 2006.

Buruma, Ian. *Inventing Japan, 1853–1964*. New York: Modern Library, 2003.

Caren, Eric, ed. *Pearl Harbor Extra: A Newspaper Account of the United States' Entry into World War II*. Edison, NJ: Castle, 2001.

Casey, Robert J. *Torpedo Junction: With the Pacific Fleet from Pearl Harbor to Midway*. Indianapolis, IN: Bobbs-Merrill, 1942.

Childs, Marquis W. *I Write from Washington*. New York: Harper, 1942.

———. *This Is Your War*. Boston: Little, Brown, 1942.

Churchill, Winston S. *The Second World War*. Vol. 3: *The Grand Alliance*. Boston: Houghton Mifflin, 1950.

———. *The Second World War*. Vol. 4: *The Hinge of Fate*. Boston: Houghton Mifflin, 1950.

Cleary, Thomas. *The Japanese Art of War: Understanding the Culture of Strategy*. Boston: Shambhala Classics, 2005.

Coletta, Paolo E. *Admiral Marc A. Mitscher and U.S. Naval Aviation: Bald Eagle*. Lewiston, NY: Edwin Mellen Press, 1997.

Colman, Penny. *Rosie the Riveter: Women Working on the Home Front in World War II*. New York: Crown Publishers, 1995.

Cooke, Alistair. *The American Home Front, 1941–1942*. New York: Atlantic Monthly Press, 2006.

Cooper, Page. *Navy Nurse*. New York: Whittlesey House/McGraw-Hill, 1946.

Costello, John. *The Pacific War*. New York: Rawson, Wade, 1981.

Cressman, Robert J. *"A Glorious Page in Our History": The Battle of Midway, 4–6 June 1942*. Missoula, MT: Pictorial Histories, 2001.

Cross, Robert F. *Sailor in the White House: The Seafaring Life of FDR*. Annapolis, MD: Naval Institute Press, 2003.

Cunningham, Winfield Scott. *Wake Island Command*. Boston: Little, Brown, 1961.

Dallek, Robert. *Franklin D. Roosevelt and American Foreign Policy, 1932–1945*. Oxford: Oxford University Press, 1995.

Davidson, Joel R. *The Unsinkable Fleet: The Politics of U.S. Navy Expansion in World War II*. Annapolis, MD: Naval Institute Press, 1996.

Davis, Kenneth S. *FDR: The War President, 1940–1943: A History*. New York: Random House, 2000.

Davis, William E. *Sinking the Rising Sun: Dog Fighting and Dive Bombing in World War II: A Navy Fighter Pilot's Story*. Minneapolis, MN: Zenith Press, 2007.

Deacon, Richard. *Kempei Tai: The Japanese Secret Service Then and Now*. Tokyo: Charles E. Tuttle Co., 1982.

Dickinson, Clarence Earle. *The Flying Guns: Cockpit Record of a Naval Pilot from Pearl Harbor Through Midway*. New York: Scribner, 1942.

Dower, John W. *War Without Mercy: Race and Power in the Pacific War.* New York: Pantheon Books, 1986.

———. *Japan in War and Peace: Selected Essays.* New York: New Press; distributed by W. W. Norton & Company, 1993.

Dull, Paul S. *A Battle History of the Imperial Japanese Navy, 1941–1945.* Annapolis, MD: Naval Institute Press, 1978.

Dunnigan, James F., and Albert A. Nofi. *Victory at Sea: World War II in the Pacific.* New York: William Morrow, 1995.

Duus, Masayo. *Tokyo Rose: Orphan of the Pacific.* New York: Kodansha International, 1979.

Dye, Bob. *Hawai'i Chronicles III: World War Two in Hawai'i, from the Pages of Paradise of the Pacific.* Honolulu: University of Hawai'i Press, 2000.

Dyer, George C. *The Amphibians Came to Conquer: The Story of Admiral Richmond Kelly Turner.* Washington, DC: Government Printing Office, 1972.

Edgerton, Robert B. *Warriors of the Rising Sun: A History of the Japanese Military.* New York: W. W. Norton & Company, 1997.

Eiler, Keith E. *Mobilizing America: Robert P. Patterson and the War Effort, 1940–1945.* Ithaca, NY: Cornell University Press, 1997.

Eisenhower, Dwight D. *Crusade in Europe.* Garden City, NY: Doubleday, 1948.

Ellis, John. *World War II, a Statistical Survey: The Essential Facts and Figures for All the Combatants.* New York: Facts on File, 1995.

Elphick, Peter. *Liberty: The Ships That Won the War.* Annapolis, MD: Naval Institute Press, 2001.

Evans, David, and Mark Peattie. *Kaigun: Strategy, Tactics, and Technology in the Imperial Japanese Navy, 1887–1941.* Annapolis, MD: Naval Institute Press, 1997.

Ewing, Steve. *Reaper Leader: The Life of Jimmy Flatley.* Annapolis, MD: Naval Institute Press, 2002.

———. *Thach Weave: The Life of Jimmie Thach.* Annapolis, MD: Naval Institute Press, 2004.

———, and John B. Lundstrom. *Fateful Rendezvous: The Life of Butch O'Hare.* Annapolis, MD: Naval Institute Press, 1997.

Feiss, Herbert. *Churchill, Roosevelt, Stalin: The War They Waged and the Peace They Sought.* Princeton, NJ: Princeton University Press, 1957.

Fisher, Clayton E. *Hooked: Tales and Adventures of a Tailhook Warrior.* Denver, CO: Outskirts, 2009.

Fuchida, Mitsuo, and Masatake Okumiya. *Midway: The Battle That Doomed Japan, The Japanese Navy's Story.* Annapolis, MD: Naval Institute Press, 1955.

Fussell, Paul. *Wartime: Understanding and Behavior in the Second World War.* New York: Oxford University Press, 1989.

Gay, George H. *Sole Survivor: The Battle of Midway and Its Effects on His Life.* Naples, FL: Midway Publishers, 1980.

Gelb, Norman. *Desperate Venture: The Story of Operation Torch, the Allied Invasion of North Africa.* New York: William Morrow, 1992.

Gilbert, Alton. *A Leader Born: The Life of Admiral John Sidney McCain, Pacific Carrier Commander.* Philadelphia: Casemate, 2006.

Gilbert, Martin. *Churchill and America.* New York: Free Press, 2005.

Gluck, Carol. *Japan's Modern Myths: Ideology in the Late Meiji Period.* Princeton, NJ: Princeton University Press, 1985.

———, and Stephen R. Graubard, eds. *Showa: The Japan of Hirohito.* New York: W. W. Norton & Company, 1992.

Goodwin, Doris Kearns. *No Ordinary Time: Franklin and Eleanor Roosevelt. The Home Front in World War II.* New York: Simon & Schuster, 1994.

Grew, Joseph C. *Report from Tokyo: A Message to the American People.* New York: Simon & Schuster, 1942.

Gruhl, Werner. *Imperial Japan's World War Two, 1931–1945.* New Brunswick, NJ: Transaction, 2007.

Halsey, William Frederick. *Admiral Halsey's Story.* New York: Whittlesey House, 1947.

Hara, Tameichi, Fred Saito, and Roger Pineau. *Japanese Destroyer Captain: Pearl Harbor, Guadalcanal, Midway—The Great Naval Battles as Seen Through Japanese Eyes.* Annapolis, MD: Naval Institute Press, 2007.

Harper, John A. *Paddles!: The Foibles and Finesse of One World War II Landing Signal Officer.* Atglen, PA: Schiffer Publishing, 2000.

Harries, Meirion, and Susie Harries. *Soldiers of the Sun: The Rise and Fall of the Imperial Japanese Army.* New York: Random House, 1991.

Hayes, Grace P. *The History of the Joint Chiefs of Staff in World War II: The War Against Japan.* Annapolis, MD: Naval Institute Press, 1982.

Holland, W. J., ed. *The Navy.* Washington, DC: Naval Historical Foundation, 2000.

Holmes, W. J. *Double-Edged Secrets: U.S. Naval Intelligence Operations in the Pacific During World War II.* Annapolis, MD: Naval Institute Press, 1979.

Hoopes, Townsend, and Douglas Brinkley. *Driven Patriot: The Life and Times of James Forrestal.* Annapolis, MD: Naval Institute Press, 2000.

Hopkins, June. *Harry Hopkins: Sudden Hero, Brash Reformer.* New York: St. Martin's Press, 1999.

Hornfischer, James D. *Ship of Ghosts: The Story of the USS Houston, FDR's Legendary Lost Cruiser, and the Epic Saga of Her Survivors.* New York: Bantam Books, 2006.

Hough, Richard Alexander. *Death of the Battleship.* New York: Macmillan, 1963.

Howard, Clive. *One Damned Island After Another: The Saga of the Seventh Air Force in World War II.* Chapel Hill: University of North Carolina Press, 1946.

Hoyt, Edwin Palmer. *How They Won the War in the Pacific: Nimitz and His Admirals.* New York: Weybright & Talley, 1970.

———. *Now Hear This: The Story of American Sailors in World War II.* New York: Paragon House, 1993.

Hynes, Samuel Lynn. *Flights of Passage: Reflections of a World War II Aviator.* New York: Penguin Books, 2003 (Naval Institute Press, 1988).

Irokawa, Daikichi. *The Age of Hirohito: In Search of Modern Japan.* New York: Free Press, 1995.

Isom, Dallas Woodbury. *Midway Inquest: Why the Japanese Lost the Battle of Midway.* Bloomington: Indiana University Press, 2007.

Jackson, Robert H. *That Man: An Insider's Portrait of Franklin D. Roosevelt.* Oxford: Oxford University Press, 2004.

Jasper, Joy Waldron, James P. Delgado, and Jim Adams. *The USS Arizona: The Ship, the Men, the Pearl Harbor Attack, and the Symbol That Aroused America.* New York: St. Martin's Press, 2003.

Jenkins, Roy. *Churchill: A Biography.* New York: Farrar, Straus & Giroux, 2001.

Johnston, Stanley. *Queen of the Flat-Tops: The U.S.S. Lexington and the Coral Sea Battle.* New York: E. P. Dutton, 1942.

Jones, Wilbur D., Jr., and Carroll Robbins Jones. *Hawaii Goes to War: The Aftermath of Pearl Harbor.* Shippensburg, PA: White Mane, 2001.

Kahn, David. *The Codebreakers: The Story of Secret Writing.* New York: New American Library, 1973.

Karig, Walter, ed. *Battle Report.* 6 vols. New York: Published for the Council on Books in Wartime by Farrar & Rinehart, 1944–52.

Karsten, Peter. *The Naval Aristocracy: The Golden Age of Annapolis and the Emergence of Modern American Navalism.* New York: Free Press, 1972.

Kase, Toshikazu. *Journey to the Missouri.* New Haven, CT: Yale University Press, 1950.

Kato, Masuo. *The Lost War: A Japanese Reporter's Inside Story.* New York: Alfred A. Knopf, 1946.

Kawahara, Toshiaki. *Hirohito and His Times: A Japanese Perspective.* Tokyo: Kodansha International, 1990.

Keegan, John. *The Second World War.* London: Hutchinson & Co., 1989.

———. *The Price of Admiralty.* New York: Penguin Books, 1990.

Kennedy, David M. *Freedom from Fear: The American People in Depression and War, 1929–1945.* New York: Oxford University Press, 1999.

———. *Freedom from Fear, Part Two: The American People in World War II.* New York: Oxford University Press, 2003.

Kennedy, Paul. *The Rise and Fall of the Great Powers.* New York: Vintage, 1989.

Kenney, George C. *General Kenney Reports: A Personal History of the Pacific War.* New York: Duell, Sloan, & Pearce, 1949.

Kernan, Alvin B. *Crossing the Line: A Bluejacket's World War II Odyssey.* Annapolis, MD: Naval Institute Press, 1994.

———. *The Unknown Battle of Midway: The Destruction of the American Torpedo Squadrons.* New Haven, CT: Yale University Press, 2005.

Kimball, Warren F. *Forged in War: Roosevelt, Churchill, and the Second World War.* New York: William Morrow, 1997.

Kimmett, Larry, and Margaret Regis. *The Attack on Pearl Harbor: An Illustrated History.* Seattle, WA: Navigator Publishers, 1991.

King, Ernest J., and Walter Muir Whitehill. *Fleet Admiral King: A Naval Record*. New York: W. W. Norton & Company, 1952.

Kinney, John F., and James M. McCaffrey. *Wake Island Pilot: A World War II Memoir*. Washington, DC: Brassey's, 1995.

Kratoska, Paul H. *South East Asia: Colonial History*. Vol. 5. London: Routledge, 2001.

Kriloff, Herbert. *Officer of the Deck: A Memoir of the Pacific War and the Sea*. Pacifica, CA: Pacifica, 2000.

Lawson, Robert. *U.S. Navy Dive and Torpedo Bombers of World War II*. Minneapolis, MN: Zenith Press, 2001.

———, and Barrett Tillman. *U.S. Navy Air Combat, 1939–46*. Osceola, WI: MBI Publishing, 2000.

Lawson, Ted W. *Thirty Seconds Over Tokyo*. New York: Random House, 1943.

Layton, Edwin T., with Roger Pineau and John Costello. *"And I Was There": Pearl Harbor and Midway—Breaking the Secrets*. New York: William Morrow, 1985.

Leach, Douglas Edward. *Now Hear This: The Memoir of a Junior Naval Officer in the Great Pacific War*. Kent, OH: Kent State University Press, 1987.

Leahy, William D. *I Was There*. New York: Whittlesey House, 1950.

Leckie, Robert. *Helmet for My Pillow*. New York: Bantam Books, 2010.

Lee, Clark. *They Call It the Pacific: An Eye-Witness Story of Our War Against Japan from Bataan to the Solomons*. New York: Viking Press, 1943.

Lee, Robert Edson. *To the War*. New York: Alfred A. Knopf, 1968.

Lingeman, Richard. *Don't You Know There's a War On? The American Home Front, 1941–45*. New York: G. P. Putnam's Sons, 1970.

Lipsitz, George. *Rainbow at Midnight: Labor and Culture in the 1940s*. Urbana: University of Illinois Press, 1994.

Livezey, William Edmund. *Mahan on Sea Power*. Norman: University of Oklahoma Press, 1947.

Lord, Walter. *Incredible Victory: The Battle of Midway*. New York: HarperCollins, 1993.

———. *Day of Infamy*. New York: Henry Holt, 2001.

Lotchin, Roger W. *The Bad City in the Good War: San Francisco, Los Angeles, Oakland, and San Diego*. Bloomington: Indiana University Press, 2003.

Lundstrom, John B. *The First South Pacific Campaign: Pacific Fleet Strategy, December 1941–June 1942*. Annapolis, MD: Naval Institute Press, 1976.

———. *The First Team: Pacific Naval Air Combat from Pearl Harbor to Midway*. Annapolis, MD: Naval Institute Press, 1984.

Madsen, Daniel. *Resurrection: Salvaging the Battle Fleet at Pearl Harbor*. Annapolis, MD: Naval Institute Press, 2003.

Mahan, Alfred Thayer. *From Sail to Steam, Recollections of Naval Life, by Capt. A. T. Mahan*. New York: Harper & Bros., 1907.

———, ed. Allan Westcott. *Mahan on Naval Warfare: Selections from the Writings of Rear Admiral Alfred T. Mahan*. Mineola, NY: Dover Publications, 1999 (Little, Brown, 1941).

Manchester, William Raymond. *American Caesar: Douglas MacArthur, 1880–1964.* Boston: Little, Brown, 1978.

———. *Goodbye, Darkness: A Memoir of the Pacific War.* Boston: Little, Brown, 1980.

Marder, Arthur J. *Old Friends, New Enemies: The Royal Navy and the Imperial Japanese Navy, 1936–1945.* Oxford: Clarendon Press; New York: Oxford University Press, 1981–90. Vols. 1–2.

Mason, Theodore C. *Battleship Sailor.* Annapolis, MD: Naval Institute Press, 1982.

———. *Rendezvous with Destiny: A Sailor's War.* Annapolis, MD: Naval Institute Press, 1997.

Matsuo, Kinoaki. *How Japan Plans to Win,* trans. Kilsoo K. Haan (published in Japan as *The Three-Power Alliance and a United States–Japanese War*). Boston: Little, Brown, 1942.

McCabe, Larry. *Pearl Harbor and the American Spirit: The World War II Generation Remembers the Tragic Event That Transformed a Nation.* Bloomington, IN: Xlibris Corp., 2004.

McIntire, Vice-Admiral Ross T. *White House Physician.* New York: G. P. Putnam's Sons, 1946.

McJimsey, George T. *Harry Hopkins: Ally of the Poor and Defender of Democracy.* Cambridge, MA: Harvard University Press, 1987.

Meacham, Jon. *Franklin and Winston: An Intimate Portrait of an Epic Friendship.* New York: Random House, 2003.

Mears, Frederick. *Carrier Combat: A Young Pilot's Story of Action Aboard the Hornet in World War II.* New York: Ballantine Books, 1967.

Michener, James A. *Tales of the South Pacific.* Greenwich, CT: Fawcett, 1947.

———. *The World Is My Home: A Memoir.* New York: Random House, 1992.

Middlebrook, Martin, and Patrick Mahoney. *Battleship: The Sinking of the Prince of Wales and the Repulse.* New York: Charles Scribner's Sons, 1979.

Miller, Edward S. *War Plan Orange: The U.S. Strategy to Defeat Japan, 1897–1945.* Annapolis, MD: Naval Institute Press, 1991.

Millot, Bernard A. *The Battle of the Coral Sea: Sea Battles in Close Up, No. 12,* trans. S. V. Whitley. Annapolis, MD: Naval Institute Press, 1974.

Morgan, Ted. *FDR: A Biography.* New York: Simon & Schuster, 1985.

Morison, Samuel Eliot. *History of United States Naval Operations in World War II.* Vol. 3: *The Rising Sun in the Pacific.* Boston: Little, Brown, 1948.

———. *History of United States Naval Operations in World War II.* Vol. 4: *Coral Sea, Midway and Submarine Actions: May 1942–August 1942.* Boston: Little, Brown, 1949.

Morita, Akio, Edwin M. Reingold, and Mitsuko Shimomura. *Made in Japan.* London: William Collins, 1987.

Morris, Ivan. *The Nobility of Failure: Tragic Heroes in the History of Japan.* Tokyo: Charles E. Tuttle Co., 1982.

Nardo, Don. *Pearl Harbor.* San Diego, CA: Greenhaven, 2003.

Nesmith, Jeff. *No Higher Honor: The USS Yorktown at the Battle of Midway.* Atlanta, GA: Longstreet, 1999.

Neu, Charles E. *An Uncertain Friendship: Theodore Roosevelt and Japan, 1906–1909.* Cambridge, MA: Harvard University Press, 1967.

Nitobe, Inazo. *Bushido: The Soul of Japan.* Tokyo: Charles E. Tuttle Co., 1969.

Okumiya, Masatake, Jiro Horikoshi, and Martin Caidin. *Zero!* New York: E. P. Dutton & Co., 1956.

Overy, Richard. *Why the Allies Won.* New York: W. W. Norton & Company, 1995.

Parshall, Jonathan, and Anthony P. Tully. *Shattered Sword: The Untold Story of the Battle of Midway.* Washington, DC: Potomac Books, 2005.

Peattie, Mark R. *Sunburst: The Rise of Japanese Naval Air Power, 1909–1941.* Annapolis, MD: Naval Institute Press, 2001.

Perkins, Francis. *The Roosevelt I Knew.* New York: Viking Press, 1946.

Perrett, Geoffrey. *Days of Sadness, Years of Triumph: The American People, 1939–1945.* Baltimore, MD: Penguin Books, 1973.

Potter, E. B. *Nimitz.* Annapolis, MD: Naval Institute Press, 1976.

———. *Bull Halsey.* Annapolis, MD: Naval Institute Press, 1985.

Prados, John. *Combined Fleet Decoded: The Secret History of American Intelligence and the Japanese Navy in World War II.* New York: Random House, 1995.

Prange, Gordon W. *God's Samurai: Lead Pilot at Pearl Harbor.* New York: Macmillan, 1990.

———, Donald M. Goldstein, and Katherine V. Dillon. *At Dawn We Slept: The Untold Story of Pearl Harbor.* New York: Penguin Books, 1982.

———. *Miracle at Midway.* New York: Penguin Books, 1983.

———. *December 7, 1941: The Day the Japanese Attacked Pearl Harbor.* New York: McGraw-Hill, 1988.

Radike, Floyd W. *Across the Dark Islands: The War in the Pacific.* New York: Presidio Press/Ballantine Books, 2003.

Regan, Stephen D. *In Bitter Tempest: The Biography of Admiral Frank Jack Fletcher.* Ames: Iowa State University Press, 1994.

Reilly, Michael F., and William J. Slocum. *Reilly of the White House.* New York: Simon & Schuster, 1947.

Reischauer, Edwin O. *The Japanese.* Cambridge, MA: Belknap Press, 1981.

———. *Japan: The Story of a Nation.* New York: McGraw-Hill, 1990.

———, and Albert M. Craig. *Japan: Tradition and Transformation.* Tokyo: Charles E. Tuttle Co., 1978.

Reynolds, Clark G. *On the Warpath in the Pacific: Admiral Jocko Clark and the Fast Carriers.* Annapolis, MD: Naval Institute Press, 2005.

Roosevelt, Eleanor. *This I Remember.* New York: Harper & Bros., 1949.

Roosevelt, Theodore. *Theodore Roosevelt; An Autobiography.* New York: Macmillan, 1913.

———. *America and the World War, by Theodore Roosevelt.* New York: Charles Scribner's Sons, 1915.

Rose, Lisle A. *The Ship That Held the Line: The USS Hornet and the First Year of the Pacific War.* Annapolis, MD: Naval Institute Press, 1995.

Rosenman, Samuel Irving. *Working with Roosevelt.* New York: Harper, 1952.

Russell, Ronald W. *No Right to Win: A Continuing Dialogue with Veterans of the Battle of Midway*. New York: iUniverse, 2006.

Sakai, Saburo, with Martin Caidin and Fred Saito. *Samurai!* New York: E. P. Dutton & Co., 1956.

Sakaida, Henry. *Imperial Japanese Navy Aces, 1937–45*. Oxford: Osprey Aerospace, 1998.

Shenk, Robert, ed. *Authors At Sea*. Annapolis, MD: Naval Institute Press, 1997.

Sherman, Frederick C. *Combat Command: The American Aircraft Carriers in the Pacific War*. New York: E. P. Dutton & Co., 1950.

Sherwood, Robert E. *Roosevelt and Hopkins: An Intimate History*. New York: Harper & Bros., 1948.

Shillony, Ben-Ami. *Revolt in Japan: The Young Officers and the February 26, 1936 Incident*. Princeton, NJ: Princeton University Press, 1973.

———. *Politics and Culture in Wartime Japan*. Oxford: Clarendon Press, 1981.

Skulski, Janusz. *The Battleship Yamato*. Annapolis, MD: Naval Institute Press, 1988.

Sloan, Bill. *Given Up for Dead: America's Heroic Stand at Wake Island*. New York: Bantam Books, 2003.

Smith, Douglas V. *Carrier Battles: Command Decision in Harm's Way*. Annapolis, MD: Naval Institute Press, 2006.

Smith, Holland M., and Percy Finch. *Coral and Brass*. New York: Charles Scribner's Sons, 1949.

Smith, Merriman. *Thank You, Mr. President: A White House Notebook*. New York: Harper & Bros., 1946.

Smith, Peter C. *Midway: Dauntless Victory*. Barnsley, UK: Pen and Sword Books, 2007.

Smyth, Robert T. *Sea Stories*. New York: iUniverse, 2004.

Spector, Ronald H. *Eagle Against the Sun: The American War with Japan*. New York: Free Press, 1984.

Sprout, Harold, and Margaret Sprout. *The Rise of American Naval Power, 1776–1918*. Annapolis, MD: Naval Institute Press, 1939.

Stafford, Edward Peary. *The Big E: The Story of the USS Enterprise*. New York: Random House, 1962.

Starr, Kevin. *Embattled Dreams: California in War and Peace, 1940–1950*. Oxford and New York: Oxford University Press, 2002.

Stimson, Henry L., and McGeorge Bundy. *On Active Services in Peace and War*. New York: Harper & Bros., 1947.

Stoler, Mark A. *Allies and Adversaries: The Joint Chiefs of Staff, the Grand Alliance, and U.S. Strategy in World War II*. Chapel Hill: University of North Carolina Press, 2000.

Storry, Richard. *The Double Patriots: A Study of Japanese Nationalism*. Boston: Houghton Mifflin, 1957.

Tagaya, Osamu. *Imperial Japanese Naval Aviator 1937–45*. Oxford: Osprey Aerospace, 2003.

Taylor, Charles Carlisle. *The Life of Admiral Mahan*. New York: George H. Doran Co., 1920.

Taylor, Theodore. *Magnificent Mitscher*. Annapolis, MD: Naval Institute Press, 1991.

Thomas, Evan. *Sea of Thunder: Four Commanders and the Last Great Naval Campaign: 1941–1945*. New York: Simon & Schuster, 2006.

Thomas, Jane. *My Hawaii, 1938–1962*. Bloomington, IN: Xlibris Corp., 2002.

Thorne, Christopher. *Allies of a Kind: The United States, Britain, and the War Against Japan, 1941–1945*. New York: Oxford University Press, 1978.

Toland, John. *But Not in Shame: The Six Months After Pearl Harbor*. New York: Random House, 1961.

———. *The Rising Sun: The Decline and Fall of the Japanese Empire, 1936–1945*. New York: Random House, 1970.

Tolischus, Otto David. *Through Japanese Eyes*. New York: Reynal & Hitchcock, 1945.

Tuchman, Barbara. *Stilwell and the American Experience in China, 1911–1945*. New York: Bantam Books, 1970.

Tully, Grace. *F. D. R.: My Boss*. New York: Charles Scribner's Sons, 1949.

Turk, Richard W. *The Ambiguous Relationship: Theodore Roosevelt and Alfred Thayer Mahan*. New York: Greenwood Press, 1987.

Urwin, Gregory. *Facing Fearful Odds: The Siege of Wake Island*. Lincoln: University of Nebraska Press, 1997.

Van der Vat, Dan. *The Pacific Campaign: World War II, the U.S.-Japanese Naval War, 1941–1945*. New York: Simon & Schuster, 1991.

———. *Pearl Harbor: The Day of Infamy—An Illustrated History*. New York: Basic Books, 2001.

Victoria, Brian Daizen. *Zen at War*. New York: Weatherhill, 1997.

Weinberg, Gerhard L. *A World at Arms: A Global History of World War II*. Cambridge, UK: Cambridge University Press, 1994.

———. *Visions of Victory: The Hopes of Eight World War II Leaders*. Cambridge, UK: Cambridge University Press, 2005.

Weintraub, Stanley. *Long Day's Journey into War: December 7, 1941*. New York: Truman Tally Books, 1991.

Wenger, J. Michael, Katherine V. Dillon, and Donald M. Goldstein. *The Way It Was: Pearl Harbor: The Original Photographs*. Washington, DC: Potomac Books, 1995.

Wheeler, Post. *Dragon in the Dust*. Hollywood, CA: Marcel Rodd, 1946.

White, William Lindsay. *They Were Expendable*. New York: Harcourt, Brace, 1942.

Wigmore, Lionel. *The Japanese Thrust*. Canberra: Australian War Memorial, 1957.

Willmott, H. P. *The Barrier and the Javelin: Japanese and Allied Pacific Strategies, February to June 1942*. Annapolis, MD: Naval Institute Press, 1983.

Winkler, Allan M. *Home Front U.S.A.: America During World War II*. Arlington Heights, IL: Harlan Davidson, 1986.

Yoshimura, Akira. *Zero Fighter*. Westport, CT: Frederick A. Praeger, 1996.

———. *Battleship Musashi: The Making and Sinking of the World's Biggest Battleship*, trans. Vincent Murphy. Tokyo and New York: Kodansha International, 1999.

Zich, Arthur, and the Editors of Time-Life Books. *The Rising Sun*. Alexandria, VA: Time-Life Books, 1977.

Zimmermann, Warren. *First Great Triumph: How Five Americans Made Their Country a World Power.* New York: Farrar, Straus & Giroux, 2002.

Articles

Asher, Harvey. "Hitler's Decision to Declare War on the United States Revisited (A Synthesis of the Secondary Literature)." Newsletter of the Society for Historians of American Foreign Relations (SHAFR), September 2000. Online at www.shafr.org/publications/newsletter/september-2000.

Eller, Ernest M. "Swords into Plowshares: Some of Fleet Admiral Nimitz's Contributions to Peace." Fredericksburg, TX: Admiral Nimitz Foundation, 1986.

Ewing, William H. "Nimitz: Reflections on Pearl Harbor." Fredericksburg, TX: Admiral Nimitz Foundation, 1985

Goldsmith, Raymond W. "The Power of Victory: Munitions Output in World War II," *Military Affairs*, vol. 10, no. 1 (Spring 1946), pp. 69–80.

Graybar, Lloyd J. "American Pacific Strategy After Pearl Harbor: The Relief of Wake Island," *Prologue* (Fall 1980), pp. 134–50.

Herbig, Katherine L. "American Strategic Deception in the Pacific: 1942–1944," in Michael I. Handel, ed., *Strategic and Operational Deception in the Second World War.* London: Cass, 1987.

Lamar, H. Arthur. "I Saw Stars." Fredericksburg, TX: Admiral Nimitz Foundation, 1985.

Layton, Edwin T. "Early Carrier Raids During World War II," in Daniel M. Masterson, ed., *Naval History: The Sixth Symposium of the U.S. Naval Academy.* Wilmington, DE: Scholarly Resources, 1987.

MacArthur, Douglas A. "MacArthur's Reminiscences: Part 5," *Life*, vol. 57, no. 2 (July 10, 1964), p. 72.

Petillo, Carol M. "Douglas MacArthur and Manuel Quezon: A Note on an Imperial Bond," *Pacific Historical Review*, vol. 48, no. 1 (February 1979), pp. 107–17.

Roosevelt, Theodore. "Washington's Forgotten Maxim." Address at U.S. Naval War College, June 2, 1897. *Naval Institute Proceedings*, vol. 23 (1897), p. 456.

Santa Fe Railway. "Along Your Way: Facts about stations and scenes on the Santa Fe," (pamphlet distributed to passengers on the Santa Fe Super Chief), 1946. Online at www.titchenal.com/atsf/ayw1946.

INDEX